W9-BLK-042

PLACEBO
Theory, Research, and Mechanisms

PLACEBO

Theory, Research, and Mechanisms

Edited by

LEONARD WHITE
State University of New York at Stony Brook
and Pilgrim Psychiatric Center

BERNARD TURSKY
State University of New York at Stony Brook

and

GARY E. SCHWARTZ
Yale University

FOREWORD BY NORMAN SARTORIUS

The Guilford Press
New York London

LIBRARY OF CONGRESS CATALOGING IN PUBLICATION DATA
Main entry under title:

Placebo: theory, research, and mechanisms.

  Includes index.
  1. Medicine and psychology—Addresses, essays, lectures. 2. Placebo (Medicine)—Addresses, essays, lectures. 3. Medicine—Philosophy—Addresses, essays, lectures. 4. Mind and body—Addresses, essays, lectures. I. White, Leonard. II. Tursky, Bernard. III. Schwartz, Gary E.
  R726.5.P59   1985   615.5   84-19829
  ISBN 0-89862-649-8

CONTRIBUTORS

Robert Ader, PhD, Division of Behavioral and Psychosocial Medicine, Department of Psychiatry, University of Rochester School of Medicine and Dentistry, Rochester, New York

Hymie Anisman, Ph.D, Department of Psychology, Unit for Behavioral Medicine and Pharmacology, Carleton University, Ottawa, Ontario, Canada

David Bakan, PhD, Department of Psychology, York University, Toronto, Ontario, Canada

Richard R. Bootzin, PhD, Department of Psychology, Northwestern University, Evanston, Illinois

D. Borkovec, PhD, Department of Psychology, The Pennsylvania State University, University Park, Pennsylvania

Joseph V. Brady, PhD, Department of Psychiatry and Behavioral Sciences, The Johns Hopkins University School of Medicine Baltimore, Maryland

Howard Brody, MD, PhD, Medical Humanities Program, Department of Family Practice, and Department of Philosophy, Michigan State University, East Lansing, Michigan

L. W. Buckalew, PhD, Department of Psychology, Alabama A & M University, Normal, Alabama

Frederick J. Evans, PhD, Carrier Foundation, Belle Mead, New Jersey; Department of Psychiatry, UMDNJ-Rutgers Medical School, Piscataway, New Jersey

Max Fink, MD, Department of Psychiatry and Behavioral Science, School of Medicine, State University of New York at Stony Brook, Stony Brook, New York

Marion J. Finkel, MD, Office of Orphan Products Development, U.S. Food and Drug Administration, Rockville, Maryland

Avram Goldstein, MD, Addiction Research Foundation and Department of Pharmacology, Stanford University, Palo Alto, California

Newton C. Gordon, DDS, Division of Oral and Maxillofacial Surgery, Department of Stomatology, University of California School of Dentistry, San Francisco, California

Priscilla Grevert, MD, Addiction Research Foundation and Department of Pharmacology, Stanford University, Palo Alto, California

Adolf Grünbaum, PhD, Departments of Philosophy and Psychiatry, University of Pittsburgh, Pittsburgh, Pennsylvania

Robert A. Hahn, PhD, Department of Psychiatry and Behavioral Sciences, University of Washington, Seattle, Washington

Jon D. Levine, MD, PhD, Section of Rheumatology and Clinical Immunology, and Division of Clinical Pharmacology and Experimental Therapeutics, Department of Medicine, University of California School of Medicine, San Francisco, California; Division of Oral and Maxillofacial Surgery, Department of Stomatology, University of California School of Dentistry, San Francisco, California

Gordon L. Paul, PhD, Department of Psychology, University of Houston-University Park, Houston, Texas

William B. Plotkin, PhD, Durango Pain Management Clinic, Durango, Colorado

Mary Crenshaw Rawlinson, PhD, Department of Philosophy, State University of New York at Stony Brook, Stony Brook, New York

Robert Rosenthal, PhD, Department of Psychology and Social Relations, Harvard University, Cambridge, Massachusetts

Sherman Ross, PhD, Department of Psychology, Howard University, Washington, D.C.

Gary E. Schwartz, PhD, Department of Psychology, Yale University, New Haven, Connecticut

Shepard Siegel, PhD, Department of Psychology, McMaster University, Hamilton, Ontario, Canada

Lawrence S. Sklar, PhD, Department of Psychology, Unit for Behavioral Medicine and Pharmacology, Carleton University, Ottawa, Ontario, Canada

Jaylan S. Turkkan, PhD, Department of Psychiatry and Behavioral Sciences, The Johns Hopkins University School of Medicine, Baltimore, Maryland

Bernard Tursky, Department of Political Science, State University of New York at Stony Brook, Stony Brook, New York

Leonard White, PhD, Department of Psychiatry and Behavioral Science, School of Medicine, State University of New York at Stony Brook, Stony Brook, New York; Piligrim Psychiatric Center, Department of Psychology, West Brentwood, New York

Ian Wickramasekera, PhD, Department of Psychiatry and Behavioral Sciences, Eastern Virginia Medical School, Norfolk, Virginia

Wallace Wilkins, PhD, Department of Psychology, Old Dominion University, Norfolk, Virginia; Virginia Consortium for Professional Psychology, Norfolk, Virginia (Present affiliation: Department of Psychology, University of Hartford, West Hartford, Connecticut)

FOREWORD

Health care is basically a human transaction. Yet, over the past few decades, biological reductionism fed by pride about recent technological achievements has gained the upper hand, and many medical schools are now producing doctors who are convinced that it is only a matter of time before machines can be entrusted with all diagnosis and most treatment. The fantasy that pharmacological substances will be prescribed by a computer once the machine is stimulated in a particular way is not seen as science fiction, but as a real option. The perspective of having illness cured without having to go through cumbersome and messy procedures, talks with patients and their relatives, rituals of reassurance, and words of doctoring is accepted by too many with pleasant anticipation.

But the essence of healing remains in the ghost on the machine, not in machines alone, the human transaction in healing continues to have, in Eisenberg's words, "an irreducible role" in medicine. Facts and opinions contained in this volume throw new light on the nature of healing and the changes in its comprehension. The history of the placebo concept reflects these changes faithfully: First understood as a "commonplace" method or medicine, given "more to please than to cure," "placebo" has become synonymous over the past few decades with an inactive, inert substance used in experiments or as a part of a charlatan's arsenal.

The change in content of the concept of "placebo" was, to an extent, an expression of the belief in the omnipotence of science. The conviction arose that the scientific method can, if applied with vigor and rigor, result in an understanding of the nature of everything including the curious effects of the encounter of two humans, one unwell and one wanting to help him (or her) from which the former often emerges feeling less ill. The encounter is sometimes complicated by a prescription of a type of behavior, a thing to avoid, a foodstuff to shun, or an injection. Examinations with complex tools and blood drawn as a price of knowing what went wrong are occasionally also part of the encounter.

The encounter plays an important role in healing; however, constituent elements of healing and the physiological or psychophysiological pathways through which action occurs are, by and large, unknown. It is therefore laudable to label some of the components of the process. Unfortunately, however, at that point, something has gone wrong. The healing process has been relegated to the position of a disturbing effect, summed up under the name of "placebo," equated to some kind of noise in the system that has to be eliminated before the "real" treatment, the action of the magic pill, can be assessed. Not even when "obecalp" reactions—a deterioration of the condition occurring during the period of administration of the placebo—have been described has there been any better acceptance of the power of the factors other than the drug in the treatment process.

Thus, the use of the "placebo" concept exposes medicine to a danger: If the medical student, the doctor, the general public, the fellow scientist is taught that evidence of pharmacological action is necessary and sufficient for treatment, and that treatment without such procedures or methods is ineffective and charlatanist, he or she will have misunderstood what medicine is all about. Most ailments tend to go away by themselves; some can be affected positively by treatment; others can be turned into more severe illnesses by doctors' actions. In most treatment, however, pharmacological substances and most other "nonplacebos" are only adjuncts to the treatment process.

It is therefore my hope that this collection of learned chapters brought together by the hard work and creative effort of the editors not only will bring a significant amount of knowledge to the reader, but will also motivate him or her to join the ranks of those who would like to see the word and current concept of "placebo" disappear altogether. To replace it, some other word or words are needed that can be used in the framework of a balanced strategy, in which the effects of all the different components of care are examined, with understanding of and respect for their interaction.

Norman Sartorius, MD, MA, DPM, PhD, FRC Psych
Director, Division of Mental Health
World Health Organization

CONTENTS

PLACEBO
Theory, Research, and Mechanisms

SECTION ONE

INTRODUCTION

1

Placebo in Perspective

LEONARD WHITE
BERNARD TURSKY
GARY E. SCHWARTZ

The role of psychological processes in the healing arts is often evaluated as a contemporary issue, but actually has a long history. In 1747, Jerome Garb, professor of medicine and chemistry at the University of Leiden, wrote the following:

> In his thoughts, to be sure, the physician can abstract body from mind and consider it separately in order to be less confused in the marshalling of ideas. Yet in the actual practice of his art, where he has to do with man as he is, should the physician devote all of his efforts to the body alone, and take no account of the mind, his curative endeavors will pretty often be less than happy and his purpose either wholly missed or part of what pertains to it neglected. (Garb, quoted in Rather, 1965, p. 70)

We have undertaken a critical examination of placebo-related issues in the spirit of Professor Garb's observations.

It has long been recognized by practicing physicians that procedures that offer patients reassurance or the expectation of help may lead to marked improvement in their clinical status. The term "placebo," derived from the Latin meaning "I shall please," has been widely used to refer to these clinical effects.

In a clinical context, "placebo" has come to denote a deceptive practice. This negative view of the term "placebo" has accrued ever since the time of Chaucer, when the term was associated with the practice of singing vespers for pay. The negative connotations of "placebo" have come to dominate contemporary thinking in large measure, due to the emergence of the double-

Leonard White. Department of Psychiatry and Behavioral Sciences, School of Medicine, State University of New York at Stony Brook, Stony Brook, New York; Department of Psychology, Pilgrim Psychiatric Center, West Brentwood, New York.

Bernard Tursky. Department of Political Science, State University of New York at Stony Brook, Stony Brook, New York.

Gary E. Schwartz. Department of Psychology, Yale University, New Haven, Connecticut.

blind placebo-controlled drug study, in which the differentiation of effects due to the pharmacological action of a compound from other unspecified "placebo" effects is a primary consideration. This methodological refinement guided by a narrowly conceived biological orientation tacitly recognizes placebo effects as a clinical reality, but dismisses them from further consideration.

Placebo effects, however, are so omnipresent that if they are not controlled for in therapeutic studies, the findings are considered unreliable. The potency of these effects may be realized by considering the number of conditions in which placebo effects have been noted: that is, cough, mood changes, angina pectoris, headache, seasickness, anxiety, hypertension, status asthmaticus, depression, common cold, lymphosarcoma, gastric motility, dermatitis, and pain symptoms from a variety of sources.

The psychobiological approach represents an alternative to the exclusionary perspective on placebo as embodied in the placebo-controlled clinical trial. Psychobiological theory allows for the possibility that the phenomena often attributed to placebo effects may be understood in psychobiological terms and incorporated as part of clinical practice. A recently proposed model for evaluating the behavioral dynamic of the placebo response emphasizes the interactive relationships between pharmacological and environmental/placebo factors (Schwartz, Shapiro, Redmond, Ferguson, Ragland, & Weiss, 1979). It has been suggested that the complex of placebo/environmental factors may then be analyzed in terms of social-psychological variables. Intrinsic to this point of view is a recognition of the limitations of a dualistic mind–body approach to disease processes, and the search for an alternative that is neither simplistic nor unverifiable.

A fundamental tenet of this approach is the recognition that placebo responses are neither mystical nor inconsequential, and that ultimately psychological and physiological processes operate through common anatomical pathways. The utility of such a model, however, remains to be demonstrated.

Although much has been written on the subject of placebo, the limits of these phenomena are not well established. In contrast to the widely held conviction that placebo effects are manifestly a potent cause of clinical improvement, a well-known authority on the subject has expressed the opinion that placebo primarily influences subjective reports and "that the amount of variance accounted for by the placebo on organic clinical conditions is minimal, and possibly even non-existent" (Shapiro, 1981).

The ambiguity regarding the magnitude of placebo effects may be due to ambiguities surrounding the definition of what is meant by "placebo," as well as issues of research design and interpretation. Although the term "placebo" has been widely used by biomedical and behavioral theorists and clinicians, most of the current literature considers placebo as an exclusionary classification, resulting in little effort directed toward definition of the term. Lacking a rigorous definition of placebo and placebo effects, there remains considerable ambiguity concerning the description and interpretation of the placebo phenomena. The main objectives of this volume are to define the term "placebo" and to assess the mechanisms, clinical significance, and limits of the included phenomena. These objectives should not be construed as mere academic pursuits, but have considerable practical significance. If some "placebo" phenomena currently being dismissed as nuisance variables are understandable as clinically significant psychobiological processes, a more comprehensive model of clinical practice may be rationalized. This more complete model may be expected to have a salutary effect upon patient care. On the other hand, the pragmatic limits of placebo phenomena must be determined if patients' needs are to be addressed realistically while the excesses of quackery are avoided.

To the degree that placebo effects vary with person, place, and time and are often considered as nuisance variables, they may provide an unreliable basis for clinical practice. On the other hand, as conceptual and experimental models of placebo are refined, previously unidentified or ignored mechanisms and incidental treatment components may take on new therapeutic value. In this process, "placebo" effects may be transformed into specified effects, and their selective incorporation into clinical practice may be rationalized. The chapters comprising the text of this volume are organized into sections that examine various aspects of the concerns alluded to above. In Section II, "Definition," there is a consideration of the areas of inquiry denoted by the term "placebo." Section III, "Research Methods," examines various methodological aspects encountered in the design and interpretation of therapeutic studies in which placebo controls are a consideration. In a sense, these two sections establish a background for the interpretation of the subsequent chapters. The chapters in Section IV, "Clinical Phenomena," have as a common focus examples of "placebo" effects that are most often of interest to the practitioner—that is, behavior change, cultural influences, and placebo analgesia. Psychobiological constructs are important considerations in accounting for placebo effects, because they demystify these effects by uniting psychological and physiological domains. The chapters in Section V, "Mediational Theory," present some of the more recent developments in conditioning models of placebo responses and psychobiological research.

The dominant view of placebo is that its use is mandatory in clinical trials, but unethical in clinical practice. These views are challenged in Section VI, "Placebo in Clinical Trials and Clinical Practice." In the final section of this volume, we have attempted to summarize the contributed material and to propose a synthesis of perspectives on placebo. Briefly, current theoretical developments and research findings have altered the traditional meaning of "placebo." There is no single placebo effect, but rather a multiplicity of effects with differential efficacy and mechanisms. We propose a systems theory approach as a synthetic heuristic model for further research and as a guide to clinical practice.

It was originally our intention to hold an invitational symposium in which participants could freely exchange information. When adequate funding for such a symposium failed to materialize, it was decided to publish a volume of collected chapters and to retain the customary role of formal discussants. The presentations by these discussants are so designated in the table of contents and the text. We wish to thank all of the contributors for their cooperation, encouragement, and contributions to this project. We wish also to acknowledge grants in support of this project from Hoffman La Roche, Inc., and Upjohn, Inc.

REFERENCES

Rather, J. L. *Mind and body in eighteenth century medicine: A study based upon Jerome Garb's De regimine mentis*. Berkeley: University of California Press, 1965.

Schwartz, G. E., Shapiro, A. P., Redmond, D. P., Ferguson, D. C., Ragland, D. R., & Weiss, S. M. Behavioral medicine approaches to hypertension: An integrative analysis of theory and research. *Journal of Behavioral Medicine*, 1979, *2*, 311–363.

Shapiro, A. K. [Review of Brody's *Placebos and the philosophy of medicine*]. *Social Science and Medicine*, 1981, *15E*, 96–97.

SECTION TWO

DEFINITION

2

Explication and Implications of the Placebo Concept

ADOLF GRÜNBAUM

INTRODUCTION

Just what is the problem of identifying an intervention or treatment *t* of one sort or another as a placebo for a target disorder *D*? One set of circumstances, among others, in which the need for such an identification may arise is the following: After the administration of *t* to some victims of *D*, some of them recover from their affliction to a significant extent. Now suppose that there is cogent evidence that this improvement can indeed be causally attributed at all to some factors or other among the spectrum of constituents comprising the dispensation of *t* to a patient. Then it can become important to know whether the therapeutic gain that ensued from *t* in the alleviation of *D* was due to *those particular factors* in its dispensation that the advocates of *t* have theoretically designated as deserving the credit for the positive treatment outcome. And one aim of this chapter is to articulate in detail the bearing of the answer to this question on whether *t* qualifies generically as a placebo or not. For, as will emerge, the medical and psychiatric literature on placebos and their effects is conceptually bewildering, to the point of being a veritable Tower of Babel.

The proverbial sugar pill is hardly the sole placebo capable of producing therapeutic benefits for ailments other than hypoglycemia and other glucose deficits. Indeed, the long-term history of medical treatment has been characterized as largely the history of the placebo effect (A. K. Shapiro & Morris, 1978). After all, it is not only the patients who can be unaware that the treatments they are receiving are just placebos for their disorders; the physicians as well may mistakenly believe that they are administering nonplacebos for their patients' ailments, when they are actually dispensing placebos, while further enhancing the patients' credulity by communicating their own therapeutic faith. For example, as we shall see, surgery for angina pectoris performed in the United States during the 1950s turned out to be a

Adolf Grünbaum. Departments of Philosophy and Psychiatry, University of Pittsburgh, Pittsburgh, Pennsylvania.

mere placebo. Unbeknownst to the physicians who practiced before the present century, most of the medications they dispensed were at best pharmacologically ineffective, if not outright physiologically harmful or even dangerous. Thus, during all that time, doctors were largely engaged in the unwitting dispensation of placebos on a massive scale. Nay, even after the development of contemporary scientific medicine some 80 years ago, "the placebo effect flourished as the norm of medical treatment" (A. K. Shapiro & Morris, 1978, p. 371).

To boot, the psychiatrist Jerome Frank (1973) has issued the sobering conjecture that those of the roughly 200 psychotherapies whose gains exceed those from spontaneous remission do *not* owe such remedial efficacy to the *distinctive* treatment factors credited by their respective therapeutic advocates, but succeed for other reasons. Nonetheless, Frank admonishes us not to disparage such placebogenic gains in therapy, at least as long as we have nothing more effective. And even in internal medicine and surgery, a spate of recent articles has inveighed against downgrading placebogenic benefits, the grounds being that we should be grateful even for small mercies. Yet the plea not to forsake the benefits wrought by placebos has been challenged on ethical grounds: The injunction to secure the patient's informed consent is a demand whose fulfillment may well render the placebo ineffective, though perhaps not always (Park & Covi, 1965).

The physician Arthur K. Shapiro is deservedly one of the most influential writers in this field of inquiry. He has been concerned with the history of the placebo effect (1960) and with the semantics of the word "placebo" (1968), no less than with current empirical research on placebogenic phenomena in medical and psychological treatments (A. K. Shapiro & Morris, 1978). Thus, in his portion of the last-cited paper, he has refined (1978, p. 371) his earlier 1971 definition of "placebo" in an endeavor to codify the current uses of the term throughout medicine and psychiatry. The technical vocabulary employed in A. K. Shapiro's earlier and most recent definitions is standard terminology in the discussion of placebo therapies and of experimental placebo controls, be it in pharmacology, surgery, or psychiatry. Yet just this standard technical vocabulary, I submit, generates confusion by being misleading or obfuscating, and indeed cries out for conceptual clarification. Hence it is my overall objective to revamp Shapiro's definition substantially so as to provide a clear and rigorous account of the placebo notion appropriate to current medicine and psychiatry.

CRITIQUE, EXPLICATION, AND REFORMULATION OF A. K. SHAPIRO'S DEFINITION

Critique

While some placebos are known to be such by the dispensing physician—though presumably not by the patient—other placebo therapies are mistakenly believed to be nonplacebos by the physician as well. Mindful of this dual state of affairs, A. K. Shapiro's definition of a placebo therapy makes it clear that, at any given stage of scientific knowledge, a treatment modality actually belonging to the genus placebo can be of the latter kind rather than of the traditionally recognized first sort. To capture both of these two species of placebo therapy, he casts his definition into the following general form, in which the expression "$=_{\text{def.}}$" stands for the phrase "is definitionally equivalent to":

Therapy t is a placebo therapy $=_{\text{def.}}$ t is of kind A OR t is of kind B.

Any definition of this "either–or" form is called a "disjunctive" definition, and *each* of the two independent clauses connected by the word "or" is called a "disjunct." For example, suppose we define a "parent" by saying:

Person X is a parent $=_{\text{def.}}$ X is a father OR X is a mother.

This is clearly a *disjunctive* definition. And it is convenient to refer to each of the separate clauses "X is a father" and "X is a mother" as a "disjunct." Thus, the sentence "X is a father" can obviously be regarded as the first of the two disjuncts, while the sentence "X is a mother" is the second disjunct. Hence, for brevity, I thus refer respectively to the corresponding two parts of Shapiro's actual disjunctive definition (A. K. Shapiro & Morris, 1978):

> A *placebo* is defined as any therapy or component of therapy that is deliberately used for its nonspecific, psychological, or psychophysiological effect, or that is used for its presumed specific effect, but is without specific activity for the condition being treated. (p. 371)

Shapiro goes on to point out at once that the term "placebo" is used not only to characterize a treatment modality or therapy, but also a certain kind of experimental control:

> A *placebo*, when used as a control in experimental studies, is defined as a substance or procedure that is without specific activity for the condition being evaluated. (p. 371)

And then he tells us furthermore that

> A *placebo effect* is defined as the psychological or psychophysiological effect produced by placebos. (p. 371)

All of the conceptual puzzlement warranted by these three statements arises in the initial disjunctive definition of a "placebo therapy." For it should be noted that this definition employs the tantalizing words "non-specific effect," "specific effect," and "specific activity" in unstated *technical* senses. Once these terms are elucidated, the further definitions of a "placebo control" and of a "placebo effect" become conceptually unproblematic. Hence let us now concentrate on the disjunctive definition of a "placebo therapy," and see what help, if any, Shapiro gives us with the technical terms in which he has expressed it. Contrary to the belief of some others, I make bold to contend that his explicit comments on their intended construal still leaves them in an unsatisfactory logical state for the purposes at hand.

In their joint 1978 paper, A. K. Shapiro and Morris elaborate quite vaguely on the key concept of "specific activity" as follows:

> Specific activity is the therapeutic influence attributable solely to the contents or processes of the therapies rendered. The criterion for specific activity (and therefore the placebo effect) should be based on scientifically controlled studies. (p. 372)

They provide this characterization as part of a longer but very rough delineation of the complementary notions denoted by the terms "specific" and "nonspecific," locutions that are as pervasive as they are misleading or confusing in the literature on placebos. Thus, they make the following comment on the definition of "placebo" given above, which I amplify within brackets:

> Implicit in this definition is the assumption that active treatments [i.e., nonplacebos] may contain placebo components. Even with specific therapies [i.e., nonplacebos] results are apt to be due to the combination of both placebo and nonplacebo effects. Treatments that are devoid of active, specific components are known as pure placebos, whereas therapies that contain nonplacebo components are called impure placebos. . . . Treatments that have specific components but exert their effects primarily through nonspecific mechanisms are considered placebo therapies. . . .
>
> The key concept in defining placebo is that of "specific activity." In nonpsychological therapies, specific activity is often equated with nonpsychological mechanisms of action. When the specific activity of a treatment is psychological [i.e., in psychotherapies that derive therapeutic efficacy from those particular factors in the treatment that the pertinent theory singles out specifically as being remedial] this method of separating specific from nonspecific activity is no longer applicable. Therefore, a more general definition of specific activity is necessary. Specific activity is the therapeutic influence attributable solely to the contents or processes of the therapies rendered [i.e., the therapeutic influence, if any, that derives solely from those component factors of the therapy that are specifically singled out by its advocates as deserving credit for its presumed efficacy]. The criterion for specific activity (and therefore the placebo effect) should be based on scientifically controlled studies. . . . In behavior therapy, some investigators have utilized "active placebo" control groups whereby some aspects of the therapy affect behavior but those aspects differ from the theoretically relevant ingredients of concern to the investigator. (pp. 371–372)

This passage calls for clarification beyond what I have supplied within brackets. Yet, as the authors emphasize further on, it is in virtue of a treatment's *lack* of so-called "specific activity" for a given target disorder that this treatment *objectively* qualifies as a placebo, regardless of whether the dispensing physician believes the treatment to have actual placebo status or not. They import this emphasis on the irrelevance of belief to generic placebo *status* into their definition. There, in its first paragraph, a disjunction makes explicit provision for the presence of such belief on the part of the dispenser, as well as for its absence. In the first disjunct, it is a placebo that the physician *believes* himself or herself to be giving the patient, and the doctor is right in so believing. In the second disjunct, the physician believes himself or herself to be administering a *non*placebo, but he or she is definitely mistaken in so believing.

In either case, a placebo is actually being dispensed, be it wittingly or unwittingly. For brevity, I distinguish between the two situations to which these disjuncts pertain by saying that the treatment is an "intentional placebo" in the former case, while being an "inadvertent placebo" in the latter. Note that if a treatment t is actually not a placebo generically while its dispenser or even the whole professional community of practitioners believes t to be one, then t is precluded from qualifying as a "placebo" by the definition. To earn the label "intentional placebo," a treatment not only must be *believed* to be a placebo by its dispenser, but must also actually *be* one generically. Thus, therapists have administered a nonplacebo in the erroneous belief that it is a placebo. For example, at one time, some psychoanalysts used phenothiazines to treat schizophrenics in the belief that these drugs were mere (anger-reducing, tranquilizing) placebos; they presumed them to be ineffective for the psychic dissociation and the pathognomonic symptoms of schizophrenia. But controlled studies showed that these medications possessed a kind of therapeutic efficacy for the disorder that was not placebogenic (Davis & Cole, 1975a, 1975b).

Incidentally, besides not being placebos for schizophrenia, the pheno-thiazines turned out to be capable of inducing the negative side effects of parkinsonism, at least transiently (Blakiston's *Gould Medical Dictionary*, 1972, p. 1130). But the motor impairment manifested in parkinsonism is attributed to a deficiency of brain dopamine. Thus the unfavorable parkinsonian side effect of the phenothiazine drugs turned out to have *heuristic* value because it suggested that these drugs block the dopamine receptors in the brain. And since the drugs were also effective nonplacebos for schizophrenia, the parkinsonian side effect raised the possibility that an excess of dopamine might be implicated in the etiology of schizophrenia. In this way, a *biochemical* malfunction of the brain was envisioned quite specifically as causally relevant to this psychosis (Kolata, 1979).

Let me now specify the terminology and notation that I employ in my rectifying explication of "placebo," using the diagram shown in Figure 2-1. Overall, there is some stated or tacit therapeutic theory, which I call "ψ." Now ψ designs or recommends a particular treatment or therapy t for a particular illness or target disorder D. In the left-hand box of Figure 2-1, I generically depict a treatment modality or therapy t. Note that it contains a spectrum of ingredients or treatment factors. For example, the theory ψ may insist that if it is to recommend surgery for the treatment of gallstones, then the surgical process must obviously include the removal of the gallstones,

THERAPEUTIC THEORY Ψ

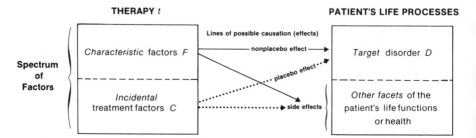

Figure 2-1. Illustration of therapeutic theory ψ, used in clarifying the definition of "placebo."

rather than a mere sham abdominal incision. I want a name for those treatment factors that a given theory ψ thus picks out as the defining characteristics of a given type of therapy *t*. And I call these factors the "characteristic factors *F*" of *t*. But ψ recognizes that besides the characteristic factors *F*, the given therapy normally also contains other factors, which it regards as just incidental. For example, a theory that deems the removal of gallstones to be therapeutic for certain kinds of pains and indigestion will assume that this abdominal surgery includes the administration of anesthesia to the patient. To take a quite different example, when Freud recommended psychoanalytic treatment, he insisted on the payment of a hefty fee, believing it to be perhaps a stimulus for overcoming the patient's neurotic resistances. Furthermore, a therapeutic theory may well allow that a given therapy includes not only known incidental factors, but also others that it has failed to recognize. And the letter *C* in the diagram, which labels "incidental treatment factors," is intended to apply to both known and unknown factors of this type.

Turning to the right-hand box in Figure 2-1, we note that the patient's life functions and activities are generically subdivided into two parts: the target disorder *D* at which the therapy *t* is aimed, and then the rest of his or her functions. But there may well be some vagueness in the circumscription of *D*. Both its pathognomonic symptoms and the presumed etiological process responsible for them will surely be included in the syndrome *D*. Yet some nosologists might include, while others exclude, certain accessory manifestations of *D* that are quite secondary, because they are also present in a number of other, nosologically distinct syndromes. Somewhat cognate conceptual problems of taxonomic circumscription arose in chemistry upon the discovery of isomerism, and even in the case of chemical isotopy.

Finally, in the middle of Figure 2-1, arrows represent some of the interesting possible causal influences or effects that may result from each of the two sets of treatment factors. Thus, one or more of the characteristic factors F may be remedial for the target disorder D, or the F factors may have no effect on D, or the F factors conceivably could make D even worse. By the same token, these factors F may have these three kinds of influence on other facets of the patient's health. And any of these latter effects—whether good or bad—will be called "side effects." Now if (and only if) one or more of the characteristic factors do have a positive therapeutic effect on the target disease D, then the therapy as a whole qualifies generically as a nonplacebo for D. This is the situation that is depicted in the diagram by the words "nonplacebo effect" in the horizontal solid arrow from F to D.

It is vital to realize that, in Figure 2-1, the causal arrows are intended to depict *possible* (imaginable) effects, such that the given treatment factors may have various sorts of positive *or* adverse effects on the target disorder, or on other facets of the patient's health. Thus, the diagram can be used to depict a nonplacebo therapy as well as a placebo therapy: In the former case, there is an actual beneficial causal influence by the characteristic factors on D, whereas in the latter case such an influence does not—as a matter of actual fact—exist, though it is imaginable (logically possible).

Similarly, the incidental treatment factors C may or may not have positive or negative effects on D. Furthermore, these factors C may have desirable or undesirable effects *outside* of D, which we again call side effects. If the incidental factors do have an effect on D, we can refer to that effect as a placebo effect, even if the therapy qualifies overall as a generic nonplacebo by containing therapeutically effective characteristic factors. For example, suppose that the characteristic factors in a certain chemotherapy are effective against a given kind of cancer, at least for a while, so that this chemotherapy is a nonplacebo for this affliction. Then this therapeutic effectiveness may well be *enhanced*, if the dispensing physician communicates his or her confidence in this therapy to the patient. And if there is such enhancement, the treatment factors C do indeed produce a positive placebo effect on D, a situation depicted in the diagram by the broken diagonal arrow. Thus we can say that *whether a given positive effect on D is or is not a placebo effect depends on whether it is produced by the incidental treatment factors or the characteristic ones*.

Let me now use the preceding informal preliminary account to give a more systematic and precise characterization of the genus placebo as well as of two of its species, thereby also revamping A. K. Shapiro's definitions.

A treatment process normally has a spectrum of constituent factors as well as a spectrum of effects when administered for the alleviation of a given target disorder D. Effects on the patient's health not pertaining to D are denominated "side effects." Though the term "side effects" often refers to *undesirable* effects outside D, there is neither good reason nor general agreement to restrict it in this way. As I soon illustrate, the therapeutic theory ψ that advocates the use of a particular treatment modality t to remedy D demands the inclusion of certain characteristic constituents F in any treatment process that ψ authenticates as an application of t. Any such process, besides qualifying as an instance of t according to ψ, will typically have constituents C, other than the characteristic ones F singled out by ψ. And when asserting that the factors F are remedial for D, ψ *may* also take cognizance of one or more of the noncharacteristic constituents C, which I denominate as "incidental." Thus, ψ may perhaps attribute certain side effects to either F or C. Indeed, it may even maintain that one or another of the incidental factors affects D—say, by enhancing the remedial effects that it claims for F. In short, if a doctor is an adherent of ψ, it may well furnish him or her with a therapeutic rationale for administering t to a patient afflicted by D, *or* for refraining from doing so.

For instance, consider pharmacological treatment, such as the dispensation of digitoxin for congestive heart dysfunction or of nitroglycerin for angina pectoris. Then it is perfectly clear that the water with which such tablets are swallowed, and the patient's awareness of the reputation of the prescribing cardiologist, for example, are incidental treatment factors, while the designated chemical ingredients are characteristic ones. But Freud also specified these two different sorts of treatment factors in the nonpharmacological case of psychoanalytic treatment, while recognizing that some of the incidental factors may serve initially as catalysts or icebreakers for the operation of the characteristic ones. Thus, he identified the characteristic constituents as the educative and affect-discharging lifting of the patient's presumed repressions, effected by means of overcoming ("working through") the analysand's resistance to their conscious recognition in the context of "resolving" his or her "transference" behavior toward the doctor. And he depicted the patient's faith in the analyst, and the derivation of emotional support from that authority figure, as mere catalysts or icebreakers in the initial stage of treatment—factors that are incidental, because they are avowedly quite incapable of extirpating the pathogenic causes, as distinct from producing merely cosmetic and temporary relief.

Hence Freud stressed tirelessly that the patient's correct, affect-discharging insight into the etiology of his or her affliction is the one quintessential ingredient that distinguishes the remedial dynamics of his treatment modality from any kind of treatment by suggestion. Treatments by suggestion, he charged, leave the pathogenic repressions intact, and yield only an ephemeral cosmetic prohibition of the symptoms (see Grünbaum, 1984). In the same vein, Freud came to maintain early in his career that the characteristic factors of Erb's electro-therapy for nervous disorders were therapeutically unavailing, and that any gains from treatment with that electric apparatus were achieved by its incidental factors.

Explications

The schematic diagram in Figure 2-1 can serve as a kind of glossary for the notations ψ, t, F, and C that I have introduced. Using this notation, I now offer the following explications, which supersede those I have offered earlier

(Grünbaum, 1981). In the first of these explications, the fourth condition (d) is somewhat tentative:

1. A treatment process *t* characterized as having constituents *F*, but also possessing other, perhaps unspecified incidental constituents *C*, will be said to be an "intentional placebo" with respect to a target disorder *D*, suffered by a victim *V* and treated by a dispensing practitioner *P*, just when the following conditions are jointly satisfied: (a) None of the characteristic treatment factors *F* are remedial for *D*; (b) *P* believes that the factors *F* indeed all *fail* to be remedial for *D*; (c) but *P* also believes that—at least for a certain type of victim *V* of *D*—t is nonetheless therapeutic for *D* by virtue of containing some perhaps even unknown incidental factors *C* different from *F*; and (d) yet *P* abets or at least acquiesces in the patient's belief that *t* has remedial efficacy for *D* by virtue of some constituents that belong to the set of characteristic factors *F* in *t*.

Note that the first of these four conditions explicates what it is for a treatment type *t* to have the objective generic property of being a placebo with respect to a given target disorder *D*. The objective property in question is just that the characteristic constituents *F* of *t* are actually not remedial for *D*. On the other hand, the remaining three of the four conditions describe the property of belonging to the species of intentional placebo, over and above being a placebo generically. And clearly these three further conditions pertain to the beliefs and intentions of the practitioners who dispense *t* and of the patients who receive it. But notice that the fourth condition would require modification, if there were enough cases, as has been claimed, in which a patient may benefit therapeutically even after being *told* that he or she is receiving a generic placebo. On the other hand, the fourth condition apparently still suffices to cover those cases in which surgeons perform appendectomies or tonsillectomies solely at the behest of their patients, who, in turn, may be egged on by their families. The need to accommodate such interventions has been stressed by Piechowiak (1982, 1983).

The caveat regarding the fourth condition (d) is occasioned by a report (Park & Covi, 1965) on an exploratory and "paradoxical" study of 15 adult neurotic outpatients, who presented with anxiety symptoms. The treating therapists did provide support and reassurance, yet "the responsibility for improvement was thrown back to the patient by means of the paradoxical statement that he needed treatment but that he could improve with a [placebo] capsule containing no drug" (p. 344). Of the 14 patients who remained willing to receive the capsules for a week, 6 *disbelieved* the purported pharmacological inertness of the capsules, and 3 of them even experienced "side-reactions," which they attributed to the pills (p. 342). But the three patients who did firmly believe in the doctor's candid disclosure of inertness improved after 1 week, no less than the "sceptics," who thought they were receiving an effective nonplacebo after all. Hence Park and Covi concluded that "unawareness of the inert nature of the placebo is not an indispensable condition for improvement on placebo" (p. 342). Yet, as these authors acknowledged at once, in so small a sample of patients, improvement may have occurred "in spite of" the disclosure as a matter of course, under *any* sort of treatment or even as a matter of spontaneous remission. And since it is quite unclear whether the moral drawn by Park and Covi is at all generalizable beyond their sample, I have let the fourth condition stand.

Piechowiak (1983) also calls attention to uses of diagnostic procedures (e.g., endoscopy, stomach X-rays) when deemed unnecessary by the physician, but demanded by the anxious patient suffering from, say, cancerphobia, who may even believe them to be therapeutic. In the latter sort of instance, the gastroenterologist may justify an invasive procedure to himself or herself and the patient, because when the expected negative finding materializes, it may alleviate the patient's anxiety as well as the vexatious somatic effects of that anxiety. In some cases (e.g., Wassermann test for syphilis), the patient may be under no illusions as to the dynamics by which this relief was wrought, any more than the doctor. But Piechowiak is concerned to point out that in other cases (e.g., angiography), the patient may well conceptualize the diagnostic intervention as *itself* therapeutic. And hence this author suggests the assimilation of these latter cases to intentional placebos. In this way, he suggests, account can be taken of the cognizance taken by doctors of the therapeutic beliefs of their patients—beliefs that are psychological realities, even if they are scientifically untutored.

As we have seen, a particular treatment modality t derives its identity from the full set of its characteristic treatment factors, as singled out by the therapeutic theory that advocates the use of t in stated circumstances. Hence therapies will be distinct, provided that they differ in at least one character-istic factor. By the same token, therapies whose distinct identities are specified in each case by two or more characteristic factors can have at least one such factor in common without detriment to their distinctness, just as they can thus share one or more incidental factors. Indeed, as I illustrate later, a shared factor that counts as characteristic of one therapy may qualify as merely incidental to another. And clearly these statements concerning factors common to distinct therapies hold for somatic medicine and psychotherapy alike.

Thus, in *either* of these two classes of healing interventions, a therapy that qualifies as a nonplacebo for a certain target D derives precisely this therapeutic status from the remedial efficacy of some or all of its character-istic factors. Yet it may share these efficacious ingredients with other, distinct therapies that differ from it in at least one characteristic factor. In fact, one or all of the common factors may count as only incidental to some of the other therapies. And it is to be borne in mind that a therapy having at least one remedial characteristic ingredient is generically a nonplacebo, even if the remaining characteristic factors are otiose. Hence a therapy t can be a nonplacebo with respect to a particular D, even if all of its efficacious characteristic treatment ingredients are common to both t and distinct other therapies!

Unfortunately, Critelli and Neumann (1984) run afoul of this important state of affairs by concluding incorrectly that "the common-factors criterion . . . appears to be the most viable current definition of the placebo for the study of psychotherapy" (p. 35). They see themselves as improving on A. K. Shapiro's explication of the placebo concept, at least for psychotherapy. Yet they actually impoverish it by advocating the so-called "common-factors definition" (for psychotherapy), which they do not even *state*, and by altogether failing to render the two species of placebo adumbrated in the 1978 definition given by A. K. Shapiro and Morris. Besides, Critelli and Neumann contend that Shapiro's explication of the notion of a generic placebo suffers from his abortive attempt to encompass somatic medicine and psychotherapy simultaneously. But once I have completed my thorough recasting of Shapiro's pioneering definition below, it will be clear that—contrary to Critelli and Neumann—his endeavor to cover medicine and psychotherapy with one definitional stroke is *not* one of the defects of his explication.

Turning now to placebo *controls*, we must bear in mind that to assess the remedial merits of a given therapy t^* for some D, it is imperative to disentangle from each other two sorts of possible positive effects as follows: (1) Those desired effects on D, if any, actually wrought by the characteristic factors of t^*; and (2) improvements produced by the expectations aroused in both the doctor and the patient by their belief in the therapeutic efficacy of t^*. To achieve just such a disentanglement, the baseline measure (2) can be furnished by using a generic placebo t in a double-blind study on a control group of persons suffering from D. For ethical reasons, informed consent has presumably been secured from a group of such patients to be "blindly" allocated to either the control group or the experimental group. By subtracting the therapeutic gains with respect to D in the former group from those in the latter, investigators can obtain the sought-after measure (1) of the incremental remedial potency of the characteristic factors in t^*. And, for brevity, one can then say that with respect to D, the generic placebo t functions as a "placebo control" in the experimental evaluation of the therapeutic value of t^* as such.

As will be recalled, the relevant definition of that term given by A. K. Shapiro and Morris (1978, p. 371) reads as follows: "A placebo, when used as a control in experimental studies, is defined as a substance or procedure that is without specific activity for the condition being evaluated." But just this characterization of a "placebo control," as used in experimental studies in medicine or psychotherapy, is in dire need of emendation. As they would have it, "the condition" D is "being evaluated" in an experimental study employing a placebo control. But surely what is being evaluated instead is the conjectured therapeuticity of a designated treatment t^* (substance, procedure) for D. And I suggest that their definition of a placebo control be recast as follows: A treatment type t functions as a "placebo control" in a given context of experimental inquiry, which is designed to evaluate the characteristic therapeutic efficacy of another modality t^* for a target disorder

D, just when the following requirements are jointly satisfied: (1) *t* is a *generic placebo* for *D*, as defined under the first condition (a) in the definition above of "intentional placebo"; (2) the experimental investigator conducting the stated controlled trial of *t** believes that *t* is not only a generic placebo for *D*, but also is generally quite harmless to those victims of *D* who have been chosen for the control group. And, as I have noted, the investigator's reason for using *t* as a placebo control when evaluating the characteristic therapeutic value of *t** for *D* is as follows: Especially if *t** is expensive or fraught with negative side effects, clinicians wish to know to what extent, if any, the beneficial effects on *D* due to its characteristic treatment factors *exceed* those produced by its incidental ones.

When schematized in this way, some of the complexities inherent in the notion of a placebo control are not apparent. To their credit, Critelli and Neumann (1984) have perceptively called attention to some of the essential refinements in psychotherapy research:

> [I]t is imperative that test procedures be compared to realistic placebo controls. Too often in the past, false claims of incremental effectiveness have resulted from the experimental use of placebos that even the most naive would not mistake for genuine therapy. There appears to be a tendency for experimental placebos to be in some sense weaker, less credible, or applied in a less enthusiastic manner than treatments that have been offered as actual therapies. At a minimum, placebo controls should be equivalent to test procedures on all major recognized common factors. These might include induced expectancy of improvement; credibility of rationale; credibility of procedures; demand for improvement; and therapist attention, enthusiasm, effort, perceived belief in treatment procedures, and commitment to client improvement. (p. 38)

Having issued this salutary caveat, these authors claim that "current [psycho]therapies have yet to meet the challenge of demonstrating incremental effects" (p. 38). Yet one of the reasons they go on to give for posing this challenge relies on their belief that treatment factors common to two or more therapies *must* be—in my parlance—incidental rather than characteristic ingredients. As I have pointed out, however, formulations invoking this belief tend to darken counsel. But here, placebo control cannot be *doubly* blind.

Suedfeld (1984) likewise addresses methodological (and also ethical) problems arising in the employment of placebo controls to evaluate psychotherapy. As he sees it, "the necessity for equating the expectancy of the active [nonplacebo] and placebo treatment groups implies the acceptance of the null hypothesis, a position that is better avoided" (p. 161). To implement this avoidance, he advocates the use of a "subtractive expectancy placebo," which he describes as follows:

> It consists of administering an active, specific therapeutic procedure but introducing it with the orientation that it is inert with respect to the problem being treated. In other words, the client is led to expect less of an effect than the treatment is known to produce. The Subtractive Expectancy Procedure avoids the need to invent or find an inert technique, attempts to create initial differences

in expectancy which can be substantiated by the rejection of the null hypothesis, and also makes it feasible to assess the specific effect of an active treatment in a design with one treated and one untreated (control) group. (p. 161)

Here I am not concerned with the pros and cons of the subtractive expectancy placebo procedure advocated by Suedfeld, *qua* alternative to the null hypothesis on which my definition above of a "placebo control" is implicitly predicated. Whatever that balance of investigative cogency, there can be little doubt that some of the ideas in Suedfeld's paper are illuminating or at least suggestive. Besides, I appreciate his several citations of my initial paper, "The Placebo Concept" (Grünbaum, 1981). There I made concrete proposals for the replacement of the standard technical vocabulary used in the placebo literature, precisely because of the Tower of Babel situation that is engendered by it, as I documented there.

Alas, in criticism of Suedfeld, I must point out that his exposition is genuinely marred by just the penalties of ambiguity, obscurity, and confusion exacted by the received placebo vocabulary, because he unfortunately chooses to retain that infelicitous terminology for the formulation of his ideas. As we shall see in due course, the terms "active," "specific," and "nonspecific" are especially insidious locutions in this context. Yet these ill-fated terms, and their cognates or derivatives, abound in Suedfeld's presentation. In any case, so much for the notion of a placebo control.

Recently there have been interesting conjectures as to the identity of the incidental constituents C that confer somatic remedial potency on medications qualifying as intentional placebos with respect to certain implicit therapeutic theories. It has been postulated (Brody, 1979) that, when present, such therapeutic efficacy derives from the placebo's psychogenic activation of the secretion of substances as follows: (1) pain-killing endorphins, which are endogenous opiate-like substances; (2) interferon, which counters viral infections; and (3) steroids, which reduce inflammations. Indeed, the physiological mechanisms involved are believed to be operative as well in the so-called miracle cures by faith healers, holy waters, and so-called quacks. As an example, there is evidence from a study of dental postoperative pain (Levine, Gordon, & Fields, 1978) that endorphin release does mediate placebo-induced analgesia. And this suggests analgesic research focusing on variables that affect endorphin activity (Levine, Gordon, Bornstein, & Fields, 1979).

So far I have explicated only the first disjunct in the misleading definition given by A. K. Shapiro and Morris (1978). Hence let me now explicate their second disjunct, which pertains to the second species of placebo.

2. A treatment process t characterized as having constituents F will be said to be an "inadvertent placebo" with respect to a target disorder D, suffered by a victim V and treated by a dispensing practitioner P, just when each of the following three conditions is satisfied: (a) None of the characteristic treatment factors F are remedial for D; (b) but—at least for a certain type of victim V of D—P credits these very factors F with being therapeutic for D, and indeed he or she deems at least some of them to be causally *essential* to the remedial efficacy of t; also (c) V believes that t derives remedial efficacy for D from constituents belonging to t's characteristic factors.

It is to be clearly understood that, as before, the first condition (a) codifies the *generic* property of being a placebo. The second condition (b) of this second explication renders the following: P denies that t's efficacy might derive mainly from its incidental constituents. Here the third condition (c) is subject to the same caveat (Park & Covi, 1965) that I have issued for the fourth condition (d) in my first explication above.

Clarifying Comments

Let me now add four sets of clarifying comments on my explications, because of questions put to me by Edward Erwin (1981), a philosopher of psychology.

1. Clearly, it was the intentional species of placebo that was denoted by the term "placebo" in its original pharmacological use. And its use in A. K. Shapiro's definition to denote as well what I have called the inadvertent species constitutes a *generalization* of the genus placebo, prompted by the sobering lessons of the history of medicine. But the tacit intuitions of many people as to what a placebo is are strongly geared to its original status in pharmacology. No wonder that these intuitions call for identifying the intentional species of placebo with the entire genus. Consequently, some people will be ruffled by the fact that in my explication of the *generalized* use of the term, the generic property of being a placebo is, of course, considerably less restrictive than the property of being an intentional placebo. For, as is clear from the codification of the generic placebo property in the first condition (a) of both of my explications, any treatment t qualifies generically as a placebo for a given target disorder D merely on the strength of the failure of *all* of its characteristic factors F to be remedial for D. But once the source of the counterintuitiveness is recognized, it should be dispelled and should occasion no objection to my explication of the generic property. Moreover, as is evident from the first paragraph in Shapiro's definition, when the term "placebo" refers to a therapy, it is frequently used in medicine and psychiatry to refer to either of the two species of my explication, rather than to its genus. Furthermore, in the generalized generic sense of "placebo," a treatment t does belong to the genus placebo even if its characteristic factors exacerbate D, since exacerbation is a particularly strong way of failing to be remedial for D. And the failure of a practitioner who dispenses *such* a treatment in good faith as an inadvertent placebo to be cognizant of this ill effect hardly detracts from t's objective status as a generic placebo. Nor does the malaise of those who would invoke the favorable etymological significance of the term "placebo" in order to forbid a generalized generic concept that fails to exclude the envisaged untoward case. Either species of placebos can *undesignedly* exacerbate D! History teaches that many treatments were worse than useless.

2. There are treatments only *some* of whose characteristic factors F are therapeutic for a given D, while the therapeutic theory ψ that advocates their dispensation claims that *all* of the factors F are thus remedial. For example, it has recently been claimed (Kazdin & Wilson, 1978) that in the systematic desensitization brand of behavior therapy, which is an effective treatment for certain phobias, only one of its three F factors is thus therapeutic, while the other two appear unavailing. What, it might be asked, is the classificatory verdict of my explication as to whether a therapy whose characteristic factors comprise both efficacious and otiose members qualifies generically as a nonplacebo?

To answer this question, note that within the class of treatments for any given D, any member t will belong to the genus placebo exactly when *none* of its characteristic factors are remedial for D. Therefore any therapy whose characteristic factors include *at least one* that is therapeutic for D will pass muster as a nonplacebo. Evidently it is not necessary for being a nonplacebo that all of the F factors be remedial. It follows that, in the absence of further information, the designation of a given therapy—such as desensitization in the example above—as a nonplacebo does not tell us whether only some of its characteristic factors are remedial or whether all of them are. But this fact hardly militates against either my explication or the usefulness of the concept of nonplacebo as rendered by it.

Upon recalling A. K. Shapiro and Morris's cited characterizations of "pure" and "impure" placebos (1978, p. 372), we see that my construal of the generic placebo notion explicates what they call a "pure placebo." Their "impure placebos" are, as they put it vaguely, "treatments that have specific components but exert their effects primarily through nonspecific mechanisms" (p. 372). This sort of treatment does count as a nonplacebo, according to my formulation. But my parlance can readily characterize their so-called impure placebos by saying the following: Although the characteristic ingredients of these therapies do make some therapeutic contribution, this remedial effect is exceeded by the therapeutic benefit deriving from the *incidental* treatment factors. This quantitative vagueness is, of course, not my problem but theirs.

3. It must not be overlooked that my explication of placebo is relativized not only to a given target disorder D, but also to those characteristic factors that are singled out from a particular treatment process by a specified therapeutic theory ψ. It is therefore not my explication but a given theory ψ that determines which treatment factors are to be classified as the characteristic factors in any one case. And by the same token, as I illustrate presently, the given therapeutic theory ψ (in medicine or psychiatry) rather than my explication determines whether any factors in the

physician–patient relationship are to count as only "incidental." Clearly, for example, a particular psychiatric theory might well designate some such factors as being characteristic. And just this sort of fact prompted A. K. Shapiro and Morris to disavow the common restriction of "specific activity" to "nonpsychological mechanisms of action," and to offer their "more general definition of specific activity" cited above.

The divergence between Jerome Frank's (1973) theory of healing as persuasion on the one hand, and such psychotherapeutic theories as Freud's or Hans Eysenck's on the other, will now serve to illustrate three important points as follows: (a) As is evident from my explication, it is the given therapeutic theory ψ rather than my explication of placebo that decides *which* treatment factors are to be respectively classified as "characteristic" and as "incidental." (b) Precisely because my analysis of the placebo concept does make explicit provision for the dependence of the memberships of these classes on the particular theory ψ at hand, it allows for the fact that rival therapeutic theories can *disagree* in regard to their classification of particular treatment factors as "characteristic," no less than in their attribution of significant therapeutic efficacy to such factors. (c) Hence, the relativization of the placebo attribute to a given theory ψ that is built into my explication provides prophylaxis against seeming inconsistencies and confusions, generated when investigators want to assess the generic placebo status of a therapy t across rival therapeutic theories and without regard to whether these theories use different characteristic factors to identify t.

In the language and notions of my explications, Jerome Frank's (1973, pp. xv–xx) view of the therapeutic status of the leading rival psychotherapies can now be outlined. For *each* of these treatment modalities t and its underlying theory ψ, he hypothesizes that t is as follows:

1. A generic placebo with respect to the characteristic treatment factors singled out by *its own* particular ψ.
2. An inadvertent placebo with respect to the beliefs of those dispensers of t who espouse ψ.
3. Therapeutically effective to the extent that the patient's hope is aroused by the doctor's healing symbols, which mobilize the patient's sense of mastery of his or her demoralization.

As is clear from the third item, Frank credits a treatment ingredient *common* to the rival psychotherapies with such therapeutic efficacy as they do possess. But his categorization of each of these therapies as a generic placebo rather than as a nonplacebo is now seen to derive just from the fact that he is tacitly classifying as "incidental," rather than as "characteristic," all those treatment factors that he deems to be therapeutic. In adopting this latter classification, he is speaking the classificatory language employed by the theories underlying the various therapies, although he denies their claim that the treatment ingredients they label "characteristic" are actually effective.

Yet in a language suited to Frank's own therapeutic tenets, it would, of course, be entirely natural to label as "characteristic" just those treatment factors that his own theory T deems remedial, even though these same ingredients count as merely incidental within each of the psychotherapeutic theories rejected by him. And if Frank were to couch his own T in that new classificatory language, then he would no longer label the leading psycho-therapies as generic placebos, although he would be holding the same therapeutic beliefs as before.

It should now be clear that by explicitly relativizing to a given ψ the classification of particular treatment factors as "characteristic" or "inci-dental," no less than by relativizing their respective therapeutic efficacy to a particular D, my explication obviates the following sort of question, which is being asked across unspecified, tacitly presupposed therapeutic theories: If the effectiveness of a placebo modality depends on its symbolization of the physician's healing power, should this ingredient not be considered a *characteristic* treatment factor?

4. In a paper devoted mainly to the ethical complexities of using placebo control groups in psychotherapy research, O'Leary and Borkovec (1978) write: "Because of problems in devising a theoretically and practically inert placebo, we recommend that the term *placebo* be abandoned in psychotherapy research" (p. 823). And they propose to "circumvent the ethical concerns inherent in placebo methodology" (p. 825) by devising alternative methods of research control. In this way, they hope to assure as well that "the confusion associated with the term *placebo* would be avoided" (p. 823).

But I hope it will become clear from my comparison of my explications above with the usual parlance in the literature that these confusions indeed can be avoided without abandoning the placebo concept in any sort of therapeutic research. Nor do I see why the theoretical identification of a particular incidental treatment factor that is effective for D rather than "inert" ever has to be detrimental to therapeutic research.

Logical Defects of Received Vocabulary

On the basis of my explications, I can now make two sets of comments on the logical defects of the key locutions commonly employed as technical terms throughout the medical and psychiatric literature on placebos.

1. We are told that any effect that a placebo has on the target disorder D is "nonspecific." But a placebo can have an effect on D that is no less sharply defined and precisely known than the effect of a nonplacebo. To take a simple example, consider two patients A and B suffering from ordinary tension headaches of comparable severity. Suppose that A unwittingly swallows the proverbial sugar pill and gets no relief from it, because it is indeed pharmacologically "inert" or useless for such a headache *qua* mere sugar pill. A stoically endures his or her discomfort. Assume further that B

consults his or her physician, who is very cautious. Mindful of the potential side effects of tranquilizers and analgesics, the doctor decides to employ a bit of benign deceit and gives B a few lactose pills without disabusing B of his or her evident belief that he or she is receiving a physician's sample of analgesics. Posit that shortly after B takes the first of these sugar pills, the headache disappears altogether. Assume further that B's headache would not have disappeared just then from mere internal causes. Both of these conditions might well apply in a given case. Thus B assumedly received the same headache relief from the mere sugar pill as he or she would have received if a pharmacologically *non*inert drug had been slipped into his food without his knowledge.

Clearly, in some such situations, the therapeutic effect of the sugar pill placebo on the headache can have attributes fully as sharply defined or "specific" as the effect that would have been produced by a so-called "active" drug like aspirin (Frank, 1973). Moreover, this placebogenic effect can be just as precisely described or known as the nonplacebogenic effect of aspirin. In either case, the effect is complete headache relief, even though the sugar pill as such is, of course, pharmacologically inert for headaches, whereas aspirin as such is pharmacologically efficacious. It is therefore at best very misleading to describe as "nonspecific" the effect that the placebo produces on the target disorder, while describing the at least qualitatively like effect of the nonplacebo as "specific." Yet just such a use of the terms "nonspecific" and "specific" as modifiers of the term "effect" is made in A. K. Shapiro's above-cited definition of "placebo," in a leading treatise on pharmacological therapeutics (Goodman & Gilman, 1975), in a German work on psychoanalysis (Möller, 1978), in a German survey article on placebos (Piechowiak, 1983), and in a very recent article on treatments to reduce high blood pressure (A. P. Shapiro, Schwartz, & Ferguson, 1977). Equally infelicitously, Schwartz (1978, p. 83) speaks of a "nonspecific placebo response." Why describe a treatment effect as "nonspecific" in order to convey that the incidental treatment factors, rather than the characteristic elements, were the ones that produced it? Relatedly, Klein (1980) points out that when a placebo counteracts demoralization in a depressed person, it is wrong-headed to describe this therapeutic outcome as a "nonspecific" effect. After all, the demoralization and the effect on it are quite specific in the ordinary sense.

Worse, as it stands, the locution "specific effect" is quite ambiguous as between the following two very different senses: (a) The therapeutic effect on D is wrought by the characteristic ("specific") factors F of the therapy t; *or* (b) the remedial effectiveness of t is specific to a quite small number of disorders, to the exclusion of a far more multitudinous set of nosologically different afflictions and of their respective pathognomonic symptoms. Most writers on placebos, though not all, intend the first construal when speaking of "specific effect." But, as we shall see in greater detail further on, according to whether the effects of a given therapy are or are not believed to be "specific" in the second sense above, Brody (1977, pp. 40–43) classifies that *therapy* as a "specific therapy" or as a "general therapy." And he wishes to allow for the fact that the placebogenic remedial efficacy of the proverbial sugar pill is presumed to range over a larger number of target ailments than the nonplacebogenic efficacy of widely used medications (e.g., penicillin). In an endeavor to make such an allowance, he uses the belief in the ability of a therapy to engender "specific effects" in the second sense above as the touchstone of its being a nonplacebo. How much better it would be, therefore, if students of placebo phenomena banished the seriously ambiguous use of "specific" as a technical term altogether.

As if this degree of technical confusion were not enough, the misleading use of "specific" in the sense of "nonplacebo" is sometimes encountered alongside the use of "specific" in the usual literal sense of "precise" or "well defined." Thus, when Miller (1980) writes that "placebo effects can be quite specific" (p. 476), the illustrations he goes on to give show that here "specific" has the force of "quantitatively precise." But in the very next paragraph, he uses the term "specific" as a synonym for "nonplacebo" when reporting that "it is only in the past 80 years that physicians have been able to use an appreciable number of treatments with specific therapeutic effects" (p. 476).

Indeed, the placebo researcher Beecher (1972), who is renowned for investigating the role of placebos in the reduction of pain, entitled one of his essays "The Placebo Effect as a Non-Specific Force Surrounding Disease and the Treatment of Disease." But even metaphorically and elliptically, it seems inappropriate to speak of the placebo effect as being a nonspecific *force*, as Beecher (1972) does repeatedly.

2. A. K. Shapiro and Morris (1978) tell us in their definition that a placebo "is without specific activity for the condition being treated." And, as we recall, they contrast "active treatments" with placebos by saying that "active treatments may contain placebo components" (p. 371). Yet they also tell us that "in behavior therapy, some investigators have utilized 'active placebo' control groups" in which "some aspects of the therapy affect behavior but those aspects differ from the theoretically relevant ingredients of concern to the investigator" (p. 372). Furthermore, in the common parlance employed by two other investigators, even placebos that are acknowledged to be "potently therapeutic" or "effective" (for angina pectoris) are incongruously dubbed "inactive" just because they are placebos (Benson & McCallie, 1979). And Beecher (1972) emphasizes that some placebos are capable of "*powerful action*" (p. 178; italics in original), while contrasting them with treatments that he and others call "active" to convey that they are indeed nonplacebos.

By contrast to Beecher's use of "active," Bok (1974) tells us that any medical procedure, "whether it is active or inactive, can serve as a placebo whenever it has no specific effect on the condition for which it is prescribed" (p. 17). Thus, in Bok's parlance, placebos may be said to be "active" (p. 17) and "placebos can be effective" (p. 18), but they must be devoid of so-called "specific effect." But just what is it for a placebo to be "active"? Clearly, a placebo therapy as a whole *might* be productive of (remedial or deleterious) effects on the target disorder while being devoid of significant (negative or positive) side effects, or it may have only side effects. On the other hand, it might have both kinds of effects. And it matters therapeutically, of course, which of these effects—if either—are produced by any particular placebo. Hence clarity will be notably served by explicitly indicating the *respect* in which a given placebo intervention is being said to be "active." Yet such explicitness is lacking when Bok tells us, for example, that there is a clear-cut "potential for damage by an active drug given as a placebo" (p. 20). Thus it is only a conjecture just what she intends the term "active" to convey in the latter context: Is it that there are pharmacologically induced side effects in addition to placebogenic effects on the target disorder D? By the same token, her usage of "inactive" is unclear when she reports that "even inactive placebos can have toxic effects" (p. 20), even though she goes on to give what she takes to be an illustration. Bok's concern with placebos focuses, however, on ethically questionable dispensations of intentional placebos.

Evidently there are divergences among writers on placebos in regard to the usage of the term "active." But they tell us in one voice, as Bok does, that a placebo procedure "has no specific effect on the condition for which it is prescribed" (p. 17). To this conceptually dissonant discourse, I say: In the case of a placebo it is, of course, recognized that incidental treatment factors *may* be potently remedial for D, although the characteristic ones by definition are not. And if some of the incidental constituents are thus therapeutic, then the actual specificity of their activity—in the ordinary sense of "specificity"—clearly does *not* depend on whether the pertinent therapeutic theory ψ is able either to specify their particular identity or to afford understanding of their detailed mode of action. Hence if some of the incidental constituents of t are remedial but presently do elude the grasp of ψ, the current inability of ψ to pick them out from the treatment process hardly lessens the objective specificity of their identity, mode of action, or efficacy. A theory's current inability to spell out certain causal factors and to articulate their mode of action because of ignorance is surely not tantamount to their being themselves objectively "nonspecific" as to their identity, over and above being unknown! At worst, the details of the operation of the incidental factors are left unspecified.

Hence, despite the assumed present inability of the pertinent theory ψ to spell out which particular incidental constituents render the given placebo remedial for D, it is at best needlessly obscure to say that these constituents are "without specific activity" for D and are "nonspecific." *A fortiori*, it is infelicitous to declare of any and every placebo treatment modality as a whole that, *qua* being a placebo, it must be devoid of "specific activity." It would seem that when speaking generically of a placebo, the risk of confusion as well as outright unsound claims can be obviated by steadfast avoidance of the term "nonspecific activity." Instead, as I have argued earlier, the objective genus property of being a placebo should be codified as follows: With respect to the target disorder D, the treatment modality t belongs to the genus placebo just when its characteristic constituents *fail* to be remedial for D. Furthermore, clarity is served by using the term "incidental" rather than "nonspecific" when speaking of those treatment constituents that differ from the characteristic ones. In short, the generic distinction between placebos and nonplacebos has nothing whatever to do with the contrast between nonspecificity and specificity, but only with whether the characteristic treatment factors do play a therapeutic role for D or not. So much for my proposed rectifications of the misleading conceptualizations conveyed by the standard locutions whose confusion I have laid bare.

CLARIFYING RAMIFICATIONS OF MY EXPLICATIONS

As is clear from my formulation, the genus property of being a placebo is altogether independent of the belief of the dispensing practitioner as to whether the treatment in question is a placebo. But, equally clearly, the species property of being an inadvertent placebo is explicitly relativized to this belief, no less than the species property of being an intentional one. Thus, a placebo treatment t that qualifies as inadvertent with respect to one school of therapeutic thought may be explicitly avowed to have intentional placebo status in the judgment of another school. By the same token, advocates of t who do not even entertain the possibility of its being a placebo will be preoccupied with its characteristic constituents, to the likely disregard of incidental factors in t that may turn out to be remedially potent for D. Consequently, if patients who received treatment t register gains, such advocates will erroneously discount any remedial efficacy actually possessed by these incidental factors. Moreover, these theoreticians will give undeserved credit to the characteristic factors for any successful results that issue from t. As recounted in Beecher's classic 1961 paper "Surgery as Placebo," which is summarized by Benson and McCallie (1979), the history of surgical treatment for angina pectoris in the United States during the mid-1950s furnishes a clear case in point.

Proponents of ligating the internal mammary artery claimed that this procedure facilitated increased coronary blood flow through collateral vessels near the point of ligation, thereby easing the ischemia of the heart muscle to which angina pectoris is due. And these enthusiasts then credited that ligation with the benefits exhibited by their surgical patients. But well-controlled, though ethically questionable, studies by skeptical surgeons in the late 1950s showed the following: When a mere sham bilateral skin incision was made on a comparison group of angina patients, then ligation of the internal mammary artery in randomly selected other angina patients yielded only equal or even less relief from angina than the sham surgery.

Furthermore, the quality of the results achieved by the intentional placebo surgery was dramatic and sustained: Apart from subjective improvement, the deceived recipients of the sham surgery had increased exercise tolerance, registered less nitroglycerin usage, and improved electrocardiographically. Moreover, a similar lesson emerges from the use of a related surgical procedure due to Vineberg, in which the internal mammary artery was implanted into a tunnel burrowed into the myocardium. The results from this Vineberg operation (Benson & McCallie, 1979) suggest that placebogenic relief occurred even in a sizeable majority of angina patients who had angiographically verified coronary artery disease. This history has a sobering moral: It bears further monitoring to what extent the positive results from coronary artery bypass surgery are placebogenic.

Now consider those who allow that such beneficial efficacy as a therapy t has could well be placebogenic. This group may thereby be led to draw the true conclusion that the characteristic factors do not merit any therapeutic credit. On the other hand, the therapeutic efficacy of a nonplacebo is enhanced if its incidental factors *also* have a remedial effect of their own. Thus, it has been found (Gallimore & Turner, 1977) that the attitudes of physicians toward chemotherapy commonly contribute significantly to the effectiveness of nonplacebo drugs. Again, Wheatley (1967) reported that in the treatment of anxiety by one particular nonplacebo drug, enthusiastic physicians got better results than unenthusiastic ones, although enthusiasm did not enhance the positive effect of tricyclic antidepressants on depression. Indeed, there may be synergism between the characteristic and incidental treatment factors, such that they potentiate each other therapeutically with respect to the *same* target disorder.

On the other hand, one and the same treatment may be a placebo with respect to the target disorder and yet may function as a nonplacebo for a secondary ailment. For example, when a viral cold is complicated by the presence of a secondary bacterial infection, a suitable antibiotic may serve as an intentional placebo for the viral cold while also acting as a nonplacebo for the bacterial infection. This case spells an important moral: It serves to discredit the prevalent stubborn refusal to relativize the placebo status of a medication or intervention to a stated target disorder, a relativization I have explicitly built into my definitions. For example, in the misguided effort to escape such relativization, Piechowiak (1983, p. 40) is driven to classify antibiotics as "false placebos." As he sees it, they are placebos because they are not pharmacologically effective for the typical sort of upper respiratory viral infection; but what makes them "false" placebos, in his view, is that they *are* pharmacologically potent (genuine medications, or, in the original German, *"echte Pharmaka"*) for other diseases (e.g., bacterial pneumonia).

But, according to this reasoning, "false" placebos are quite common. A telling illustration is provided by the following story reported by Jennifer Worrall, a British physician (Worrall, 1983). One of her patients, a middle-aged woman, complained of a superficial varicose leg ulcer. As Worrall relates,

> [The patient] was very demanding and difficult to please and claimed to suffer continuous agony from her ulcer (although there were none of the objective signs of pain, such as sleep disturbance, increased heart rate and blood pressure, pallor and sweating). All of the many mild-to-moderate analgesics were "useless" [according to the patient] and I did not feel opiates were justified, so I asked the advice of my immediate superior. [The superior, here referred to as "W.,"] saw the patient, discussed her pain and, with a grave face, said he wanted her to try a "completely different sort of treatment." She agreed. He disappeared into the office, to reapper a few minutes later, walking slowly down the ward and holding in front of him a pair of tweezers which grasped a large, white tablet, the size of [a] half-dollar. As he came nearer, it became clear (to me, at least) that the tablet was none other than effervescent vitamin C. He dropped the tablet into a glass of water which, of course, bubbled and fizzed, and told the patient to sip the water carefully when the fizzing had subsided. It worked—the new medicine completely abolished her pain! W. has used this method several times, apparently, and it always worked. He felt that the single most important aspect was holding the tablet with *tweezers*, thereby giving the impression that it was somehow too powerful to be touched with bare hands!

Some may find this episode amusing. Yet it has a devastating moral for the claim that without regard to a *specified* target disorder, a pharmacological agent can qualify as a generic and even as an intentional placebo. Assume that, for the varicose leg ulcer that afflicted the given patient, vitamin C is a generic placebo even in high doses; this assumption allows that, in such large doses, it may have negative side effects. And furthermore, relying on W.'s findings, grant that for at least some patients suffering from a superficial leg ulcer, the administration of vitamin C as an intentional placebo in W.'s ceremonious manner ("with tweezers"!) is therapeutic for such an ulcer. Then surely such a placebo status for leg ulcer hardly detracts from the fact that, at least in sufficient doses, vitamin C is a potent nonplacebo for scurvy. And if Linus Pauling is to be believed, sufficiently high doses of this vitamin can even afford prophylaxis for certain cancers. In short, only conceptual mischief results from the supposition that the property of being a (generic) placebo is one that a treatment—be it pharmacological or psychiatric—can have per se, rather than only with respect to a stated target disorder.

Ironically, none other than the much-maligned proverbial sugar pill furnishes a *reductio ad absurdum* of the notion that a medication can be generically a placebo *simpliciter*, without relativization to a target disorder. For even a lay person knows that the glucose in the sugar pill is anything but a generic placebo if given to a victim of diabetes who is in a state of insulin shock, or to someone suffering from hypoglycemia. But if an antibiotic were a "false placebo" on the strength of the properties adduced by Piechowiak (1983), then—by parity with his reasoning—so also is the notorious sugar pill, the alleged paradigm of a "true" nonrelativized placebo. Even the diehards among the antirelativizers will presumably regard this consequence of their view as too high a price to pay. Nor would they ever think someone's Uncle Charlie to be a "false" uncle merely because Charlie is not also somebody else's uncle!

Suppose that, for specified types of diseases, a certain class of afflicted victims does derive placebogenic remedial gain from the use of a particular set of therapeutic interventions. Then it may become important, for one reason or another, to ascertain—*within* the classes of incidental treatment factors picked out by the pertinent set of therapeutic theories—which particular kinds of factors are thus remedial. And this quest for identification can proceed across various sorts of treatment modalities (e.g., chemotherapy, radiation therapy, surgery), or may be focused more narrowly on factors within such modalities (e.g., surgery). Research during the past three decades has envisioned (1) that such placebogenic treatment gain may require a so-called "placebo reactor" type of victim of disease, characterized by a specifiable (but as yet unspecified) personality trait or cluster of such traits; or (2) that the therapeutic success of placebos may depend on certain kinds of characteristics or attitudes possessed by the treating physician. It should be noted that my explications of both the intentional and inadvertent species of placebo have made provision for these two possibilities: Both explications are relativized to disease victims of a specifiable sort, as well as to therapists (practitioners) of certain kinds. As it turns out, for some two dozen or so of proposed patient-trait correlates of placebo responsiveness, the first hypothesis named above—that of placebo reactivity—has been largely unsuccessful empirically, except for the following: Generalized chronic anxiety has been frequently and reliably found to correlate with placebo responsivity, notably in the treatment of pain (Gallimore & Turner, 1977). Yet in a 25-year series of studies of placebo responsiveness in psychotherapy, Frank (1974) found reason to discount the role of enduring personality factors in the patient (see also Liberman, 1964). As for the second hypothesis, which pertains to the therapeutic relevance of the physician's communicated attitudes, I have already commented on the demonstrated role of physician variables among incidental treatment factors in enhancing the therapeutic efficacy of nonplacebo drugs.

Having explicated the placebo concept by reference to A. K. Shapiro and Morris' proposed definition, I ought to comment on the divergences between theirs and the one offered by Brody (1977), which I have mentioned preliminary above (see p. 27).

A. K. Shapiro and Morris's definition appeared in 1978 in the *second* edition of the Garfield and Bergin *Handbook of Psychotherapy and Behavior Change*. But in the first edition of this *Handbook*, which appeared in 1971, Shapiro alone had published an only slightly different definition. This 1971 definition is not discussed by Brody (1977). But Brody claims rough consistency between Shapiro's (1968) definition of "placebo effect" and his own account of that notion. Hence I am concerned to point out that there are several important divergences between the construals of "placebo" given by Shapiro and Morris on the one hand, and Brody on the other. And these differences are such, I claim, that A. K. Shapiro and Morris render the generic placebo concept implicit in the medical and psychiatric literature far more adequately than Brody, notwithstanding the important respects in which I have found Shapiro and Morris's definition wanting.

The reader is now asked to recall my earlier remarks as to the consideration that seems to have prompted Brody's introduction of his notion of a "specific therapy": the putative fact that the placebogenic remedial efficacy of the proverbial sugar pill is presumed to range over a larger number of target ailments than the nonplacebogenic efficacy of widely used medications (e.g., of penicillin). Then the essence of his account becomes quite clear from his proposed definitions of the following terms: "therapy"; "specific therapy," which Brody avowedly contrasts with "general therapy" (1977, p. 41); and finally, "placebo." Let me first cite these definitions and Brody's comment on them. (For the sake of consistency, I am substituting the abbreviations used up to this point in this chapter for Brody's here.)

> (i) $[t]$ is a therapy for condition $[D]$ if and only if it is believed that administration of $[t]$ to a person with $[D]$ increases the empirical probability that $[D]$ will be cured, relieved, or ameliorated, as compared to the probability that this will occur without $[t]$. (Brody, 1977, p. 38)
> (ii) $[t]$ is a specific therapy for condition $[D]$ if and only if:
>   (1) $[t]$ is a therapy for $[D]$.
>   (2) There is a class A of conditions such that $[D]$ is a subclass of A, and for all members of A, $[t]$ is a therapy.
>   (3) There is a class B of conditions such that for all members of B, $[t]$ is not a therapy; and class B is much larger than class A.
>
> For example, consider how the definition applies to penicillin used for pneumococcal pneumonia. Penicillin is a therapy for this disease, since it increases the empirical probability of recovery. Pneumococcal pneumonia is one of a class of diseases (infectious diseases caused by penicillin-sensitive organisms) for all of which penicillin is a therapy; but there is a much larger class of diseases (noninfectious diseases and infectious diseases caused by penicillin-resistant organisms) for which penicillin is not a therapy. (Brody, 1977, pp. 40–41)

It will be noted that Brody presumably intends the third requirement in the second definition to implement his stated objective of contrasting "specific therapy" with "general therapy"—an aim that, as we have seen, does *not* govern A. K. Shapiro and Morris's construal of "specific." For Brody's third requirement here makes the following demand: The membership of the class B of disorders for which t is believed to be *ineffective* has to be numerically greater than the membership of the class A of target disorders for which t is deemed to be remedial. But clearly, Shapiro and Morris's cited account of what it is for t to possess "specific activity" for D does *not* entail logically Brody's third restriction on the relative number of disorders for which t is (believed to be) therapeutic! For example, just think of how Shapiro and Morris would analyze the claim that aspirin is not a placebo for arthritis or tension headaches and that it affords nonplacebogenic prophylaxis for blood clotting and embolisms. Nor would Brody's third restriction seem to be implicit in the medical and psychiatric usage of "specific therapy."

Yet Brody does deserve credit for pointing out, in effect, that the placebogenic efficacy of intentional placebos is believed to range over a larger number of target ailments, as a matter of empirical fact, than the nonplacebogenic efficacy of such medications as penicillin. This is much less significant, though, than he thinks: After all, the old sugar pill and penicillin alike have *placebogenic* efficacy, such that the sugar pill does not excel in regard to the number of target disorders!

The third of Brody's definitions reads:

(iii) A placebo is:
    (1) a form of medical therapy, or an intervention designed to simulate medical therapy, that at the time of use is *believed* not to be a specific therapy for the condition for which it is offered and that is used for its psychological effect or to eliminate observer bias in an experimental setting,
    (2) (by extension from 1) a form of medical therapy now believed to be inefficacious, though believed efficacious at the time of use.

Clause 2 is added to make sense of a sentence such as, "Most of the medications used by physicians one hundred years ago were actually placebos." (Brody, 1977, p. 43; italics added)

A further major divergence between Brody's and A. K. Shapiro and Morris's definitions of "placebo" derives from the *multiple* dependence of Brody's generic placebo concept on therapeutic beliefs, in contrast to Shapiro and Morris's explicit repudiation of any such dependence of the generic notion of placebo. As shown by Brody's definition of "therapy" above, what renders a treatment a "therapy" in his construal is that "it is believed" to be remedial (by its advocates or recipients). Consequently, this dependence on therapeutic belief enters into Brody's definition of "specific therapy" via each of the three requirements that he lays down in his definition of that term above. On the other hand, no such belief dependence is present in Shapiro and Morris's counterpart notion of "specific activity." As if this were not enough, Brody's definition of "placebo" invokes yet another layer of belief by requiring that "at the time of use," a placebo treatment be "believed not to be a specific therapy" for the target disorder, presumably by the doctor but not by the patient.

It is patent, therefore, that A. K. Shapiro and Morris's construal of the *generic* placebo notion, which we have seen to be objective rather than dependent on therapeutic beliefs, makes incomparably better sense than Brody's of such claims as "most of the medications used by physicians a century ago were actually placebos," a claim that Brody avowedly hopes to accommodate via the second requirement of his definition of "placebo." For on Shapiro and Morris's construal, physicians can in fact be *objectively* mistaken in deeming a treatment modality to be a nonplacebo. But on Brody's definition, it is merely a matter of a change in their therapeutic beliefs. For this reason alone, I have made Shapiro and Morris's definition rather than Brody's the focus of my explication.

I hope it is now apparent that the customary notions and terminology of placebo research foster conceptual confusion, and that the adoption of the conceptualizations and vocabulary I have proposed would obviate the perpetuation of such confusion.

ACKNOWLEDGMENTS

I thank Dr. Thomas Detre and Dr. Arthur K. Shapiro for useful expository comments on the first draft of this chapter. And I am indebted to the Fritz Thyssen Stiftung, Cologne, West Germany, for the support of research. Furthermore, I am grateful to Dr. Jennifer Worrall as well as to Dr. John Worrall, who offered some perceptive suggestions for clarifying some of the formulations in my earlier publication on this subject, "The Placebo Concept," *Behaviour Research and Therapy*, 1981, *19*, 157–167. Sections from this earlier paper are reprinted by permission of Pergamon Press, Ltd.

REFERENCES

Beecher, H. K. The placebo effect as a non-specific force surrounding disease and the treatment of disease. In R. Janzen, J. P. Payne, R. A. T. Burt (Eds.), *Pain: Basic principles, pharmacology, therapy*. Stuttgart: Thieme, 1972.

Benson, H., & McCallie, D. P. Angina pectoris and the placebo effect. *New England Journal of Medicine*, 1979, *300*, 1424–1429.

Blakiston's *Gould medical dictionary* (3rd ed.). New York: McGraw-Hill, 1972.

Bok, S. The ethics of giving placebos. *Scientific American*, 1974, *231*, 17–23.

Brody, H. *Placebos and the philosophy of medicine*. Chicago: University of Chicago Press, 1977.

Brody, J. Placebos work, but survey shows widespread misuse. *New York Times*, April 3, 1979, p. C 1.

Critelli, J. W., & Neumann, K. F. The placebo. *American Psychologist*, 1984, *39*, 32–39.

Davis, J. M., & Cole, J. O. Antipsychotic drugs. In S. Arieti (Ed.), *American handbook of psychiatry* (Vol. 5, 2nd ed.). New York: Basic Books, 1975. (a)

Davis, J. M., & Cole, J. O. Antipsychotic drugs. In A. M. Freedman, H. T. Kaplan, & B. J. Sadock (Eds.), *Comprehensive textbook of psychiatry* (Vol. 2, 2nd ed.). Baltimore: Williams & Wilkins, 1975. (b)

Erwin, E. Personal communication, 1981.

Frank, J.D. *Persuasion and healing* (Rev. ed.). Baltimore: Johns Hopkins University Press, 1973.

Frank, J. D. Therapeutic components of psychotherapy. *Journal of Nervous and Mental Disease*, 1974. *159*, 325–342.

Gallimore, R. G., & Turner, J. L. Contemporary studies of placebo phenomena. In M. E. Jarvik (Ed.), *Psychopharmacology in the practice of medicine*. New York: Appleton-Century-Crofts, 1977.

Goodman, L. S., & Gilman, A. (Eds.). *The pharmacological basis of therapeutics* (5th ed.). London: Macmillan, 1975.

Grünbaum, A. The placebo concept. *Behaviour Research and Therapy*, 1981, *19*, 157–167.

Grünbaum, A. *The foundations of psychoanalysis: A philosophical critique*. Berkeley: University of California Press, 1984.

Kazdin, A. E., & Wilson, G. T. *Evaluation of behavior therapy*. Cambridge, Mass.: Ballinger, 1978.

Klein, D. V. *Diagnosis and drug treatment of psychiatric disorders* (2nd ed.). Baltimore: Williams & Wilkins, 1980.

Kolata, G. B. New drugs and the brain. *Science*, 1979, *205*, 774–776.

Levine, J. D., Gordon, N. C., & Fields, H. L. The mechanism of placebo analgesia. *Lancet*, 1978, *2*, 654–657.

Levine, J. D., Gordon, N. C., Bornstein, J. C., & Fields, H. L. Role of pain in placebo analgesia. *Proceedings of the National Academy of Sciences USA*, 1979, *76*, 3528–3531.

Liberman, R. An experimental study of the placebo response under three different situations of pain. *Journal of Psychiatric Research*, 1964, *2*, 233–246.

Miller, N. E. Applications of learning and biofeedback to psychiatry and medicine. In A. M. Freedman, H. T. Kaplan, & B. J. Sadock (Eds.), *Comprehensive textbook of psychiatry* (Vol. 1, 3rd ed.). Baltimore: Williams & Wilkins, 1980.

Möller, H-J. *Psychoanalyse*. Munich: Wilhelm Fink, 1978.

O'Leary, K. D., & Borkovec, T. D. Conceptual, methodological, and ethical problems of placebo groups in psychotherapy research. *American Psychologist*, 1978, *33*, 821–830.

Park, L. C., & Covi, L. Nonblind placebo trial. *Archives of General Psychiatry*, 1965, *12*, 336–345.

Piechowiak, H. Die namenlose Pille. Über Wirkungen und Nebenwirkungen im therapeutischen Umgang mit Plazebopräparaten. *Internistische Praxis*, 1982, *22*, 759–772.

Piechowiak, H. Die Schein-Heilung: Welche Rolle spielt das Placebo in der ärztlichen Praxis? *Deutsches Ärzteblatt*, March 4, 1983, pp. 39–50.

Schwartz, G. E. Psychobiological foundations of psychotherapy and behavior change. In S. L. Garfield & A. E. Bergin (Eds.), *Handbook of psychotherapy and behavior change* (2nd ed.). New York: Wiley, 1978.

Shapiro, A. K. A contribution to a history of the placebo effect. *Behavioral Science*, 1960, 5, 109–135.

Shapiro, A. K. Semantics of the placebo. *Psychiatric Quarterly*, 1968, *42*, 653–696.

Shapiro, A. K., & Morris, L. A. The placebo effect in medical and psychological therapies. In S. L. Garfield & A. E. Bergin (Eds.), *Handbook of psychotherapy and behavior change* (2nd ed.). New York: Wiley, 1978.

Shapiro, A. P., Schwartz, G. E., & Ferguson, D. C. Behavioral methods in the treatment of hypertension. *Annals of Internal Medicine*, 1977, *86*, 626–636.

Suedfeld, P. The subtractive expectancy placebo procedure: A measure of non-specific factors in behavioural interventions. *Behaviour Research and Therapy*, 1984, *22*, 159–164.

Wheatley, D. Influence of doctors' and patients' attitudes in the treatment of neurotic illness. *Lancet*, 1967, *2*, 1133–1135.

Worrall, J. Personal communication, 1983.

3

Placebo Effect: An Examination of Grünbaum's Definition

HOWARD BRODY

Philosophers, bless their souls (to paraphrase Aunt Betsey Trotwood in *David Copperfield*), would define terms by the ream, even if it were a capital offense. And so the first impulse of any philosopher approaching the topic of this book is to clarify definitions of "placebo" and related concepts. Adolf Grünbaum has vigorously pursued this problem, and has also demonstrated its practical importance: " ... formulations employing this unfortunate terminology engender conceptual confusion in therapeutic research, instead of being just linguistically inept or inelegant" (Grünbaum, 1981, p. 157). Further examples of the dangers lurking in possible conceptual confusion may be found in a recent paper coauthored by one of the most prestigious authors on the placebo effect (Shapiro & Shapiro, 1982), which seeks to "deromanticize" the allegedly overrated estimates of placebo efficacy. But lurking under the Shapiro analysis seems to be an unrecognized circularity. What is "real" in medicine is taken to be that which can be proven by a controlled double-blind experiment. Proven efficacy in such an experiment is taken to be the equivalent of "having been shown to be more active than placebo." But it then seems to follow that the placebo effect is not "real," since no placebo can be shown to be superior to placebo in a controlled study. So improved definitions that help to resolve such riddles ought to be welcome.

Grünbaum has defined "intentional placebo" and "inadvertent placebo," and in the process introduced the concept of the "genus" placebo. He has also, in passing, criticized some definitions that I have previously proposed. I wish to argue in this chapter that Grünbaum's definitions offer important advantages and clarify some issues, and generally move use forward in our attempts to understand the placebo effect. But I also argue that Grünbaum's definitions leave untouched some equally important dimensions of the placebo effect, and that this arises less from the specifics of

Howard Brody. Medical Humanities Program, Department of Family Practice, and Department of Philosophy, Michigan State University, East Lansing, Michigan.

Grünbaum's definitions than from the overall strategy with which he approaches the problem.

REVIEW OF PROPOSED DEFINITIONS

It is useful to begin by juxtaposing the various proposed definitions for ready reference. Both Grünbaum and I (Brody, 1980; Grünbaum, 1981) review representative definitions from medical and scientific papers and note their various deficiencies, so I need not repeat this exercise here. I do, however, take the liberty to rephrasing Grünbaum's definitions (which he might prefer to call corrected explications, rather than definitions in the formal sense) in a tabular form for easier comparison and analysis, while retaining, I hope, his meaning unaltered. I rely here on Grünbaum's original (1980, 1981) formulations; his chapter in this volume modifies these only slightly in ways that do not affect my analysis. One must first accept a table of abbreviations:

D = target disorder
t = particular treatment modality
ψ = therapeutic theory (which advocates the use of t for D)
F = characteristic constituents of t according to ψ
C = incidental constituents of t according to ψ (i.e., for a certain treatment process to be viewed by ψ as an authentic example of t, F needs to be present, but C need not be present)
P = dispensing practitioner

Grünbaum's definitions then follow:

G:1. t is an "intentional placebo" with respect to D and P if and only if:
   a. None of F are remedial for D;
   b. P believes that none of F are remedial for D;
   c. P believes that t is remedial for D by virtue of C;
   d. P causes or allows the patient to believe that t is remedial for D by virtue of F. (Adapted from Grünbaum, 1981, p. 159)
G:2. t is an "inadvertent placebo" for D and P if and only if:
   a. None of F are remedial for D;
   b. P believes that t is remedial for D by virtue of F;
   c. the patient believes that t is remedial for D by virtue of F. (Adapted from Grünbaum, 1981, p. 160)

Noting that the first condition (a) is shared by both definitions, Grünbaum labels as the generic objective property of being a placebo the property of failing to be remedial for the target disorder by virtue of any of the constituents that the governing biomedical theory regards as characteristic.

Grünbaum offers no definition of "remedial." He also offers no definition of "placebo effect." Presumably he feel that once one has satisfactorily elucidated the definitions of "placebo," one may simply define "placebo effect" as Shapiro and Morris (1978) do: "A *placebo effect* is defined as the psychological or psychophysiological effect produced by placebos" (p. 371).

My own earlier definitions include, in order, "therapy," "specific therapy," "placebo effect," and "placebo." They are as follows, with alterations where appropriate so as to use the same abbreviations used by Grünbaum:

B:1. t is a "therapy" for D if and only if it is believed that the administration of t to a person with D increases the empirical probability that D will be cured, relieved, or ameliorated, as compared to the probability that this will occur without t. (Adapted from Brody, 1980, p. 38)

B:2. t is a "specific therapy" for D if and only if:
a. t is a therapy for D;
b. there is a class A of conditions such that D is a subclass of A and that for all members of A, t is a therapy;
c. there is a class B of conditions such that for all members of B, t is not a therapy; and class B is much larger than class A. (Adapted from Brody, 1980, pp. 40–41)

B:3. A "*placebo effect*" occurs for person V if and only if:
a. V has condition D;
b. V believes that he or she is within a healing context (i.e., the socioculturally approved settling, with its associated rituals and practitioners, that is identified with healing for V);
c. V is administered t as part of that context, where t is either the total active intervention or some component of that intervention;
d. D is changed;
e. the change in D is attributable to the symbolic import of t and not to any specific therapeutic effect of t or to any known pharmacological or physiological property of t. (Adapted from Brody, 1980, p. 84)

B:4. A "placebo" is:
a. a form of medical therapy, or an intervention designed to simulate medical therapy, that at the time of use is believed not to be a specific therapy for the condition for which it is offered and that is used either for its psychological effect or to eliminate observer bias in an experimental setting;
b. (by extension from a) a form of medical therapy now believed to be inefficacious, though believed efficacious at the time of use. (Adapted from Brody, 1980, p. 43)

The major difference in strategy (to be addressed below at length) is apparent from the fact that I define "placebo" and "placebo effect" independently (although both depend upon the definition of "specific therapy"). "Placebo effect" is *not* defined as "the effect produced by placebos," and indeed its definition makes no reference to placebos. By contrast, Grünbaum seems to feel that once he has defined "placebo," he has done away with any complexities in the notion of "placebo effect." Furthermore, in criticizing my definitions, he focuses on B:4 and on B:2 (which defines a key term in B:4) but totally ignores B:3, despite my clear statement (Brody, 1980, pp. 41–43) that B:3 is the central definition and that B:4 is appended more or less as an afterthought.

In essence, then, Grünbaum conceives of "placebo effect" in such a way that it is irreducibly bound up with the notion of "placebo." I conceive of "placebo effect" more as a historical term: that is, the effect that investigators first became aware of as an outgrowth of the application and study of placebos, but that then on reflection and further research turned out to be a much more broadly based phenomenon—indeed, a phenomenon that seems to play some role in virtually all encounters between healer and patient in all cultures. I contend that the term "placebo effect" in medicine should be seen as somewhat analogous to the "Edison effect" in physics, which one could define in a completely satisfactory manner without having any idea who Edison was. Since this contention implies an assertion about the historical development of the concept of "placebo effect," this should next be spelled out.

HISTORICAL SKETCH OF THE PLACEBO PHENOMENON

Our purposes for the present discussion will be served by a very sketchy historical account, which I hope to flesh out with adequate supporting documentation on another occasion.

Both prescientific and scientific physicians throughout medical history have been confronted with the problem of explaining why a patient gets better (or worse) after a particular healing intervention is administered (or withheld). As Grünbaum's definitions suggest, one may view the history of medicine as a succession of therapeutic theories that have attempted to account for the change in terms of some predictable and repeatable properties or characteristics of the healing intervention. A new theory supplanted an older one if it offered a more persuasive account of which properties were most predictably tied in with healing (depending on what criteria were then in force that judged a scientific theory to be more or less "persuasive"). But besides these particular therapeutic theories, at least two alternative general accounts seem to have had a rather marked staying power, at least from Hippocratic days to the present.

One such account was that postulated as the *vis medicatrix naturae*, or the healing power of nature, which has been thoroughly reviewed (Neuberger, 1932). This account calls attention to the natural organisms's marked recuperative powers, and to its ability to restore balanced function by somehow drawing on its own inner resources in the face of illness. This view would give the skeptical critic of any of the then-popular therapeutic theories reason to doubt whether any cure was due to the physician's healing intervention. At best, the patient might simply have been destined to get better anyway, even if he or she had never visited the physician; at worst, the physician's drastic potion might have upset the delicate balance of nature and simply placed additional obstacles in the way of the *vis medicatrix*. A typical expression of the worst-case view comes from a letter from Thomas Jefferson to a physician friend in 1807. Jefferson admitted that medical science had in some cases identified a specific cause for a disease, thus explaining the efficacy of a specific remedy; but he held in most cases that no such cause was known. He argued that the physician should, in those cases, desist from offering a heroic and potentially harmful treatment: "Having been so often a witness to the salutary efforts which nature makes to re-establish the disordered functions, he should rather trust to their action, than hazard the . . . greater derangement of the system" (Ford, Vol. 9, 1898, pp. 78–85).

Another account could be labeled as that of the healing power of the imagination. This can be traced back at least to Greek medicine, although the concept is better described in some writings of Plato than in the Hippocratic corpus (Lain Entralgo, 1970). By this account, it is admitted that the intervention by the physician might make a real difference in the outcome of the disease; but it is argued that the positive emotions prompted by that intervention in the mind of the patient, and not the specific properties of that treatment according to the therapeutic theory, make the difference. This account gained support over centuries from the dominance of humoral theory, which had a strong psychosomatic slant and postulated specific ways in which a change in one's emotional state could alter body chemistry (and vice versa):

> [T]here is no virtue in such [commonly used folk remedies], but a strong conceit and opinion alone, as Pomponatius holds, "which forceth a motion of the humours, spirits, and blood, which take away the cause of the malady from the parts affected." . . . An empiric oftentimes, or a silly chirurgeon, doth more strange cures than a rational physician . . . because the patient puts his confidence in him. (Burton, 1621/1924, p. 168)

Late in the 18th century, some elegant experiments utilizing single-blind controls (notably Franklin's inquiry into animal magnetism and Haygarth's experiments with "Perkins's tractors") revealed that it was the emotional effect of the treatment on the subject, and not its postulated physiological properties, that accounted for the changes observed. But the dictionary definitions of "placebo," which began to appear in medical dictionaries about that time, reveal an ongoing tension between the *vis medicatrix* and the imagination as the favored explanation of why diseases were cured after the patient took bread pills or some other "inert" remedy. Most definitions from 1810 to 1860 emphasized the *vis medicatrix* by defining "placebo" as a remedy given to please the patient without any hope that it will exercise curative powers (Shapiro, 1968). But later evidence, bolstered further by psychosomatic research in the mid-20th century, swung the decision over to the imagination camp by demonstating that placebos indeed could change the natural history of an illness via psychological or psychophysiological mechanisms. Finally, the modern age of placebo research began in the late 1940s with the ascendency of the double-blind controlled study as the gold standard of medical research. Recent studies of the effect of emotional arousal on endogenous levels of endorphins, interferon, and catecholamines hold promise for elucidating the connecting links in the postulated psychosomatic chain.

While throughout medical history the emotional or symbolic impact of treatment has been recognized as an alternative explanation for many medical phenomena, it has thus only been recently that the placebo effect has been viewed as a variable open to direct experimental manipulation. It is this experimental aspect of the placebo concept, its role in theory building and theory testing, which most intrigues Grünbaum—with good reason, as we shall see below, since the placebo problem raises several very interesting issues for philosophy of science. But the historical and descriptive aspect of the placebo effect is equally important, especially from the perspective of the medical practitioner, and an adequate definition must deal with both aspects.

ISSUES IN DEFINING PLACEBO EFFECT

Today's physician, coming out of the historical tradition briefly sketched above, is faced with three different possibilities in explaining why a certain patient showed improvement after receiving a certain therapy:

1. The patient got better due to the "natural history" of the condition in an organism with intact healing and recuperative powers (the *vis medicatrix*).
2. The patient got better due to the symbolic effect of the treatment— that is, its impact on his or her imagination, beliefs, and/or emotions.
3. The patient got better due to some "specific" or "characteristic" feature of the treatment that can be studied, isolated, and predicted within the context of contemporary medical theory.

Whether these three categories are jointly exhaustive is discussed below. For now, it should be noted that each must be expanded before it can be determined whether they are mutually exclusive. For example, if by 1 one intends that the treatment administered must be therapeutically inefficacious, then to assert 1 is simultaneously to assert not-2. But one may instead include under the heading of "natural recuperative powers" of the human organism a "potential to respond with positive bodily changes to factors in the environment which alter one's beliefs and/or emotions," in which case 2 may be viewed as a subcategory of 1.

Those who promote a systems approach to biological and psychosocial phenomena as a defense against the absurdities of mind–body dualism (e.g., Hahn, 1983) might argue that any separation of these three categories (e.g., as if a drug that exerts a specific biochemical effect cannot at the same time exert a symbolic effect) amounts to an inadmissable reductionism. It should be remembered that 1, 2, and 3 are *types of explanations*, and as such may comfortably be assigned to discrete levels of the hierarchy, while events or phenomena in the real world manifest themselves simultaneously at various hierarchical levels. (Implications of the systems approach for the placebo concept are considered further below.)

The physician engaged in clinical research wants to know which one of the three explanations apply (or which combination of the three), so that he or she can be *objectively* correct in his or her account of the observed phenomena, and does not make the error of mistaken ascription to 3 of a change actually due to 1 or 2. The practitioner wants to know which of the three accounts for changes under which circumstances, so that he or she can make effective use of all three as part of his or her therapeutic armamentarium. (This is especially true due to the frequency of toxic reactions and side effects, as well as expense, when complex therapeutic maneuvers are employed; one does not wish to use such maneuvers where 1 or 2 would serve as well.)

This analysis therefore suggests that we can test the adequacy of a proposed definition of "placebo" or "placebo effect" by asking questions like the following: Does this definition aid the investigator or practitioner in distinguishing among 1, 2, and 3? Does the definition guide further research into, and application of, the mechanisms involved in 1, 2, and 3? I now try to answer these sorts of questions for the various definitions summarized above.

Grünbaum claims that one of the major strengths of his definitions relates to the problem of the researcher who is trying to make an objectively correct causal ascription. Looking back on the remedies employed by physicians 100 or 150 years ago, we want to state *objectively* that those physicians were wrong in attributing their cures to those remedies, and to say that if the treatment had any beneficial affect at all, it was via the placebo route. Grünbaum states,

For on Shapiro and Morris's construal [the construal he claims to have explicated more satisfactorily in his definitions], physicians can in fact be *objectively* mistaken in deeming a treatment modality to be a nonplacebo. But on Brody's definition, it is merely a matter of a change in their therapeutic beliefs. For this reason alone, I have made Shapiro and Morris's definition rather than Brody's the focus of my explication. (Grünbaum, Chapter 2, p. 35; see also 1981, p. 167)

However, Grünbaum makes this objectivity claim not for his definitions of intended and inadvertent placebos, but rather for the generic property of being a placebo. This generic property is a somewhat difficult concept and is admitted by Grünbaum to be counterintuitive at first glance. Since a generic placebo is anything that *fails* to be remedial for the target disorder by virtue of any of its characteristic constituent properties, one has the puzzling conclusion that potassium cyanide is a "generic placebo" for the common cold. Now, it is by virtue of the way in which the generic property of placebo is defined that Grünbaum's definitions allow for negative as well as positive placebo reactions, which most authorities (e.g., Shapiro & Morris, 1978) accept as an adequacy test of a placebo definition. But the effect of cyanide on a cold sufferer is not what is generally meant when one talks about a "negative placebo response," since the change due to cyanide is one's well-being falls under category 3 and is readily explainable by the known pharmacological ("characteristic") properties of cyanide. (Noting that in its original Latin "placebo" means "I shall please," many have objected to the apparent self-contradiction in "negative placebo" and have urged adoption of the term "nocebo" instead; however, the concept has traveled so far already from its etymological origins that I see no particular advantage in this change.)

The relativity that seems to bother Grünbaum in the definition of "placebo" is of three sorts: what the dominant therapeutic theory ψ claims for the treatment; what the physician believes accounts for the treatment's efficacy; and what the patient believes. Grünbaum claims a higher degree of "objectivity" for the generic property of placebo, on the grounds that it is relative only in the first way. But while the generic placebo property has the advantage of making reference only to this first sort of relativity, we have seen that it is a strongly counterintuitive notion that becomes useful in practice only when combined with the other terms of Grünbaum's definitions (which state *exactly* which t's that fail to be remedial for D by virtue of F are intentional or inadvertent placebos). And those other terms of the definitions reintroduce both of the remaining sorts of relativity, physician belief and patient belief.

My definition B:3 of "placebo effect" makes reference directly to the relativity of patient belief, and indirectly to theory relativity as the latter is implied in definition B:1 of "therapy." Definition B:4 of "placebo" is flawed because it includes the vague phrase, "at the time of use is believed not to be" and thus fails to distinguish between the relativiity of theory and that of physician belief. If B:4 were revised to correct this deficiency, so as to parallel Grünbaum's definitions more closely in this regard, it would include all three sorts of relativity. Each of Grünbaum's definitions, G:1 and G:2, includes all three sorts of relativity. Thus it is hard to see where the purported "objectivity" advantage lies.

Grünbaum, in Chapter 2, openly acknowledges the theory relativity of his construal of "placebo" and makes a number of important observations that follow from this feature. I find this acceptance of theory relativity very congenial with my own views, as I discuss below in greater detail; I take this to be one of the signal advances in Grünbaum's present statement, as contrasted to his earlier accounts (1980, 1981).

Joseph Hanna has pointed out to me that Grünbaum has a way of sidestepping the potassium cyanide counterexample. There is one attribute besides the "generic placebo property" that is common to the definitions of both "intentional" and "inadvertent" placebo—the stipulation that "P believes that t is remedial for D" (by some means or other). If Grünbaum were to expand his "generic placebo property" to include this stipulation of physician belief, then potassium cyanide would cease to be a generic placebo. But, as I interpret his strategy, this is precisely the sort of move that Grünbaum is loath to make, since it would seem to introduce an additional nonobjective element into a definition, the objectivity of which seems to him to be one of its chief virtues.

A word should be added, incidentally, about the relativity of patient belief. Grünbaum acknowledges (1981, p. 159) that his first condition (a) of definition G:1 would need modification if it were the case that patients showed a positive response from placebo even after being told of its "inert" content. I believe that the evidence this can occur, while limited, is compelling (Park & Covi, 1965; Vogel, Goodwin, & Goodwin, 1980). Accordingly, I have tried to include in my definition B:3 the minimally specified belief state of the patient that would suffice—the belief that one is in a healing context. If this condition were not included, any form of autosuggestion or self-fulfilling prophecy, whether or not connected with disease or healing, would count as an instance of the placebo effect; this would seem to make the term impossibly broad. But this formulation still leaves open exactly what role various patient beliefs might play as a matter to be settled by empirical investigation, not by definition.

By focusing on the so-called generic placebo property, Grünbaum has usefully called attention to a crucial question: Within what more inclusive class of phenomena is the placebo effect to be located? Grünbaum assumes that the conceptually clearest answer is to locate "placebo" as a species within the genus of noncharacteristic therapies—that is, everything that fails to be a therapy by virtue of its characteristic properties. Hence the inclusion of cyanide and the resultant counterintuitiveness of the generic placebo property. For reasons explained at some length (Brody, 1980, pp. 29–44), I have opted for a different approach, trying to locate the placebo effect within the larger reference class of "general" therapies. The assumption is that one of the most striking features of the placebo phenomenon, which somehow must be accounted for in any adequate definition, is the ability of placebos to effect change in virtually any potentially reversible disease or disorder in medicine, while contemporary theories of pathophysiology and therapeutics lead us to expect a "specific" or "characteristic" remedy to be efficacious for only a small number of disorders. We anticipate that a "specific"/"characteristic" remedy has roughly a 75–95% probability of being efficacious for a very small number of disorders, while a placebo has a 30–40% probability of being efficacious for almost any disorder (Beecher, 1955). This feature suggests that placebos are somehow analogous to "general" therapies, such as diet, exercise, rest, and the like, and should be considered as part of the same class of phenomena. There are, of course, a number of complexities that must be sorted out. For one thing, therapies like diet and exercise are ambiguous among categories 1, 2, and 3 above. Given in advance of the disorder, so as simply to strengthen the body's general level of fitness and the natural defense mechanisms, they fall under 1. Given as part of the treatment for a specific disorder, they seem more to resemble 3, if one assumes that 1 implies that the patient would have gotten better whether or not a healing intervention had been administered. And, of course, whenever a diet or exercise plan is prescribed as part of an explicit act of healing, there is a symbolic element in addition to any physiological response, thus including 2 in the bargain. (We may assume that 2 *alone* is not involved, as we could theoretically improve the health status of a comatose patient via better tube feedings and passive physical therapy maneuvers, even though no symbolic exchange was occurring.) But despite these difficulties, the notion of some class of general therapies makes more sense to me than Grünbaum's generic placebo property, which is yet another attempt to define "placebo" merely by reference to what it is not.

"SPECIFIC" OR "CHARACTERISTIC"?

One of the major values of Grünbaum's treatment is his criticism of the unclear or self-contradictory ways in which many medical writers have used the terms "specific" and "nonspecific" (1981, pp. 162–163). He criticizes, for example, calling a placebo effect a "nonspecific response," when the response itself is as specific as one would desire and what one really means is a response to a so-called nonspecific therapy. Many of these criticisms could be applied with profit to my own definitions B:1 and B:2 as well. Grünbaum's careful distinction between two different uses of "specific" (see Chapter 2 of this volume) is especially valuable in showing how my approach, outlined above, differs from that of most medical authors (e.g., Shapiro & Morris, 1978).

However, attempts to avoid this sort of problem by switching attention to the notion of a "characteristic" therapy create new difficulties that Grünbaum appears not to have appreciated. The difficulties are illustrated by my categories of explanatory accounts, 1, 2, and 3. By locating placebo effects within the general category of "effects that aren't characteristic according to the dominant theory," one simply asserts that placebo effects cannot be explained under 3 and leaves open the equally important question of whether they fall under 1 or 2.

Grünbaum's definition G:1 of "intentional placebo" also makes reference to C, the incidental constituents of the treatment. It may thus be inferred that category 1 is excluded; if the patient would have improved whether or not treatment was administered, there would be no need to mention any constituents of the treatment, incidental or otherwise. But C is mentioned in the definition only by way of specifying the belief state of the practitioner, not by way of specifying any objective property of the treatment. Furthermore, merely identifying the constituents in question as "incidental" does little to indicate what sorts of properties are intended. For example, suppose a particular physician believes that sugar pills emit radiation on a portion of the electromagnetic spectrum that, according to currently accepted biomedical theories, ought to exert no biological activity. The physician believes, however, that it is by virtue of this radiation, viewed as an "incidental" constituent of the treatment, that some patients experience symptom relief when given sugar pills. By Grünbaum's definition, this physician when giving sugar pills is using an "intentional placebo," but it seems wrong to suggest that this physician is attributing the success of his or her treatment measures to explanatory category 2. (The physician could more accurately be depicted as alleging a flaw in the existing biomedical theories; this matter is discussed in more detail in the next section.) By definition B:3, in contrast, the fact that a treatment works by a symbolic mechanism is given as an *objective* feature of the placebo effect, so there can be no question that category 2 is the reference category.

Having said all this, one may still find considerable fault with definition B:2 and its use of an apparently arbitrary quantitative measure to distinguish specific from nonspecific therapies. This crudity could be eliminated if a more suitable definition of "general therapy" were proposed, which would include, along with the placebo effect and treatment modalities which promote it, such measures as diet, rest, and exercise. As noted above, these treatments, depending on circumstances, may be explained by all three categories. We could then define "placebo" as a subclass of the class of general therapies—that is, those whose activity is best explained by category 2 sorts of explanations. I am not so bold at this time as to suggest an adequate definition of "general therapy" that avoids all the criticisms that may be directed at definition B:2 in its present form. But I do submit that such a line of inquiry will ultimately be more fruitful than a further elaboration of "characteristic" versus "incidental" constituents of treatments, despite the value that Grünbaum's terminology has for calling attention to theory relativity and differences among theories.

THE DISAPPEARANCE PROBLEM

The "characteristic" versus "incidental" issue leads into another area of difficulty with the definitions proposed by clinical investigators. This is the possibility that in the future, as new theories are developed or as old theories are expanded, the effects of symbolism, expectation, and emotional arousal are included as the "characteristic" constituents of therapy by the now-dominant biomedical theories. There will then be no more placebos and no more placebo effect. Grünbaum, in Chapter 2 of this volume, is careful to dissociate himself from this viewpoint, pointing out that questions about the "disappearance" of placebos are necessarily raised *across rival therapeutic theories*, and his observations about the theory relativity of the placebo concept render such questions pointless. Yet the disappearance viewpoint has been raised by enough medical authors (e.g., Shapiro & Shapiro, 1982) to be worth extended comment.

It must be emphasized that the "disappearance" would not necessarily mean that, because of the loss of placebo terms from our vocabulary, our ability to explain medical phenomena would be lessened; it might be that the enlarged explanatory powers of the new theories would more than make up for the gap. One practical issue at stake here is the predictability of the placebo response. The contemporary placebo literature suggests that one may predict with confidence only that 30–40% of subjects administered a placebo will show a positive response, and few or no measurements exist to determine with any accuracy *which* 30–40% will be the responders in any given situation. But, both for research and for therapeutic aims, more reliable predictions would appear desirable. (This is especially true since the observation that "35% of the subjects improved after taking a placebo" does *not* by itself distinguish between explanatory categories 1 and 2; by contrast, the assertion that "these subjects improved because of a placebo effect" [defined as per B:3] *does* postulate that 2 rather than 1 is the correct explanatory model.) Accordingly, it might be argued that in order for our biomedical theories to advance to the point where the factors responsible for the placebo effect can be identified as "characteristic" constituents of a treatment, it would be necessary for us to be able to isolate these precise factors and to predict their causal outcomes with much better reliability than is now possible. This increase in the predictive power of the revised biomedical theory would far outweigh the semantic inconvenience of having the term "placebo" disappear from the vocabulary.

But, against this argument, it might be suggested that some medical phenomena simply fail to adhere to the Newtonian model of 100% cause-

and-effect predictability. The need to expand our thinking so as to allow for the existence of probabilistic phenomena, describable by statistical accounts but not predictable in any exact fashion, has of late been persuasively argued (Bursztajn, Feinbloom, Hamm, & Brodsky, 1981). If any medical phenomena must be understood by a probabilistic rather than a Newtonian or mechanistic paradigm, it should be those modalities labeled above as "general therapies," including the placebo effect. One would then have to ask whether the proposal to remove "placebo" and "placebo effect" from our vocabulary, to be replaced with accounts in terms of more predictable characteristic factors, is not just a disguised positivism, which smuggles in assumptions about the appropriate structure of biomedical theories so as to exclude from consideration any theory that takes a probabilistic rather than a mechanistic form. If this is what is meant by talk of "characteristic" factors, then there is reason to fear that any new biomedical theory following such a model will fail to do justice to the placebo phenomenon. (I have suggested elsewhere that proper understanding of the placebo effect as well as other psychosomatic and culturally mediated medical phenomena may require different senses of "causation" from those dominant in the Newtonian physical sciences; see Brody, 1980, pp. 81–84.)

The brief historical sketch given above suggests that, while various biomedical theories have come and gone over the centuries, the general explanatory category of the "healing power of the imagination" has had rather remarkable staying power. Changes in biomedical theories have produced differing concepts of the intermediate mechanisms by virtue of which the imagination was able to produce bodily changes, from the humors of Galen and Pomponatius to today's endorphins. It is even possible that for brief periods, and in particular cultures, especially rigid biomedical theories were held, according to which it was impossible for the imagination to exert any effect on the body. But such episodes have been the exception rather than the rule. When an understanding of this tradition is coupled with a sympathetic reading of the contemporary placebo literature, it seems hard to defend the position that explanatory category 2 will drop out of medical thinking without suggesting a much more radical revolution in the body of biomedical theory than the shift from "incidental" to "characteristic" factors would seem to indicate.

The disappearance problem links up at a deeper level to the problems of the objectivity of placebo ascriptions and their theory relativity, as the following example may help illustrate. Consider a primitive healing practice, first ascribed to the placebo effect and then reascribed by Western scientists to a "specific" pharmacological mechanism. Perhaps a disease from which the natives suffer—say, a type of rash associated with chronic diarrhea—was initially classified by Western physicians as an autoimmune disorder. The healing ritual includes ingesting a concoction made from leaves of a certain native plant, which, on first investigation by the Western scientists, revealed no substances of antihistamine- or corticosteroid-like properties. The scientists thus concluded that only a placebo response could account for the cures observed as a result of the healing ritual. The natives themselves, let us say, explain the cures by pointing out that the disease is caused by demon possession, and that the leaves of the plant in question are characterized by sharply pointed edges. These sharp points, by magical association, result in the pricking and stabbing of the demons as if by knives, forcing them to let go of the sufferer and removing the malady. The Western scientists assumed after their initial investigation that the positive belief/emotional state induced in the sick person as a result of this cultural belief system is what actually effects the cure.

Now suppose that there has been a further investigation of the disease, again within the framework of Western medicine, which has resulted in a reclassification. It has been discovered that this disease is not really autoimmune in nature, but is instead an acquired variant of acrodermatitis enteropathica, the pathology of which is related to abnormal zinc metabolism, and which has been shown in empirical studies to respond to zinc supplementation therapy. The plant leaves have been reinvestigated and found to contain significant amounts of zinc salts. This leads the Western scientists to abandon the old explanation in terms of a placebo effect (category 2) and to offer instead an explanation in terms of specific pharmacological properties (category 3). These scientists need not be so simple-minded as to assume that categories 2 and 3 are mutually exclusive: It is simply the case that previously, 2 was the *only* explanatory category that seemed relevant, whereas now, 3 appears to be the *principal* explanation in terms of explanatory and predictive power. A symbolic effect may be occurring at the same time and may contribute to healing, but this now appears to be a secondary or subsidiary explanation. As far as the natives are concerned, they are quite content with their own explanation in terms of demons, even if they somehow learn of the Western reclassification.

A number of interesting points now emerge. First, what are we to make of the first Western explanation, which was based on a theory of disease caustion later viewed as faulty? It might be argued that the example reveals that the categories 1, 2, and 3 are not jointly exhaustive. As we look back on the explanation given from the perspective of our current knowledge, we see that the cure was not due to 1, and it was not due to 2 even though the observers at the time mistakenly thought it was. But neither was it due to 3 if by 3 we mean to include those pharmacological and physiological factors *then known in the light of currently accepted medical theory*.

This problem requires that we further clarify the sense of theory relativity that has been alluded to in the proposed definitions for "placebo effect." How narrow or how general are the theories that we are alluding to here? If theory is construed narrowly, so that the theory in question is something like "Such-and-such a disease is caused by an autoimmune reaction (abnormal zinc metabolism) and can be treated by immunosuppressive (zinc supplement) therapy," then the "dominant biomedical theory" underwent a major change between the two studies of the native healing ritual carried out by the Western scientists. By all definitions we have been considering, what counts as a placebo effect, a specific or characteristic feature of a therapy, and so on, is dependent upon the dominant theory; and what can be asserted *objectively* about these phenomena depends upon the theory of reference.

But "theory" might be construed much more broadly as shorthand for the entire system of physiological, pathophysiological, and therapeutic theories that characterize medical science in a specific culture and historical period. The relevant "dominant theory," by this interpretation, is more like this: "The human organism functions by means of such-and-such physiological mechanisms; these mechanisms can become deranged in such-and-such ways, resulting in diseases $w, x, y, z, \ldots$; and the derangements can be compensated for by administration of physically or chemically active substances $a, b, c, \ldots$ which interact with the physiological mechanisms in such-and-such ways." This sense of "theory" corresponds with what Thomas Kuhn originally labeled a paradigm (Kuhn, 1970) and then delineated more carefully as a "disciplinary matrix" (Kuhn, 1977b)—that is, the set of theories, laws, models, and exemplars (crudely put, the world view) that is shared by a community of scientists and by virtue of which they can readily agree on what counts as good experimental design, what sort of evidence is most persuasive, and so forth. The hypothetical sketch previously given has been intended to show that modern medical science has evolved a disciplinary matrix that favors explanations from category 3 but also allows room for those from 1 and 2. This disciplinary matrix did not change in between the two studies of the healing ritual. Within this disciplinary matrix, the "correct" answer was a 3-type explanation all along; the first scientific study was *objectively* wrong in ascribing the cures solely or primarily to a 2-type explanation. Even though the role of zinc metabolism was not known at the time, the same basic sort of explanation is envisioned, whether we are talking about autoimmune disease or abnormal zinc metabolism; the scientists at that earlier time, had they been presented with the zinc hypothesis, would readily have recognized it as the *same sort of* explanation, even though the details would be different.

The situation is very different when one compares either of the two Western scientific explanations with the native explanation. It might at first seem that the native account is simply a different sort of 3-type explanation, with certain kinds of leaves being a "specific therapy" for diseases caused by demon possession. But this presupposes that the natives' disciplinary matrix is sufficiently like the Western one so as to have explanatory categories corresponding to the present 1, 2, and 3 so that the natives and the Western scientists could agree on what sorts of treatment were examples of each type of explanatory category, differing only in the names or labels applied descriptively. However, it is much more likely that the two disciplinary matrices differ at a much more radical level, so that there is nothing in the natives' explanatory system remotely resembling 1, 2, and 3. In that case, and still assuming that what counts as placebo effect, specific therapy, and so on is disciplinary-matrix-dependent, it will make little sense to say that the Western scientists are objectively correct in ascribing the cure to the zinc contained in the leaves, while the natives are objectively wrong in ascribing it to the magical properties. This statement presupposes that there are two competing explanations being offered for the *same event*, whereas the radical difference in the disciplinary matrices assures that observers in the different cultures cannot even agree on what event is occurring. That is, it is fundamental to the Western explanation that the native ingesting the leaf concoction is *doing the same sort of thing as* some Westerner who takes a zinc supplement purchased in the drug store; however, the native healer would not recognize these two actions as being even remotely connected.

This extended example, then, has illustrated both a relatively superficial shift of theory within a constant disciplinary matrix (autoimmune disease vs. zinc deficiency disease), and also a more radical disagreement across rival disciplinary matrices (Western scientific pathophysiology vs. demon possession). How are such issues to be handled according to Grünbaum's strategy for approaching the definition of "placebo"? Grünbaum appears to recognize two aspects to the problem. In asserting his "generic placebo property," Grünbaum seems to be identifying a sense in which the placebo concept is independent of shifts in disciplinary matrix; on this interpretation not only the individual scientists, but also the entire disciplinary matrix itself, may be objectively mistaken about whether event X is a placebo effect. Then, in his additional terms that fill out the definitions for "intentional placebo" and "inadvertent placebo," Grünbaum recognizes the sense in which what counts as a placebo depends upon the beliefs and theories of the particular scientist or practitioner, and in turn is dependent upon the disciplinary matrix in which he works.

Underlying Grünbaum's assertion of the disciplinary-matrix-independent sense of "placebo" may be some version of the logical positivist tradition in philosophy of science and its assumption of the existence of a theory-neutral observation language. But much of the work in contemporary philosophy of science, both by Kuhn and by many who reject Kuhn, has been aimed at refuting these traditional assumptions, by noting that observations and theories mutually infect one another and cannot be simplistically separated (see Suppe, 1977). Even if it were acceptable in other scientific fields, the idea of a theory-neutral observation language is especially suspect in medicine, where the "facts" observed—"disease" states—are heavily value-laden (Caplan, Engelhardt, & McCartney, 1981; Clouser, Culver, & Gert, 1981).

The most acceptable alternative stance if the search for a disciplinary-matrix-independent concept is to be abandoned is to acknowledge freely that the placebo concept is given meaning only within a disciplinary matrix, which establishes what counts as "therapy," what categories of explanations are acceptable (e.g., categories 1, 2, and 3), and what counts as evidence for or against the various categories. True, a *definition* of "placebo effect" must to some extent cross disciplinary-matrix lines; else one could not ask the question about how different or how similar are the ideas of placebo effect that prevail in two different disciplinary matrices. But the full *meaning* of the concept—at least those aspects of it that are likely to be philosophically interesting and useful in guiding research—can be comprehended only within the context of a given disciplinary matrix, when one sees how the term "placebo effect" is used in relation to other concepts, theories, and models within that overall scheme. The meaning stays the same over superficial shifts in theory, such as reclassifying a so-called autoimmune disease as a zinc deficiency disease. But the meaning must be radically altered for a concept like "placebo effect" to be translated from a Western scientific disciplinary matrix into a demon possession matrix, if indeed one can make any useful sense at all of the "translation." (It should be emphasized that this sort of disciplinary-matrix relativity can coexist comfortably with the argument that we have sound rational criteria for preferring the Western scientific matrix over the demon one; see Kuhn, 1977a.) To return to Grünbaum's favored example (1981, pp. 158–159), it would not make good sense to say that the psychoanalysts who thought they were giving placebos when they administered phenothiazines to schizophrenics were objectively mistaken. Within their disciplinary matrix, phenothiazines could function only as placebos; a psychoanalyst who later comes to accept the therapeutic efficacy of chemotherapy in psychosis has not so much "realized the earlier mistake" as he or she has shifted to a radically different disciplinary matrix, within which "placebo effect" *means* something very different compared to its role in the psychoanalytic matrix.

An alternative that is not acceptable is to waffle on the issue of matrix dependence and simply assume that the dominant Western scientific matrix is the reference point; some of my earlier statements have suggested confusion on this issue (e.g., see Brody, 1980, pp. 38–39). To the extent that such a sloppy and half-hearted relativism has come to affect definitions B:1, B:2, and B:3, Grünbaum is fully correct in criticizing them. Proper refinement of all these definitions would make clear the disciplinary-matrix-dependent character of the concepts; the definition of "therapy" (B:1) is probably the one most in need of such a cleanup. Perhaps Grünbaum's strategy in leaving "remedial" undefined is wisest after all.

These observations on the matrix dependence of the placebo concept place the disappearance problem in perspective. The basic question has to do with the projected new discoveries in neurophysiology, neurochemistry, and other fields, which will offer improved explanations of the phenomena we now classify as "symbolic healing." If the changes in our scientific world view that result are on the order of minor changes in theory, analogous to the autoimmune–zinc shift, then "placebo effect" may be refined in its application, but will retain essentially the same meaning and will not disappear in any sense. On the other hand, if the changes are more radical, they will lead to a revolutionary matrix shift more analogous to the demon–Western medicine transition. If this occurs, the placebo effect will not disappear, if what is meant by that is that the *same event* that was formerly called a placebo response is now explained on a different basis; along with the scientific revolution will have come totally new criteria for which events are the same and which are different, making any sort of cross-matrix debate on the issue pointless. Radical shifts in disciplinary matrix are essentially unpredictable, but it is worth noting that recent developments, which have been interpreted by some observers to be the first signs of a placebo disappearance, do not really seem at all indicative of such a revolutionary change. A commonly cited instance is the link between placebo response and endorphin release (Levine, Gordon, & Fields, 1978). Even if the current Western biomedical disciplinary matrix is as irremediably Cartesian and dualist as some insist, it must still accept the notion that a change in an individual's belief state, if it is to affect the rest of the body, must have accompanying neurophysiological phenomena (whether these are referred to as "connecting links" in a dualist model or "features" or "aspects" in a systems-hierarchical model). The explanatory problem, insofar as the placebo concept is concerned, has simply been relocated from asking why certain situations of a healing character produce positive bodily changes to asking why those situations promote the release of endorphins. And this does not in any way seem to suggest the imminent disappearance of the placebo concept.

Up till now I have been assuming (and have introduced the historical account of the three explanatory categories to support the assumption) that the dominant Western biomedical matrix does include room for the placebo effect in the sense that we mean the term. New discoveries about the power of belief states to alter bodily function and about the cultural dimensions of the healing process expand the matrix's set of theories, and in some ways lead it to a rediscovery of its too-readily-forgotten historical roots, but do not augur a radical disciplinary-matrix shift. By contrast, the criticism of my definition by Hahn (1983) seems to presuppose the idea that the dominant biomedical matrix is immovably materialistic and mechanistic, and can never adequately take into account psychological, let alone sociocultural, phenomena (cf. Hahn, 1982). This debate is of great interest to the philosophy of medicine as well as the philosophy of science. A definition of "placebo effect" that points out its disciplinary-matrix-dependent character seems more likely to promote and enhance this debate than does one that identifies the core sense of the placebo concept as matrix-independent.

To review, Grünbaum's definitions, while far advanced in clarity over many previous medical definitions, still define the placebo effect essentially by exclusion, as the effect not explainable by characteristic constituents of the treatment; thus no distinction is made between categories 1 and 2. Definition B:3 defines the placebo effect as a general therapeutic effect attributable to symbolic means, thus specifying category 2 and defining "placebo effect" by inclusion. (Again, definition B:4 of "placebo" fails to distinguish between categories 1 and 2, but this feature captures the actual role of the placebo control in a double-blind study, and reveals once again the need to define "placebo effect" independently from "placebo.") It is possible also to criticize definition B:3 from the other direction, and to contend that any definition that merely makes reference to "symbolic import" is overly vague and does not do justice to what we now know about the placebo effect. For example, Hahn (1983) has suggested that "placebo effect" ought to be defined in terms of "the pathogenic and therapeutic powers of expectation." This proposal is quite plausible and incorporates the theory of placebo causation that finds the widest support in the contemporary literature. There is, however, a problem with a definition that tries to be this specific, as shown by the possibility of significant counterexamples. One study of faith healing at Lourdes suggested that intensity of feeling was a better predictor of response to treatment than was content of belief: Those who felt strongly that they would improve and those who were most skeptical both had better healing rates than those with weaker convictions (Frank, 1974, pp. 71–72). An assumption underlying definition B:3 is that the precise role of expectation, emotional arousal, cultural behavior patterns, and the like in producing a placebo response needs still to be clarified by empirical research, and that the term "symbolic import" is sufficiently precise to serve as a guide to this research but not so precise as to appear to answer the empirical questions in advance.

CONCLUSIONS

A sound definition, by itself, will not take us far in understanding the placebo effect. We certainly require a definition that avoids conceptual confusion and that locates the placebo effect within a larger reference class of medical phenomena. But we also need a *model* that can serve as a background set of assumptions to tell us which theoretical approaches to the problem are most likely to be adequate and productive, and a *theory* that links the placebo effect to physician, patient, and illness variables in ways that are potentially falsifiable by empirical study.

I have been arguing that the most adequate definition is one that locates the placebo effect clearly within explanatory category 2 by making explicit reference to healing via the imagination or via symbolism; that relates the placebo effect to other "general" therapies by virtue of its all-pervasive presence within the healing practice; and that recognizes the triple relativity of the placebo effect to the tenets of the dominant biomedical theory, to physician beliefs, and to patient beliefs. I have suggested further that any definition, to accomplish these, will define "placebo effect" as the primary concept and "placebo" as a secondary concept. My criticisms of

Grünbaum's definitions have been aimed at the places where his approach deviates from this strategy.

Within contemporary medical thinking, the model best suited to explicating placebo phenomena is the systems-hierarchical model (Brody, 1973; Brody & Sobel, 1979), which has recently been refined and popularized as the "biopsychosocial model" (Engel, 1977). This approach fits comfortably within the probabilistic paradigm (Bursztajn et al., 1981) and thus allows for explanations in terms of statistical connections among complex networks of factors, instead of simplistically relying upon a linear cause-and-effect model. Since it locates physiological, psychological, and sociocultural phenomena as occurring at different levels of complexity within a hierarchy of homeostatically interrelated natural systems, it allows for the study of psychosomatic and culturally mediated events without interjecting the conceptual crudities of Cartesian mind–body dualism.

I have urged elsewhere the adoption of a "meaning model" as a suitable and testable working theory for the further investigation of the placebo effect (Brody, 1980; Brody & Waters, 1980). This theory asserts that a positive placebo response will be most likely to occur when three factors are optimally present: the meaning of the illness experience for the patient is altered in a positive manner, given the patient's preexisting belief system and world view; the patient is supported by a caring group; and the patient's sense of mastery and control over the illness is restored or enhanced. This theory attempts to refine the notion of "expectation" so as to yield more easily falsifiable predictions, and also highlights the cultural dimensions of the phenomena, so that the pertinence of cross-cultural studies in medical anthropology to placebo research can be shown more clearly.

Furthermore, the view of the placebo effect resulting from this definition–model–theory combination can be assessed from distinct practical contexts. Grünbaum approaches the problem primarily from the perspective of clinical research; his main interest is in the extent to which a psychotherapeutic theory such as psychoanalysis is actually falsifiable, which in turn raises the question of what would be the suitable control group against which such a theory could be tested (e.g., whether there can be such a thing as "placebo psychoanalysis"; see Grünbaum, 1980). This set of questions is of course of major importance for research in psychiatry and psychology. The great bulk of contemporary literature on the placebo effect (since 1945) has grown out of the role of placebos as controls in research. So there are undoubted advantages to adopting this perspective, and, as noted above, Grünbaum has succeeded admirably in clarifying some previously obscure points.

But other practical contexts place slightly different demands on a definition of "placebo effect." One such context is that of day-to-day medical practice. The scientifically informed practitioner will be aware that virtually every healing action he performs will have a symbolic effect, as well as a physiological or pharmacological effect, upon the patient; he or she will naturally wish to become more aware of those effects and to use them consciously, where possible, to the advantage of the patient. The physician is also aware, indeed, that placebo responses can be negative as well as positive, and so he or she will want especially to avoid any symbolic intervention that may make the patient's condition worse (e.g., by failing to make clear to a cancerphobic patient that the mole on the skin is probably benign, thereby allowing the patient to suffer from an increased state of anxiety). Now, as noted above, it does not matter for the investigator in a controlled, double-blind trial whether the cures in the control group are due to natural recuperative forces or to the symbolic effects of the placebo treatment (categories 1 and 2, respectively). But the practitioner has a much greater stake in sorting out those effects due directly to his or her interventions (either via symbolic or via physiological means) from those consequences that would have occurred anyway due to the patient's illness state and its natural history. Furthermore, modern scientific practitioners are aware of the placebo effect as a pervasive force in all of their activities, whereas they hardly ever employ placebos in pure form as a therapeutic modality (Goodwin, Goodwin, & Vogel, 1979); thus, an accurate definition of the former concept is much more useful to them than the latter.

Finally, there are ethical considerations. By Grünbaum's definition of "intentional placebo," it seems impossible to use a placebo without deceiving the patient and hence engaging in an ethically questionable practice. But it is possible to use a placebo such as a sugar pill as an effective therapeutic device while disclosing its precise contents to the patient (Vogel et al., 1980), as Grünbaum has been willing to recognize by offering to reconsider the fourth term of his definition G:1. And more significantly, the multitude of ways in which the practitioner can employ the placebo effect for the benefit of the patient, without ever using a placebo per se, seems to remove almost all impulse toward deception of patients (Brody, 1982). Defining "placebo effect" independently from "placebo" drives this ethical point home.

Ideally, the important insights to be gained from Grünbaum's analysis of the placebo concept can be integrated into the strategy that I have outlined in this chapter so as to enhance future research into the placebo effect.

ACKNOWLEDGMENTS

I am indebted to Joseph Hanna and Robert A. Hahn for extensive and thoughtful criticisms of an earlier draft of this chapter.

REFERENCES

Beecher, H. K. The powerful placebo. *Journal of the American Medical Association*, 1955, *176*, 1102–1107.

Brody, H. The systems view of man: Implications for medicine, science, and ethics. *Perspectives in Biology and Medicine*, 1973, *17*, 71–92.

Brody, H. *Placebos and the philosophy of medicine*. Chicago: University of Chicago Press, 1980.

Brody, H. The lie that heals: The ethics of giving placebos. *Annals of Internal Medicine*, 1982, *97*, 112–118.

Brody, H., & Sobel, D. S. A systems view of health and disease. In D. S. Sobel (Ed.), *Ways of health*. New York: Harcourt Brace Jovanovich, 1979.

Brody, H., & Waters, D. B. Diagnosis is treatment. *Journal of Family Practice*, 1980, *10*, 445–449.

Burton, R. *The anatomy of melancholy*. New York: Empire State Book Company, 1924. (Originally published, 1621.)

Bursztajn, H., Feinbloom, R. I., Hamm, R. M., & Brodsky, A. *Medical choices, medical chances*. New York: Delacorte Press, 1981.

Caplan, A. L., Engelhardt, H. T., & McCartney, J. J. (Eds.). *Concepts of health and disease: Interdisciplinary perspectives*. Reading, Mass.: Addison-Wesley, 1981.

Clouser, D. K., Culver, C. M., & Gert, B. Malady: A new treatment of disease. *Hastings Center Report*, 1981, *11*(3), 29–37.

Engel, G. L. The need for a new medical model: A challenge for biomedicine. *Science*, 1977, *196*, 129–136.

Ford, P. L. (Ed.). *The writings of Thomas Jefferson* (Vol. 9). New York: Putnam, 1898.

Frank, J. D. *Persuasion and healing*. New York: Schocken Books, 1974.

Goodwin, J. S., Goodwin, J. M., & Vogel, A. V. Knowledge and use of placebos by house officers and nurses. *Annals of Internal Medicine*, 1979, *91*, 106–110.

Grünbaum, A. Epistemological liabilities of the clinical appraisal of psychoanalytic theory. *Nous*, 1980, *14*, 307–385.

Grünbaum, A. The placebo concept. *Behaviour Research and Therapy*, 1981, *19*, 157–167.

Hahn, R. A. "Treat the patient, not the lab": Internal medicine and the concept of "person." *Culture, Medicine and Psychiatry*, 1982, *6*, 219–236.

Hahn, R. A. *Rethinking the placebo phenomenon*. Manuscript in preparation, 1983.

Kuhn, T. S. *The structure of scientific revolutions*. Chicago: University of Chicago Press, 1970.

Kuhn, T. S. Objectivity, value judgment, and theory choice. In T. S. Kuhn (Ed.), *The essential tension*. Chicago: University of Chicago Press, 1977. (a)

Kuhn, T. S. Second thoughts on paradigms. In F. Suppe (Ed.), *The structure of scientific theories* (2nd ed.). Urbana: University of Illinois Press, 1977. (b)

Lain Entralgo, P. *The therapy of the word in classical antiquity* (L. J. Rather & J. M. Sharp, Eds. and trans.). New Haven: Yale University Press, 1970.

Levine, J. D., Gordon, N. C., & Fields, H. L. The mechanism of placebo analgesia. *Lancet*, 1978, *2*, 654–657.

Neuberger, M. *The doctrine of the healing power of nature throughout the course of time*. New York: Linn J. Boyd, 1932.

Park, L. C., & Covi, L. Nonblind placebo trial: An exploration of neurotic outpatients response to placebo when its inert content is disclosed. *Archives of General Psychiatry*, 1965, *12*, 336–345.

Shapiro, A. K. Semantics of the placebo. *Psychiatric Quarterly*, 1968, *42*, 653–696.

Shapiro, A. K., & Morris, L. A. The placebo effect in medical and psychological therapies. In S. L. Garfield & A. E. Bergin (Eds.), *Handbook of psychotherapy and behavior change* (2nd ed.). New York: Wiley, 1978.

Shapiro, A. K., & Shapiro, E. The placebo effect: Art or science? *Medical Times*, June 1982, pp. 45s–52s.

Suppe, F. (Ed.). *The structure of scientific theories* (2nd ed.). Urbana: University of Illinois Press, 1977.

Vogel, A. V., Goodwin, J. S., & Goodwin, J. M. The therapeutics of placebo. *American Family Physician*, 1980, *22*, 105–109.

4

Discussion

Placebo: Defining the Unknown

T. D. BORKOVEC

The opportunity to read the thoughts of two authors who have devoted considerable thought to the perplexing issue of placebo has been a humbling and educational experience. Logic was, unfortunately, my worst subject in college. My strengths (or biases) of background, however, are twofold: (1) a love for linear, cause-and-effect, scientific inquiry into human behavior, and (2) an appreciation for the awesomeness of human behavior that derives from devoting one's professional life to its investigation. I do not have much to say about the latter here. It is worthwhile to point out, however, that for me the placebo effect represents one of those amazing "realities" that on my pessimistic side indicates how little we know about human behavior, despite our painstakingly slow progress in learning how to relieve human suffering; and on my optimistic side hints at what incredible potential may exist within human psychological abilities. The possibility that what one believes to be true may actually influence what does become true is nothing short of spectacular in its implications. If I had been asked to write about theories of placebo, I would have become quite expansive and speculative. Fortunately for this book, I was not asked to do this.

I was asked to comment on the two authors' definitional approaches to placebo. It is clear from these two chapters that agreed-upon definitions of placebo and placebo effect are, in the main, not forthcoming. Sincere and serious disagreements remain. I am in no position to offer any greater clarity, so I do two things here by way of commentary. First, I mention some comments contained in the chapters to which I have particularly strong reactions. Second, I assume the position of devil's advocate and argue that in the last analysis we should probably abandon the placebo concept. I do the latter in the face of Brody's arguments to the contrary, in the hope of

T. D. Borkovec. Department of Psychology, The Pennsylvania State University, University Park, Pennsylvania.

generating multiple viewpoints to facilitate others' critical thinking and for the sake of remaining consistent with past statements I have made.

Grünbaum has made a particularly useful argument regarding the relativity of the concept of placebo. His definitions divide the therapeutic universe of procedural elements into those predicted by a specific theory to be active in the treatment of a disorder versus those elements left unmentioned or considered irrelevant by the theory. This approach wisely leaves an open system for the specification of what will be considered placebo and what will be identified as active treatment. A further advantage to this view is made explicit later in Chapter 2, when he notes that a placebo effect is without question mediated by a specific mechanism. Part of the confusion in past literature is thus eliminated, and our eyes are pointed toward the logical next step. The term "nonspecific" has at times simply meant elements of a therapy that are not unique to that therapy but are common across many therapies. Unfortunately, the term has at times been applied to effects rather than to procedural elements. Replacing "nonspecific" with "incidental" helps to keep us focused on procedural elements and their theory-relative characteristics, rather than on effects that are surely specifiable. The logical next step is to concentrate research efforts into isolating empirical relationships between procedural elements and behavioral effects and into identifying the specific mechanisms whereby such effects occur. Such a strategy seems appropriate whether we are investigating "active" therapy procedures (i.e., procedures demonstrated to be superior to a placebo procedure for a given disorder) in order to learn more about its principles and the principles of human behavior underlying its effectiveness, or the placebo effect itself in order to elucidate its nature and thus shed light on another aspect of the nature of human beings.

One further point might be useful to emphasize regarding characteristic and incidental factors in therapy procedures. The active elements of a therapy may be the very factors considered to be characteristic by a particular theory of mode of action, but that theory, while correctly identifying the characteristics, may be mistaken about mode of action. For example, in the anxiety area, certain learning theories and subsequent research have identified exposure to a feared stimulus as an active procedural ingredient in the treatment of phobias. But whether the mode of action is best described by extinction, counterconditioning, cognitive restructuring, or any other perspective remains debatable. A theory may thus be partially correct because it has identified characteristic factors or because it has specified a valid description of mode of action.

Grünbaum's emphasis on the specific nature of placebo mechanisms also serves to remind us to avoid myopia with regard to human change, whether it is physical or psychological/behavioral in its outcome. The fact that a particular drug is specifically efficacious in eliminating a specific disease process does not imply that such a disease process might not be eliminated by a wholly different, specific mechanism, be it physical or psychological according to our current ways of categorizing procedures. For example, to pick just one potentially dramatic area, if Hall's (1983) demonstration of the possible influence of imagery and hypnotic procedures on the immune system holds up under further experimental scrutiny, then Brody's comments about the healing power of imagination must be taken seriously as an alternative vehicle of cure, in addition to surgical or medicinal approaches to some diseases. More familiarly, aspirin and relaxation techniques employing pleasant imagery may both be efficacious in reducing tension headaches. I as a psychologist may see a disorder at one level of analysis, while my medical colleagues may see the same disorder from another perspective. This is the beauty of many of Brody's arguments pointing to the disciplinary-matrix dependency of world views. The human being is not constructed according to any one myopic view, so that several relatively true perspectives on explanation can coexist, and there may be several paths with their own specific or overlapping mechanisms by which an outcome takes place.

The strength of Brody's comments resides for me not so much in the specifics of his definitions as in (1) the elaboration of the notion of levels of explanation within and across disciplinary matrices, and (2) the centrality of the patient in his definition of placebo. We Western scientists will have very red faces if indeed it turns out that diabolic possession has a validity conceptually closer to that imagined by Brody's hypothetical non-Western shamans than to our own medical theories. But this example reminds us to avoid becoming overly comfortable with our own theories and to look periodically outside of ourselves as we continue to go deeply into investigations within our chosen perspective. Within medical theory, Brody suggests the possible relevance of natural history, symbolic effects, and specific, characteristic treatment effects as types of explanations. My only disagreement with this classification would suggest that placing placebo effects into the category of symbolic effects may mistakenly force our attention away from Grünbaum's emphasis on the specificity of the placebo effect. I heartily agree, however, with Brody's conviction that the patient's imagination, belief, and emotion play a crucial role. At the present time, it seems unwise to consider the concept of placebo without an appreciation for the significance of the patient's construction of his or her world. In a legitimate sense, especially in psychotherapy research, the identification of an "objective" stimulus has less to do with a subject's response than does the subject's interpretation of the meaning or significance of that stimulus. Whether the guiding theory couches that fact in classical conditioning terms (e.g., the central evaluative response; see Levey & Martin, 1983) or in cognitive processes (e.g., belief systems; see Beck, 1976), future discoveries concerning the mechanisms of placebo action will unquestionably lead us in that direction.

By stating these three types of explanations for curative processes and by concluding in his chapter that definition without model and theory will not advance our understanding of placebo very far, Brody sets the stage for the notions I wish to present.

"Placebo" is a word used to label a procedure (1) that produces a positive or negative therapeutic effect, or no effect at all; and/or (2) for whose possible outcomes we have no current theoretical model. When stated in this way—and, indeed, this seems to be the common ground in both of the preceding chapters—one wonders how conceptual confusion regarding a construct whose essential meaning is currently grounded in ignorance can ever be satisfactorily defined. The issue is reminiscent of the concept of "idiopathic illness" (i.e., an illness that has an unknown cause and is not secondary to some other identifiable process). Knowing what it is not is useful, but knowing what it is eludes us. When faced with concepts specifically invented to label our ignorance, it seems that our best choice is to pursue the investigation of the phenomenon, so that its meaning continually emerges within a growing context of empirical and theoretical networks developed from such investigation.

Because I sometimes hold such a view, it is my purpose to argue that the concept of placebo should in large part be abandoned. The remaining small part is as follows: We will always find ourselves in partial ignorance about the causes of human behavior. Our theories are indeed only metaphorical expressions of consistencies we observe in our world and the meanings we associate with them within our "disciplinary matrices." In some circumstances (e.g., those conditions eloquently outlined by Grünbaum and Brody in their attempts to clarify the terms surrounding the concept of placebo) and in the absence of existing theories, we certainly may choose to look up from our bewildered mental state and say the effect was due to "placebo." But we probably would benefit from avoiding a feeling of satisfaction from so doing. Our real task is to continue exploring effects that we do not understand. Conceptual and definitional clarity will certainly help, and in this the two authors have provided us with improvements and thought-provoking debate. It is, on the other hand, advantageous to realize that definitional chapters can sometimes ring a note of finality, as if satisfactory definition has been achieved, when in fact such is impossible with an ignorance-based concept like placebo. We do not know what we do not know. The task of defining what we do not know will always fail.

The same comments in general form are, of course, applicable to existing theories of effective therapy techniques (i.e., nonplacebos), or indeed of any human phenomenon. Theories are in a constant process of change due to new empirical relationships or new, superior, subsuming theories. Each theory has its restricted domain and its area of ignorance beyond that domain. A current theory has pragmatic value for providing a useful feeling of understanding; for providing a somewhat accurate basis for making a prediction or modifying a behavior; or for guiding new and profitable research that further increases understanding, prediction, or control. But the theory is false in an ultimate sense, soon to be replaced by something better. So to say that a placebo effect has no relevant existing theory for its explanation, whereas the therapeutic effectiveness of repeated exposure to a feared stimulus given to a phobic individual does have such theory, should not imply that the latter theory is in any way absolutely true and accurate. Further research will show this not to be the case. The point is that existing theory at least gives us a basis for pursuing a phenomenon and learning more about it. In the absence of placebo theory, specific definition seems futile. The two authors appear to appreciate this, inasmuch as theoretical notions clearly enter into their definitions (e.g., Brody's "symbolic import" and Grünbaum's "patient beliefs").

Having momentarily realized that I do not have an explanation for a phenomenon, and having called it a placebo effect because it fits within someone's definition of such an effect, what remains for me to do? For the researcher, the commitment is to the elucidation of the meaning of the phenomenon via scientific inquiry. There are, of course, choices here, from Newtonian cause-and-effect models to the probabilistic models that Brody feels may be more heuristic. But the bottom line is the same. Scientific approaches, as one source of knowledge about the world, can provide information on relationships among variables, and by so doing can produce the fodder for the theory construction that guides further empirical work.

I happen to be a proponent of the strong-inference approach (Platt, 1964) to therapy research. The essence of strong inference is the disconfirmation of crucial rival hypotheses and the recycling of such experimentation upon remaining, unrejected hypotheses. Our own approach (Borkovec & Bauer, 1982) has been to apply this procedure not only to competing theories and hypotheses about treatment procedures, but also to competing procedural elements within or across therapies. The latter application is particularly useful in the absence of good theory. Procedural elements can be divided or interactively combined, contrasted with one another, and eliminated as irrelevant to therapeutic effect. Such a component control approach is simply an extension to therapy ingredients of the customary placebo comparison design, wherein we wish to control for all of those known and unknown contributions of the general healing context. The same component control strategy can be applied to the ingredients of a "placebo" procedure itself if we wish to identify relationships between the stimuli contained therein and patient change. Thus, for example, placebo elements may be manipulated in terms of any number of variables thought to possibly underlie the placebo effect (e.g., patient expectation, physician belief, payment of fees, attention to the problem, physician suggestions of relief), with empirical evidence ruling out the relevance of some variables and encouraging further exploration of variables surviving disconfirmation.

Contrasting theories of surviving variables may be pitted against one another, or further testing of subingredients within a single variable may be performed.

While many may reject such an approach as overly mechanistic, reductionistic, or linear, the resulting data will at least give us more information about relationships among things we do as therapists and changes that occur in patients, and at best will provide an identification of important functional aspects of what we call "placebo" and a network of relationships upon which to build theories about the specific mechanisms of placebo. Either outcome results in the ultimate definition of "placebo," either as a case of a more general law of behavior (and so the term "placebo" disappears within that researched domain) or within a growing theoretical network surrounding the concept of placebo itself. But, in terms of the latter case, notice that when Brody introduces such notions as "the healing power of imagination," experimental analysis of the effects of imagination on psychological and physical processes becomes an example of a possible research focus, and the outcome of such activity will be the specification of relationships between those two domains. What will emerge will be theories about a specific mechanism reflective of a general principle of behavior. And, of course, we will no doubt find in the future more than one such mechanism accounting for the broad and no doubt heterogeneous class of phenomena now called placebo effects.

Despite the counterargument that this research process simply shifts from one type of explanation to another type, our advantage is that we will have specific, functional, and empirically meaningful definitions of processes once attributed to the vague placebo notion. Those definitions will be better because less will be unknown, even though the unknown is ridiculously large.

REFERENCES

Beck, A. T. *Cognitive therapy and emotional disorders*. New York: International Universities Press, 1976.

Borkovec, T. D., & Bauer, R. Experimental design in group outcome research. In A. Bellack, M. Hersen, & A. Kazdin (Eds.), *International handbook of behavior modification and therapy*. New York: Plenum, 1982.

Hall, H. R. Hypnosis and the immune system: A review with implications for cancer and the psychology of healing. *American Journal of Clinical Hypnosis*, 1983, *25*, 92–103.

Levey, A. B., & Martin, I. Cognitions, evaluations and conditioning: Rules of sequence and rules of consequence. *Advances in Behavior Research and Therapy*, 1983, *4*, 177–223.

Platt, J. R. Strong inference. *Science*, 1964, *146*, 347–353.

RESEARCH METHODS

5

Placebo Agentry: Assessment of Drug and Placebo Effects

SHERMAN ROSS

L. W. BUCKALEW

In our modern society, one more closely than ever attuned to the advances of medical science and technology (Byerly, 1976), the quest for a "magic bullet" capable of dealing with everything from a hangnail to a cancer is heightened by each new announcement of a "miracle" drug or advanced technique. Pills, capsules, and injections have become closely associated with relief from pain, discomfort, and many ailments and diseases. Unfortunately, the same popularity may be ascribed to drug preparations used to escape from the very reality that so proficiently provides these medications, as attested to by the rising drug abuse problem. People have become accustomed to the belief that a drug represents potential relief from any undesirable psychological or physiological state, with at least three major sources of such drugs: the medical doctor, the corner drug store, and the illegal distributor. It may be hypothesized that drugs, however obtained, spell relief, with little specific interest in or concern for the actual pharmacological properties of the preparation. This leaves the stage set for deception, predicated on the needs of a drug user or recipient.

A different perspective, albeit no less scientific, is the concept of a medicinal drug preparation, the concern for which is centrally in terms of its pharmacological action on a living organism. Medicine strives to develop and perfect safe and effective drug preparations designed to relieve or ameliorate specific physiological or psychological conditions. Such an interest is primarily concerned with the efficacious alteration of structure or function in an organism. Such alterations are both desirable and necessary in restoring or maintaining the validity of the organism. At some point, a trained professional makes the decision that a given drug preparation is indicated and that this drug is needed by the patient for therapeutic reasons. However, the very recognition that an individual equates drugs and relief, hence acknow-

Sherman Ross. Department of Psychology, Howard University, Washington, D.C.

L. W. Buckalew. Department of Psychology, Alabama A & M University, Normal, Alabama.

ledging need and belief, again sets the stage for deception, be it deliberate or unwitting.

Clearly, drugs can be miracles or menaces depending on their purpose and use, but we would suggest that all drugs inherently incorporate an element of deception. However, this deception should not necessarily be considered as negative or harmful, nor is it necessarily intentional. Indeed, it may be deliberate, self-motivated, or a combination of both. If we rename "deception" as "psychological factors directly related to prescribing, obtaining, using, and believing in a preparation," a clearer picture of this central concept emerges. To argue the ethics of using these factors (Bok, 1974; Carter & Allen, 1973; Liberman, 1962; O'Leary & Borkovec, 1978), assuming positive intent, is beyond the scope of this chapter. Similarly, it is not our intent to trace the history of the use of these factors in medical treatment.[1] Our purpose is to introduce the reader to the nature and extent of these psychological factors associated with drugs and to provide an overview of how such "nonspecific factors," as they are called, have been and should be treated in drug research. To accomplish this goal, we have segmented our discussion into two topical presentations. One topic, for which we provide only an overview, is "Placebo Agentry"; under this heading, we discuss some of the known factors, both physical and mental, that are responsive to placebo manipulation. The second topic, "Drug Research and the Placebo," presumes recognition of agentry and is devoted to methods of separating the effects of nonspecific factors from the true drug effects. A supplementary purpose of this chapter is to provide the interested reader with a representative and relatively extensive reference base to facilitate more detailed exploration of specific topics, issues, and phenomena. In combination, we hope to provide a clearer understanding and appreciation of the placebo and its use in drug research.

PLACEBO AGENTRY

It has been argued that the history of the placebo and that of medicine are inseparable (Shapiro, 1960). Indeed, we might extend this analogy by suggesting that medical therapeutics and placebo effects are inherently entwined (Bok, 1974), though we do not mean to imply that medical treatment itself is a placebo. "To please" and "to placate" are short definitions of "placebo" that appear frequently in the literature. To integrate these thoughts, it might be appropriate to consider a placebo as any treatment

1. Attention is directed to Shapiro (1968), who has provided a detailed and extensive historical treatment of the placebo. Also, we (Ross & Buckalew, 1983) have elsewhere provided a tabularized list of additional contributions to historical development of placebos.

or preparation given a patient or client that does not provide any direct pharmacological or psychotherapeutic effect for the specific condition being treated. Again, our purpose is not to argue the semantics of the word "placebo," as so eloquently addressed by Shapiro (1968) and Beecher (1955), but rather to offer a conceptual framework for the discussion to follow. In essence, the general concept of a placebo portrayed here is that it represents the personification of a myriad of nonspecific drug/therapy factors.

While the scope of our attention does not allow due consideration of all known nonspecific factors, attention is directed to previous reviews and discussions that provide more detailed coverage of this topic (Buckalew & Ross, 1981; Fisher, 1970; Kissel & Barrucand, 1964; Nash, 1960; Ray, 1978). It may be appropriate, in a representative and illustrative fashion, to touch on some of the most important and best-acknowledged nonspecific factors. Remember, these nonspecific factors are as integral a part of the treatment of a client or patient as is pharmacokinetics, surgery, or active therapeutic intervention. Indeed, some researchers as well as practitioners have argued, perhaps not too popularly, that a large part of patients' improvement or recovery in many cases is the product of nonspecific or placebo factors (Byerly, 1976). A wide range of research efforts has been devoted to the empirical identification and exeprimental manipulation of particular nonspecific factors. Many of these efforts have produced rather dramatic alterations of behavior or condition, giving rise to the formal consideration of placebo agentry.

Just what operations and conditions constitute recognized nonspecific factors? That is, what are the supportive components of a placebo effect or response? Most pharmacological and medical texts acknowledge the existence of nonspecific factors, though typically in subdued fashion. Indeed, one researcher (Evans, 1974a) has indicted the placebo effect as a medical nuisance, and Benson and Epstein (1975) contend that the prevalent attitude in medicine for the placebo effect is disdain. Apparently, some disciplines, or at least some of its practitioners, fear that recognition of placebo effects and the powerful influence a placebo can have detracts from their power, authority, and expertise, and ultimately serves as a source of embarrassment (Rachman & Philips, 1975). We would suggest that, to the contrary, recognition and appreciation of the "powerful placebo" (Beecher, 1955) can add appreciably to the efficacy of any indicated therapeutic treatment. Let us consider some of these factors, with the understanding that appropriate manipulations thereof can serve as aids, rather than impediments, to the fullest, most efficacious, and most beneficial therapeutic treatment of a patient or client.

As we consider an overview of nonspecific factors, keep in mind that these are the very same variables responsible for or involved in the placebo effect. For the interested researcher, we provide for each noted nonspecific factor a list of references facilitating further exploration. Perhaps the most important, or at least the most researched, nonspecific factors are these:

1. The doctor–patient relationship (Gelbman, 1967; Sleisenger, 1958).
2. The patient's expectations and needs (Affleck, 1966; Aletky & Carlin, 1975; Beecher, 1952; Ehrenwald, 1974; Hurst, Weidner, Radlow, & Ross, 1973; Rosenthal & Frank, 1956; Tetreault & Bordeleou, 1971).
3. Suggestion (Buckalew, 1969, 1972).
4. The patient's personality and psychological state (Buckalew, Ross, & Starr, 1981; Ray, 1978).
5. Symptom or discomfort severity (Aletky & Carlin, 1975; Ray, 1978).
6. Instructions (Buckalew, 1972; Lyerly, Ross, Krugman, & Clyde, 1964; Ross et al., 1962).
7. Preparation characteristics (Buckalew & Coffield, 1982a, 1982b; Buckalew & Ross, 1981; Jacobs & Nordan, 1979; Morris & O'Neal, 1974).
8. Environmental milieu (Beck, 1977; Fisher, 1970).

Each one of these factors may be manipulated to produce an optimal level or effect, though the picture becomes more complicated experimentally when considering the potential interactive processes, as some degree or state of each variable exists in any client or patient relationship. Research involving these factors has sought to determine the relative importance of each variable in terms of its contribution to a placebo response or effect. Again, remember that a placebo response or effect is inherent in any drug or therapy response (Berg, 1977; Bok, 1974; Vrhovac, 1977). Indeed, the ultimate research problem in this area—to be addressed later in this chapter—is to be able to separate effects directly attributable to the drug or therapy from those associated with a placebo response or effect.[2]

Now that we have, in cursory fashion, established the nature and importance of nonspecific factors in therapeutic intervention, all of which constitute precipitant, predisposing, or supportive variables, we may shift our attention to effects. We have chosen to approach this topic under the rubric of "agentry." This concept of agentry assumes that the placebo, whatever its operational form, functions as an agent in the process of bringing a patient or client from condition A to condition B. However, prior to delving into agentry, a semantic distinction must be made and appreciated involving "response" and "effect." As argued by several investigators (Buckalew,

---

2. Liberman (1962, 1964) directed early attention to the important distinction between "response" and "effect," and we (Ross & Buckalew, 1983) have offered a careful delineation of these terms, along with a detailed rationale for appreciating this distinction.

1972; Fisher, 1970; Liberman, 1962, 1964; Ross & Buckalew, 1983), "response" and "effect" are different words bearing quite different connotations. Indeed, it might be argued that considerably more clarity would be lent to drug and placebo research if more attention were paid to this distinction.

For some 20 years, it has been argued that a drug or placebo response is quite different from a drug or placebo effect. Fisher (1970) approached this semantic problem, which can ultimately lead to drug research misinterpretation, by carefully noting that what follows the administration of a drug is a drug response. This is different from saying that the observed therapeutic change is due to the effect of the drug. In essence, the inference is that a response to a drug is not necessarily a drug effect. As we have noted, drug responses may occur solely due to nonspecific factors, with the drug itself literally having no effect. More recently, we (Ross & Buckalew, 1983) have approached the response versus effect dichotomy in terms of the degree of behavioral or therapeutic change associated with a drug or placebo. Inherent in this perspective is the assumption that, at least for placebos, any alteration in behavior or condition constitutes a response, while the term "effect" is appropriate only to such change when it significantly exceeds that witnessed in an appropriate control group. Implicit in both Fisher's (1970) and our (Ross & Buckalew, 1983) perspectives is the idea that "response" constitutes a large and potentially nondescript domain, while "effect" represents that portion of the response domain that can be directly attributed to the specific action of a drug or placebo. We would further argue that if a drug "effect" in a well-controlled study was insufficient to differ significantly from an appropriate standard of comparison, the drug's efficacy would certainly be questionable.

With this resolution of an important problem, let us explore the realm of placebo agentry. This adventure is not necessarily intended to impress one with the vast range of human functions and conditions that have been influenced by simply the administration of a placebo, but rather to develop an appreciation that many organismic states, functions, and capabilities thought to be relatively impervious to anything but direct pharmacological influence are not necessarily so. Let there be little doubt that the administration of a placebo, as a pharmacologically or therapeutically inert preparation, when coupled with careful attention to major nonspecific factors, can constitute a very powerful and influential treatment. Further, we must recognize that placebos can come in many forms, and are certainly not limited to pills or capsules. To extend this thought, simply think about such phenomena as self-fulfilling prophecy (Rosenthal, 1963), the Hawthorne effect[3] (Mayo, 1933; Snow, 1927), and some of the various forms of meditation and self-discipline. While we make no suggestions as to their validity or invalidity,

3. An interesting reevaluation and potential explanation of this phenomenon is provided by Parsons (1974, 1978).

faith healing and some cathartic religious phenomena certainly also lend themselves to consideration from a placebo effect perspective. Lastly, it would seem that the relatively high incidence of spontaneous remission of symptoms in some physical and many mental disorders might suggest that many therapeutic approaches constitute little more than placebo treatments (Brodeur, 1965; Demarr & Pelikan, 1955; O'Leary & Borkovec, 1978; Silbergeld, Manderscheid, & Soeken, 1976).

The literature abounds with admonishments to recognize and appreciate the placebo, along with testimonials of its power. Ironically, as noted by Shapiro (1960) and Brodeur (1965), few papers were written about the placebo before the 1950s; during and following this decade, a proliferation of research demonstrating the placebo phenomenon began (Pihl & Altman, 1971). Particularly good reviews of early placebo work are available (Haas, Fink, & Hartfelder, 1959; Shapiro, 1968), and Turner, Gallimore, and Fox-Henning (1980) have provided a compilation of nearly 1000 articles dealing with placebos. Similarly, pleas for the formal recognition and respect of placebos as potentially significant manipulators of behavior continue to invade the literature (Ehrenwald, 1974; Goldstein, 1962; Rachman & Philips, 1975; Ross & Buckalew, 1979; Rubin, 1963). Ultimately, there is little room in either medicine or psychology for ignorance of placebo phenomena, or for failure to recognize and appreciate their efficacy in altering internal condition or behavior. Shapiro (1968) was able to find references to the placebo in medical literature as early as 1691, and it seems ironic, particularly considering the massive amount of material on placebos reported by Turner et al. (1980), that it has taken our disciplines nearly 300 years to do justice formally and comprehensively to what has been characterized by Evans (1974b) and Martin (1964) as essential to medicine.

But glowing attempts to extol the power and virtues of placebos would be void without specific documentation, an overview of which we offer under the rubric of placebo agentry. Just what are the behaviors and conditions that lend themselves to placebo manipulations? We (Ross & Buckalew, 1979) have suggested that the need exists for a comprehensive review, analysis, and evaluation of the placebo as a precursor to a more accurate conceptualization and more effective use of its properties. From this suggestion, several review efforts have followed, designed to summarize available knowledge on specific aspects of the placebo: personality variables and placebo responsivity (Buckalew et al., 1981), perceptual characteristics of placebos (Buckalew & Coffield, 1982a, 1982b; Buckalew & Ross, 1981), and placebo agentry (Ross & Buckalew, 1983). Of appreciable aid in obtaining a sense of the many diverse effects placebos can have is the comprehensive compilation of placebo research summaries spanning nearly 80 years by Turner et al. (1980). While placebos are perhaps best known as control agents in drug research, prescribed "pacifiers" in some medical cases, and successful modulators in an embarrassingly large number of pain complaints, there are many cognitive, physiological, affective, psychomotor, and clinical behaviors or conditions for which placebos have been shown to be influential.

As noted (Ross & Buckalew, 1979), it is quite evident that placebos, by design or inadvertently, constitute viable experimental manipulations involving a range of behavioral or psychological variables. Good examples of earlier efforts to explore the range of potential manipulations are the studies of multiple tasks by Lehmann and Knight (1960) and Nash (1962). Most recently, we (Ross & Buckalew, 1983) have provided an overview of representative studies that used placebos in attempts to influence some specific response. This review includes tabularized results of some 50 different studies reporting on attempts to manipulate at least 70 different variables. In summary, the following conclusions have been offered (Ross & Buckalew, 1983). In studies involving psychomotor abilities, reaction time and grip strength seemed sensitive to placebo manipulation, while tapping speed seemed less so. Among physiological variables, pulse rate, blood pressure, and pain appeared manipulable. With cognitive measures, placebos appeared more likely to influence short-term rote memory, as most complex performances were not appreciably altered. For affective measures, self-perceptions of relaxation and activation seemed conducive to placebo manipulation, though changes in general mood appeared less reliably altered. While clinical indices of placebo manipulations were numerous, lack of replication and differences in evaluation clouded conclusions; nevertheless, strong evidence exists for the suggestion that the physical nature of the placebo may be a significant factor in determining its effect. The measures surveyed ranged from anxiety to writing speed, from angina pain to ward activity, and from functions mediated by the autonomic nervous system to clearly higher-level mental processes. Naturally, there are appreciable problems in any attempt to draw firm conclusions about the nature and extent of variables responsive to placebo effects, due to the lack of comparability between and replications of studies, different modes of evaluation, and different control conditions. We (Ross & Buckalew, 1983) have concluded that both psychology and medicine are necessarily and increasingly accepting that the placebo, traditionally used as a control, can constitute a powerful treatment over a wide range of variables—psychological as well as physiological.

As evidence on the agentry of placebos mounts, and as we become more knowledgeable about the manipulation potentials of a placebo treatment, a number of methodological issues and considerations that are particularly relevant to the use of placebos in drug research emerge. These concerns range from the nature of the placebo itself as a stimulus to the mimicry of a drug response complete with side effects. These issues, along with others, ultimately emphasize the fundamental consideration of the placebo as a control and the adequacy of currently used drug research designs. With a clearer appreciation of the power and potentials of the placebo, let us now turn our attention to these thorny problems.

DRUG RESEARCH AND THE PLACEBO

Perhaps the best way to establish a theme for what follows is to refer to the pointed, succinct, and dramatic statement of Ross, Krugman, Lyerly, and Clyde (1962) that a placebo group does not necessarily constitute a fully controlled condition. As has been recently reiterated (Buckalew & Coffield, 1982b; Buckalew & Ross, 1981), the placebo itself represents a manipulable variable, the characteristics of which may provide distinct consequences. Even with this recognition, there remain many questions of the adequacy of conventional drug research designs: single-, double-, and triple-blind studies, with or without crossover. But before dealing specifically with research designs, let us first gain a more thorough understanding and appreciation of the placebo itself as an "inert" pharmacological or therapeutic treatment.

There should be little argument with the statement that the placebo has an indispensable role in the control of drug research (Kurland, 1957). As noted by Rubin (1963), any therapeutic maneuver must be properly controlled, though we must respect the fact that the placebo has distinct and recognized power and properties. While the placebo has enjoyed a position as the control of choice in drug studies, evidence casting doubt on the purity of such practices has been accumulating for many years. Most recently, Schindel (1978) pointed out that the placebo has been used since about 1950 in drug evaluations, though definite problems connected with such use exist.

It was long ago established by Lasagna, Laties, and Dohan (1958) that placebos may be shown to have demonstrable peak, cumulative, and carry-over effects, just as would be presumed of an active drug, and Beecher (1955) even made reference to possible toxic effects. In a review of over 60 papers, Pogge (1963) found numerous side effects and toxic effects from placebos, the most common of which were drowsiness, headache, nervousness, insomnia, nausea, and constipation. Buckert and Niederberger (1963) cautioned that placebo side effects should not be confused with those of the actual drug, and Green (1964) found that placebos accentuated the severity of side effect symptoms present prior to treatment. Given the knowledge that placebo side effects do occur, it remained to be suggested that drug research use placebos that mimic the side effects of active drugs being tested (Blumenthal, Burke, & Shapiro, 1974; Dinnerstein & Halm, 1970). There is an associated suggestion that the use of "impure" or "active" placebos (i.e., mild pharmacological agents without specific remedy for a given ailment) might be desirable (Fellner, 1958; Schindel, 1962). The current status of such considerations appears to be characterized by Dinnerstein and Halm's (1970) suggestion that placebos should be used that produce transient feelings of internal change as amplifiers of any placebo effect. In essence, people given an active drug typically expect some physiological indication of drug action. If a drug is to be compared with a placebo for evaluation, and we are concerned that only the pharmacology of the active drug be allowed to vary in a well-controlled study, use of an "impure" placebo that is likely to produce discernible effects, though not specific to the condition being treated, seems plausible and proper.

Haas *et al* (1959) suggested that subjective sensory qualities may play an important part in the placebo effect, and Shapiro, Wilensky, and Struening (1968) stated that the nature of the placebo stimulus is crucial in the measurement of placebo effects. In response to these concerns, we (Buckalew & Ross, 1981) reviewed the available experimental findings relative to placebo perceptual characteristics, including route of administration, dosage, taste, and color. We reported a paucity of empirical information about these concerns, suggesting that personal preference and/or tradition probably served as the basis for selecting a placebo. Buckalew and Coffield (1982a, 1982b) investigated the specific placebo variables of color, size, and preparation form, and found several significant color effects relating capsule color to perceived drug action, a definite preference for capsules over tablets in perceived strength, and relationships between preparation size and perceived strength. Such data, along with those of Jacobs and Nordan (1979), argue rather strongly for differential placebo–drug effects based on perceptual characteristics of the preparation. In essence, people appear to have many definable biases related to drugs and their anticipated effects, and adequately controlled research must be cognizant of and responsive to these "built-in" mental sets. While considerations for the use of a standardized placebo (Atkinson, 1958; Blumenthal *et al.*, 1974) can be appreciated for their intent, adequately controlled drug research appears to necessitate the use of "matching" placebos long ago suggested by Travell (1955). Interestingly, Blumenthal *et al.* (1974) found medical students to be very successful in distinguishing active drugs from placebos based on perceptual characteristics, even when "identical matching placebos" were used. Obviously, the importance of using placebos that are in every way except pharmacologically identical to the active drug can not be underestimated.

Given the efficacious value of true "matching" placebos and strong consideration of an "impure" placebo to effect a control condition in the elevation of a drug, it is appropriate now to center attention on the concept and traditional employment of conventional drug research designs. The discussion that follows is also appropriate to placebo effect research in which the true effects of the placebo per se are delineated.

There would be little disagreement with Hailman's (1953) statement of the need for a "blind" placebo control in clinical trials. This blind condition can be single, double, or in some cases triple, depending on how many or few persons directly responsible for or involved with drug administration (physician, patient, drug administrator/dispenser) know of the true conditions permeating the situation. An interesting discussion of the pros and cons of placebo disclosure is offered by Kirkendall (1967), and a very relevant warning of a potential fallacy in the apparently well-entrenched double-blind condition—physician discovery of the situation by virtue of side effects—is provided by Snyder (1974). There are numerous thoughtful reviews available of the principles and features of drug research design and methodology (Carter & Allen, 1973; Hoch, 1971; Modell, 1959; Nash, 1960), as well as more specific considerations of conventional designs (Jus, 1967; Marks, 1962; Shapiro, 1976). Specific comments on the use of placebos in controlled evaluations of drugs have been provided by Tetreault and Bordeleau (1970). Provocative discussions of the fate of the double-blind procedure, in light of informed consent requirements in research efforts, are offered by several investigators (Brownell & Stunkard, 1982; Loftus & Fries, 1979; Ross & Buckalew, 1983). There are very appreciable consequences for the integrity of drug research, given placebo control groups, by this movement.

Quite obviously, the formal recognition in modern research literature of the placebo effect (conventionally dated in the mid-1950s), which opened the floodgates to controversy and confirmation, is closely correlated with articles extolling a double-blind design (Demarr & Pelikan, 1955; Lasagna, 1955; Travell, 1955). Prior to this era, a single- or "patient"-blind standard was common, though this design now seems reserved for practice rather than research. Its adequacy within the research setting was seriously jeopardized by greater appreciation for the effects of nonspecific factors—primarily experimenter bias and psychological variables, as noted by Modell and Houde (1958) and Travell (1955). Since this time, relatively few mentions of the single-blind technique have appeared in the literature, though several reviews have discussed it (Meyer-Bisch, 1967; Schindel, 1962; Shapiro, 1976).

Initially, the double-blind condition appeared to offer salvation to drug research; it was heralded as an effective control procedure for many contaminations of nonspecific factors. As members of each dyad (doctor–patient, therapist–client, researcher–subject) were "blind" as to the true treatment being administered, conceivably any inherent bias and subtle suggestion would be controlled for. However, not long after its adoption as the conventional mode of drug research, problems and deficiencies in the design began to be recognized (Barsa, 1963; Lehmann, 1964; Schor, 1966), and Tuteur (1958) described some of the typical faults and needs associated with the design. For the last 20 years, it has become increasingly evident that the double-blind design, even though lauded as a major advance in drug research (Lorber, 1975), suffers from some potentially serious flaws. For example, Sleisenger (1958) warned of the dangers associated with differential doctor–patient relationships; Park and Covi (1965) found that even patients informed that they had taken an inert tablet reported improvement; Engelhardt, Margolis, Rudorfer, and Paley (1969) cautioned about effects of "guess bias" by the doctor or researcher; and Snyder (1974) noted that design integrity was destroyed when the doctor detected side effects. Most of these criticisms, while valid, are not necessarily problems associated distinctively with the double-blind design, and must be guarded against in any research effort involving human interaction.

We recognize that the double-blind technique certainly constitutes a major advance in drug research, though it does not necessarily constitute a fully controlled experiment. We agree with Nash (1962) that the design has both limitations and potentialities, and with Plutchik, Platman, and Fieve (1969) that the design is not indispensable and workable alternatives do exist. Perhaps the least heralded but most important suggestion for design improvement is the addition of a crossover condition, which was suggested long ago (Hoffer & Osmond, 1961; Marks, 1962; Travell, 1955). In this modification, each subject serves under both drug and placebo conditions, hence becoming his or her own control. Most certainly, this practice would appreciably decrease contamination of evaluation through placebo effects.

Given the appraisal that a double-blind design with crossover does represent a viable drug evaluation paradigm, the major residual problem remains as to the adequacy of a placebo or placebo group as a control (Ross & Buckalew, 1979). The suggestion that this concept needs to be seriously examined is certainly substantiated by recognition of the following: (1) The placebo can constitute a powerful agent of manipulation of an ever-expanding range of behaviors; (2) even slight differences between placebos and active drugs in their appearance can act as influential variables; (3) there may be definitive expectations by subjects based only on preparation characteristics; (4) placebo treatments have often been found to mimic even side effects of active preparations, (5) just the knowledge that placebos may be incorporated in the research can differentially influence both researcher/doctor and subject/patient; and (6) a placebo group incorporates numerous variables (nonspecific) which may, independently and/or through interaction, differentially influence response. These distinctions are relevant considerations, not just for conventional drug evaluations, but also for research specifically dedicated to investigating placebo responses and effects.

While it would be convenient to terminate discussion at this point, in the conviction that some contribution has been made by simply calling attention to facts, issues, and problems associated with placebo and drug research, diagnosis without therapeutic recommendations can prove frustrating. More efficacious than just the statement and discussion of a problem would be the provision of some tenable hypothesis regarding solution. We would like to introduce some considerations and ideas directed toward the purification and enhanced integrity of drug and placebo research. If nothing more, what follows constitutes a reference point from which refinements may ensue.

We (Ross & Buckalew, 1979) have suggested that, in consideration of the mounting evidence illustrating the placebo as an active and significant agent in behavioral manipulations, the placebo must be appreciated as a distinctive agent with complex consequences. The content and discussion offered in this chapter would certainly not indicate differently. The point must follow that evaluation research, be it of drug or placebo effects, must respect and respond to the complexity of the placebo. As noted long ago by Ross et al. (1962), conventional drug studies typically contrast a drug group with a placebo group; both groups are given a preparation and supporting instrutions. It is presumed in the conventional experiment (drug–placebo group contrast) that a drug's effects are represented by the pharmacological properties of the agent (drug group) minus the placebo effect (placebo group). As noted by Ross et al. (1962), the research task in psychopharmacology is to isolate experimentally and estimate quantitatively the specific pharmacological effects of a drug separated from nonspecific factors—a task complicated in adult human subjects by the interplay of these factors. Particularly in view of the number and complexity of nonspecific factors, the question of the adequacy of a placebo group as a single-group control clearly emerges. However, due credit must be accorded the more experimentally sound but less frequently used design in which an untreated control group is employed.

We emphatically contend that the factor of expectation, inherently involving suggestion and instructions, constitutes a major and complex variable per se and commands specific experimental design consideration. Very clear support for this contention may be found in the studies of Barrios and Karoly (1983), Buckalew (1972), Lent (1983), and Lyerly et al. (1964). We must staunchly support the suggestion of Ross et al. (1962) and Lyerly et al. (1964) that a drug-disguised group be added to drug study design, along with an untreated control group, while maintaining a double-blind condition. Hence, drug evaluation research would encompass (1) a conventional drug group, (2) a drug-disguised group, (3) a placebo group, and (4) an untreated control group. Differences between the untreated and placebo groups would reflect the effect of the placebo per se; deliberately vague and nondirective instructions would be given the "pill" groups in order to avoid influence by "implanted" expectations. Differences between the drug and drug-disguised groups would reflect the effect of instruction/suggestion/expectation, and comparison of the drug-disguised and placebo groups would reflect pharmacological drug effects. Both conceptual and empirical support for the proposed design, incorporating an untreated control and a drug-disguised group, may be found in the studies of Buckalew (1972), Hurst et al. (1973), Lyerly et al. (1964), and Ross et al. (1962); a concise explanation and a discussion of this design are provided by Ross (1968).

The efficacy of the proposed design is further enhanced from a more quantitative perspective. The addition of a no-treatment group, as a true control, and a drug-disguised group facilitates more specific partitioning of the variance encountered in drug evaluations, ultimately leading to more exact statements and conclusions about drug effects. In essence, the information value or potential of the proposed design is appreciably enhanced and more definitive, as are opportunities for more sensitive statistical analysis. Further, application of crossover procedures facilitating additional accountability of intraindividual variation is not precluded. An example of the advantages and opportunities offered by this design, modified appropriately for specific and definitive study of the placebo effect, is an investigation by Buckalew (1972) in which specific variables of the placebo itself, instructional suggestion, and reinforcement were quantified as to their individual and collective contribution to a placebo effect. Ultimately, we proffer that the design discussed, as applied to drug evaluation (Ross, 1968) or placebo effect research (Buckalew, 1972), would enhance the purity, analytical potential, and clarity of findings and would facilitate a more exact understanding of both drug and placebo effects.

REFERENCES

Affleck, D. C. The action of a medication and the physician's expectations. *Nebraska State Medical Journal*, 1966, *51*(8), 331–334.

Aletky, P. J., & Carlin, A. S. Sex differences and placebo effects: Motivation as an intervening variable. *Journal of Consulting and Clinical Psychology*, 1975, *43*, 278.

Atkinson, E. C. Dummy tablets. *British Medical Journal*, 1958, *1*, 1478.

Barrios, F. X., & Karoly, P. Treatment expectancy and therapeutic change in treatment of migraine headache: Are they related? *Psychological Reports*, 1983, *52*, 59–68.

Barsa, J. A. The fallacy of the "double-blind." *American Journal of Psychotherapy*, 1963, *119*, 1174–1175.

Beck, F. M. Placebos in dentistry: Their profound potential effects. *Journal of the American Dental Association*, 1977, *95*, 1122–1126.

Beecher, H. K. Experimental pharmacology and measurement of the subjective response. *Science*, 1952, *116*, 157–162.

Beecher, H. K. The powerful placebo. *Journal of the American Medical Association*, 1955, *159*, 1602–1606.

Benson, H., & Epstein, M. D. The placebo effect: A neglected asset in the care of patients. *Journal of the American Medical Association*, 1975, *232*, 1225–1227.

Berg, A. O. Placebos: A brief review for family physicians. *Journal of Family Practice*, 1977, *5*, 97–100.

Blumenthal, D. S., Burke, R., & Shapiro, K. The validity of "identical matching placebos." *Archives of General Psychiatry*, 1974, *31*, 214–215.

Bok, S. The ethics of giving placebos. *Scientific American*, 1974, *231*, 17–23.

Brodeur, D. W. A short history of placebos. *Journal of the American Pharmaceutical Association*, 1965, *5*, 642, 662.

Brownell, K. D., & Stunkard, A. J. The double-blind in danger: Untoward consequences of informed consent. *American Journal of Psychiatry*, 1982, *139*, 1487–1489.

Buckalew, L. W. The placebo effect in the 60s: Status and direction. *Southern Journal of Educational Research*, 1969, *3*, 119–124.

Buckalew, L. W. An analysis of experimental components in a placebo effect. *Psychological Record*, 1972, *22*, 113–119.

Buckalew, L. W., & Coffield, K. E. Drug expectations associated with perceptual characteristics: Ethnic factors. *Perceptual and Motor Skills*, 1982, *55*, 915–918. (a)

Buckalew, L. W., & Coffield, K. E. An investigation of drug expectancy as a function of capsule color and size and preparation form. *Journal of Clinical Psychopharmacology*, 1982, *2*, 245–248. (b)

Buckalew, L. W., & Ross, S. Relationship of perceptual characteristics to placebo efficacy. *Psychological Reports*, 1981, *49*, 955–961.

Buckalew, L. W., Ross, S., & Starr, B. J. Nonspecific factors in drug effects: Placebo personality. *Psychological Reports*, 1981, *48*, 3–8.

Buckert, A., & Niederberger, W. The placebo problem and its importance in the clinical evaluation of drugs. *Schweizerische Medizinische Wochenschrift*, 1963, *93*, 344–349.

Byerly, H. Explaining and exploiting placebo effects. *Perspectives in Biology and Medicine*, 1976, *19*, 423–436.

Carter, D. B., & Allen, D. C. Evaluation of the placebo effect in optometry. *American Journal of Optometry*, 1973, *50*, 94–104.

Demarr, E. W. J., & Pelikan, E. W. Use of placebos in therapy and in clinical pharmacology. *Modern Hospital*, 1955, *84*, 108–118.

Dinnerstein, A. J., & Halm, J. Modification of placebo effects by means of drugs: Effects of aspirin and placebos on self-rated moods. *Journal of Abnormal Psychology*, 1970, *75*, 308–314.

Ehrenwald, J. Placebo: Ploy, psi effect, research tool or psychoactive agent? *Parapsychology Review*, 1974, *5*, 1–4.

Engelhardt, D. M., Margolis, R. A., Rudorfer, L., & Paley, H. M. Physician bias and the double-blind. *Archives of General Psychiatry*, 1969, *20*, 315–320.

Evans, F. J. The placebo response in pain reduction. *Advances in Neurology*, 1974, *4*, 289–296. (a)

Evans, F. J. The power of a sugar pill. *Psychology Today*, April 1974, pp. 55–59. (b)

Fellner, C. H. Tranquilizing drugs in general practice or the triumph of the impure placebo. *American Practitioner and Digest of Treatment*, 1958, *9*, 1265–1268.

Fisher, S. Nonspecific factors as determinants of behavioral response to drugs. In A. DiMascio & R. I. Shader (Eds.), *Clinical handbook of psychopharmacology*. New York: Science House, 1970.

Gelbman, F. The physician, the placebo and the placebo effect. *Ohio State Medical Journal*, 1967, *63*, 1459–1461.

Goldstein, A. P. *Therapist–patient expectancies in psychotherapy*. New York: Macmillan, 1962.

Green, D. M. Preexisting conditions, placebo reactions, and "side effects." *Annals of International Medicine*, 1964, *60*, 255–265.

Haas, H., Fink, H., & Hartfelder, G. Das placeboproblem. *Fortschritte der Arzneimittelforschung*, 1959, *1*, 279–454.

Hailman, H. F. The "blind placebo" in the evaluation of drugs. *Journal of the American Medical Association*, 1953, *151*, 1430.

Hoch, E. L. *Experimental contributions to clinical psychology*. Belmont, Calif.: Brooks/Cole, 1971.

Hoffer, A., & Osmond, H. Double blind clinical trials. *Journal of Neuropsychiatry*, 1961, *2*, 221–227.

Hurst, P. M., Weidner, M. F., Radlow, R., & Ross, S. Drugs and placebos: Drug guessing by normal volunteers. *Psychological Reports*, 1973, *33*, 683–694.

Jacobs, K. W., & Nordan, F. M. Classification of placebo drugs: Effect of color. *Perceptual and Motor Skills*, 1979, *49*, 367–372.

Jus, K. Assessment of methods used to examine placebo response in modern psychopharmacotherapy. *Psychiatria Polska*, 1967, *17*, 609–613.

Kirkendall, W. M. The placebo and clinical investigation. *Journal of Clinical Pharmacology*, 1967, *7*, 245–247.

Kissel, P., & Barrucand, D. *Placebos and the placebo effect in medicine*. Paris: Masson et Cie, 1964.

Kurland, A. A. The drug placebo—its psychodynamic and conditional reflex action. *Behavioral Science*, 1957, *2*, 101–110.

Lasagna, L. The controlled clinical trial: Theory and practice. *Journal of Chronic Diseases*, 1955, *1*, 353–367.

Lasagna, L., Laties, V. G., & Dohan, J. L. Further studies on the "pharmacology" of placebo administration. *Journal of Clinical Investigation*, 1958, *37*, 533–537.

Lehmann, H. E. The placebo response and the double-blind study. In P. H. Hoch & J. Zubin (Eds.), *The evaluation of psychiatric treatment*. New York: Grune & Stratton, 1964.

Lehmann, H. E., & Knight, D. A. Placebo-proneness and placebo-resistance of different psychological functions. *Psychiatric Quarterly*, 1960, *34*, 505–516.

Lent, R. W. Perception of credibility of treatment and placebo by treated and quasi-control subjects. *Psychological Reports*, 1983, *52*, 383–386.

Liberman, R. An analysis of the placebo phenomenon. *Journal of Chronic Diseases*, 1962, *15*, 761–783.

Liberman, R. An experimental study of the placebo response under three different situations of pain. *Journal of Psychiatric Research*, 1964, *2*, 233–246.

Loftus, E. F., & Fries, J. F. Informed consent may be hazardous to health. *Science*, 1979, *204*, 11.

Lorber, M. Delaying double-blind drug evaluation in usually fatal diseases. *New England Journal of Medicine*, 1975, *293*, 508–509.

Lyerly, S. B., Ross, S., Krugman, A. D., & Clyde, D. J. Drugs and placebos: The effects of instructions upon performance and mood under amphetamine sulphate and chloral hydrate. *Journal of Abnormal and Social Psychology*, 1964, *68*, 321–327.

Marks, J. Placebomania. *Journal of New Drugs*, 1962, *2*, 71–77.

Martin, G. J. The myth of the magic bullet. *Experimental Medicine and Surgery*, 1964, *22*, 199–211.

Mayo, E. *The human problems of an industrial civilization*. Boston: Harvard University Graduate School of Business Administration, 1933.

Meyer-Bisch, R. Réflexions sur le problème des placébos et de leurs deux méthodes d'application. *Annales de Thérapeutique Psychiatrique*, 1967, *3*, 138–143.

Modell, W. Problems in the evaluation of drugs in man. *Journal of Pharmacy and Pharmacology*, 1959, *11*, 577–594.

Modell, W., & Houde, R. W. Factors influencing clinical evaluation of drugs with special reference to the double-blind technique. *Journal of the American Medical Association*, 1958, *167*, 2190–2199.

Morris, L. A., & O'Neal, E. C. Drug-name familiarity and the placebo effect. *Journal of Clinical Psychology*, 1974, *30*, 280–282.

Nash, H. The design and conduct of experiments on the psychological effects of drugs. In L. Uhr & J. G. Miller (Eds.), *Drugs and behavior*. New York: Wiley, 1960.

Nash, H. The double-blind procedure: Rationale and empirical evaluation. *Journal of Nervous and Mental Disease*, 1962, *134*, 34–47.

O'Leary, K. D., & Borkovec, T. D. Conceptual, methodological, and ethical problems of placebo groups in psychotherapy research. *American Psychologist*, 1978, *33*, 821–830.

Park, L. C., & Covi, L. The non-blind placebo trial. *Archives of General Psychiatry*, 1965, *12*, 336.

Parsons, H. M. What happened at Hawthorne? *Science*, 1974, *183*, 922–932.

Parsons, H. M. What caused the Hawthorne effect?: A scientific detective story. *Administration and Society*, 1978, *10*, 259–283.

Pihl, R. O., & Altman, J. An experimental analysis of the placebo effect. *Journal of Clinical Pharmacology*, 1971, *11*, 91–95.

Plutchik, R., Platman, S. R., & Fieve, R. R. Three alternatives to the double-blind. *Archives of General Psychiatry*, 1969, *20*, 428–432.

Pogge, R. C. The toxic placebo. Part I—Side and toxic effects reported during the administration of placebo medicine. *Medical Times*, 1963 *91*(8), 1–6.

Rachman, J., & Philips, C. A new medical psychology. *New Scientist*, 1975, *65*, 518–520.

Ray, O. *Drugs, society, and human behavior* (2nd ed.). St. Louis: C. V. Mosby, 1978.

Rosenthal, R. On the social psychology of the psychological experiment: The experimenter's hypothesis as unintended determinant of experimental results. *American Scientist*, 1963, *51*, 268–283.

Rosenthal, D., & Frank, J. Psychotherapy and the placebo effect. *Psychological Bulletin*, 1956, *53*, 294–302.

Ross, S. Psychopharmacology. In *International encyclopedia of the social sciences*. New York: Macmillan, 1968.

Ross, S., & Buckalew, L. W. On the agentry of placebos. *American Psychologist*, 1979, *34*, 277–278.

Ross, S., & Buckalew, L. W. The placebo as an agent in behavioral manipulations: A review of problems, issues, and affected measures. *Clinical Psychology Review*, 1983, *3*, 457–471.

Ross, S., Krugman, A. D., Lyerly, S. B., & Clyde, B. J. Drugs and placebos: A model design. *Psychological Reports*, 1962, *10*, 383–392.

Rubin, W. Placebo effect in relation to drug evaluation. *Archives of Otolaryngology*, 1963, *77*, 6–9.

Schindel, L. E. Placebo in theory and practice. *Antibiotica et Chemotherapia Advances*, 1962, *10*, 398–430.

Schindel, L. The placebo dilemma. *European Journal of Clinical Pharmacology*, 1978, *13*, 231–235.

Schor, S. S. The mystic statistic: The double-blind study. *Journal of the American Medical Association*, 1966, *195*, 1094.

Shapiro, A. K. A contribution to a history of the placebo effect. *Behavioral Science*, 1960, 5, 398–430.

Shapiro, A. K. Semantics of the placebo. *Psychiatric Quarterly*, 1968, *42*, 653–695.

Shapiro, A. K. Psychochemotherapy. In R. G. Grenell & S. Gabay (Eds.), *Biological foundations of psychiatry*. New York: Raven Press, 1976.

Shapiro, A. K., Wilensky, H., & Struening, E. L. Study of the placebo effect with a placebo test. *Comprehensive Psychiatry*, 1968, *9*, 118–137.

Silbergeld, S., Manderscheid, R. W., & Soeken, D. R. Issues at the clinical–research interface: Placebo effect control groups. *Journal of Nervous and Mental Disease*, 1976, *163*, 147–153.

Sleisenger, M. H. The double-blind test in the evaluation of the therapeutic effect of drugs. *American Journal of Digestive Diseases*, 1958, *3*, 411–415.

Snow, C. E. A discussion of the relation of illumination intensity to productive efficiency. *Technical Engineering News*, November 1927, pp. 257–282.

Snyder, S. H. *Madness and the brain*. New York: McGraw-Hill, 1974.

Tetreault, L., & Bordeleau, J. M. On the usefulness of placebo and of the double-blind technique for the evaluation of psychotropic drugs. *L'Encephale*, 1970, *59*, 5–24.

Travell, J. Assessment of drugs for therapeutic efficacy. *American Journal of Physical Medicine*, 1955, *34*, 129–140.

Turner, J. L., Gallimore, R., & Fox-Henning, C. An annotated bibliography of placebo research. *JSAS Catalog of Selected Documents in Psychology*, 1980, *10* (MS. No. 2063).

Tuteur, W. The "double-blind" method: Its pitfalls and fallacies. *American Journal of Psychiatry*, 1958, *114*, 921–922.

Vrhovac, B. Placebo and its importance in medicine. *International Journal of Clinical Pharmacology*, 1977, *15*, 161–165.

6

Placebo Controls and Concepts in Chemotherapy and Psychotherapy Research

WALLACE WILKINS

INTRODUCTION

The focus of this chapter is on the utility of placebo procedures and their underlying concepts in applied research. Given the conceptual, professional, ethical, and practical problems they create (Beecher, 1966; Bok, 1974; Brody, 1980; Leslie, 1954; O'Leary & Borkovec, 1978; Rawlinson, Chapter 22, this volume; Shapiro, 1960a; Tuteur, 1958), it is important to evaluate the benefits provided by placebo procedures for different research purposes. This chapter is organized into three domains of inquiry: chemotherapy research, placebo research, and psychotherapy research. Within those three domains, placebo designs have been developed for the two complementary purposes of (1) demonstrating the efficacy of therapy procedures and (2) identifying the mechanisms through which those procedures cause improvement.

The purpose of efficacy research is to determine whether an intervention actually causes improvement. Questions and answers that guide efficacy research can be stated exclusively in observable terms. The basic, unidimensional question is "Do the observable operations that define treatments (independent variables) cause observable changes (dependent variables)?" The more precise, multidimensional question is "Which procedures, delivered in which settings to which clients, by which therapists under which conditions, cause change on which criteria?" Efficacy questions can also be asked to determine which observable components of a treatment package are important and which combinations of treatment packages maximize improvement. In efficacy research, it is not necessary to ask why an

Wallace Wilkins. Department of Psychology, Old Dominion University, Norfolk, Virginia; Virginia Consortium for Professional Psychology, Norfolk, Virginia. (Present affiliation: Department of Psychology, University of Hartford, West Hartford, Connecticut.)

83

intervention causes improvement. A reliable association between independent and dependent variables is sufficient to determine that a treatment procedure is effective.

For scientific and professional reasons, it is also important to identify why a procedure is effective. This is asked by adding the phrase " ... by which processes or mechanisms (intervening variables)?" to the efficacy question (e.g., Paul, 1969). Questions and answers in mechanism research are not limited to observable operations. Rather, they involve unobservable, hypothetical phenomena inferred from observable events. While efficacy research and mechanism research are distinct endeavors, often a single experiment can be designed to serve both purposes.

PLACEBO DESIGNS IN CHEMOTHERAPY RESEARCH

Chemotherapy research has been guided, in part, by the doctrine of specific causation, a goal of which is to identify specific physiochemical treatments for specific biological maladies (Beecher, 1972; Dubos, 1954). Table 6-1 depicts a progression of placebo methodologies designed to eliminate artifacts in order to establish that a drug is efficacious and that it operates via physiochemical mechanisms.

Chemotherapy Efficacy Research

Chemotherapy experiments are designed to answer the basic, unidimensional question (e.g., Paul, 1969). Questions and answers in mechanism research plaining of an ailment visit a physician's office, receive a drug, and report satisfaction, it would not be possible to conclude that the drug causes improvement. Many plausible, alternative explanations for symptom remis-

Table 6-1. Artifacts and Controls in Chemotherapy and Psychotherapy Research

	Controls	
Artifacts	Chemotherapy research	Psychotherapy research
Efficacy artifacts		
Spontaneous remission	Waiting list	Waiting list
Client traits	Random assignment	Random assignment
Professional attention	Attention control	Nonspecific therapy
Treatment per se	Passive placebo	Pseudotherapy
Client awareness	Single-blind	None
Therapist awareness	Double-blind	None
Mechanism artifacts		
Side effects and cognitive changes	Triple-blind and active placebo	Equated credibility

sion have been argued, one of which is the possibility of spontaneous remission. Since symptoms increase and then decrease during the normal course of an ailment, improvement that coincides with taking the drug may have occurred, whether or not a physician was even consulted.

There are professional and political, as well as scientific, reasons for ruling out this rival hypothesis. Physicians have been politically antagonistic to herbalists, charlatans, and quacks, who presumably proffer remedies that have no specific medicinal effects on specific diseases (Burrow, 1977; Cabot, 1906; Griggs, 1981; Shapiro, 1964, 1968; Young, 1961). Unless chemotherapy researchers can demonstrate that the drug is effective, the treatment may not be distinguishable from quackery.

WAITING-LIST CONTROL

The passage of time and other spontaneous influences can be ruled out by designing experiments in which some patients complaining of the ailment are asked to wait, while other patients receive the normal routine of examination, conference, and drug. Superiority of drug patients over waiting-list patients means that something other than the passage of time produces recovery.

Ruling out spontaneous influences, however, is not sufficient to enable investigators to claim that the drug causes improvement. An alternative possibility is that there are differences between patients assigned to the treatment and waiting-list groups. Differential improvement may be due to differences in patient characteristics, rather than the drug.

RANDOM ASSIGNMENT

To avoid systematic bias in group membership, chemotherapy researchers make assignments on a random basis (Zelen, 1979). Random assignment precludes either spontaneous influences or patient characteristics from contaminating outcome differences between groups.

This is still not sufficient to permit researchers to conclude that the drug causes improvement. It is possible that reports of relief are caused by professional attention received during the examination, the office conference, and repeated testing, regardless of whether or not a drug is delivered. At this point, the chemotherapy researchers still have not demonstrated that the causal factors involved in delivering professional services are any different than those of a quack who would offer professional attention, concern, interest, and brief companionship in a healing setting.

ATTENTION CONTROL

To eliminate the latest rival hypothesis, the standard examination, testing, conference, and drug are offered to one randomized group of patients. Instead of assignment to a waiting list, other patients receive the professional attention involved in the examination, testing, and conference in the same treatment milieu, but no drug is delivered. By precluding contamination from spontaneous influences, patient characteristics, and professional attention, it may be concluded that improvement is caused by the delivery of the drug.

The finding that *drug delivery* is effective is not sufficient to permit the investigators to conclude that the *drug delivered* is effective. Since no treatment is delivered to patients in the attention control group, it is plausible that differences in improvement may be due to the drug patients' knowledge that they are being treated, while control patients know that treatment is omitted. Also, demand characteristics (Orne, 1962) involved in pill delivery may cause drug patients to report more improvement, even if biological differences in symptom reduction have not occurred (e.g., Hurst, Weidner, Radlow, & Ross, 1973; M. Ross & Olson, 1981). The drug itself still has not been demonstrated to be different from ineffective potions and concoctions used by quacks and physicians in centuries past (Shapiro, 1959, 1960b, 1978; Shapiro & Morris, 1978; Young, 1961).

PASSIVE PLACEBO CONTROL

To rule out the effects of treatment per se, the examination, the testing, the conference, and the drug are delivered to one randomized group, while another group receives the examination, the testing, and the conference in the professional setting, plus a "passive," or "pure," placebo (Shapiro, 1959; Shapiro & Morris, 1978)—a pill containing a pharmacologically inert substance, such as sucrose, lactose, saline, or starch, that has no known effect on the ailment. Differences in symptom reduction will not be confounded by differential knowledge that treatment per se is being delivered.

However, on the basis of different colors, sizes, or markings on the pills, patients can become aware that the treatments are different, particularly if they have opportunities to make direct comparisons (Blumenthal, Burke, & Shapiro, 1974; Tuteur, 1958). These superficial differences between the pills could possibly produce different improvement between groups. Alternatively, these superficial differences could elicit different reports of improvement where none has actually occurred. These rival hypotheses prevent the conclusion that the drug itself causes improvement.

SINGLE-BLIND CONTROL

Possible effects of these superficial differences can be eliminated by delivering the drug and the inert substance in pills or capsules that are identical in size, shape, color, markings, and taste (Molitch & Eccles, 1937). In the metaphorical language of experimental research, the patients are "blind," since they are kept in the dark as to their treatment condition (Haas, Fink, & Hartfelder, 1959).

However, while patients are unaware of their treatment condition, the chemotherapist and staff members may not be unaware. If evaluators are aware of assignments of patients to groups, their ratings of improvement could be biased (Breuning, Ferguson, & Cullari, 1980; Loranger, Prout, &

White, 1961). If staff members are aware of group assignments, they may behave differently to the different groups of patients. Chemotherapists may behave in a more confident and enthusiastic manner when delivering the drug than when delivering the placebo (Feldman, 1956). These possibilities mean that the causes of improvement may not be different from those through which confident, enthusiastic, motivated quacks bring about relief. The rival hypotheses prevent the conclusion that improvement is caused by the drug.

DOUBLE-BLIND CONTROL

To rule out the possibility of bias from therapists and staff, the administrative activities involving group assignment and record keeping are performed by people other than those who deliver the drugs and placebos, those who interact with the patients, and those who evaluate improvement. This metaphorically "blinds" the service providers and evaluators, so that any effects they have will be randomly distributed across patient groups. Since neither patients nor professionals are aware of the contents of the capsules, the experiment is called a "double-blind" design. The history and utility of double-blind designs have been discussed by Barsa (1963), Chassan (1979), Finkel (Chapter 23, this volume), Gadow, White, and Ferguson (in press-a), Haas et al. (1959), Honigfeld (1964), and Tuteur (1958).

There are several ways in which the blind on patients, chemotherapists, staff members, and evaluators may be broken and thus allow psychosocial variables to influence eventual treatment outcome. Some are relevant to this section on efficacy, while others are discussed in the next section concerning the mechanisms of change. Concerning efficacy, as a consequence of receiving efficacious drugs, drug patients differ from placebo patients in the relief experienced when symptoms begin to remit. The psychological effects of initial improvement, as well as differences in the manner in which staff and family members treat improved and unimproved patients, preclude the claim that only physiochemical events affect ultimate outcome (Whalen & Henker, 1976). As pointed out by Henker, Whalen, and Collins (1979), the only way in which staff members can be kept completely blind throughout an experiment is when ineffective drugs are compared with placebos. While psychological factors cannot be ruled out from the entire sequence of improvement, they can be ruled out until initial improvement begins to differentiate drug and placebo patients. Therefore, breaking the blind on the basis of differential symptom change is an indirect, but legitimate, criterion for concluding drug efficacy (Rickels, Lipman, Fisher, Park, & Uhlenhuth, 1970).

Double-blind designs are capable of ruling out contamination from time, other spontaneous influences, patient characteristics, professional attention in a healing setting, patient knowledge about treatment per se, and client and therapist biases during initial treatment delivery. With those rival hypotheses ruled out, differences between patient groups mean that the drug is efficacious. At least at the initial point of a cause–effect sequence, causality can be attributed to the physiochemical differences between the drug and the placebo, which define the independent variable of a chemotherapy experiment.

Chemotherapy Mechanism Research

While double-blind controls allow the attribution of causality to independent variables, they do not preclude rival hypotheses at the intervening variable position of cause–effect sequences. In addition to improvement, drugs produce psychological changes, which are artifacts according to the doctrine of specificity. Possible psychological mechanisms that rival physiochemical explanations include (1) patient interpretations of drug side effects and (2) patient cognitive changes.

It is possible that improvement is caused by symptom-irrelevant sensations produced by efficacious drugs, which are interpreted by patients to mean that the drug is working. Patients who receive the passive placebo would not experience those sensations (Adelman & Compas, 1977; Baker & Thorpe, 1957; Lyerly, Ross, Krugman, & Clyde, 1964; Molitch & Eccles, 1937; Orne, 1962; Tuteur, 1958). Evidence presented by Hurst et al. (1973), and Lipman, Park, and Rickels (1966) has shown that recipients can detect differences between the side effects of drugs and placebos.

In addition to initial improvement and side effects, the effects of some drugs may possibly be due to changes in personality, cognitive, and information-processing characteristics of drug recipients that are not changed by inert placebos (e.g., Dinnerstein, 1968). The possibility that these side effects and cognitive changes could break the patient blind increases if patients have opportunities to interact and compare their reactions. Differences in patient reactions following drug delivery could also break the blind on chemotherapists and staff members (Adelman & Compas, 1977; Barsa, 1963; Honigfeld, 1964; Lipman et al., 1966; Wing, 1956).

It is important to recognize that the latest concern is qualitatively different from those raised previously. The purpose of the control procedures described earlier is to ascertain whether or not the drug is efficacious. In double-blind experiments, when patients who receive a drug improve more than patients who receive a placebo, it may be concluded that the drug is efficacious. Rather than addressing efficacy, the concerns about side effects and cognitive changes pertain to the mechanisms through which the drug is efficacious. Psychological and social possibilities function as rival hypotheses challenging the conclusion that improvement occurs via physiochemical pathways. The possibility remains that the mechanisms of improvement from the drug are no different from those of a quack's concoction that produces subterfuge sensations irrelevant to the physiochemical pathways involving the ailment.

Mechanisms are investigated through two complementary strategies in chemotherapy research. In the first approach, efforts are made to rule out all psychological mechanisms, so that the indirect inference can be drawn that the causal mechanisms are physiochemical. The second approach is to specify the physiochemical mechanisms directly.

ANTIPSYCHOLOGICAL MECHANISM RESEARCH

This mechanism question is "Can all nonphysiochemical mechanisms be ruled out as explanations for the drug's efficacy?" McGlynn, Kinjo, and Doherty (1978) applied the term "net effects" to the indirect inferential strategy. By subtracting the nonspecific effects of placebo delivery from the total effects of drug delivery, the remaining net effects are attributed to physiochemical aspects of the drug.

Since the physiochemical mechanisms are not actually specified when psychological mechanisms are ruled out, the indirect approach is anti-psychological. Antipsychological scientific efforts parallel antiquackery political efforts. The ability to conclude that mechanisms are nonpsychological would mean that the mechanisms of efficacious drugs are different from the sources of change involved in quackery.

Two control procedures that have been implemented to reduce differences in interpretations of side effect sensations and other cognitive changes are (1) the triple-blind control and (2) the active placebo control.

Triple-Blind Control. Knowledge by patients, chemotherapists, and staff members that a research project involving a particular drug is under way can have an obtrusive effect on their behavior (Chassan, 1979; Henker et al., 1979; Loranger et al., 1961). Curious patients and staff may direct attention to their sensations, perhaps to outguess the experimenter and to determine their group assignment (Baker & Thorpe, 1957; Gadow, Ferguson, & White, in press-b). These psychological differences confound attributions of causality to physiochemical mechanisms.

Control of these possibilities has been attempted through several strategies collectively called "triple-blind controls." While the term has been used inconsistenly, a composite of triple-blind strategies means that neither patients, nor chemotherapists, nor staff members, nor evaluators (Haas et al., 1959; Hoffer & Osmond, 1961) are informed of the name of the active drug, its probable effects, or even the fact that a drug experiment is being conducted (Baker & Thorpe, 1957; Gadow et al., in press-a, in press-b; Henker et al., 1979; Paul, Tobias, & Holly, 1972). The probability of discovering side effect differences could be reduced by introducing medications and placebos unobtrusively or "silently"—for example, in orange juice consumed normally (Gadow et al., in press-b; Gottschalk, 1961; Lyerly et al., 1964). Complete ignorance on the part of all possible participants is a hyperbole described by Hoffer and Osmond (1961) as a "deca-blind" study.

Triple- or deca-blind designs, however, do not reduce side effect differences between drugs and placebos. They just reduce the probability that side effects will be discovered. Even if all participants are completely unaware of the research project, and even if all social comparison activities are prevented, the possibility still exists that improvement and reports of improvement are influenced by interpretations of side effects and other cognitive changes produced by the drug, but not produced by the passive placebo. The rival hypothesis allowed in triple-blind designs is basically the same as that in double-blind investigations with passive placebos.

Active Placebo Control. To eliminate contamination from psychological events, patients in the placebo group receive a chemical that is presumed not to affect the ailment in question, but that produces sensations intended to mimic the side effects or cognitive changes produced by the drug (Greiner, 1958). Since these chemicals are not completely inert, they are called "active," or "impure," placebos (Shapiro, 1959, 1963). For example, atropine has been used as an active placebo to mimic the autonomic side effects, such as dry mouth, of the drug amitriptyline in the treatment of depression (Friedman, 1975).

This control tactic used to deal with the rival hypothesis at the intervening variable position is qualitatively different from the control tactics used to deal with rival hypotheses at the independent variable position. Ruling out the influence of side effect sensations and cognitive changes would require measurement and validation that the states produced by the drug and the placebo were psychologically identical. However, the current status of psychological measurement prevents that conclusion. Statistically, to conclude that the psychological experiences of different groups are identical is to accept the null hypothesis. When the null hypothesis is accepted, it may only be concluded that no differences have been detected by the measurements, not that no differences have occurred. As a consequence, there is little assurance either that the sensations and cognitions produced by the active placebo are the same as those produced by the drug or that patient interpretations of the respective sensations are the same. The possibility remains that the improvement of drug patients is influenced by interpretations of side effect sensations, particularly if patients have opportunities to compare reactions.

Even assuming that psychological factors can be completely ruled out, the most that can be claimed from the net effects strategy is that part of the drug action occurs somewhere on the physiochemical level. That indirect approach does not identify the actual physiochemical mechanisms responsible for symptom reduction.

PROPHYSIOCHEMICAL RESEARCH

Antipsychological mechanism research is complemented by direct investigations into the physiochemical pathways that account for drug action. This mechanism question is "What are the actual physiochemical mechanisms that account for the drug's efficacy?" Prophysiochemical experiments are conducted in pharmacological laboratories, guided by findings from applied research. In turn, information about components and combinations of drugs tested in the pharmacological laboratory leads to further testing in the applied chemotherapy setting. Standard pharmacological and psychopharmacological texts may be consulted for reviews of this extensive literature, which interfaces with applied chemotherapy research (Bowman & Rand, 1980; Clark & del Guidice, 1978; Gilman, Goodman, & Gilman, 1980; Lipton, DiMascio, & Killam, 1978).

PLACEBO RESEARCH

The psychological factors that are artifacts in chemotherapy research are the main focus in placebo research. While placebos are used in chemotherapy research to eliminate all psychological factors indiscriminately, they are used in placebo research to explicate psychological causes in the "pill-giving ritual" (Honigfeld, 1964, 1968) and in the healing context (Brody, 1980).

Placebo Efficacy Research

The basic efficacy question in placebo research complements the unidimensional efficacy question posed in chemotherapy research: "Does the delivery of a placebo cause improvement?" Without proper controls, it may not be concluded that improvement during the delivery of a placebo is actually due to the delivery of the placebo (Fisher, 1970; Honigfeld, 1968; Loranger et al., 1961; M. Ross & Olson, 1981). Repeated testing, client traits, and spontaneous influences correlated with the passage of time function as rival hypotheses. Their possible effects must be ruled out if causality is to be attributed to the pill-giving ritual or the healing setting.

Random assignment to waiting-list and placebo groups can be used to eliminate change due to repeated testing, client traits, or spontaneous influences. Superiority of placebo procedures over waiting-list procedures means that the causes of improvement are located somewhere in the healing setting. The effects of the pill-giving ritual can be assessed independently of the healing setting by comparing patients who receive a pill with patients who receive no pill during their contact with a therapist in that setting (Klerman, DiMascio, Weissman, Prusoff, & Paykel, 1974; S. Ross, Krugman, Lyerly, & Clyde, 1962; Weissman, Klerman, Paykel, Prusoff, & Hanson, 1974).

In addition to simply demonstrating that placebo delivery causes improvement, the multidimensional conditions of improvement from placebos can be specified by asking, "Which activities, delivered by which therapists in which settings, to which patients receiving which placebos, cause improvement for which complaints?" Consideration has been given to

(1) characteristics of the pill, such as its size, color, taste, and name (Baker & Thorpe, 1957; Blumenthal *et al.*, 1974); (2) the method of delivery (Leslie, 1954); (3) instructions accompanying placebo delivery (Loranger *et al.*, 1961; Morris & O'Neal, 1974; Storms & Nisbett, 1970); and (4) characteristics of the patient, such as the nature of the ailment, personality traits, stress, and psychiatric status (Beecher, 1960; Freedman, Cutler, Englehardt, & Margolis, 1967). Detailed reviews of factors influencing the efficacy of placebo delivery are available in this volume and elsewhere (Gadow *et al.*, in press-b; Jospe, 1978; Shapiro & Morris, 1978).

Placebo Mechanism Research

Placebo researchers explore mechanisms that are dismissed in chemotherapy research. They do not address the mechanisms through which the placebo causes improvement, since the placebo is inert. Rather, the basic mechanism question is "What are the mechanisms through which the *delivery* of a placebo causes improvement?" Both physiochemical and psychological events have been implicated as placebo mechanisms.

PHYSIOCHEMICAL MECHANISMS

Recent clinical investigations have implicated an intervening variable of endorphin release at central nervous system sites of placebo reactors (Levine, Gordon, & Fields, 1978). Just as pharmacological laboratory methods are used to elucidate the mechanisms of drug action, so can they be used to identify the physiochemical sequelae of placebo delivery.

PSYCHOLOGICAL MECHANISMS

Psychological factors that are summarily ruled out as artifacts in chemotherapy research play a complementary role as mechanisms in placebo research (Gadow *et al.*, in press-b; Peek, 1977; S. Ross *et al.*, 1962). Bourne (1971) described transference and conditioning mechanisms of placebo delivery. Similarly, Byerly (1976) classified placebo mechanisms as mentalistic and conditioning interpretations.

Mentalistic Theories. Plotkin (Chapter 14, this volume), Bootzin (Chapter 10, this volume), and M. Ross and Olson (1981) have described the roles of faith, expectancy, and attribution as placebo mechanisms. Theories involving expectancy and faith weave a common thread among such diverse phenomena as placebos, withcraft, and religious miracle cures (Fish, 1973; Frank, 1959, 1973).

Conditioning Theories. Ader (Chapter 17, this volume), Herrnstein (1962), Siegel (Chapter 16, this volume), and Wickramasekera (1980; Chapter 15, this volume) have described the classical conditioning model of placebo. When paired with ingredients that have produced healing and relief, conditioned stimuli involving the setting, the therapist, and the treatment ritual acquire the capacity to produce subsequent relief.

Interdomain Designs: Chemotherapy and Placebo Research

Just as components of the treatment setting and the pill delivery process can be studied when inert placebos are delivered, so can those nonphysio-chemical events be manipulated as independent variables when drugs are delivered. Complementarity between chemotherapy research and placebo research is evident in research designs in which both physiochemical and psychological independent variables are manipulated. Interdomain research identifies nonphysiochemical characteristics of settings, capsules, instructions, therapists, and patients that moderate the effects of active drugs (Dinnerstein & Halm, 1970; Downing & Rickels, 1973, 1978; Fisher, 1970; Honigfeld, 1964; Klett & Moseley, 1965; Lipman et al., 1966; Lyerly et al., 1964; Raskin, Schulterbrandt, Reatig, & McKeon, 1970; Rickels, 1977; Rickels & Cattell, 1969; Schapira, McClelland, Griffiths, & Newell, 1970; Uhlenhuth, Canter, Neustadt, & Payson, 1959).

PLACEBO DESIGNS IN PSYCHOTHERAPY RESEARCH

Research designs with placebo groups have proven to be so useful in chemotherapy research that they have been generalized to investigate the efficacy and mechanisms of psychotherapy. A network of terms, concepts, and inferential practices involving placebos has also been generalized from chemotherapy research (Thorne, 1952). In spite of differences in the phenomena investigated by chemotherapy and psychotherapy researchers (Peek, 1977), placebo groups represent the epitome of sophistication in psychotherapy research (O'Leary & Borkovec, 1978), just as they do in chemotherapy research. The actual utility of placebo designs in efficacy and mechanism research is evaluated in the following sections.

Psychotherapy Efficacy Research

The basic psychotherapy efficacy question is "Does the psychotherapy technique cause improvement?" As indicated in Table 6-1, up to the point of dealing with client and therapist biases, the controls in psychotherapy efficacy research provide benefits similar to those in chemotherapy efficacy research.

RANDOM ASSIGNMENT TO WAITING-LIST CONTROLS

In psychotherapy research, waiting-list control procedures play similar roles and raise similar ethical and practical issues to those in chemotherapy and placebo research (O'Leary & Borkovec, 1978). Random assignment of clients to treatment, waiting-list, and/or minimal contact procedures (Imber, Frank, Nash, Stone, & Gliedman, 1957) rule out potential artifacts from the passage of time, spontaneous remsision, and client traits. Superiority of a psychotherapy procedure over a waiting-list procedure warrants the conclusion that the process of visiting a psychotherapist is better than not visiting a therapist.

However, the psychological factors that cause improvement may not be part of the psychotherapy procedures delivered when improvement takes place. Paul (1966), for example, showed the beneficial effects of an initial interview and assessment over no contact. Improvement can be caused by the effects of the client–therapist relationship formed during psychotherapy, which may not be different from the effects of any other relationship (Strupp, 1973). In Grünbaum's (1981) terminology, the causes may be incidental constituents, rather than characteristic constituents of psychotherapy procedures.

NONSPECIFIC THERAPY

A. P. Goldstein's (1960, 1962) nonspecific therapy plays a role in psychotherapy research analogous to that of attention control procedures in chemotherapy research. Nonspecific therapy consists of initial interviews and psychological assessment, but no formal psychotherapy. It is used to rule out rival hypotheses involving professional attention and repeated testing, in addition to those ruled out with waiting lists. Superiority of a psychotherapy procedure over nonspecific therapy is sufficient to conclude that the process of psychotherapy is beneficial over and above initial visits to a therapist.

However, since nonspecific treatment consists only of pretherapy activities, it does not control for the delivery of a treatment per se. Nor does it necessarily control for the amount of client contact with a therapist during therapy. As a consequence, causality cannot be attributed to the psychotherapy technique itself.

PSEUDOTHERAPY

The role played by pseudotherapy is similar to that of a passive palcebo in chemotherapy research. Clients do not receive formal therapy, but are involved in conversational interviews for the same frequency and duration as clients who receive psychotherapy (Lang, Lazovik, & Reynolds, 1965; Paul, 1966). Since intervention concerning client problems is avoided, pseudotherapy is theoretically inert.

Pseudotherapy controls for the quantity of contact that clients receive. However, after a few sessions of avoiding therapeutic intervention, pseudotherapy clients may conclude that treatment is not being offered, particularly if they have opportunities to compare their experiences with those of other clients. In addition, the therapists involved in the delivery of psychotherapy and pseudotherapy are not blind as to which treatment they are delivering. Biases resulting from client awareness and therapist awareness preclude the conclusion that the therapy procedure itself causes improvement, even if it is superior to pseudotherapy.

BROKEN CLIENT BLINDS

Single-blind experiments are used in chemotherapy research to rule out patients' awareness of superficial differences between pills. Drugs and placebos can be delivered in identical capsules and with identical chemotherapist behaviors. However, psychotherapy treatments and controls cannot be made to appear identical. Psychotherapists must behave in different ways in order to meet the boundary conditions defining different treatments and placebos. Different therapist behaviors provide information that different treatments are being delivered. Even without opportunities for clients to compare their reactions, the behaviors of therapists delivering control procedures can break the client blind by failing to meet clients' criteria of treatment.

The pivotal difference between the benefits of placebos in chemotherapy and psychotherapy efficacy research is the point at which the client blind is broken. In chemotherapy efficacy research, there is nothing inherent in the chemotherapy delivery process that breaks the client blind. The blind might be broken *after* the delivery of drugs and placebos and *after* differential effects begin to occur. Even so, efficacy can be attributed to the chemicals that produce initial improvement, independently of patient awareness of treatment differences. On the other hand, in psychotherapy efficacy research, inherent differences in the delivery process break the client blind *during* treatment delivery and *before* differential improvement occurs. Efficacy cannot be attributed to psychotherapy procedures independently of possible client awareness of treatment differences.

The problem of observable differences between psychotherapy treatments and placebos can be attenuated somewhat by tape recordings. The superficial appearance of two tapes containing different messages can be made identical, just as two identical capsules may contain different chemicals. However, unlike patients who cannot observe the chemical contents of a capsule, psychotherapy clients do observe the contents of a tape. This can break the client blind and prevent investigators from attributing causality to the taped messages independently of client awareness.

BROKEN THERAPIST BLINDS

Double-blind procedures are employed in chemotherapy research to keep therapists unaware of which treatments and placebos are being delivered. This rules out unintentional differences in therapist enthusiasm or confidence during treatment delivery. However, psychotherapy research has no equivalent control to assure therapist blindness. When a psychotherapist delivers a treatment or a placebo procedure, it is impossible to keep the therapist unaware of which procedure is being delivered (Gadow *et al.*, in press-a).

Again, the pivotal difference in the benefits of placebo groups in chemotherapy and psychotherapy efficacy research is the point at which the therapist blind is broken. In chemotherapy efficacy research, the therapist blind can be maintained until *after* initial effects of drugs occur. Initial improvement can be attributed to drugs independently of therapist bias. In psychotherapy efficacy research, however, breaking the psychotherapist blind is inherent in the delivery of therapy and control procedures *before* differential change begins. Initial improvement cannot be attributed to psychotherapy procedures independently of therapist bias.

Tape recordings may reduce the problem of therapist bias somewhat. Delivering two messages via headphones could preclude bias on the part of the individual actually interacting with the client. However, tapes would not preclude differences in confidence or enthusiasm on the part of the person whose behaviors were recorded on the tapes.

While placebo procedures in chemotherapy research rule out therapist bias, psychotherapy placebo procedures may actually increase therapist bias. Psychotherapists are more likely to be biased when a treatment is compared to a placebo than when two different forms of psychotherapy are compared to each other without a placebo.

Psychotherapy Mechanism Research

Paralleling antipsychological and prophysiochemical mechanism research in chemotherapy, psychotherapy researchers have developed tactics to rule out psychological factors and to identify what the mechanisms of psychotherapy actually are.

ANTIPSYCHOLOGICAL MECHANISM RESEARCH: CREDIBLE CONTROLS

In chemotherapy research, differences in the side effects produced by different substances may lead to differences in confidence in the treatments being delivered. Active placebos are employed to reduce differences in the symptom-irrelevant side effects produced by drugs and placebos.

Similarly, it is possible that psychotherapy groups improve more than placebo groups because the therapy procedure is more credible and instills greater faith, confidence, or expectancy of improvement (Borkovec & Nau, 1972; Kazdin & Wilcoxon, 1976; Lick & Bootzin, 1975). Rosenthal and Frank (1956) contended that clients must have equal faith in the therapy procedures they receive before causality can be attributed to theoretical mechanisms. Kazdin and Wilcoxon (1976) described an empirically derived control tactic designed to rule out expectancies. This tactic requires the construction of placebo procedures that are rated as equal in credibility to therapy procedures (Lent, Crimmings, & Russell, 1981; Lent, Russell, & Zamostny, 1981; McReynolds & Grizzard, 1971; Walter & Gilmore, 1973; Wilson, 1973).

The problems with inferring equal credibility between psychotherapy and placebo procedures, however, are similar to those involved in validating that a drug and an active chemotherapy placebo instill identical side effects and cognitions. In the empirical equation strategy, psychotherapy and control procedures are judged to be equivalent if no significant differences occur on expectancy measures. Unfortunately, this is to accept the null hypothesis. It may only be concluded that possible differences have not been detected by the measures employed. The acceptance of the null hypothesis does not assure that no differences have occurred. Also, measured equivalence on one occasion does not mean that procedures remain equated throughout an experiment. Etringer, Cash, and Rimm (1982), A. P. Goldstein (1960), and Lick and Heffler (1977) showed marked changes in credibility and expectancies over time.

McGlynn, Mealiea, and Landau (1981) described attempts to equate expectancies as antiexperiments with regard to expectancies. As in the case of antipsychological mechanism research in the chemotherapy setting, ruling out such psychological factors as faith, expectancy, or credibility does not specify the actual mechanisms through which improvement does occur.

PROPSYCHOLOGICAL MECHANISM RESEARCH

Mechanisms of psychotherapy have been identified by reinterpreting chemotherapy artifacts, and derived from the psychological research laboratory.

Reinterpretation of Chemotherapy Artifacts. Since the phenomena investigated in chemotherapy and psychotherapy research are different, artifacts are not necessarily the same in the two research settings.

Expectancies are rival hypotheses in chemotherapy research, since they are nondrug factors. In addition to conceptualizing expectancies in psychotherapy research as rival hypotheses (Kazdin & Wilcoxon, 1976), which they are in chemotherapy research, expectancies and other cognitive events have been conceptualized as theoretical mechanisms and intervening variables in their own right (Bernstein & Nietzel, 1977; Bootzin & Lick, 1979; Lick & Bootzin, 1975). Expectancies serve dual roles as either artifacts or mechanisms, depending upon the hypothesis of a particular psychotherapy experiment.

Psychological Laboratory Research. Just as applied chemotherapy research and placebo research have counterparts in the basic pharmacological laboratory, so does applied psychotherapy research have counterparts in the basic psychological laboratory. Mechanisms of psychotherapy involve (1) physiochemical and (2) psychosocial factors.

1. Physiochemical mechanisms. Basic research on physiochemical mediators of psychotherapeutic change, such as muscle relaxation and autonomic activity, are studied in psychological laboratories. The theoretical mechanism of reciprocal inhibition (Wolpe, 1958) was derived, in part, from basic laboratory research that interfaced with applied research activities. Physiochemical mechanisms involved in sex therapy and biofeedback are also examples of mechanisms derived from basic research.

2. *Psychosocial mechanisms.* In addition to the analogy that Rosenthal and Frank (1956) drew from the chemotherapy setting to shed new light on psychotherapy, A. P. Goldstein (1962) drew analogies from the social-psychological laboratory. Such theoretical processes as self-efficacy, attributions, and expectancies have been examined in the social-psychological laboratory (Bandura, 1982; Brehm, 1976; Darley & Fazio, 1980; Strong, 1978; Wilkins, 1977). The psychotherapy setting functions as a specific instance of those general principles of change. In turn, the psychotherapy setting provides opportunities to test the ecological validity of the principles examined in laboratory research.

Interdomain Designs: Chemotherapy and Psychotherapy Research

Just as placebos have been compared with drugs, so have psychotherapies been compared with drugs (Craighead, Stunkard, & O'Brien, 1981; Gadow et al., in press-a; Hogarty, Ulrich, Goldberg, & Schooler, 1976; Hollon & DeRubeis, 1981; Rush, Beck, Kovacs, & Hollon, 1977; Weissman et al., 1974). In addition, multidimensional designs can be used to study the interactive effects of chemotherapy, psychotherapy, client traits, outcome criteria, and other variables of interest (Extein & Bowers, 1979; Friedman, 1975; M. J. Goldstein, Rodnick, Evans, May, & Steinberg, 1978; Hollon & Beck, 1978; Klerman et al., 1974). Not only have relative efficacies been assessed, but new theoretical advances are emerging from the interface of chemotherapy–psychotherapy comparisons (Karasu, 1982; Schwartz, Shapiro, Redmond, Ferguson, Ragland, & Weiss, 1979).

DISCUSSION

Chemotherapy researchers, placebo researchers, and psychotherapy researchers share a network of common terms, common research designs, and common inferential practices. These commonalities and analogies are intended to facilitate communication and to increase the generalization of concepts across domains. However, the resulting language system is cumbersome and has promoted conceptual confusion (Grünbaum, 1981; Wilkins, 1979a, 1979b). For example, a claim such as "the placebo effect ... can be quite powerful" (Rosenthal & Frank, 1956, p. 296) illustrates professional jargon that cannot be interpreted literally. First, it is not placebo *effects* that are powerful; only *causes* are powerful. Second, the phrase "placebo effect" is an oxymoron—an expression that contradicts itself. Placebos are inert substances employed precisely because they are known *not* to cause the placebo effect. The causes of the placebo effect could be located almost anywhere in the pill-giving ritual or in the healing context *except* in the inert placebo. Consequently, the definition of placebo effect as the "effect produced by placebos" (Shapiro & Morris, 1978, p. 371) is a unique case of a circular definition that is literally false.

These basic linguistic imperfections have not posed much of a problem to chemotherapy researchers who attempt to eliminate placebo influences. However, the language problems have obfuscated important paradigmatic issues for psychotherapy researchers and for placebo researchers who search for causes among psychological factors ruled out by chemotherapy researchers. An examination of definitions and variables investigated within each of the three domains suggests new directions for psychotherapy research.

Variables and Definitions

A common terminology creates an illusion that analogous phenomena are investigated across the three domains of inquiry. This is not the case, however. Chemotherapy researchers, placebo researchers, and psychotherapy researchers are interested in qualitatively different cause–effect sequences.

CHEMOTHERAPY RESEARCH

For scientific and professional reasons, the *independent* variables that define the domain of chemotherapy research are limited to physiochemical manipulations. It would be scientifically meaningful to study psychological mechanisms of physiochemical independent variables; however, it is politically important that *intervening* variables also be limited exclusively to physiochemical events at some point in the process of improvement. At the *dependent* variable position of cause–effect sequences, either physiochemical or psychological events may be employed. Patients' verbal reports function as legitimate dependent variables, whether or not improvement on the physiochemical level is validated.

Brody (1980) has distinguished between paradigm-dependent and culture-dependent definitions of placebo, which are relevant to chemotherapy research and placebo research, respectively. Placebo factors in chemotherapy research are paradigm-dependent. They refer to phenomena outside the boundaries of the paradigms through which physiochemical causes are investigated. Since placebo factors in chemotherapy research are treated as artifacts, there is no need for clear, articulate definitions of placebo. Consequently, chemotherapy definitions tend to be negative and exclusionary, such as "nonspecific," "nondrug" (Peek, 1977; Rickels, 1968, 1977), or "any effect attributable to a pill, potion, or procedure, but not to its pharmacodynamic or specific properties" (Wolf, 1959, p. 689). Another aspect of paradigm-dependent definitions is that design flaws, methodological errors, and spontaneous remission have been included as placebo factors in chemotherapy research (Loranger *et al.*, 1961; Shapiro, 1960b), presumably since they are nondrug and constrain the attribution of causality to physiochemical factors.

PLACEBO RESEARCH

While it is appropriate to interpret design flaws and spontaneous remission as evidence against the physiochemical independent variables studied in chemotherapy research, it would be a mistake to interpret them as evidence for the psychological independent variables studied in placebo research (Fisher, 1970). When placebo factors are the primary focus, it is important to have positive, inclusionary definitions to guide research. In Brody's (1980) schema, definitions to the placebo researcher are culture-dependent. They involve the culturally acquired, symbolic meaning of healing activities for a person in a sick role. Placebo factors are defined as constituents of the pill-giving ritual and the healing context.

Placebo research is fundamentally different from chemotherapy research at the independent and intervening variable positions of cause–effect sequences. Unlike chemotherapy research, *independent* variables in placebo research involve the manipulation of psychological factors. Whereas *intervening* variables in chemotherapy research are limited to physiochemical events, in placebo research they can be either physiochemical or psychological. Endorphins and expectancies are respective examples. Placebo research and chemotherapy research are similar at the *dependent* variable position of cause–effect sequences. Either psychological or physiochemical events are acceptable.

PSYCHOTHERAPY RESEARCH

When the terms, concepts, and inferential practices found to be so useful in chemotherapy research were generalized to psychotherapy research, the terms retained their connotative meanings. However, their denotative meanings were altered dramatically. For example, in psychotherapy research, placebo groups are used in the name of ruling out nonspecific influences in order to attribute causality to specific factors, just as they are in chemotherapy research. However, in psychotherapy research, the term "placebo" no longer denotes a pharmacologically inert substance. Rather, the term denotes psychological procedures that are not inert, except in a metaphorical sense (Critelli & Neumann, 1984; Kazdin, 1979b; O'Leary & Borkovec, 1978).

Also, the denotative meanings of "specific" and "nonspecific" were altered when the terms were transferred from chemotherapy research to psychotherapy research. Specific factors in psychotherapy are completely excluded from the category of specific factors in chemotherapy. In fact, since "specific" and "nonspecific" no longer distinguish between physiochemical and psychological events in psychotherapy research, there may be no fundamental difference between them (Bernstein & Nietzel, 1977). Likewise, Grünbaum's (1981) "characteristic constituents" and "incidental constituents" denote qualitatively different events in chemotherapy research; however, there may be no fundamental difference between them in psychotherapy research.

Using placebo designs to rule out placebo factors in psychotherapy research implies that chemotherapy and psychotherapy research are similar to each other and are different from placebo research. However, in re-examining the phenomena investigated, there is a greater analogy between psychotherapy research and placebo research, both of which are different from chemotherapy research. At the *dependent* variable position of cause–effect sequences, chemotherapy research, placebo research, and psychotherapy research are similar. In all three domains, dependent variables may be either physiochemical or psychological. Fundamental differences occur at the independent variable and intervening variable positions. While *independent* variables in the chemotherapy research paradigm are restricted to physiochemical events, those in placebo research and in psychotherapy research are restricted to psychological events. *Intervening* variables in chemotherapy research are physiochemical events. In psychotherapy research and placebo research, intervening variables may be either psychological or physiochemical.

New Directions for Psychotherapy Research

The terms, research designs, and inferential practices involving the placebo concept were originated in chemotherapy research and have served chemotherapy researchers well in demonstrating the efficacy and mechanisms of physiochemical substances. However, the dissimilarity between chemotherapy research and psychotherapy research calls for a change in the inferential practices and placebo procedures used in psychotherapy research.

CONCEPTUAL MODELS

While some theorists have argued against analogies between chemotherapy and psychotherapy (Kirsch, 1978; Peek, 1977), others have promoted analogies between psychotherapy and placebos (Evans, 1977; Frank, 1959; Gliedman, Nash, Imber, Stone, & Frank, 1958; A. P. Goldstein, 1962). Early formulations about psychotherapy were derived from phenomena involving chemotherapy placebos (Rosenthal & Frank, 1956). Shapiro (1964) argued that effective psychotherapies are possibly placebo treatments. Frank (1973) considered the delivery of inert chemicals to be a form of psychotherapy. Viewed from the chemotherapy paradigm, psychotherapy treatments are grouped with chemotherapy placebos, since both involve nonphysiochemical causes. In psychotherapy research, there would be greater merit in deriving conceptual models from placebo research and from social-psychological research, in which psychological factors are considered to be legitimate causes (Brehm, 1976; A. P. Goldstein, 1962; Mischel, 1973, 1977; Strong, 1978), rather than borrowing strategies from chemotherapy research, in which psychological factors are summarily ruled out.

EFFICACY–MECHANISM REVERSAL

Efficacy research and mechanism research are distinct scientific endeavors. There is a logical order for the formulation of efficacy conclusions and mechanism conclusions: Conclusions about the mechanisms of a therapy procedure presume, first, that the therapy procedure is efficacious. Otherwise, the mechanisms identified would be those of ineffective procedures. However, chemotherapists have reversed that logic, preferring not to claim efficacy until there is evidence that the mechanisms are physiochemical. This preference reflects professional, rather than scientific, concerns. It would be scientifically legitimate to identify drugs that cause improvement via psychological mechanisms. However, if chemotherapists claim efficacy before nonpsychological mechanisms are inferred, there is a possiblity that the efficacious drugs may operate via the same sources of improvement as those employed by quacks. As an illustration, the therapy procedure of mesmerism was not discredited because of efficacy issues, but because its proponents failed to substantiate their claim that magnetic fluids were the physical mechanism that accounted for the efficacy of the procedure (Glasscheib, 1963; Orne, 1977). To be able to retain exclusive legal authority over drugs, chemotherapists prefer not to claim that a drug is efficacious until its mechanisms have been demonstrated to be independent of possible psychological mechanisms.

Psychotherapy researchers appear to have generalized the preference from chemotherapy research of not inferring efficacy until mechanism issues are settled. To illustrate, Rosenthal and Frank (1956) concluded that equivalent client faith, a mechanism, was necessary before efficacy was attributed to therapy techniques. The error here was to confuse efficacy issues with mechanism isues. Kazdin (1979a, 1979b) later clarified that equal faith is not necessary for efficacy conclusions. Efficacy can be established exclusively on the basis of manipulating independent variables, regardless of whatever mechanisms may be operating as intervening variables.

Reversing the logic does not provide the same benefits to psychotherapists. In fact, it is self-defeating. As a consequence of confusing efficacy and mechanism issues, the suggestion that nonspecific psychological factors are theoretical mechanisms has been misinterpreted to mean that psychotherapy procedures are ineffective (Critelli & Neumann, 1984; Frank, 1973). In order to avoid efficacy–mechanism confusion, it is important for psychotherapy reesarchers to maintain the distinction between the two research purposes and to retain their logical order.

PLACEBO GROUPS

In chemotherapy research, placebo groups are employed to make gross discriminations between physiochemical and psychological events in order to eliminate all possible psychological causes. In contast, in placebo research and in psychotherapy research, the same research tactic is called upon to make more refined discriminations among psychological factors in order to elucidate psychological causes. The use of placebo groups to elucidate psychological causes is also self-defeating for the psychotherapy researcher. An analogy would be for chemotherapy researchers to borrow strategies from some other area of inquiry that were designed specifically to rule out all physiochemical causes.

As previously discussed, and as depicted in Table 6-1, placebo procedures do not provide the same benefits to the psychotherapy researcher that they do to the chemotherapy researcher in ruling out client and therapist biases. In all probability, there will be less client and therapist bias when two forms of therapy are compared to each other than when a therapy is compared with a placebo. Throughout the history of psychotherapy research, many authors have recommended other forms of psychotherapy rather than placebo groups to control for the placebo effect (A. P. Goldstein, 1960, 1962; A. P. Goldstein, Heller, & Sechrest, 1966; Kazdin, 1979b; Kirsch, 1978; O'Leary & Borkovec, 1978; Rosenthal & Frank, 1956; Thorne, 1952; Wilkins, 1983). Knowing that one psychotherapy procedure is more effective than another provides more proscriptive information than knowing that a psychotherapy procedure is better than nothing. It is recommended that the net effects tactic with placebo groups be abandoned in favor of the relative effects tactic, in which two or more therapy procedures are compared with each other without placebo groups.

REFERENCES

Adelman, H. S., & Compas, B. E. Stimulant drugs and learning problems. *Journal of Special Education*, 1977, *11*, 377–416.

Baker, A. A., & Thorpe, J. G. Placebo response. *Archives of Neurology and Psychiatry*, 1957, *78*, 57–60.

Bandura, A. Self-efficacy mechanism in human agency. *American Psychologist*, 1982, *37*, 122–147.

Barsa, J. A. The fallacy of the "double blind." *American Journal of Psychiatry*, 1963, *119*, 1174–1175.

Beecher, H. K. Increased stress and effectiveness of placebos and "active" drugs. *Science*, 1960, *132*, 91–92.

Beecher, H. K. Ethics and clinical research. *New England Journal of Medicine*, 1966, *274*, 1354–1360.

Beecher, H. K. The placebo effect as a non-specific force surrounding disease and the treatment of disease. In R. Janzen, W. D. Keidel, A. Herz, C. Steichele, J. P. Payne, & R. A. P. Burt (Eds.), *Pain: Basic principles—pharmacology—therapy*. Baltimore: Williams & Wilkins, 1972.

Bernstein, D. A., & Nietzel, M. T. Demand characteristics in behavior modfiication: The natural history of a "nuisance." In M. Hersen, R. M. Eisler, & P. M. Miller (Eds.), *Progress in behavior modification* (Vol. 4). New York: Academic Press, 1977.

Blumenthal, D. S., Burke, R., & Shapiro, A. K. The validity of "identical matching placebos." *Archives of General Psychiatry*, 1974, *31*, 214–215.

Bok, S. The ethics of giving placebos. *Scientific American*, 1974, *231*(5), 17–23.

Bootzin, R. R., & Lick, J. R. Expectancies in therapy research: Interpretive artifact or mediating mechanism? *Journal of Consulting and Clinical Psychology*, 1979, *47*, 852–855.

Borkovec, T. D., & Nau, S. D. Credibility of analogue therapy rationales. *Journal of Behavior Therapy and Experimental Psychiatry*, 1972, *3*, 257–260.

Bourne, H. R. The placebo—A poorly understood and neglected therapeutic agent. *Rational Drug Therapy*, 1971, *5*, 1–6.

Bowman, W. C., & Rand, M. J. *Textbook of pharmacology* (2nd ed.). Oxford: Blackwell Scientific Publications, 1980.

Brehm, S. S. *The application of social psychology to clinical practice*. Washington, D.C.: Hemisphere, 1976.

Breuning, S. E., Ferguson, D. G., & Cullari, S. Analysis of single–double blind procedures, maintenance of placebo effects, and drug-induced dyskinesia with mentally retarded persons. *Applied Research in Mental Retardation*, 1980, *1*, 175–192.

Brody, H. *Placebos and the philosophy of medicine: Clinical, conceptual, and ethical issues*. Chicago: University of Chicago Press, 1980.

Burrow, J. G. *Organized medicine in the progressive era: The move toward monopoly*. Baltimore: Johns Hopkins University Press, 1977.

Byerly, H. Explaining and exploiting placebo effects. *Perspectives in Biology and Medicine*, 1976, *19*, 423–436.

Cabot, R. C. The physician's responsibility for the nostrum evil. *Journal of the American Medical Association*, 1906, *47*, 982–983.

Chassan, J. B. *Research design in clinical psychology and psychiatry* (2nd ed.). New York: Irvington, 1979.

Clark, W. G., & del Guidice, J. (Eds.). *Principles of psychopharmacology* (2nd ed.). New York: Academic Press, 1978.

Craighead, L. W., Stunkard, A. J., & O'Brien, R. M. Behavior therapy and pharmacotherapy for obesity. *Archives of General Psychiatry*, 1981, *38*, 763–768.

Critelli, J. W., & Neumann, K. F. The placebo: Conceptual analysis of a construct in transition. *American Psychologist*, 1984, *39*, 32–39.

Darley, J. M., & Fazio, R. H. Expectancy confirmation processes arising in the social interaction sequence. *American Psychologist*, 1980, *35*, 867–881.

Dinnerstein, A. J. Marijuana and perceptual style: A theoretical note. *Perceptual and Motor Skills*, 1968, *26*, 1016–1018.

Dinnerstein, A. J., & Halm, J. Modification of placebo effects by means of drugs: Effects of aspirin and placebos on self-rated moods. *Journal of Abnormal Psychology*, 1970, *75*, 308–314.

Downing, R. W., & Rickels, K. Predictors of response to amitriptyline and placebo in three outpatient treatment settings. *Journal of Nervous and Mental Disease*, 1973, *156*, 109–129.

Downing, R. W., & Rickels, K. Nonspecific factors and their interaction with psychological treatment in pharmacotherapy. In M. A. Lipton, A. DiMascio, & K. F. Killam (Eds.), *Psychopharmacology: A generation of progress*. New York: Raven Press, 1978.

Dubos, R.J. The gold-headed cane in the laboratory. *Public Health Reports*, 1954, *69*, 365–371.

Etringer, B. D., Cash, T. F., & Rimm, D. C. Behavioral, affective, and cogitive effects of participant modeling and an equally credible placebo. *Behavior Therapy*, 1982, *13*, 476–485.

Evans, F. J. The placebo control of pain: A paradigm for investigating non-specific effects in psychotherapy. In J. P. Brady, J. Mendels, M. T. Orne, & W. Rieger (Eds.), *Psychiatry: Areas of promise and advancement.* New York: Spectrum, 1977.

Extein, I., & Bowers, M. B. State and trait in psychiatric practice. *American Journal of Psychiatry*, 1979, *136*, 690–693.

Feldman, P. E. The personal element in psychiatric research. *American Journal of Psychiatry*, 1956, *113*, 52–54.

Fish, J. M. *Placebo therapy.* San Francisco: Jossey-Bass, 1973.

Fisher, S. Nonspecific factors as determinants of behavioral response to drugs. In A. DiMascio & R. I. Shader (Eds.), *Clinical handbook of psychopharmacology.* New York: Jason Aronson, 1970.

Frank, J. D. The dynamics of the psychotherapeutic relationship: Determinants and effects of the therapist's influence. *Psychiatry*, 1959, *22*, 17–39.

Frank, J. D. *Persuasion and healing: A comparative study of psychotherapy* (Rev. ed.). Baltimore: Johns Hopkins University Press, 1973.

Freedman, N., Cutler, R., Englehardt, D. M., & Margolis, R. On the modification of paranoid symptomatology. *Journal of Nervous and Mental Disease.* 1967, *144*, 29–36.

Friedman, A. S. Interaction of drug therapy with marital therapy in depressive patients. *Archives of General Psychiatry*, 1975, *32*, 619–637.

Gadow, K. D., White, L., & Ferguson, D. G. Placebo controls and double-blind conditions: Experimenter bias, conditioned placebo response, and drug–psychotherapy comparisons. In S. E. Breuning, A. D. Poling, & J. L. Matson (Eds.), *Applied psychopharmacology: Methods for assessing medication effects.* New York: Grune & Stratton, in press. (a)

Gadow, K. D., White, L., & Ferguson, D. G. Placebo controls and double-blind conditions: Placebo theory in experimental design. In S. E. Breuning, A. D. Poling, & J. L. Matson (Eds.), *Applied psychopharmacology: Methods for assessing medication effects.* New York: Grune & Stratton, in press. (b)

Gilman, A. G., Goodman, L. S., & Gilman, A. (Eds.). *The pharmacological basis of therapeutics* (6th ed.). New York: Macmillan, 1980.

Glasscheib, H. S. *The march of medicine: The emergence and triumph of modern medicine.* New York: G. P. Putnam's Sons, 1963.

Gliedman, L. H., Nash, E. H., Imber, S. D., Stone, A. R., & Frank, J. D. Reduction of symptoms by pharmacologically inert substances and by short-term psychotherapy. *Archives of Neurology and Psychiatry*, 1958, *79*, 345–351.

Goldstein, A. P. Patient's expectancies and non-specific therapy as a basis for (un)spontaneous remission. *Journal of Clinical Psychology*, 1960, *16*, 399–403.

Goldstein, A. P. *Therapist–patient expectancies in psychotherapy.* New York: Pergamon Press, 1962.

Goldstein, A. P., Heller, K., & Sechrest, L. B. *Psychotherapy and the psychology of behavior change.* New York: Wiley, 1966.

Goldstein, M. J., Rodnick, E. H., Evans, J. R., May, P. R. A., & Steinberg, M. R. Drug and family therapy in the aftercare of acute schizophrenics. *Archives of General Psychiatry*, 1978, *35*, 1169–1177.

Gottschalk, L. A. The use of drugs in interrogation. In A. B. Biderman & H. Zimmer (Eds.), *The manipulation of human behavior.* New York: Wiley, 1961.

Greiner, T. Problems of methodology in research with drugs. *American Journal of Mental Deficiency*, 1958, *64*, 346–352.

Griggs, B. *Green pharmacy: A history of herbal medicine.* New York: Viking, 1981.

Grünbaum, A. The placebo concept. *Behaviour Research and Therapy*, 1981, *19*, 157–167.

Haas, H., Fink, H., & Hartfelder, G. [The placebo problem.] *Fortschritte der Arzneimittelforschung*, 1959, *1*, 279–454. (Available in *Psychopharmacology Service Center Bulletin*, 1963, *2*, 1–65.)

Henker, B., Whalen, C. K., & Collins, B. E. Double-blind and triple-blind assessments of medication and placebo responses in hyperactive children. *Journal of Abnormal Child Psychology*, 1979, *7*, 1–13.

Herrnstein, R.J. Placebo effect in the rat. *Science*, 1962, *138*, 677–678.

Hoffer, A., & Osmond, H. Double blind clinical trials. *Journal of Neuropsychiatry*, 1961, *2*, 221–227.

Hogarty, G. E., Ulrich, R., Goldberg, S., & Schooler, N. Sociotherapy and the prevention of relapse among schizophrenic patients: An artifact of drug? In R. L. Spitzer & D. F. Klein (Eds.), *Evaluation of psychological therapies: Psychotherapies, behavior therapies, drug therapies, and their interactions*. Baltimore: Johns Hopkins University Press, 1976.

Hollon, S. D., & Beck, A. T. Psychotherapy and drug therapy: Comparison and combinations. In S. L. Garfield & A. E. Bergin (Eds.), *Handbook of psychotherapy and behavior change: An empirical analysis* (2nd ed.). New York: Wiley, 1978.

Hollon, S. D., & DeRubeis, R. J. Placebo–psychotherapy combinations: Inappropriate representations of psychotherapy in drug–psychotherapy comparative trials. *Psychological Bulletin*, 1981, *90*, 467–477.

Honigfeld, G. Non-specific factors in treatment: II. Review of social-psychological factors. *Diseases of the Nervous System*, 1964, *25*, 225–239.

Honigfeld, G. Specific and non-specific factors in the treatment of depressed states. In K. Rickels (Ed.), *Non-specific factors in drug therapy*. Springfield, Ill.: Charles C Thomas, 1968.

Hurst, P. M., Weidner, M. F., Radlow, R., & Ross, S. Drugs and placebos: Drug guessing by normal volunteers. *Psychological Reports*, 1973, *33*, 683–694.

Imber, S. D., Frank, J. D., Nash, E. H., Stone, A. R., & Gliedman, L. H. Improvement and amount of therapeutic contact: An alternative to the use of no-treatment controls in psychotherapy. *Journal of Consulting Psychology*, 1957, *21*, 309–315.

Jospe, M. *The placebo effect in healing*. Lexington, Mass.: Heath, 1978.

Karasu, T. B. Psychotherapy and pharmacotherapy: Toward an integrative model. *American Journal of Psychiatry*, 1982, *139*, 1102–1113.

Kazdin, A. E. Nonspecific treatment factors in psychotherapy outcome research. *Journal of Consulting and Clinical Psychology*, 1979, *47*, 846–851. (a)

Kazdin, A. E. Therapy oucome questions requiring control of credibility and treatment-generated expectancies. *Behavior Therapy*, 1979, *10*, 81–93. (b)

Kazdin, A. E., & Wilcoxon, L. A. Systematic desensitization and nonspecific treatment effects: A methodological evaluation. *Psychological Bulletin*, 1976, *83*, 729–758.

Kirsch, I. The placebo effect and the cognitive–behavioral revolution. *Cognitive Therapy and Research*, 1978, *2*, 255–264.

Klerman, G. L., DiMascio, A., Weissman, M., Prusoff, B., & Paykel, E. S. Treatment of depression by drugs and psychotherapy. *American Journal of Psychiatry*, 1974, *131*, 186–191.

Klett, C. J., & Moseley, E. C. The right drug for the right patient. *Journal of Consulting Psychology*, 1965, *29*, 546–551.

Lang, P. J., Lazovik, A. D., & Reynolds, D. J. Desensitization, suggestibility, and pseudo-therapy. *Journal of Abnormal Psychology*, 1965, *70*, 395–402.

Lent, R. W., Crimmings, A. M., & Russell, R. K. Subconscious reconditioning: Evaluation of a placebo strategy for outcome research. *Behavior Therapy*, 1981, *12*, 138–143.

Lent, R. W., Russell, R. K., & Zamostny, K. P. Comparison of cue-controlled desensitization, rational restructuring, and a credible placebo in the treatment of speech anxiety. *Journal of Consulting and Clinical Psychology*, 1981, *49*, 608–610.

Leslie, A. Ethics and practice of placebo therapy. *American Journal of Medicine*, 1954, *16*, 854–862.

Levine, J. D., Gordon, N. C., & Fields, H. L. The mechanism of placebo analgesia. *Lancet*, 1978, *2*, 654–657.

Lick, J., & Bootzin, R. Expectancy factors in the treatment of fear: Methodological and theoretical issues. *Psychological Bulletin*, 1975, *82*, 917–931.

Lick, J. R., & Heffler, D. Relaxation training and attention placebo in the treatment of severe insomnia. *Journal of Consulting and Clinical Psychology*, 1977, *45*, 153–161.

Lipman, R. S., Park, L. C., & Rickels, K. Paradoxical influence of a therapeutic side-effect interpretation. *Archives of General Psychiatry*, 1966, *15*, 462–474.

Lipton, M. A., DiMascio, A., & Killam, K. F. (Eds.). *Psychopharmacology: A generation of progress*. New York: Raven Press, 1978.

Loranger, A. W., Prout, C. T., & White, M. A. The placebo effect in psychiatric drug research. *Journal of the American Medical Association*, 1961, *176*, 920–925.

Lyerly, S. B., Ross, S., Krugman, A. D., & Clyde, D. J. Drugs and placebos: The effects of instructions upon performance and mood under amphetamine sulphate and chloral hydrate. *Journal of Abnormal and Social Psychology*, 1964, *68*, 321–327.

McGlynn, F. D., Kinjo, J., & Doherty, G. Effects of cue-controlled relaxation, a placebo treatment, and no treatment on changes in self-reported test anxiety among college students. *Journal of Clinical Psychology*, 1978, *34*, 707–714.

McGlynn, F. D., Mealiea, W. L., & Landau, D. L. The current status of systematic desensitization. *Clinical Psychology Review*, 1981, *1*, 149–179.

McReynolds, W. T., & Grizzard, R. H. A comparison of three fear reduction procedures. *Psychotherapy: Theory, Research and Practice*, 1971, *8*, 264–268.

Mischel, W. Toward a cognitive social learning reconceptualization of personality. *Psychological Review*, 1973, *80*, 252–283.

Mischel, W. On the future of personality assessment. *American Psychologist*, 1977, *32*, 246–254.

Molitch, M., & Eccles, A. K. The effect of benzedrine sulfate on the intelligence scores of children. *American Journal of Psychiatry*, 1937, *94*, 587–590.

Morris, L. A. & O'Neal, E. C. Drug-name familiarity and the placebo effect. *Journal of Clinical Psychology*, 1974, *30*, 280–282.

O'Leary, K. D., & Borkovec, T. D. Conceptual, methodological, and ethical problems of placebo groups in psychotherapy research. *American Psychologist*, 1978, *33*, 821–830.

Orne, M. T. On the social psychology of the psychological experiment: With particular reference to demand characteristics and their implications. *American Psychologist*, 1962, *17*, 776–783.

Orne, M. T. The search for specific treatments in psychiatry. In J. P. Brady, J. Mendels, M. T. Orne, & W. Rieger (Eds.), *Psychiatry: Areas of promise and advancement*. New York: Spectrum, 1977.

Paul, G. L. *Insight versus desensitization in psychotherapy: An experiment in anxiety reduction*. Stanford, Calif.: Stanford University Press, 1966.

Paul, G. L. Behavior modification research: Design and tactics. In C. M. Franks (Ed.), *Behavior therapy: Appraisal and status*. New York: McGraw-Hill, 1969.

Paul, G. L., Tobias, L. L., & Holly, B. L. Maintenance psychotropic drugs in the presence of active treatment programs: A "triple-blind" withdrawal study with long-term mental patients. *Archives of General Psychiatry*, 1972, *27*, 106–115.

Peek, C. J. A critical look at the theory of placebo. *Biofeedback and Self-Regulation*, 1977, *2*, 327–335.

Raskin, A., Schulterbrandt, J. G., Reatig, N., & McKeon, J. J. Differential response to chlorpromazine, imipramine, and placebo: A study of subgroups of hospitalized depressed patients. *Archives of General Psychiatry*, 1970, *23*, 164–173.

Rickels, K. Non-specific factors in drug therapy of neurotic patients. In K. Rickels (Ed.), *Non-specific factors in drug therapy*. Springfield, Ill.: Charles C Thomas, 1968.

Rickels, K. Non-specific factors in drug treatment. In J. P. Brady, J. Mendels, M. T. Orne, & W. Rieger (Eds.), *Psychiatry: Areas of promise and advancement*. New York: Spectrum, 1977.

Rickels, K., & Cattell, R. B. Drug and placebo response as a function of doctor and patient type. In P. R. A. May & J. R. Wittenborn (Eds.), *Psychotropic drug response: Advances in prediction*. Springfield, Ill.: Charles C Thomas, 1969.

Rickels, K., Lipman, R. S., Fisher, S., Park, L. C., & Uhlenhuth, E. H. Is a double-blind clinical trial really double-blind?: A report of doctors' medication guesses. *Psychopharmacologia*, 1970, *16*, 329–336.

Rosenthal, D., & Frank, J. D. Psychotherapy and the placebo effect. *Psychological Bulletin*, 1956, *53*, 294–302.

Ross, M., & Olson, J. M. An expectancy-attribution model of the effects of placebos. *Psychological Review*, 1981, *88*, 408–437.

Ross, S., Krugman, A. D., Lyerly, S. B., & Clyde, D. J. Drugs and placebos: A model design. *Psychological Reports*, 1962, *10*, 383–392.

Rush, A. J., Beck, A. T., Kovacs, M., & Hollon, S. Comparative efficacy of cognitive therapy and pharmacotherapy in the treatment of depressed outpatients. *Cognitive Therapy and Research*, 1977, *1*, 17–37.

Schapira, K., McClelland, H. A., Griffiths, N. R., & Newell, D. J. Study on the effects of tablet colour in the treatment of anxiety states. *British Medical Journal*, 1970, *2*, 446–449.

Schwartz, G. E., Shapiro, A. P., Redmond, D. P., Ferguson, D. C. E., Ragland, D. R., & Weiss, S. M. Behavioral medicine approaches to hypertension: An integrative analysis of theory and research. *Journal of Behavioral Medicine*, 1979, *2*, 311–363.

Shapiro, A. K. The placebo effect in the history of medical treatment: Implications for psychiatry. *American Journal of Psychiatry*, 1959, *116*, 298–304.

Shapiro, A. K. Attitudes toward the use of placebos in treatment. *Journal of Nervous and Mental Disease*, 1960, *130*, 200–211. (a)

Shapiro, A. K. A contribution to a history of the placebo effect. *Behavioral Science*, 1960, *5*, 109–135. (b)

Shapiro, A. K. Psychological aspects of medication. In H. I. Lief, V. F. Lief, & N. R. Lief (Eds.), *The psychological basis of medical practice*. New York: Harper & Row, 1963.

Shapiro, A. K. A historic and heuristic definition of the placebo. *Psychiatry*, 1964, *27*, 52–58.

Shapiro, A. K. Semantics of the placebo. *Psychiatric Quarterly*, 1968, *42*, 653–695.

Shapiro, A. K. The placebo effect. In W. G. Clark & J. del Guidice (Eds.), *Principles of psychopharmacology* (2nd ed.). New York: Academic Press, 1978.

Shapiro, A. K., & Morris, L. A. The placebo effect in medical and psychological therapies. In S. L. Garfield & A. E. Bergin (Eds.), *Handbook of psychotherapy and behavior change: An empirical analysis* (2nd ed.). New York: Wiley, 1978.

Storms, M. D., & Nisbett, R. E. Insomnia and the attribution process. *Journal of Personality and Social Psychology*, 1970, *16*, 319–328.

Strong, S. R. Social psychological approach to psychotherapy research. In S. L. Garfield & A. E. Bergin (Eds.), *Handbook of psychotherapy and behavior change: An empirical analysis* (2nd ed.), New York: Wiley, 1978.

Strupp, H. H. Toward a reformulation of the psychotherapeutic influence. *International Journal of Psychiatry*, 1973, *11*, 263–327.

Thorne, F. C. Rules of evidence in the evaluation of the effects of psychotherapy. *Journal of Clinical Psychology*, 1952, *8*, 38–41.

Tuteur, W. The "double-blind" method: Its pitfalls and fallacies. *American Journal of Psychiatry*, 1958, *114*, 921–922.

Uhlenhuth, E. H., Canter, A., Neustadt, J. O., & Payson, H. E. The symptomatic relief of anxiety with meprobamate, phenobarbital and placebo. *American Journal of Psychiatry*, 1959, *115*, 905–910.

Walter, H. I., & Gilmore, S. K. Placebo versus social learning effects in parent training procedures designed to alter the behavior of aggressive boys. *Behavior Therapy*, 1973, *4*, 361–377.

Weissman, M. M., Klerman, G. L., Paykel, E. S., Prusoff, B., & Hanson, B. Treatment effects on the social adjustment of depressed patients. *Archives of General Psychiatry*, 1974, *30*, 771–778.

Whalen, C. K., & Henker, B. Psychostimulants and children: A review and analysis. *Psychological Bulletin*, 1976, *83*, 1113–1130.

Wickramasekera, I. A conditioned response model of the placebo effect: Predictions from the model. *Biofeedback and Self-Regulation*, 1980, *5*, 5–18.

Wilkins, W. Expectancies in applied settings. In A. S. Gurman & A. M. Razin (Eds.), *Effective psychotherapy: A handbook of research*. New York: Pergamon Press, 1977.

Wilkins, W. Getting specific about nonspecifics. *Cognitive Therapy and Research*, 1979, *3*, 319–329. (a)

Wilkins, W. Heterogeneous referents, indiscriminate language, and complementary research purposes. *Journal of Consulting and Clinical Psychology*, 1979, *47*, 856–859. (b)

Wilkins, W. Failure of placebo groups to control for nonspecific events in therapy outcome research. *Psychotherapy: Theory, Research and Practice*, 1983, *20*, 31–37.

Wilson, G. T. Effects of false feedback on avoidance behavior: "Cognitive" desensitization revisited. *Journal of Personality and Social Psychology*, 1973, *28*, 115–122.

Wing, L. The use of reserpine in chronic psychotic patients: A controlled trial. *Journal of Mental Science*, 1956, *102*, 530–541.

Wolf, S. The pharmacology of placebos. *Pharmacological Review*, 1959, *11*, 689–704.

Wolpe, J. *Psychotherapy by reciprocal inhibition*. Stanford, Calif.: Stanford University Press, 1958.

Young, J. H. *The toadstool millionaires: A social history of patent medicines in America before federal regulation*. Princeton, N.J.: Princeton University Press, 1961.

Zelen, M. A new design for randomized clinical trials. *New England Journal of Medicine*, 1979, *300*, 1242–1245.

7

Designing, Analyzing, Interpreting, and Summarizing Placebo Studies

ROBERT ROSENTHAL

INTRODUCTION

There are strong methodological reasons and strong substantive reasons for the widespread interest in placebo effects. The methodological reasons center around the placebo effect as a plausible rival hypothesis to the hypothesis of a "true" treatment effect. This methodological application is so well established that there is scarcely a treatment condition that would be claimed effective in the absence of a placebo control, whether the "treatment" is biomedical, psychological, educational, or organizational. In addition to the methodological interest, there is also strong substantive interest in the placebo effect. This substantive interest includes both psychological (Ross & Olson, 1981) and physiological aspects (Watkins & Mayer, 1982).

The purposes of the present chapter include the following: briefly to outline some issues in the design and analysis of studies employing placebo conditions, whether for methodological or for substantive purposes; briefly to consider some issues in the interpretation of the practical meaning of the results of studies employing placebo conditions; and briefly to describe some procedures for summarizing multiple studies employing placebo conditions.

DESIGNING PLACEBO STUDIES

Placebo Control versus Placebo Effect

Imagine an experiment to evaluate a new treatment procedure. We randomly assign patients, clients, or students to one of three conditions:

Robert Rosenthal. Department of Psychology and Social Relations, Harvard University, Cambridge, Massachusetts.

T = The new treatment condition
P = The placebo control condition
O = The baseline control condition

The comparison T-P tells the extent to which the new treatment is superior to the placebo regarded as the control. That is, how much better is the treatment than patients' simply believing that they have been given the new treatment? This is the comparison of interest to the investigator employing placebo as *control*.

The comparison P-O tells the extent to which the placebo condition is superior to the baseline condition—say, treatment as usual prior to the development of the new treatment. This is the comparison of interest to the student of placebo *effect*.

The comparison T-O is the uncontrolled-for-placebo index of the benefit of the new treatment. It is the practical clinician's query: How much better is the new treatment than the baseline control condition, granting that the treatment effect may have been augmented by the placebo effect?

Single- versus Double-Expectancy Control

A popular and efficient experimental design that permits the simultaneous assessment of treatment effects and placebo effects is the 2 × 2 factorial design, wherein the treatment variable is crossed by the patient expectancy variable (e.g., Berg, Laberg, Skutle, & Öhman, 1981). This is a useful procedure, just as a "single-blind" experiment is a useful procedure (Rosenthal, 1966, 1976). However, the evidence suggests that patients' expectations are only part of what is involved in the placebo effect. The work of Beecher (1961, 1966), for example, showed how important the clinician's or researcher's expectations could be in contributing to the placebo effect (Rosenthal & Jacobson, 1968).

On the basis of this work, it seems wiser to employ controls not only for patients' expectations, but for clinicians' (or researchers') expectations as well. This added control is the experimental design analogue to the employment of the "double blind." It is not, however, the same thing as a double-blind study, since in the latter there is no experimental manipulation of clinician or researcher expectation. Table 7-1 shows the design of a study with controls for both patient and clinician expectancies; it is called a "double-expectancy control design."

The top half of Table 7-1 shows four conditions, none of which is administered the treatment of interest. The bottom half shows four conditions, each of which is administered the treatment of interest. Each of these two halves of the table is arranged as a 2 × 2 factorial design in which patients' expectancies are crossed by clinicians' (or researchers') expectancies. A brief description of each of the eight conditions is given in Table 7-1.

Table 7-1. Design of An Experiment with Double-Expectancy Control

	Patient expectancy	
Clinician expectancy	Control	Treatment
Treatment not administered		
Control	A. Pure control condition	B. Pure patient expectancy
Treatment	C. Pure clinician expectancy	D. Double-expectancy condition
Treatment actually administered		
Control	E. Pure treatment condition	F. Patient-augmented treatment
Treatment	G. Clinician-augmented treatment	H. Doubly augmented treatment

Condition H is the typical clinical application in which a new treatment is administered by a clinician (this can be a physician, nurse, psychologist, teacher, researcher, etc.) who believes that a new treatment is being administered. Condition E might involve a so-called "smuggled treatment," in which both the clinician and the patient are unaware that the treatment is being administered. Conditions F and G require that one but not both of the treatment dyad correctly believe that the treatment is being administered.

Condition D requires that both members of the treatment dyad believe the treatment is being administered when it is not. Conditions B and C require that one but not both of the treatment dyad believe the treatment is being administered when it is not. Condition A is the typical non-treatment condition; no treatment is administered, and neither member of the treatment dyad believes a treatment is being administered.

ANALYZING PLACEBO STUDIES

Tables 7-2 and 7-3 show the results of a hypothetical experiment employing the design of Table 7-1. For each of the eight conditions A through H, the

Table 7-2. Hypothetical Results of an Experiment with Double-Expectancy Control: Means

	Actual control		Actual treatment	
	Patient– control	Patient– treatment	Patient– control	Patient– treatment
Clinician–control	(A) 1	(B) 2	(E) 2	(F) 3
Clinician–treatment	(C) 2	(D) 3	(G) 3	(H) 8

Table 7-3. Hypothetical Results of an Experiment with Double-Expectancy Control: Analysis of Variance

Source	df	MS	F (1, 40)	p	r
Treatment	1	48	1.60	>.20	.20
Clinician expectancy	1	48	1.60	>.20	.20
Patient expectancy	1	48	1.60	>.20	.20
Treatment × clinician expectancy	1	12	.40	—	.10
Treatment × patient expectancy	1	12	.40	—	.10
Clinician expectancy × patient expectancy	1	12	.40	—	.10
Treatment × clinician expectancy × patient expectancy	1	12	.40	—	.10
Within conditions	40	30			

mean benefit score is shown in Table 7-2 for the six patients that have been randomly assigned to that condition. Table 7-3 shows the results of the $2 \times 2 \times 2$ analysis of variance. None of the three main effects and none of the interactions approach the customary level of significance (.05).

Design-Driven versus Theory-Driven Contrasts

It seems natural on seeing a set of eight conditions that can be arranged as a 2^k factorial to analyze this arrangement as a set of $2^k - 1$ orthogonal contrasts. The seven sources of variance of Table 7-3 are just such a set of $2^3 - 1$ orthogonal contrasts. However, just because one *can* analyze data by means of a 2^k factorial analysis of variance is no reason why one *should* analyze data by means of a set of such "canned contrasts." It would serve us far better to plan precisely the questions we want to put to the data, and to design our contrasts specifically to address those questions. It would increase our theoretical precision, our statistical power, the accuracy of our effect size estimation, and often our morale if we substituted planned contrasts for canned contrasts.

CONTRASTS: A BRIEF REVIEW

Contrasts are comparisons, employing two or more groups, set up in such a way that the results obtained from the several conditions involved in the research are compared (or "contrasted") to the predictions based on theory, hypothesis, or hunch. These predictions are expressed as weights (called λ), and they can take on any convenient numerical value so long as the sum of the weights ($\Sigma\lambda$) is 0 for any given contrast. Contrasts are quite easy to compute within the context of the analysis of variance. The following formula (Snedecor & Cochran, 1967, p. 308) shows the computation of a contrast in terms of a sum of squares for the single *df* test being made. Because contrasts are based on only one *df*, the sum of squares (*SS*) is identical to the mean square (*MS*) and needs only to be divided by the appropriate mean square for error to yield an *F* test for the contrast

$$MS \text{ contrast} = SS \text{ contrast} = \frac{L^2}{n\Sigma\lambda^2}$$

where $L =$ sum of all condition totals (T), each of which has been multiplied by the weight (λ) called for by the hypothesis, or

$$L = \Sigma[T\lambda] = T_1\lambda_1 + T_2\lambda_2 + T_3\lambda_3 \ldots T_k\lambda_k$$

where $k =$ number of conditions; $n =$ number of observations in each condition, given equal n per condition; and $\lambda =$ weights required by the hypothesis such that the sum of the weights equals 0.

The top half of Table 7-4 shows the contrast weights (λ's) for each of the canned or "wired-in" contrasts of our $2 \times 2 \times 2$ factorial design. We consider the first of these contrasts—that for treatment—in enough detail to serve the purpose of this review. The four groups receiving no treatment are each assigned weights of -1, while the four groups receiving the treatment are each assigned weights of $+1$; the sum of the weights is 0 as required (i.e., $\Sigma\lambda = 0$). We want to compute L, which requires that we line up the condition *totals* (i.e., mean $\times$ n per condition) along with the λ for each condition. For our example we have:

Condition:	A	B	C	D	E	F	G	H	Σ
Total (mean × 6):	6	12	12	18	12	18	18	48	144
Weight (λ):	−1	−1	−1	−1	+1	+1	+1	+1	0
Total × λ:	−6	−12	−12	−18	12	18	18	48	48

Therefore,

$$MS \text{ contrast} = \frac{L^2}{n\Sigma\lambda^2} = \frac{(48)^2}{6(8)} = 48$$

This is precisely the value of the MS for treatment obtained by the more traditional analysis-of-variance computational procedures and reported in Table 7-3. Although the contrasts for treatment, for clinician expectancy, and for patient expectancy are all quite sensible as planned contrasts, examination of the contrast weights for the four interactions raises serious questions of just what hypothesis could sensibly be addressed by these contrasts. Although even high-order interactions are sometimes of central theoretical interest, such seems not to be the case here (Rosenthal & Rosnow, 1984). These four interactions are simply (and literally) the products of the three main effects that would be of theoretical interest.

THEORY-DRIVEN CONTRASTS

At the bottom of Table 7-4, we have half a dozen contrasts to serve as illustrations of theory-driven contrasts that might have been planned by the investigators of our eight-condition experiment.

The first planned contrast is designed to test the following simple additive model. We give 1 point if the treatment is actually administered, 1 point if the clinician believes it to be actually administered, and 1 point if the patient believes it to be actually administered. Therefore we have one condition with 0 points, three conditions with 1 point, three conditions with 2 points, and one condition with 3 points. We cannot use these point values directly in our contrast, however, because they do not add up to 0. They will add up to 0 if we first subtract the mean number of points per condition from each condition. Thus, the total number of points $[12 = (1 \times 0) + (3 \times 1) + (3 \times 2) + (1 \times 3)]$ when divided by the number of groups (8) is 1.5. Subtracting 1.5 from each condition's theory-derived weight yields one condition with $\lambda = -1.5$, three with $\lambda = -0.5$, three with $\lambda = 0.5$, and one with $\lambda = 1.5$. To get rid of decimals, we can multiply these weights by 2, yielding the λ's shown for the simple additive model contrast of Table 7-4.

The second theory-based contrast of Table 7-4 tests the model that although all three factors will make a difference, the treatment effect will be greater (2 points) than the effect of either clinician (1 point) or patient (1 point) expectancy. The third contrast assigns 3 points to treatment and 2 points and 1 point to patient and clinician expectancy, respectively.

The fourth contrast addresses the clinician's query: How much does the new treatment, accompanied (as it usually is in a clinical context) by the favorable expectation of both the patient and the clinician, benefit the patient compared to treatment as usual? Since this contrast involves the direct comparison of two groups, we could have employed the ordinary t test. In this case,

$$t = \frac{M_1 - M_2}{\sqrt{(\frac{1}{n_1} + \frac{1}{n_2})MS\text{ error}}} = \frac{8 - 1}{\sqrt{(\frac{1}{6} + \frac{1}{6})30}} = 2.21, p < .04, \text{ two-tailed}$$

Table 7-4 shows that using the contrast procedure yields $F(1, 40) = 4.90, p < .04$; this is an identical result, since for F with a single df in the numerator, $\sqrt{F} = t$ and $\sqrt{4.90} = 2.21$.

The fifth contrast tests the hypothesis of complete synergy: that is, that only when the treatment is accompanied by favorable expectations of both patient and clinician will there be any benefit. The sixth and final contrast tests a modified synergy hypothesis: that is, that treatment alone is somewhat better than no treatment, but that the full benefits of treatment

Table 7-4. Design-Determined and Theory-Determined Contrasts

	Contrast weights for eight conditions								Contrast-based results		
									Significance tests		Effect size
	A (M=1)	B (M=2)	C (M=2)	D (M=3)	E (M=2)	F (M=3)	G (M=3)	H (M=8)	$F(1, 40)$	p	r
Design-determined contrasts											
1. Treatment	−1	−1	−1	−1	+1	+1	+1	+1	1.60	>.20	.20
2. Clinician expectancy	−1	−1	+1	+1	−1	−1	+1	+1	1.60	>2.0	.20
3. Patient expectancy	−1	+1	−1	+1	−1	+1	−1	+1	1.60	>.20	.20
4. Treatment × clinician expectancy	+1	+1	−1	−1	−1	−1	+1	+1	.40	—	.10
5. Treatment × patient expectancy	+1	−1	+1	−1	−1	+1	−1	+1	.40	—	.10
6. Clinician expectancy × patient expectancy	+1	−1	−1	+1	+1	−1	−1	+1	.40	—	.10

7. Treatment × clinician expectancy × patient expectancy	−1	+1	+1	−1	+1	−1	−1	+1	.40	—	.10

Theory-determined contrasts

1. Simple additive model	−3	−1	−1	+1	−1	+1	+1	+3	4.80	.04	.33
2. Treatment > expectancy model	−2	−1	0	0	0	+1	+1	+2	4.27	.05	.31
3. Treatment > patient expectancy > clinician expectancy	−3	−1	−2	0	0	+2	+1	+3	4.11	.05	.31
4. All against none	−1	0	0	0	0	0	−1	+1	4.90	.04	.33
5. Complete synergism	−1	−1	−1	−1	−1	−1	−1	+7	5.71	.02	.35
6. Modified synergism	−1	−1	−1	−1	0	0	0	+4	5.76	.02	.35

occur only when accompanied by the favorable expectations of both clinician and patient.

For all of the contrasts shown, Table 7-4 provides a test of significance and an estimate of effect size, r. Some estimate of effect size should be reported with every test of significance, and r is a convenient index (Cohen, 1977; Rosenthal, 1982; Rosenthal & Rubin, 1982c). For the particular results shown, a not implausible set of results, the F's and r's associated with the theory-driven contrasts are appreciably larger than were those associated with the design-driven contrasts, those "wired into" the 2^3 factorial analysis of variance.

If competing theories yield the theory-driven contrasts of Table 7-4, all will be confronted by good news and by bad news. The good news is that their theory is supported by the significant F and the substantial effect size r (see the following section on the interpretation of results). The bad news is that their theory (any of the theory-driven contrasts 1 to 6) does not fare especially better than any of the other theories. Although the results of such comparative evaluations are not always definitive, one of the most valuable uses of theory-driven contrasts is that they permit the head-to-head confrontation of competing theories. All the theorists of our example do about equally well, though the synergistic theorists have a tiny edge. A much more detailed discussion of the use of contrasts can be found elsewhere (Rosenthal & Rosnow, 1984, 1985; see especially 1985).

INTERPRETING THE RESULTS OF PLACEBO STUDIES

In the preceding section, it has been noted that some estimate of effect size should be reported for each significance test reported. Here I want to evaluate more usefully the practical meaning of any effect size estimate we obtain from our placebo studies.

Despite the growing awareness of the importance of estimating effect sizes, there is a problem in evaluating various effect size estimators from the point of view of practical usefulness (Cooper, 1981). It was found (Rosenthal & Rubin, 1979b, 1982c) that neither experienced behavioral researchers nor experienced statisticians had a good intuitive feel for the practical meaning of such common effect size estimators as r^2, omega^2 (ω), epsilon^2 (ε), and similar estimates.

The Binomial Effect Size Display

Accordingly, Rubin and I introduced an intuitively appealing general-purpose effect size display whose interpretation is perfectly transparent: the Binomial Effect Size Display (BESD). There is no sense in which we claim to have resolved the differences and controversies surrounding the use of various effect size estimators, but the BESD is useful because it is (1) easily understood by researchers, students, and lay persons; (2) applicable in a wide variety of contexts; and (3) conveniently computed.

The question addressed by the BESD is this: What is the effect on the success rate (e.g., survival rate, cure rate, improvement rate, selection rate, etc.) of the institution of a new treatment procedure? It therefore displays the change in success rate (e.g., survival rate, cure rate, improvement rate, selection rate, etc.) attributable to the new treatment procedure. An example shows the appeal of the display.

In one of their meta-analyses of psychotherapy outcome studies, Smith and Glass (1977) summarized the results of some 400 studies. An eminent critic (Rimland, 1979) stated that the results of their analysis sounded the "death knell" for psychotherapy because of the modest size of the effect. This modest effect size was calculated to be equivalent to an r of .32 accounting for "only 10% of the variance."

Table 7-5 is the BESD corresponding to an r of .32 or an r^2 of .10. The table shows clearly that it is absurd to label as "modest indeed" an effect size equivalent to increasing the success rate from 34% to 66% (e.g., reducing a death rate from 66% to 34%). Even so small an r as .20, accounting for "only 4% of the variance," is associated with an increase in success rate from 40% to 60% (e.g., a decrease in death rate from 60% to 40%)—hardly a trivial effect. It might be thought that the BESD can be employed only for dichotomous outcomes (e.g., alive vs. dead) and not for continuous outcomes (e.g., scores on a Likert-type scale of improvement due to psychotherapy). Fortunately, however, the BESD works well for *both* types of outcomes under a wide variety of conditions (Rosenthal & Rubin, 1982c).

A great convenience of the BESD is how easily we can convert it to r (or r^2) and how easily we can go from r (or r^2) to the display. Table 7-6 shows systematically the increase in success rates associated with various values of r^2 and r. For example, an r of .30, accounting for "only 9% of the variance," is associated with a reduction in death rate from 65% to 35%, or, more generally, with an increase in success rate from 35% to 65%. The last column of Table 7-6 shows that the difference in success rates is identical to r. Consequently, the experimental group's success rate in the BESD is computed as $.50 + r/2$, whereas the control group's success rate is computed as $.50 - r/2$.

Table 7-5. The Binomial Effect Size Display (BESD) for an r of .32 That "Accounts for Only 10% of the Variance"

Condition	Treatment outcome		
	Alive	Dead	Σ
Treatment	66	34	100
Placebo	34	66	100
Σ	100	100	200

Table 7-6. Changes in Success Rates (BESD) Corresponding to Various Values of r^2 and r

Effect sizes		Equivalent to a success rate increase		Difference in success rates[a]
r^2	r	From	To	
.00	.02	.49	.51	.02
.00	.04	.48	.52	.04
.00	.06	.47	.53	.06
.01	.08	.46	.54	.08
.01	.10	.45	.55	.10
.01	.12	.44	.56	.12
.02	.14	.43	.57	.14
.03	.16	.42	.58	.16
.03	.18	.41	.59	.18
.04	.20	.40	.60	.20
.05	.22	.39	.61	.22
.06	.24	.38	.62	.24
.07	.26	.37	.63	.26
.08	.28	.36	.64	.28
.09	.30	.35	.65	.30
.16	.40	.30	.70	.40
.25	.50	.25	.75	.50
.36	.60	.20	.80	.60
.49	.70	.15	.85	.70
.64	.80	.10	.90	.80
.81	.90	.05	.95	.90
1.00	1.00	.00	1.00	1.00

[a]The difference in success rates in a BESD is identical to r.

Obtaining r from Test Statistics

Cohen (1965) and Friedman (1968) provide useful discussions of finding r from a variety of significance test statistics. The three most frequently used equivalences show how to compute r given t, F, and χ^2. If the test statistic is t, we get r as follows:

$$r = \sqrt{\frac{t^2}{t^2 + df}}$$

If the test statistic is F as for a contrast, as described earlier, we get r as follows:

$$r = \sqrt{\frac{F}{F + df(\text{error})}}$$

If F has more than one df in the numerator, r cannot be computed. Other indices of effect size, such as eta, could be computed; however, their use is not recommended because of the diffuse, unfocused hypotheses addressed by F's of $df > 1$ in the numerator (Rosenthal & Rosnow, 1984, 1985). The same situation prevails when χ^2 is our test statistic. The use of χ^2 with $df > 1$ is not recommended because of the diffuse, unfocused hypothesis addressed. When diffuse F's or χ^2's are obtained, they should ordinarily be decomposed into more focused contrasts, such as those described earlier. If our test statistic, however, is $\chi^2(1)$ (i.e., when $df = 1$), we can get r as follows:

$$ r = \sqrt{\frac{\chi^2}{N}} $$

The r in this case is sometimes called phi (ϕ), but ϕ is nothing more than r computed on dichotomously scored data.

The following results serve as an illustration of this last equation. On October 29, 1981, the National Heart, Lung and Blood Institute officially discontinued its placebo-controlled study of propranolol, because the results were so favorable to the treatment that it would be unethical to keep the placebo control patients from receiving the treatment (Kolata, 1981). The 2-year data for this study were based on 2108 patients, and $\chi^2(1)$ was approximately 4.2. What, then, was the size of the effect that led the Institute to break off its study? Was the use of propranolol accounting for 90% of the variance in death rates? Was it 50% or 10%, the "modest indeed" effect size that should prompt us to give up psychotherapy? We find the proportion of variance accounted for (r^2) as follows:

$$ r^2 = \frac{\chi^2}{N} = \frac{4.2}{2108} = .002 $$

Thus, the propranolol study was discontinued for an effect accounting for 1/5 of 1% of the variance! To display this result as a BESD, we take the square root of r^2 to obtain the r we use for the BESD. That r is about .04, which displays as follows:

	Alive	Dead	Σ
Propranolol	52	48	100
Placebo	48	52	100
Σ	100	100	200

As behavioral researchers, we are not accustomed to thinking of r's of .04 as reflecting effect sizes of practical importance. If we were among the 4 per 100 who moved from one outcome to the other, we might well revise our view of the practical import of small effects!

Concluding Note on Interpreting Effect Sizes

Rubin and I (Rosenthal & Rubin, 1982c) proposed that the reporting of effect sizes could be made more intuitive and more informative by using the BESD. It was our belief that the use of the BESD to display the increase in success rate due to treatment would more clearly convey the real-world importance of treatment effects than would the commonly used descriptions of effect size based on the proportion of variance accounted for.

One effect of the routine employment of a display procedure such as the BESD to index the practical meaning of our research results would be to provide us as clinicians with more useful and realistic assessments of how well we are doing in placebo research and in the behavioral sciences more generally. Employment of the BESD has, in fact, shown that we are doing considerably better than we thought we were.

SUMMARIZING SERIES OF PLACEBO STUDIES

There is a kind of pessimism among placebo researchers and behavioral scientists more generally that, when compared to the natural sciences, our progress has been depressingly slow, if indeed there has been any progress at all. One of the sources of this pessimism is the finding that many of our well-replicated results show only "small" effect sizes. I have discussed this problem of "small effects" in the last section. In the present section, I discuss another source of pessimism—the problem of "poor cumulation." This refers to the observation that the behavioral sciences do not show the orderly progress and development shown by such older sciences as physics and chemistry. The newer work of the physical sciences is seen to build directly upon the older work of those sciences. The behavioral sciences, on the other hand, seem nearly to be starting afresh with each succeeding volume of scientific journals.

Poor cumulation does not seem to be primarily due to lack of replication or to failure to recognize the need for replication. Indeed, the clarion calls for further research with which we so frequently end our articles are carried wherever our scholarly journals are read. It seems, rather, that we have been better at issuing such calls than at knowing what to do with the answers. There are many areas of the behavioral sciences for which we do have available the results of many studies that all address essentially the same question. Our summaries of the results of these sets of studies, however, have not been nearly as informative as they might have been, either with respect to summarized significance levels or with respect to summarized effect sizes. Even the best reviews of research by the most sophisticated workers have rarely told us more about each study in a set of studies than the direction of the relationship between the variables investigated and whether or not a given *p* level was attained. This state of affairs is beginning to change. More and more reviews of the literature are moving from the traditional, literary format to the quantitative format (for overviews, see Glass, McGaw, & Smith, 1981; Rosenthal, 1980, 1984).

The purposes of this section relevant to the problem of poor cumulation include the following: (1) providing a general framework for conceptualizing the quantitative summary of research domains; and (2) illustrating the quantitative procedures within this framework so they can be applied by the reader and/or understood more clearly when applied by others.

A Framework for Summarizing Series of Studies

Table 7-7 provides a summary of four types of procedures for summarizing series of studies for the special case where just two studies are to be evaluated. It is useful to list the two-study case separately, because there are some especially convenient computational procedures for this situation. The two columns of Table 7-7 show that there are two major ways to evaluate the results of research studies—in terms of their statistical significance (e.g., p levels), and in terms of their effect sizes (e.g., the difference between means divided by the common standard deviation σ or S—indices employed by Cohen, 1977, and by Glass, 1980—or the Pearson r). The two rows of Table 7-7 show that there are two major analytic processes applied to the set of studies to be evaluated, comparing and combining. The cell labeled A in Table 7-7 represents the procedure that evaluates whether the significance level of one study differs significantly from the significance level of the other study. The cell labeled B represents the procedure that evaluates whether the effect size (e.g., d or r) of one study differs significantly from the effect size of the other study. Cells C and D represent the procedures that are used to estimate the overall level of significance and the average size of the effect, respectively. Illustrations of these procedures are given below.

Table 7-8 provides a more general summary of six types of summarizing procedures that are applicable to the case where three or more studies are to be evaluated. The columns are the same as in Table 7-7, but the row labeled "Comparing studies" in Table 7-7 has now been subdivided into two rows— one for the case of diffuse tests, and one for the case of focused tests.

Table 7-7. Four Types of Procedures for Summarizing a Set of Two Studies

	Outcomes defined in terms of	
Analytic process	Significance testing	Effect size estimation
Comparing studies	A	B
Combining studies	C	D

Table 7-8. Six Types of Procedures for Summarizing a Set of Three or More Studies

	Outcomes defined in terms of	
Analytic process	Significance testing	Effect size estimation
Comparing studies: Diffuse tests	A	B
Comparing studies: Focused tests	C	D
Combining studies	E	F

When studies are compared as to their significance levels (Cell A) or their effect sizes (Cell B) by diffuse tests, we learn whether they differ significantly among themselves with respect to significance levels or effect sizes respectively, but we do not learn how they differ or whether they differ according to any systematic basis. When studies are compared as to their significance levels (Cell C) or their effect sizes (Cell D) by focused tests, or contrasts, we learn whether the studies differ significantly among themselves in a theoretically predictable or meaningful way. Thus, important tests of hypotheses can be made by the use of focused tests. Cells E and F of Table 7-8 are simply analogues of Cells C and D of Table 7-7, representing procedures used to estimate overall level of significance and average size of the effect, respectively.

Summarizing Procedures: Two Studies

Even when we have been quite rigorous and sophisticated in the interpretation of the results of a single study, we are often prone to err in the interpretation of two or more studies. For example, Smith may report a significant effect of some social intervention, only to have Jones publish a rebuttal demonstrating that there is no such effect. A closer look at both their results may show the following:

Smith's study: $t(78) = 2.21, p < .05, d = .50, r = .24$

Jones's study: $t(18) = 1.06, p > .30, d = .50, r = .24$

Smith's results are more significant than Jones's, to be sure, but the studies are in perfect agreement as to their estimated sizes of effect defined by either d or r. A comparison of their respective significance levels reveals, furthermore, that these p's are not significantly different ($p = .42$). Clearly Jones is quite wrong in claiming that he failed to replicate Smith's results. I begin this section by considering some procedures for comparing quantitatively the results of two independent studies (i.e., studies conducted with different research participants). The examples I examine in this chapter are in most cases hypothetical, constructed specifically to illustrate a wide range of situations that occur when working on meta-analytic problems—not only in the domain of placebo studies, but in any other domain as well.

COMPARING STUDIES

Significance Testing. Ordinarily, when we compare the results of two studies, we are more interested in comparing their effect sizes than their p values. However, sometimes we cannot do any better than comparing their p values, and here is how we do it (Rosenthal & Rubin, 1979a): For each of the two test statistics, we obtain a reasonably exact one-tailed p level. (All of the procedures described in this chapter require that p levels be recorded as one-tailed. Thus $t(100) = 1.98$ is recorded as $p = .025$, not $p = .05$.) Then, as an illustration of being "reasonably exact," if we obtain $t(30) = 3.03$, we give p as .0025, not as "$< .05$." Extended tables of the t distribution are helpful here (e.g., Federighi, 1959; Rosenthal & Rosnow, 1984). For each p, we find Z, the standard normal deviate corresponding to the p value. Since both p's must be one-tailed, the corresponding Z's will have the same sign if both studies show effects in the same direction, but different signs if the results are in the opposite direction. The difference between the two Z's when divided by $\sqrt{2}$ yields a new Z corresponding to the p value that the difference between the Z's could be so large, or larger, if the two Z's did not really differ. In short,

$$\frac{Z_1 - Z_2}{\sqrt{2}} \text{ is distributed as } Z \qquad (1)$$

Example 1. Placebo studies A and B yield results in opposite directions, and neither is "significant." One p is .06, one-tailed; the other is .12, one-tailed but in the opposite tail. The Z's corresponding to these p's are found in a table of the normal curve to be $+1.56$ and -1.18 (note the opposite signs to indicate results in opposite directions). Then, from the preceding equation (1), we have

$$\frac{Z_1 - Z_2}{\sqrt{2}} = \frac{(1.56) - (-1.18)}{1.41} = 1.94$$

as the Z of the difference between the two p values or their corresponding Z's. The p value associated with a Z of 1.94 is .026 one-tailed or .052 two-tailed. The two p values thus may be seen to differ significantly; this suggests that we may want to draw different inferences from the results of the two placebo studies.

Effect Size Estimation. When we ask whether two studies are telling the same story, what we usually mean is whether the results (in terms of the estimated effect size) are reasonably consistent with each other or whether they are significantly heterogeneous. For the purposes of the present chapter, the discussion is restricted to r as the effect size indicator, but analogous procedures are available for comparing such other effect size indicators as Cohen's (1977) d or differences between proportions (Hedges, 1982; Rosenthal & Rubin, 1982a).

For each of the two studies to be compared, we compute the effect size r and find for each of these r's the associated Fisher z, defined as $\frac{1}{2} \log_e [(1 + r)/(1 - r)]$. Tables to convert our obtained r's to Fisher z's are available in most introductory textbooks of statistics. Then, when N_1 and N_2 represent the number of sampling units (e.g., subjects) in each of our two studies, the quantity

$$\frac{Z_1 - Z_2}{\sqrt{\dfrac{1}{N_1 - 3} + \dfrac{1}{N_2 - 3}}} \text{ is distributed as } Z \text{ (Snedecor \& Cochran, 1967, 1980)}$$

$$(2)$$

Example 2. Placebo studies A and B yield results in opposite directions, with effect sizes of $r = .60$ ($N = 15$) and $r = -.20$ ($N = 100$), respectively. The Fisher z's corresponding to these r's are .69 and $-.20$, respectively (note the opposite signs of the z's to correspond to the opposite signs of the r's). Then, from the preceding equation (2), we have

$$\frac{Z_1 - Z_2}{\sqrt{\dfrac{1}{N_1 - 3} + \dfrac{1}{N_2 - 3}}} = \frac{(.69) - (-.20)}{\sqrt{\dfrac{1}{12} + \dfrac{1}{97}}} = 2.91$$

as the Z of the difference between the two effect sizes. The p value associated with a Z of 2.91 is .002 one-tailed or .004 two-tailed. These two effect sizes, then, differ significantly.

COMBINING STUDIES

Significance Testing. After comparing the results of any two independent studies, it is an easy matter also to combined the p levels of the two studies. Thus, we get an overall estimate of the probability that the two p levels might have been obtained if the null hypothesis of no relationship between X and Y were true. Many methods for combining the results of two or more studies are available and have been summarized elsewhere (Rosenthal, 1978, 1980). Here it is necessary to give only the simplest and most versatile of the procedures, the method of adding Z's called the

"Stouffer method" by Mosteller and Bush (1954). This method, just like the method of comparing p values, asks us first to obtain accurate p levels for each of our two studies and then to find the Z corresonding to each of these p levels. Both p's must be given in one-tailed form, and the corresponding Z's will have the same sign if both studies show effects in the same direction. They will have different signs if the results are in the opposite direction. The sum of the two Z's when divided by $\sqrt{2}$ yields a new Z. This new Z corresponds to the p value that the results of the two studies combined, or results even further out in the same tail, could have occurred if the null hypothesis of no relationship between X and Y were true. In short,

$$\frac{Z_1 + Z_2}{\sqrt{2}} \text{ is distributed as } Z \tag{3}$$

Should we want to do so, we could weight each Z by its df (Rosenthal, 1978, 1980).

Example 3. Placebo studies A and B yield results in opposite directions, and both are significant. One p is .05, one-tailed; the other is .0000001, one-tailed but in the opposite tail. The Z's corresponding to these p's are found in a table of normal deviates to be -1.64 and 5.20, respectively (note the opposite signs to indicate results in opposite directions). Then, from the preceding equation (3), we have

$$\frac{Z_1 + Z_2}{\sqrt{2}} = \frac{(-1.64) + (5.20)}{1.41} = 2.52$$

as the Z of the combined results of studies A and B. The p value associated with a Z of 2.52 is .006 one-tailed or .012 two-tailed. Thus, the combined p supports the more significant of the two results. If these were actual results, we would want to be very cautious in interpreting our combined p, both because the two p's are significant in opposite directions and because the two p's are so very significantly different from each other. We would try to discover what differences between studies A and B might have led to results so significantly different.

Effect Size Estimation. When we want to combine the results of two studies, we are as interested in the combined estimate of the effect size as we are in the combined probability. As in the case when two effect size estimates are compared, we shall consider r as our effect size estimate in the combining of effect sizes. However, it should be noted that many other estimates are possible (e.g., Cohen's d or differences between proportions).

For each of the two studies to be combined, we compute r and the associated Fisher z and have

$$\frac{z_1 + z_2}{2} = \bar{z} \qquad (4)$$

as the Fisher z corresponding to our mean r. We use an r-to-z or z-to-r table to look up the r associated with our mean $\bar{z}$. Tables are handier than computing r from z, but, if necessary, this can be done with the following equation: $r = (e^{2z} - 1)/(e^{2z} + 1)$. Should we want to do so, we could weight each z by its df (Snedecor & Cochran, 1967, 1980).

Example 4. Placebo studies A and B yield results in opposite directions, one $r = .80$, the other $r = -.30$. The Fisher z's corresponding to these r's are 1.10 and -0.31, respectively. From the preceding equation (4), we have

$$\frac{z_1 + z_2}{2} = \frac{(1.10) + (-0.31)}{2} = .395$$

as the mean Fisher z. From a z-to-r table, we find a z of .395 associated with an r of .38.

Summarizing Procedures: Three or More Studies

Although we can do quite a lot in the way of comparing and combining the results of sets of studies with just the procedures given so far, it does happen often that we have three or more studies of the same relationship that we want to compare and/or combine. The purpose of this section is to present generalizations of the procedures given in the last section so that we can compare and combine the results of any number of studies. Again, the examples are hypothetical, constructed to illustrate a wide range of situations occurring in meta-analytic work on placebo research or any other domain. Often, of course, the number of studies entering into our analyses will be larger than the number required to illustrate the various meta-analytic procedures.

COMPARING STUDIES: DIFFUSE TESTS

Significance Testing. Given three or more p levels to compare, we first find the standard normal deviate, Z, corresponding to each p level. All p levels must be one-tailed, and the corresponding Z's will have the same sign if all studies show effects in the same direction, but different signs if the results are not all in the same direction. The statistical significance of the heterogeneity of the Z's can be obtained from a χ^2 computed as follows (Rosenthal & Rubin, 1979a):

$$\Sigma(Z_j - \bar{Z})^2 \text{ is distributed as } \chi^2 \text{ with } K - 1 \ df \qquad (5)$$

In this equation Z_j, is the Z for any one study, $\bar{Z}$ is the mean of all the Z's obtained, and K is the number of studies being combined.

Example 5. Placebo studies A, B, C, and D yield one-tailed p values of .15, .05, .01, and .001, respectively. Study C, however, shows results opposite in direction from those of studies A, B, and D. From a normal table we find the Z's corresponding to the four p levels to be 1.04, 1.64, −2.33, and 3.09. (Note the negative sign for the Z associated with the result in the opposite direction.) Then, from the preceding equation (5), we have

$$\Sigma(Z_j - \bar{Z})^2 = [(1.04) - (0.86)]^2 + [(1.64) - (0.86)]^2 \\ + [(-2.33) - (0.86)]^2 + [(3.09) - (0.86)]^2 = 15.79$$

as our X^2 value, which for $K - 1 = 4 - 1 = 3$ df is significant at $p = .0013$. The four p values we have compared, then, are clearly significantly heterogeneous.

Effect Size Estimation. Here we want to assess the statistical heterogeneity of three or more effect size estimates. The discussion is again restricted to r as the effect size estimator, though analogous procedures are available for comparing such other effect size estimators as Cohen's (1977) d or differences between proportions (Hedges, 1982; Rosenthal & Rubin, 1982a).

For each of the three or more studies to be compared, we compute the effect size r, its associated Fisher z, and $N - 3$, where N is the number of sampling units on which each r is based. Then the statistical significance of the heterogeneity of the r's can be obtained from a χ^2 computed as follows (Snedecor & Cochran, 1967, 1980):

$$\Sigma(N_j - 3)(z_j - \bar{z})^2 \text{ is distributed as } \chi^2 \text{ with } K - 1 \ df \qquad (6)$$

In this equation z_j is the Fisher z corresponding to any r, and $\bar{z}$ is the weighted mean z; that is,

$$\bar{z} = \Sigma(N_j - 3) z_j / \Sigma(N_j - 3) \qquad (7)$$

Example 6. Placebo studies A, B, C, and D yield effect sizes of $r = .70$ ($N = 30$), $r = .45$ ($N = 45$), $r = .10$ ($N = 20$), and $r = -.15$ ($N = 25$), respectively. The Fisher z's corresponding to these r's are found from tables of Fisher z to be .87, .48, .10, and −.15, respectively. The weighted mean z is found from Equation 7 above to be

$$[27(.87) + 42(.48) + 17(.10) + 22(-.15)]/[27 + 42 + 17 + 22] \\ = 42.05/108 = .39$$

Then, from the equation for χ^2 above (6), we have

$$\Sigma(N_j - 3)(z_j - \bar{z})^2 = 27(.87 - .39)^2 + 42(.48 - .39)^2$$
$$+ 17(.10 - .39)^2 + 22(-.15 - .39)^2 = 14.41$$

as our χ^2 value, which for $K - 1 = 3$ df is significant at $p = .0024$. The four effect sizes we have compared, then, are clearly significantly heterogeneous.

COMPARING STUDIES: FOCUSED TESTS

Significance Testing. Although we know how to answer the diffuse question of the significance of the differences among a collection of significance levels, we are often able to ask a more focused and more useful question. For example, given a set of p levels for studies of placebo effects in children, we might want to know whether results from younger children show greater degrees of statistical significance than do results from older children (Rosenthal, 1983c; Rosenthal & Rubin, 1978).

As in the case for diffuse tests, we begin by finding the standard normal deviate, Z, corresponding to each p level. All p levels must be one-tailed, and the corresponding Z's will have the same sign if all studies show effects in the same direction, but different signs if the results are not all in the same direction. The statistical significance of the contrast testing any specific hypothesis about the set of p levels can be obtained from a Z computed as follows (Rosenthal & Rubin, 1979a):

$$\frac{\Sigma \lambda_j Z_j}{\sqrt{\Sigma \lambda_j^2}} \text{ is distributed as } Z \qquad (8)$$

In this equation λ_j is the theoretically derived prediction or contrast weight for any one study, chosen such that the sum of the γ_j's will be zero, and Z_j is the Z for any one study.

Example 7. Placebo studies A, B, C, and D yield one-tailed p values of $1/10^7$, .0001, .21, and .007, respectively, all with results in the same direction. From a normal table, we find the Z's corresponding to the four p levels to be 5.20, 3.72, .81, and 2.45. Suppose that studies A, B, C, and D involved differing amounts of placebo administration, such that studies A, B, C, and D involved 8, 6, 4, and 2 placebo capsules per day, respectively. We might, therefore, ask whether there is a linear relationship between number of daily capsules and statistical significance of the result favoring placebo effects. The weights of a linear contrast involving four studies are 3, 1, -1, and -3. (These are obtained from a table of orthogonal polynomials.) Therefore, from the preceding equation (8), we have

$$\frac{\Sigma \lambda_j Z_j}{\sqrt{\Sigma \lambda_j^2}} = \frac{(3)5.20 + (1)3.72 + (-1).81 + (-3)2.45}{\sqrt{(3)^2 + (1)^2 + (-1)^2 + (-3)^2}}$$

$$= \frac{11.16}{\sqrt{20}} = 2.50$$

as our Z value, which is significant at $p = .006$, one-tailed. The four p values, then, tend to grow linearly more significant as the number of capsules of placebo per day increases.

Effect Size Estimation. Here we want to ask a more focused question of a set of effect sizes. For example, given a set of effect sizes for studies of placebo effect, we might want to know whether these effects are increasing or decreasing linearly with the number of capsules administered. The discussion is again restricted to r as the effect size estimator, though analogous procedures are available for comparing other effect size estimators (Rosenthal & Rubin, 1982a).

As in the case for diffuse tests, we begin by computing the effect size r, its associated Fisher z, and $N - 3$, where N is the number of sampling units on which each r is based. The statistical significance of the contrast, testing any specific hypothesis about the set of effect sizes, can be obtained from a Z computed as follows (Rosenthal & Rubin, 1982a, 1982b):

$$\frac{\Sigma \lambda_j Z_j}{\sqrt{\Sigma \dfrac{\lambda_j^2}{w_j}}} \text{ is distributed as } Z \qquad (9)$$

In this equation λ_j is the contrast weight determined from some theory for any one study, chosen such that the sum of the γ_j's will be zero. The z_j is the Fisher z for any one study, and w_j is the inverse of the variance of the effect size for each study. For Fisher z transformations of the effect size r, the variance is $1/(N_j - 3)$, so $w_j = N_j - 3$.

Example 8. Placebo studies A, B, C, and D yield effect sizes of $r = .89$, .76, .23, and .59, respectively, all with $N = 12$. The Fisher z's corresponding to these r's are found from tables of Fisher z to be 1.42, 1.00, .23, and .68, respectively. Suppose that studies A, B, C, and D involved differing amounts of placebo administration, such that studies A, B, C, and D involved 8, 6, 4, and 2 placebo capsules per day, respectively. We might, therefore, ask whether there is a linear relationship between number of daily capsules and size of effect favoring placebo effects. As in Example 7, the appropriate weights, or λ's, are 3, 1, −1, and −3. Therefore, from the preceding equation (9), we have

$$\frac{\Sigma\lambda_j z_j}{\sqrt{\Sigma\dfrac{\lambda_j^2}{w_j}}} = \frac{(3)1.42 + (1)1.00 + (-1).23 + (-3).68}{\sqrt{\dfrac{(3)^2}{9} + \dfrac{(1)^2}{9} + \dfrac{(-1)^2}{9} + \dfrac{(-3)^2}{9}}}$$

$$= \frac{2.99}{\sqrt{2.222}} = 2.01$$

as our Z value, which is significant at $p = .022$, one-tailed. The four effect sizes, therefore, tend to grow linearly larger as the number of capsules of placebo per day increases.

Before leaving the topic of focused tests, it should be noted that their use is more efficient than the more common procedure of counting each effect size or significance level as a single observation (e.g., Eagly & Carli, 1981; Hall, 1980; Rosenthal & Rubin, 1978; Smith, Glass, & Miller, 1980). In that procedure, we might, for example, compute a correlation between the Fisher z values and the λ's of Example 8 to test the hypothesis of greater effect size being associated with greater placebo dosages. Although that r is substantial (.77), it does not even approach significance because of the small number of df upon which the r is based. The procedures employing focused tests, or contrasts, employ much more of the information available, and therefore are less likely to lead to Type II errors.

COMBINING STUDIES

Significance Testing. After comparing the results of any set of three or more studies, it is an easy matter also to combined the p levels of the set of studies in order to get an overall estimate of the probability that the set of p levels might have been obtained if the null hypothesis of no relationship between X and Y were true. Of the various methods available and described elsewhere in detail (Rosenthal, 1978, 1980), I present here only the generalized version of the method presented earlier in the discussion of combining the results of two groups.

This method requires only that we obtain a one-tailed Z for each of our p levels. Z's disagreeing in direction from the bulk of the findings are given negative signs. Then, the sum of the Z's divided by the square root of the number (K) of studies yields a new statistic distributed as Z. In short,

$$\Sigma Z_j / \sqrt{K} \text{ is distributed as } Z \tag{10}$$

Should we want to do so, we could weight each of the Z's by its df (Rosenthal, 1978, 1980).

Example 9. Placebo studies A, B, C, and D yield one-tailed p values of .15, .05, .01, and .001, respectively. Study C, however, shows results opposite in direction from the results of the remaining studies. The four Z's associated with these four p's, then, are 1.04, 1.64, −2.33, and 3.09. From the preceding equation (10), we have

$$\Sigma Z_j/\sqrt{K} = \frac{(1.04) + (1.64) + (-2.33) + (3.09)}{\sqrt{4}} = 1.72$$

as our new Z value, which has an associated p value of .043 one-tailed or .086 two-tailed. This combined p supports the results of the majority of the individual studies. However, even if these p values (.043 and .086) were more significant, we would want to be very cautious about drawing any simple overall conclusion, because of the very great heterogeneity of the four p values we are combining. Example 5, which employs the same p values, shows that this heterogeneity is significant at $p = .0013$.

Effect Size Estimation. When we combine the results of three or more studies, we are as interested in the combined estimate of the effect size as we are in the combined probability. We follow here our earlier procedure of considering r as our effect size estimator, while recognizing that many other estimates are possible. For each of the three or more studies to be combined, we compute r and the associated Fisher z and have

$$\Sigma z/K = \bar{z} \qquad (11)$$

as the Fisher $\bar{z}$ corresponding to our mean r (where K refers to the number of studies combined). We use a table of Fisher z to find the r associated with our mean z. Should be want to give greater weight to larger studies, we could weight each z by its df (Snedecor & Cochran, 1967, 1980).

Example 10. Placebo studies A, B, C, and D yield effect sizes of $r =$ .70, .45, .10, and −.15, respectively. The Fisher z values corresponding to these r's are .87, .48, .10, and −.15, respectively. Then, from the preceding equation (11), we have

$$\Sigma z/K = \frac{(.87) + (.48) + (.10) + (-.15)}{4} = .32$$

as our mean Fisher z. From a table of Fisher z values, we find a z of .32 to correspond to an r of .31. Just as in the preceding example of combined p levels, however, we would want to be very cautious in our interpretation of this combined effect size. If the r's we have just averaged are based on substantial sample sizes, as is the case in Example 6, they would be significantly heterogeneous. Therefore, averaging without special thought and comment would be inappropriate.

SUMMARY

In this chapter, some issues in the design and analysis of studies employing placebo conditions are outlined. Placebo controls are distinguished from placebo effects, and single-expectancy controls are distinguished from the more comprehensive double-expectancy controls. The value of contrasts is emphasized; their use is reviewed; and design-driven ("wired-in") contrasts are distinguished from theory driven (planned) contrasts.

Issues in the interpretation of the practical meaning of the results of studies employing placebo conditions are also considered. The widespread error of underestimating the importance of so-called "small effects" is illustrated, and a method for helping avoid this error is presented.

Finally, some issues in the summarizing of series of placebo studies are discussed. A general framework is provided to help conceptualize the enterprise of summarizing series of placebo studies. Within this framework, a variety of quantitative procedures are described and illustrated to permit their direct application to series of studies of placebo effect.

ACKNOWLEDGMENTS

Preparation of this chapter was supported in part by the National Science Foundation. It is based, in part, on material presented in Rosenthal (1982, 1983a, 1983b, 1984) and in Rosenthal and Rubin (1982c).

REFERENCES

Beecher, H. K. Surgery as placebo. *Journal of the American Medical Association*, 1961, *176*, 1102–1107.
Beecher, H. K. Pain: One mystery solved. *Science*, 1966, *151*, 840–841.
Berg, G., Laberg, J. C., Skutle, A., & Öhman, A. Instructed versus pharmacological effects of alcohol in alcoholics and social drinkers. *Behaviour Research and Therapy*, 1981, *19*, 55–66.
Cohen, J. Some statistical issues in psychological research. In B. B. Wolman (Ed.), *Handbook of clinical psychology*. New York: McGraw-Hill, 1965.
Cohen, J. *Statistical power analysis for the behavioral sciences*. New York: Academic Press, 1969. (Rev. ed., 1977.)
Cooper, H. M. On the significance of effects and the effects of significance. *Journal of Personality and Social Psychology*, 1981, *41*, 1013–1018.
Eagly, A. H., & Carli, L. L. Sex of researchers and sex-typed communications as determinants of sex differences in influenceability: A meta-analysis of social influence studies. *Psychology Bulletin*, 1981, *90*, 1–20.
Federighi, E. T. Extended tables of the percentage points of Student's t-distribution. *Journal of the American Statistical Association*, 1959, *54*, 683–688.
Friedman, H. Magnitude of experimental effect and a table for its rapid estimation. *Psychological Bulletin*, 1968, *70*, 245–251.

Glass, G. V. Summarizing effect sizes. In R. Rosenthal (Ed.), *New directions for methodology of social and behavioral science: Quantitative assessment of research domains* (No. 5). San Francisco: Jossey-Bass, 1980.

Glass, G. V, McGaw, B., & Smith, M. L. *Meta-analysis in social research*, Beverly Hills, Calif.: Sage, 1981.

Hall, J. A. Gender differences in nonverbal communication skills. In R. Rosenthal (Ed.), *New directions for methodology of social and behavioral science: Quantitative assessment of research domains* (No. 5). San Francisco: Jossey-Bass, 1980.

Hedges, L. V. Estimation of effect size from a series of independent experiments. *Psychological Bulletin*, 1982, *92*, 490–499.

Kolata, G. B. Drug found to help heart attack survivors. *Science*, 1981, *214*, 774–775.

Mosteller, F. M., & Bush, R. R. Selected quantitative techniques. In G. Lindzey (Ed.), *Handbook of social psychology* (Vol. 1, *Theory and method*). Reading, Mass.: Addison-Wesley, 1954.

Rimland, B. Death knell for psychotherapy? *American Psychologist*, 1979, *34*, 192.

Rosenthal, R. *Experimenter effects in behavioral research*. New York: Appleton-Century-Crofts, 1966.

Rosenthal, R. *Experimenter effects in behavioral research* (Enlarged ed.). New York: Irvington, 1976.

Rosenthal, R. Combining results of independent studies. *Psychological Bulletin*, 1978, *85*, 185–193.

Rosenthal, R. (Ed.). *New directions for methodology of social and behavoral science: Quantitative assessment of research domains* (No. 5). San Francisco: Jossey-Bass, 1980.

Rosenthal, R. Valid interpretation of quantitative research results. In D. Brinberg & L. H. Kidder (Eds.), *Forms of validity in research*. San Francisco: Jossey-Bass, 1982.

Rosenthal, R. Assessing the statistical and social importance of the effects of psychotherapy. *Journal of Consulting and Clinical Psychology*, 1983, *51*, 4–13. (a)

Rosenthal, R. Methodological issues in behavioral sciences. In B. B. Wolman (Ed.), *Progress volume I of the international encyclopedia of psychiatry, psychology, psychoanalysis, and neurology*. New York: Aesculapius Publishers, 1983. (b)

Rosenthal, R. Improving meta analytic procedures for assessing the effects of psychotherapy versus placebo. *Behavioral and Brain Sciences*, 1983, *6*, 298–299. (c)

Rosenthal, R. *Meta-analytic procedures for social research*. Beverly Hills, Calif.: Sage, 1984.

Rosenthal, R., & Jacobson, L. *Pygmalion in the classroom*. New York: Holt, Rinehart & Winston, 1968.

Rosenthal, R., & Rosnow, R. L. *Essentials of behavioral research: Methods and data analysis*. New York: McGraw-Hill, 1984.

Rosenthal, R., & Rosnow, R. L. *Contrast analysis: Focused comparisons in the analysis of variance*. New York: Cambridge University Press, 1985.

Rosenthal, R., & Rubin, D. B. Interpersonal expectancy effects: The first 345 studies. *Behavioral and Brain Sciences*, 1978, *3*, 377–415.

Rosenthal, R., & Rubin, D. B. Comparing significance levels of independent studies. *Psychological Bulletin*, 1979, *86*, 1165–1168. (a)

Rosenthal, R., & Rubin, D. B. A note on percent variance explained as a measure of the importance of effects. *Journal of Applied Social Psychology*, 1979, *9*, 395–396. (b)

Rosenthal, R., & Rubin, D. B. Comparing effect sizes of independent studies. *Psychological Bulletin*, 1982, *92*, 500–504. (a)

Rosenthal, R., & Rubin, D. B. Further meta-analytic procedures for assessing cognitive gender differences. *Journal of Educational Psychology*, 1982, *74*, 708–712. (b)

Rosenthal, R., & Rubin, D. B. A simple, general purpose display of magnitude of experimental effect. *Journal of Educational Psychology*, 1982, *74*, 166–169. (c)

Ross, M., & Olson, J. M. An expectancy-attribution model of the effects of placebos. *Psychological Review*, 1981, *88*, 408–437.

Smith, M. L., & Glass, G. V. Meta-analysis of psychotherapy outcome studies. *American Psychologist*, 1977, *32*, 752–760.

Smith, M. L., Glass, G. V, & Miller, T. I. *The benefits of psychotherapy*. Baltimore: Johns Hopkins University Press, 1980.

Snedecor, G. W., & Cochran, W. G. *Statistical methods* (6th ed.). Ames: Iowa State University Press, 1967.

Snedecor, G. W., & Cochran, W. G. *Statistical methods* (7th ed.). Ames: Iowa State University Press, 1980.

Watkins, L. R., & Mayer, D. J. Organization of endogenous opiate and nonopiate pain control systems. *Science*, 1982, *216*, 1185–1192.

8

Discussion

Can Pregnancy Be a Placebo Effect?: Terminology, Designs, and Conclusions in the Study of Psychosocial and Pharmacological Treatments of Behavioral Disorders

GORDON L. PAUL

After 20 years' immersion in research, practice, training, and consultation in the clinical treatment of people who display the full range of disordered behavior, I continue to be impressed with the exquisite complexity of the area and with the sheer volume of material produced. The foregoing chapters on research methods and placebo phenomena by Ross and Buckalew, by Wilkins, and by Rosenthal amply demonstrate the richness in meaning and fertile quality of ideas effected by consideration of the placebo concept. In combination, these thought-provoking works fulfill the supplmentary purpose noted by Ross and Buckalew—to provide the reader with a reference base to facilitate more detailed exploration of specific topics. All three chapters recommend experimental designs to disentangle various placebo phenomena from those of other psychological or pharmacological treatments. They illustrate the extent to which terminological or semantic problems contribute to misconceptions and slowing of progress. All three also provide "mini-summaries" of substantive conclusions from more extensive reviews or of analytic procedures.

A most important contribution of the combined chapters is the extent to which they reflect salient issues in our progress toward discovering, accumulating, and applying knowledge with regard to effective clinicial treatments. In the brief space available, I must confine my comments to only a few of these issues, without attempting a thorough coverage of major topics

Gordon L. Paul. Department of Psychology, University of Houston–University Park, Houston, Texas.

concerning research methods and placebo phenomena. Rather, I restrict my exposition to those aspects of the clinical research enterprise that have been stimulated by these authors and that seem especially deserving of further discourse. Such a focus clearly emphasizes my own perspective, biases, and cautions, without a balanced coverage of the fertile ideas of others or of those issues that I consider to be equally important, but not directly stimulated by the foregoing chapters.

RELEVANT QUESTIONS, DOMAINS AND CLASSES OF VARIABLES, AND RESEARCH STRATEGIES

A major aspect of the enterprise that is brought to mind by all three chapters is the commonality of questions to be answered, as well as of the domains and classes of variables that are relevant to research and practice with clinical treatments—whether psychosocial or pharmacological. Before commenting on issues reflected in the chapters, a reminder of these commonalities is needed for orientation. As Wilkins notes, some years ago I proposed the ultimate question(s) to be answered by research on clinical interventions as follows: "What treatment, by whom, is most effective for this individual with that specific problem, under which set of circumstances, and how does it come about?" (Paul, 1969a, p. 44). Of course, no single investigation can provide all the answers to this question for any class of variables. Posing it, however, provides a framework for specifying the aspect of the question for which a given study seeks answers, as well as a basis for judging the study's adequacy in providing them. The "how does it come about?" part refers to the principles or mechanisms that best account for changes obtained as a result of different interventions—parallel to Wilkins's "mechanism identification" purpose, which may or may not be included in studies whose purpose is to determine absolute or comparative efficacy. All other parts of the question point to the domains and classes of variables that should be measured, manipulated, described, or controlled to establish the internal validity of *any* investigation in the area, and to the levels of those variables that should be defined in any study to provide guidance in judging the generalizability of findings. Such specification and measurement can also provide a basis for the systematic accumulation of knowledge over several studies by allowing the identification of studies or of their components that constitute replications and quasi-replications of one another.

The analysis of the domains and classes of variables that led to the formulation of the "ultimate question" was originally based on research needs for evaluating the outcome of psychotherapies (Paul, 1967b), and was later elaborated, with design considerations emphasizing psychosocial treatments more broadly defined (Paul, 1969a). Their applicability has since been expanded and applied to research with pharmacological treatments and with both inpatient and community psychosocial programs (e.g., Paul &

Lentz, 1977; Paul, Tobias, & Holly, 1972), as well as to the operation of mental health facilities and systems (Mariotto & Paul, 1984; Paul, Mariotto, & Redfield, in press-a). As developed in these sources, the domains of variables within which information is minimally necessary for addressing aspects of the "ultimate question" include the following: clients (or patients)—the individuals or groups targeted for change; staff members (or therapists)—the individuals or groups responsible for producing or maintaining change; and time.

Specific classes of variables within each domain must be described, manipulated, and/or controlled to maximize progress in the discovery, accumulation, or application of knowledge regarding effective clinical treatments. Within the client domain, these classes of variables are as follows:

1. *Problem behaviors*—those aspects of client motoric, emotional, or ideational functioning that are distressing to the clients or others, due to their excesses, deficits, or inappropriateness of timing, and to which interventions should be directed.
2. *Relatively stable personal–social characteristics*—those attributes other than problem behaviors on which clients may differ that can define role behavior and/or can interact with responsiveness to treatment, such as demographics, diagnostic classifications, personality traits, educational–vocational history, physical status, motivation, and expectancies regarding conditions of intervention.
3. *Physical–social life environments*—those settings and events external to the treatment context that provide intercurrent life experiences and that may set the time or place for the occurance of problem behaviors or interact with responsiveness to treatment, such as the nature of economic and social resources, family, friends, work, and school situations.

Within the staff domain, these classes of variables include the following:

1. *Therapeutic techniques*—the specific interventions through which improvement in client problem behaviors is attempted, including discrete somatic treatments (e.g., drugs) and planned or unplanned psychosocial procedures defined by the nature, frequency, content, and timing of verbal and nonverbal acts delivered by staff to clients.
2. *Relatively stable personal–social characteristics*—those attributes other than therapeutic techniques on which staff members may differ that can interact with the effectiveness of specific techniques for given classes of clients, problem behaviors, and environments, such as demographics, personality traits, physical status, experience,

        prestige, theoretical orientation, confidence, attitudes, and opinions
        regarding conditions of intervention.

3. *Physical–social treatment environments*—those characteristics of
        the settings in which interventions are carried out that may interact
        with variables in other classes, such as size, age, location, reputation,
        "plushness," staffing levels, public versus private, and institutional
        versus *in vivo.*

The third major domain, time, serves to specify further the "set of
circumstances" for assessing other classes of variables and to determine the
focus and nature of measurement needed within and between treatment
periods, depending on the aspect of the "ultimate question" to be answered.
Both the moment in time, or the "time window" at which information should
be obtained, and the period of time to which such information applies must be
explicit in order for valid conclusions to be drawn (see Paul, Mariotto, &
Redfield, in press-a, in press-b).

The means of obtaining partial answers to the "ultimate question" in a
study or research program is a matter of design and tactics for discovering
causal relationships between specified treatment techniques and changes in
specified problem behaviors, as well as the manner in which these
relationships are moderated by client and staff personal–social characteristics and respective physical–social environments. Existing knowledge
regarding the intricacies of particular problem behaviors and treatment
techniques will, of course, suggest differences in the aspect of the "ultimate
question" to which investigations are directed and will require varying
methods, particularly for research on the identification of principles or
mechanisms mediating change from psychosocial as distinct from pharmacological treatment techniques. However, the same domains and classes of
variables are relevant for any clinical research study of interventions for
behavioral disorders. Similarly, for investigations of efficacy, the same
domains and classes of variables *and* the same considerations of design and
tactics apply, whether the studies are called "outcome evaluations" (e.g.,
Mahoney, 1978); "outcome research" and "comparative studies" (e.g.,
Kiesler, 1971; Paul, 1969a), "clinical trials" (e.g., Wortman, 1981),
"program evaluation" (e.g., Cronbach, 1982), or "experimental" and
"quasi-experimental studies" (e.g., Campbell & Stanley, 1966; Cook &
Campbell, 1979). There is one fundamental design principle: Ask a question
in such a way that the effects of independent variables (i.e., specified
treatment techniques) on dependent variables (i.e., specified problem
behaviors) can be unambiguously determined. For investigators to be able to
draw conclusions about the causal influence of any given variable, it must be
manipulated alone somewhere in the design. As in other areas, the greatest
problems in clinical research come from "research errors"—that is,
discrepancies between what *is* concluded and what *can* be concluded as a

consequence of the data base and operations involved (Underwood, 1957).

Because knowledge from clinical research should ultimately be applied in practice, research errors that threaten either internal or external validity are of concern (Campbell & Stanley, 1966). "Internal validity" refers to the degree to which *plausible* rival hypotheses can be ruled out of conclusions about cause–effect relationships in a single study. Greatest threats to internal validity are confounds between variables from the different domains or classes described above, since there is no way that a scientifically meaningful conclusion can be reached from the operations. A study with such confounds is fundamentally flawed with "lethal" research errors. Confounds within classes of variables, such as the planned and unplanned psychosocial aspects of treatment techniques, may also result in research errors, but the resulting threat to internal validity is less "lethal" and may still allow some meaningful conclusions other than the ones drawn by the investigator. It is here that the precise separation of "nonspecific" and/or placebo factors from "specific" psychosocial or pharmacological factors is called for. "External validity" refers to the generalizability of findings from an investigation to different samples or populations of variables in other investigations and in clinical practice. Drawing conclusions about the generalizability of findings is a rational–empirical undertaking, in which hypotheses are strengthened to the extent that a study provides strong internal validity and thorough measurement and description of the domains and classes of variables over which generalization could be expected on the basis of knowledge from other sources (see Paul, 1969a; Paul & Licht, 1978).

As I have argued elsewhere (Paul, 1969a; Paul & Lentz, 1977), due to the complex, multivariate, and interactive classes of relevant variables, the only designs capable of establishing cause–effect relationships attributable to specific psychosocial or pharmacological treatments within a single study are factorial or partial-factorial group designs including "untreated" and "nonspecific treatment" controls. "Untreated" controls provide the necessary comparison for the state of affairs in the absence of the treatments to be evaluated, and might consist of conditions such as no contact, no treatment, a waiting list, minimal treatment, or custodial treatment, depending on the nature of problem behaviors and what would otherwise happen to clients in the normal course of events. "Nonspecific treatment" controls serve to partial out the effects of common therapeutic features involved in clients "receiving treatment" within the particular class of intervention techniques— that is, features that are "nonspecific" (common) to any treatment technique in the class. Such "nonspecific treatment" controls might consist of conditions such as a placebo, an attention placebo, pseudotreatment, component treatment, or alternative treatment, depending on the nature of the problem behaviors and treatments to be evaluated. The basic model of such a research design is similar to that presented by Rosenthal and would include three conditions (the treatment to be evaluated, a nonspecific control treatment, and untreated control conditions) with clients drawn from the same population, assessed and equated by the same criteria over the same time periods, with the levels of all classes of variables factorially equated or controlled over all conditions. However, there is no single factorial design, but as many different and complex designs as are required by the number and nature of aspects of the "ultimate question" that are asked in a given study. Factors, levels of factors, and different treatment and control conditions are added as required by the nature of the cause–effect relationships to be investigated. The crucial points are that the aspect of the given variable whose effects are to be evaluated occur at one or more levels in treatment groups; that it not occur in at least one control group; and that all other features occur in both treatment and control groups.

Although factorial or partial-factorial designs are the most efficient approach to the ultimate question—and the only way to precisely determine the comparative effectiveness of different treatment techniques—an inverse relationship exists between the level of product of findings from a single study and the time, money, and personnel required for its conduct. Also, situational constraints often place limits on feasibility. The tactical use of different levels of research design is, therefore, important for the entire enterprise. Lower-level between-group designs, continuous "systems monitoring," within-group designs, and accumulated single-subject experimental analyses all have an important role when they are strategically employed on the basis of their possible level of product in relation to the knowledge already established for the phenomena of interest (see Paul, 1969a; Paul & Lentz, 1977). To the extent that such designs measure all relevant classes of variables and systematically replicate particular treatment and control conditions across studies in a programmatic way, a series of such studies can result in the same level of product as a factorial design. Experimental analysis of the single case is unquestionably the most rigorous method for determining the functional relationships and parameters of treatment techniques for the individual client (see Hersen & Barlow, 1976). Similarly replicated within-subject designs can be exceptionally useful before and after comparative factorial studies for investigating mechanisms of change, establishing that change does or does not come about, and extending findings over variations of clients, problems, staff and settings. Strategically, continuous systems monitoring aided by time-series analysis, within-subject group designs, and lower-level between-group designs can also be useful in the evaluation of systematic modifications to the procedures found most effective from factorial comparative studies, as well as for testing the limits of generalizability of findings over other classes of variables. Before comparative studies, these designs can also be helpful in developing and narrowing hypotheses and in "polishing" procedures. Thus, in the clinical research area as in any other—whether laboratory-based or field-based—the utility of a particular research design is a function of the questions, or aspects of the "ultimate question" asked, the measurement and control of relevant classes of variables, and the relationship to knowledge from other sources.

UNIFORMITY ASSUMPTIONS, CONCEPTUAL RELEVANCE, AND ABSOLUTE DESIGN REQUIREMENTS

With this orientation to the commonality of the questions to be answered and of the relevant domains and complex classes of variables involved, attention may be directed to a particularly salient set of issues for the clinical research enterprise. Although the earlier chapters in this section address some aspects of these issues, the recommended designs and control groups, definitions or lack of definitions of terms, or "minisummaries" of other literature contained in these chapters reflect continuing problems that contribute to less than optimal progress in the area. These have to do with differences between the commonalities of relevant variables, research strategies, and design logic, on the one hand; and unwarranted assumptions of uniformity, semantic problems, and the conceptual relevance of labeled concepts, procedures, and research practices on the other.

As noted earlier, the "ultimate question" and the domains and classes of variables summarized therein appear to be of universal relevance to any research study of clinical interventions for the behavioral disorders. The design logic and desirable research strategies for establishing cause–effect relationships, and the knowledge of moderating factors for specific treatment procedures that derives from a consideration of the "ultimate question" (excluding the "how does it come about?" part), seem equally applicable to all clinical research areas. These commonalities do not, however, automatically translate into uniform designs, controls, or other procedures for one or more studies. Rather, each study should be designed to answer the specific questions (or aspects of the "ultimate question") asked, and each control condition should be constructed to control for specific sources of influence pertinent to the questions asked and to the particular treatment techniques and problem behaviors of concern. Rosenthal notes that reliance on "canned contrasts" may lessen the precision, power, and accuracy of data analyses. Similarly, reliance on "canned designs," "canned treatments," "canned controls," or any other "absolute" or "cookbook" solution to the design required in a specific study runs a high risk of introducing unwarranted uniformity assumptions. Such unwarranted assumptions are compounded by the language imperfections in the field, noted by Wilkins, in which the same terms often signify quite different concepts and procedures. When these misplaced uniformity assumptions are added to the "uniformity assumption myths" first summarized by Kiesler (1966) in regard to the presumed commonality of relevant classes of variables that are not precisely described in any study, conditions are ripe for confusion, research errors, cult-like arguments, and decisions based on "words" rather than on the phenomena the words represent.

Some examples stimulated by the foregoing chapters should be illustrative and should offer a note of caution to readers, apropos of either the unguarded acceptance of conclusions from the work of others or the mechanical application of designs and control conditions in their own. Wilkins addresses the problem of changed denotative meanings of terms transferred from pharmacological research to psychotherapy research. Although other chapters in this book focus on definitions per se, Ross and Buckalew's definition of "placebo" typifies the difficulty in both pharmacological and psychosocial research—that is, "any treatment or preparation given a patient or client that does not provide any direct pharamacological or psychotherapeutic effect for the specific condition being treated" (see pp. 68–69). Ross and Buckalew, like other authors, also use "nonspecific" and "placebo" more or less interchangably in their discussion, which leads to additional lack of precision in summarizing findings. Although Grünbaum's (1981) differentiation of "characteristic" and "incidental" constituents may add some clarification to pharmacological research, it continues to blur concepts in psychosocial research, as does Wilkins's discussion of "nonspecific treatment" and "pseudotherapy" controls.

In all of the cases cited above, unwarranted uniformity assumptions are applied to concepts, procedures, and practices signified by the shorthand descriptive terms of different commentators. These unwarranted assumptions might start with mere surplus meaning being attached to the words taken out of their operational contexts, but ultimately result in totally different meanings and complete misinterpretations in specific instances. As an example of the latter, the "theoretically inert" aspects of placebo definitions originally applied only to the specific chemical compound or the specific psychotherapeutic procedures to be evaluated. In my own formulations, as summarized earlier, "nonspecific treatment" controls are conceived *neither* as "theoretically inert" *in toto, nor* as failing to provide "direct effects for the specific conditions being treated." Rather, such "nonspecific treatment" controls in general, and the "attention placebo" treatment (Paul, 1966) to which Wilkins refers in his discussion of pseudotherapy, are viewed as active treatment conditions applying theoretically potent intervention techniques that are common to a particular set of treatment approaches, which are expected to have direct effects on the problem behaviors being treated. Such common features may even be necessary rather than "incidental" constituents of treatment for a specific technique to be effective. It is precisely because of the potency of common features within the class of therapeutic techniques that they become pertinent sources of influence to be disentangled or controlled in the evaluation of the effectiveness of particular therapeutic techniques with specific, "not-common" features or combinations of features. When the "theoretically inert" concept becomes overgeneralized from, and is misapplied to concepts and research purposes with much more specific delineation, conceptual relevance is lost; confusion and unnecessary arguments about the presumed ethical and methodological desirability of "nonspecific treatment" controls are the results, as seen in Wilkins's chapter and in other publications (e.g., O'Leary & Borkovec, 1978; Wilkins, 1983).

Although the confusions and unnecessary arguments noted above are drawn from discussions of psychotherapy research, parallel problems appear in discussions of pharmacological research. From my perspective, Wilkins's entire discussion of artifacts in his sections on "antipsychological mechanism research" for both chemotherapy and psychotherapy does not refer to mechanism research at all, but to threats to the internal validity of efficacy studies for the respective classes of treatment techniques. It is not that outcome studies of pharmacological and psychosocial interventions constitute basically different undertakings; rather, pharmacological researchers have simply not been attuned, historically, to conceptualizing sources of influence from the class of environmental variables within either client or staff domains. Pharmacological investigators, as well as some psychotherapy investigators, have also tended to blur distinctions between the personal-social characteristics of clients or staff and the variables within the class of problem behaviors or psychosocial aspects of treatment techniques, respectively. The result is that conclusions often fail to distinguish justifiable cause–effect relationships from moderating variables or outright confounds. Hundreds of studies, for example, have drawn conclusions about the effectiveness of neuroleptic drugs for treating "schizophrenia" (a relatively stable personal–social characteristic of clients) on the basis of measured change in "positive symptoms" (excess problem behaviors), without even assessing the "negative symptoms" (deficit problem behaviors) that are often more predictive of relapse or rehospitalizaton for this class of clients (see Keith, 1984; Paul et al., in press-a; Schooler & Severe, 1984). Similarly, hundreds of outcome studies on pharmacological interventions have been conducted in custodial treatment environments, or have simply failed to consider environmental and staff personal–social characteristics or psychosocial components of treatment techniques as potential influencing factors, beyond those that may be controlled by the inclusion of a "double-blind placebo group." When these additional classes of variables have been included in pharmacological research, conclusions from prior studies have been enhanced, nullified, or reversed, but seldom simply supported (see Carroll, Miller, Ross, & Simpson, 1980; Liberman, Falloon, & Wallace, 1984; Paul et al., 1972; Schooler & Severe, 1984). As Varela (1977) points out in the first "Law of Serendipity," "In order to find anything—you must be looking for something" (p. 921). Systematic progress in the accumulation of solid knowledge on the effectiveness of pharmacological interventions seems more likely to occur with conceptually relevant designs that manipulate both pharmacological and psychosocial treatment techniques, with ongoing assessment of all relevant classes of variables (see Hollon &

DeRubeis, 1981; Liberman *et al.*, 1984; Licht, 1979; Paul *et al.*, in press-b; Power, 1984).

Potential unwarranted assumptions of uniformity in desirable research designs and control conditions, and semantic difficulties concerning what sources of influence are to be controlled or investigated, are also worthy of comment. Since investigators tend to duplicate one another's designs and operations, caution is required concerning the need to maintain the conceptual relevance of designs to the aspect of the "ultimate question" addressed (see Yeaton & Sechrest, 1981a, 1981b). For example, both the four-group design (including a drug-disguised group) recommended by Ross and Buckalew and the "double-expectancy control design" proposed by Rosenthal may be desirable for some investigations of "how changes come about," but are generally inappropriate for studies of efficacy or comparative outcomes. Most studies with intent to generalize findings to clinical practice would find neutral or negative "expectancy" manipulations conceptually *irrelevant*, if not misleading, since client participation and compliance with procedures should be maximized to maintain the integrity of treatments. In my estimation, such manipulations also have limited utility for the investigation of mechanisms for the same reasons. "Smuggled treatments," "disguised treatments," and "triple-blind control" designs, in fact, appear practical and ethical only for withdrawal studies in which clients have already been receiving pharmacological interventions whose effects are to be evaluated by removing the existing intervention.

Warranting even greater caution than the adoption of conceptually irrelevant "canned designs" is the adoption of "canned controls" that may be conceptually irrelevant to the pertinent sources of influence. A major part of the problem is, once again, semantic: Our shorthand descriptive terms for referencing various phenomena—often metaphorically—become reified, with the result that the phenomena are lost. Control conditions tend to be automatically applied, so that investigators lose sight of what is to be controlled. Although these tendencies are apparent in all of the previous chapters, as well as other writings in the area, a few examples from Table 6-1 in Wilkins's chapter should illustrate my concerns. "Spontaneous remission," for instance, is not likely to be "spontaneous" at all, but a response to events occurring in time within the classes of environmental variables, or other variables that are not planned components of the treatment techniques being evaluated. Consideration of these pertinent sources of potential influence might well lead to other "untreated" control conditions beyond the "waiting list," such as those I have listed in the preceding section. "Awareness," "expectancy," "bias," and "interpretation" as explanatory artifacts or threats to internal validity, particularly on the part of staff or therapists, are clear instances of category mistakes in most discussions. It is not therapist or staff awareness, expectancy, or bias per se that constitutes a threat to internal validity, but differential biasing actions on the part of therapists or staff. "Blinding" is, therefore, not the only or best control procedure to guard against such threats. Staff selection, training, and ongoing monitoring of the integrity and precision of implementation of both "legitimate" and control treatment conditions (combined with client single blinds or explanatory rationales) can serve as appropriate controls for all of the "none" control conditions in Wilkins's Table 6-1, and may be an even better research strategy than "blinding" when there is a choice. Differential therapist and staff attitudes or biases toward treatments, and differential expectancies regarding outcomes, have *not* predicted comparative treatment effectiveness when strong treatments were involved and the integrity of treatments was maintained by thorough training and ongoing monitoring of staff in their application (e.g., Paul, 1966; Paul & Lentz, 1977). In fact, therapist attitudes and expectancies toward different treatments more accurately follow rather than precede changes in client functioning in the latter circumstances.

CONCEPTUAL RELEVANCE, STRENGTH, AND INTEGRITY OF PROCEDURES AND CONVERGING EVIDENCE

The field would obviously benefit from increased specification and precision in the description and measurement of relevant classes of variables, phenomena, and procedures. In addition, the entire clinical research enterprise would profit by re-emphasizing a construct validity approach (see Campbell & Stanley, 1966; Cook & Campbell, 1979) to the design, conduct, analysis, and interpretation of individual studies in order to reduce threats of research errors to both internal and external validity, as well as to accumulate knowledge over a number of studies (see also Borkovec & Bauer, 1982). Yeaton and Sechrest's (1981a, 1981b) emphasis on the importance of the conceptual relevance, strength, and integrity of treatment and control conditions and the precision of implementation of procedures is an elaboration of this approach—whether involving "pseudotherapies," "placebo treatments," or "legitimate" psychosocial techniques and pharmacological compounds. Such an approach requires that the procedures, conditions, and assessment operations within a study be designed to provide converging evidence regarding the phenomena under investigation and the effects obtained, rather than relying on a single measure, "canned contrasts," "canned designs," "canned treatments," or "canned control conditions" to yield conclusions. Of course, the same features of the approach should be considered when generalizing findings from one study to another.

   Failure to attend to the conceptual relevance, strength, and integrity of treatment and control conditions, combined with reliance on unwarranted uniformity assumptions, has slowed progress in many clinical research areas touched upon in the earlier chapters. Nowhere, however, are these effects more apparent than in the series of papers and investigations, noted in Wilkins's chapter, dealing with "expectancy–credibility" issues in research on systematic desensitization. Several of my own investigations, reviews, and comments have directly addressed these issues (see Bernstein & Paul, 1971; Paul, 1969a, 1969b, 1969c; Paul & Bernstein, 1976). Although my recent research efforts involve the assessment and treatment of chronic psychoses, I have maintained practice, teaching, and currency with the literature concerning treatment of less severe disorders, particularly anxiety-related problems, systematic desensitization, and related treatment techniques. In 1969, I summarized a review of all reports and controlled investigations of systematic desensitization treatment up to that time by stating, "[F]or the first time in the history of psychological treatments, a specific therapeutic package reliably produced measurable benefits for clients across a broad range of distressing problems in which anxiety was of fundamental importance" (Paul, 1969c, p. 159). Since the early review, recent conclusions regarding the effectiveness of systematic desensitization range from Emmelkamp's statement, "It is still questionable whether systematic desensitization is not merely a highly effective placebo procedure" (1982, p. 356), to McGlynn, Mealiea, and Landau's conclusion, "There is no reason in 1981 to challenge Paul's verdict" (1981, p. 150).

The papers and investigations appearing in the late 1960s and 1970s that have allowed such disparate conclusions to be reached constitute a veritable guidebook showing the sequential effects of ignoring the conceptual relevance, strength, and integrity of designs, treatments, and controls while relying on "canned" experimental procedures reflecting unwarranted uniformity assumptions. By 1971, Bernstein and I had become so alarmed by the lack of relevance of huge numbers of "laboratory-analogue" investigations of systematic desensitization and other techniques for treating anxiety-related problems that we detailed common errors of analogue research in hopes of improving the situation (Bernstein & Paul, 1971). I agree with Kazdin (1978) that the "analogue research" versus "clinical research" distinction in studies of psychological interventions should not be construed as a dichotomy, but as a multivariate continuum, based upon the extent to which the essential characteristics of each of the relevant classes of variables summarized earlier are shared between a given research study and the situations and phenomena to which findings are meant to apply. However, I do not agree that the generality of findings for all classes of variables within a study is a matter for empirical determination, and it is these research errors based on the absence of conceptual relevance about which Bernstein and I were most concerned.

For example, an evaluation of fetal monitoring techniques conducted on men, or on women who were not pregnant, is conceptually irrelevant and would not need an empirical test of the generality of findings to pregnant women. Similarly, "analogue" studies conducted on students who do not view anxiety as a central life problem and who have been enlisted as "clients" to receive course credit for participation without documenting the presence of clinically significant increases in anxiety in the presence of presumed eliciting stimuli are *ipso facto* conceptually irrelevant to the treatment of anxiety-related disorders. The essential phenomena for the class of problem behaviors may be totally absent in such investigations. (Note that the opposite conceptual error also occurs, as when Luborsky, Singer, & Luborsky, 1975, or Emmelkamp, 1982, categorize all studies of "student volunteers" as not involving "bona fide patients," and exclude them from review. Students can have "bona fide" problems, and there is no basis for considering clients who request treatment in response to an announcement of its availability to be essentially different in the character of problem behaviors than those who seek treatment at other times, as long as the intensity and extent of problem behaviors are documented; see Ullmann & Krasner, 1975.) Although we (Bernstein & Paul, 1971) viewed the absence of documented anxiety as the most "lethal" error, several other errors in analogue research were noted that made most such studies conceptually irrelevant to systematic desensitization as evaluated in other clinically relevant studies or as applied in practice. These errors largely had to do with violations of the strength or integrity of the treatment packages, as, for example, in employing inexperienced and minimally trained "therapists" to conduct treatment in nonclinical laboratory settings. Often, blatant changes in aspects of treatment procedures were involved, as in having therapists read various aspects of instructions or training to clients, presenting treatment procedures via tape recordings, and employing a variety of parametric variations that were not accurate replicas of the treatment packages.

Our (Bernstein & Paul, 1971) comments might have served to stop or improve the quality of such conceptually irrelevant "analogue" desensitization studies, but for the publication of a study by Borkovec and Nau (1972) whose findings were overgeneralized and gave renewed impetus to this approach. Borkovec and Nau had college undergraduates read rationales of systematic desensitization and several nonspecific treatment conditions abstracted from prior research studies, and rate them for "expectancy" of improvement and "credibility." Their findings that students in a classroom rated the abstracted systematic desensitization rationale that they read as higher in "expectancy–credibility" than the abstracted nonspecific treatment rationales that they read resulted in several more "analogue" research studies including such ratings in the designs. Of no surprise to those who took our (Bernstein & Paul, 1971) comments seriously, a batch of studies demonstrating lethal analogue research errors, but now including "expectancy–credibility" ratings, resulted in some differences in outcome" among various treatment and control procedures related to such ratings, but mostly found "no differences," without converging evidence to verify the conceptual relevance and internal validity of studies. Unfortunately, reviewers then uncritically accepted these conceptually irrelevant and flawed studies (e.g., Bootzin & Lick, 1979; Lick & Bootzin, 1975), according them equal weight to those appearing earlier (Paul, 1969b, 1969c). Even worse, Kazdin and Wilcoxon (1976) concluded that the absence of such expectancy–credibility ratings in comparative outcome studies of systematic desensitization precluded determination of the specific effectiveness of systematic desensitization beyond nonspecific factors. They also proposed the "empirically derived control strategy" noted by Wilkins as the necessary and sufficient condition for an appropriate nonspecific treatment. Such unwarranted assumptions perhaps contributed to the fact that later reviewers, such as Emmelkamp (1982), have failed even to reference (or read?) the prior reviews and controlled studies, except for selectively including some flawed "analogue" studies to bolster their opinions.

Although expectancy–credibility ratings as employed by Borkovec and Nau (1972) and proposed by Kazdin and Wilcoxon (1976) may have some utility for the clinical research enterprise, such ratings are neither necessary nor sufficient for establishing the viability of nonspecific treatments or cause–effect conclusions regarding specific treatment techniques within a given study. In addition to the logical limitations noted by Wilkins, such ratings are no substitutes for a strong emphasis on converging evidence and construct validity in the interpretation of findings, and they appear to constitute an unwarranted uniformity assumption in methodology. For example, one of the studies supposedly indicted by the absence of "expectancy–credibility" ratings was one of my own (Paul, 1966, 1967a)—a factorial comparative investigation of competing techniques for reducing interpersonal performance anxiety. (A detailed summary, including converging evidence pertinent to the present issue, is included in Paul, 1969c, pp. 111–117.) In this study, experienced professional therapists all individually conducted their own preferred type of insight-oriented psychotherapy, systematic desensitization, and a stylized attention-placebo treatment, concurrently, with an equal number of clients who were equated before treatment on relevant classes of variables. Both waiting-list and no-contact control groups were included. Multiple ratings by clients and therapists assessed various process components, and therapists were trained and monitored in the conduct of all treatments. Standardized behavioral, physiological, and cognitive assessments were obtained to equate client groups before treatment, and to assess change after treatment and at follow-ups.

Pertinent to the "expectancy–credibility" issue, all clients were documented to experience social evaluation anxiety as a central life problem. Prior to meeting with assigned therapists, each client met with an experienced clinician who presented the rationale and course of the specific treatment to be undergone, scheduled meeting times, and presented "positive-expectancy" inductions regarding the specific therapist to be seen. The latter were conducted in a standardized but personalized fashion. Although "ratings" were not obtained, any client was reassigned who indicated a lack of acceptance of the treatment rationale or whose expectations of treatment differed from that assigned. This was necessary for only two clients. Each of the experienced therapists similarly personalized treatment and rationale to each client, and included specific procedures to maintain credibility and to reinforce expectations of improvement throughout the course of treatment.

Overall outcomes on standardized assessment measures found desensitization to be clearly superior to attention-placebo and insight-oriented treatments, with the latter generally producing equivalent results that showed improvement over untreated control groups. The patterning of results showed that the greatest effects of the attention-placebo treatment were on measures susceptible to "expectancies," but *real* changes equal to those produced by insight-oriented treatment were also obtained. Significant differences in therapist ratings of client improvement parralleled the objective and standardized assessments, while therapists rated clients in all three groups as equally likeable and responsive. Clients rated therapists in all three conditions as equally competent and likeable and rated themselves as equally improved at the end of the treatment. Clients in all three groups completed treatment and returned data at 6-week and 2-year follow-ups. In addition, correlational analyses within and among treatment conditions provided converging evidence of the strength and integrity of treatment conditions and of the consistency of outcomes. To equate the "expectancy–credibility" ratings of abstracted rationales read by or to nonanxious individuals with the strength of evidence provided by the above-described construct validity approach to decision making appears to extend research errors to "analogues of analogues."

META-ANALYSIS AND INDICES OF THE MAGNITUDE OF TREATMENT EFFECTS

Another particularly salient set of issues for the clinical research enterprise has to do with the manner of interpreting and integrating the results of empirical studies. The bulk of Rosenthal's chapter is devoted to a summary of statistical techniques of potential value as quantitative aids to those undertakings. Ways of measuring the magnitude of the effect of an intervention to provide an index that can be compared across conditions and studies, or one that reflects the importance of obtained effects, has been a matter of concern for several decades (Mintz, 1983; Sechrest & Yeaton, 1982). However, the recent publications of Glass, Smith, and their colleagues, in which such quantitative techniques (dubbed "meta-analysis" for "analysis of analyses") were applied to outcome studies of psychotherapy and psychotropic drugs, have been the major impetus for increased attention to this approach in the clinical research area (e.g., Glass & Kliegl, 1983; Smith & Glass, 1977; Smith, Glass, & Miller, 1980). The timeliness and importance of the issues involved is reflected in the publication of a special section on meta-analysis in the February 1983 issue of the *Journal of Consulting and Clinical Psychology* (Vol. 51, No. 1).

The publication of this special section (including an article by Rosenthal covering the same material as his chapter in this book, plus articles by Fiske; Glass & Kliegl; Mintz; Shapiro & Shapiro; Strube & Hartmann; and Wilson & Rachman), combined with recent publications of Sechrest and Yeaton (Sechrest & Yeaton, 1981, 1982; Yeaton & Sechrest, 1981a, 1981b), provides such a thorough coverage of the issues and techniques concerning meta-analyses and interpreting the importance of effect size that I refer the reader directly to those works. Unfortunately, the supercilious and sardonic style of Glass and his coauthors flavors the subject with an unpleasand *ad hominem* aspect, which has been reciprocated by several authors. To my knowledge, neither Rosenthal nor I have engaged in the more sullied emotional debates, although his contributions have focused on furthering the applications of meta-analysis while mine have concentrated on empirical findings that have been included (or excluded) in meta-analytic reviews or on methodological recommendations that have been characterized as the antithesis of the approach. Because of the thoroughness of the previously cited sources in providing a basis for more intensive study of meta-analysis, I present only a brief overview of my perspective here—first the general approach, and later the interpretation of the importance of effects; I also emphasize a few cautions, some of which are mentioned by Rosenthal.

I see statistical techniques such as those presented in Rosenthal's chapter, and the meta-analytic approach in general, as potentially useful tools to aid in ordering, integrating, and examining the results of clinical treatment studies. Standardized effect sizes calculated on purportedly identical treatment and control conditions with the same measures of problem behaviors can clarify differences between studies. The approach also appears to offer a methodological advance over purely intrepretive ones for integrating a large number of studies, *to the extent* that a precise and accurate data base can be retrieved, and that reliable procedures are made explicit for selecting studies and contrasts, coding variables, calculating comparable effect sizes, and aggregating or disaggregating the information according to meaningful classification schemes. In fact, from my perspective, such a meta-analytic approach offers promise of contributing a more sensitive accumulation of answers to aspects of the "ultimate question" noted earlier regarding research on clinical interventions than has resulted from the majority of other approaches to research integration. The domains and classes of variables described earlier as relevant components for measurement, manipulation, description, or control for precise knowledge to be forthcoming from individual studies also appear to be of equal or greater relevance to the systematic accumulation of knowledge from a series of studies.

Although I view the meta-analytic approach to the review and integration of subparts of the clinical research literature as a promising one, it is as yet, a promise unfulfilled. In the same way that "canned designs" fail to insure valid or useful conclusions to be forthcoming from individual studies, so do rigorous statistical calculations and meta-analytic approaches fail to insure valid or useful conclusions to be forthcoming from a collection of studies. The logical and thoughtful analysis required by an emphasis on converging evidence and construct validity in the design, conduct, statistical analyses, and interpretation of individual studies appears to be even more important when conclusions are to be drawn from a collection of studies. As with individual studies, the aspect of the question posed for a meta-analytic review needs to be specified in a way that does not result in "research errors"—that is, discrepancies between what is concluded and what can be concluded from the data base and operations undertaken. Thus, for precise knowledge to accumulate, the meta-analytic review should consider all of the domains and classes of variables of importance to individual studies, plus a number of other considerations. Beyond the conceptual relevance, strength, and integrity of the treatment and control conditions, the "time window" of assessments, the adequacy of individual studies, the conceptual relevance with which the measures from individual designs are indexed in the meta-analysis, and the statistical characteristics of the indices employed all become additional sources of potential research errors in a meta-analytic review.

Even when research errors are not blatantly involved, a considerable amount of subjective interpretation enters the conclusions drawn from a meta-analytic summary of findings. For example, in one of the first empirical evaluations of the conclusions drawn from meta-analytic combinations of data, Cooper and Rosenthal (1980) reported 19 respondents to cover the full range of conclusions from "definite no" to "probably yes" regarding perceived support for the hypothesis in question, and from "none" to "large" regarding the perceived magnitude of effect. Of even greater concern are the judgments that enter meta-analysis *before* the final analyses. The extensive discussions in the recent literature leave no doubt that meta-analytic reviews involve a series of complex, subjective, and often arbitrary judgments prior to the time that the computer objectively aggregates or disaggregates the data—according to a program selected on the basis of human decisions. Although the sophisticated mathematical operations applied in meta-analytic reviews may *appear* to be more rigorous and objective than other means of integrating empirical studies, that appearance can be illusory. Meta-analytic reviews are subject to all of the problems and potential biases of any other means of literature review, but they may at least be more explicit, so that some of the problems are easier to identify.

One problem for any review has to do with the adequacy of the data base. Flawed studies with absent information, or those in which the results are confounded, are a problem for any systematic integration. I believe that a series of investigations—each differing in the nature of missing information or in within-class and within-domain confounds—can contribute more valid hypotheses than any one of them in isolation. I am further convinced (1) that most studies in any clinical research area tend to share similar confounds and missing information for long time periods, such that errors do *not* "balance out"; (2) that one well-designed study with high conceptual relevance and internal validity that separates important confounds can cast doubt on 100 or more flawed studies with similar confounds or design problems; and (3) that the inclusion of seriously flawed studies in either the "box score," "vote-counting" approach to summarizing literature (i.e., tallying the number of studies in which similarly labeled treatment techniques show "better," "worse," or "not different" outcomes from some other procedures), or in meta-analyses in which "effects" or studies are given equal weights to be aggregated statistically, yields inconclusive results at best, and misleading results based on "research" errors most of the time. The problem of an inadequate data base in individual studies, and the inability of any known statistical procedure to untangle information from inherently flawed data, have been well covered in the previous literature, especially by Strube and Hartmann (1983), Shapiro and Shapiro (1983), Wilson and Rachman (1983), Fiske (1983), and Mintz (1983).

Two other potential errors in meta-analytic reviews have received less attention, and are worthy of extreme caution because the subjective decisions involved directly affect the computation of indices from which all other operations proceed. They are also less obvious and may therefore be masked in the final report. These potential errors involve (1) the conceptual relevance with which the results from individual designs are entered into meta-analyses; and (2) the influence of designs, statistical models, and calculation formulas employed in deriving the effect size index. Concern for the first of these errors was brought to my attention by the Smith *et al.* (1980) report of a meta-analysis of psychotherapy outcome research, which included two of my earlier empirical studies (Paul, 1966; Paul & Shannon, 1966), although the 2-year follow-ups to those investigations were not included (Paul, 1967a, 1968). Since I have earlier provided more detail on one study (Paul, 1966), some data from that study may exemplify the problem. As in most carefully designed outcome studies, specific measurement instruments and conditions of assessment were established to gather information for a variety of purposes, only some of which were conceptually relevant to the practical outcome of treatment. Other standardized scales and ratings were included to examine different questions, and were gathered as pretreatment and/or posttreatment outcome and follow-up measures—with their purposes in the design being clearly specified. How have such careful measurement and design considerations been treated by meta-analysts? According to Smith *et al.* (1980), "Each outcome measurement listed by the experimenter was used in the meta-analysis. Each measure was weighted equally; however, redundant measures were eliminated. If, for example, a second measure matched the first in outcome type, degree of reactivity, follow-up time, and approximate size of effect, the second measure was deemed redundant" (p. 66).

The extent to which such subjective decisions may totally misrepresent the conceptual integrity of results from specific studies should be clear with a couple of examples. Since the study described here (Paul, 1966) was a comparative study of the differential effectiveness of competing treatment techniques for reducing interpersonal performance anxiety, the most stringent test of effects came from measures taken in standardized stress conditions designed to elicit the distressing anxiety before and after the treatment period. In order to tap each of the three relevant domains (motoric, cognitive, physiological) for measuring anxiety (see Paul & Bernstein, 1976), standardized assessments included objective measures of overt behavior during the stress performance and self-report and physiological measures immediately prior to each client's performance. Table 8-1 presents effect size indices for these stress condition measures, calculated by one of the methods used by Smith *et al.* (1980). Only two of the treatment groups are included for this example. Examination of the effect sizes for each individual domain of measurement fairly reflects the original analyses, showing the attention-placebo treatment to have produced improvements over those obtained by untreated clients in observable behavior and self-report, but not in physiological responsiveness. Systematic desensitization produced improvements in all three domains over untreated clients, and improvements over nonspecific treatment effects on overt behavior and physiological responsiveness.

These findings provide useful information on the differential nature of improvements obtained by systematic desensitization and by active, effective "nonspecific" psychological treatment. However, for assessing the practical outcome of these treatments on the reduction of anxiety, the three assessment domains need to be aggregated into a composite measure for *each individual*

Table 8-1. Example of How Arbitrary Meta-Analytic Decisions (Individual or Mean Effect Size) Can Misrepresent the Conceptual Relevance (Composite Effect Size) of Findings for the Basic Data to Compare Outcomes

Measure	Treatment effect size[a]		Advantage of desensitization over nonspecific treatment effects
	Systematic desensitization	Attention placebo	
Overt behavior effect size	2.19	.88	1.31
Self-report effect size	1.24	.94	.30
Physiological effect size	1.24	.17	1.07
Mean effect size	1.56	.66	.90
Composite effect size	2.88	.83	2.05

[a]Effect sizes calculated as the difference between treatment group and no-treatment control group means divided by the common standard deviation for stress condition measures from Paul (1966).

in order to maintain their conceptual integrity—resulting in the composite effect size presented in Table 8-1. The mean effect sizes presented in Table 8-1 would presumably reflect the outcome of the Smith *et al.* combination procedures, and would constitute the basic data for other meta-analysts (e.g., Shapiro & Shapiro, 1983). Although both mean and composite effect sizes reflect a similar patterning *within* the study, meta-analytic procedures require effect size indices that are portable *across* studies. Therefore, failing to take into account the conceptual relevance of the measures in this instance would grossly underestimate the size of effect produced by both the systematic desensitization and the attention-placebo treatments—even if other studies included in the meta-analyses employed similar measures and testing conditions. Of course, if other studies employed only one of the measures in Table 8-1 to be compared with the combination of measures from this study, quite different conclusions would be forthcoming, depending on the preponderance of the particular measurement domain included.

An even greater misrepresentation of design-relevant findings by meta-analysts is shown in Table 8-2. Within the design, a battery of standardized self-report scales was included at 6-week and 2-year follow-ups. Of those scales administered at the 6-week follow-up, one was directly relevant to the outcome of the treated problem—a focal scale of anxiety experienced in an outside performance required of all respondents; another was related to a different aspect of outcome—a focal scale assessing anxiety "expected" in a hypothetical performance situation. The remaining scales were included only to aid in identifying the sample of clients and to assess other changes in client behavior predicted by the competing theoretical models underlying the insight-oriented psychotherapy ("symptom substitution" for desensitization and attention placebo clients) and systematic desensitization treatments ("generalization" or "no change" in nonfocal areas for all clients). Thus, to represent the conceptual integrity of the design-relevant measures, only the "focal-experienced" scale (or, at most, the two focal scales) should be included in a meta-analysis of treatment outcomes. As shown in Table 8-2, inclusion of "all" scales, as was presumably done by Smith *et al.*, enters indices as basic data for the meta-analysis that totally misrepresent the valid findings from the design.

The second potential source of additional error in meta-analytic reviews calling for extreme caution has to do with the influence of designs, statistical models, and calculation formulas employed in deriving and combining statistical indices. Rosenthal's hypothetical examples and cautionary notes should alert the careful reader to the importance of these factors, not only in deriving average indices across studies, but in the derivation of individual indices as well. There is considerable controversy among statisticians about the appropriate means of deriving, combining, and interpreting estimates of effect size (see Fiske, 1983; Rosenthal, 1980; Sechrest & Yeaton, 1981; Strube & Hartmann, 1983). It seems that all of the statistical techniques for indexing the magnitude of effects—including r, d, variations of z, percentage

Table 8-2. Example of How Arbitrary Meta-Analytic Decisions (Including and Equally Weighting All Scales) Can Misrepresent the Conceptual Integrity of Design-Relevant Findings (Including Only "Focal-Experienced" or "Focal" Scales) for the Basic Data to Compare Outcomes

| Measure | Treatment effect size[a] | | Advantage of desensitization over nonspecific treatment effects |
	Systematic desensitization	Attention placebo	
1. Focal Scale of Experienced Performance Anxiety	2.71	1.92	.79
2. Focal Scale of Expected Performance Anxiety	1.43	1.32	.11
3. Situational Anxiety Scales to Test Symptom Substitution versus Generalization Predictions			
(a)	.25	.69	−.44
(b)	.41	.22	.19
(c)	.74	.77	−.03
4. Personality and General Anxiety Scales to Test Symptom Substitution versus Generalization Predictions			
(a)	.50	.46	.04
(b)	.35	.34	.01
(c)	.53	.70	−.17
(d)	.34	.49	−.15
Mean focal scales (1 & 2)	2.07	1.62	.45
Mean other scales (3 & 4)	.45	.52	−.07
Mean all scales (1–4)	.81	.77	.04

[a]Effect sizes calculated as the difference between treatment group and no-contact group means divided by the common standard deviation for 6-week follow-up scales from Paul (1966).

of variance accounted for, and so on—can be so influenced by sample size, the metric of the measures, assumptions of underlying statistical models, or the nature of designs from which primary statistics are derived that the *decisions* made by a meta-analyst are capable of producing almost contradictory results from the same data (see Glass, 1980; Hedges, 1983; Kraemer & Andrews, 1982; O'Grady, 1982; Sechrest & Yeaton, 1982).

Since I have no expertise as a theoretical statistician, my usual approach to things statistical is to read what the experts say (especially results of parametric and Monte Carlo studies), get consultation from trusted quantitative colleagues, and then apply various procedures to concrete clinical research data with which I have familiarity. Experimenting with various ways of calculating effect sizes served to sharpen my reservations concerning ready acceptance of the conclusions from meta-analytic reviews. Applying only five different ways of calculating effect sizes—from the many employed by Smith *et al.* (1980)—to the *identical* data set from any single study regularly resulted in five different effect sizes, and the differences among obtained indices were substantial. For example, limiting the data set to the overt behavioral measure under stress conditions for systematic desensitization and no-treatment groups included in Table 8-1 resulted in effect size indices for systematic desensitization ranging from 1.93 to 3.06. These different effect size indices depended simply upon whether pooled variances were used to obtain the standardizing standard deviation and whether the data entered were posttest data only, pre–post change data, or improvement scores. Thus, the index of effect size on a single measure for the same treatment groups in the same study differed by a magnitude that was larger than 88% of the standard deviations of effect sizes for different groups and measures included in Smith *et al.*'s (1980, p. 89) meta-analyses, simply as a function of the calculations employed. Using r to index effect size on the same data, as recommended by Rosenthal, similarly resulted in five different indexes ranging from .68 to .82. Within the interpretation of the Rosenthal and Rubin Binomial Effect Size Display (BESD), this range of r is equivalent to 14 people in 100 moving from "failure" to "success" in treatment outcomes, simply as a result of the particular test statistic that was available or chosen to calculate effect size from the same data set. In large meta-analytic reviews, the marked influence of these subjective choices and/ or available primary test statistics may be buried in a morass of computations rather than being public and explicit. Such a masking of lethal errors certainly warrants extreme caution in the conduct and interpretation of large-scale meta-analyses.

A final caution has to do with the interpretation of the importance of various effect size indices in outcome studies of psychosocial, pharmacological, and placebo or nonspecific clinical treatments. The extreme variability in the values of effect size indices derived from the same data set within a single study, as noted above, should forewarn against unguarded interpretation of the importance of measures that may have been obtained from a "rubber yardstick." Most of the proposed means of interpreting the practical clinical importance of treatment effects are also subject to more constraints than is readily apparent. Kraemer and Andrews (1982) point out (1) that the Cohen d statistic calculated on standardized differences between treatment and control group means, as used by Glass and his coworkers, varies in value as a function of the measure, metric, variances, and type of design from which it is derived; and (2) that its interpretation as reflecting the percentile rank of the typical treated patient compared to controls is accurate only in limited conditions. Those conditions are restricted to "the case of normally distributed control measures and under conditions in which the treatment effect is additive and uncorrelated with pretreatment and control treatment responses" (1982, p. 407). Such conditions are rare in clinical research.

Rosenthal's summary of the Friedman r statistic as an effect size estimate, and of its interpretation via the Rosenthal and Rubin BESD as the effect on success rate, is appealing for the reasons presented in his chapter.

However, its ease of computation and its intuitive appeal as "equivalent to" an increase in success rate from X to Y could easily lead to misapplication. Strictly speaking, the BESD appears to be an accurate respresentation of treatment effects only when a treatment group and a control group of equal size have dichotomous outcome measures with equal variance and means equally distributed above and below .5 (Rosenthal & Rubin, 1982). As violations of those assumptions occur in the data, adjustments and/or cautions in the interpretation of the BESD become necessary. Rosenthal and Rubin (1982) note that equal groups with equal variances on a continuous outcome measure should adjust the value of r for BESD interpretation— differently, depending on the shape of the distributions. For example, an obtained r of .55 would be adjusted downward to .49 if the distributions were normal, and upward to .66 with asymmetrical distributions of opposite shapes. A difference equivalent to 17 clients in 100 moving from "failure" to "success" in treatment outcomes does indicate the desirability of such adjustments. The r to be entered into BESD is a phi coefficient in the two-group case with dichotomous outcome measures, and appears to be equal to the square root of partial eta-squared in more complex designs (Sechrest & Yeaton, 1982). Therefore, the influences of unequal group sizes and variances on the ϕ coefficient, and the additional design-specific influences on components-of-variance measures, would also affect r and the accuracy of BESD interpretation (Cohen, 1977; O'Grady, 1982; Sechrest & Yeaton, 1982). For example, in the hypothetical experiment presented by Rosenthal in Tables 7-2, 7-3, and 7-4 of his chapter, the obtained r for the effect size of the "all against none" contrast in Table 7-4 is .33. The obtained r to reflect effect size for the *identical data* obtained from a t-test in a two-group-only study would be .57, and increasing the size of the groups without changing means or variances would systematically increase r. Thus, a difference "equivalent to" 24 more clients in 100 moving from "failure" to "success" in treatment outcomes could occur by the unthoughtful application of BESD interpretation.

Similar variations can occur in the representativeness of BESD interpretations of true dichotomous outcomes as the data depart from assumptions. For example, in a study employing equated groups of 28 beds each (Paul & Lentz, 1977), we reported an actual discharge success rate of 93% for 40 chronically hospitalized schizophrenics treated by a comprehensive social learning program, as compared to 42% of 31 patients receiving the usual hospital treatment during the same time period. The r calculated on the actual data equals .55, "equivalent to" the social learning program's increasing discharge success from 23% to 78% over usual hospital treatment, according to BESD interpretation—in the ballpark, but certainly not an accurate reflection of the actual increase from 42% to 93% success. However, the same actual success rates of 42% and 93% would be reflected quite differently if the size of the treatment and control groups were to be more disparate: Increasing the size of the control group could result in r

= .38 (BESD success = 31% to 69%); increasing the size of the treatment group could result in r = .45 (BESD success = 28% to 73%). In contrast to the actual gain of 51 more patients in 100 moving from continuous hospitalization to successful community tenure, the latter changes in group size would "lose" 13 and 6 of those patients, respectively, in BESD displays of practical importance. Additionally, all of the "success rates" fail to reflect the greater efficiency of the social learning program. Overall, I find myself in agreement with Yeaton and Sechrest (1981b) that purely statistical approaches for indicating the importance of treatment effects rely so heavily on specific features of the design of each study and its implementation that they cannot be relied upon as a generalizable solution.

CONCLUSION

I have added my comments and, I hope, clarifications to several salient issues in the clinical research enterprise that have been stimulated by the chapters on research methods and placebo phenomena by Ross and Buckalew, by Wilkins, and by Rosenthal. These issues include the commonalities of questions, domains and classes of variables, and research strategies in the area; concerns about uniformity assumptions and absolute design requirements; and the need for conceptual relevance, strength, integrity, and converging evidence in order to provide valid conclusions; and some details of meta-analyses and indices of the magnitude of treatment effects. The general solution to improving our progress in discovering, accumulating, and applying knowledge with regard to effective clinical treatments appears to lie in a re-emphasis on the construct validity approach, with better-designed and better-executed individual studies in which the questions asked are clearly specified and the relevant domains and classes of variables are explicitly described and measured—including data on the social importance and clinical relevance of findings. Can pregnancy be a placebo effect? For those readers who have responded to my editorial ploy by wading through the entire chapter in search of an answer, the answer is obviously "yes"—if the secondary definitions of "pregnant" as "rich in meaning" or "prolific of ideas" are adopted. Such a condition has been effected by consideration of the placebo concept in the foregoing chapters and, perhaps, in this one. I hope that careful study of them will result in some readers' "giving birth" to new and better clinical research.

REFERENCES

Bernstein, D. A., & Paul, G. L. Some comments on therapy analogue research with small animal "phobias." *Journal of Behavior Therapy and Experimental Psychiatry*, 1971, *2*, 225–237.

Bootzin, R. R., & Lick, J. R. Expectancies in therapy research: Interpretive artifact or mediating mechanism? *Journal of Consulting and Clinical Psychology*, 1979, *47*, 852–855.

Borkovec, T. D., & Bauer, R. M. Experimental designs in group outcome research. In A. S. Bellack, M. Hersen, & A. E. Kazdin (Eds.), *International handbook of behavior modification and therapy*. New York: Plenum, 1982.

Borkovec, T. D., & Nau, S. D. Credibility of analogue therapy rationales. *Journal of Behavior Therapy and Experimental Psychiatry*, 1972, *3*, 257–260.

Campbell, D. T., & Stanley, J. C. *Experimental and quasi-experimental designs for research*. Chicago: Rand McNally, 1966.

Carroll, R. S., Miller, A., Ross, B., & Simpson, G. M. Research as an impetus to improved treatment. *Archives of General Pscyhiatry*, 1980, *37*, 377–380.

Cohen, J. *Statistical power analysis for the behavioral sciences* (Rev. ed.). New York: Academic Press, 1977.

Cook, T. D., & Campbell, D. T. *Quasi-experimentation: Design and analysis for field settings*. Chicago: Rand McNally, 1979.

Cooper, H. M., & Rosenthal, R. Statistical versus traditional procedures for summarizing research findings. *Psychological Bulletin*, 1980, *87*, 442–449.

Cronbach, L. J. *Designing evaluations of educational and social programs*. San Francisco: Jossey-Bass, 1982.

Emmelkamp, P. M. G. Anxiety and fear. In A. S. Bellack, M. Hersen, & A. E. Kazdin (Eds.), *International handbook of behavior modification and therapy*. New York: Plenum, 1982.

Fiske, D. W. The meta-analytic revolution in outcome research. *Journal of Consulting and Clinical Psychology*, 1983, *51*, 65–70.

Glass, G. V. Summarizing effect sizes. In R. Rosenthal (Ed.), *New directions for methodology of social and behavioral science: Quantitative assessment of research domains* (No. 5). San Francisco: Jossey-Bass, 1980.

Glass, G. V., & Kliegl, R. M. An apology for research integration in the study of psychotherapy. *Journal of Consulting & Clinical Psychology*, 1983, *51*, 28–41.

Grünbaum, A. The placebo concept. *Behaviour Research and Therapy*, 1981, *19*, 157–167.

Hedges, L. V. A random effects model for effect sizes. *Psychological Bulletin*, 1983, *93*, 388–395.

Hersen, M., & Barlow, D. H. *Single case experimental designs: Strategies for studying behavior change*. New York: Pergamon Press, 1976.

Hollon, S. D., & DeRubeis, R. J. Placebo–psychotherapy combinations: Inappropriate representations of psychotherapy in drug–psychotherapy comparative trials. *Psychological Bulletin*, 1981, *90*, 467–477.

Kazdin, A. E. Evaluating the generality of findings in analogue therapy research. *Journal of Consulting and Clinical Psychology*, 1978, *46*, 673–686.

Kazdin, A. E., & Wilcoxon, L. A. Systematic desensitization and nonspecific treatment effects: A methodological evaluation. *Psychological Bulletin*, 1976, *83*, 729–758.

Kiesler, D. J. Some myths of psychotherapy research and the search for a paradigm. *Psychological Bulletin*, 1966, *65*, 110–136.

Kiesler, D. J. Experimental designs in psychotherapy research. In A. E. Bergin & S. L. Garfield (Eds.), *Handbook of psychotherapy and behavior change*. New York: Wiley, 1971.

Keith, S. J. Psychosocial and psychopharmacological treatments: Realistic expectations. In M. Mirabi (Ed.), *The chronically mentally ill: Research and services*. New York: SP Medical & Scientific Books, 1984.

Kraemer, H. C., & Andrews, G. A nonparametric technique for meta-analysis effect size calculation. *Psychological Bulletin*, 1982, *91*, 404–412.

Liberman, R. J., Falloon, I. R. H., & Wallace, C. J. Drug–environmental interactions in schizophrenic patients. In M. Mirabi (Ed.), *The chronically mentally ill: Research and services*. New York: SP Medical & Scientific Books, 1984.

Licht, M. H. The Staff–Resident Interaction Chronograph: Observational assessment of staff performance. *Journal of Behavioral Assessment*, 1979, *1*, 185–197.

Lick, J., & Bootzin, R. Expectancy factors in the treatment of fear: Methodological and theoretical issues. *Psychological Bulletin*, 1975, *82*, 917–931.

Luborsky, L., Singer, B., & Luborsky, L. Comparative studies of psychotherapies. *Archives of General Psychiatry*, 1975, *32*, 995–1008.

Mahoney, M. J. Experimental methods and outcome evaluation. *Journal of Consulting and Clinical Psychology*, 1978, *46*, 660–672.

Mariotto, M. J., & Paul, G. L. The utility of assessment for different purposes. In M. Mirabi (Ed.), *The chronically mentally ill: Research and services*. New York: SP Medical & Scientific Books, 1984.

McGlynn, F. D., Mealiea, W. L., & Landau, D. L. The current status of systematic desensitization. *Clinical Psychology Review*, 1981, *1*, 149–179.

Mintz, J. Integrating research evidence: A commentary on meta-analysis. *Journal of Consulting and Clinical Psychology*, 1983, *51*, 71–75.

O'Grady, K. E. Measures of explained variance: Cautions and limitations. *Psychological Bulletin*, 1982, *92*, 766–777.

O'Leary, K. D., & Borkovec, T. D. Conceptual, methodological, and ethical problems of placebo groups in psychotherapy research. *American Psychologist*, 1978, *33*, 821–830.

Paul, G. L. *Insight versus desensitization in psychotherapy: An experiment in anxiety reduction*. Stanford, Calif.: Stanford University Press, 1966.

Paul, G. L. Insight vs. desensitization in psychotherapy two years after termination. *Journal of Consulting Psychology*, 1967, *31*, 333–348. (a)

Paul, G. L. The strategy of outcome research in psychotherapy. *Journal of Consulting Psychology*, 1967, *31*, 109–118. (b)

Paul, G. L. Two-year follow-up of systematic desensitization in therapy groups. *Journal of Abnormal Psychology, 1968, 73*, 119–130.

Paul, G. L. Behavior modification research: Design and tactics. In C. M. Franks (Ed.), *Behavior therapy: Appraisal and status*. New York: McGraw-Hill, 1969. (a)

Paul, G. L. Outcome of systematic desensitization I: Background, procedures and uncontrolled reports of individual treatment. In C. M. Franks (Ed.), *Behavior therapy: Appraisal and status*. New York: McGraw-Hill, 1969. (b)

Paul, G. L. Outcome of systematic desensitization II: Controlled investigations of individual treatment, technique variations, and current status. In C. M. Franks (Ed.), *Behavior therapy: Appraisal and status*. New York: McGraw-Hill, 1969. (c)

Paul, G. L., & Bernstein, D. A. Anxiety and clinical problems. In J. T. Spence, R. C. Carson, & J. W. Thibaut (Eds.), *Behavioral approaches to therapy*. Morristown, N.J.: General Learning Press, 1976.

Paul, G. L., & Lentz, R. J. *Psychosocial treatment of chronic mental patients: Milieu versus social-learning programs*. Cambridge, Mass.: Harvard University Press, 1977.

Paul, G. L., & Licht, M. H. The resurrection of uniformity assumption myths and the fallacy of statistical absolutes in psychotherapy research. *Journal of Consulting and Clinical Psychology*, 1978, *46*, 1531–1534.

Paul, G. L., & Shannon, D. T. Treatment of anxiety through systematic desensitization in therapy groups. *Journal of Abnormal Psychology*, 1966, *71*, 123–135.

Paul, G. L., Mariotto, M. J., & Redfield, J. P. Assessment purposes, domains, and utility for decision making. In G. L. Paul (Ed.), *Assessment in residential treatment settings*. Cambridge, Mass.: Harvard University Press, in press. (a)

Paul, G. L., Mariotto, M. J., & Redfield, J. P. The potential utility of different sources and methods of formal assessment. In G. L. Paul (Ed.), *Assessment in residential treatment settings*. Cambridge, Mass.: Harvard University Press, in press. (b)

Paul, G. L., Tobias, L. L., & Holly, B. L. Maintenance psychotropic drugs in the presence of active treatment programs: A "triple-blind" withdrawal study with long-term mental patients. *Archives of General Psychiatry*, 1972, *27*, 106–115.

Power, C. T. Ongoing assessment of staff and program functioning in residential treatment settings. In M. Mirabi (Ed.), *The chronically mentally ill: Research and services*. New York: SP Medical & Scientific Books, 1984.

Rosenthal, R. On telling tails when combining results of independent studies. *Psychological Bulletin*, 1980, *88*, 496–497.

Rosenthal, R. Assessing the statistical and social importance of the effects of psychotherapy. *Journal of Consulting and Clinical Psychology*, 1983, *51*, 4–13.

Rosenthal, R., & Rubin, D. B. A simple, general purpose display of magnitude of experimental effect. *Journal of Educational Psychology*, 1982, *74*, 166–169.

Schooler, N. R., & Severe, J. A. Efficacy of drug treatment for chronic schizophrenic patients. In M. Mirabi (Ed.), *The chronically mentally ill: Research and services*. New York: SP Medical & Scientific Books, 1984.

Sechrest, L., & Yeaton, W. H. Empirical bases for estimating effect size. In R. F. Boruch, P. M. Wortman, & D. S. Cordray (Eds.), *Reanalyzing program evaluations*. San Francisco: Jossey-Bass, 1981.

Sechrest, L., & Yeaton, W. H. Magnitudes of experimental effects in social science research. *Evaluation Review*, 1982, *6*, 579–600.

Shapiro, D. A., & Shapiro, D. Comparative therapy outcome research: Methodological implications of meta-analysis. *Journal of Consulting and Clinical Psychology*, 1983, *51*, 42–53.

Smith, M. L., & Glass, G. V. Meta-analysis of psychotherapy outcome studies. *American Psychologist*, 1977, *32*, 752–760.

Smith, M. L., Glass, G. V., & Miller, T. I. *The benefits of psychotherapy*. Baltimore: Johns Hopkins University Press, 1980.

Strube, M. J., & Hartmann, D. P. Meta-analysis: Techniques, applications, and functions. *Journal of Consulting and Clinical Psychology*, 1983, *51*, 14–27.

Ullmann, L. P., & Krasner, L. *A psychological approach to abnormal behavior* (2nd ed.). Englewood Cliffs, N.J.: Prentice-Hall, 1975.

Underwood, B. J. *Psychological research*. New York: Appleton-Century-Crofts, 1957.

Varela, J. S. Social technology. *American Psychologist*, 1977, *32*, 914–923.

Wilkins, W. Failure of placebo groups to control for nonspecific events in therapy outcome research. *Psychotherapy: Theory, Research, and Practice*, 1983, *20*, 31–37.

Wilson, G. T., & Rachman, S. J. Meta-analysis and the evaluation of psychotherapy outcome: Limitations and liabilities. *Journal of Consulting and Clinical Psychology*, 1983, *51*, 54–64.

Wortman, P. M. Randomized clinical trials. In P. M. Wortman (Ed.), *Methods for evaluating health services*. Beverly Hills, Calif.: Sage, 1981.

Yeaton, W. H., & Sechrest, L. Critical dimensions in the choice and maintenance of successful treatments: Strength, integrity, and effectiveness. *Journal of Consulting and Clinical Psychology*, 1981, *49*, 156–167. (a)

Yeaton, W. H., & Sechrest, L. Estimating effect size. In P. M. Wortman (Ed.), *Methods for evaluating health services*. Beverly Hills, Calif.: Sage, 1981. (b)

CLINICAL PHENOMENA

9

A Sociocultural Model of Illness and Healing

ROBERT A. HAHN

INTRODUCTION

This chapter explores the multiple ways in which human societies, their variant beliefs, customs, and relations, are involved in the creation of both sickness and healing. These effects are both powerful and pervasive. Yet they present a profound anomaly for the paradigm (Kuhn, 1962) of our medicine, Biomedicine. It is proposed that a (medical) anthropological paradigm that embraces Biomedical knowledge within a broader, essentially interdisciplinary framework gives ample room for the exploration of the range of sociocultural phenomena.

Three interrelated modes of the sociocultural creation of events of sickness and healing may be distinguished: I have called these modes "construction," "production," and "mediation." They do not preclude, but rather persistently accompany and complement, the pathogenic and therapeutic modes recognized and addressed by Biomedicine.

This chapter begins by defining some elements for an anthropological theory of sociocultural effects. It then surveys these effects in schematic fashion. It explores the placebo phenomenon as a prime exemplar of sociocultural causation. Finally, it returns to review the place of sociocultural causation in the paradigm of Biomedicine and to propose a radically different, anthropological paradigm in which such phenomena have a central, though not exclusive, place.

THE SOCIOCULTURAL CREATION OF SICKNESS AND HEALING: THEORETICAL FOUNDATIONS

Humans who regularly interact establish among themselves organized (though not necessarily static) systems of symbols, beliefs, sentiments, and

Robert A. Hahn. Department of Psychiatry and Behavioral Sciences, University of Washington, Seattle, Washington.

167

rules and standards for interaction, to which anthropologists have applied the term, "culture." The patterned interactions of persons and the cultural rules by which actions are guided and judged are commonly termed "society." Boundaries between one society and another are more or less loose, for even the inhabitants of isolated islands may interact with others, manifesting social divisions on their islands as well. Within such relative boundaries, the interactions of societal members differentially distribute social positions (or "statuses"), cultural beliefs, sentiments, and various other products, so that different persons in a society will partake of this culture in different ways. A society is an intricate system of exchange, a complex economy.

Social analysts have denominated as "socialization" the process by which societal members interact with the purpose and effect of inculcating in others the society's culture; by this process, societal members learn how to think and feel, how to behave, and how to judge the behaviors of others. While observation of socialization usually focuses on neonates and children, this process is a consequence of all interaction throughout the life cycle; culture is continuously reproduced and altered in ongoing interaction. Thus, the interactional rules of a culture shape interactions, which at the same time affect the ongoing economics of culture itself—its production, distribution, and consumption (Giddens, 1976).

As general anthropologists have applied the prefix, "ethno-," to parts of a society's culture and social order concerned with particular issues (e.g., "ethnobotany" and "ethnohistory"), so medical anthropologists have distinguished the part of a society and its culture concerned with medical matters as its "ethnomedicine." Biomedicine is an ethnomedicine, as are traditional and contemporary Chinese medicines (Kleinman, 1980; Porkert, 1974), African systems of healing (e.g., Turner, 1967), and Amazonian curing (e.g., Reichel-Dolmatoff & Reichel-Dolmatoff, 1961). More specifically, ethnomedicines are comprised of conceptualizations of healthy and unhealthy conditions, moral and ethical evaluations of them, theories of their causation and alteration, and rules of interaction, including the "sick role" (Parsons, 1951) and the responses of consociates and of medical professionals. A society's ethnomedicine thus comprehends all of its medically oriented concerns, understandings, sentiments, and actions. An ethnomedicine may be more or less clearly and explicitly distinguished from other sectors of a society—for example, its polity, its economy, and its religion.

Through their ethnomedicines, societies and their cultures are causally involved in processes of pathology and healing in three essential ways:

First, the conditions of health and suffering are defined as elements of a culture. Societal members inform each other about how these conditions are called; what (they believe) causes and alters them; what they might signify in a larger, perhaps a moral or cosmological sense; and how to respond to them. The world created in this way by Biomedicine (Hahn & Kleinman, in press) is very different from what anthropologists have observed in other societies (e.g., Landy, 1977; Leslie, 1976). Any society may manifest a range of variant ethnomedical sectors—for example, professional, folk, and popular (Kleinman, 1980); theories and practices from each sector may influence those of the other sectors, and patients may resort to different sectors for the same or for different conditions, at the same time or sequentially.

Along with phenomenological sociologists (e.g., Berger & Luckmann, 1967), I refer to this form of social definition as "construction"; in this sense, a society constructs the reality it lives in. In noting that medical realities are socially constructed, I do not deny that their referents are real—that there is a physical, biological, and so on, reality from (and by means of) which they are constructed. Medical realities are not social fictions, as some social observers have argued (Sedgwick, 1981). But neither are they simply facts of nature, as the ideology of Biomedicine assumes. Pathology and its relief accord with the interests and values of sufferers (Hahn, 1984); they are at once physiological *and* cultural (and psychological, biochemical, etc.) in origin, course, and consequence. Medical realities are constructed from nature by cultural plan.

A second mode of sociocultural influence on events of sickness and healing is one of "mediation." The concepts, ideas, and values of an ethnomedicine and its broader culture, along with a society's rules of social interaction, guide the acts of societal members, distributing them in time, space, and activity. There is thus an economy of activity in which persons as well as impersonal things are literally moved around. By such socioculturally guided movement, societal members may be brought into greater or lesser contact with both pathogenic and therapeutic sources; thus disease may be fostered or prevented, and cured (or palliated) or not. Mediation may be regarded as a form of transportation of persons, pathogens, and therapeutic agents.

Mediation is perhaps the simplest, most widely acknowledged, and best understood of sociocultural influences on sickness and healing. Such disciplines as public health and occupational medicine recognize the ways in which societal organization may be pathogenic or preventive, by withholding or providing "health services" of various sorts. The culturally guided course that patients take when they or consociates begin to diagnose an illness has been described as "the health-seeking process" (Chrisman, 1977). The "sick role" and "illness behavior" (Mechanic, 1962) are the ways in which the patient responds to his or her own condition; these are thought of as responses to rather than as central elements in the illness itself. The process generally begins in the popular health care sector; it may lead to the Biomedical professional sector, and then back to the broader society. The diagnosis and felt significance of the patient's condition may be radically transformed along the way (e.g., Helman, 1985). "The doctor–patient relationship," an idealized understanding, is often regarded as the central stage of the mediational process, whose ideal outcome is "compliance."

Least recognized and understood among sociocultural modes—indeed, an anomaly to the Biomedical paradigm—is "production." Ethnomedicines,

the cultures that include them, and socially organized interpersonal relationships not only construct our medical worlds and guide participants into
different forms of contact with pathogens and medicines (i.e., therapeutic
agents); beliefs and patterned relations may themselves *be* pathogens and
medicines in the same logical sense as are commonly acknowledged
pathogens and medicines.[1] That is, given host and environmental conditions,
pathogenesis and healing follow beliefs and relations with consistent
regularity. This form of causation argues for a conception of pathogenesis
and therapeutics very different from that assumed in our medicine; indeed, it
fits with a radically different understanding of the world, its metaphysics, and
its praxis.

The Cartesian premises hidden in our language and thought hinder
appropriate discussion of these issues. Conception of belief and relations as
pathogens and medicines requires understanding of these human phenomena
as corporeal ones, literally embodied. Beliefs are not simply propositional
attitudes about the world; as humans maintain and profess them, they are a
part of, and inseparable from, human physiology. Likewise, as humans
interact, in culturally patterned ways, their relations are also embodied;
interpersonal relations, too, have a physiology. Conversely, the human body
is not only a natural entity; it is at the same time a mindful entity (in
conscious, functioning persons), socially and culturally imbued. The bodies
of persons are social as well as natural artifacts. This understanding, further
explored below, is anomalous to the paradigm of Biomedicine; it threatens
the paradigm logically and is the source of a strong and ambivalent
reaction.

While construction, mediation, and production are analytically separ-
able aspects of the sociocultural influence on events of sickness and health,
they commonly occur together. Their interaction merits more extensive
exploration, but is only briefly mentioned here.

Those same beliefs and relations that engender (i.e., produce) disease
(or health) may also hinder (or facilitate) transportation and effective
response to therapeutic resources. That is, disease etiology (and therapeutic
processes) may affect the way in which the pathology (or cure) is presented,
received and further treated. Societal stigmatization of psychiatric illness, for
example, commonly leads to "somatization," in which psychological distress
may be experienced in bodily terms and presented in medical rather than

1. It might be argued, reductionistically, that what I have called "production" is ultimately a
form of mediation in which symbols and relations alter and transport pathogenic and salubrious
substances in the body. For example, loss of a valued relationship may be discovered to affect
neurotransmitters significantly, thus causing depression, a physiological as well as a psychological condition. I recommend below an alternative ontology in which symbols and
relationships, insofar as persons maintain and engage in them, are themselves corporeal. Thus
they have bodily *concomitants* rather than bodily *consequences*.

psychiatric or psychological therapeutic settings (Katon, Kleinman, & Rosen, 1982); the etiology of a condition affects the means of its experience and treatment. Biomedical practitioners (e.g., Ries, Bokan, Katon, & Kleinman, 1981) have labeled as "health care abuse" a variety of similar presentations, in which patients appear in medical settings expressing concerns and interpretations at odds with those of medical practitioners. I (Hahn, 1984) have referred to this pathological form as "meta-disease"—a disturbed presentation of disturbance.

The sociocultural construction of medical reality affects both mediation and production in general by representing the world to which societal members respond. Thus, as noted, a society's ethnomedicine may guide societal members to avoid certain activities, places, and contacts as sources of sickness, and to seek others as sources of health; these are mediational effects of the sociocultural construction of medical reality.

A society's construction of its medical reality (or realities) affects the production of sickness and health in a variety of other ways. In its guidance of activity, it organizes relationships among persons that may themselves be pathogenic and/or healthful. Perhaps the most striking examples of the direct consequence of sociocultural construction on the production of pathological and therapeutic events are the nocebo and placebo phenomena, in which ethnomedical constructions produce the reality to which they refer (e.g., fear of death producing death). But beliefs may also have other effects that are less well recognized and not as spectacular. That is, it is likely that beliefs of certain kinds affect (or effect) not only the conditions they refer to, but other tangential conditions. It may be, for example, that fear of cancer produces not cancer, but sniffles or headaches. Such tangential effects of beliefs differ from placebo–nocebo phenomena.

Mediational and productive effects reciprocally influence a society's construction of its medical reality as well, in two ways. For one, etiological and therapeutic processes themselves may alter the ratiocinative and affective processes of patients, and thus their understanding of, use of, and attitudes regarding everyday constructions (Young, 1981). That is, people who are becoming sick, who are sick, and who are healing are likely to react differently to their conditions than others do and than they themselves would in healthy states. In addition, a person who has or has had some condition may experience this condition very differently from a person who has not had it.

Second, the medical reality socioculturally effected by production and mediation provides a testing ground for society's construction of reality. While social constructions need not perfectly explain the empirical world they confront, still the empirical hold provides an objective tension. At one limit, constructions that are too far off empirical realities may lead their proponents to self-harm, if not to self-destruction.

Figure 9-1 presents a classification of findings of sociocultural effects in sickness and healing.

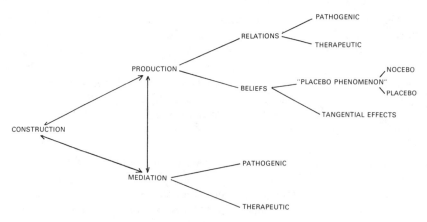

Figure 9-1. A classification of sociocultural effects on sickness and healing.

THE SOCIOCULTURAL CREATION OF SICKNESS AND HEALING: A REVIEW

I now review, in a most cursory fashion, evidence for the great range of sociocultural effects in sickness and healing. I begin with the person and his or her immediate environment as a locus, medium, and source of both pathology and healing, then move through ever-expanding social environments—family, social networks, social classes and workplaces, societal segments, national society, and international relations.

Events of sickness and healing are affected by relations at all of these levels. Again, the workings of any one level do not exclude simultaneous and parallel workings of other levels. "Smaller" levels commonly mediate the relations of "larger" ones; "larger" levels are comprised of interacting "smaller" ones. In fact, the attribution of causal efficacy to one level rather than another—for example, self or social environment—is somewhat arbitrary, depending on the time frame examined. The self is in good part a product of the interactions in a social environment; in turn, the self in part recreates its own environment. Symbolic interactionists (Lindesmith & Strauss, 1968; Mead, 1956), though they have tended to ignore the seemingly harder facts of human physiology, have successfully argued that the selves and environments of persons continuously recreate one another. Thus, when we talk of the pathogenic and therapeutic powers of self, we are talking of the residues of broader social fields.

Self as Pathogen and Healer

The ways in which persons construct, confront, and "cope" or deal with the difficulties and successes in their lives—rapid changes, including migration, unemployment, marriage, separation, and divorce, childbearing, deaths of others, and so on—significantly influence their health.

With great methodological clarity, and a combination of epidemiology and depth interviewing, G. W. Brown and Harris (1978) present evidence for a model of clinically defined depression among women, in which personal characteristics of the subject, including her beliefs, values, and psychological coping devices, play a causal role in the onset and chronicity of depressive illness. This model (see Figure 9-2), well substantiated for depressive illness, has very broad applications and resembles that implied by Rabkin and Struening (1976) and by Rahe and Arthur (1978). It distinguishes historical events in a person's life that hinder or foster later adjustment capacities from contemporary events that evoke relative failure or success in adjustment. The capacities of self are historically produced.

Similarly, Engel (1968) describes and documents the "giving-up–given-up complex," in which people react strongly to events in their symbolic and relational environments, and consequently suffer severe disease. In its most extreme form, patients die very suddenly, often from grief. The pathogen here is symbolic and social. The breadth of such reactions is documented in the vast and recent literature on "stress" (Rahe, 1979; for critiques, see Lumsden, 1981; Rabkin & Struening, 1976; Young, 1980). The phenomenon should be viewed in terms of the person's capacity to deal with such social and symbolic traumas, and in terms of both the relationships that

Figure 9-2. A model of clinically defined depression among women. (From *Social Origins of Depression* by G. W. Brown and T. Harris. London: Tavistock, 1978. Reprinted by permission.)

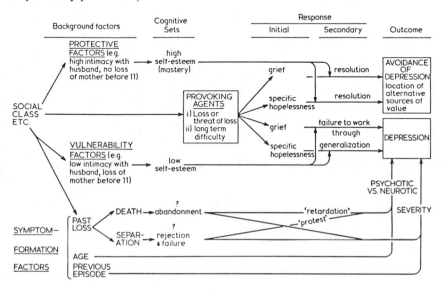

foster his or her capacity and those that precipitate (or mitigate) given crises.

Corresponding to the evidence for the psychological and social etiology of the depressive syndrome, defined both by mental and by physiological symptoms, Kovacs (1980) has reviewed evidence for the therapeutic effects of cognitive, behavioral, and combined cognitive and behavioral psychiatric therapies. In a wide variety of studies, many therapies have shown effectiveness in the alleviation or reduction of depressive symptoms. Beck (1971) has argued and shown evidence that the reordering of the depressed patient's (culturally constructed) cognitive world significantly improves his or her depressed condition.

Finally, whether or not one wishes to classify suicide as a "disease," it is by definition a most serious event of persons. If a disease, it is the most extreme form of self as pathogen. Suicide has been probably underestimated as the ninth leading cause of death in the United States, and the fourth leading cause among adolescents. (The definition of "suicide" is itself problematic, since a variety of human acts may be regarded as slowly self-destructive.) Suicide has been shown to have a variety of social and psychological causes and precipitants. (For an excellent summary and criticism of social, economic, and political causes, see Hopper & Guttmacher, 1979; for a psychiatric perspective, see Baechler, 1979.)

Family and Social Network as Pathogen and Therapy: Beyond the Contextual View

The people who live closely and are closely related, in "positive" and "negative" ways, with a given person, causally influence this person's sickness and health. I discuss here two principal modes of influence: the production and the mediation of pathology and healing. Family and networks cause or partly cause and prevent or mitigate pathological conditions; they may frustrate or satisfy psychological and social needs, as well as detracting from or providing physically sanitary environments. Family and social networks may also facilitate or obstruct the movement of the sick person to, within, and from the variety of both pathogenic and healing sources. The "contextual" view of the relevance of society and culture regards social life as mediating but not as significantly generating pathological or therapeutic events. This view is inadequate. I seek to restore social and psychological considerations of etiology and therapeutics to the core of medicine, alongside physiology.

THE PRODUCTION OF ILLNESS AND HEALING

Meyer and Haggerty (1962) observed 100 persons in 16 families for the period of a year, recording streptococcal manifestations and changing personal and family characteristics at regular intervals. They found *no correspondence* between streptococcal episodes and the number and type of streptococci present, allergic history, presence or absence of tonsils, weather changes, housing, or family size. They did find a correspondence of streptococcal episodes with closeness of contact in sleeping arrangements, age, season, and penicillin treatment. Moreover, streptococcal and other respiratory infections were four times as likely to be preceded as to be followed by acute family and personal stress. The causal (or predispositional) mechanism is not explored here, but the association is strong and remarkable. The study of Gruchow (1979) suggests one such mechanism by demonstrating that elevated catecholamines regularly precede the onset of respiratory symptoms.

While subject to a number of conceptual and methodological difficulties (Rabkin & Struening, 1976; Thoits, 1982; Young, 1980), there has accumulated over the past 20 years a vast amount of information on the relations between natural and social environmental "stress" and the onset, course, and outcome of disease conditions. This literature should be considered in conjunction with the research on "coping" (Cohen & Lazarus, 1973; Lazarus, 1981; Nuckolls, Cassel, & Kaplan, 1972) and that on "support networks" (McKinlay, 1981; see Thoits, 1982). Different people cope with or respond differently to the "same" stress environments, with different disease consequences. Similarly, the different social environments or "support networks" differentially order the effects of stressful environments on given persons. In other words, the characteristics both of self and of social environment can be shown to be either or both sources or channels of stress and/or the means by which stress is avoided or deflected. That is, self and society can themselves *be* stress, or they may mitigate or amplify the effects of other stress.

Rahe and Arthur (1978) review a wide range of influences of stressful situations on human disease, beginning with prenatal events, through parturition, infancy, youth, adulthood, and old age. Not only are these effects manifest through the human life cycle; they, and the coping and support system effects, may also be seen as working at all levels of psychological and social organization, from the psychodynamic "defenses" of individuals through wider and wider contexts of social relations surrounding individuals.

Based on a major survey of research, Kagan and Levi (1974) cautiously review some mechanisms of psychological effects on physiology; they find strong evidence for central nervous system influences, and at least some evidence for the influence of stress on thyroid, cardiac, hypertensive, and gastrointestinal pathologies. Similarly, Sterling and Eyer (1981) propose a physiological mechanism to account for the pathological effects of chronic stress.

Rahe (1979; see also Mueller, 1980) reviews evidence for the relations between life change events and the onset of mental illness, including such studies as the G. W. Brown and Harris (1978) project mentioned above. Rahe claims that environmental events can be stressful, regardless of the affected person's perception and evaluation of these events. Other social scientists reviewing this area have come to the opposite conclusion (Dohrenwend & Dohrenwend, 1974; Lumsden, 1981; Mechanic, 1978): What counts as stressful will vary according to the premises and values of one's culture (Spradley & Phillips, 1972) and one's personal experience.

There is a wide range of evidence—clinical, epidemiological, and experimental—on the psychosocial pathology and the psychosocial therapeutics even of such seemingly physiological conditions as coronary disease. Sudden cardiac death is, by common classification, the leading cause of death in the industrially developed world (Lown, DeSilva, Reich, & Murawski, 1980). Medalie, Kahn, Newfeld, Riss, and Goldbourt (1973) have made an extensive and careful study of the 5-year incidence of myocardial infarction among an Israeli immigrant population of 10,000 male government workers. Beyond possible hereditary factors, and such physiological factors as weight, blood pressure, and serum cholesterol, Medalie and his coworkers found significant relationships between the incidence of myocardial infarction and smoking, and a possible relationship with exertion in leisure activity. Most striking in Medalie's study is a strong inverse relationship between the incidence of myocardial infarction and a history and continuity of good relations with a superior at work and a wife. The latter findings are close to those disclosed for depressive illness in the research of Brown and Harris (1978). The strength of these relationships is persuasive and argues for the social and psychological bases of important and seemingly discrete "physiological" events.

In a clinical vein, Engel (1980) explains and illustrates the "biopsychosocial" model in the case of a patient, "Mr. Glover," who suffers a myocardial infarction. Engel examines the range of co-occurring events on the chemical, physiological, psychological, social, and symbolic levels. Engel demonstrates how Mr. Glover's personal qualities affect his own response to his early symptoms as well as the responses of those around him, including his supportive employer. Engel also describes how the behavior of the physicians who treat Mr. Glover, under the "Biomedical" approach, severely exacerbates the pathology of his condition. The physicians' training fosters a posture that contributes to the disease in the attempt to alleviate it. Engel describes the contrasting "biopsychosocial" approach as one that is concerned, in a scientific manner, with *persons* and their psychological and social environments.

Lown et al. (1980) survey a large body of research on the coronary effects of mental events. Given the condition of coronary artery disease, psychologically stressful events will set off ventricular fibrillation by means of central nervous system mechanisms. "The neuroeffector sequence is the summated expression emanating from complex interactions between sensory perception, recall of past emotional events, preexisting conditioned reflex pathways, concentration of neurochemical precursors at various brain sites, and a host of other factors as yet to be identified" (Lown et al., 1980, p.

1333). One study (Jarvinen, 1955) gives anecdotal evidence that ward rounds conducted by chiefs of surgery initiate cardiac complications, including sudden death. These findings correspond with the clinical example of "Mr. Glover."

Psychosocial effects are both short-term and long-term (Kagan & Levi, 1974). Moreover, not only do cardiac pathologies have psychosocial causes; they also have well-documented psychosocial consequences, including depression, which, if not treated, may have further coronary implications (Hackett & Cassem, 1975). Cohen and Lazarus (1973) have explored psychosocial factors that differentiate those who recover well from surgery from those who do poorly. They find that those patients who are "vigilant," who know and are most concerned about their conditions, do less well on several measures than those who are "avoidant."

To examine a severe pathological condition with more obvious psychological as well as physiological involvement, take the case of anorexia nervosa, a condition mostly affecting adolescent girls from higher socio-economic classes. Bruch (1978) has argued persuasively that anorexia originates in families in which parents have extremely high expectations of their children (especially daughters), while at the same time failing to respect the daughters' individual qualities. Through diet these daughters assume a tyrannical control over their bodies, as a means of gaining irrefutable authority in at least this one domain. The condition becomes cyclical as the weak physical state of these girls precludes their escape from their beliefs and their corresponding regimens; productive effects modify both construction and mediation. The therapy that Bruch employs involves both physiological restoration and family therapy. Minuchin, Rosman, and Baker (1978) have had success with a similar therapeutic approach.

Incidents of disease need not result from environmental stresses, since the way in which the stress is dealt with—indeed, perceived—may deflect serious impact: "[T]o relate stress to adaptation requires emphasis not so much on stressors as on the cognitive and coping processes mediating the reaction" (Lazarus, 1981, p. 48). There is some evidence, for example, that primagravida women who sustain life crises preceding and/or during their pregnancies have fewer delivery complications if they have had stronger coping devices and supportive social relations (Nuckolls et al., 1972).

Cobb (1976) and McKinlay (1981) summarize a great range of literature on the morbidity and mortality consequences of social networks and support systems. Mueller (1980) reviews suggestive studies of the role of social networks in both the etiology and the remedy of several psychiatric disorders. Cobb emphasizes the importance of the person's *perception* of support. He minimizes the causal relationship by talk of "moderating" and "facilitating" (as others write of "buffering"), rather than of simply causal effects, within a system of causes. Cobb cites evidence of the moderating effects of social support in life stresses, beginning before birth and continuing in infancy and childhood, through illness episodes and hospitalization, to mourning and old age. He cites his own collaborative research on the social mitigation of the effects of unemployment, in which he found that, following dismissal from employment, serum cholesterol and uric acid levels as well as symptom complaints were higher among men with less supportive networks (Cobb, 1974; see also Gore, 1978; Henderson, 1977).

Berkman and Syme (1979) report on a study of almost 7000 adults over a 9-year period, demonstrating that age-adjusted relative risk of mortality is 2.3 for men and 2.8 for women with fewer social contacts. This association of increased mortality rates associated with decrease in social connections is independent of common risk factors, including use of preventive health services.

FROM THE PRODUCTION TO THE MEDIATION OF ILLNESS AND HEALING

The same social ties that may support a person, thus preventing disease, or that may "stress" a person, thus causing or facilitating the onset of disease—this same social nexus may also exert significant influence on the subsequent therapeutic (or nontherapeutic) responses to the pathological condition once generated. Personal characteristics and social relations affect one's movement to, through, and following the variety of sources of healing.

Chrisman (1977) has conceptually distinguished five steps in the "health-seeking process": symptom definition, illness-related shifts in role behavior, lay consultation and referral, treatment action, and adherence. A "sick" person may exhibit these, but need not exhibit all; nor do the steps always appear in the listed sequence. The different steps may also be simultaneous. There is evidence that persons commonly experience on the average one symptom during a week, and that the majority of these are dealt with outside of medical institutions (Demers, Altamore, Mustin, Kleinman, & Leonardi, 1980; Hulka, Kupper, & Cassell, 1972; Kleinman, 1980; Zola, 1972a, 1972b). The discrimination among symptoms by various criteria (Mechanic, 1968) leads the sufferer to respond in different ways; these reactions are part of an essential *culture of medicine* of the person who suffers and those around him or her.

Within medical settings, personal and social characteristics also influence both the patient's response and "compliance" with the practitioner's advice and the practitioner's own behavior (Zola, 1981). A variety of studies collected by Harwood (1981) usefully explores the range of understandings and responses by different cultural groups to the dominant culture of Biomedicine. The Biomedical notion of "compliance" is highly medicocentric, assuming that the physician's viewpoint is exclusively correct (and even value-free), and that the patient would only be "wrong" or "bad" were he or she not to comply. Katon and Kleinman (1981) elaborate a negotiation strategy of patient care to maximize effectiveness and satisfaction. By this approach, the physician elicits the patient's understanding of what is and what should occur; the physician explains his or her own understanding; and both patient and physician attempt to achieve a common understanding. The negotiation strategy transforms the doctor-centered view into a patient-centered approach. Evidence is accumulating that this clinical method and similar approaches are associated with improved health care outcomes (Inui, Yourtee, & Williamson, 1976; Katon & Kleinman, 1981; Kleinman, 1980; Lazare, Eisenthal, & Wasserman, 1975).

Society and the Production of Disease and Healing

Berkman (1981) reviews a broad body of evidence indicating that a person's position in the larger society significantly affects his or her morbidity and mortality. Such effects are commonly independent of other risk factors—for example, smoking, alcoholism, and high-fat diet. Though much more research is needed, there is reason to suspect that these pathological effects are more directly psychological and symbolic—perhaps related to a sense of autonomy (i.e., control in one's own life), which in turn affects central nervous system function (see Sterling & Eyer, 1981).

Berkman (1981) cites the research of Kitagawa and Hauser (1973) demonstrating that in the United States, lower social class, as evaluated either by income, education, or occupation, corresponds with dramatically higher mortality from most causes of disease for which data are available. She cites other evidence that this relationship can only in part be accounted for by the recognized risk factors.

Berkman also cites a large variety of evidence concerning migration, the movement within society or between societies, as a cause of disease; she focuses on cardiovascular disease. It has been shown, for example, that the morbidity and mortality of migrants to more industrial societies is higher than that of resident nonimmigrants, and that the morbidity and mortality of second-generation offspring of migrants is less than that of their grandparents. There is also some evidence that the blood pressure of migrants is lower before than after migration, and that migrants who live with people of similar origin have a smaller risk of heart disease than those who live with the members of the "new" society. While there are methodological difficulties with this research with regard to self-selection and the nature and priority of antecedents and consequents, these results are nevertheless suggestive and concordant with other research.

Waitzkin (1981) analyzes the literature on the relationships among medical institutions, occupation, and morbidity and mortality. He cites research demonstrating that for many major infectious diseases, the rate of decline of mortality has been little affected by the advent of specific antibiotic therapies. Nor has the recent and rapidly increasing expense of health care led to corresponding decline of morbidity or mortality. Waitzkin cites prospective random control studies demonstrating that coronary patients with adequate home care do slightly better than similar patients in cardiac care units (Mather et al., 1971). McDermott, Deuschle, and Barnett (1972) have shown that great efforts at introducing technological medicine in a

Navaho community had little effect on the infantile diarrhea–pneumonia complex of diseases, presumably because broader social conditions were not changed at the same time.

Like Waitzkin, I do not argue that our medicine is of no therapeutic value; I do claim, however, that technological medicine, administered without consideration of the social and psychological bases of pathology, is of limited value, and often iatrogenic. Its important positive effects could be multiplied.

Waitzkin cites the striking case of "farmworker's back" in which, by the employers' "economy" in buying shorter- rather than longer-handled hoes, farm workers develop back disease. He surveys other occupational diseases as well. Even in such white-collar occupations as flight control, there is evidence of morbidity in excess of that of pilots (Cobb & Rose, 1973). A society and an economy with different divisions of labor and systems of rewards might produce different patterns of morbidity and mortality. Garfield (1980) suggests that much research on occupations, stress, and disease (again, coronary disease) can be explained by the notion of "alienation," resembling the Durkheimian notion of "anomie."

Brenner (1981) has compiled a large body of data from the United States and Great Britain, demonstrating that morbidity and mortality are associated in several ways with national economic characteristics and fluctuations. Brenner shows that national morbidity and mortality decrease with long-range, gradual economic growth and employment. (For a conflicting interpretation, see Eyer, 1977.) However, morbidity and mortality, including chronic disease (e.g., cardiovascular), increase sharply in periods following sharp fluctuations in economic movement, both in periods of rapid growth and in recessions—that is, in periods of instability. Moreover, like Berkman (1981), Brenner shows that rapid fluctuation more severely affects those of lower social economic status. He suggests that "countries with the higher real per capita income in their poorest populations in conjunction with the most stable economic growth rates should, and typically do, show the lowest mortality rates" (p. 390). As an example, one might cite the great improvement of morbidity and mortality rates in China that has taken place since the revolution of 1949. Complementing this argument, others (e.g., Basch, 1978) have suggested the improvement of public health, diet, and sanitation as sources of the secular decline in mortality.

Finally, there is evidence to suggest that the pathogenic and therapeutic effects of human social relations and their political and economic determinants do not stop at national boundaries, but extend to international relations in the same manner. Navarro (1976), for example, presents evidence that the underdevelopment of health resources in Latin America parallels the general underdevelopment of resources in Latin America (see also E. R. Brown, 1976). Health resources are more available to the wealthy than to the vast majority of the population. As in the United States, medicine is more accessible in urban than in rural areas. And this medicine does not address the prevention of widespread infectious disease and malnutrition, but rather, as in the United States, focuses on cure. Such widespread underdevelopment is the product of the interests of both national and international economic powers seeking to maximize their own capital growth.

Hughes and Hunter (1970) detail the devastating disease consequences of "development" in Africa, where pathogenic side effects work principally by means of movement of pathogens, either by water projects or by the migration of human or animal hosts. Basch (1978) cites broader evidence on relationships between "development" and disease. We should note also the extensive "dumping" in the Third World of pharmaceuticals and other chemical products, banned in the United States for reasons of health (Cultural Survival, 1981).

The seemingly extreme history of the Ivory Coast (Lasker, 1977), from the colonial era to contemporary times of independence, illustrates the power of international interests in the promotion of health and disease. In the colonial period of this region—called with morbid paradox, "the white man's grave"—colonial medicine served primarily the interests of the military in establishing its control throughout the country; the scanty medicine administered to the black population served to reinforce this power. In an exploitative phase of economic development, the institution of broad-scale medicine "for the indigenous population" served, in the words of a French colonial minister, "especially, in our most immediate and practical interest." The minister stated that "human capital" was used to make money capital work better. During a subsequent period of political change and movements toward independence, the allocation of health resources was used in response to specific political situations to promote political stability. Even following independence, while direct international power is no longer obvious, the nation's leaders assert the necessity of subordinating long-term health wants to the prior, purportedly necessary "creation of wealth."

THE PLACEBO–NOCEBO PHENOMENON: EXEMPLAR OF SOCIOCULTURAL EFFECTS IN HEALING AND SICKNESS

Universal and most likely common in all events of human pathology and healing is the so-called "placebo phenomenon." It is claimed that the placebo phenomenon has been the dominant mode of healing throughout the history of human medicine (Shapiro, 1960). It might also be claimed that in the contemporary nonindustrial world, the placebo phenomenon and placebo-like phenomena persist as the major force in healing. Finally, it has also been claimed that even in contemporary, Western, so-called "scientific" medicine (see Dunn, 1976), the placebo phenomenon accounts for one-third of all healing in a great variety of conditions (Beecher, 1955).

To distinguish pleasing, salubrious effects that accord with the etymology of "placebo" from semantically discordant noxious effects, Kissel and Barrucand (1964) have cleverly nominated the "nocebo" effect. I claim here that the nocebo and placebo phenomena comprise a whole in which the culturally fostered expectations of persons (causally) effect what is expected. Simply put, belief sickens; belief kills; belief heals.

The Range and Depth of Ethnomedicogenic Phenomena

PATHOGENIC EFFECTS

Ethnomedical pathogenesis is widely documented, though under disparate labels. Cannon (1942) surveyed the variety of extreme ethnomedicogenic phenomena found in tribal, "traditional" societies: from Australia, where, among some aboriginal peoples, pointing a bone at someone induces quick death in that person, to Latin America and Africa, where belief that one is bewitched also leads to one's rapid "voodoo death." Cannon explained this mortality as a result of prolonged and heightened emotional stress and the concomitant activation of the sympathetic nervous system. He believed that the phenomenon was far more likely to be found among "primitive people, because of their profound ignorance and insecurity in a haunted world, than among educated people living in civilized and well protected communities" (1942, p. 174). For our own society, however, Engel (1971) has described and analyzed the similar phenomenon of "sudden and rapid death during psychological stress" (p. 771), denying conclusive evidence of a causal relationship, but suggesting a physiologism of "rapid shifts between sympathetic and parasympathetic cardiovascular effects" (p. 780). (Engel and others appear to be more cautious in ascribing "psychological" causes than they are in ascribing physical or physiological ones.)

Lex (1974) similarly explains the pathogenesis of voodoo death and the therapy of curing rituals in terms of three stages of "tuning" of the sympathetic and parasympathetic processes of the autonomic nervous system. "Suggestion" passes a lowered threshold of analytic judgment to effect what is suggested. Lex also explains the common requirement of traditional medical systems that healers have suffered the conditions that they come to treat: Their prior illness gives these healers first-hand acquaintance with and sensitivity to the vagaries of the autonomic nervous system.

Lewis (1977) has accurately pointed out that the evidence for "voodoo death," early reviewed by Mauss (1926), is anecdotal—unaccompanied by any report of the victims' other pathology or autopsy. Fuller evidence, however, would be difficult to obtain, since it would require extensive medical records for populations at risk for sorcery or like curses. With such evidence, other pathological causes of death might be evaluated. Fuller evidence would also require autopsy, socially difficult under the charged circumstances of purported "voodoo death." Since "voodoo death" is comparable to our own society's "sudden death," for which much anecdotal material is complemented by some clinical and pathophysiological assessment, the "voodoo death" heuristic does seem to refer to an empirical phenomenon whose complex dimensions are receiving more adequate description.

States of thought, emotion, and expectations are also associated with and precede a great range of morbid conditions short of death. As noted, Engel (1968) has described the "giving-up–given-up complex" in which, generally following an event perceived as stressful, a person "feels unable to cope" and "has no expectations that any change in the environment is possible or will help" (p. 297). This cognitive and emotional complex affects "neurally regulated biological emergency patterns" (p. 293), which in turn facilitate the onset of a variety of morbid conditions. Culturally formed and symbolically mediated "stressful life events" seem to be a common provocation of the "giving-up–given-up complex"—an intellectual and emotional frame of mind that facilitates disease.

Beliefs and expectations sicken and kill. It is difficult to calculate the extent of these morbid effects, but they are far more extensive than is commonly recognized in our medicine.

THERAPEUTIC EFFECTS

Beliefs and expectations also heal. This phenomenon extends beyond those commonly denoted in the literature (Brody, 1977)—that is, the "physical" but "inert" medicines or interventions that are administered either for therapeutic ends or to test the powers of "pharmacologically active" therapies. The common Biomedical perception construes the ambivalent terms "medication" and "administration" as physical "things" rather than as relations; that is, medication is regarded as a concrete object rather than as the social act of giving this "thing." English gerunds allow and mask both possibilities; our medicine has chosen the seemingly more physical and concrete.

The pleasing effects of the placebo phenomenon are not illusory: The placebo effect works to relieve a great variety of pathological conditions of persons, both those with recognized psychological and those with recognized physical signs. Beecher (1955), summarizing a sample of a large number of studies (of even limited "physical" placebo therapies), concludes that for a great variety of conditions, placebo therapies have "an average significant effectiveness of 35.2% ± 2.2%" (p. 1603) (i.e., the percentage of patients for whom there is satisfactory relief).

The placebo response parallels that of "pharmacologically active" drugs. Brody (1977) summarizes these parallels: Placebo effects peak after a certain number of hours following administration; there is a cumulative effect as the placebo is continued over time, a lingering effect after the placebo is stopped, and a decreasing efficacy with increasing severity of symptoms. Placebo drugs (or their administrations) also have toxic "side effects." And they can be addictive, causing withdrawal symptoms when discontinued.

These effects should be surprising only according to a Cartesian principle that regards mental events as nonphysical and physical events as mindless. A recent, somewhat painful experiment on dental patients whose teeth were extracted indicates a physiological concomitant of the placebo effect (Levine, Gordon, & Fields, 1978). In this double-blind study, patients whose pain was significantly diminished on administration of a placebo experienced increased pain (almost at the level of "nonresponders") when then administered naloxone, an opiate antagonist, thought to bind to natural opiate receptors in the brain. It is thus strongly suggested that placebo phenomena are effected through opiate-like substances, which are thus inhibited by "opiate antagonists." An expectation has a corresponding physiological concomitant. (Like many others, this study ignores placebo effects that underlie the physical pills administered—effects that may be common for experimental and control subjects. The experiment measures effects beyond the act of administration itself, those effects that are shared by virtue of experimental design itself. More comprehensive research would control for the effects of administration itself.)

Both Brody (1977) and Jospe (1978) discern great inconsistency in the literature on "placebo responders." It is unclear what kinds of people respond to placebos, or even whether there are kinds who do and kinds who do not. It is uncertain also in what circumstances, including the beliefs of the healer, placebos work. I suggest that the focus of these studies on this *or* that feature of persons or circumstances is insufficient to clarify this phenomenon; especially neglected are the systems of beliefs and expectations of patients, the system of "socialization" by which these are incorporated, and the sociocultural situations in which they are called forth. It is only in an anthropological framework of this breadth that these phenomena will be comprehended.

In the nocebo–placebo phenomenon, what I have earlier distinguished as "construction" becomes a primary element in "production." Since both pathological and therapeutic expectations comprise what we have called an "ethnomedicine," I describe the nocebo–placebo phenomenon as "ethno-medicogenic." Its contents and specifics vary significantly from society to society. It exemplifies the power of culture in human events.

I propose an ethnomedicogenic thesis (Hahn & Kleinman, 1983a; see Figure 9-3), for which much evidence already exists, though more is needed. In a dialectical process, systems of belief and expectation causally effect the reality to which they refer, while this causal efficacy perceptually reinforces the referring ethnomedical system by confirming its beliefs. There is a concentration of events in the belief–reality space toward an axis corresponding to and correlating two ethnomedical divisions—that between pathological and healthy *outcomes*, and that between pathogenic and saludogenic *expectations* concerning these outcomes. The thesis may be graphically, though crudely, represented with "positive" (hopeful) and "negative" (fearful) beliefs and expectations on the vertical axis, and with

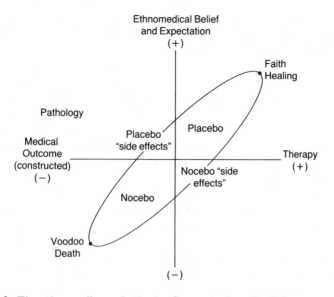

Figure 9-3. The ethnomedicogenic thesis: Concentration of relief–outcome events. (From "Belief as Pathogen, Belief as Medicine, 'Voodoo Death' and the Placebo Phenomenon in Anthropological Perspective" by R. A. Hahn and A. Kleinman. *Medical Anthropological Quarterly*, 1983, *14*(4), 3, 16–19. Reprinted by permission.)

pathological and therapeutic outcomes on the horizontal axis, forming a space of ethnomedical belief–reality possibilities.Waxler (1977) and others have claimed that discriminatory "labeling" of normal variation accounts for the prevalence of psychiatric conditions (see Hahn, 1978). Ethnomedicogenesis defines the limiting powers of "labeling" to effect what is labeled.

It is unlikely that belief in the healing power of large doses of arsenic would transform this chemical into a healing agent; yet I submit, though I will not attempt to prove it, that such a belief would retard its poisonous effects. Likewise, lack of faith in antibiotics may diminish the potency of these drugs, and faith or skepticism about "pharmacologically inert" materials or practices may shift the results in expected directions.

THE SOCIOCULTURAL CAUSATION OF SICKNESS AND HEALTH: FROM BIOMEDICAL ANOMALY TO ANTHROPOLOGICAL PARADIGM

I contend that sociocultural causation in sickness and health, epitomized in the nocebo and placebo phenomena, represents a profound anomaly to the paradigm of Biomedicine. I propose a (medical) anthropological paradigm encompassing Biomedicine within a broader, interdisciplinary understanding in which this anomaly may be resolved.

Brody, in his perspicacious and insightful analysis of the placebo phenomenon (Brody, 1977), goes so far as to explain and *define* the placebo phenomenon as an anomaly for the Biomedical paradigm. As one defining criterion, for example, he specifies, "the change in C [patient's condition] is attributable to I [active intervention], but not to any specific therapeutic effect of I or to any known pharmacologic or physiologic property of I" (p. 41). The logical effect of such a definition is to make the placebo phenomenon and known pharmacological or physiological properties forever incompatible. As the phenomenon falls to the pharmacological or physiological knowledge, so it disappears; as it is known, so it does not exist. It seems strange to define a phenomenon in terms of current nescience. It seems more reasonable and perhaps less dualistic to regard the placebo (and nocebo) phenomena as inexplicable by contemporary psychological or pharmacological knowledge, yet necessarily as compatible with them and likely to be discovered.

The premises of Biomedical thought are seldom made explicit, nor are they uniform among Biomedical specialties or their practitioners (Hahn & Gaines, 1985). Nevertheless, analysis of medical texts and institutions, social relations, symbolism, and practice reveals a strong tendency toward a cultural paradigm (Engel, 1977; Hahn, 1982; Hahn & Kleinman, 1983b) that makes explanation of the powerful placebo and nocebo and other sociocultural phenomena difficult, if not impossible.

Biomedicine manifests seemingly contradictory philosophical premises regarding bodily and nonbodily "things." In one direction, it makes the dualistic, Cartesian assumption that body and mind are fundamentally different sorts of entities. (Descartes [see 1955] believed that bodies had "extension without spirit," and that mind had "spirit without extension," and that these two corporeal and incorporeal "substances" interacted closely through the pineal gland.) This form of dualism allows for the possibility of mutual effects; it also allows for the possibility that the phenomena of each of these two domains may be significantly isolated, and thus may be known and treated in isolation.

In the opposite direction, Biomedicine seems to make the more radical, monistic assumption that while bodily and nonbodily phenomena appear different, this appearance is deceptive: Nonbodily phenomena are in fact essentially reducible to true and real physical and material ones. Until such reductions have been demonstrated, such seemingly nonmaterial occurrences as beliefs and social relations may simply serve as convenient (or inconvenient) labels for phenomena that are not yet well explained. Reduction of this sort is inherently monistic rather than dualistic, for it denies essential reality to one sort of (apparent) "thing."

According to both of these positions, mental and social phenomena are troublesome to the theory and practice of medicine, for they threaten either causative interference from a different realm and/or the engagement of phenomena not well understood. Mental and sociocultural phenomena are most often regarded as peripheral, if not obstructive to the core of medical work—that is, the maintenance or restoration or physiological integrity.

A recent study (Goodwin, Goodwin, & Vogel, 1979) of placebo use by physicians and nurses in a hospital shows that the placebo phenomenon is commonly misunderstood, its powers underestimated. Consistent with a sharply dualistic theory of body and nonbody (i.e., mind), placebos are often administered to show that the patient has nothing "really" wrong, that the purported "pain" is rather "all in his (or her) head." Paradoxically, placebos may be given not only to prove the patient wrong, but also as punishment, thus not to please but to hurt; the patient is thought to receive a "dummy," inert medicine rather than a "real," specific one. Concomitantly, physicians may give placebos to vent their own frustrations at the recalcitrance of patients themselves or their problems. It seems likely that the combined power of the placebo phenomenon and its anomalous position in medical theory make it a highly ambivalent issue; it is applied with ambivalence in situations that are themselves uncertain and ambiguous.

The Biomedical disregard for sociocultural and psychological conditions extends not only to the patient, but to the enterprise and practice of medicine itself. Biomedical work is thought to follow some sort of logic of nature in reaction to statistical deviations from empirically determined, perhaps universal norms (see Boorse, 1977). Biomedical *knowledge* may thus be contrasted with the *belief*, if not the superstition, of patients and practitioners of other ("folk") medicines. Judgment, following cultural values, is often regarded as not essential to the work of medicine; rather, it may be seen as a troublesome hindrance (Hahn, 1985).

The paradigm of (medical) anthropology builds an understanding on premises radically different from those of Biomedicine itself. It does not deny the enormous contributions of Biomedicine to our understanding of human physiology, pathophysiology, and therapeutics. Rather, it situates this understanding within a sociocultural context; it restores human experience, suffering, mental life, social relations, and institutions to the core of medicine; and it insists on the simultaneous engagement of multiple levels, including the physical, the mental, and the social, in the workings of human affairs, health, and disease. By these essential expansions, the anthropological paradigm embraces the Biomedical one while resolving a crucial anomaly.

The model developed here is not widely recognized either as well validated or as radically different from that of Biomedicine itself. In the course of a caustic critique of "holistic health" movements, Glymour and Stalker (1983) have recently argued that medicine should ideally be a scientifically based engineering applied to persons; that behavioral sciences have made only scientifically weak contributions to medicine; that these contributions are in no way excluded from the theory or practice of our medicine; and that "holistic" medicines, presumably including the bio-psychosocial model as well, thus do not constitute paradigmatic (or successful) revolutions against Biomedicine. While much of their critique of holistic medicines is reasonable, I would argue that they have misunderstood the underlying principles and institutions of our medicine, Biomedicine, and in doing so, have underestimated the difference between this paradigm and the holistic form I have supported here.

Though not central to my argument here, I would first suggest that, though perhaps they do not regard such workers as ideals, physicians more closely approximate service, maintenance, or repair personnel than engineers: While each of these may work with great skill, concern, and even love of their subjects, none of the subjects of these crafts (e.g., bridges, vacuum cleaners, elevators) itself has concerns of its own. But more important here, there is much evidence that the theory and institution of our medicine, its forms of socialization and practice, overwhelmingly converge on bodily concerns. Other "matters" are regarded as secondary and marginal; they are denied, avoided, stigmatized, and shunned. Clearly there are exceptions and new directions, but these are clearly exceptions.

Glymour and Stalker (1983) also grossly underestimate the range of scientific evidence connecting mind and society and sickness and health. They focus on mediational effects, and they seem dualistically to relegate "consoling" to a secondary role of physicians (thus essentially an extra-medical role). When they mock the thesis that "mental states affect physical states, and physical states affect mental states" (p. 961) as both undoubted and "trivial," they touch on one of the basic theoretical and research questions of contemporary physiological psychology; neither our language nor the philosophy of mind have even given us good ways to talk or think of this subject.

The model I have developed here builds upon the strong foundations laid by Engel (1977; see also Engel, 1960) in the "biopsychosocial model" and by Brody and Sobel (1979; see also Brody, 1973). I have referred to the model as "sociocultural" because I am exploring and elaborating these aspects of sickness and healing; I have similarly described this model as "anthropological" not to exclude its essential integration of "biopsychosocial' understandings, but to emphasize the multiple roles of cultural definition of the most basic issues of all ethnomedicines and of social organization in the production and mediation of all medical events. My labels are antidotes to some (iatrogenic) Biomedical remedies.

The position I have proposed modifies those explored by Engel and Brody by removing hints of dualism still implicit in their notions of causality, by distinguishing among three forms of sociocultural influence, by insisting on the variety and importance of human culture in the very definition of medical issues, and by formulating the nature of reality (i.e., ontology) and its disciplines that accord with this new position.

Brody and Sobel (1979) apply systems and information theory to the understanding of sickness and healing. They distinguish hierarchical levels (e.g., organs, persons, and societies) of interacting phenomena, as I have recommended here. The elements within levels interact in terms of information; levels also interact with one another by means of information exchanges. In this scheme, Brody and Sobel define health as the "ability of a system (for example, cell, organism, family, society) to respond adaptively to a wide variety of environmental challenges (for example, physical, chemical, infectious, psychological, social)" (pp. 92–93). While they do not define "adaptation," they do note the importance of culture and personal judgment in determining what counts as health. They accordingly define "disease" as "a failure to respond adaptively to environmental challenges resulting in a disruption of the overall equilibrium of the system" (p. 93).

This scheme appears to be not monistic, or even dualistic, but multiplex; while levels interact, each seems to have its distinct reality. While Brody and Sobel claim to eliminate "the sharp distinction between mind and body which has plagued medical thought" (p. 95), their position is still at least Cartesian in that different levels retain fundamentally distinct ontological characteristics. Thus they suggest, "we might expect that psychological disruptions can cause tissue or biochemical manifestations and vice versa" (p. 95).

Engel writes:

> Thus, while the diagnosis of diabetes is first suggested by certain core clinical manifestations, for example, polyuria, polydypsia, polyphagia, and weight loss, and is then confirmed by laboratory documentation of relative insulin deficiency, how these are experienced and how they are reported by any one individual, and how they affect him, all require considerations of psychological, social, and cultural factors, not to mention other concurrent or complicating biological factors. (1977, pp. 131–132)

Psychological, social, and cultural factors are consequences rather than causes of diabetes; they affect their hosts' response. Thus, "psychophysiologic responses to life changes may interact with existing somatic factors to alter susceptibility and thereby influence the time of onset, and severity, and the course of a disease" (Engel, 1977, p. 132), and "Thus, the biochemical defect may determine certain characteristics of the disease, but not necessarily the point in time when the person falls ill or accepts the sick role or the status of patient" (Engel, 1977, p. 132). Most of the effects described here are mediational. While Engel writes of "the role of psychosocial variables in disease causation" and of indirect effects on "underlying biochemical processes," the causation considered seems to be an attenuated one of altering "susceptibility," and then time of onset, severity, and course. It is as if the real disease were truly caused by biochemical and physiological events that were modified by sociocultural events. These modifying events must be taken into account, but they seem to be of a different order of reality.

The position I advocate is more thoroughly monistic, but very different from the monism of Biomedical reductionism. Its central element is the human event rather than human physics or physiology; it is multidisciplinary rather than exclusively natural–scientific. Human events, segmented in time by units of significance (or meaning) that vary from culture to culture, each have multiple aspects or systemic levels, including those of atomic physics, chemistries (inorganic, organic, and biochemistry), physiology, psychology, anthropology, international relations, and even cosmological events (insofar as these affect human existence). Most human events share simultaneous, concurrent interactions at all of these levels. Occurrences at one level do not *cause* occurrences at other levels; rather, they are co-occurrences, different aspects of a common event.

The anthropological paradigm insists that Biomedical interventions, relations, institutions, and so on are social acts—elements of a culture and social system of Biomedicine. Biomedicine is an ethnomedicine. Its thoughts and actions, even its most medical ones, are not logically implied in or induced from nature; rather, Biomedicine is a culturally shaped reaction to and interpretation of nature. As an ethnomedicine, Biomedicine selectively constructs nature; natural resources are employed to cultural ends. While the ethnomedicines constructed by patients and by the healers of other traditions manifest very different qualities, still they share with Biomedicine their nature as ethnomedical versions of the world. They represent and vitally affect our worlds of sickness and healing.

ACKNOWLEDGMENTS

This chapter unites and expands upon two studies undertaken in collaboration with Arthur Kleinman (Hahn & Kleinman, 1981; Kleinman & Hahn, in press). The first was prepared for a symposium on "Symbols, Meaning, and Efficacy in the Healing Process" at the Edinburgh meeting of the Society for Applied Anthropology (April 1981); the second was prepared for a Rockefeller Foundation Conference on "Competing Definitions of Health" (New York, January 1981). Kleinman has been a seminal founder in medical anthropology; his support has been invaluable.

I thank Noel Chrisman for a constructive reading of a draft of this chapter.

REFERENCES

Baechler, J. *Suicides.* New York: Basic Books, 1979.
Basch, P. F. *International health.* New York: Oxford University Press, 1978.
Beck, A. T. Cognition, affect, and psychopathology. *Archives of General Psychiatry,* 1971, *24,* 485–500.

Beecher, H. K. The powerful placebo. *Journal of the American Medical Association*, 1955, *159*, 1602–1606.

Berger, P. & Luckmann, T. *The social construction of reality*. Garden City, N.Y.: Doubleday, 1967.

Berkman, L. Physical health and the social environment: A sound epidemiological perspective. In L. Eisenberg & A. Kleinman (Eds.), *The relevance of social science for medicine*. Dordrecht, The Netherlands: D. Reidel, 1981.

Berkman, L. F., & Syme, S. L. Social networks, host resistance, and mortality: A nine-year follow-up study of Alameda County residents. *American Journal of Epidemiology*, 1979, *109*(2), 186–204.

Boorse, C. Health as a theoretical concept. *Philosophy of Science*, 1977, *44*, 542–573.

Brenner, H. Importance of the economy to the nation's health. In L. Eisenberg & A. Kleinman (Eds.), *The relevance of social science for medicine*. Dordrecht, The Netherlands: D. Reidel, 1981.

Brody, H. The systems view of man: Implications for medicine, science, and ethics. *Perspectives in Biology and Medicine*, 1973, *17*, 71–92.

Brody, H. *Placebos and the philosophy of medicine*. Chicago: University of Chicago Press, 1977.

Brody, H., & Sobel, D. A systems view of health and disease. In D. Sobel (Ed.), *Ways of health* New York: Harcourt Brace Jovanovich, 1979.

Brown, E. R. Public health in imperialism: Early Rockefeller Programs at home and abroad. *American Journal of Public Health*, 1976, *66*(9), 897–903.

Brown, G. W., & Harris, T. *Social origins of depression*. London: Tavistock, 1978.

Bruch, H. *The golden cage*. New York: Random House, 1978.

Cannon, W. B. Voodoo death. *American Anthropologist*, 1942, *44*(2), 169–181.

Chrisman, N. The health-seeking process: An approach to the natural history of illness. *Culture, Medicine and Psychiatry*, 1977, *1*, 351–377.

Cobb, S. Physiologic changes in men whose jobs were abolished. *Journal of Psychosomatic Research*, 1974, *18*, 245–258.

Cobb, S. Social support as a moderator of life stress. *Journal of Psychosomatic Medicine*, 1976, *38*(5), 300–314.

Cobb, S., & Rose, R. M. Hypertension, peptic ulcer, and diabetes in air traffic controllers. *Journal of the American Medical Association*, 1973, *244*(4), 489–492.

Cohen, F., & Lazarus, R. S. Active coping process, coping disposition, and recovery from surgery. *Journal of Psychosomatic Medicine*, 1973, *35*(5), 375–389.

Cultural Survival. Hazardous substances in the Third World. *Cultural Survival Newsletter*, Fall 1981, pp. 2–4.

Descartes, R. *Selections* (R. M. Gaton, Ed.). New York: Charles Scribner's Sons, 1955.

Demers, R. Y., Altamore, R., Mustin, H. Kleinman, A., & Leonardi, D. An exploration of the depth and dimensions of illness behavior. *Journal of Family Practice*, 1980, *11*, 1085–1092.

Dohrenwend, B. S. & Dohrenwend, B. P. *Stressful life events: Their nature and effects*. New York: Wiley, 1974.

Dunn, F. Traditional Asian medicine and cosmopolitan medicine as adaptive systems. In C. Leslie (Ed.), *Asian medical systems*. Berkeley: University of California Press, 1976.

Engel, G. A unified concept of health and disease. *Perspectives in Biology and Medicine*, 1960, *3*, 459–485.

Engel, G. A life setting conducive to illness: The giving-up–given-up complex. *Annals of Internal Medicine*, 1968, *69*(2), 292–300.

Engel, G. Sudden and rapid death during psychological stress: Folklore or folkwisdom? *Annals of Internal Medicine* 1971, *74*, 771–782.

Engel, G. The need for a new medical model: A challenge for biomedicine. *Science*, 1977, *196*, 129–136.

Engel, G. The clinical application of the biopsychosocial model. *American Journal of Psychiatry*, 1980, *137*(5), 535–544.

Eyer, J. Prosperity as a cause of death. *International Journal of Health Services*, 1977, *7*, 125–150.

Garfield, J. Alienated labor, stress, and coronary disease. *International Journal of Health Services*, 1980, *10*(4), 551–561.

Giddens, A. *New rules of the sociological method*. New York: Basic Books, 1976.

Glymour, C., & Stalker, D. Engineers, cranks, physicians, magicians. *New England Journal of Medicine*, 1983, *308*, 960–964.

Goodwin, J. S., Goodwin, J. M., & Vogel, J. M. Knowledge and use of placebo by house officers and nurses. *Annals of Internal Medicine*, 1979, *91*, 106–110.

Gore, S. The effect of social support in moderating the health consequence of unemployment. *Journal of Health and Social Behavior*, 1978, *19*, 157–165.

Gruchow, H. W. Catecholamine activity and infectious disease episode. *Journal of Human Stress*, 1979, *5*(3), 11 17.

Hackett, T. P., & Cassem, N. H. Psychological management of the myocardial infarction patient. *Journal of Human Stress*, 1975, *1*(3), 25–28.

Hahn, R. A. "Is mental illness cured in traditional societies? A theoretical analysis" and "Culture and mental illness: Social labeling perspective": A critique of the work of N. Waxler. *Transcultural Psychiatric Research Review*, 1978, *15*, 157–165.

Hahn, R. A. Treat the patient, not the lab: Internal medicine and the concept of "person." *Culture, Medicine and Psychiatry*, 1982, *6*(3), 219–236.

Hahn, R. A. Rethinking "illness" and "disease." In E. V. Daniel & J. Pugh (Eds.), *South Asian systems of healing* (special issue). *Contributions to Asian studies*, 1984.

Hahn, R. A. A world of internal medicine: Portrait of an internist. In R. A. Hahn & A. D. Gaines (Eds.), *Physicians of Western medicine*. Dordrecht, The Netherlands: D. Reidel, 1985.

Hahn, R. A., & Gaines, H. D. (Eds.). *Physicians of Western medicine*. Dordrecht, The Netherlands: D. Reidel, 1985.

Hahn, R. A., & Kleinman, A. *Belief as pathogen, belief as medicine, "voodoo death" and the placebo phenomenon in the anthropological perspective*. Paper presented at Symbols, meaning, and efficacy in the healing process, a symposium conducted at the meeting of the Society for Applied Anthropology, Edinburgh, April 1981.

Hahn, R. A., & Kleinman, A. Belief as pathogen, belief as medicine, "voodoo death" and the placebo phenomenon in the anthropological perspective. *Medical Anthropological Quarterly*, 1983, *14*(4), 3, 16–19. (a)

Hahn, R. A., & Kleinman, A. Biomedical practice and anthropological theory. In B. J. Siegal, A. R. Beals, & S. A. Tyler (Eds.), *Annual review of anthropology* (Vol. 12). Palo Alto, Calif.: Annual Reviews, 1983. (b)

Hahn, R. A., & Kleinman, A. Biomedicine as a cultural system. In M. Piatelli-Palmarini (Ed.), *The social history of the biomedical sciences*. Milan: Franco Maria Ricci, in press.

Harwood, A. (Ed.). *Ethnicity and medical care*. Cambridge, Mass.: Harvard University Press, 1981.

Helman, C. Disease and pseudo-disease: A case history of pseudo angina. In R. A. Hahn & A. D. Gaines (Eds.), *Physicians of Western medicine*. Dordrecht, The Netherlands: D. Reidel, 1985.

Henderson, S. The social network, support and neurosis: The function of attachment in adult life. *British Journal of Psychiatry*, 1977, *131*, 185–191.

Hopper, K., & Guttmacher, S. Rethinking suicide: Notes toward a critical epidemiology. *International Journal of Health Services*, 1979, *9*(3), 417–438.

Hughes, C. C., & Hunter, J. M. Disease and "development" in Africa. *Social Science and Medicine*, 1970, *3*, 443–493.

Hulka, B. S., Kupper, L. L., & Cassell, J. C. Determinants of physician utilization. *Medical Care*, 1972, *10*, 300–309.

Inui, T., Yourtee, E. L., & Williamson, J. W. Improved outcomes in hypertension after physician tutorials. *Annals of Internal Medicine*, 1976, *84*, 646–651.

Jarvinen, K. A. J. Can ward rounds be a danger to patients with myocardial infarctions? *British Medical Journal*, 1955, *1*, 318–320.

Jospe, M. *The placebo effect in healing*. Lexington, Mass.: Lexington Books, 1978.

Kagan, A., & Levi, L. Health and environment—psychosocial stimuli: A review. *Social Science and Medicine*, 1974, *8*, 225–241.

Katon, W., & Kleinman, A. Doctor–patient negotiation and other social science strategies in patient care. In L. Eisenberg & A. Kleinman (Eds.), *The Relevance for Social Science for Medicine*. Dordrecht, The Netherlands: D. Reidel, 1981.

Katon, W., Kleinman, A., & Rosen, G. Depression and somatization: A review, Parts I and II. *American Journal of Medicine*, 1982, *72*, 127–135, 241–247.

Kissel, P., & Barrucand, D. *Placébos et effet-placébo en médecine*. Paris: Masson, 1974.

Kitagawa, E. M., & Hauser, P. M. *Differential mortality in the United States*. Cambridge, Mass.: Harvard University Press, 1973.

Kleinman, A. *Patients and healers in the context of culture*. Berkeley: University of California Press, 1980.

Kleinman, A., & Hahn, R. A. *The sociocultural model of illness and healing: Rockefeller Foundation working papers*. New York: Rockefeller Foundation, in press.

Kovacs, M. The efficacy of cognitive and behavior therapies for depression. *American Journal of Psychiatry*, 1980, *137*(12), 1495–1501.

Kuhn, T. S. *The structure of scientific revolutions*. Chicago: University of Chicago Press, 1962.

Landy, D. (Ed.). *Culture, disease, and healing*. New York: Macmillan, 1977.

Lasker, J. N. The role of health services in colonial rule: The case of the Ivory Coast. *Culture, Medicine and Psychiatry*, 1977, *1*(3), 277–297.

Lazare, A., Eisenthal, S., & Wasserman, L. The customer approach to patienthood. *Archives of General Psychiatry*, 1975, *32*, 553–558.

Lazarus, R. S. The stress and coping paradigm. In C. Eisdorfer, D. Cohen, A. Kleinman, & P. Maxim (Eds.), *The critical evaluation of behavioral paradigms for clinical psychopathology*. New York: Spectrum, 1981.

Leslie, C. (Ed.). *Asian medical systems*. Berkeley: University of California Press, 1976.

Levine, J. D., Gordon, N. C., & Fields, H. L. The mechanism of placebo analgesia. *Lancet*, 1978, *23*, 654–657.

Lewis, G. Fear of sorcery and the problem of death by suggestion. In J. Blacking (Ed.), *The anthropology of the body*. New York: Academic Press, 1977.

Lex, B. W. Voodoo death: New thoughts on an old explanation. *American Anthropologist*, 1974, *76*, 818–823.

Lindesmith, A., & Strauss, A. L. *Social psychology*. New York: Holt, Rinehart & Winston, 1968.

Lown, B., DeSilva, R., Reich, P., & Murawski, B. Psychophysiologic factors in sudden cardiac death. *American Journal of Psychiatry*, 1980, *137*(11), 1325–1335.

Lumsden, P. Is the concept of stress of any use anymore? In D. Randall (Ed.), *Contributions to primary prevention in mental health*. Toronto: Canadian Mental Health Association National Office, 1981.

Mather, H. G., Pearson, N. G., Read, K. L. Q., Shaw, D. B., Steed, G. R., Thorne, M. G., Jones, S., Guerrier, C. J., Eraut, C. B., et al. Acute myocardial infarction: Home and hospital treatment. *British Medical Journal*, 1971, *3*, 334–338.

Mauss, M. Effet physique chez l'individu de l'idée de mort suggérée par la collectivité (Australie, Nouvelle-Zelande). *Journal de Psychologie Normale et Pathologique*, 1926, *23*, 652–659.

McDermott, W., Deuschle, K. W., & Barnett, C. R. Health care experiment in many farms. *Science*, 1972, *175*, 23–28.

McKinlay, J. B. Social network influences on morbid episodes and the career of help seeking. In L. Eisenberg & A. Kleinman (Eds.), *The relevance of social science for medicine*. Dordrecht, The Netherlands: D. Reidel, 1981.

Mead, G. A. *On social psychiatry* (A. Strauss, Ed.) Chicago: University of Chicago Press, 1956.

Mechanic, D. The concept of illness behavior. *Journal of Chronic Diseases*, 1962, *15*, 180–194.

Mechanic, D. *Medical sociology* (2nd ed.). New York: Free Press, 1978.

Medalie, J. H., Kahn, H. A., Neufeld, H., Riss, E., & Goldbourt, G. Five-year myocardial infarction incidence—II. Association of single variables to age and birthplace. *Journal of Chronic Disease*, 1973, *26*, 329–349.

Meyer, R. J., & Haggerty, R. J. Streptococcal infections in families. *Pediatrics*, 1962, *29*(4), 539–549.

Minuchin, S., Rosman, B. L., & Baker, L. *Psychosomatic families*. Cambridge, Mass.: Harvard University Press, 1978.

Mueller, D. P. Social networks: A promising direction for research on the relationship of the social environment to psychiatric disorder. *Social Science and Medicine*, 1980, *14A*, 147–161.

Navarro, V. *Medicine under capitalism*. New York: Prodist, 1976.

Nuckolls, K. B., Cassel, J., & Kaplan, B. H. Psychosocial assets, life crises and the prognosis of pregnancy. *American Journal of Epidemiology*, 1972, *95*(5), 431–441.

Parsons, T. *The social system*. Glencoe, Ill.: Free Press, 1951.

Porkert, M. *The theoretical foundations of Chinese medicine*. Cambridge, Mass.: MIT Press, 1974.

Rabkin, J. G., & Struening, E. L. Life events, stress, and illness. *Science*, 1976, *194*, 1013–1020.

Rahe, R. H. Life changes and mental illness. *Journal of Human Stress*, 1979, *5*(3), 2–10.

Rahe, R. H., & Arthur, R. Life changes and illness studies. *Journal of Human Stress*, 1978, *4*(1), 3–15.

Reichel-Dolmatoff, G., & Reichel-Dolmatoff, A. *The people of Aritama*. London: Routledge & Kegan Paul, 1961.

Ries, R., Bokan, J., Katon, W., & Kleinman, A. The medical care abuser, differential diagnosis and management. *Journal of Family Practice*, 1981, *13*(2), 257–265.

Sedgwick, P. Illness—mental and otherwise. In A. Caplan, H. T. Engelhardt, Jr., & J. J. McCartney (Eds.), *Concepts of health and disease*. Reading, Mass.: Addison-Wesley, 1981.

Shapiro, A. K. A contribution to the history of the placebo effect. *Behavioral Science*, 1960, *5*, 109–135.

Spradley, J. P., & Phillips, M. Culture and stress: A quantitative analysis. *American Anthropologist*, 1972, *74*, 518–529.

Sterling, P., & Eyer, J. Biological bases of stress-related mortality. *Social Science and Medicine*, 1981, *15E*, 3–42.

Thoits, P. Conceptual, methodological, and theoretical problems in studying social support as a buffer against life stress. *Journal of Health and Social Behavior*, 1982, *23*(2), 145–159.

Turner, V. *The forest of symbols*. Ithaca, N.Y.: Cornell University Press, 1967.

Waitzkin, H. A Marxist analysis of the health care systems of advanced capitalist societies. In L. Eisenberg & A. Kleinman (Eds.), *The relevance of social science for medicine*. Dordrecht, The Netherlands: D. Reidel, 1981.

Waxler, N. Is mental illness cured in traditional societies? *Culture, Medicine and Psychiatry*, 1977, *1*, 223–253.

Young, A. The discourse on stress and the reproduction of conventional knowledge. *Social Science and Medicine*, 1980, *14B*, 133–146.

Young, A. When rational men fall sick. *Culture, Medicine and Psychiatry*, 1981, *5*(4), 317–335.

Zola, I. K. The concept of trouble and sources of medical assistance. *Social Science and Medicine*, 1972, *6*, 673–679. (a)

Zola, I. K. Studying the decision to see a doctor. *Advances in Psychosomatic Medicine*, 1972, *8*, 216–236. (b)

Zola, I. K. Structural constraints in the doctor–patient relationship: The case of non-compliance. In L. Eisenberg & A. Kleinman (Eds.), *The relevance of social science for medicine*. Dordrecht, The Netherlands: D. Reidel, 1981.

10

The Role of Expectancy in Behavior Change

RICHARD R. BOOTZIN

In the past few years, there has been an increased emphasis on expectancy as an explanatory variable in behavior change. Some of the reasons for this change are (1) an increased awareness that placebo manipulations change behavior; (2) a revolution within psychology in which explanatory models of behavior have increasingly relied upon cognitive variables; and (3) a renewed focus on the common ingredients of psychotherapy. I discuss each of these trends in turn and their implications for the investigation of expectancy.

EFFECTIVENESS OF PLACEBOS

This volume is a testament to the current interest in placebo effects. Such interest has not always existed. Placebo effects and expectancy as an explanatory variable have followed the typical course of an artifact described by McGuire (1969). They were first ignored, then treated as contaminants to be controlled, and finally investigated as variables of interest in their own right. Within the behavior change literature, placebos have typically been in the second category—that is, as contaminants to be controlled (e.g., Wilkins, 1979).

The primary method in the therapy literature to control this contaminant has been through the use of placebo control groups. There has been controversy, however, about their function. To some, placebos set a minimum standard of effectiveness that "legitimate" treatments must surpass (e.g., Prioleau, Murdock, & Brody, 1983). For example, the standard methodology in the evaluation of new drugs is to compare the drug against a placebo. The drug must result in more improvement than the placebo in order for the drug to be considered an effective treatment for a particular problem.

Richard R. Bootzin. Department of Psychology, Northwestern University, Evanston, Illinois.

However, it is not really the effectiveness of the drug that is being evaluated, but rather its mechanism of action. The assumption of the model being tested is that the effect of a drug consists of two components, a specific physiological and a nonspecific psychological component, whereas the effect of a placebo consists of only one, the nonspecific psychological component. Thus, it is not total effectiveness that is being evaluated, but the extent to which the physiological component adds significantly to the psychological component.

One problem with this type of model is that it assumes that physiological and psychological components are independent of each other and involve different mechanisms. Such a simple, dualistic model does not accurately describe the interrelatedness of physiological and psychological mechanisms. There are many instances in which psychological stimuli produce or moderate physiological effects, and vice versa. This should not be surprising. Psychological events must have some physical representation in the central nervous system. Thus, experiences that change the psychology of individuals also change their physiology.

To illustrate the subtle interactions that are possible, investigators have found that uncontrollable as compared to controllable stress is associated with faster growth and poorer rejection of cancerous tumors (Sklar & Anisman, 1979; Visintainer, Volpicelli, & Seligman, 1982). Thus, a psychological variable, the controllability of stress, has been found to affect physiological mechanisms involving the immune system (Laudenslager, Ryan, Drugan, Hyson, & Maier, 1983). Another example is the fact that impressive physiological changes can be achieved in response systems once thought to be beyond voluntary control by a psychological intervention, biofeedback (N. E. Miller, 1969). It follows from these illustrations that the so-called "nonspecific" psychological component of taking medication for a particular problem could affect the same specific physiological mechanisms that are affected by pharmacologically active agents.

Despite the inadequacies of the underlying model, drug outcome studies have served reasonably well in identifying drugs that have pharmacological effects. However, there is considerable variability in drug study results, often produced by the "surprising" viability of the placebo. Nevertheless, experimental designs using placebo control groups constitute the standard design in drug outcome research and have similarly been adopted to evaluate the effectiveness of psychological treatment interventions. In psychological treatment research, the control groups are often called "attention placebo controls" to indicate that the attention received from the therapist is being controlled, in addition to other nonspecific or unspecified variables associated with the receipt of treatment.

As in drug studies in which the placebo control groups provide a means to identify the mechanism of action, the attention placebo control groups are used to identify why treatments are effective, not whether they are effective (Cordray & Bootzin, 1983). Although a partition into physiological and psychological components is not relevant, an attempt to distinguish the *specific* effects dictated by theory from the *nonspecific* effects associated with all therapy is relevant. For example, there is substantial evidence that systematic desensitization (SD) is an effective treatment of anxiety disorders (Kazdin & Wilson, 1978; Paul, 1969). Attention placebo control groups are used to evaluate not whether SD is effective, but whether its effectiveness is due to counterconditioning or to the ingredients common to all therapy (Bootzin & Lick, 1979).

Parenthetically, it should be noted that there are experimental designs available to evaluate mechanisms of treatment that do not rely on attention placebo control groups. In fact, because of the practical and ethical problems in developing credible placebo interventions, some have suggested that researchers use alternate experimental designs to evaluate psychological interventions (e.g., O'Leary & Borkovec, 1978). Among the alternate possibilities are (1) the component or element control in which the full treatment is compared to components of the treatment; (2) dose–response designs in which the amount of treatment is varied; and (3) designs in which assessment of the degree of realization of treatment is related to subsequent change. However, evaluations of psychological interventions, particularly behavior therapy, have frequently employed placebo control groups. Thus, it is possible to evaluate the effectiveness of placebo control groups as compared to other psychological treatments.

Early behavior therapy research typically found that SD was superior to the attention placebo control, indicating that SD was effective because of principles from counterconditioning theory (Davison, 1968; Lang, Lazovik, & Reynolds, 1965; Paul, 1966). As many have pointed out, however, the placebo must be as credible as the treatment to which it is being compared (e.g., Baker & Kahn, 1972; Borkovec & Nau, 1972; Lick & Bootzin, 1975).

There are many factors that influence the credibility of an attention placebo therapy, including therapy rationale, therapeutic instructions, experiences during therapy implying improvement, subtle cues from the therapist, the context of the evaluation, and the apparent appropriateness of the treatment for the problem. For example, placebos in drug studies have been found to differ in effectiveness and in the extent to which they produce side effects, depending upon the drugs to which they were being compared (A. K. Shapiro & Morris, 1978). Credibility and effectiveness may also vary for different problems. Thus, an attention placebo treatment found to be effective for phobias (Lick, 1975; Marcia, Rubin, & Efran, 1969) has been ineffective as a treatment for insomnia (Lick & Heffler, 1977).

Whereas attention placebo controls in early behavior therapy research tended to be ineffective, in later research credible attention placebo controls were developed that were as effective for some problems as traditional behavior therapies such as SD (Kazdin & Wilcoxon, 1976; Kirsch, Tennen, Wickless, Saccone, & Cody, 1983; Lick, 1975; Lick & Bootzin, 1975).

More generally, Smith, Glass, and Miller (1980), in a meta-analysis of 475 psychotherapy outcome studies, found an average effect size of .56 for placebo treatment compared to an average effect size of .80 for psychotherapy. They concluded that their findings indicated "the surprisingly strong showing of placebo treatments" (p. 186).

Although attention placebo controls have sometimes been found to be very effective, two qualifications should be noted. First, the treatment to which the placebo is being compared may be a weak implementation. For example, in order to keep the amount of therapy constant in all groups, treatments are often limited to a set number of sessions. This could limit the effectiveness of therapy if a substantial number of subjects did not reach a theoretically relevant criterion (e.g., completing the hierarchy in SD). Further, even a fully implemented SD is not the most effective treatment available for many specific fears and phobias. With animal phobias, treatments that involve *in vivo* exposure and performance feedback, such as participant modeling, have been found to be substantially more effective than SD (Bandura, Blanchard, & Ritter, 1969; Leitenberg, 1976; Marks, 1978). Thus, the apparently remarkable effectiveness of placebos may in part be due to comparisons with weak and weakly implemented treatments. While it is important to understand the mechanisms involved in the placebo effects, it is also essential to continue to search for more effective treatments. For example, in a review of outcome studies of insomnia, I (Bootzin, 1977) found that placebos resulted in a mean reduction in sleep latency of only 25%, compared to mean reductions of 45% and 75% for relaxation treatments and stimulus control instructions, respectively.

The second qualification regarding the effectiveness of placebos involves the severity of the problem. Specific treatments may be more effective than placebos only with severely disabled patients. For example, it was found (Murphy & Bootzin, 1973) that even repeated testing resulted in substantial improvement in mildly snake-fearful children. Participant modeling was found to be significantly superior to repeated testing only with those children who were moderately or severely fearful. Similarly, Nicolis and Silvestri (1967), in a two-night evaluation of hypnotics for the treatment of insomnia, found that a placebo was as effective as phenobarbital with mild and moderate insomniacs. Only with severe insomniacs was phenobarbital more effective than the placebo.

As mentioned at the beginning of this section, most earlier research on placebos dealt with placebo effects as contaminants to be eliminated in evaluating legitimate therapeutic interventions. In the process, however, evidence accumulated that placebos were often themselves very effective, and thus deserved investigation in their own right. Although there are qualifications that must be made in evaluating the evidence, a large body of literature indicates that placebos frequently have substantial effects. Thus, much is to be gained by attempting to understand the mechanisms involved in the effectiveness of placebos.

COGNITIVE THEORIES

A second reason for an increased emphasis on expectancy has been the extension of the cognitive revolution to theories of behavior change. During the 1950s and 1960s, the behavioral perspective drew primarily upon theories of learning for the theoretical underpinnings for behavior therapy interventions. The contrasting cognitive model in psychotherapy was not a learning model, but a psychodynamic model in which insight was considered an important, if not a necessary, feature of subsequent change.

Increasingly, however, it became apparent that the explanatory power of traditional learning explanations of behavior change could be increased by including cognitive mediating mechanisms. Thus, there have been cognitive challenges and subsequent modifications of learning theory. In one of the first studies of cognitive mediation, N. E. Miller (1935) demonstrated that a physiological response could be conditioned to a cognitive stimulus. Miller shocked subjects to the letter "T" but not the number "4" read out loud. Subjects were then instructed to think "T" and "4," alternately, in a series of trials. Subjects had galvanic skin responses when they thought "T," but not when they thought "4."

Although Miller's research expanded Pavlovian conditioning to include cognitive stimuli, it did not challenge the basic model. Conditioned responses (CRs) would be elicited by conditioned stimuli (CSs), whether the stimuli were cognitive or overt. However, contemporaries of Miller, such as Tolman (1948), proposed a more explicit cognitive learning theory. According to Tolman, learning resulted in a new cognitive organization, which in turn mediated subsequent performance. In experiments on latent learning, Tolman (1948) proposed that rats learned the map of a maze during unreinforced exploratory trials. Reinforcement affected the speed of performance, but not the degree of learning. Learning took place without reinforcement.

Research in modeling and observational learning is the modern descendent of Tolman's research on latent learning. Just as Tolman's research demonstrated that reinforcement is not necessary for learning, so do modeling and observational learning experiments. It has been repeatedly found that individuals can learn by observing others being reinforced. The person observing does not overtly engage in the response to be learned and is not directly reinforced for the response. Thus, observational learning must involve symbolic processes. There is evidence that observational learning occurs both in skill acquisition and in the acquisition and extinction of emotional responses (Rosenthal & Bandura, 1978).

Similar demonstrations of the capacity of symbolic processes to elicit emotional and behavioral changes have been documented by research on hypnosis, autogenic training (Schultz & Luthe, 1959), verbally induced anxiety (Lang, 1977; Sipprelle, 1967), verbally induced depression and elation (Velten, 1968), and aversive conditioning procedures such as covert sensitization that employ imagined pairs of CSs and unconditioned stimuli (UCSs) (Cautela, 1967).

Symbolic processes are also involved in the transmission of information about feared objects or events. Although there is little formal evidence, experience from everyday life clearly indicates that anxiety can be induced by information alone (Rachman, 1978). Information and instructions are constantly used—by parents, for example—to teach distinctions between situations that are not dangerous and situations that are dangerous and, therefore, to be feared. A person walking alone at night in parts of a city that he or she has been told are dangerous may become anxious even if he or she has never previously been mugged or observed a mugging. The anticipation of feared consequences is likely to lead to cognitive rehearsal of the feared event, thereby inducing emotional arousal.

Because of the important role that modeling, information, imagery, and language have in mediating behavior, it is plausible that emotional reactions and defensive behavior are centrally controlled. In contrast, from a traditional Pavlovian conditioning view, images and language are covert stimuli that have acquired their capacity to elicit emotional responses through prior conditioning (Wolpe, 1978). However, there have been cognitive challenges to Pavlovian conditioning as well. For example, individuals improve in their ability to verbally induce elation, depression, and emotional arousal. If symbolic stimuli are covert CSs, then repeated practice (without the presentation of a UCS) should lead to extinction of the emotional reaction. That this does not happen indicates that emotional responses are at least partially centrally controlled rather than purely the result of prior Pavlovian conditioning (Bootzin & Max, 1980).

Additionally, recent theories of Pavlovian conditioning have focused on the information contained in the stimulus rather than on the traditional association of CS and UCS through contiguity. For example, Wagner and Rescorla (1972) proposed that Pavlovian conditioning of a CS depends on the new information that the CS provides about the magnitude or occurrence of the UCS. This model explains findings such as the Kamin blocking effect that are contradictory to contiguity theories. Kamin (1969) found that if an animal is given a series of conditioning trials in which a particular CS (B) is always followed by a UCS, and then another series of conditioning trials with a compound CS (A and B) followed by the UCS, a CR is not elicited by A alone. According to the Wagner and Rescorla information model, A does not acquire associative strength when it is paired with B because it provides no new information about the occurrence of the UCS.

Reiss (1980) proposed an expectancy model of fear acquisition in humans that derived from Wagner and Rescorla's information model. According to Reiss, Pavlovian conditioning is itself a cognitive process: " . . . what is learned in Pavlovian conditioning is an expectation regarding the occurrence or nonoccurrence of a US onset or a change in US magnitude or duration" (p. 387). However, conditioning is only one way to change expectancies. Cognitive learning and the observation of models change expectancies just as associative learning and covert conditioning do.

In applying this model to phobias, Reiss (1980) identified two types of expectancies, danger and anxiety expectancies. Danger expectancy is the anticipation of physical danger or social rejection. Anxiety expectancy is the anticipation of anxiety, or the person's fear of becoming anxious. According to this model, different therapeutic interventions may be required for the different types of expectancies.

Attention placebo treatments may be particularly effective at ameliorating anxiety expectancies. For example, Kirsch et al. (1983) found that a highly credible expectancy modification procedure was of equivalent effectiveness to SD in the modification of fear of snakes in a clinical population. In addition, expected anxiety was highly correlated with fear both before and after treatment. As a result, the authors concluded that both the attention placebo treatment and SD were effective because of their effects on the patients' expectancy, which in turn primarily affected anticipatory anxiety.

Reiss's theory is not the only current theory of behavior change to focus on expectancies. Without attempting a comprehensive review, suffice it to say that of the different types of expectancies investigated, many are variations of expectancies of predictability and control. Both predictable aversive events and aversive events over which the organism can exert control are experienced as less stressful than those that are unpredictable and/or uncontrollable (Thompson, 1981). Controllability, in particular, has been found to have wide-ranging psychological and physiological effects. For example, as described earlier, uncontrollable aversive events can affect the immune system and facilitate the growth of cancerous tumors (Laudenslager et al., 1983). The organism's response to uncontrolled aversive events has also been used as a model for the psychological as well as the neurobiochemical features of depression (W. R. Miller, Rosellini, & Seligman, 1977; Weiss, 1982). Further, Bandura (1977, 1982) has made expectations of control (efficacy expectations) the central concept in his theory of behavior change.

Bandura (1977) distinguishes between two types of expectations: outcome expectancies, the belief that a given behavior will lead to particular outcomes; and efficacy expectancies, the belief that "one can successfully execute the behavior required to produce the outcomes" (p. 193). Thus, a person who is afraid of flying may have high outcome expectancies (the plane will make it to the destination) but low efficacy expectancies (the person may not expect to be able to manage his or her distress sufficiently in order to get on the plane). In addition, high efficacy expectations are related to perseverance of effort at a task and the maintenance of therapeutic improvement (Bandura, 1982). As can be seen in this example, there are similarities between Reiss's anxiety expectancies and Bandura's efficacy expectancies. Bandura's concept is broader, however, and is not limited to an analysis of phobias. Efficacy expectancy would also apply in situations in which anxiety is not elicited, such as performing a new task. In Bandura's view, efficacy expectations—and not anxiety—are the primary determinants of coping and defensive behavior, since people who are anxious sometimes do continue to engage in coping behavior despite emotional arousal.

An important feature of Bandura's theory that distinguishes it from other expectancy theories is a subtheory of how efficacy expectations are developed. According to Bandura (1977), efficacy expectations are derived from four types of information. The major determinant of efficacy expectations is performance feedback from prior experiences. Thus, therapeutic interventions that change performance directly and provide experiences of mastery will have the strongest effect on efficacy expectations and on subsequent behavior. Vicarious experience, verbal persuasion, and feedback from autonomic arousal also affect efficacy expectations, but not as strongly as performance feedback. From this theory, it would not be expected that placebos would have as powerful an effect on either efficacy expectations or subsequent behavior as would interventions that directly provide mastery experiences.

COMMON INGREDIENTS OF PSYCHOTHERAPY

During the past few years, there has been a renewed interest in the commonalities of psychotherapy. One indication of this interest has been the growth of eclectic psychotherapy (Garfield, 1980). Most clinical psychologists identify themselves as eclectic rather than as belonging to a particular school of psychotherapy. They are inclined to believe that they take the best from all therapies. This movement has also led to an emphasis on ingredients common to all therapy. Among the most central of these ingredients is the patient's expectation of benefit (Garfield, 1982), which is also frequently assumed to be the variable responsible for the effectiveness of placebos.

Parenthetically, I have called this a *renewed* focus on the common ingredients of therapy, because there is an earlier literature that emphasized that experienced, as opposed to novice, therapists from different schools of therapy treated patients very similarly (Fiedler, 1950). There has also been a continuing emphasis on the client's expectation of benefit as one of the central common ingredients (Goldstein, 1962). For example, Frank (1961, 1983) has repeatedly proposed that the central ingredient in much psychotherapy is that the client's hopes are inspired by the therapist and help to combat the client's demoralization. This help can even be transmitted during the initial interview.

A major impetus for the focus on the common ingredients of psychotherapy was the large-scale meta-analysis of therapy outcome studies by Smith *et al.* (1980). In an analysis of 475 therapy outcome studies, they found that psychotherapy was more effective than no treatment and that different types of therapy had about equivalent effectiveness. Effectiveness was measured by the average effect size for each therapy across all measures from comparisons of treatment with no-treatment control groups. Smith *et al.* (1980) concluded that their analysis emphasized the need for attention to the commonalities shared by all therapies.

It is not necessary to endorse Smith *et al.*'s methodology or conclusions to recognize the influence their study has had upon the therapy outcome literature. It is beyond the scope of this chapter to discuss meta-analytic methodology, but it should be noted that there is a burgeoning literature discussing its advantages, disadvantages, and possible solutions (e.g., Light, 1983). Nevertheless, the Smith *et al.* (1980) study has become a sort of watershed with regard to psychotherapy research. It was published at a time when psychotherapists were coming under increased demand from third-party payers (such as insurance companies and the U.S. government) to demonstrate the effectiveness of their interventions. Therapists could point to the Smith *et al.* findings to indicate that psychotherapy was indeed effective, and, furthermore, that all therapies were approximately equivalent and thus should all be reimbursable.

Not everyone who has evaluated the therapy outcome literature has concluded that the commonalities are most important. For example, Andrews and Harvey (1981) reanalyzed only the studies from the larger Smith *et al.* (1980) data set in which "neurotics" had sought or been referred for treatment. They found that behavioral therapies had a significantly higher average effect size than verbal dynamic psychotherapies.

To avoid the problem in a meta-analysis of giving equal weight to both strong and weak studies, Kazdin and Wilson (1978) reviewed only methodologically strong outcome studies that directly compared different treatments. They found that most studies showed behavior therapy to be the most effective treatment. Although a number of studies found no difference between treatments, none found any other type of treatment to be more effective than behavior therapy. Behavior therapy was also found be be more effective than alternative treatments in many problem areas not included by Smith *et al.* (1980), such as the treatment of addiction, the institutional management of psychotic disorders, and the treatment of such childhood disorders as bedwetting and hyperactivity.

Since behavior therapists have typically prided themselves on developing interventions based on specific learning principles, it is tempting to conclude that any superiority of behavioral interventions must be due to specific principles of behavior change rather than to the factors common to all therapies. However, the therapy outcome literature does not address this question directly. Effectiveness and expectancy are typically confounded. It may be that interventions differ in effectiveness because they differentially elicit expectancy of benefit.

D. A. Shapiro (1981) has called this the "expectancy arousal hypothesis"; that is, "treatments differ in effectiveness only to the extent that they arouse in clients differing degrees of expectation of benefit" (p. 112). In support of this hypothesis, Shapiro (1981) found that the rationales of therapies that had been demonstrated in the literature to differ in effectiveness differed similarly in ratings of credibility. Although consistent with an expectancy arousal hypothesis, this is by no means definitive evidence. First, as Shapiro (1981) acknowledges, the credibility ratings were not obtained from the same populations as those receiving therapy. Thus, client expectations might be very different than those obtained by Shapiro. Second, and more importantly, there is the question of the determinants of the credibility ratings themselves. It may be that raters can accurately predict which among broad classes of therapies are going to be most effective, based on their previous experience with similar treatments or parts of treatments. Thus, it may not be that expectancies cause subsequent change as much as that they are a prediction of subsequent change based upon previous experience. For example, expectations of benefit obtained in the middle or at the end of therapy have been found to reflect the degree of improvement already experienced (Lick, 1975).

While the concern with common ingredients of therapy has focused attention on expectancy, this literature has not disentangled mechanisms of effectiveness from expectancy. It is as likely that they are reciprocally related as that one has causal precedence over the other.

HOW DOES EXPECTANCY CHANGE BEHAVIOR?

The previous sections have described the convergence of emphasis on expectancy as an explanatory variable in behavior change. In this section, I discuss the relationship between expectancy and behavior. Expectancy has both direct cognitive effects and indirect mediated effects that change behavior.

Direct Cognitive Effects

A number of theories described earlier propose that behavior change is mediated directly by changes in expectancy (Bandura, 1977; Reiss, 1980; D. A. Shapiro, 1981). If a person expects to be able to cope with a problem, he or she will be better able to cope. If a person expects anticipatory anxiety to be diminished, emotional reactivity will be diminished. According to these theories, the final common pathway to predicting subsequent therapeutic change is the person's expectancy. However, not all expectancy manipulations are equally effective. Expectancy theories acknowledge that there are many ways in which expectancies can be changed, including performance feedback, associative learning, observational learning, information, persuasion, feedback from autonomic responses, and other symbolic processes. The more reliable the information upon which the expectancies are based, such as performance feedback (Bandura, 1977) or associative learning over many trials (Reiss, 1980), the stronger the expectancy and the more likely that subsequent behavior will correspond to it.

Expectancy is only one of many cognitive variables that have been investigated. Others include goals, plans, strategies, motives, and values (e.g., Mischel, 1973, 1979). Rather than limit discussion to one cognitive variable, expectancy, and its relationship to behavior, it may be useful to consider the broader context of cognitive organization. One way of conceptualizing the relationship of cognitive variables and behavior is by means of schemas. A "schema" is a knowledge structure that specifies the defining features of some stimulus domain. Schemas "help to structure, organize, and interpret new information; they facilitate encoding, storage, and retrieval of relevant information; they can affect the time it takes to process information, and the speed with which problems can be solved" (Crocker, Fiske, & Taylor, 1984, p. 201).

One type of schema that may have particular relevance to the present discussion is the self-schema. "Self-schemas are knowledge structures about the self that derive from past experience and organize and guide the processing of the self-relevant information contained in the individual's social experiences" (Markus, 1983, p. 547). They not only describe the past self, but also define future possible selves (Markus, 1983). Performance feedback and other experiences that influence expectancy are modulated by self-schemas (Goldfried & Robins, 1982). Thus, self-schemas are active cognitive structures that frame situations, encode experience, and include generalizations about the self, such as expectancies, values, and plans.

To illustrate, a common goal of therapy is to help change the patients' views of themselves from people who are victims of a problem to people who are capable of coping with the problem. The self-schemas of "victim" versus "coper" would have different implications regarding efficacy expectations, anticipatory affect, and willingness to confront the problem. Thus, from this perspective, expectancy is just one of a number of associated features of a schema, rather than the sole determinant of behavior. Current research on schemas has focused primarily on the information-processing effects of schemas. However, as the illustration indicates, it may be useful to consider the schema as the organizing structure determining the interrelationships among cognitive structure, affect, and behavior.

Mediated Cognitive Effects

A theory regarding expectancy manipulations must account for the cognitive, behavioral, and autonomic changes that constitute improvement. Although some of these changes may be produced by direct cognitive effects, it may be that changes in expectancy lead to changes in behavior that bring into play other behavior change principles, such as extinction through exposure, self-reinforcement, and covert conditioning (Bootzin & Lick, 1979; Lick & Bootzin, 1975).

Perhaps the major effects of changes in expectancy are changes in motivation. Patients with increased expectancies regarding their ability to cope are likely to confront their problems in order to test the hypothesis that they are better able to cope. Exposure to feared stimuli has been found to be therapeutic, while avoidance has not (Greist, Marks, Berlin, Gournay, & Noshirvani, 1980). Increased exposure is likely to result in both fear extinction and self-reinforcement for behavioral improvement.

In a recent study of dental fear, Bernstein and Kleinknecht (1982) found that five treatments, including an attention placebo control, were equivalently effective. The authors concluded that all treatments shared two elements that were essential for therapeutic gain. First, the treatments decreased anticipatory anxiety and enabled patients to enter dental care with decreased stress reactivity. As mentioned earlier, the effects of placebo treatments may be particularly focused on anticipatory anxiety (Reiss, 1980). Second, the treatments allowed for direct exposure to dental care that was minimally aversive, allowing for extinction of fear.

Another way in which expectancy may mediate behavior change is through changes in covert rehearsal. We have already seen that it is possible to induce changes in anxiety and mood through verbal and imagery techniques. The person receiving a supposedly effective therapy may reduce the number of self-defeating thoughts and images in which he or she engages and may increase the frequency of coping self-statements and positive images. This analysis suggests that greater attention should be paid to the patient's encounters with phobic stimuli outside of the therapy session, including cognitive activity occurring before, during, and after such encounters.

The preceding analysis of how expectancy changes behavior just scratches the surface regarding a theoretical understanding of placebos. While most research on placebos has been directed at evaluating their effectiveness or eliminating placebo effects as contaminants, it is time to focus our efforts on attempting to understand the mechanisms underlying their effectiveness. In the process, we may further our understanding of the general relationships among cognition, affect, and behavior.

REFERENCES

Andrews, G., & Harvey, R. Does psychotherapy benefit neurotic patients?: A reanalysis of the Smith, Glass, and Miller data. *Archives of General Psychiatry*, 1981, *38*, 1203–1208.

Baker, B. L., & Kahn, M. A reply to "Critique of 'Treatment of insomnia by relaxation training': Relaxation training, Rogerian therapy, or demand characteristics." *Journal of Abnormal Psychology*, 1972, *79*, 94–96.

Bandura, A. Self-efficacy: Toward a unifying theory of behavioral change. *Psychological Review*, 1977, *84*, 191–215.

Bandura, A. Self-efficacy mechanism in human agency. *American Psychologist*, 1982, *37*, 122–147.

Bandura, A., Blanchard, E. B., & Ritter, B. Relative efficacy of desensitization and modeling approaches for inducing behavioral, affective, and attitudinal changes. *Journal of Personality and Social Psychology*, 1969, *13*, 173–199.

Bernstein, D. A., & Kleinknecht, R. A. Multiple approaches to the reduction of dental fear. *Journal of Behavior Therapy and Experimental Psychiatry*, 1982, *13*, 287–292.

Bootzin, R. R. Effects of self-control procedures for insomnia. In R. Stuart (Ed.), *Behavioral self-management: Strategies and outcomes*. New York: Brunner/Mazel, 1977.

Bootzin, R. R., & Lick, J. R. Expectancies in therapy research: Interpretive artifact or mediating mechanism? *Journal of Consulting and Clinical Psychology*, 1979, *47*, 852–855.

Bootzin, R. R., & Max, D. Learning and behavioral theories. In I. L. Kutash & L. B. Schlesinger (Eds.), *Handbook on stress and anxiety*. San Francisco: Jossey-Bass, 1980.

Borkovec, T. D., & Nau, S. D. Credibility of analogue therapy rationales. *Journal of Behavior Therapy and Experimental Psychiatry*, 1972, *3*, 257–260.

Cautela, J. R. Covert sensitization. *Psychological Reports*, 1967, *20*, 459–468.

Cordray, D. S., & Bootzin, R. R. Placebo control conditions: Tests of theory or effectiveness? *Behavioral and Brain Sciences*, 1983, *6*, 286–287.

Crocker, J., Fiske, S. T., & Taylor, S. E. Schematic bases of belief change. In J. R. Eiser (Ed.), *Attitudinal judgment*. New York: Springer, 1984.

Davison, G. C. Systematic desensitization as a counterconditioning process. *Journal of Abnormal Psychology*, 1968, *73*, 91–99.

Fiedler, F. E. A comparison of therapeutic relationships in psychoanalytic, nondirective, and Adlerian therapy. *Journal of Consulting Psychology*, 1950, *14*, 436–445.

Frank, J. D. *Persuasion and healing: A comparative study of psychotherapy*. Baltimore: Johns Hopkins University Press, 1961.

Frank, J. D. The placebo is psychotherapy. *Behavioral and Brain Sciences*, 1983, *6*, 291–292.

Garfield, S. L. *Psychotherapy: An eclectic approach*. New York: Wiley, 1980.

Garfield, S. L. Eclecticism and integration in psychotherapy. *Behavior Therapy*, 1982, *13*, 610–623.

Goldstein, A. P. *Therapist–patient expectancies in psychotherapy*. New York: Macmillan, 1962.

Goldfried, M. R., & Robins, C. On the facilitation of self-efficacy. *Cognitive Therapy and Research*, 1982, *6*, 361–380.

Greist, J. H., Marks, I. M., Berlin, F., Gournay, K., & Noshirvani, H. Avoidance versus confrontation of fear. *Behavior Therapy*, 1980, *11*, 1–14.

Kamin, L. J. Predictability, surprise, attention, and conditioning. In B. A. Campbell & R. M. Church (Eds.), *Punishment and aversive behavior*. New York: Appleton-Century-Crofts, 1969.

Kazdin, A. E., & Wilcoxon, L. A. Systematic desensitization and nonspecific treatment effects: A methodological evaluation. *Psychological Bulletin*, 1976, *83*, 729–759.

Kazdin, A. E., & Wilson, G. T. *Evaluation of behavior therapy: Issues, evidence and research strategies*. Cambridge, Mass.: Ballinger, 1978.

Kirsch, I., Tennen, H., Wickless, C., Saccone, A. J., & Cody, S. The role of expectancy in fear reduction. *Behavior Therapy*, 1983, *14*, 520–533.

Lang, P. J. Imagery in therapy: An information processing analysis of fear. *Behavior Therapy*, 1977, *9*, 962–886.

Lang, P. J., Lazovik, A. D., & Reynolds, D. J. Desensitization, suggestibility, and pseudotherapy. *Journal of Abnormal Psychology*, 1965, *70*, 395–402.

Laudenslager, M. L., Ryan, S. M., Drugan, R. C., Hyson, R. L., & Maier, S. F. Coping and immunosuppression: Inescapable but not escapable shock suppresses lymphocyte proliferation. *Science*, 1983, *221*, 568–570.

Leitenberg, H. Behavioral approaches to treatment of neuroses. In H. Leitenberg (Ed.), *Handbook of behavior modification and behavior therapy*. Englewood Cliffs, N.J.: Prentice-Hall, 1976.

Lick, J. Expectancy, false galvanic skin response feedback, and systematic desensitization in the modification of phobic behavior. *Journal of Consulting and Clinical Psychology*, 1975, *43*, 557–567.

Lick, J., & Bootzin, R. Expectancy factors in the treatment of fear: Methodological and theoretical issues. *Psychological Bulletin*, 1975, *82*, 917–931.

Lick, J. R., & Heffler, D. Relaxation training and attention placebo in the treatment of severe insomnia. *Journal of Consulting and Clinical Psychology*, 1977, *45*, 153–161.

Light, R. J. (Ed.). *Evaluation studies review manual* (Vol. 8). Beverly Hills, Calif.: Sage, 1983.

McGuire, W. J. Suspiciousness of experimenter's intent. In R. Rosenthal & R. L. Rosnow (Eds.), *Artifact in behavioral research*. New York: Academic Press, 1969.

Marcia, J. E., Rubin, B. M., & Efran, J. S. Systematic desensitization: Expectancy change or counterconditioning? *Journal of Abnormal Psychology*, 1969, *74*, 382–387.

Marks, I. Behavioral psychotherapy of adult neurosis. In S. L. Garfield & A. E. Bergin (Eds.), *Handbook of psychotherapy and behavior change: An empirical analysis*, (2nd ed.). New York: Wiley, 1978.

Markus, H. Self-knowledge: An expanded view. *Journal of Personality*, 1983, *51*, 543–565.

Miller, N. E. *The influence of past experience upon the transfer of subsequent training*. Unpublished doctoral dissertation, Yale University, 1935.

Miller, N. E. Learning of visceral and glandular responses. *Science*, 1969, *163*, 434–445.

Miller, W. R., Rosellini, R. A., & Seligman, M. E. P. Learned helplessness and depression. In J. D. Maser & M. E. P. Seligman (Eds.), *Psychopathology: Experimental models*. San Francisco: W. H. Freeman, 1977.

Mischel, W. Toward a cognitive social learning reconceptualization of personality. *Psychological Review*, 1973, *80*, 252–283.

Mischel, W. On the interface of cognition and personality: Beyond the person–situation debate. *American Psychologist*, 1979, *34*, 740–754.

Murphy, C. M., & Bootzin, R. R. Active and passive participation in the contact desensitization of snake fear in children. *Behavior Therapy*, 1973, *4*, 203–211.

Nicolis, F. B., & Silvestri, L. G. Hypnotic activity of placebo in relation to severity of insomnia: A quantitative evaluation. *Clinical Pharmacology and Therapeutics*, 1967, *8*, 841–848.

O'Leary, K. D., & Borkovec, T. D. Conceptual, methodological, and ethical problems of placebo groups in psychotherapy research. *American Psychologist*, 1978, *33*, 821–830.

Paul, G. L. *Insight versus desensitization in psychotherapy: An experiment in anxiety reduction*. Stanford, Calif.: Stanford University Press, 1966.

Paul, G. L. Outcome of systematic desensistization II: Controlled investigation of individual treatment technique variations and current status. In C. M. Franks (Ed.), *Behavior therapy: Appraisal and status*. New York: McGraw-Hill, 1969.

Prioleau, L., Murdock, M., & Brody, N. An analysis of psychotherapy versus placebo studies. *Behavioral and Brain Sciences*, 1983, *6*, 275–310.

Rachman, S. *Fear and courage*. San Francisco: W. H. Freeman, 1978.

Reiss, S. Pavlovian conditioning and human fear: An expectancy model. *Behavior Therapy*, 1980, *11*, 380–396.

Rosenthal, T., & Bandura, A. Psychological modeling: Theory and practice. In S. L. Garfield & A. E. Bergin (Eds.), *Handbook of psychotherapy and behavior change: An empirical analysis* (2nd ed.). New York: Wiley, 1978.

Schultz, J. H., & Luthe, W. *Autogenic training: A physiologic approach in psychotherapy.* New York: Grune & Stratton, 1959.

Shapiro, A. K., & Morris, L. A. Placebo effects in medical and psychological therapies. In S. L. Garfield & A. E. Bergin (Eds.), *Handbook of psychotherapy and behavior change: An empirical analysis* (2nd ed.). New York: Wiley, 1978.

Shapiro, D. A. Comparative credibility of treatment rationales: Three tests of expectancy theory. *British Journal of Clinical Psychology*, 1981, *20*, 111–122.

Sipprelle, C. Induced anxiety. *Psychotherapy: Theory, Research, and Practice*, 1967, *4*, 36–40.

Sklar, L. S., & Anisman, H. Stress and coping factors influence tumor growth. *Science*, 1979, *205*, 513–515.

Smith, M. L., Glass, G. V., & Miller, T. J. *The benefits of psychotherapy.* Baltimore: Johns Hopkins University Press, 1980.

Thompson, S. C. Will it hurt less if I control it?: A complex answer to a simple question. *Psychological Bulletin*, 1981, *90*, 89–101.

Tolman, E. C. Cognitive maps in rats and men. *Psychological Review*, 1948, *55*, 189–208.

Velten, E. A laboratory task for induction of mood states. *Behaviour Research and Therapy*, 1968, *6*, 473–482.

Visintainer, M. A., Volpicelli, J. R., & Seligman, M. E. P. Tumor rejection in rats after inescapable or escapable shock. *Science*, 1982, *216*, 437–439.

Wagner, A. R., & Rescorla, R. A. Inhibition in Pavlovian conditioning: Applications of a theory. In R. A. Boakes & M. S. Halliday (Eds.), *Inhibition and learning.* New York: Academic Press, 1972.

Weiss, J. M. *A model for neurochemical study of depression.* Paper presented at the annual meeting of the American Psychological Association, Washington, D.C., August 1982.

Wilkins, W. Expectancies in therapy research: Discriminating among heterogeneous nonspecifics. *Journal of Consulting and Clinical Psychology*, 1979, *47*, 837–845.

Wolpe, J. Cognition and causation in human behavior and its therapy. *American Psychologist*, 1978, *33*, 437–446.

11

Discussion

The Apprehension of the Placebo Phenomenon

DAVID BAKAN

The chapters by Bootzin and by Hahn are exercises in the apprehension of the placebo phenomenon. Apprehension is an extremely important feature of the development of science. Thus, for example, the shift from apprehending the sun as moving across the sky to apprehending it as an apparent motion resulting from the revolution of the earth constituted a profoundly important step in the history of science. Both chapters are also important steps toward the development of a *theory* of the placebo. Both chapters respond to the placebo as a phenomenon in search of context of meaning.

Both chapters are also very empirical. In reading them, I thought of an older view of empiricism, in which "empirical" is *constrasted* with "scientific." Today "empirical" and "scientific" are virtually synonymous. Yet there was a time when they were not. The distinction was often made within medicine, in which empirical physicians, on the basis of their own experience, stood opposed to the scientific information that they could only accept on authority, since they did not have access to either the laboratories or the esoteric theorizing of those who were involved in scientific enterprises. The connection to the issue at hand may even be closer, since it may well have been precisely the placebo effect that historically buttressed the obstinacy of the empirical physicians.

One of the things that makes the placebo phenomenon problematic is that while there is ample evidence of its existence, there is almost no place into which it fits easily and comprehensibly within established scientific contexts. Both of these chapters attempt to make a place for the placebo phenomenon within scientific contexts. Bootzin's chapter identifies expectancy as the critical feature of the phenomenon, and attempts to show that it is equally a critical feature in the psychology of learning and of psychotherapy. Hahn's chapter takes expectancy as a phenomenon that rests more

David Bakan. Department of Psychology, York University, Toronto, Ontario, Canada.

comfortably in a culturological than in a biological view of health and sickness, and it takes the very existence of the placebo phenomenon as an argument for the appropriateness of the former view.

The problem lies in our metaphysics, in our view of the nature of reality. The commonest, best established, and most readily comprehensible metaphysical view is that the ultimate reality consists of material particles and their motions in time, with all other phenomena resulting from the interactions among these particles. Mental phenomena constitute *empirical* challenges to this metaphysical view. Various versions of dualism, interactionism, double aspectism, dualism with materialistic reductionism, and dualism with mentalistic reductionism (such as solipsism) have all sought to make some metaphysical accommodation to the patently empirical dual reality of the physical and the mental. The fact of the matter is that, to this day, no fully satisfactory metaphysical position has been developed, in spite of the many claims in the philosophical and scientific literature that the mental–physical duality problem has been solved or satisfactorily circumvented.

We can easily accommodate ourselves to a situation of metaphysical uncertainty. My own conviction is that we can make progress in science without solving ultimate questions first. Biology has made great progress without solving the problem of what life is. Physicists have learned a great deal about light without having knowledge of the ultimate nature of light. It is quite possible to learn a great deal about the placebo phenomenon without having to answer the question of how mental events can possibly have an effect upon physical events. *Empirically* they do, however much some metaphysical orientations might indicate that such effects are impossible.

In both of these chapters, I find a sense of obligation on the part of the authors to have solved the metaphysical problem as a precondition. Bootzin, for example, seems compelled to say that "Psychological events must have some physical representation in the central nervous system" (see p. 197). This proposition, of course, does not arise from observations of representations of psychological events in the central nervous system. It results from a metaphysical point of view that demands that there be some physical representation somewhere in the physical organism, with the central nervous system being regarded as a likely locus. This view comes to us not from Descartes originally, but goes back at least to Plato's *Timaeus*, a book from which we also got the idea that hysteria is the result of a wandering uterus. Similarly, Hahn's excellent defense of the significance of the sociocultural in the "construction, production, and mediation" of medical events stands quite well on the basis of empirical observations, and inferences from them. It does not require entry into the metaphysical question of the relationship between the mental and the physical.

There is, however, a major feature intrinsic to the placebo phenomenon that I believe should have been dealt with in such theoretical contexts as these chapters seek to provide, and that I fail to find dealt with. This is the element of *falsity* that is associated with the placebo phenomenon. If we allow, as both authors indicate, that expectancy is a critical feature of the placebo phenomenon, the placebo entails expectancy that, even within the cultural context that Hahn emphasizes, is *groundless*. For the placebo effect is one in which the effect takes place quite precisely in cases in which the expectancy is falsely grounded. What makes the placebo effect interesting, of course, is that an expectancy that is not adequately grounded should indeed have any effect at all, let alone a positive effect.

It is the groundlessness that makes the placebo phenomenon interesting. The tablet is a placebo because, say, it gets rid of the pain when there is no ground for believing that the tablet has the pharmacological property of reducing pain. The problem is more complex in connection with religious healing. The phenomena of contemporary healings by Jesus constitute manifestations of the placebo only if one thinks that there are no grounds for the heavenly Jesus interceding in response to prayer. Dealing with this— especially from the relentlessly culturological point of view of Hahn, who even sees the effect of culture as mitigating the poisonous effects of arsenic—has its own difficulties. The placebo becomes the placebo not out of culture as such, but out of cultural diversity.

It is important to recognize that the history of science itself is a history of struggle with respect to beliefs, of struggle over questions of the *grounds* of belief, and of struggle over eliminating falsity. The possibility that one might advocate the use of the placebo as a therapy is met by a scientific sensitivity conditioned by centuries of the struggles of science to win acceptability. Currently the medical profession, having won its modern respect on the grounds of its scientism, and even maintaining its monopoly among healing approaches because of its scientism, would understandably resist allowing legitimacy to something that, in its essence, is grounded in groundlessness.

Let us allow, as Bootzin suggests, that we think of the placebo phenomenon as in a class with psychotherapy in general. As such, we then have to contend with the deepest feature of one of the major psychotherapies, psychoanalysis. Falsity has a major place in psychoanalysis. It is falsity that is, in psychoanalytic theory, the cause of the psychological disturbance. Overcoming the falsity is regarded as the major means of therapy. The difficulty that the person experiences, according to the psychoanalytical point of view, results from the repression of truths and memories. Restoration of accurate apprehension, achieving "insight," is the working aim of psychoanalysis. There is a contradiction between the image of exploration and discovery as the appropriate mode of therapy that comes from psychoanalysis, and the conjuring to produce expectations that are known to be groundless that is associated with the possible advocacy of the use of placebos.

Lastly, the problem of falsity of the placebo has to be considered together with the role of trust in therapy. We allow that trust itself has to be considered as an important part of any therapeutic relationship. Not least, the trust that a patient might have is associated with the reduction of stress, and with the greater compliance in the modes of treatment that are being prescribed. The deliberate use of the placebo effect—that is, the deliberate building up of an expectation on a foundation known to be groundless—introduces the possibility of a reduction of trust, when and if the groundlessness should become known. This could be a seriously deleterious "side effect" of placebo treatment.

12

Expectancy, Therapeutic Instructions, and the Placebo Response

FREDERICK J. EVANS

INTRODUCTION

Although the placebo response in medicine has been widely recognized (Shapiro, 1970), it has generally been regarded as a nuisance variable. The routine inclusion of a control group receiving an inert or nonspecific medication has been considered an essential methodological control, particularly in evaluating the pharmacologically active components of psychoactive drugs. The double-blind methodology was designed as a powerful method of controlling "demand characteristics" (Orne, 1970)— those inadvertent cues that emanate from the investigator, the hypotheses of the subject about what is being investigated, and clues derived from the procedure itself that influence the behavior of the subject in any investigation. The placebo control methodology implicitly recognizes that the interaction among the doctor, the patient, and the drug-taking ritual has powerful effects on response to medication and treatment.

A quite different interpretation should be given to the placebo effect. The placebo effect should be considered as a potent therapeutic intervention in its own right, rather than merely a nuisance variable. The placebo can be understood as if it were another active (pharmacological) agent whose positive (and sometimes negative) effects can be independently evaluated, and whose mode of action is worthy of independent investigation. Two questions are addressed here: (1) How powerful is the placebo in terms of clinical efficacy? (2) To what extent is the placebo effect mediated by verbal and nonverbal expectational factors?

Frederick J. Evans. Carrier Foundation, Belle Mead, New Jersey; Department of Psychiatry, UMDNJ–Rutgers Medical School, Piscataway, New Jersey.

UBIQUITOUS PLACEBO

The history of the placebo response is almost the history of pharmacy. In 1952, Dunlop, Henderson, and Inch reviewed 17,000 British medical prescriptions and concluded that 30% of the drugs prescribed were placebos, in the sense that they were even then known to have no specific effects on the conditions for which they were prescribed.

The anecdotal and empirical accounts of the potency of the placebo effect are legion. For example, in one study, 30% of a large number of patients reported decreased sex drive, 17% increased headache, 14% increased menstrual pain, and 8% increased nervousness and irritability. These were all side effects of the administration of a *placebo* in a double-blind study of oral contraceptives (Aznar-Ramos, Giner-Velazquez, Lara-Ricalde & Martinez-Manautou, 1969). In a double-blind study of a cold vaccine, 7% of patients in both groups reported toxic side effects requiring additional medical intervention. Double-blind studies will often list iatro-genic side effects found in the placebo group, but these symptoms will differ markedly from study to study. In contrast to the study of oral contraceptives, it is not surprising that in double-blind studies with antihistamines, fatigue and sleepiness are reported. Obviously the target symptoms monitored are different. In an antihistamine study, it is unlikely that the investigators would inquire about decreased sex drive and headaches among females.

Significant placebo effects have been found in studies of adrenal gland secretion, angina, blood cell counts, blood pressure, common cold, cough reflex, fever, gastric secretion and motility, headache, insomnia, oral contraceptives, various kinds of pain, pupil dilation and constriction, respiration, rheumatoid arthritis, vaccines, vasomotor function, and warts (Haas, Fink, & Hartfelder, 1959). Placebos have inhibited gastric acid secretion, bleeding ulcers, and the effects of ipecac, and have reduced adrenocortical activity and serum lipoproteins (Bush, 1974). Placebo effects can be shown in addiction and withdrawal programs. Boleloucky (1971) showed chronic dependence with withdrawal symptoms for several years on a placebo after it has been substituted for morphine. The substitution of placebo during gradual withdrawal of multiple medications using the pain cocktail method (Fordyce, 1976) is a standard procedure in many chronic pain inpatient programs.

Placebo effects have certainly not been limited to pharmacological studies. For example, Dimond, Kittle, and Crockett (1960) evaluated the placebo effect of a surgical procedure for the treatment of angina pain involving the ligation of the mammary arteries. There was no difference between the real and sham surgery on the angina pain: Physiological changes, including the inverted T wave, were found in both groups.

The pharmaceutical industry has recognized that important expecta-tional variables and components of the pill-taking ritual themselves have profound effects on the efficacy of their products. Red or pink stimulants work better than blue ones; multiple-colored capsules or large brown–green or small red–orange or pink pills work better than other color combinations, particularly the traditional small white tablet. Brand-name-labeled aspirin, and an identical-appearing placebo, give better results than either combination labeled generically (Shapiro, 1970).

THE EFFICACY OF PLACEBO ANALGESIA

Although placebo responses have been observed in studies of almost all pharmacological agents, they have been most extensively studied in comparison with analgesic drugs for clinical pain control. Reviewing 15 double-blind studies of active analgesic drugs, Beecher (1959) concluded that about 35% of 1082 patients suffering from a wide variety of severe traumatic and postoperative pains could be significantly relieved by the double-blind administration of placebo medication. In a review of similar studies from 1959 to 1974 (F. J. Evans, 1974), Beecher's conclusions were confirmed: In 11 double-blind studies involving 908 pain patients, an average of 36% achieved at least 50% relief from pain following placebo medication. Thus, placebos are effective in reducing severe clinical pain to about half of its original intensity for about a third of suffering patients.

This result needs to be reinterpreted, since it is recognized that potent analgesic drugs do not necessarily relieve pain completely. The efficacy of placebo must be evaluated relative to the efficacy of the active drug with which it is being compared. A standard dose of morphine, for example, will successfully reduce subjective pain intensity by half in only about 75% of patients. Even when the dose is increased, 10–15% of patients will not obtain significant relief. A better way to evaluate the effectiveness of placebo relative to morphine is to allow for the fact that a standard injection of morphine is sometimes unsuccessful in reducing pain. This can be achieved by comparing placebo as a drug of unknown potency with a standard drug (morphine) of known effectiveness. The efficacy of an unknown analgesic can be determined by calculating an index of drug efficiency, expressed as the ratio:

$$\frac{\text{Reduction in pain with unknown active drug}}{\text{Reduction in pain with known analgesic}}$$

For example, if a mild analgesic such as codeine is compared with morphine, the index of efficiency for codeine compared to morphine is less than 1.00, but if codeine is compared with aspirin, the index is likely to be greater than 1.00; this indicates that codeine is less powerful than morphine, but more powerful than aspirin. What is the efficiency of placebo compared to morphine? From six available double-blind studies (excluding crossover

Table 12-1. Illustration of Calculation of Index of Drug Efficiency for Evaluating Placebo Efficiency Compared to Analgesic Drugs

---

Index of analgesic drug efficiency:

$$\frac{\text{Reduction in pain with unknown drug}}{\text{Reduction in pain with known analgesic (typically morphine)}}$$

Pain criterion:

Reduction in pain by 50% of initial level over drug level,
or
change in pain of 50% on rating scale (typically 10- or 5-point)

Index of placebo efficiency for morphine:
(averaged across six double-blind non-crossover-design studies)

$$\frac{\text{Reduction in pain with placebo}}{\text{Reduction in pain with morphine}} = 56\%$$

---

trials), the index of placebo efficiency compared to a standard dose of morphine averaged .56. Thus, on the average, placebo is 56% as effective as a standard injection of morphine in reducing severe clinical pain of various kinds (see Table 12-1).

There are nonspecific factors involved in the process of giving an injection or a pill that have no known active pharmacological effects on the patient, but that nevertheless produce salutary therapeutic effects, and even increase the potency of the drug itself. What mechanisms account for these impressive therapeutic changes?

MECHANISMS OF PLACEBO RESPONSE

Three factors have usually been discussed when accounting for the placebo response: (1) suggestion; (2) anxiety; and (3) the expectancy-mediated attributes of the doctor–patient relationship. A fourth explanation, specific to pain control, suggests the placebo response may be mediated by endorphins; this explanation will be briefly discussed first.

Placebo Analgesia Mediation by Endorphins

Some recent studies (Levine, Gordon, & Fields, 1978) have suggested that the placebo response may be based on physiological and biochemical actions specifically related to the endorphins. They have reported that the narcotic antagonist naloxone may block the pain-killing effects of morphine, and (perhaps more controversially) the endorphins themselves. Naloxone may have effects other than as a narcotic antagonist, such as mild arousal and increased systolic blood pressure. Unfortunately, there are a number of problems, untested assumptions, and failures to replicate (F. J. Evans, 1981b; Goldstein & Grevert, 1978; Gracely, 1983; Grevert, 1983; Grevert & Goldstein, 1977; Mihic & Binkert, 1978; Sjolund & Ericksson, 1978), which raise serious questions about these provocative studies.

Placebo, Suggestibility, and Hypnosis

Historically, many investigators have equated "placebo" and "suggestion" without specifying precisely what they mean by either term. In general, however, the few available clinical and experimental studies have found no consistently significant relationship between the placebo response and a variety of measures of suggestibility (reviewed in F. J. Evans, 1969, 1974). In addition, the placebo response is uncorrelated with susceptibility to hypnosis. However, even in subjects who are incapable of experiencing deep hypnosis, the context of hypnosis itself may (like any other powerful therapeutic intervention) produce a placebo effect. The placebo effect of the hypnotic situation is an expectational effect, which must be distinguished from whatever specific effects hypnosis itself may produce in deeply hypnotizable individuals.

This conclusion was supported (F. J. Evans, 1977, 1981a; McGlashan, Evans, & Orne, 1969; Orne, 1974) by administering an ischemic muscle pain task during three sessions: (1) during highly motivated baseline conditions; (2) following the induction of hypnotic analgesia; (3) after ingestion of a placebo capsule (presented to the subjects as an experimental pain-killing drug), serving as a control procedure against which to evaluate the effects of hypnosis. In the placebo session, the experimenter believed subjects were randomly given placebo or Darvon compound in double-blind fashion. Half of the 24 subjects were selected from the top 5% of the hypnotic responsivity distribution and half from the bottom 5% of the range of hypnotic ability. A simple but compelling deception procedure was used to legitimize an expectancy of analgesia for the unhypnotizable subjects. An independent experimenter induced a "glove" analgesia, using a hypnotic relaxation induction geared to each subject's prior minimal hypnotic experiences. This was tested by administering a brief electric shock to the fingers. These unhypnotizable subjects experienced the analgesia because the experimenter surreptitiously turned down the shock intensity from the preanalgesic test level. The logic of this study was to maximize the placebo response, as is done in the clinic, rather than to control or eliminate it, as is done in traditional studies.

The improvement shown by these extremely hypnotizable and un-hypnotizable subjects in tolerating excruciating ischemic muscle pain under suggestions of hypnotic analgesia, and subsequently after ingesting a placebo, is illustrated in Figure 12-1. Three aspects of the results should be noted:

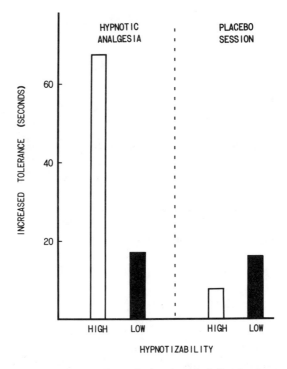

Figure 12-1. Improved ability to tolerate ischemic pain following hypnotic analgesia and following a placebo pill in extremely high- and low-hypnotizable subjects ($n = 24$).

1. There was a dramatic increase in pain tolerance for deeply hypnotizable subjects during hypnotically induced analgesia. This was presumably an effect directly attributable to the dissociative aspects of the hypnotic condition when it occurred in highly responsive hypnotic virtuoso subjects.

2. The much smaller but significant placebo-induced pain reduction was equal in magnitude for both highly hypnotizable and unhypnotizable subjects. Thus, there was no correlation between response to placebo and hypnotic responsivity.

3. Of most theoretical importance, the hypnotic analgesia suggestions significantly reduced pain even for unhypnotizable subjects who did not have the ability to enter hypnosis. This can be labeled as a "placebo component" of the hypnotic situation. Indeed, for these hypnotically insusceptible subjects, the pain relief produced by the placebo component of the hypnotic context and that produced by the placebo component of ingesting a pill were about equal and highly correlated (.76, $n = 12$). The expectation that hypnosis can be helpful in reducing pain produced similar significant reductions in pain as the expectations derived from taking a pain-killing pill, particularly in those individuals who otherwise had no special hypnotic skills.

From this study and other evidence, it can be concluded that there are placebo components not only in drug studies, but in any treatment situation. Nonspecific factors are always present with any treatment modality— acupuncture, biofeedback, behavior therapy, hypnosis, psychotherapy, surgery, or even Grandmother's special potion. Any method of treatment occurs in a context in which the specific techniques are viewed by the patient as plausible, and by the therapist as likely to be effective.

Anxiety and Placebo

Placebo effects are often attributed to anxiety reduction. Administering a placebo may lead to a reduction of anxiety, which may in turn be accompanied by a decrease in the perception of suffering. It is important to distinguish between two types of anxiety. Some people chronically experience relatively high levels of anxiety as a personality trait or a stable characteristic of their life style. However, there are specific occasions involving stress in which even a relatively nonanxious person may temporarily feel highly anxious. The day before surgery is a good example of a time in which anxiety is both adaptive and appropriate to the specific situation, but is nevertheless relatively transitory.

In the study described above (F. J. Evans, 1977; McGlashan, Evans, & Orne, 1969), chronic (Taylor, 1953) and situational (Zuckerman, 1960) anxiety were measured several times during the session in which 24 subjects were administered the ischemic muscle pain task after ingesting a placebo. The results are presented in Figure 12-2. Chronic anxiety was not directly related to the increased ability to tolerate the ischemic pain following the ingestion of a placebo. However, changes in situationally relevant anxiety led to important placebo-induced changes in pain tolerance. Anxiety levels increased substantially in 10 subjects after taking the placebo; for these fearful subjects, the excruciating dull aching pain was tolerated significantly less well. In contrast, for 14 subjects, anxiety levels decreased between the time they took the placebo and the time they performed the pain task. Their ability to tolerate pain longer was significantly improved.

This study found that if a subject was a chronically anxious person who temporarily found his or her anxiety level reduced, the improvement in pain tolerance was quite extensive. Even if he or she was not a chronic worrier, the subject's feeling of calm and well-being after ingesting a placebo, which had been legitimized as an effective treatment, led to a significant increase in the ability to tolerate pain. These results, along with other recent studies, suggest that a placebo-induced reduction in suffering can be expected in a context in which anxiety is concomitantly reduced.

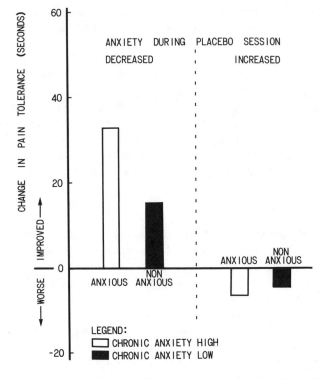

Figure 12-2. Relationship among placebo response (change in ischemic pain tolerance), chronic (trait) anxiety, and situational (state) anxiety ($n = 24$).

Expectation, Belief, and the Doctor–Patient Relationship

It appears that placebo response is mediated by expectancies generated within the context of the doctor–patient relationship. The mediation of belief systems about the plausibility of treatment and anticipated clinical change can be shown in a review of double-blind studies evaluating the effectiveness of a placebo in reducing pain compared to other standard analgesic medications. As noted above, placebo has been found to be 56% as effective as a standard dose of morphine in reducing clinical (postoperative) pain in a number of double-blind studies. Using the same procedures, it is possible to evaluate the effectiveness of placebo compared to presumably less potent analgesics, such as aspirin, Darvon, and codeine. Table 12-2 shows the results of such an evaluation.

Surprisingly, the index of placebo efficiency from nine studies for aspirin, 54%, is virtually the same as the index for morphine from six studies, 56%! It is also nearly the same for the intermediate-strength analgesics Darvon and codeine (54% and 56%, respectively, from two studies each)

Table 12-2. Index of Placebo Efficiency Comparing Placebo with Morphine, Aspirin, Darvon, and Zomax (Derived from Available Single-Trial Double-Blind Published Studies)

Number of double-blind studies	Placebo efficiency for	%
6	Morphine	56
9	Aspirin	54
2	Darvon	54
2	Codeine	56
3	Zomax	55

and Zomax (55% from three studies). In other words, the effectiveness of a placebo compared to standard doses of different analgesic drugs under double-blind circumstances seems to be relatively constant. This is indeed a rather remarkable and unique characteristic for any therapeutic agent! The effectiveness of the placebo is proportional to the apparent effectiveness of the active analgesic agent.

It is worth noting that this 56% effectiveness ratio is not limited to comparing placebo with analgesic drugs. It is also found in double-blind studies of nonpharmacological insomnia treatment techniques (58% from 13 studies) and psychotropic drugs for the treatment of depression such as tricyclics (59% from 93 studies reviewed by Morris & Beck, 1974) and lithium (62% from 13 studies reviewed in Marini, Sheard, Bridges, & Wagner, 1976). Thus, it appears that placebo is about 55–60% as effective as active medications, irrespective of the potency of these active medications.

Expectancy Effects in Drug–Placebo Studies: Some Examples

There are many other studies in the pain, psychiatric, and medical literature showing that patient/subject expectancies and the hope for relief mediated by doctor/experimenter cues and expectations can account for the pervasiveness of the placebo response (Frank, 1973). For example, placebos are more effective when the pain is more severe (Beecher, 1956). In one study, Beecher (1956) reported that severe pain was relieved by morphine and by placebo in 52% and 40% of the patients, respectively; for moderate pain, 62% and 35%, respectively; for mild pain, 77% and 26%, respectively. In addition, effects of drugs and placebo are interactive rather than additive. For placebo reactors, the likelihood of responding to morphine was 95%; however, for placebo nonreactors, only 55% of patients responded to morphine (Lasagna, Mosteller, von Felsinger, & Beecher, 1954). Hankoff, Freedman, and Engelhardt (1958) reported that among schizophrenic placebo responders, only 20% required subsequent rehospitalization when treated with neuroleptic drugs, but 80% of placebo nonresponders required rehospitalization. A recent unpublished study by Melzack, Jeans, Taenzer, and Kinch (1982) confirmed the 56% effect—but only for the more potent of two analgesic agents in a double-blind study involving a placebo and two different analgesics (diflunisal and acetaminophen). They concluded that in a double-blind study of more than one drug, the placebo value is determined by the most effective drug.

Lyerly, Ross, Krugman, and Clyde (1964) showed that subjects reported either stimulant or depressant effects, according to the experimenter's instructions, after taking amphetamine. Both stimulant and depressive effects, depending on instructions, were obtained after taking a depressant medication (chloral hydrate). Similarly, when two habitual LSD users believed they received LSD but got a placebo, typical hallucinogenic experiences were reported, but no effects were obtained when they were actually given LSD under the belief that it was a placebo (Reed & Witt, 1965). A newspaper report ("New 'Thrill Drug,'" 1967) indicated extensive hallucinogenic experiences at a shore resort when analysis indicated that the substance being ingested was an inert peppermint-flavored sugar cube.

In a series of seven consecutive studies of the treatment of schizophrenic patients, Bishop and Gallant (1966) showed that chlorpromazine was significantly better than placebo. The effects of drug and placebo were in the same relative proportion, but the absolute effect of both declined in each study. Presumably the interaction created by the changes in expectations of the observers, as the powerful, newly released "wonder" drug was gradually found to be less effective clinically and produced fewer side effects, led to lowered vigilance and monitoring and to a consequent "weakening" of the nonspecific expectations. In a similar vein, Engelhardt, Margolis, Rudorfer, and Paley (1969) were perhaps the first to document that more powerful clinical effects were obtained when patients were perceived by raters as having received psychoactive medication, even though they received placebo. Conversely, poorer clinical results were obtained if the patients actually ingested active medication, but were perceived by the doctors or themselves as having ingested placebo. Not surprisingly, the placebo effect is highest in double-blind studies, is lower in single-blind studies, and is lower still in nonblind or open-label studies (Batterman & Lower, 1968).

If we can generalize from these studies, it appears that when the patient as well as the physician believe that a powerful drug is being used, a strong placebo effect is obtained in a double-blind administration. If, however, it is assumed that the medication is less effective, a much smaller placebo effect is obtained, even though it is still proportionately about half as effective as the actual analgesic. The conviction of the therapist about the drug's potency—which presumably communicates itself to the hopeful patient in terms of the plausibility and expectation that it will work, and the consequent reduction of anxiety—seems to be a powerful mediator of therapeutic effectiveness.

CLINICAL IMPLICATIONS AND USE OF PLACEBOS

Clinically, the question is often asked about when (if ever) it is justified to knowingly administer a placebo to reduce a patient's pain, symptoms, or suffering. Space precludes discussion of issues of ethics and informed consent with placebo (Silber, 1979), except to say that if the implicit treatment contract is to help the patient to get better, and if placebos are considered as active treatment, then the issues are no different from those involved in informed consent for any other form of treatment.

A trial on placebo may be warranted where active medication is contraindicated, or where the active medication is too slow in working. Some patients accept the pill-giving ritual as sufficiently indicative of promised relief that the anxiety-reducing nature of the ritual itself is symptom-alleviating. Placebo can occasionally be substituted successfully in a drug withdrawal program. This is difficult, though not impossible, when withdrawal symptoms are likely. Placebo can be used effectively as a substitute for an active drug that is no longer needed or medically safe for a chronically ill patient. A rationale is presented to the patient in terms of substituting a "new powerful medication without side effects that will help reduce your pain." When this approach is supported by other behavioral and cognitive treatment strategies, it can be very effective clinically—for example, in the development of the "pain cocktail" approach to chronic pain (Fordyce, 1976).

The most important single use of placebo, however, is diagnostic. A trial on placebo that is accompanied by significant, even if transient, symptom relief gives powerful leverage for developing a meaningful therapeutic program. Unfortunately, response to placebo, particularly in pain patients, is usually incorrectly interpreted as evidence that the symptom is not "real"; it is psychological and functional, rather than real and organic (from the patient's point of view, all pain is "real"). Instead, positive response to placebo not only indicates that, for the patient, expectancy and hope for further success in therapy is realistic; for the therapist, it indicates that the patient, at some cognitive level, has the resources to be able to influence, modulate, and control his or her pain (or other symptom). Of course, similar leverage can be obtained from other adjuncts, such as hypnosis or biofeedback, as well as from "pills." If handled skillfully, the combined faith and self-control capacity is a positive indication of therapeutic success.

Some of these principles are illustrated in a case (B. J. Evans, 1978) of a 9-year-old girl who complained of pains in the left temple, abdomen, and both knees. This had persisted for about 5 years, and she was taking at least four aspirins per day, which usually controlled the pain for about 40 minutes. She lived in a remote, rural area, which was visited by a pediatric neurologist once every other month. She was referred for underachievement at school. She was the oldest of three. At birth, she had had a tracheoesophageal fistula and two bouts of pneumonia. Possibly due to unconfirmed interference with ganglia in the tracheal and laryngeal areas, she sweated only on the right side of the face. She did not discriminate salt or sugar on either side of the tongue—an anomalous finding, as this neurological deficit should have led to lack of discrimination only on the left side. There was no evidence that these neurological signs had anything to do with the headaches, and all other neurological test results, including X-ray and EEG, were normal.

Because of the neurologist's infrequent visits, permission was obtained from the mother, with the girl's enthusiastic consent, to try a "new, more powerful medication" that would not produce the side effects she was experiencing from the aspirin. She was allowed to take one of the "powerful" new pills as needed. At 2 and 6 months afterward, the headaches had virtually stopped, and the school problems were being rapidly resolved. Use of placebo in this situation seemed well indicated because of the potential medical risk of the continued excessive use of aspirin and the lack of any apparent medical reason for the headaches. The brief, powerful intervention involved the visiting specialist from the city with the newest in medical treatment, and this was apparently sufficient to set in motion those expectancies of change that allowed the young girl to give up her debilitating symptoms and make a readjustment to her family and educational circumstances.

SUMMARY

The reported findings have implications for understanding how a pharmacologically inactive substance can produce marked therapeutic effects. The conviction of the therapist about an analgesic drug's potency presumably communicates itself to the anxious patient, and legitimizes a plausibility and expectation that it will work. Belief creates its own promise of relief when the patient learns that he or she has nothing to fear but fear itself. The reduction of fear through the shared expectations and beliefs that the doctor's "special medicine" will work—even if it is a placebo—mediates powerful therapeutic effects.

ACKNOWLEDGMENT

I wish to thank Helen M. Pettinati, Kenneth S. Mathisen, Julie Wade, Sarah Robin, and Leslie Martin for their help during the preparation of this chapter.

REFERENCES

Aznar-Ramos, R., Giner-Velazquez, J., Lara-Ricalde, R., & Martinez-Manautou, J. Incidence of side effects with contraceptive placebo. *American Journal of Obstetrics and Gynecology*, 1969, *105*, 1144–1149.

Batterman, R. C., & Lower, W. R. Placebo responsiveness—influence of previous therapy. *Current Therapeutic Research*, 1968, *10*, 136–143.

Beecher, H. K. Evidence for increased effectiveness of placebos with increased stress. *American Journal of Physiology*, 1956, *187*, 163–169.

Beecher, H. K. *Measurement of subjective responses: Quantitative effect of drugs.* New York: Oxford University Press, 1959.

Bishop, M. P., & Gallant, D. M. Observations of placebo response in chronic schizophrenic patients. *Archives of General Psychiatry*, 1966, *14*, 497–503.

Boleloucky, Z. A contribution to the problems of placebo dependence: Case report. *Activitas Nervosa Superior*, 1971, *13*, 190–191.

Bush, P. J. The placebo effect. *Journal of the American Pharmaceutical Association*, 1974, *NS14*, 671–672.

Dimond, E. G., Kittle, C. F., & Crockett, J. E. Comparison of internal mammary artery ligation and sham operation for angina pectoris. *American Journal of Cardiology*, 1960, 5, 483–486.

Dunlop, D., Henderson, T., & Inch, R. Survey of 17,301 prescriptions of Form Ec 10. *British Medical Journal*, 1952, *1*, 292–295.

Engelhardt, D. M., Margolis, R. A., Rudorfer, L., & Paley, H. M. Physician bias and the double-blind. *Archives of General Psychiatry*, 1969, *20*, 315–320.

Evans, B. J. Personal communication, 1978.

Evans, F. J. Placebo response: Relationship to suggestibility and hypnotizability. *Proceedings of the 77th Annual Convention of the American Psychological Association*, 1969, *4*, 889–890.

Evans, F. J. The power of a sugar pill. *Psychology Today*, April 1974, pp. 55–59.

Evans, F. J. The placebo control of pain: A paradigm for investigating non-specific effects in psychotherapy. In J. P. Brady, J. Mendels, W. R. Reiger, & M. T. Orne (Eds.), *Psychiatry: Areas of promise and advancement.* New York: Spectrum, 1977.

Evans, F. J. Hypnosis, placebo, and the control of pain. *Svensk Tidskrift for Hypnos*, 1981, *8*, 69–76. (a)

Evans, F. J. The placebo response in pain control. *Psychopharmacology Bulletin*, 1981, *17*, 72–76. (b)

Fordyce, W. E. *Behavioral methods for control of chronic pain and illness.* St. Louis: C. V. Mosby, 1976.

Frank, J. D. *Persuasion and healing.* Baltimore: Johns Hopkins University Press, 1973.

Goldstein, A., & Grevert, P. Placebo analgesia, endorphins, and naloxone. *Lancet*, 1978, *2*, 1385.

Gracely, R. H. *Evidence for opioid and non-opioid mechanisms of placebo analgesia.* Paper presented at the Fourth General Meeting of the American Pain Society, Chicago, November 1983.

Grevert, P. *Opioid involvement in placebo analgesia in response to experimental pain.* Paper presented at the Fourth General Meeting of the American Pain Society, Chicago, November 1983.

Grevert, P., & Goldstein, A. Effects of naloxone on experimentally induced ischemic pain and on mood in human subjects. *Proceedings of the National Academy of Sciences USA*, 1977, *74*, 1291–1294.

Haas, H., Fink, H., & Hartfelder, G. Das placeboproblem. *Fortschritte der Arzneimittelforschung*, 1959, *1*, 279–454.

Hankoff, L. D., Freedman, N., & Engelhardt, D. M. The prognostic value of the placebo response. *American Journal of Psychiatry*, 1958, *115*, 549–550.

Lasagna, L., Mosteller, F., von Felsinger, J. M., & Beecher, H. K. A study of the placebo response. *American Journal of Medicine*, 1954, *16*, 770–779.

Levine, J. D., Gordon, N. C., & Fields, H. L. The mechanism of placebo analgesia. *Lancet*, 1978, *2*, 654–657.

Lyerly, S. B., Ross, S., Krugman, A. D., & Clyde, D. J. Drugs and placebos: The effects of instructions upon performance and mood under amphetamine sulphate and chloral hydrate. *Journal of Abnormal and Social Psychology*, 1964, *68*, 321–327.

Marini, J. L., Sheard, M. H., Bridges, C. I., & Wagner, E. An evaluation of the double-blind design in a study comparing lithium carbonate with placebo. *Acta Psychiatrica Scandinavica*, 1976, *53*, 343–354.

McGlashan, T. H., Evans, F. J., & Orne, M. T. The nature of hypnotic analgesia and placebo response to experimental pain. *Psychosomatic Medicine*, 1969, *31*, 227–246.

Melzack, R., Jeans, M. E., Taenzer, P., & Kinch, R. A. *Masking effects of analgesic drugs with differing potencies: Some properties of placebos in double-blind experiments.* Unpublished manuscript, 1982.

Mihic, D., & Binkert, E. *Is placebo analgesia mediated by endorphin?* Paper presented at the meeting of the Second World Congress on Pain, Montreal, August 1978.

Morris, J. B., & Beck, A. T. The efficacy of antidepressant drugs: A review of research (1958 to 1972). *Archives of General Psychiatry*, 1974, *30*, 667–674.

New "thrill drug" at shore is only peppermint sugar. *The Evening Bulletin*, Philadelphia, 1967, *121*(135), pp. 1, 3.

Orne, M. T. Hypnosis, motivation, and the ecological validity of the psychological experiment. In W. J. Arnold & M. M. Page (Eds.), *Nebraska Symposium on Motivation*. Lincoln: University of Nebraska Press, 1970.

Orne, M. T. Pain suppression by hypnosis and related phenomena. In J. J. Bonica (Ed.), *Pain*. New York: Raven Press, 1974.

Reed, C. F., & Witt, P. N. Factors contributing to unexpected reactions in two human drug–placebo experiments. *Confina Psychiatrica*, 1965, *8*, 57–68.

Shapiro, A. K. Placebo effects in psychotherapy and psychoanalysis. *Journal of Clinical Pharmacology*, 1970, *10*, 73–78.

Silber, T. J. Placebo therapy: The ethical dimension. *Journal of the American Medical Association*, 1979, *242*, 245–246.

Sjolund, B. H., & Ericksson, M. B. E. *Endorphins and analgesia produced by peripheral conditioning stimulation.* Paper presented at the meeting of the Second World Congress on Pain, Montreal, August 1978.

Taylor, J. A. A personality scale of manifest anxiety. *Journal of Abnormal and Social Psychology*, 1953, *48*, 285–290.

Zuckerman, M. The development of an affect adjective check list for the measurement of anxiety. *Journal of Consulting Psychology*, 1960, *24*, 457–462.

13

Discussion

The 55% Analgesic Effect: Real or Artifact?

BERNARD TURSKY

The chapter by Evans suggests that the placebo response has generally been regarded as a nuisance variable necessary for the evaluation of specific pharmacological and clinical treatments. Evans argues that the onus of nuisance variable should be removed from the placebo response and that it should instead be considered as a possible potent therapeutic intervention that can be independently evaluated for clinical efficacy. This is not a novel argument. Benson and Epstein (1975) have suggested that "the placebo effect is a neglected and berated asset of patient care," and that it is "imperative we recognize the value of the placebo effect so that provisions can be made for its proper use" (p. 225).

The possible importance of the clinical use of placebo treatment in health care calls for a careful analysis of the therapeutic effect of placebo treatment. Evans emphasizes this idea by suggesting that two important questions related to the placebo response must be answered: (1) How powerful is the clinical effect of placebo treatment? (2) To what extent is the placebo effect mediated by expectancy?

Evans attempts to answer these questions by briefly examining the report of placebo effects in several clinical areas; however, the major emphasis of his chapter is related to the analgesic effectiveness of placebo treatment. Evans points out that anecdotal and experimental evidence indicates that placebo treatments can be as effective as most over-the-counter analgesics in the control of pain. He also reviews evidence that placebos have been demonstrated to produce 50% pain relief in 36% of the treated populations. The potency of this effect is amplified by the knowledge that proven analgesics such as morphine produce a 50% report of pain relief in only 75% of the treated population.

Bernard Tursky. Department of Political Science, State University of New York at Stony Brook, Stony Brook, New York.

Evans discusses suggestion, anxiety, and expectancy as mechanisms that may control the therapeutic effect of the placebo treatment. He provides data that demonstrate the effect of analgesic suggestion in high- and low-susceptible hypnosis subjects. The presented evidence suggests that the analgesic placebo effect due to suggestion occurs at all levels of hypnotic susceptibility.

Evans also points out that anxiety reduction may often enhance the analgesic placebo effect. Evidence is presented of a direct relationship between experimental pain tolerance and an increase or decrease in situationally relevant anxiety.

The most provocative information discussed in this chapter is related to the role of expectancy and belief as analgesic placebo response mechanisms. Evans reviews evidence of the role of expectancy in double-blind studies that compare the effectiveness of a placebo to a standard analgesic medication. One of the most perplexing points covered in this discussion is the consistent 55% report of pain reduction produced when a placebo response is compared to the pain relief response of any of several different-strength analgesic medications (morphine, codeine, and aspirin). The extreme congruency of the relationship between pain relief achieved by these active analgesics of different proven strengths and the pain relief response to placebo treatment raises several important questions about the methodology used to evaluate the pain reduction effect of both the analgesic and the placebo. It is possible that the 55% effect may be due to a lack of understanding of the pain evaluation process, as well as to the use of poor measurement techniques.

One major problem is assessing human pain responses is that both clinicians and patients lack understanding of the multidimensionality of the pain experience. Many of the pain evaluation studies summarized in Evans's chapter deal with pain as a unidimensional phenomenon. Thus an increase or reduction in pain tolerance or the relief of pain due to the administration of an analgesic or placebo is often reported in unidimensional pain terms. In his chapter, Evans discusses pain and pain reduction in terms of pain and suffering, indicating his recognition of at least two major dimensions in the human pain experience. The recent pain literature clearly supports a multidimensional concept of human pain. Beecher (1956b) introduced the notion of two separate but interacting dimensions (intensity and reactivity) in the pain response. Beecher (1956a) was also able to demonstrate that the reactive component was more manipulable by psychological variables than the intensity dimension. These findings are supported by studies indicating that the reactive component of the pain experience can be altered by such psychological variables as suggestion and instruction, or by providing the subject with control of the onset of the pain stimulus (Staub, Tursky, & Schwartz, 1971), as well as by ethnic and cultural attitudes toward the expression of pain (Sternbach & Tursky, 1965).

Beecher's two-dimensional definition of pain was amplified by Melzack and Torgerson (1971) into a multidimensional picture. They sorted and category-scaled a large number of pain descriptors into several major categories: the temporal–spatial pressure and thermal properties of pain; the affective qualities of pain, such as tension and fear; and the subjective intensity of the pain experience. These descriptors have been incorporated into the McGill Pain Questionnaire, which is a popular instrument in the evaluation of human pain. I (Tursky, 1976) have defined three similar dimensions of pain: intensity (how strong the pain is), reactivity (how unpleasant the pain is), and sensation (what the pain feels like).

The research of Beecher, Melzack and Torgerson, myself, and others clearly demonstrates the multidimensional properties of the human pain experience and thus may reduce the explanatory effectiveness of the results of many unidimensional analgesic–placebo comparison studies. Several clinical studies have demonstrated that much of the reduction in pain associated with behavioral treatment (biofeedback and relaxation) are reflected primarily in an alteration of the reactive component of the pain experience. Elmore and I (Elmore & Tursky, 1981) demonstrated that temporal artery blood flow biofeedback was clinically more effective than hand temperature biofeedback, but this alteration was primarily demonstrated in the reactive (unpleasantness) component of the pain experience. Similar results have been reported by Gracely, McGrath, and Dubner (1978) in evaluating the use of diazepam, a mild tranquilizer. It seems reasonable to argue that evaluation of the placebo effect should take into account which of the major dimensions of the pain experience are being altered by the administration of placebo.

The second major problem in the placebo–analgesic evaluation process is related to the use and abuse of data generated by 4- and 5-point category scales to evaluate the effectiveness of analgesics (Beaver, 1983) and to compare the placebo response to the analgesic effect. Huskisson (1974) summarizes the methods available for measurement of pain in disease. These range from the simplistic quantal method to the use of more complex analogue-visual scales. Beaver (1983) demonstrates the use of these category scales in the measurement of analgesic efficacy in humans. Though both these discussions are reasonably comprehensive, neither author addresses the major problems inherent in the use of most types of category scales. Lodge and I (Lodge & Tursky, 1979) spell out the shortcomings of category scaling in the quantification of social and behavioral assessment variables. We clearly identify three major problems related to the use of category scaling:

1. Most category-scaling techniques provide at best ordinal information.
2. Information is often lost or distorted through the limited resolution of category scales. Category scaling forces the respondent to make a similarity–difference judgment for each item and thus to place items that are only more or less alike in the same categories.

3. Category scales artificially constrain or expand the range that can be used by the respondent by expanding or reducing the number of categories in the scale.

Some of the category scales used to evaluate the pain reducing effects of analgesic and placebo treatments may be major offenders in these three problem areas. The 4-point pain relief scale can serve as an example. This scale defines relief in four categories, and each item is arbitrarily assigned an equally spaced numerical value: 1 (no relief), 2 (slight relief), 3 (moderate relief), or 4 (complete relief).

It can be argued that the two extreme categories (no relief and complete relief) are not often designated, since almost any treatment (real or imagined) will produce at least some indication of slight relief, and complete pain relief is almost never achieved by analgesics. Thus we are left with the two middle categories, slight relief (2) and moderate relief (3). By arbitrarily assigning all categories equally spaced scale values, this process almost insures a 50% group-averaged difference in judgment between an active and a passive treatment. A similar scenario can be written for the usual 4- or 5-point pain intensity scale. How can these category-scaling problems be solved?

My colleagues and I (Lodge & Tursky, 1979; Tursky, 1976; Tursky, Jamner, & Friedman, 1982) suggest that the use of psychophysical scaling methods and cross-modality matching procedures developed by Stevens (1975) can substantially reduce the major problems inherent in the use of category scales. Magnitude estimation using number or line production to assess pain or relief of pain directly in each pain dimension can produce interval rather than ordinal response data and can substantially reduce the problems of limited resolution and artificial constraint.

If verbal report of pain intensity or pain relief is preferred, similar direct scaling techniques can be utilized to psychophysically scale a prothetic series of pain descriptors in each of the three major dimensions of pain. This procedure can provide a proportional scale value for each descriptor that can be utilized as interval information if that word is used in a category scale. The use of more than one response measure (lines and numbers production) can be utilized in a cross-modality matching procedure to demonstrate the validity of these scale values. I (Tursky, 1976) was able to demonstrate that a discrete set of pain descriptors could be identified and psychophysically scaled to provide validated scale values representing the relative strength of each descriptor in each of the three major pain dimensions: intensity, reactivity, and sensation.

Gracely et al. (1978) replicated and validated the evaluation of three similar sets of pain descriptors, and my colleagues and I (Tursky et al., 1982) incorporated these descriptors into a comprehensive pain perception profile. A major component of the Tursky Pain Perception Profile is the use of a Pain Diary, which enables the pain patient to utilize the scale descriptors to evaluate each of the three dimensions of pain for every pain episode. The diary format enables the patient to concentrate on and delineate the judgments in each of these pain dimensions. It can be argued that unless the dimensions of pain are clearly separated, the respondent may switch dimensions between responses, and the clinician may not be able to clearly identify the pain dimension the patient is referring to in any pain evaluation response.

It has been stated (Benson & Epstein, 1975) that the placebo effect can play an important role in the treatment of disease. The overall effect of placebo treatment may begin when the patient decides to seek medical assistance, and this effect may continue through the entire therapeutic relationship. Recent evidence of placebo biochemical alterations similar to the changes produced by powerful analgesics indicates that placebo may indeed be more than a nuisance variable. It is therefore important to evaluate the true analgesic effect of placebo treatment. Care must be taken to reduce the possible artifacts of dimensionality and measurement error. I suggest that the measurement and validation powers of psychophysical scaling and cross-modality matching are two powerful evaluation techniques that can be utilized for this purpose.

The suggestion by Evans that placebo treatment and effect be removed from the category of nuisance variable and given the status of an effective clinical treatment can only be justified by a clear demonstration that the therapeutic effects claimed for the placebo treatment response are free of artifacts and meet the standards of scientific investigations.

ACKNOWLEDGMENT

I wish to thank Larry D. Jamner for his great help in the preparation of this discussion.

REFERENCES

Beaver, W. T. Measurement of analgesic efficacy in man. In J. L. Bonica, J. C. Liebeskind, & D. G. Albe-Fessard (Eds.), *Advances in pain research and therapy.* New York: Raven Press, 1983.

Beecher, H. K. Evidence for increased effectiveness of placebos with increased stress. *American Journal of Physiology,* 1956, *187,* 163–169. (a)

Beecher, H. K. The subjective response and reaction to sensations. *American Journal of Medicine,* 1956, *20,* 107–112. (b)

Benson, H., & Epstein, M. D. The placebo effect: A neglected asset in the care of patients. *Journal of the American Medical Association,* 1975, *232,* 1225–1227.

Elmore, A. M., & Tursky, B. A comparison of two psychophysiological approaches to the treatment of migraine. *Headache,* 1981, *21,* 93–101.

Gracely, R. H., McGrath, P., & Dubner, R. Validity and sensitivity of ratio scales of sensory and affective verbal pain descriptors: Manipulation of affect by diazepam. *Pain,* 1978, *5,* 19–29.

Huskisson, E. C. Measurement of pain. *Lancet,* 1974, *2,* 1127–1131.

Lodge, M., & Tursky, B. Comparisons between category and magnitude scaling of political opinion employing SCR/CPS items. *American Political Science Review*, 1979, *73*(1), 50–66.

Melzack, R., & Torgerson, W. S. On the language of pain. *Anesthesiology*, 1971, *34*, 50–59.

Staub, E., Tursky, B., & Schwartz, G. E. Self-control and predictability: Their effects on reactions to aversive stimulation. *Journal of Personality and Social Psychology*, 1971, *18*, 157–162.

Sternbach, R. A., & Tursky, B. Ethnic differences among housewives in psychophysical and skin potential response to electric shock. *Psychophysiology*, 1965, *1*, 241–246.

Stevens, S. S. *Psychophysics: Introduction to its perceptual, neural, and social prospects*. New York: Wiley, 1975.

Tursky, B. Development of a Pain Perception Profile. In M. Weisenberg & B. Tursky (Eds.), *Pain: New perspectives in therapy and research*. New York: Plenum, 1976.

Tursky, B., Jamner, L., & Friedman, R. The Pain Perception Profile: A psychophysical approach to the assessment of pain report. *Behavior Therapy*, 1982, *13*(4), 376–394.

MEDIATIONAL THEORY

14

A Psychological Approach to Placebo: The Role of Faith in Therapy and Treatment

WILLIAM B. PLOTKIN

Psychotherapists and physicians are taking a closer look at the placebo effect (Bernstein & Nietzel, 1977; Goldstein, 1962, 1966; Kirsch, 1978; Lick & Bootzin, 1975; O'Leary & Borkovec, 1978; Peek, 1977; A. K. Shapiro & Morris, 1978; Wilkins, 1979), and for good reason. Consider, for example, the following comment of A. K. Shapiro and Morris (1978), who have made a comprehensive study of the subject matter:

> Psychotherapy is commonly believed to be a modern treatment based on scientific principles while the placebo effect is believed to be a superstitious response to a sugar pill. . . . However, the placebo effect is an important component and perhaps the entire basis for the existence, popularity, and effectiveness of numerous methods of psychotherapy. (p. 369)

Shapiro and Morris go on to review thoroughly the large and often striking body of evidence that persuasively demonstrates the therapeutic effectiveness of "placebo treatments" for a wide range of psychological and physiological disorders. They dramatically conclude that "the history of both physiological and psychologic treatment is largely the history of the placebo effect" (p. 397). Likewise, in an earlier review of the evidence, Rosenthal and Frank (1956) concluded:

> The placebo effect, in short, can be quite powerful. It can significantly modify the patient's physiological functioning even to the extent of reversing the normal pharmacological action of drugs; and . . . it may be enduring. Placebo effects cannot be dismissed as superficial or transient. (p. 296)

These are strong and compelling conclusions. They indeed enjoin us to take a closer look at the variety of phenomena identified by the phrase "placebo effects." However, prior to asking, "How does it work?" we shall do well to first articulate, pre-empirically, what it is that we wish to understand more thoroughly. We cannot hope to design or conduct successful empirical

William B. Plotkin. Durango Pain Management Clinic, Durango, Colorado.

studies to discover how a given instance of a placebo effect takes place (e.g., its physiological or psychosocial parameters) until we are able to identify clearly and explicitly what is or is not an instance of a placebo effect in the first place. (How would we know we were finding out about the placebo effect—rather than something else—if we did not have a pre-empirical basis for determining whether what we were empirically investigating *was* a placebo effect?)

The primary task of this chapter is to introduce a pre-empirical articulation of the concept of "placebo effect." Doing so should be contrasted with merely identifying those antecedent variables that result in more or less of a placebo effect; we already know quite a bit about the causes—both formal (personality) and efficient (situational)—of placebo effects (see the review by A. K. Shapiro & Morris, 1978). What we need now is to understand better why these various variables have the positive therapeutic outcomes that they so often do; we need a comprehensive conceptual framework for integrating the otherwise disparate conclusions and inconsistent approaches; we require an understanding of *what* the placebo effect is, not merely a technical understanding of how to enhance it, suppress it, or predict it.

My second goal is to show how the placebo effect, as conceptualized here, is a special case of an intransitive phenomenon that I call "self-healing," and how this understanding of the placebo effect reflects what may become a major transformation in the healing arts—one that places the responsibility for cure or change squarely on the client's own shoulders.

I argue that the placebo effect is primarily and fundamentally a psychological phenomenon, as opposed to a biological or even a "psycho-biological" one. When a placebo effect does have physiological parameters or consequences (as is often but by no means always the case), we are left with the intriguing empirical question (among others) of precisely what physiological events or processes constitute that particular occurrence or class of occurrences of the placebo effect. However, we must remember that just because a given physiological process has constituted part of the occurrence of a placebo effect on one or several occasions, there is thereby no implication that a placebo effect in another person or at another time need take place physiologically in a manner that is any way similar. It is based on this reasoning that I argue that what makes a placebo effect a placebo effect is not how it takes place physiologically, but rather the fact that it is an instance of a certain sort of psychological phenomenon, to be articulated below. It does not make sense to search for "*the* physiological mechanism" of the placebo effect (no matter how centrally we reach into the central nervous system) if what we mean by "placebo effect" is a psychological phenomenon (whose relationship to physiological occurrences is comparable to the relationship of a process to one version or instantiation of that process). Such a search would be somewhat analogous to looking for "*the* physiological mechanism" of flight in the anatomy or biochemistry of a bird's wing, or perhaps in the aerodynamic engineering of a jet.

A CONCEPTUALIZATION OF PLACEBO

It is important that the reader understand that what follows in this section is not a theory or hypothesis—and it is not *about* the placebo effect (e.g., about how it is caused, assessed, or predicted). Rather, it is a pre-empirical conceptualization of what I take the placebo effect to be; it is an explicit and systematic articulation of the sort of phenomenon I would look for in order *then* to be able to empirically investigate the placebo effect. This is a critically important distinction that is typically unfamiliar to psychologists and physicians who are not well versed in modern philosophy (see Davis, 1981; Ossorio, 1973, 1978). What is offered in the following section is not something that requires, or is even eligible for, empirical substantiation (since nothing is claimed or asserted, even when declarative sentences are used); rather, it is something that can only be used or not used as a conceptual framework—a means of identifying a subject matter, a range of possible facts about persons. In particular, it is important to understand that what follows is not a theory or description of how the placebo effect might be "mediated," psychologically or otherwise. It is a conceptual articulation of the phenomenon itself, not of its mediation.

I begin with a summary of the discerning perspective on the placebo effect introduced by Peek (1977). Readers who are interested in a more thorough presentation of his ideas are referred to Peek's article.

Peek's Conceptualization

The popular definition of a placebo[1] amounts to saying that it is any therapeutic treatment whose effects are not explained or explainable in physiological, biochemical, or medical language. There is a major problem with such a definition: It implies that only direct physiological and biochemical effects are "real" or efficacious ones, and that others are "artifacts," "unreal," or insubstantial. This classifies the effects of such procedures as psychotherapy and biofeedback as artifactual, since they are explained in the language of, for example, psychodynamics, learning, or conditioning. However, there is in principle nothing unreal or artifactual about the outcomes of these procedures (see also Kirsch, 1978):

---

1. A. K. Shapiro (1971), for example, defines a placebo as "any therapy . . . that is deliberately used for its nonspecific, psychologic, or psychophysiologic effect, or that is used for its presumed specific effect on a patient, symptom, or illness, but which, unknown to patient and therapist, is without specific activity for the condition treated" (p. 440). See Wilkins (1979) for a critique of the use of the term "nonspecific."

What is fact and artifact for a given observer depends on his conceptualization of the phenomena. For example, if a person is a biologist talking biology, then what counts for him *in his role as a biologist* are accounts of phenomena that employ the conceptual system of biology and that are couched in the language of biology. Conceptualizations outside the biological domain are irrelevant to his work *as a biologist* and are unreal for him *as a biologist*. In contrast, a psychologist talking psychology conceptualizes in the theoretical domain of psychology, and consequently what is fact or real to him *as a psychologist* lies in that domain. (Peek, 1977, p. 330; original italics)

The placebo effect is neither artifactual nor unreal. It is a psychological phenomenon and requires a psychological conceptualization in psychological language. Toward this end, Peek (1977) offers the following articulation of the concept of "faith" as the central concept and component of a psychological explanation of what are usually considered placebo effects:

A person is said to "have faith" that something is the case when it doesn't cross his mind to doubt it. Inversely, a person is said to "lack faith" that something is the case if it does cross his mind to doubt it, even if he eventually decides it *is* the case. (Peek, 1977, p. 332)

Thus, to say "a person has faith in X" is to say that, for that individual, the question of whether or not X really is the case never arises.

The general importance in life of faith—or lack of it (doubt)—is that it determines (formally, not causally) the manner in which equivocal or irregular occurrences are treated. With doubt in a given procedure (e.g., following a recipe, riding a bicycle, writing a manuscript, participating in a new therapy), irregularities in that procedure—even minor ones—are treated as evidence that the procedure is infeasible or that one does not have the competence to succeed at it. Such appraisals give the person reason not to begin, to give up, or not to try as hard. With doubt, the person focuses on the details and mechanisms of the process (with the expectation that something will go wrong), so that he or she is not unlikely to find something that can be interpreted as evidence of failure or hopelessness. Even if the person does not find a major problem, the very act of focusing on the details and mechanisms of the process is likely to trip him or her up.

In contrast, with faith, irregularities are treated as only minor deviations to be ignored or corrected for; difficulties are merely technical problems, not in-principle infeasibilities. The person who has faith in a procedure does not question whether that procedure will work—it is a "foregone conclusion." The importance, then of having faith is that, other things being equal (e.g., competence, task difficulty), persons who have faith in their course of action are more likely to succeed than those who do not have that faith. To put it more succinctly, having faith frees a person to do as well as he or she can. Hence, therapists routinely attempt to evoke their clients' faith in therapy in order to increase their clients' chances of succeeding at therapeutic tasks (Fish, 1973).

Employing the concept of faith described above, the placebo effect can be conceptualized in either or both of the following two related ways (Peek, 1976). First, consider a group of persons who have faith in a given procedure that they appraise to be therapeutic for their condition. On the basis of their faith in this procedure, they will be strongly motivated to engage in any actions that they understand to be components of the therapeutic procedure, since, if they do not lack faith in that procedure, there are no questions in their minds as to whether they will be cured by it. Some or all of these actions may result in or be expressions of therapeutic improvement.

The second way in which faith may facilitate therapeutic improvement is more general, direct, and powerful, and applies as well to therapeutic treatments that do not include any client action as explicitly identified or recognized components of the treatment. (In medical practice, for example, patients are often fully passive—non-agents—relative to the treatment, and thus have no behavioral role in the treatment.) As soon as the treatment is believed to have commenced, persons who have faith in that treatment will begin, on the basis of that faith, to *treat themselves as persons whose problems have been cured.* The reason, again, is that if they do not lack faith in the treatment, there is no question in their minds as to whether it will succeed; if they see themselves as being in the process of being cured, and if they have the necessary competence to act accordingly, then we can say that they have already started to be persons who *are* cured—they are treating themselves that way and acting appropriately (not merely going through the motions). They have already begun to behave as persons who are cured, since they do not lack faith that they have started on a process that is going to end that way. If these acts of behaving as a cured person either result in or directly express a cure, we would usually speak of a "placebo effect."

During the course of this process of coming to act as cured persons, patients may also strengthen those skills that are relevant to therapeutic improvement. Through practice and experience in acting as cured persons, they may improve at those behaviors that aid or express a cure.

It should be noted that the person who has faith in a therapeutic procedure is even more likely to improve than one who merely has "positive expectancies," "conviction," or "hope": If an individual does not merely expect to be cured, but takes it for granted that he or she *has* been cured or is well on the road to a cure, then that individual is less likely to see things as evidence to the contrary, and, accordingly, is more likely to act in a manner consistent with and facilitative of cure.

As an illustration of an explanation of a placebo effect employing Peek's concept of faith, consider a man who suffers from chronic muscle contraction headaches. If he is given a prescription of placebo pills, and if he has faith in the efficacy of the putative medicine, he will take it for granted that his headache problem has been cured and will treat himself accordingly. He may no longer expect to be stricken with headaches; he may cease to worry about being regularly incapacitated; he may experience a lifting of a tremendous burden, and may perhaps celebrate by spending his newly "won" time in pursuing various pleasurable and relaxing endeavors for which he previously felt ineligible; and he may no longer present himself to others (or to himself) as a headache sufferer, with a consequent reduction in social pressure to behave (and experience) accordingly. (Of course, all "placebo cures" presuppose that the individual is willing to give up the "secondary gains" that may accompany his or her role as a patient.)

The outcome of a successful placebo intervention is an individual who no longer suffers as much or at all because (1) he or she no longer engages in those behaviors that previously created or expressed the problem, and/or (2) he or she now engages in behaviors that prevent or counteract the problem, and/or (3) he or she now engages in health-promoting and health-maintaining behaviors.

A Definition of the Placebo Effect

The following definition of the placebo effect is based upon Peek's (1977) concept of faith. This definition formally identifies what I mean when I speak of the "placebo effect" in the remainder of this chapter. It also serves as a systematic and explicit articulation of a pre-empirical conceptual framework that can be used to create and/or identify actual instances of the placebo effect for the purpose of empirically investigating this phenomenon. (However, it is not to be confused with an operational definition.)

A placebo effect is the occurrence of any therapeutic change that is caused and/or expressed by the patient's own intentional actions[2] when the decision to engage in those actions is an expression of his or her faith in a therapeutic procedure whose mode of effectiveness is not (fully) understood or is misunderstood by the patient.

PLACEBO AS AN OBSERVER'S CONCEPT

There are several points of clarification and exemplification that need to be made about this definition. Most importantly, the definition presents "placebo effect" as an observer's concept, as opposed to an actor's concept (Ossorio, 1973). That is, "placebo effect" is paradigmatically a concept that an observer employs to describe some *other* person's behavior, rather than his or her own. Ordinarily, the person (actor) exemplifying a placebo effect, as defined above, is not in a position at the time to know that that is the case. (Notice that if a person did know and thus correctly understood that his or her therapeutic change was caused and/or expressed by some of his or her

---

2. A resolution of some of the mysteries surrounding the placebo effect requires a concept of behavior as intentional, voluntary action (Ossorio, 1973), as opposed to merely mechanistic re-action, and a concept of persons as deliberate actors or agents (Abelson, 1977; Davis, 1981; Harré & Secord, 1973; Mischel, 1969; Ossorio, 1964, 1969; Strawson, 1959), as opposed to cognizant automatons.

own actions, and that he or she engaged in those actions for that reason, then most observers would not want to speak of a "placebo effect"; they would simply refer to it as a case of "self-administered treatment" or "self-healing.") Furthermore, whether or not a given therapeutic change is considered to be a placebo effect, as defined above, depends upon the *observer's* explanation of the change as well as the *observer's* description of the patient's understanding of the change. (Implicit in the definition is that the observer and the actor have different explanations of the change, and that the observer appraises the actor to be either mistaken or uninformed.) Of course, the explanation for a given therapeutic change may vary from one observer to the next, or even for a single observer from time to time; whether or not that change is considered a placebo effect varies accordingly. (In addition, whether or not a given change during or following a treatment is considered to be therapeutic at all—either negatively or positively—depends upon the observer's standards for and judgments of therapeutic changes. This definition of the placebo effect is independent of any particular notions of what constitutes a therapeutic change, and may thereby be used in conjunction with any and all such notions.) In short, the observer is an intrinsic and necessary component of the psychosocial framework that informs the placebo effect. No specific treatments are intrinsically placebos. It depends upon the observer's understanding and description of the treatment and the patient.

These comments allow us to understand why most people would consider it a joke if a person were to say, while swallowing a pill, that he or she was self-administering a "placebo treatment." For the person to call it such would be to imply that he or she understood why it was effective (viz., through the evocation of health-promoting or health-expressing behaviors) and at the same time to imply that he or she did not understand why it was effective (since the absence of understanding is one feature of what is usually suggested by "placebo"). Also, if the person believed that it was not the pill per se that was important, he or she would not have a reason to take it *as* a form of treatment.

THE RELEVANCE OF FAITH

A second point of clarification is that faith is relevant to and facilitative of a wide variety of therapeutic and other behavioral phenomena beyond those involved in placebo effects. In general, faith-inducing moves by therapists are ways of increasing a person's eligibility to succeed in ways in which the therapist wants him or her to succeed. The placebo effect, as defined here, is instantiated only by that subclass of "faith cures" identified in the definition given above. Moreover, faith cures constitute only one subclass of self-healing effects (see below).

PATIENTS' BELIEFS ABOUT THEIR BEHAVIORS

A third point is that in order for a therapeutic change to qualify as a placebo effect in terms of the definition given above, the patient need not believe that his or her own behaviors are incidental to the therapeutic event. At one extreme—with the case of placebo *medications*, for example—the patients typically do not see themselves as in any way involved as agents of change. At the other extreme, however, the patients may believe that the improvements result from their own behavior. The latter case is nevertheless correctly termed a placebo effect by the present definition if either the patients are mistaken about *which* of their behaviors caused or expressed the changes, or the patients do not understand in what *way* their behaviors are involved. For example, consider a successful biofeedback intervention in which a woman believes that her improvement has resulted from her success at physiological self-control. If the observer (based on research evidence or otherwise) sees the improvement as being due to the patient's *belief* in her new ability of physiological self-regulation, and not to her actual success at physiological control (which may in fact be minimal and clinically insignificant), then that observer would speak of a "placebo effect" according to the present definition.

THE PLACEBO EFFECT AS A PSYCHOLOGICAL PHENOMENON

A fourth point to note is that the placebo effect, as defined here, is fundamentally and primarily a psychological phenomenon. Its explication is found within the domain of psychology, in terms of psychological concepts such as "faith," "(mis)understanding," and "intentional action." Even when a placebo effect involves a physiological change as a primary outcome (as with psychosomatic medicine or biofeedback therapy), the explanation is primarily psychological. Physiological language fits in only as a specification of how that particular physiological change is an effect or parameter of the therapeutic intentional actions evoked by faith. Thus, it would be misleading to speak of the placebo effect, as defined here, as being, in a primary sense, either "biobehavioral" or "psychophysiological": A placebo effect need not in any important way involve physiological change (e.g., in psychotherapy it often does not); in those cases when it does, physiological language is only a component of the explanation of how that instance of the placebo effect occurred—not a component of what we *mean* by "placebo effect."

RELATIONSHIP BETWEEN CHANGE AND CLIENTS' ACTIONS

A fifth point of clarification concerns the component of the definition that states that the therapeutic change may be "caused and/or expressed" by the client's actions. Why not simply "caused"? It is tempting to think that the therapeutic change is always an event that is the *result* of the client's actions. However, the relationship between the change and the client's actions need not be one of cause–effect. Alternately, the client's actions themselves may be a manifestation or expression of change. In the latter case, the placebo effect simply lies in the client's coming to act in a "cured" manner, as opposed to his or her acting in a way that will thereby result in a cure. For example, if a woman with a snake phobia has faith in the efficacy of a pseudohypnotic treatment and consequently treats herself as cured, her subsequent behavior of holding a snake without fear is a direct expression of the cure, not a cause of it (although this behavior may lead to additional therapeutic effects).

Four additional elements of the definition that require expansion are the roles of the patient, faith, the therapist, and the therapeutic procedure in the placebo effect.

THE ROLE OF THE PATIENT

To whatever extent a therapeutic improvement is attributed to a placebo effect, that improvement, by the definition above, is the direct achievement of the patient himself or herself. That is, it is the patient, through the exercise of personal competence, who directly achieves the therapeutic outcome. It is for this reason that I have used the language of "intentional action" in the definition. (However, in the case of placebo effects, although the patient's action is intentional, he or she is not aware of the fact that the action is the cause of the improvement and/or of the fact that that action is an active and independent expression of improvement.)

In general, whenever we speak of a placebo effect, it is always the patients themselves who are the immediate therapeutic agents: They are doing something that they have the competence to do, and that they have always had the competence to do (except for those cases in which the competence is acquired *during* the faith-enhancing procedure). It is for this reason that I speak of placebo effects as a subclass of self-healing. Patients are, in essence, healing themselves through the exercise of competence.

Note that even with successful faith enhancement, a placebo treatment will fail if the individual does not in fact have the competence to self-heal the particular disorder. However, the major empirical lesson from the vast number of successful demonstrations of placebo effects (A. K. Shapiro & Morris, 1978) can only be that persons have a significantly greater capacity for self-healing than they are willing or prepared to recognize.

One reason why the placebo-treated individuals may not have previously exercised their self-healing competence outside of a treatment context can be understood in terms of the self-concept—the person's understanding of his or her behavioral eligibilities. Specifically, many persons may not have seen themselves as being eligible to affect the physiological or behavioral outcomes in question, so that they either never tried, or if they did, they took early or minor deviations as in-principle infeasibilities and gave up. As is well understood, one's self-concept can restrict one's behavioral repertoire significantly below the level otherwise determined by one's competence.

THE ROLE OF FAITH

The role of faith in the placebo effect is precisely to circumvent the restriction that the self-concept often imposes upon the effective exercise of self-healing competence. With faith in a therapeutic procedure, the patient has no reason (i.e., doubt in competence) to refrain from engaging in the sorts of behaviors that will cause or express a therapeutic outcome. However, it is important to emphasize that faith is not to be understood as a causal agent. Faith does not *do* anything; the patient does. "Having faith" is a personal characteristic that *allows* for the full expression of competence.

THE ROLE OF THE THERAPIST

The role of the therapist (or physician), if there is one at all, is to arrange the context appropriately to induce or enhance the patient's faith in the therapeutic procedure. Thus, placebo effects are commonly instances of therapist-evoked self-healing.

However, in order for a placebo effect to occur, there need not be an actual therapist who intends to induce or enhance the patient's faith. The therapist may evoke that faith unintentionally, or there may be no therapist at all. In the latter case, the patient's faith may be evoked by his or her own experimentation or experience, by reading or hearing about a purportedly therapeutic procedure from a neutral source, or by a friend who is simply relating his or her own experience with the procedure.

Note also that when there is a therapist, it is not necessarily the case that he or she intentionally deceives the patient about the mode of effectiveness of the therapeutic procedure. It is equally possible that the therapist believes the treatment to be effective for reasons unrelated to faith enhancement.

THE ROLE OF THE THERAPEUTIC PROCEDURE

The role of the therapeutic procedure in the placebo effect is primarily as a "stage setting." The therapeutic procedure is that in which the patient must have faith if the placebo treatment is to be a success. If there is a therapist, he or she attempts to choose or create a purportedly therapeutic procedure that the particular patient will see as most credible. (Of course, the patient's faith in the procedure may simply follow from his or her faith in the therapist.)

The therapeutic procedures that are components of placebo effects are not limited to the ingestion of sugar pills or the use of other bogus medications. Any course of action whatsoever in whose therapeutic effectiveness the patient has faith may qualify (see Fish, 1973).

Note also that the fact that a given therapeutic procedure is successfully employed in a placebo treatment in no way precludes the possibility that that procedure may also have direct therapeutic results that are independent of or complementary to any placebo effects. Faith-inducing maneuvers in therapy will always facilitate change, whether or not they are employed in conjunction with direct therapeutic interventions. A major implication of this chapter is that a psychological conceptualization of "faith" and "placebo effect" can lead to a more explicit appreciation of the client's or patient's role in the therapy process, and that taking that role explicitly into account can only enhance the ultimate effectiveness and validity of medical and psychotherapeutic intervention.

THE PLACEBO EFFECT AND PSYCHOSOMATIC DISORDERS

In earlier discussions of the placebo effect in the medical treatment of psychosomatic disorders, the causal agent was thought to be the sugar pill (or whatever inert substance was administered). This implicit belief led to the associated notion that placebo treatments do not have *specific* effects on persons or their physiology (hence, the popular misleading reference to placebo effects as "nonspecific"; see footnote 1). After all, how *could* a sugar pill have a specific effect on, for example, blood pressure? The answer is that of course it cannot, but the notion of the pill as causal agent was as incorrect as it was misleading; it prevented us from seeing that the active agent all along has been the patient, and that the patient's choice of behaviors can have specific effects on his or her physical well-being. As has been well established, it is often the patient's habitual behavioral repertoire (e.g., "Type A" behaviors; Friedman & Rosenman, 1974) that leads to specific psychosomatic and stress-related illnesses in the first place (Pelletier, 1977). Thus, it should not be surprising when the patient's decision to behave differently (see footnote 2) results in a reversal or alleviation of that condition. As Lazarus (1977) has noted:

> We . . . do a great deal of active regulating of our emotional reactions. To some extent, the person selects the environment to which he/she must respond; plans, chooses, avoids, tolerates, postpones, escapes, demolishes, manipulates his/her attention; and he/she also deceives him/herself about what is happening, as much as possible casting the relationship in ways that fit his/her needs and premises about him/herself in the world. *In regulating one's emotional life, a person is also thereby affecting the bodily reactions that are an integral part of any emotional state.* (p. 77; italics added)

It is precisely the sorts of behaviors and choices described above (which are involved in regulating one's emotional life) that may be altered as an expression of faith in a therapeutic treatment—with accompanying *specific* changes in physiological and psychological conditions (see Lazarus, 1966).

Moreover, there is no longer any doubt that it is possible for persons to exercise remarkable degrees of control over their autonomic and central nervous systems. Many researchers, working in such contexts as placebo administration, suggestion, and hypnosis, have empirically demonstrated that individuals can unconsciously regulate very specific systems within their own bodies, including such diverse processes as stomach motility (Sternbach, 1964), dermatitis (Ikemi & Nakagawa, 1962), hypertension (D. T.

Graham, Kabler, & Graham, 1962), visual acuity (C. Graham & Liebowitz, 1972), skin temperature (Maslach, Marshall, & Zimbardo, 1972), and various other physiological alterations (Barber, 1970; Erickson, 1945; Sarbin & Slagle, 1972). In addition, the entire field of biofeedback stands as further confirmation that such phenomena of self-regulation can occur voluntarily and consciously (e.g., Yates, 1980).

MANIFESTATIONS OF FAITH IN THERAPY

Since faith is one of the essential features of the placebo effect, as defined here, it is important to understand the ways in which faith may be manifested in therapy. These considerations form a foundation for the development of explicit procedures for the empirical assessment of the presence or absence of faith in clients.

We would expect successful faith inducement (such as in the placebo effect) to be reflected in a change in the description that patients give of where they are in relation to their problems. Before treatment, the individual characteristically sees himself or herself as a passive victim of some infliction or incapacity: "I have a splitting headache," "I'm all wound up," "I'm worried sick," "I'm in great pain," "I'm unable to do X." Such persons are preoccupied with their problems and act accordingly (e.g., by imposing certain social and/or physical limits upon their behavioral repertoires; by excusing themselves from certain activities; and, in general, by "playing the part" of an invalid or patient, or of a diseased or imbalanced person).

After the start of treatment, however, the description should change (assuming that faith in the treatment has been successfully induced) to one implying active intervention and progress: "I've taken two aspirins," "I'm relaxing now," "The pain is under control," "I'm free to do X now." The patients are no longer preoccupied with their problems, since, from their perspective, all that is required for the cure has been accomplished or set in motion by a drug or some other therapeutic procedure. In many cases, such as headache, the elimination of the preoccupation may have been all that was needed for the alleviation of the problem.

Successful faith enhancement should also be reflected in the form of the description that patients give of the therapy that is in progress. The mark of faith is that patients give a straightforward description of what they are doing or have done as therapy. In contrast, the mark of persons who lack faith in the treatment is seen in their descriptions of what they and/or their physicians are "trying" to accomplish, of what they "hope" to accomplish but may or may not. In the case of faith, doubts of success do not arise. (See Kirsch, 1978, for a related analysis within the context of psychotherapy research.)

These remarks form the foundations of an approach to the empirical assessment of the presence or absence of faith. Notice that one would not, of course, directly ask a patient if he or she has faith, due to the implication that perhaps there is a reason to have doubt (which may destroy the very phenomenon one has set out to assess). Instead, one would ask, "How were you cured?" or "What form of treatment did you receive?" or "How do you feel about the treatment you received/are receiving?" The form of the answers should indicate the presence or absence of faith, as discussed above.

It can be seen that the curative process of the placebo treatment, as conceptualized here, consists of the patients' public and/or private redescriptions of where they are in relation to their problems, along with the changes in behavior that reflect those redescriptions.

FAITH-ENHANCING METHODOLOGIES

The conceptualization given above of the placebo effect (as a special case of "faith cures") is consistent with and effectively integrates what is known about the procedures that are effective in generating successful placebo outcomes. A. K. Shapiro and Morris (1978) and Wickramasekera (1977) have published reviews of these procedures. In essence, all of these procedures can be seen as methods of enhancing and/or employing a person's faith in a subsequent or ongoing treatment. For example, it is well known that the strength of a placebo is closely related to the strength of both the patient's and the therapeutic staff's expectations and enthusiasm, and to the degree to which they have positive attitudes toward the treatment. "Positive attitudes" can readily be seen as a reflection of faith, as conceptualized here. The contexts within which placebo effects have been found to be strongest (e.g., clinic vs. lab, supportive vs. impersonal, harmonious vs. discordant) are also those that one would expect to be most faith-enhancing. The conceptualization of the placebo effect in terms of faith is similarly consistent with the findings that placebos work best with persons who are highly motivated to improve, that the most effective treatment procedures are those that are closest to what the patient desires, and that new therapies and presitigious therapists are especially effective.

The several "concepts of placebogenesis" reviewed by A. K. Shapiro and Morris (1978) also fit in with the present formulation. For example, such social influence procedures as suggestion and persuasion are clearly relevant to the therapist's efforts at faith inducement through context redefinition. A major way of inducing a patient's faith in a therapeutic procedure is to describe (to the patient) that procedure and/or the patient in such a way that (1) the patient will see no basis for doubting the efficacy of the treatment and/or (2) the patient sees his or her most natural course of action to be one that the therapist (at least) recognizes to be therapeutic (see the discussions of "therapeutic double binds" and "reframing" in this regard: Watzlawick, 1978; Watzlawick, Beavin, & Jackson, 1967; Watzlawick, Weakland, &

Fisch, 1974). These carefully constructed therapeutic descriptions and the patient's use of them for decision making can be seen as the essence of suggestion and persuasion in therapy (Erickson, Rossi, & Rossi, 1976; Fish, 1973).

Other researchers see the placebo effect as the outcome of a transference relationship in which the patient becomes "archaically" involved with the therapist, like a child with a parent. The archaic transference relationship is one in which a cure by the omnipotent parent figure is taken for granted (faith), and one in which the role of a cured patient has an explicit place, form, and desirability. The concept of "role demands" and the role of the "good patient" are also relevant here: The therapist and other patients often communicate the proper behavior of the cured patient.

The relationship between faith induction and "expectancy effects" is also straightforward. Indeed, A. K. Shapiro and Morris (1978) include "faith, . . . trust, confidence, and the strength of belief" as expectancy effects.

SELF-HEALING: THE CHALLENGE TO MODERN MEDICINE

The successes of modern scientific medicine have been widely impressed upon the populace by the mass media. . . . The public has come to expect a "magic-bullet" pill or a "sixty-minute TV-doctor cure" by an omnipotent physician who allegedly possesses a vast armamentarium of infallible cures. . . . According to this modern prescription, the doctor has become solely responsible for the cure, not the patient. It is true that once tissue pathology has occurred, . . . external intervention by modern medicine to patch the defect is often impressive and largely beyond the subjective control of the patient. However, the vast majority of ills and the illness-onset situation itself, are clearly not beyond subjective control. These cannot be the private domain of the doctor-scientists, but are a matter of responsibility for each individual. (Stroebel & Glueck, 1973, p. 31)

Better health care will not depend on some new therapeutic standard, but on the level of willingness and competence to engage in self-care. (Illich, 1976, p. 270)

From the point of view of general health maintenance and improvement, a major problem with most placebo treatments (as well as most other traditional medical treatments) is that they foster the impression on the part of both the patient and the therapist that the cure is entirely a result of the *therapist's* competency or of the *therapy's* potency, thereby affecting a cure at the cost of reducing the patient's sense of self-control and competence. While patients may frequently be cured of their illnesses, there is the danger of creating a population that is increasingly dependent upon—if not addicted to—expensive drugs and a professional elite. Our contemporary medical and health care institutions may be unintentionally teaching us to treat ourselves as helpless consumers of health care that we neither understand nor control (Carlson, 1975; Illich, 1976).

However, the history of the placebo effect teaches us that the tremendous acceleration in the incidence of addiction to prescription drugs and of stress-related illnesses may be as unnecessary as it is undesirable. Clearly, the challenge for the modern healing arts is to develop methods for freeing persons to exercise their self-healing competencies *without* reducing their sense of self-control and responsibility. From this point of view, it is not good enough that patients in fact have that control and are exercising it; they must also recognize that fact. The potential benefits and ramifications of developing competence-mobilizing procedures that also enhance our *sense* of competence, autonomy, and self-control are enormous and wide-reaching:

1. Our dependency upon expensive physician and hospital care can be substantially reduced.
2. Likewise, our dependency upon expensive medicines can be reduced—chemicals that include pharmacologically active drugs as well as placebo pills, which can be equally addicting (A. K. Shapiro & Morris, 1978).
3. Unlike drug treatments, self-healing would be expected to be subject to less (or no) tolerance, and should transfer to problems other than those to which it was originally applied.
4. A population that is cognizant of its considerable powers of self-healing and knowledgeable in their employment would be expected to stay healthier and to reverse developing illnesses earlier in their course.

Clearly, programs designed for the development of such self-healing skills and attitudes belong in a prominent and early place in our educational and health-promoting systems.

Fortunately, many programs and techniques have appeared in recent years that may prove to be effective in the realization of this goal. These include some traditional psychotherapeutic approaches (see Bandura, 1977, for a discussion of psychotherapy as a means of enhancing "perceived self-efficacy"), as well as the tools recently brought together under the labels of "behavioral medicine" (Pomerleau & Brady, 1979; D. Shapiro, 1979), "holistic health" (Benson, 1975; Pelletier, 1977; Samuels & Samuels, 1975), and "high-level wellness" (Ardell, 1977), such as relaxation techniques, physical exercise, improved nutrition, self-hypnosis, imagery and visualization techniques, autogenic training, some "self-help" programs, environmental and behavioral change, meditation, and biofeedback. These techniques and programs have in common the provision of a framework or context that gives both form and legitimacy to the explicit exercise of the individual's own self-healing abilities. That is, the practice of these techniques does not necessarily result in the acquisition of *new* skills; they may have their effectiveness simply by providing people with a format for consciously exercising the self-healing skills that they already possess and that they would otherwise be "covertly" exercising under the guise of "placebo treatments" or other treatments in which the therapist is appraised to be the active agent. The importance of such a framework cannot be overemphasized. The typical response to the claim that human beings can cure themselves of many, if not most, common (e.g., stress-related) illnesses can be expected to be a skeptical "How?" even among the open-minded. An answer can be an introduction to the set of self-healing practices mentioned above, which can be seen partly as a collection of techniques for developing self-healing skills, and partly as a set of rituals that simply give structure, pattern, or form to the exercise of latent self-healing skills. As a bonus, many of them (e.g., exercise and nutritional improvement) make direct contributions to the individual's well-being independently of new skills or self-concept change (or even the degree of faith). Moreover, if appropriately "packaged" for particular cultural settings and age groups, these frameworks can provide a legitimization for the manifest exercise of these skills, which, in many contemporary contexts, may otherwise appear silly, futile, or pretentious.

REFERENCES

Abelson, R. *Persons: A study in philosophical psychology.* London: Macmillan, 1977.

Ardell, D. B. *High-level wellness: An alternative to doctors, drugs, and disease.* Emmaus, Pa.: Rodale Press, 1977.

Bandura, A. Self-efficacy: Toward a unifying theory of behavioral change. *Psychological Review,* 1977, *84,* 191–215.

Barber, T. X. *LSD, marijuana, yoga, and hypnosis.* Chicago: Aldine, 1970.

Benson, H. *The relaxation response.* New York: Avon, 1975.

Bernstein, D. A., & Nietzel, M. T. Demand characteristics in behavior modification: The natural history of a "nuisance." In M. Hersen, R. M. Eisler, & P. M. Miller (Eds.), *Progress in behavior modification.* New York: Academic Press, 1977.

Carlson, R. J. *The end of medicine.* New York: Wiley, 1975.

Davis, K. E. (Ed.), *Advances in descriptive psychology* (Vol. 1). Greenwich, Conn.: JAI Press, 1981.

Erickson, M. H. Hypnotic investigation of psychosomatic phenomena: Psychosomatic interrelations studied by experimental hypnosis. *Psychosomatic Medicine,* 1945, *5,* 51–58.

Erickson, M. H., Rossi, E., & Rossi, S. *Hypnotic realities.* New York: Irvington, 1976.

Fish, J. M. *Placebo therapy.* San Francisco: Jossey-Bass, 1973.

Friedman, M., & Rosenman, R. H. *Type A behavior and your heart.* Greenwich, Conn.: Fawcett-Crest, 1974.

Goldstein, A. P. *Therapist–patient expectancies in psychotherapy.* New York: Macmillan, 1962.

Goldstein, A. P. Prognostic and role expectancies in psychotherapy. *American Journal of Psychotherapy,* 1966, *20,* 35–44.

Graham, C., & Liebowitz, H. W. The effects of suggestion on visual acuity. *International Journal of Clinical and Experimental Hypnosis,* 1972, *20,* 169–186.

Graham, D. T., Kabler, J. D., & Graham, F. K. Physiological response to the suggestion of attitudes specific for hives and hypertension. *Psychosomatic Medicine,* 1962, *24,* 159–167.

Harré, R., & Secord, P. F. *The explanation of social behavior.* Totowa, N.J.: Littlefield, Adams, & Co., 1973.

Ikemi, Y., & Nakagawa, S. A psychosomatic study of contagious dermatitis. *Kyushu Journal of Medical Science,* 1962, *13,* 335–350.

Illich, I. *Medical nemesis: The expropriation of health.* New York: Random House, 1976.

Kirsch, I. The placebo effect and the cognitive–behavioral revolution. *Cognitive Therapy and Research,* 1978, *2,* 255–264.

Lazarus, R. S. *Psychological stress and the coping process.* New York: McGraw-Hill, 1966.

Lazarus, R. S. A cognitive analysis of biofeedback control. In G. E. Schwartz & J. Beatty (Eds.), *Biofeedback: Theory and research.* New York: Academic Press, 1977.

Lick, J., & Bootzin, R. Expectancy factors in the treatment of fear: Methodological and theoretical issues. *Psychological Bulletin,* 1975, *82,* 917–931.

Maslach, C., Marshall, G., & Zimbardo, P. Hypnotic control of peripheral skin temperature. *Psychophysiology,* 1972, *9,* 600–605.

Mischel, T. *Human action: Conceptual and empirical issues.* New York: Academic Press, 1969.

O'Leary, K. D., & Borkovec, T. D. Conceptual, methodological, and ethical problems of placebo groups in psychotherapy research. *American Psychologist,* 1978, *33,* 821–830.

Ossorio, P. G. *Persons.* Boulder, Colo.: Linguistic Research Institute, 1964.

Ossorio, P. G. *Meaning and symbolism.* Boulder, Colo.: Linguistic Research Institute, 1969.

Ossorio, P. G. Never smile at a crocodile. *Journal for the Theory of Social Behavior,* 1973, *3,* 121–140.

Ossorio, P. G. *What actually happens: The representation of real world phenomena.* Columbia: University of South Carolina Press, 1978.

Peek, C. J. *Placebo: Faith and skepticism.* Lecture presented at University of Colorado at Boulder, April 27, 1976.

Peek, C. J. A critical look at the theory of placebo. *Biofeedback and Self-Regulation,* 1977, *2,* 327–335.

Pelletier, K. R. *Mind as healer, mind as slayer: A holistic approach to preventing stress disorders.* New York: Delta, 1977.

Pomerleau, O. F., & Brady, J. P. (Eds.). *Behavioral medicine: Theory and practice.* Baltimore: Williams & Wilkins, 1979.

Rosenthal, D., & Frank, J. D. Psychotherapy and the placebo effect. *Psychological Bulletin,* 1956, *55,* 294–302.

Samuels, M., & Samuels, N. *Seeing with the mind's eye: The history, techniques, and uses of visualization.* New York: Random House, 1975.

Sarbin, T. R., & Slagle, R. W. Hypnosis and psychophysiological outcomes. In E. Fromm & R. E. Shor (Eds.), *Hypnosis: Research developments and perspectives.* Chicago: Aldine, 1972.

Shapiro, A. K. Placebo effects in medicine, psychotherapy, and psychoanalysis. In A. E. Bergin & S. L. Garfield (Eds.), *Handbook of psychotherapy and behavior change: An empirical analysis.* New York: Wiley, 1971.

Shapiro, A. K., & Morris, L. A. The placebo effect in medical and psychological therapies. In S. L. Garfield & A. E. Bergin (Eds.), *Handbook of psychotherapy and behavior change: An empirical analysis* (2nd ed.). New York: Wiley, 1978.

Shapiro, D. Biofeedback and behavioral medicine in perspective. *Biofeedback and Self-Regulation,* 1979, *4,* 371–381.

Sternbach, R. A. The effects of instructional sets of autonomic responsivity. *Psychophysiology,* 1964, *1,* 67–72.

Strawson, P. F. *Individuals.* London: Methuen, 1959.

Stroebel, C. F., & Glueck, B. C. Biofeedback treatment in medicine and psychiatry: An ultimate placebo? In L. Birk (Ed.), *Biofeedback: Behavioral medicine.* New York: Grune & Stratton, 1973.

Watzlawick, P. *The language of change.* New York: Basic Books, 1978.

Watzlawick, P., Beavin, J. H., & Jackson, D. D. *Pragmatics of human communication: A study of interactional patterns, pathologies, and paradoxes.* New York: Norton, 1967.

Watzlawick, P., Weakland, J. H., & Fisch, R. *Change.* New York: Norton, 1974.

Wickramasekera, I. E. The placebo effect and biofeedback for headache pain. *Proceedings of the San Diego Biomedical Symposium,* 1977, *16,* 191–201.

Wilkins, W. Getting specific about nonspecifics. *Cognitive Therapy and Research,* 1979, *3,* 319–329.

Yates, A. J. *Biofeedback and the modification of behavior.* New York: Plenum, 1980.

15

A Conditioned Response Model of the Placebo Effect: Predictions from the Model

IAN WICKRAMASEKERA

THE PLACEBO EFFECT

A "placebo" may be defined as a presumably inert or neutral substance or procedure that elicits a therapeutic response (Beecher, 1959; Evans, 1974a, 1974b; Shapiro, 1971). Reviews of 26 double-blind studies covering 1991 patients found that approximately 35% of patients have severe *clinical* pain reduced by at least half of its original intensity by an inert substance or placebo drug. The placebo rate for *experimentally* induced laboratory pain, however, is considerably lower (Evans, 1974a). This discrepancy between the placebo rate in experimental and clinical pain strongly suggests that the psychological significance of the therapy situation is a major determinant of the magnitude of the placebo effect.

Placebo effects are not limited to chemical treatments, but may include surgical and psychological therapies. In a classic paper, "Surgery as a Placebo," Beecher (1961) compared the results of enthusiastic and skeptical surgeons performing the once popular internal mammary artery ligation for angina pectoris. Two independent skeptical teams (Cobb, Thomas, Dillard, *et al.*, 1959; Dimond, Kittle, & Crockett, 1958), using a single-blind procedure, performed a bilateral skin incision on all patients under local anesthesia, and in randomly selected patients the internal mammary artery was ligated. Dimond *et al.* (1958) found that 100% of the nonligated and 76% of the ligated patients reported decreased need for nitroglycerin and increased exercise tolerance. All nonligated patients showed improvement for more than 6 weeks, and followed patients remained improved 6 to 8 months later. Neither the ligated nor the nonligated group showed any improvement on electrocardiography. Cobb *et al.* (1959) team reported that 6 months after surgery five ligated and five nonligated patients reported more

Ian Wickramasekera. Department of Psychiatry and Behavioral Sciences, Eastern Virginia Medical School, Norfolk, Virginia.

255

than 40% subjective improvement. Two nonligated patients showed dramatic improvement in exercise tolerance, and one nonligated patient even showed improved electrocardiographic results after exercise. These studies demonstrated that ligation of the internal mammary artery was no better than a skin incision, and that skin incision could generate a dramatic and sustained therapeutic effect.

Placebo effects are not limited to the relief of acute pain. Placebos may be useful in the therapy of coughs, headaches, asthma, multiple sclerosis, the common cold, diabetes, ulcers, arthritis, emesis, seasickness, cancer, parkinsonism, and other ailments (Beecher, 1955; Haas, Fink, & Hartfelder, 1959; Horningfeld, 1964a, 1964b; Wolf, 1950). Nor are placebo effects limited to chemical and surgical treatments; in fact, a review of controlled studies of systematic desensitization (Kazdin & Wilcoxon, 1976) and a pioneering credible double-blind study of clinical biofeedback (Cohen, Graham, Fotopoulos, & Cook, 1977) have also found equally high rates of placebo response for these psychological treatments. For example, in the Cohen *et al.* (1977) study, subjects who received false feedback (the placebo treatment) improved clinically as much as those who received true feedback under double-blind conditions. In fact, an early study by Schwitzgebel and Traugott (1968) found that mechanical devices (like medical instruments) can also generate placebo effects, and I (Wickramasekera, 1977c) have elsewhere discussed the placebo effect of medical instruments in biofeedback.

The review above suggests that a therapeutic phenomenon like the placebo, which occurs across such a wide range of clinical treatment modalities (drugs, surgery, psychotherapies, biofeedback) and across such a wide range of physical and mental symptoms (pain, anxiety, edema, tachycardia, emesis, fever, vasoconstriction, phobias, depressions, etc.) to people who are physically or psychologically immobilized by symptoms or in a state of health deprivation, must be a true *general* ingredient in *all clinical* situations.

A review of the placebo literature leads to several conclusions: (1) A subset of patients show a significant therapeutic response to "inert" or "placebo" substances, procedures, and objects in any clinical study. (2) No reliable procedure exists to date to identify in advance this subset of patients. (3) The same subset may not reliably respond to placebos. (4) Any object or procedure offered with therapeutic intent can under the "right" conditions generate placebo effects. (5) The mechanism of the effect is unknown, and all the "right" conditions are unclear.

It has been found that a placebo can potentiate, attenuate, or negate the active ingredients in a drug (Shapiro, 1971). Placebos can have powerful effects on organic illness and malignancies, and can even mimic the effects of active drugs (Shapiro, 1971). Studies have found that dose–response and time–effect curves for an active drug and a placebo can be similar and that the side effects of an active drug and a placebo can be similar (Evans, 1974a).

Clearly we are dealing with a real effect that has been regarded as a "nuisance," for several reasons previously discussed (Wickramasekera, 1976b, 1977b, 1977c), and that has been summarized as follows: (1) Its action is not logically related to the known etiology of the disease or condition. (2) The mechanism of its action is unknown. (3) The effect is unreliable. (4) The effect may not be durable. (5) It is an effect that can occur in any therapeutic situation.

The effect has been called "nonspecific" because our ignorance of its parameters has limited our ability to manipulate the effect systematically. One purpose of the present chapter is to contribute toward the specification of what is now "nonspecific," and toward a technology that will enable us to use some "nonspecified" effects in controlled, reliable, and specific ways. Eventually, perhaps, some placebo effects can be attenuated or negated in laboratory studies, and systematically manipulated to potentiate other specific effects in clinical studies. Such a psychological technology can increase the reliability of positive clinical outcome when active ingredients are used in routine clinical practice.

Many hypotheses have been advanced to explain the mechanism of the placebo response. Shapiro (1971) and T. X. Barber (1959) appear to favor a suggestion hypothesis, and Evans (1974a) appears to favor an anxiety reduction hypothesis. Frank (1973) and Stroebel and Glueck (1973) have stressed the role of expectancy in potentiating therapeutic response. In fact, Stroebel and Glueck (1973) have proposed a clinically useful way of approaching expectancy. For reasons of brevity, these analyses are not presented here; they are discussed elsewhere (Wickramasekera, 1976b, 1977b, 1977c). The present chapter offers a new model[1,2] of the placebo

---

1. After this chapter was written and submitted for publication, one of the reviewers drew my attention to a relevant paper by Gleidman, Gantt, and Teitelbaum (1957). I located and read this paper in July 1979. It was very exciting to note that Gleidman et al. advanced one of the central components of the present theory over 20 years ago. Their brief and excellent paper "summarizes some experiences in conditional reflex studies in dogs that relate placebo reactivity to established learning concepts" (Gleidman et al., 1957). The observations are cited in informal anecdotal style and deal with three groups of "unpublished" studies. The first group of studies "demonstrates that the effect of a person" can be conditioned. The second series stresses the importance of "central excitatory states" in conditioning. The third group of studies is "a miscellaneous one," which pertains to the general state of the organism and the general setting with respect to placebo effects. Their thoughts with respect to the first point are almost identical to mine, and with respect to the second and third points, there is substantial implicit agreement. But there is no elaboration with respect to hypnotizability, brain lateralization, and the possibility that the UCSs can be nonchemical behavioral events.

2. After this chapter was written and accepted for publication, the editor of Biofeedback and Self-Regulation, Dr. J. Stoyva, drew my attention (on October 29, 1979) to a study by R. J. Herrnstein (1962). In this controlled study of the disruptive effects of scopalamine hydrobromide on lever pressing in the rat, physiological saline is shown to mimic the effects of scopalamine hydrobromide. Based on this study, Herrnstein infers that the placebo effect appears to be an instance of simple Pavlovian conditioning.

response, traces the predictions from this model, and presents the relevant subject, therapist, and procedural variables. This analysis points out that intrinsic to *all unconditioned stimuli (UCSs) or reliably effective interventions or events* (physiochemical, behavioral/psychological, or surgical) is the potential for Pavlovian conditioning (Pavlov, 1927) and therefore placebo learning.

This suggests that reliable mechanisms of pathophysiology that have clearly and sharply defined onsets and offsets can operate as UCSs. Chemicals and procedures that reliably and clearly turn on or off such pathophysiology can also operate as UCSs. Hence mechanisms of disease and healing may not be insulated from conditioning effects. The unconditioned response (UCR) is a function not only of the UCS, but also of an associated CS. The symptomatically immobilized and dependent patient in a state of health deprivation (not unlike food deprivation) is an ideal candidate for conditioning. Counterintuitively, it predicts that therapists who use *active* ingredients will get stronger placebo effects than those who use *inert* ingredients. The model also paradoxically predicts that progress in isolating active ingredients will inevitably lead to more and stronger placebo effects!

There is no systematic human evidence to support this model. But there is some strong controlled animal evidence (Ader, 1981; Drawbraugh & Lal, 1974; Goldberg & Schuster, 1967, 1970; Schuster & Thompson, 1969; Siegel, 1978; Wilker & Pesor, 1970) that supports the view that *neutral* stimuli can elicit complex biological and biochemical changes as postulated by the conditioned response (CR) model of the placebo.

ORIGINS OF THE CONDITIONED RESPONSE MODEL

Early in 1970 during clinical work (Wickramasekera, 1972a, 1973a) with patients with diagnosed chronic and continuous muscle contraction headaches of over 20 year's duration in electromyograph (EMG) feedback therapy, I made some puzzling observations. A subset of these patients reported relief of headache pain with startling rapidity. Often this occurred after no more than one or two sessions of EMG feedback therapy, and several sessions before they demonstrated any measurable ability to reduce the muscle tension levels in their head and neck. Since the etiology and mechanisms of muscle contraction headache are presumed to involve sustained contraction of muscles of the head and neck, changes in the verbal report of the intensity and frequency of headache pain should correlate with or follow, not *precede*, a drop in frontal EMG levels.

I wondered if this very short-latency therapeutic response was not a placebo response to the impressive and highly "credible" biofeedback instruments in anticipation of actual healing. It is well known that CRs mediated by the central nervous system (CNS) can have a shorter latency than a UCR, or, in this case, the actual reduction in muscle tension levels in the head and neck. I conceptualized the positive short-latency therapeutic response of this subset of patients as a type of fractional anticipatory goal response (Hull, 1952) or CR to the impressive electronic medical instruments used in this therapy (Wickramasekera, 1977c). This rapid therapeutic response (CR) to the sight of the biofeedback instruments (CS) was like conditioned salivation (CR), a *fractional* component of actual eating of food (UCR) that occurs in *anticipation* of food (UCS). The rapidity of this response reminded me of the well-known clinical observation that ingestion of aspirin often relieves the headache long before its pharmacological effect can occur. This placebo response group suggested that respondent or Pavlovian conditioning was one factor that could account for a portion of the positive therapeutic outcome in EMG feedback therapy for headache. At that time, the mechanism of therapeutic response in EMG feedback therapy for headaches was considered to be exclusively operant or Skinnerian conditioning of reduced frontal EMG.

THE CLINICAL SITUATION AND CONDITIONING PHENOMENA

This analysis predicts (1) that psychological responses (CRs) that were previously relegated to the realm of "nonspecific" factors can come to reliably *attenuate* or *potentiate* both health and illness; (2) that initially neutral stimuli (CSs) can come to either directly or indirectly influence the underlying physiochemical and cellular mechanisms (pathophysiology) of health and illness; and (3) that, theoretically, the influence of such variables on the symptom and mechanism of disease can be demonstrated in appropriately controlled double-blind studies in which the UCS (e.g., active chemical ingredient) is withheld.

Till as recently as the first two decades of this century, physicians had only a few active ingredients or UCSs (digitalis, opium) with which they could reliably *control* certain disease or disorder mechanisms. Yet for centuries physicians have inspired confidence in patients, and individual physicians have enjoyed high credibility and high social status. Physicians occupied positions of confidence long before they could reliably and effectively control pathophysiological mechanisms (UCRs) in any significant number of disorders. The CR model of the placebo can illuminate at least a part of this historical paradox. The perceived potency of a healer can stem not only from his or her ability to *control* pathophysiological mechanisms, but also from his or her ability to make an accurate and precise *prediction* of the time course, the specific changing symptoms, and the antecedents of disease. The ability to predict or prophesy requires only careful observation, recognition of the descriptive features of symptoms, access to medical records of prior observations, and a knowledge of the base rates of certain deviant biological events.

It is likely that patients frightened by the eruption of unfamiliar symptoms on their bodies and uncertain about their future were not prone to think analytically about their physicians' behavior. Consequently, they confused the ability to *predict* biological symptoms accurately with the ability to *control* disease mechanisms, and attributed therapeutic potency to the physicians who reduced their fear and uncertainty by identifying and labeling their diseases and accurately predicting their symptomatic course. A physician's predictive knowledge replaces disorganizing fear and uncertainty with a sense of familiarity, illusory control, and security. For centuries physicians have carefully observed, recorded, and labeled multiple common diseases and disorders. They were often also knowledgeable about the likely antecedents (e.g., hereditary or familial antecedents, dietary and environmental antecedents) of some of these disorders. A learned physician could easily recognize the specific symptoms a patient was currently experiencing, and could predict specific symptoms the patient would develop within 12 to 48 hours, as well as the sequence of symptomatic changes that would occur as the disease progressed. Such a physician also knew the death rate and sometimes the rate of spontaneous remission for the disease. This enabled the knowledgeable practitioner, after a brief physical examination, to make to the patient and his or her family uncannily accurate predictions about the patient's current experiences and future experiences. As a specific disease (e.g., gonorrhea) progressed and the physician's predictions about the symptoms were verified, the physician's credibility escalated in the patient's and the community's perception. In addition, a knowledge of the likely antecedents of a disease or disorder (diet, hereditary factors, environmental exposure or trauma) could not only enable the physician to predict the future, but also to reveal to the patient the precursors of his or her illness from out of his or her past. In short, accurate *prediction* and *postdiction* have been and can be the basis of great perceived therapeutic potency and the basis of the illusion of control over the disease process. In the field of clinical practice, a physician is never asked to reinstate a cured disease ("do that again") to demonstrate his or her control over the mechanisms of disease. Clinical practice never requires experimental replication of unpleasant illness.

This conditioning analysis of the historical health care situation demonstrates how perceived therapeutic potency can be acquired by simply being a good observer and having a detailed knowledge of the sequence of onset of specific symptoms of common diseases. The ability to recognize that one has confused prediction and description with control of pathophysiological mechanisms requires a level of analytic thought that is unlikely in a fearful and aroused patient.

These speculations lead to the more general notion that all stimuli in the clinical therapeutic situation (the therapist and his or her behavior, the staff, the tools and procedures, the physical environment and furnishings, etc.) can be conveniently divided into two classes of events: (1) UCSs and (2) CSs or discriminative stimuli. This analysis assumes that all people who are sick as a result of disease, injury, or dysfunction are in a state of health deprivation that selectively sensitizes their attentional process to stimuli (UCSs and CSs) labeled "therapeutic" by their culture. The disruptive, uncomfortable, and perhaps life-threatening predicament of patients focuses their attention on stimuli that *in vivo* or vicarious social learning has shown to reduce the unpleasant drive stimuli associated with illness.

Unconditioned Stimuli

UCSs (physiological/chemical or behavioral/psychological) are a class of events that reliably elicit or increase the probability of therapeutic responses (UCRs) by altering the mechanisms of pathophysiology. An example of such stimuli would be behavioral responses (UCSs) that reduce the elevated frontal EMG levels that are presumed (Ostfeld, 1962; Wolff, 1963) to be etiological to muscle contraction headache pain. Theoretically, the definitive feature of UCSs in this analysis is their ability to reliably (within the limits of adaptation at the receptor or reflex level) alter the underlying response mechanism (sustained contraction of muscles of head and neck, or UCR) of disease, injury, or dysfunction, and eventually its observable physical and/or behavioral symptoms. Some UCRs (e.g., emesis, eyeblink) can be triggered by multiple physical stimuli (UCSs). For example, both a puff of air and a loud noise may elicit an eyeblink. Emesis may be elicited by both ipecac and mechanical methods like fingers in throat. But other UCRs may be elicited only by a narrow class of UCSs. For example, some acute infectious diseases are responsive only to a narrow class of antibiotics (UCSs), while most modern chronic diseases (e.g., cardiovascular disease, respiratory disease) are reliably responsive only to a combination of several interventions (UCSs), such as diet, medication, exercise, and life style change (e.g., smoking cessation, alcohol ingestion cessation, etc.). The onset or offset of many chronic diseases appear to be determined by multiple UCSs. Some UCSs, or reliable elicitors or reinforcers of the mechanisms of disease or dysfunction, are easier to see and specify in medicine than in psychology—for example, the effect of appropriate doses of insulin (UCS) on the glucose metabolism response (UCR) of diabetics, or the effects of morphine (UCS) on the pain response (UCR) of the postsurgical patient, or the effects of penicillin (UCS) on pneumococcal pneumonia. Such UCSs (morphine, penicillin, insulin, etc.) are believed to operate directly or indirectly on the theoretical mechanism of the illness or its pathophysiology. In the original Pavlovian laboratory analogue, which is not obscured by presumed theoretical etiological mechanisms, the UCS, food in the mouth or the sight of food, will reliably elicit salivation (UCR), particularly if the animal is hungry (selectively sensitized to certain classes of stimuli by food deprivation). Similarly, the sight of a socially sanctioned healer ("doctor," swami, or shaman) will reliably elicit "hope," particularly if the person is health-deprived. "Health deprivation" is a general state of reduced physical and psychological mobility and dependency induced in sick people by the eruption of unpleasant and unfamiliar physical symptoms (e.g., changes in skin color, edema, fever, pain on movement, boils and pus, respiratory distress, etc.). The state of health deprivation selectively sensitizes the patient to a class of stimuli (the healer, his or her substances, and his or her rituals) that have previously reduced unpleasant and unfamiliar symptoms. A state of health deprivation appears to be an important precondition for the learned component of disease or dysfunction.

Conditioned Stimuli

CSs are certain neutral stimuli that initially do not elicit a UCR (e.g., change in glucose metabolism, emesis), but that as a function of repeated association with an appropriate UCS (e.g., insulin, ipecac) can come to *inhibit* even temporarily the symptoms and/or underlying mechanism of the disease, either directly or indirectly. The neutral CS, as a function of contiguity with the UCS, can now elicit a fractional anticipatory component of the UCR. Neutral stimuli (CSs) may also be associated with the onset of the underlying mechanisms or symptoms of disease or injury (UCSs). Such CSs may actually potentiate the disease or illness. CSs are ineffective with vertebrates if the UCR is elicited by a route other than the CNS (Hilgard & Marquis, 1940). CSs may alter some disease mechanisms indirectly by modifying, for example, neuroendocrine or other CNS mechanisms that can inhibit immunocompetence (Ader, 1981; Ader & Cohen, 1982; Bovbjerg, Ader, & Cohen, 1982) or that can theoretically disinhibit or potentiate immuno-competence. If, on the other hand, the UCR (depression, anxiety, pain, etc.) is elicited directly through CNS activity, then CSs may act directly on the presumed mechanism of the disorder (e.g., excessive sympathetic activation, depletion of norepinephrine, activation of endorphins, etc.) and rapidly cause a positive clinical outcome. For example, the ingestion of a tablet of aspirin is frequently reported to relieve headache pain long before the active ingredient (pharmacological effect) working peripherally can alter pain.

CSs may also operate as "safety signals" (Mowrer, 1960) to potentiate healing. Mowrer (1960) indicated that neutral stimuli associated with the offset of pain or fear can be termed "safety signals" because they are associated with the reduction of anxiety or equivalently with the arousal of "hope." They indicate that the period of suffering is over. Neutral stimuli (CSs) in the health care situation can become conditioned by their association with either the *onset* of the mechanisms and symptoms of health or the *offset* of the symptoms and mechanisms of disease. Certain CSs or discriminative stimuli in the medical situation are repeatedly associated with the onset of potent UCSs (morphine, antibiotics, insulin). For example, CSs like syringes, stethoscopes, white coats, and certain behavioral procedures (cleaning the skin with alcohol swabs, physical examinations) are routinely paired with potent UCSs like morphine, insulin, and antibiotics.

Also, culture-specific cognitive verbal labels for places ("hospital," "laboratory," "emergency room," "clinic", procedures ("medical," "scientific," "graphing," "measuring") and persons ("medical," "professor," "doctor") can also be associated with potent UCSs or active ingredients, and come to acquire conditioned properties. CSs reliably associated with the *offset* of aversive stimuli (electric shock, childbirth, ugly skin eruptions, headache, painful injury, etc.) can acquire conditioned positive reinforcing properties (Mowrer, 1960). In other words, these CSs come to operate like "safety signals" (Mowrer, 1960). These phenomena are well established in the laboratory (Kimble, 1961) and are discussed below.

THE PLACEBO AS A CONDITIONED RESPONSE

I propose that a variety of inert, neutral, or nonspecific substances, procedures, persons or places can come to function as CSs (Pavlov, 1927) or discriminative stimuli (Skinner, 1953) for the alleviation of anxiety, pain, dysfunction, trauma, and disease, if such CSs or discriminative stimuli have been repeatedly associated with the *onset* (see footnote 2) of powerful UCSs (e.g., like penicillin, nitroglycerine, insulin, morphine, etc.) that reliably relieve both the mechanisms and overt symptoms of illness (e.g., pneumococcal pneumonia, angina pectoris, diabetes, postsurgical pain).

Mowrer's (1960) analysis of secondary reinforcement based on negative primary reinforcement points to other ways in which neutral stimuli can come to acquire both "nocebo" and placebo effects. Unfamiliar reactions (skin eruptions, pus discharges, etc.) and unpleasant symptoms (fever, pain, insomnia, etc.) are naturally occurring aversive reactions (UCRs) that are triggered by some underlying disease process, injury, or dysfunction (UCS). Neutral stimuli (CSs) associated with the *onset* and course of the disease reactions (UCRs) may become negative CSs. These CSs may elicit CRs that potentiate the UCRs or disease reactions, by either directly or indirectly inhibiting mechanisms of immunocompetence (Ader, 1981). Such CSs can be termed "nocebos" and the learned response to them a "nocebo response." In fact, it is sometimes observed that simply changing the patient's physical environment (deleting those CSs or nocebos) will potentiate spontaneous remissions, when other variables (e.g., medication ingestion, degree of environmental structure, etc.) are held constant. This phenomenon is most often observed with the hospitalization of mental patients.

Neutral stimuli associated with the *offset* (due to spontaneous remission or delivery of an active drug) and diminution of unpleasant symptoms and/or painful disease processes (UCSs) may come to acquire *positive* conditioned properties for healing and anxiety reduction, and may operate as "safety signals" as discussed above. Instances of such neutral stimuli may be the arrival of the physician/therapist, the physical examination, the prescription of medication, and the rituals of medication ingestion.

Mediational Theory

Hence, CSs for pain reduction and healing can be produced in at least two ways: (1) by association with the *onset* of an active ingredient for healing (e.g., morphine, insulin, nitroglycerine, penicillin); (2) by association with the *offset* of the symptoms of an unfamiliar, unpleasant, and painful disease or injury. Finally, neutral stimuli associated with the onset of the symptoms (UCRs) of a painful and unfamiliar disease process may come to elicit conditioned anxiety and/or a fractional anticipatory disease response components, and may be called nocebos.

In view of the analysis above, the labels "inert" and "nonspecific" appear to be less heuristic today. Because this analysis suggests that a variety of neutral substances or procedures that are initially inert or do not reliably alter the underlying presumed mechanisms of disease can, if repeatedly associated with appropriate UCSs, come either to attenuate or to potentiate the disease process and pathophysiology, based on conditioning mechanisms.[3] This analysis predicts (1) that psychological responses (CRs) that were previously relegated to the realm of "nonspecific" factors can come to reliably *attenuate* or *potentiate* health and illness; (2) that initially neutral stimuli (CSs) can come to influence the underlying physiochemical and cellular mechanisms (pathophysiology) of health and illness, either directly or indirectly; and (3) that, theoretically, the influence of such variables on the symptom and mechanism of disease can be demonstrated in appropriately controlled double-blind studies in which the UCS (active chemical ingredient) is witheld.

The notion of active ingredients in a drug or procedure has generally been that which the relevant therapeutic theory singled out as specifically remedial for the condition. For example, penicillin is the active ingredient for pneumococcal pneumonia, according to therapeutic theory, because the disease is caused by pneumococcus, which is sensitive to penicillin. The notion of "specific activity" (Wickramasekera, 1977b, 1977c, 1980) in medicine has traditionally meant (1) that the therapeutic mechanism of action was exclusively a physiochemical one; (2) that the action of the active ingredient was logically related to the presumed etiology (pathophysiology) of the disease; (3) that the therapeutic effect was reliable; and (4) that the therapeutic effect was durable.

Clearly, the CR analysis given above of the placebo effect, and the new psychobiological models (Engel, 1977; Lipowski, 1977; Weiner, 1977) of disease and dysfunction, render the traditional notion of "specific activity" outmoded. On both theoretical and empirical grounds, it is clear that most modern chronic illness is *multiply* determined, and the present analysis

---

3. There are a few exceptional instances in which the CR and the UCR are in opposite directions (e.g., the UCR to atropine is a dry mouth, and the CR is salivation; the UCR to small doses of insulin is hypoglycemia, but the CR is hyperglycemia).

points out that every disease process (UCR) may have a CR component and is therefore psychophysiological in nature. The Pavlovian concept of a UCS (physiochemical or psychological) as an independent variable may be more heuristic today than the notion of "specific activity." As this analysis points out, illness and disease mechanisms are not insulated from conditioning effects. The UCR is a function not only of the UCS (specific ingredient), but also of any associated CS. This learning or conditioning effect is inevitable, given an intact complex CNS. The present analysis indicates that intrinsic to all *effective* interventions or events (chemical, surgical, psychological, or psychophysiological) is the potential for learning or Pavlovian conditioning. Learning that is initially electrical in nature and later physiochemical in character can lead to neuroendocrine and neuroimmunological changes that alter biological structures. Current models of disease (Engel, 1977; Weiner, 1977) suggest that changes in the dependent variable, or health (UCR), can be accounted for by several specifiable independent variables (UCSs) operating either directly or indirectly on the UCR, and that some of these independent variables (CSs) may be psychological in nature.

The literature of respondent conditioning clearly demonstrates that the response to a UCS (e.g., nitroglycerine) will inevitably involve two components. The first component will be a UCR (nonplacebo response) elicited by the active ingredient or UCS (e.g., nitroglycerine). The second component is a CR or learned fractional component of the UCR, elicited by neutral events surrounding the delivery of the drug. The latency and magnitude of these two response components may be different. The CR will have a shorter latency because it is centrally mediated. The CR will also be of smaller magnitude than the UCR. Hence, the UCS inevitably elicits two response components, a CR and a UCR. This analysis saliently points out that intrinsic to all effective interventions (physiochemical, surgical, or behavioral) is the potential for Pavlovian conditioning (Pavlov, 1927), and therefore for placebo learning. Counterintuitively, it predicts that therapists who use UCSs or active ingredients will get stronger placebo effects than those who use only CSs or neutral ingredients, because regular UCS-CS association strengthens the CR. This model also paradoxically predicts that progress in isolating UCSs or active physiochemical, surgical, or behavioral procedures will inevitably lead to more and stronger placebo effects. Thus, therapists who routinely use UCSs or active ingredients will eventually enjoy escalating placebo effects and may be perceived as "miracle workers," when in fact only a part of their "miracles" can be directly traced to their use of UCSs or active pharmacological or surgical techniques. In this analysis, then, medical science emerges as a uniquely human historical endeavor to isolate UCSs or reliably effective ingredients (nitroglycerine, digitalis, etc.). Hence, the potential for respondent conditioning exists in all human situations (not just medical ones) in which UCSs are used or reliably effective events occur.

COMPONENTS OF THE CONDITIONED PLACEBO RESPONSE

The nature of the conditioned placebo response in healing is unknown today. It is probably a complex patterned psychophysiological response (Schwartz, 1976) that is a composite of (1) cognitive–verbal, (2) motor, and (3) physiochemical responses.

The Cognitive–Verbal Component

The cognitive–verbal component may be recognized subjectively as an emotion like "Hope" (Frank, 1973; Mowrer, 1960). But not all cognitive and emotional information processing is explicitly verbally mediated or conscious. There is now evidence from several converging experimental and empirical sources that a salient amount of cognitive and emotional information processing continues in the absence of conscious awareness (Davidson, 1980, in press; Nisbett & Wilson, 1977; Shevrin & Dickman, 1980). In fact, in the case of overlearned behaviors that are critical to survival, or where channel space for conscious information processing is limited, unconsciousness and automaticity in response may be very adaptive features of behavior. Mowrer (1956) has proposed that neutral stimuli associated with the *onset* of pain (e.g., a common symptom of disease, dysfunction, or injury) will acquire drive (e.g., anxiety) properties, and that stimuli associated with the *offset* (cessation) of pain will acquire reinforcing properties ("hope") or will operate as "safety signals." CSs (cognitions, visual impressions, tactile–kinesthetic sensations) associated with the onset of the injury or unpleasant symptoms of disease (UCSs) will come to elicit conditioned anxiety. The visit to the "doctor," the prescription and ingestion of medication, and the like are neutral events ("safety signals") that have previously (in health care history) been associated with active pharmacological agents or UCSs and the offset or reduction of pain and discomfort. Hence, these "safety signals" (CSs) may have acquired anxiety- and/or uncertainty-reducing properties or even fractional anticipatory healing properties (the physiochemical correlates of which remain unspecified today). Neutral events like the visit to the doctor and the "prescription" can operate as conditioned "safety signals" that can inhibit the aversive conditioned anxiety (CR) from cognitions (CSs) and sensations (CSs) associated with the disease onset and maintenance. "Safety signals" like a white coat (CS) and a prescription (CS) can indicate that the period of pain, uncertainty, fear, and depression is over, and that the period of relief and healing is here. The safety signals can both inhibit anxiety and disinhibit the subjective emotion of hope.

The Motor Component

The motor component of the placebo response is probably strongly controlled by the patient's mood (emotions) and current environmental reinforcement contingencies. Current reinforcement contingencies may sometimes be able to override mood and alter motor behavior temporarily, prior to stable and positive changes in emotion. But generally, as the patient's mood starts to "feel better" and as the inhibition of motor activity by emotions like pain and depression recede, the patient may expand his or her behavioral repertoire by resuming such normal activities as eating, copulating, and returning to work. These adaptive activities then fill the temporal and behavioral vacuums that were previously occupied by maladaptive uncertainty, fear, pain, and depressive cognitive–affective ruminations. These conditioned aversive cognitive–affective ruminations (occurring both consciously and unconsciously) probably potentiated the unconditioned components (UCRs) of the disease or injury. This analysis may be particularly relevant to chronic diseases and functional disorders (e.g., low back pain, diabetes, cardiovascular disorders, musculoskeletal disorders, cancer, etc.) where the long-term and *intermittent* reinforcement nature of the UCS (disease process, injury, or dysfunction) enhances the probability of conditioning effects. It is a well-established fact that intermittent reinforcement by the UCS will make a maladaptive cognitive, motor, or affective habit maximally resistant to extinction. The chronic intermittent activation of the disease mechanism by the UCS (physiochemical cause) may lead to increasingly pervasive aversive anticipatory cognitive and affective responses, markedly resistant to extinction, that inhibit the motor system even when the UCS is dormant or inactive in chronic diseases.

The Physiochemical Component

The physiochemical component of the placebo response probably involves at least two subcomponents: psychoneuroendocrine and psychoneuroimmunological components.

PSYCHONEUROENDOCRINE SYSTEM

It now appears that there are descending pain inhibitory pathways from the medial brain stem to the dorsal horn of the spinal cord (Cannon, Liebeskind, & Frank, 1978; Mayer, Wolfe, Akil, Carder, & Liebeskind, 1971). These pathways may involve both opiate and nonopiate mechanisms. The opiate mechanisms can be activated by endogenous morphine-like substances termed "endorphins," and apparently also by electrical stimulation of certain brain sites (e.g., periaqueductal gray matter, etc.). Whether certain types of state-specific cognitive–affective activity (e.g., hypnotic analgesia) can stimulate these brain sites is not known. It appears that the opiate mechanism can be activated within seconds of CNS stimulation; that the analgesic effects extend beyond the period of stimulation; and that the stimulation is particularly effective with clinical as opposed to experimental pain. It appears that other rapidly activated nonopiate pain inhibitory systems (e.g., hypnotic analgesia) are not blocked by naloxone (J. Barber & Mayer, 1977; Goldstein & Hilgard, 1975; Mayer, Prince, Barber, & Rafii, 1976). A recent study (Levine, Gordon, & Fields, 1978) and two extensive literature reviews Basbaum & Fields, 1978; Verebey, Volavka, & Clouet, 1978) suggest that the activation of the endorphin system may be one of the primary chemical mechanisms of pain reduction in the placebo response. However, other cognitively initiated (hypnotic analgesia) but chemically mediated psychoneuroendocrine pain inhibitory systems may also exist (Sternbach, 1982).

There is good evidence that depression potentiates chronic clinical pain (Merskey & Hester, 1972; Taub & Collins, 1974), and it has been suggested that decreased functional activity in the endogenous opioid system may be linked to the pathophysiology of depression (Gold, Pottash, Sweeney, Martin, & Extein, 1982). Both pain sensitivity and deficits in pleasure (depression susceptibility) may be mediated through the catecholamines serotonin, norepinephrine, and dopamine, which are known to alter opiate action. Hence, one rapidly activated psychoneuroendocrine mechanism through which a placebo stimulus may reduce both depression and pain sensitivity is through the recruitment of the endorphin system.

PSYCHONEUROIMMUNOLOGICAL SYSTEM

There is now evidence that the immune system, the primary mechanism of healing, is not totally independent of the CNS and the psychosocial environment. At least three lines of evidence (hypothalamic lesions, adrenocorticotropic hormone [ACTH] and the adrenal cortical axis, and classical conditioning) suggest that the CNS events can potentially and reliably alter the immune system (Ader, 1981; Hirsch, 1982). More specifically, there is now evidence that anxiety and depression can inhibit the immune system (Rogers, Dubey, & Reich, 1979). There is also good experimental evidence that Pavlovian or respondent conditioning procedures can modestly but reliably reduce immunocompetence (Ader, 1981). Theoretically, respondent conditioning procedures may also be able to significantly *potentiate* immunocompetence, but this remains to be experimentally demonstrated. The clinical implications of this prediction are quite profound. Hence, through such CNS mechanisms as emotion and expectancy learning (Pavlovian conditioning), even the immune system may be influenced by placebo stimuli (CSs).

In summary, *the placebo response is probably a composite of patterned, interacting verbal–subjective, motor, neuroendocrine, and neuroimmunological response systems that can attenuate or potentiate both the underlying mechanisms of pathophysiology and overt clinical symptoms.*

DEVELOPMENTAL ASPECTS OF THE CONDITIONED
PLACEBO RESPONSE

Historical Aspects

Developmentally, the child or immature organism, in a stage of dependency and deprivation, is the ideal candidate for conditioning or placebo learning. The reliable delivery of food, clothing, and shelter to dependent immature organisms is in the final analysis associated with the strength and intelligence of the adult parent. In the developmental history of the immature organism, the effective and reliable satisfaction of needs may be associated with certain neutral (CS) features of persons (height, weight, color), response styles (authoritarian, permissive), and places. The ability of an adult caretaker to intervene effectively and reliably to reduce discomfort, uncertainty, fear, and pain, or to produce specific changes (pain, fear) in the individual, the tribe, or the physical environment, is the original basis of the notion of active ingredients or UCSs. For example, a dominant adult male baboon who loses his teeth (UCS), or a political leader who loses his or her wits (UCS) due to senility, is likely to be pushed aside eventually by younger, stronger, and more intelligent members of the group, who can more reliably and effectively consequate (punish or reward) the older, weaker, and less intelligent group members. Both the dominant baboon and the leader will eventually encounter "placebo sag" (Wickramasekera, 1977b, 1977c) or "credibility extinction" as their active ingredients or UCSs (teeth, muscles, claws, IQ) fade with senility. The potency of their "packaging" or neutral features (CSs) cannot be sustained without at least intermittent demonstrations of strength and intelligence (UCSs). From this analysis, general intelligence, a UCS, emerges as a potent and highly generalizable new (on the evolutionary scale) behavioral UCS. A complex active ingredient or UCS such as general intelligence can produce specific and reliable changes in both physiochemical and psychological domains. General intelligence, then, coupled with pertinent information, can be a potent behavioral UCS, on a par with other active ingredients (e.g., physiochemical) and capable of producing respondent conditioning effects. "High credibility" in this analysis is a quality of any behaviors (stimulus events) that reliably produce precise and potent physical, biological, and/or psychological changes in the environment for one's own benefit or the benefit of others. Hence, baboons, leaders, and therapists who come to lean increasingly on their CSs or packaging (neutral features) will inevitably encounter "placebo sag" as their active ingredients (muscles, teeth, IQ) or UCSs fade. They will be discovered to be "impostors" and historically identified as "quacks." On the other hand, those who use primarily UCSs or active ingredients will get stronger placebo effects than quacks, will enjoy escalating credibility, and will be seen as miracle workers, when in fact only half of their miracles can be traced to their active ingredients or UCSs. The other half will be a function of the subjects' anticipatory responses (CRs) elicited by neutral features (CSs) of the "miracle workers." Science in this analysis emerges as a uniquely human quest to identify, isolate, and manipulate UCSs, so that our physical, biological, and psychosocial environments may be rendered more predictable, more reliably controllable, and more nearly explainable.

Acquisition Phase

A dependent organism is a prerequisite for effective conditioning. The physical and psychological immobilization of the organism by health deprivation (injury, infection, tissue, damage, high fever, disorientation, unpleasant and unusual symptoms, fear, and depression) creates both the prerequisite dependent patient role (Mechanic, 1972) and the opportunity for conditioning.

Fear, anxiety, and uncertainty can be inhibited and the attentional process brought to focus in expectant arousal, when parents or caretaker surrogates (doctors, priests, etc.) enter the health-deprived person's environment. The focusing of the attentional mechanism on the physician, and the inhibition of anxiety and fear by a psychophysiological attitude of expectant arousal (hope), are based on prior primitive and infantile social learning (operant, respondent, vicarious) in which parental entry and intervention are associated with the reliable *offset* of aversive events (danger and deprivation) and the *onset* of reinforcing events (food, protection from danger and pain, etc.). Parental figures have acquired the properties of "safety signals" (Mowrer, 1960) that inhibit fear and anxiety and disinhibit an attitude of expectant arousal (hope).

During the acquisition or credibility formation phase, the placebo stimulus and response to be conditioned probably involve (1) awareness of the CS-UCS and the response–reinforcement contingency; (2) implicit or explicit verbal mediation of this contingency; and (3) conscious awareness of several culture-specific, socially learned credible "safety signals" (discriminative stimuli). These culture-specific credible safety signals (e.g. rattles, syringes, pills, potions, wands, stethoscopes, etc.) may or may not be verbally encoded as safety signals. The CSs or safety signals can inhibit worry, doubt, and skepticism. Worry can interfere with the operation of natural homeostatic healing mechanisms. For example, worry and doubt can cause sleep onset or psychophysiological insomnia, thereby inhibiting sleep onset and its healing neuroendocrine consequences. It is clear that the bulk of insomnia is psychophysiological and is caused by cognitive or physiological hyperactivity stimulated by anxiety and worry that is conscious or unconscious. There is also growing evidence that anxiety can inhibit the immune system (Rogers *et al.*, 1979).

The inhibition of worry and doubt by conditioned safety signals (e.g., a placebo pill, an ointment) can make the patient more receptive to healing instruction suggestions given by a physician or therapist. Safety signals may potentiate the instructional signal by inhibiting "noise" or worry, and by improving reception of mesasges. For example, the migraine patient may be given suggestions to constrict cerebral arteries in the second (pain) phase of the disorder by relaxing and reducing sympathetic outflow. The patient with asthma may be given suggestions for bronchodilation. A study by Luparello, Leist, Lourie, and Sweet (1970) in fact demonstrated that the pharmacological action of a bronchodilating drug (UCS) could be doubled on a measure of airway resistance if bronchodilating suggestions (CSs) were associated with the delivery of the drug (UCS). Hence, safety signals may also potentiate the action of active pharmacological agents (UCSs) by inhibiting "noise" or cognitions of uncertainty and doubt. Cognitions of uncertainty and doubt may operate as negative CSs that attenuate the effects of a UCS (active drug).

These discriminative stimuli or CSs may also influence the rate of acquisition of the placebo response by potentiating attentional and arousal mechanisms. These credible signals may be quite diverse: (1) The labeling of the therapist (e.g., "doctor," "swami," "professor," etc.) can influence his or her attention and arousal stimulus value in a given culture. (2) The credibility of the therapeutic setting (e.g., emergency room of a hospital, temple, university medical center, park bench) can also influence the above-described mechanisms of learning. The university medical center, in North American culture, is the new temple of healing. (3) The credibility of the placebo per se (e.g., size, shape, color, taste) and the credibility of the (4) administration ritual (e.g., oral vs. injection, a single dramatic or startling episode like surgery) can also influence attention and arousal conditions. (5) Finally and very saliently, the nature of the interpersonal relationship between the patient and the therapist (e.g. accurate empathy, confidence, warmth, authoritarianism) can influence the attention and arousal properties of these events. The attention and arousal value of these CSs can be directly related to the extent to which they have previously been reliably associated with specific and effective interventions on behalf of the patient when he or she was an immature and dependent organism.

In the acquisition of most new materials (e.g., math) or tasks (e.g., driving a car), it is likely that the specification of component responses facilitates conditioning. The sequential specification of the emission or elicitation of these component responses and the accurate verbal mediation of these component responses will reduce errors in the acquisition phase of learning. During this first phase, large individual differences in pertinent subject characteristics (e.g., autonomic nervous system lability, hypnotizability, general intelligence), a subject's history of reinforcement and punishment, and the culture-specific context of learning can influence placebo learning through the determination of attentional and arousal mechanisms and the specification of what is a "credible" CS for a given subject.

Consolidation Phase

After the placebo response is well established through repeated association with potent UCSs or active ingredients, it probably (1) becomes increasingly abbreviated, (2) involves minimal or no awareness, (3) becomes rapid and automatic, (4) involves a bypass of the verbal or dominant hemisphere, and (5) preferentially involves the minor hemisphere. Hypnosis, like the consolidated placebo response, also appears to involve the nondominant hemisphere preferentially. Indeed, the conditioned placebo response may be potentiated or attenuated by some of the same variables that determine hypnotic responsivity; these variables are specified later. The importance of bypassing the dominant hemisphere is that the lack of verbal mediation, and the very rapid, automatic elicitation of the placebo response, make it relatively independent of the critical, skeptical, analytic mode of information processing that is typical of the dominant hemisphere. Hence, the short-latency placebo response occurs before doubt and skepticism ("noise") can inhibit or attenuate the response or "signal." Stimulus events can directly elicit physiochemical or visceral changes without the interference of the critical, skeptical, filtering mode of information processing that is typical of the dominant hemisphere. This may be similar to the profound visceral and neuroendocrine changes that can occur in response to a CNS event (e.g., being charged by a lion in a dream) when there is an inhibition of critical, analytic brain functions during sleep.

Developmentally, the placebo response may begin as what Spence and Taylor (1951) and others (Cerekwicki, Grant, & Porter, 1968; Grant, 1972) have called a "V form" of classical conditioning, but it can develop into a "C form" of conditioning. The basis of this distinction is the degree of verbal mediation and volition involved in the CR. The mechanism of placebo responding is probably most effective when, in the "C" or second stage, it is increasingly automatic and involves a bypass of the dominant verbal hemisphere's critical, analytic mode of information processing. In the "C" phase it is probably a short-latency, automatic response that can be labeled an "unconscious" response. Currently, the bulk of experimental evidence from several fields of empirical research (selective attention, cortical evoked potentials, subliminal perception) supports the position that the registration of perceptual stimulation can occur outside of conscious awareness (Dixon, 1971; Erdelyi, 1974; Kahneman, 1973; Nisbett & Wilson, 1977; Shevrin & Dickman, 1980) and may be consciously recognized only as a change in behavior or a subjective change in mood or feeling. There is also evidence unrelated to psychodynamic clinical speculation that many of the determinants of social behavior are not open to conscious inspection or specification (Nisbett & Wilson, 1977) and that a large part of cognitive and emotional activity occurs without conscious awareness (Davidson, 1980). It appears that overlearned and less conscious information processing is preferentially localized in the nondominant hemisphere (Luria & Simernitskaya, 1977) and that the frontal lobes are preferentially involved in emotional arousal (Davidson, in press).

PLACEBO RESPONDING

Health Deprivation, Anxiety, Dependency, and Placebo Responding

The eruption of strange physical symptoms on the patient's body, pain, and discomfort all induce uncertainty and anxiety, from which the patient craves relief. This situation of physical immobilization (health deprivation) by symptoms like pain and fear reactivates earlier or regressive dependent attitudes, which increase the patient's receptivity to direction from caretakers or credible healers. In other words, health deprivation makes the good placebo reactor particularly dependent and receptive to help from others. Effective conditioning requires a deprived, anxious, and dependent subject. Anxiety has been shown (Evans, 1974a; Thorn, 1962) to be reliably related to placebo responding. The acquiescence tendency or the tendency to agree ("yea-saying") has been reliably but modestly and positively correlated with both placebo responding (Jospe, 1978) and hypnotizability (Hilgard, 1965). Hence, the results of several experimental and empirical studies reviewed by Jospe and Hilgard point to the role of anxiety, dependency, and the noncritical, nonskeptical mode (the nondominant-hemisphere or hypnotic mode) of information processing in placebo responding and hypnosis.

Placebo Responding and Hypnotizability

Shapiro (1971) has pointed out that laboratory tests of hypnotic susceptibility show an unreliable relationship to placebo responding. Several other analyses have also cast doubt on the existence of a reliable relationship between hypnotizability and the placebo response (Evans, 1969; Katz, Kao, Spiegel, & Katz, 1974; Moore & Berk, 1976; Thorn, 1962). It is possible that this unreliability is due to the activity of other moderating variables (e.g., low credibility, health deprivations, accurate empathy, authoritarianism, levels of attention and arousal, potency of instructional signals), which were not systematically manipulated in the studies relating hypnotic susceptibility and placebo responding. The observation of reliable and orderly relationships between complex events in the empirical world awaits attention to all the relevant variables.

The strongest evidence to date showing a lack of relationship between hypnotizability and placebo responding is a study by McGlashan, Evans, and Orne (1969). This study found the degree of hypnotizability to be unrelated to the magnitude of the placebo response. However, there are several problems with making inferences and generalizing to a clinical situation from this laboratory study, and, therefore, any conclusion may be premature. First, the McGlashan *et al.* (1969) study was a study of experimental pain, and in several areas the paremeters of experimental and clinical pain do not overlap (Melzack, 1973). Caution is necessary in generalizing from this otherwise excellent study to the phenomena of clinical pain. Second, in the McGlashan *et al.* study, there was a failure to use strong, extended, and specific instructions of dominant arm analgesia to mobilize the full potential of the highly hypnotizable subjects in the placebo analgesia session. The presentation of a rationale for a "drug" (placebo) can cognitively mobilize the hypnotic ability of the patient and can function as a hypnotic induction (Wickramasekera, 1976b). A study by Glass and Barber (1961) found that a placebo administered as a "hypnosis"-inducing drug was as effective as an actual trance induction in eliciting enhanced suggestibility. A more recent study of experimental pain by Knox and Gekoski (1981) has shown clearly that a subject's level of hypnotizability is related to the placebo response. Evans (1967) reviewed two nonpatient and five patient studies of the relationship between suggestibility and placebo responding. In neither of the nonpatient studies, and in all but one of the patient (clinical) studies, there was a positive relationship between suggestibility and placebo responding.

I predict that with increased attention to those variables mentioned above as moderating the relationship between hypnotizability and placebo responding, more reliable and stronger relationships between suggestibility and placebo responding will emerge in clinical studies.

If the mechanism of the placebo response is conditioning, and if conditioning is enhanced by the degree of bypass of dominant-hemisphere functions (Saltz, 1973), then it is clear why good placebo responders, like good hypnotic subjects, inhibit the critical, analytic mode of information processing that is characteristic of the dominant verbal hemisphere. Good placebo responders will tend to be individuals who are prone to see conceptual or other relationships between events that seem randomly distributed to others. They will inhibit the interfering signals of doubt and skepticism, which are consequences of the more analytic mode of information processing typical of the dominant (left) hemisphere. Like good hypnotic subjects, good placebo responders are likely to embroider or elaborate on the given stimulus properties of a drug potentiating it, out of their own rich subjective repertoires. Alternatively, they may negate or attenuate the effects of a UCS (drug) through negative attributions.

Shapiro (1971) describes placebo nonresponders as "rigid and stereo-typic and not psychologically minded" (p. 445). There is a striking similarity between this description and that of a poorly hypnotizable subject. There is increasing evidence (Bakan, 1969; K. Graham & Pernicano, 1976; Gur & Gur, 1974; Lachman & Goode, 1976) that hypnotizability or suggestibility is predominantly a right-hemisphere (nondominant or minor-hemisphere) function for right-handed people. Minor-hemisphere functions include holistic and imaginative mentation with diffuse, relational, and simultaneous processing of information (Ornstein, 1973; Sperry, 1964); the tendency to "see" some relationship or "meaning" in data, however randomly generated (e.g., a Rorschach inkblot), would appear to be an aspect of creative mentation that is posited to be a property of the nondominant hemisphere. This explanation can account for the common features of good placebo responders and good hypnotic subjects.

In the second phase (the consolidation phase) of placebo learning, the placebo response may become regnant in the right hemisphere, which appears to be the hemisphere mainly involved in the hypnotic or suggestible mode of information processing. I hypothesize that at this stage the same variables that can influence hypnotic responding can also influence placebo responding. I predict that the placebo response can be potentiated through strong implicit or explicit verbal instructions (Wickramasekera, 1976b) if the following hypnosis-potentiating conditions are also systematically manipulated: (1) Low-arousal states, or training procedures (e.g., biofeedback) that induce low arousal, appear to increase hypnotic responsivity temorarily (Arons, 1976; Engstrom, 1976; Schacter, 1976; Wickramasekera, 1971, 1973b, 1977a). (2) Procedures that induce high arousal appear to increase hypnotic responsivity temporarily (Gur, 1974; Wickramasekera, 1972b, 1976a). (3) Sensory deprivation procedures also appear to increase hypnotic responsivity temporarily (Pena, 1963; Sanders & Reyher, 1969; Wickramasekera, 1969, 1970). (4) The subject's level of attention to relevant stimuli appears to influence hypnotic responsivity (C. Graham & Evans, 1977; Krippner & Bindler, 1974; Mitchell, 1967; Van Nuys, 1973). (5) The baseline suggestibility or hypnotizability of the individual subject (T. X. Barber, 1969; Hilgard, 1965) has a profound effect on hypnotic responsivity.

PARAMETERS OF PLACEBO LEARNING

The Interstimulus Interval (CS-UCS)

Contemporary research (Kimble, 1973) on conditioning and learning clearly demonstrates that interstimulus (CS-UCS) intervals are not immutable, particularly with human subjects, and that they can exceed .5 milliseconds. A positive UCS in the health care situation can be defined as a stimulus that *reliably* elicits a set of specific therapeutic changes (UCRs) in the verbal–subjective, physiochemical, and motor response systems of a human subject. The UCS alters not only the overt symptoms, but also the pathophysiology of the disease or disorder. The CSs are initially neutral features of the physician, the context, and the procedures. There are several ways in which the CS-UCS association can occur in the health care situation.

SIMULTANEOUS CONDITIONING

If the onset and offset of the CS and UCS occur simultaneously, the procedure is called "simultaneous conditioning." This situation is unlikely to occur, except perhaps in the association of a neutral CS with the relief of acute pain with a powerful, fast-acting analgesic (UCS).

DELAYED CONDITIONING

"Delayed conditioning" is a procedure in which CS onset occurs prior to the UCS and lasts at least until the UCS appears. Historically, an example of this would be the arrival of the physician (CS) prior to the onset of spontaneous remission, and his or her departure timed to occur with the onset of the physiochemical events (UCSs) that precede or correlate with symptomatic improvement. This is not unlikely, since for hundreds of years physicians have observed and tracked the natural invariable symptomatic course of several common diseases; therefore, they could predict or prophesy the sequential progression and resolution of symptoms long before they could control these symptomatic events. It is probable that sagacious physicians timed their arrivals and departures to coincide with visible symptomatic changes in the patient. For example, physicians who were good observers and were knowledgeable about the progression and timing of symptoms could time the delivery of their rituals (CSs) to coincide clearly and dramatically with the onset of the spontaneous remission of obvious symptoms. On a simple correlation basis, this could be a dramatic demonstration of therapeutic power. But prediction and correlation are not control. It would be control if they could turn the disease process on and off again at will. Fortunately, early physicians were not told, "Do that again."

TRACE CONDITIONING

"Trace conditioning" occurs when the CS comes on briefly and goes off before the onset of the UCS. A physician with a very detailed and confident knowledge of the course of an illness could arrive late, stay briefly, and leave long before the onset of spontaneous remission, accurately prophesying the course of the patient's symptoms even in his or her absence. Before leaving, the physician might order the performance of some inert rituals and leave, confidently predicting a cure within a specified time interval.

BACKWARD CONDITIONING

"Backward conditioning" occurs when the CS follows the UCS, or the physician (CS) arrives after the recovery (UCR) has started. It is unlikely that too many smart physicians in the early days of medicine used this conditioning procedure. It is now known to lead to weak and unreliable conditioning.

TEMPORAL CONDITIONING

"Temporal conditioning" is a situation in which a specific time interval functions as a CS. A UCS occurs or is presented at regular time intervals, and during the test period the UCS is omitted on a portion of the trials. Under these conditions, a CR will occur at the time the UCS typically occurs. This form of conditioning may occur with some chronic diseases that have a fairly reliable intermittent onset. For example, primary dysmenorrhea may be caused part of the time by physiochemical (endocrine) stimuli (UCSs) of varying magnitude. But the chronic maintenance of severe symptoms of unvarying or increasing intensity may be in part related to psychoneuro-endocrine events (CSs), such as temporarily conditioned anticipatory dysmenorrhea responses.

Phenomena of Conditioning

ADAPTATION

Repeated presentations of even potent UCSs can lead to the failure to evoke the UCR and to an absent or extinguishing CR. This phenomena is particularly likely to occur in the treatment of chronic functional problems treated symptomatically. In this instance, even initially potent but non-specific drugs, such as Valium given for classic migraine headaches, can become less effective over time. For example, the physician and most aspects of his or her practice can lose the ability to elicit conditioned therapeutic responses. The physician has encouenred "placebo sag" and becomes a "quack" in the eyes of the patient. Hence, even a careful CS–UCS analysis of the therapy situation would focus attention on the clear and urgent need for therapeutic stimuli to be targeted on the known or presumed etiology of the disorder, and not simply on peripheral symptoms.

SUMMATION

When two or more CSs are presented together, the strength of the CR will be stronger than to either CS alone. This implies that the presence of several "safety signals" or CSs will lead to a stronger placebo response (e.g., not 36% but perhaps 60%). The *humane* use of diagnostic electrical–medical high technology (e.g., CAT scans) (CSs) and efficacious drugs (UCSs) and/or effective surgical procedures (UCSs) may inflate the size of the placebo component in healing. When high technology and irrelevant (nonspecific) state-of-the-art diagnostic and therapy procedures are used withuot sacrificing humane patient care, by practitioners even with minimal UCSs, a large placebo component will be found. This situation probably occurs in large and prestigious tertiary care medical centers to which many patients with functional disorders journey over long distances, as if on a pilgrimage to temples of healing.

TWO-COMPONENT RESPONSE

A UCS will always elicit two components, a CR and a UCR. This is predicted because it is probably impossible to deliver a pure UCS isolated from a CS to a conscious vertebrate.

RESPONSE GENERALIZATION

A person who has learned to respond therapeutically to physician A or procedure A has also learned to respond therapeutically to almost equivalent stimului (e.g., physician B and procedure B). This phenomenon is often clearly observable in the medical management of acute illness. Acute illness is effectively treated by the health care system, and psychosocial factors seldom have enough time to interfere with healing. In the case of chronic illness, however, we often observe attenuated therapeutic effects even to active therapeutic ingredient (UCSs), due to generalization of negative CRs from previous illness episodes or ineffective therapy.

GENERALIZATION OF EXTINCTION

When physicians use ineffective UCSs to treat chronic conditions, we often observe extinction of the placebo response—not only to the original primary care physician, but to all subsequent physicians. This extinction of the placebo component to even an effective UCS may jeopardize even a rational and effective treatment program, because it has been found that the placebo response may not only potentiate or attenuate a UCS (active drug), but may also *negate* its effects.

THE IMPACT OF EXPLICIT OR IMPLICIT VERBAL INSTRUCTIONS AND "INFORMATION" ON CONDITIONED RESPONSES

There is good evidence that "awareness" of contingence can potentiate the acquistion of CRs (Bandura, 1969). The patient's conscious recognition of the association between the physician and efficacious UCSs (e.g., penicillin) will enhance the acquisition of learning of placebo responses. Also, information about the physician's credentials, reputation among colleagues, and therapeutic record can potentiate or attenuate the placebo component of the healing. There is a large, well-established, experimentally based literature documenting the fact that instructions and information can potently influence both respondent and operant conditioning procedures (Bandura, 1969).

PREDICTIONS FROM THE MODEL

The following predictions appear consistent with the CR model of the placebo, and empirical data disconfirming any of these predictions will cast doubt on the theory.

1. Therapists who routinely use active ingredients (UCSs) will get stronger placebo effects (CRs) than those who do not. This procedure creates and reinforces the CS-UCS relationship that optimizes the conditions for "hope" (Frank, 1973). Intrinsic to all interventions with active ingredients (UCSs) is the potential for Pavlovian conditioning, and therefore for placebo learning. Hence, the stronger the active ingredient (UCS) or drug used, the stronger the placebo effect; the weaker the active ingredient or UCS intensity, the weaker the placebo response.

2. The response to any active ingredient (UCS) will come to include two components (CR + UCR): a placebo (CR) and an active component (UCR). In other words, a fraction of the response to a UCS will always include a CR—for example, the response to the sight of the syringe (CS) or the ingestion per se (CS) of the pill. In fact, it is very likely that the fractional anticipatory response (CR) will have a shorter latency than the response (UCR) to the UCS (e.g., morphine). The shorter latency of the CR will be due to the posited central mediation of conditioning effects, as opposed to the initial peripheral mediation of some drug effects.

3. Therapists who frequently use inert or placebo medication or procedures (CSs) will get weaker placebo responses over time. This is an extinction procedure because withdrawal of the UCS (active ingredient) will eventually lead to extinction of the CR, or "placebo sag." Therapists who have the "right packaging" (CSs) but who lack a science or truly efficacious UCSs will eventually collapse under the weight of their own incompetence.

4. Numerous repeated presentations of the UCS in drug therapy can lead to temporary tolerance or habituation. But temporary withdrawal of the UCS will abolish "placebo sag." CSs alone will not reliably show this recovery feature.

5. Dose–response and time–effect curves for a placebo and an active medication will be similar but not identical. Literature review (Evans, 1974a) supports this prediction. The response to CS is like the response to UCS but of shorter latency.

6. Patients higher on *trait* anxiety will be stronger placebo responders. It is known that trait anxiety is related to the acquisition and magnitude of CRs (Spence & Taylor, 1951). This model can comfortably embrace the anxiety reduction data reviewed by Evans (1974a).

7. The placebo response is predicted to be stronger under modified double-blind conditions. This implies that neither patient nor therapist should know that an inert or CS procedure is being used. In fact, they should both be told that only an active ingredient or a UCS is used. In general, there will be less inhibition of the expectancy mechanism when this modified double-blind procedure is used. Credibility will be optimal with this modified double blind. Orne (1974) and Frank (1973) have stressed the role of expectancy and credibility in their analyses of the placebo.

8. The use of several placebo (inert or neutral) stimuli (CS_1, CS_2, CS_3) can lead to a stronger placebo response (higher than the typical 35% rate) than the use of one placebo stimulus (CS_1). It is known that when two (CS_1 + CS_2) or more CSs are presented together, the strength of the CR is often greater than to either CS alone. This phenomenon is called "summation" (Kimble, 1961).

9. In the final analysis, there can be no CR if there are no UCS (active ingredients). Pardoxically, progress in isolating and manipulating active ingredients (UCSs) will inevitably lead to more and stronger placebo effects (CRs). In other words, "faith" will grow with progress in "science," and it may be increasingly difficult to separate out the effects of CSs and UCSs.

10. If the baseline suggestibility of the patient is mobilized with specific explicit or implicit instructions, then the CR can be potentiated or attenuated.

11. Children, highly hypnotizable adults, and early adolescents can be stronger placebo responders because of their inherently higher baseline suggestibility (Hilgard, 1965).

12. Treatment procedures that use systematic (a) attentional manipulations, (b) induction of low or high arousal, and (c) sensory restriction can potentiate placebo components (CSs) plus any active ingredients (UCSs) in a procedure or substance.

13. Neutral persons, places, and procedures can operate as both positive or negative CSs. This may explain iatrogenic illness and may suggest ways of arranging the conditions for iatrogenic health. Nocebo effects can arise out of associating neutral stimuli with negative UCSs.

14. Patients whose childhood histories combine firm discipline with warm and effective relief of needs, plus an ability to entertain themselves alone, will be the best placebo responders. Patients whose childhood histories include few or no instances of predictable, reliable, and effective (positive or negative) interventions in their environment or on their behalf will demonstrate weak placebo responses to culture-specific, socially sanctioned health rituals. For example, austistic children will be poor placebo responders.

15. Skeptical, critical, analytic modes of thinking or information processing (typical of the dominant hemisphere) will attenuate or negate placebo responding (CR).

16. The placebo response will not occur if the healing ritual involves bypass of consciousness and the CNS.

17. The placebo response will occur maximally under conditions of strong motivation or real personal health deprivation (e.g., escape from life-threatening illness, pain, or fear). In clinical situations with sick patients, the threat to well-being is real, intense, cross-situational, and of unknown duration, whereas with nonpatients in experimental studies, the threat to well-being is superficial, situation-specific, reversible, and of known duration. The magnitude of the placebo response will generally be weaker with nonpatients. In general, the placebo response will be most potent in life-threatening medical situations, and not in personally trivial social-psychological experiments in university laboratories.

TESTING THE MODEL

The model must be tested under conditions of ecological validity. "Ecological validity" refers to the extent to which we may generalize from controlled laboratory studies of a phenomena to similar phenomena in nonexperimental situations (clinical or natural environments). For example, it is well known that the parameters of clinical and experimental pain are different (Melzack, 1973; Sternbach, 1978). The placebo rate in double-blind experimental pain studies is small and ranges between 9% and 16% (Evans, 1974a) whereas the average placebo rate in double-blind clinical pain (postsurgical) studies is 36%, and thus substantially larger (Beecher, 1959). A sick or health-deprived person is in several psychological and physical respects different from a well person in an experimental study. A sick person is often immobilized by his or her symptoms cross-situationally. An experimental subject is only immobilized by experimental pain in a situation-specific (laboratory) sense. An experimental subject exposed to a physical stressor (radiant heat, ischemic pain, etc.) is a voluntary subject involved in an episodic and reversible stressful event, which does not intrude on the rest of the subject's life. A sick person is immobilized cross-situationally in an involuntary situation, whose outcome is uncertain and which intrudes on all social, personal, and vocational aspects of his or her life. Uncertainty about the consequences of diagnosis and therapy, dependency on others, and lost mobility cause loss of self-esteem over the erosion of important social roles (income provider, caretaker, adult). Sometimes the impatience and progressive withdrawal of loved ones from the patient cause frustration, anger, and depression. These psychological reactions are often superimposed on the pain and physical discomfort caused by the physiological disease process. Therefore, both physically and psychologically, a sick person is not like a typical experimental laboratory subject. The CR model has been developed to predict behavior in a *clinical* situation and should be tested on sick patients in therapy.

CONCLUSION

Since this model of the placebo effect is formulated in terms of experimental psychology and learning, it may have some heuristic value, because it may lead us to the design of experiments that raise different questions about treatment and may lead us to interpret the responses in unexpected ways. This model makes several specific counterintuitive and paradoxical predictions that may be worth testing empirically. A large body of precise and empirically validated principles from learning theory can now be related to the nebulous field of the placebo. This conceptual translation may stimulate new, sharper, and more focused thought and empirical investigation into this neglected psychobiological realm.

This realm includes psychological effects that are powerful but unreliable, rapid but not always durable, and clearly worthy today of investigation in their own right. It may even turn out that this realm includes the only therapeutic effects that are primarily psychological. It is perhaps time that we settled down to the tedious business of making these "nonspecific" effects specific by isolating, explicating, and specifying the type of subject, the type of therapist, and the situational and procedural conditions under which these effects can be negated, attenuated, or potentiated. It seems unlikely that all the phenomena today lumped under the label "placebo effects" can be comprehended within the present CR model. But we can no longer continue to dismiss these effects with impatience and embarrassment as "nonspecific," "placebo," or plain "nuisance" effects. It appears to me that these effects reside at and regulate the intersections of all psychobiological actions and transactions.

ACKNOWLEDGMENTS

A version of this chapter was first presented at the San Diego Biomedical Symposium (invited paper), San Diego, California, November 1977. Later it was presented at a symposium on Non-Specific Effects in Biofeedback, Biofeedback Society of America, Albuquerque, New Mexico, February 1978. It has been published in abbreviated form in *Proceedings of the San Diego Biomedical Symposium* (New York: Academic Press, 1977) and the *Journal of Clinical Engineering* (1977, 2, 227–230). I would like to thank G. E. Schwartz for encouraging me to repackage this model for left-brain (critical, analytic) consumers, and particularly for his encouragement and critical comments during the review process.

REFERENCES

Ader, R. (Ed.). *Psychoneuroimmunology.* New York: Academic Press, 1981.
Ader, R., & Cohen, N. Behaviorally conditioned immunosuppression and murine systemic lupus erythematosus. *Science,* 1982, *215,* 1534–536.
Arons, L. Sleep assisted instructions. *Psychological Bulletin,* 1976, *83,* 1–40.
Bakan, P. Hypnotizability, laterality of eye movements and functional brain asymmetry. *Perceptual and Motor Skills,* 1969, *28,* 927–932.
Bandura, A. *Principles of behavior modification.* New York: Holt, Rinehart & Winston, 1969.
Barber, J., & Mayer, D. Evaluation of the efficacy and neural mechanism of a hypnotic analgesia procedure and experimental and clinical dental pain. *Pain,* 1977, *4,* 41–48.
Barber, T. X. Toward a theory of pain: Relief of chronic pain by prefrontal leucotomy, opiates, placebos, and hypnosis. *Psychological Bulletin,* 1959, *56,* 430.
Barber, T. X. Hypnosis: A scientific approach. New York: Van Nostrand Reinhold, 1969.

Basbaum, A. I., & Fields, H. L. Endogenous pain control mechanisms: Review and hypothesis. *Annals of Neurology*, 1978, *4*(5), 451–462.

Beecher, H. K. The powerful placebo. *Journal of the American Medical Association*, 1955, *159*, 1602–1606.

Beecher, H. K. *Measurement of subjective responses: Quantitative effects of drugs.* New York: Oxford University Press, 1959.

Beecher, H. K. Surgery as a placebo. *Journal of the American Medical Association*, 1961, *176*, 1102–1107.

Bowbjerg, D., Ader, R., & Cohen, N. Behaviorally conditioned suppression of a graft-versus-host response. *Proceedings of the National Academy of Sciences USA*, 1982, *79*, 583–585.

Cannon, J. T., Liebeskind, J. C., & Frank, H. Neural and neurochemical mechanisms of pain inhibition. In R. A. Sternbach (Ed.), *The psychology of pain.* New York: Raven Press, 1978.

Cerekwicki, L. E., Grant, D., & Porter, E. C. The effect of number and relatedness of verbal discriminanda upon differntial eyelid conditioning. *Journal of Verbal Learning and Verbal Behavior*, 1968, *7*, 847–853.

Cobb, L. A., Thomas, G. I., Dillard, D. H., *et al.* An evaluation of internal-mammary-artery ligation by a double blind technic. *New England Journal of Medicine*, 1959, *260*, 1115–1118.

Cohen, H. D., Graham, C., Fotopoulos, S. S., & Cook, M. R. A double-blind methodology for biofeedback research. *Psychophysiology*, 1977, *14*, 603–608.

Davidson, R. J. Consciousness and information processing: A biocognitive perspective. In J. M. Davidson & R. J. Davidson (Eds.), *The psychobiology of consciousness.* New York: Plenum, 1980.

Davidson, R. J. Affect, cognition and hemispheric specialization. In C. E. Izard, J. Kagan, & R. Zajonc (Eds.), *Emotion, cognition and behavior*, in press.

Dimond, E. G., Kittle, C. F., & Crockett, J. E. Evaluation of internal mammary artery ligation and sham procedure in angina pectoris. *Circulation*, 1958, *18*, 712–713.

Dixon, N. F. *Subliminal perception: The nature of a controversy.* London: McGraw-Hill, 1971.

Drawbraugh, R., & Lal, H. Reversal by narcotic antagonist of a narcotic action elicited by a conditioning stimulus. *Nature*, 1974, *247*, 65–67.

Engel, G. L. The need for a new medical model: A challenge for biomedicine. *Science*, 1977, *196*, 129–136.

Engstrom, D. R. Hypnotic susceptibility, EEG-alpha and self-regulation. In G. E. Schwartz & D. Shapiro (Eds.), *Consciousness and self-regulation.* New York: Plenum Press, 1976.

Erdelyi, M. H. A new look at the new look: Perceptual defense and vigilance. *Psychological Review*, 1974, *81*, 1–25.

Evans, F. J. Suggestibility in the normal working state, *Psychological Bulletin*, 1967, *67*(2), 114–129.

Evans, F. J. Placebo response: Relationship to suggestibility and hypnotizability. *Proceedings of the 77th Annual Conention of the American Psychological Association*, 1969, *4*, 889–890.

Evans, F. J. The placebo response in pain reduction. In J. J. Bonica (Ed.), *Advances in neurology* (Vol. 4, *Pain*). New York: Raven Press, 1974. (a)

Evans, F. J. The power of a sugar pill. *Psychology Today*, April 1974, p. 32. (b)

Frank, J. D. *Persuasion and healing: A comparative study of psychotherapy.* Baltimore: Johns Hopkins University Press, 1973.

Glass, L. B., & Barber, T. X. A note on hypnotic behavior, the definition of the situation and the placebo effect, *Journal of Nervous and Mental Disease*, 1961, *132*, 539–541.

Gleidman, L. H., Gantt, W. H., & Teitelbaum, H. A. Some implications of conditional reflex studies for placebo research. *American Journal of Psychiatry*, 1957, *113*, 1103–1107.

Gold, M. S., Pottash, A. C., Sweeney, D., Martin, D., & Extein, I. Antimanic, antidepressant and anti-panic effects of opiates: Clinical, neuroanatomical and biochemical evidence. In K. Verebey (Ed.), *Opioids in mental illness*. New York: New York Academy of Sciences, 1982.

Goldberg, S. R., & Schuster, C. R. Conditioned suppression by a stimulus associated with nalorphine in morphine dependent monkeys. *Journal of the Experimental Analysis of Behavior*, 1967, *10*, 235–242.

Goldberg, S. R., & Schuster, C. R. Conditioned nalorphine induced abstinence changes: Persistence in post-morphine dependent monkeys. *Journal of the Experimental Analysis of Behavior*, 1970. *14*, 33–46.

Goldstein, A., & Hilgard, E. R. Failure of the opiate antagonist naloxone to modify hypnotic analgesia. *Proceedings of the National Academy of Sciences USA*, 1975, *72*, 2041–2043.

Graham, C., & Evans, F. Hypnotizability and the development of waking attention. *Journal of Abnormal Psychology*, 1977, *86*, 631–638.

Graham, K., & Pernicano, K. *Laterality, hypnosis and the autokinetic effect*. Paper presented at the meeting of the American Psychological Association, Washington, D.C., 1976.

Grant, D. A. A preliminary model for processing information conveyed by verbal conditioned stimuli in classical conditioning. In A. Black & W. Prokasy (Eds.), *Classical conditioning II: Current research and theory*. New York: Meredit, 1972.

Gur, R. C. An attention-controlled operant procedure for enhancing hypnotic susceptibility. *Journal of Abnormal Psychology*, 1974, *83*, 644–650.

Gur, R. C., & Gur, R. E. Handedness, sex, eyedness, and moderating variables in relation to hypnotic susceptibility and functional brain symmetry. *Journal of Abnormal Psychology*, 1974, *83*, 635–643.

Haas, H., Fink, H., & Hartfelder, G. Das placeboproblem. *Fortschritte der Arzneimittelforschung*, 1959, *1*, 279–454.

Herrnstein, R. J. Placebo effect in the rat. *Science*, 1962, *138*, 677–678.

Hilgard, E. R. *Hypnotic susceptibility*. New York: Harcourt, Brace, 1965.

Hilgard, E. R., & Marquis, D. G. *Conditioning and learning*. New York: Appleton, 1940.

Hirsch, J. Current state of research in psychoneuroimmunology and cancer. In J. Holland (Ed.), *Current concepts in psychosocial oncology*. New York: Sloan–Kettering Memorial Cancer Center, 1982.

Horningfeld, G. Nonspecific factors in treatment: I. Review of placebo reactions and placebo reactors. *Diseases of the Nervous System*, 1964, *25*, 145–156. (a)

Horningfeld, G. Nonspecific Factors in Treatment: II. Review of social-psychological factors. *Diseases of the Nervous System*, 1964, *25*, 225–239. (b)

Hull, C. L. *A behavioral system*. New Haven: Yale University Press, 1952.

Jospe, M. *The placebo effect in healing*. Lexington, Mass.: Lexington Books, 1978.

Kahneman, D. *Attention and effort*. Englewood Cliffs, N.J.: Prentice-Hall, 1973.

Katz, R. L., Kao, C. Y., Spiegel, H., & Katz, G. J. Pain, acupuncture, hypnosis. In J. J. Bonica (Ed.), *Advances in neurology* (Vol. 4, *Pain*). New York: Raven Press, 1974.

Kazdin, A. E., & Wilcoxon, L. A. Systematic desensitization and nonspecific treatment effects: A methodological evaluation. *Psychological Bulletin*, 1976, *83*(5), 729–758.

Kimble, G. *Conditioning and learning*. New York: Appleton-Century-Crofts, 1961.

Kimble, G. Scientific psychology in transition. In F. McGuigan & D. Lumsdan (Eds.), *Contemporary approaches to conditioning and learning*. New York: Wiley, 1973.

Knox, V. J., & Gekoski, W. L. *Analgesic effect of acupuncture in high and low hypnotizables*. Paper presented at the meeting of the Society for Clinical and Experimental Hypnosis, Portland, Oregon, October 1981.

Krippner, S., & Bindler, P. R. Hypnosis and attention: A review. *American Journal of Clinical Hypnosis*, 1974, *16*, 166–177.

Lachman, S., & Goode, W. J. *Hemispheric dominance and variables related to hypnotic susceptibility*. Paper presented at the meeting of the American Psychological Association, 1976.

Levine, J. D., Gordon, N. C., & Fields, H. L. The mechanism of placebo analgesia. *Lancet*, 1978, *2*, 654–657.

Lipowski, Z. J. Psychosomatic medicine in the seventies: An overview. *American Journal of Psychiatry*, 1977, *134*, 233–244.

Luparello, T. J., Leist, N., Lourie, C. H., & Sweet, P. The interaction of psychologic stimuli and pharmacologic agents on airway reactivity in asthmatic subjects. *Psychosomatic Medicine*, 1970, *32*, 509–513.

Luria, A. R., & Simernitskaya, E. G. Interhemispheric relations and functions of the minor hemisphere. *Neuropsychologia*, 1977, *15*, 175–178.

Mayer, D. J., Wolfe, T. L., Akil, H., Carder, B., & Liebeskind, J. C. Analgesia from electric stimulation in the brainstem of the rat. *Science*, 1971, *174*, 1351–1354.

Mayer, D. J., Prince, D. D., Barber, J., & Rafii, A. Acupuncture analgesia: Evidence for activation of a pain inhibitory system as a mechanism of action. In J. J. Bonica & D. Albe-Fessard (Eds.), *Advances in pain research and therapy* (Vol. 1). New York: Raven Press, 1976.

McGlashan, T. H., Evans, F. J., & Orne, M. T. The nature of hypnotic analgesia and placebo response to experimental pain. *Psychosomatic Medicine*, 1969, *31*, 227–246.

Mechanic, D. Social psychological factors affecting the presentation of bodily complaints. *New England Journal of Medicine*, 1972, *286*, 1132–1139.

Merskey, H., & Hester, R. A. The treatment of chronic pain with psychotropic drugs. *Postgraduate Medicine Journal*, 1972, *48*, 594–598.

Melzack, R. *Puzzle of pain*. New York: Basic Books, 1973.

Mitchell, M. G. *Hypnotic susceptibility and response to distraction*. Unpublished doctoral dissertation, Claremont Graduate School, 1967.

Moore, M. E., & Berk, S. M. Acupuncture for chronic shoulder pain: An experimental study with attention to the role of placebo and hypnotic susceptibility. *Annals of Internal Medicine*, 1976, *84*, 381–384.

Mowrer, O. H. Two factor learning theory reconsidered, with special reference to secondary reinforcement and the concept of habit. *Psychological Review*, 1956, *63*, 114–128.

Mowrer, O. H. *Learning theory and behavior*. New York: Wiley, 1960.

Nisbett, R. E., & Wilson, T. D. Telling more than we can know: Verbal reports on mental processes. *Psychological Review*, 1977, *84*, 231–259.

Orne, M. T. Pain suppression by hypnosis and related phenomena. In J. J. Bonica (Ed.), *Advances in neurology* (Vol. 4, *Pain*). New York: Raven Press, 1974.

Ornstein, R. *The psychology of consciousness*. New York: Viking, 1973.

Ostfeld, A. M. *The common headache syndromes: Biochemistry, pathophysiology, therapy*. New York: Grune & Stratton, 1962.

Pavlov, I. P. *Conditioned reflexes* (G. V. Anrep, trans.). London: Oxford University Press, 1927.

Pena, F. *Perceptual isolation and hypnotic susceptibility*. Unpublished doctoral dissertation, Washington State University, 1963.

Rogers, M. P., Dubey, D., & Reich, P. The influence of the psyche and the brain on immunity and disease susceptibility: A critical review. *Psychosomatic Medicine*, 1979, *41*(2), 147–164.

Saltz, E. Higher mental processes as the bases for the laws of conditioning. In F. McGuigan & D. Lumsden (Eds.), *Contemporary approaches to conditioning and learning*. New York: Wiley, 1973.

Sanders, S., & Reyher, J. Sensory deprivation and the enhancement of hypnotic susceptibility. *Journal of Abnormal Psychology*, 1969, *74*, 375–381.

Schacter, D. L. The hypnogogic state: A critical review of the literature. *Psychological Bulletin*, 1976, *83*, 452–481.

Schuster, C., & Thompson, T. Self administration of and behavioral dependence on drugs. *Annual Review of Pharmacology*, 1969, *9*, 483–502.

Schwartz, G. E. Self-regulation of response patterning: Implications for psychophysiological research and therapy. *Biofeedback and Self-Regulation*, 1976, *1*, 7–30.

Schwitzgebel, R., & Traugott, M. Initial note on the placebo effect of machines. *Behavioral Science*, 1968, *13*, 267–273.

Shapiro, A. Placebo effects in medicine, psychotherapy and psychoanalysis. In A. Bergin & S. Garfield (Eds.), *Handbook of psychotherapy and behavior change*. New York: Wiley, 1971.

Shevrin, H., & Dickman, S. The psychological unconscious. *American Psychologist*, 1980, *35*(5), 421–434.

Siegel, S. A Pavlovian conditioning analysis of morphine tolerance. In N. A. Krasnegor (Ed.), *Behavioral tolerance: Research and treatment implications* (National Institute on Drug Abuse Monograph No. 18; U.S. DHEW Publ. No. ADM 78-551). Washington, D.C.: U.S. Government Printing Office, 1978.

Skinner, B. F. *Science and human behavior*. New York: Macmillan, 1953.

Spence, K., & Taylor, J. A. Anxiety and the strength of the UCS as determiners of the amount of eyelid conditioning. *Journal of Experimental Psychology*, 1951, *42*, 183–188.

Sperry, R. The great cerebral commissure. *Scientific American*, 1964, *210*, 42–52.

Sternbach, R. A. *The psychology of pain*. New York: Raven Press, 1978.

Sternbach, R. A. On strategies for identifying neurochemical correlates of hypnotic analgesia. *International Journal of Clinical and Experimental Hypnosis*, 1982, *30*(3), 251–256.

Stroebel, C. F., & Glueck, B. C. Biofeedback treatment in medicine and psychiatry: An ultimate placebo. In L. Birk (Ed.), *Biofeedback: Behavior medicine*. New York: Grune & Stratton, 1973.

Taub, A., & Collins, W. F., Jr. Observations on the treatment of denerveral dysthesia with psychotropic drugs: Posttherapeutic neuralgia, anesthesia dolorosa, and peripheral neuropathy. In J. J. Bonica (Ed.), *Advances in Neurology* (Vol. 4, *Pain*). New York: Raven Press, 1974.

Thorn, W. F. The placebo reactor. *Australian Journal of Pharmacy*, 1962, *43*, 1035–1037.

Van Nuys, D. Meditation, attention, and hypnotic susceptibility: A correlational study. *International Journal of Clinical and Experimental Hypnosis*, 1973, *21*, 59–69.

Verebey, K., Volavka, J., & Clouet, D. Endorphins in psychiatry. *Archives of General Psychiatry*, 1978, *35*, 877–888.

Weiner, H. *Psychobiology and human disease*. New York: Elsevier/North-Holland, 1977.

Wickramasekera, I. The effects of sensory restriction on susceptibility to hypnosis: A hypothesis and some preliminary data. *International Journal of Clinical and Experimental Hypnosis*, 1969, *17*, 217–224.

Wickramasekera, I. Effects of sensory restriction on susceptibility to hypnosis: More data. *Journal of Abnormal Psychology*, 1970, *76*, 69–75.

Wickramasekera, I. Effects of EMG feedback training on susceptibility to hypnosis: Preliminary observations. In J. Stoyva, T. Barber, L. V. DiCara, J. Kamiya, N. E. Miller, & D. Shapiro (Eds.), *Biofeedback and self-control*. Chicago: Aldine, 1971.

Wickramasekera, I. EMG feedback training and tension headache: Preliminary observations. *American Journal of Clinical Hypnosis*, 1972, *15* (2), 83–85. (a)

Wickramasekera, I. A technique for controlling a certain type of sexual exhibitionism. *Psychotherapy: Theory, Research and Practice*, 1972, *9*, 207–210. (b)

Wickramasekera, I. The application of verbal instructions and EMG feedback training to the management of tension headache. *Headache*, 1973, *13*(2), 74–76. (a)

Wickramasekera, I. The effects of EMG feedback on susceptibility to hypnosis. *Journal of Abnormal Psychology*, 1973, *82*, 174–177. (b)

Wickramasekera, I. Aversive behavior rehearsal for secaul exhibitionism. *Behavior Thereapy*, 1976, *7*, 167–176. (a)

Wickramasekera, I. (Ed.). *Biofeedback, behavior therapy and hypnosis*. Chicago: Nelson-Hall, 1976. (b)

Wickramasekera, I. On attempts to modify hypnotic susceptibility: Some psychophysiological procedures and promising directions. *Annals of the New York Academy of Sciences*, 1977, *296*, 143–153. (a)

Wickramasekera, I. The placebo effect and biofeedback for headache pain. In *Proceedings of the San Diego Biomedical Symposium*. New York: Academic Press, 1977. (b)

Wickramasekera, I. The placebo effect and medical instruments in biofeedback. *Journal of Clinical Engineering*, 1977, *2*, 227–230. (c)

Wickramasekera, I. A conditioned reponse model of the placebo effect: Predictions from the model. *Biofeedback and Self-Regulation*, 1980, *5*, 5–18.

Wilker, A., & Pesor, F. T. Persistence of relapse tendencies of rats previously made physically dependent on morphine. *Psychopharmacologia*, 1970, *16*, 375–384.

Wolf, S. Effects of suggestion and conditioning on the action of chemical agents in human subjects: The pharmacology of placebos. *Journal of Clinical Investigation*, 1950, *29*, 100–109.

Wolff, H. G. *Headache and other pain*. New York, Oxford University Press, 1963.

16
Drug-Anticipatory Responses in Animals

SHEPARD SIEGEL

THE PHARMACOLOGICAL CONDITIONING SITUATION

Living organisms not only respond reflexively to stimuli; they also respond in anticipation of stimuli. The analysis of such anticipatory responding uses procedures and terminology developed by Ivan Pavlov, and is called "Pavlovian" (or "classical") conditioning (Pavlov, 1927).

In the Pavlovian conditioning situation, a contingency is arranged between two stimuli; typically, one stimulus reliably predicts the occurrence of the second stimulus. Using the usual terminology, the second of these paired stimuli is termed the "unconditional stimulus" (UCS). The UCS, as the name implies, is selected because it elicits relevant activities from the outset (i.e., unconditionally), prior to any pairings. The stimulus signaling the presentation of the UCS is "neutral" (i.e., it elicits little relevant activity prior to its pairing with the UCS), and is termed the "conditional stimulus" (CS). The CS, as the name implies, becomes capable of eliciting new responses as a function of (i.e., conditional upon) its pairing with the UCS.

In Pavlov's well-known conditioning research, the CS was a conveniently manipulated exteroceptive stimulus (bell, light, etc.), and the UCS was either food or orally injected dilute acid (both of which elicited a conveniently monitored salivary response). After a number of CS-UCS pairings, it was noted that the subject salivated not only in response to the UCS, but also in anticipation of the UCS (i.e., in response to the CS). The subject was then said to display a "conditional response" (CR).

A wide range of exteroceptive and interoceptive stimuli have been used in Pavlovian conditioning experiments (Razran, 1961). Drugs constitute a particularly interesting class of UCSs. After some number of drug administrations, each administration reliably signaled by a CS, pharmacological CRs can be observed in anticipation of the actual drug administration. It was Pavlov who first demonstrated that a drug could be an effective UCS:

Shepard Siegel. Department of Psychology, McMaster University, Hamilton, Ontario, Canada.

288

A dog was given a small dose of apomorphine subcutaneously and after one or two minutes a note of a definite pitch was sounded during a considerable time. While the note was still sounding the drug began to take effect upon the dog: the animal grew restless, began to moisten its lips with its tongue, secreted saliva and showed some disposition to vomit. After the experimenter had reinforced the tone with apomorphine several times it was found that the sound of the note alone sufficed to produce all the active symptoms of the drugs, only in a lesser degree. (Pavlov, 1927, p. 35)

Additional research by Krylov (reported by Pavlov, 1927, pp. 35–37) indicated that even if there is not an explicit CS (such as an auditory cue), naturally occurring predrug cues (opening the box containing the hypodermic syringe, cropping the fur, etc.) could serve as CSs. In Krylov's experiments, a dog was repeatedly injected with morphine; each injection elicited a number of responses, including copious salivation. After five or six such injections, it was observed that "the preliminaries of injection" (Pavlov, 1927, p. 35) elicited many morphine-like responses, including salivation.

FORM OF CONDITIONAL DRUG RESPONSES

Subsequent to Pavlov's initial demonstrations, the effectiveness of many drugs as UCSs in the Pavlovian conditioning situation has been evaluated (see reviews by Loucks, 1937; Lynch, Stein, & Fertziger, 1976; Siegel, 1977a). Generally, the obtained results may be divided into two categories: (1) studies (like Pavlov's) demonstrating drug CRs that appear to mimic the response unconditionally elicited by the drug (the UCR), and (2) studies demonstrating drug CRs that appear to mirror (or be opposite to) the drug UCR.

Drug-Mimicking CRs

As illustrated in the previously described research with apormorphine and morphine, pharmacological CRs often appear to be replicas of the drug-induced UCR; other examples of such drug-mimicking CRs are provided by studies of dogs repeatedly injected with anticholinergic drugs. The mydriatic response elicited by the drug may eventually be seen in response to the presentation of predrug cues (e.g., Lang, Brown, Gershon, & Korol, 1966). Similarly, the convulsive behavior elicited in rats by repeated injections of high doses of insulin may be displayed as a CR (Reiss, 1958; Siegel, 1975a).

Drug-Mirroring CRs

Drugs have many effects. For example, in addition to mydriasis, anticholinergic drugs inhibit salivation. Similarly, in addition to eliciting convulsions, insulin also induces hypoglycemia. It has been noted that the salivary effects of anticholinergic drugs, and the glycemic effects of insulin, are often expressed as drug-mirroring CRs. That is, the animal with a history of atropine administration displays a CR of *hyper*salivation (e.g., Lang *et al.*, 1966; Mulinos & Lieb, 1929), and the animal with a history of insulin administration displays a CR of *hyper*glycemia (Siegel, 1972, 1975a). Many other examples of such drug-mirroring CRs have been noted; indeed, one of the earliest studies of pharmacological conditioning (Subkov & Zilov, 1937) reported that dogs repeatedly injected with epinephrine (each injection eliciting tachycardia) displayed a bradycardiac CR when presented with the usual predrug cues but administered a placebo. These investigators cautioned "against the widely accepted view that the external modifications of the conditioned reflex must always be identical with the response of the organism to the corresponding unconditioned stimulus" (Subkov & Zilov, 1937, p. 296). Subsequent research has revealed other examples of such drug-mirroring CRs in animals. For example, in addition to its bradycradiac effect, epinephrine also decreases gastric secretion and induces hyper-glycemia. Rats with a history of epinephrine administration display an *increase* in gastric secretion (Guha, Dutta, & Pradhan, 1974) and *hypo*-glycemia (Russek & Piña, 1962). Summaries of pharmacological condi-tioning studies demonstrating drug-mirroring CRs may be found elsewhere (Siegel, 1983a).

Determination of Pharmacological CR Topography

Although both drug-mimicking and drug-mirroring CRs have been noted, the conditions that favor the expression of the two CR forms are not yet entirely clear. However, an imporant analysis of pharmacological conditioning has recently been presented by Eikelboom and Stewart (1982) that may elucidate the area. They suggest that there is a fundamental confusion concerning the identification of pharmacological UCSs and UCRs. This confusion arises because the observed effects of drugs, in contrast to the observed effects of most peripherally applied stimuli, may occur without the participation of the central nervous system (CNS).

In the typical (nonpharmacological) Pavlovian conditioning prepara-tion, the UCS is an event with an afferent site of action; that is, the UCS stimulates receptors that initiate activity in the CNS. It is the effects of this CNS activity that constitute the UCR. In such a conditioning situation, the CR usually mimicks the UCR. Eikelboom and Stewart (1982) suggest that for those drugs whose effects are mediated in a similar manner (i.e., drugs with an afferent site of action), the CR will similarly mimick the UCR.

In contrast with this situation, however, many chemical UCSs have an *efferent* site of action; the observed drug effect may be due to direct pharmacological stimulation of the effector system. In such cases, it is accurate to consider the drug effect as the UCS (not the UCR), since it elicits (rather than results from) a CNS response. It is this central response to the drug effect that constitutes the UCR. For example, parenterally administered glucose causes a rise in blood glucose concentration, and the CR seen in the animal trained with glucose is a depression in blood glucose concentration (Deutsch, 1974; Mityushov, 1954). These results have been presented as examples of a pharmacological CR (hypoglycemia) that mirrors the pharmacological UCR (hyperglycemia) (e.g., Siegel, 1975b; Woods & Kolkosky, 1976). In fact, the hyperglycemia noted following glucose administration is the *UCS* (not the UCR), with this UCS initiating CNS activities that act to compensate for the hyperglycemia; the correctly conceptualized UCR, then, is the CNS-mediated response to the glucose (i.e., homeostatic corrections for the glucose-induced hyperglycemia).

Speaking casually, it is the UCS-elicited activities of the brain that get associated with the CS. These activities may be initiated via direct afferent stimulation, or via efferent stimulation that engages feedback mechanisms to counteract the drug effect. In both cases, according to Eikelboom and Stewart (1982), the CR will mimic the UCR. In the case of pharmacological conditioning, the CR will be in the same direction as the drug effect if the drug has an afferent site of action, and the CR will be opposite in direction to the drug effect if the drug has an efferent site of action. In the case of those drugs with multiple effects, the various components of the CR would be expected either to mimic or to mirror the drug effect, depending on the mechanism by which the effect results.

Eikelboom and Stewart (1982) have presented an important analysis of the stimulus and response characteristics of drugs. It is likely that their discussion is relevant to apparant discrepancies concerning the relationship between the pharmacological CR and UCR. Nevertheless, the "site-of-action" argument offered by Eikelboom and Stewart (1982) does not appear to be readily applicable to some reports concerning pharmacological CR topography. For example, using apparently very similar procedures involving conditioning of insulin effects in rats, Woods, Makous, and Hutton (1969) reported an insulin-like hypoglycemic CR, and Siegel (1972) reported an insulin-compensatory hyperglycemic CR. Indeed, more recently, Flaherty, Uzwiak, Levine, Smith, Hall, and Schuler (1980) reported both insulin-mimicking and insulin-mirroring anticipatory responding, depending on the characteristics of the CS. Such findings suggest that additional work is necessary to fully delineate the conditions favoring the expression of the various forms of pharmacological CRs.

Assessment of Conditional Pharmacological Responses

As summarized elsewhere (Siegel, 1977a), there are several ways of determining whether the organism has learned the association between the predrug CS and the pharmacological UCS.

NEW RESPONSES IN CS-UCS INTERVAL

The CR may be detected in the interval between the presentation of the CS and the administration of the UCS. For example, in experiments by Yakovlevich (described by Genes, 1955, p. 213), dogs were brought into a distinctive room (the CS) before they were injected with insulin (the UCS). After a number of such pairings, merely bringing the dog into the room where it had previously been injected induced the motor behavior, salivation, respiratory changes, and other responses initially elicited by the insulin. Similarly, Rikki (research described by Bykov, 1959) placed a dog on a table to administer a choleretic agent on two or three occasions when "a sudden and dramatic increase in bile formation was observed when the animal was placed on the experimental table, preparatory to receiving the cholagogue" (Bykov, 1959, p. 61).

CS-ALONE TEST

Pharmacological conditioning may be revealed on a test session in which a subject with a history of drug administration is presented with the usual drug-signaling CS, but no substance (or an inert substance) is administered. For example, Bykov (1959, pp. 77–78) described an experiment in which a dog received 100 pairings of an auditory stimulus (a "bicycle horn") and nitroglycerine. Subsequently, when the horn was sounded, but no drug injected, the dog displayed an altered elctrocardiogram similar to that induced by nitroglycerine (diminished QRS complex and an increase in P- and T-wave magnitude). Similarly, it has been reported that an auditory stimulus presented simultaneously with bulbocapnine administration can evoke a bulbocapnine-like cataleptic state when it is sounded but no drug administered (Konradi, 1960; Perez-Cruet & Gantt, 1964).

PHARMACOLOGICAL "CHALLENGE"

Recently, it has been suggested that pharmacological CRs may not be readily detectable in some response systems because of the inertial characteristics of these systems (Hinson, Poulos, & Cappell, 1982). A *tendency* to manifest a CR may result in an observable CR only if the responding system is "challenged" or "primed." For example, Hinson, Poulos, and Cappell (1982) reported that rats presented with a pentobarbital-paired CS did not display any overt CR. However, a drug-mirroring CR (opposite to the behaviorally sedating effect of pentobarbital) was noted when these rats received a stimulant challenge (cocaine) in conjunction with the pento-barbital-signaling stimulus; there was an augmented reaction to the motor-simulatory effects of cocaine. Poulos and Hinson (1984) describe another example of such pharmacologial "priming" of a pharmacological CR. Rats with a history of scopolomine administration (and its adipsic consequences) displayed a drug-mirroring CR of excessive polydipsia (relative to control subjects) when confronted with scopolomine-associated cues and adminis-tered phenobarbital, a drug that increases water consumption. It is possible that the use of a pharmacological challenge would reveal pharmacological CRs in situations where they are otherwise not readily observable (Demellweek & Goudie, 1983; LaHoste, Cison, Olson, & Kastin, 1980; Tiffany, Petrie, Baker, & Dahl, 1983).

MODULATION OF PHARMACOLOGICAL UCR

As suggested by Bykov (1959, pp. 82–83), drug CRs displayed in anticipation of the actual pharmacological assault should be expected to interact with the drug-induced UCR, and thus pharmacological conditioning may be evidenced by the modulation of the unconditional effect of the drug over the course of successive administrations. Thus, a drug-mimicking CR would be expected to augment the drug effect, and a drug-mirroring CR would be expected to attenuate the drug effect. In fact, many of the effects of a variety of drugs do either increase or decrease over the course of successive administrations (such changes are termed "sensitization" and "tolerance," respectively). Although such progressive alterations in drug effects have not typically been attriubted to learning, results of recent research implicate Pavlovian conditioning in drug sensitization and tolerance. This research is discussed in the next section.

SIGNIFICANCE OF PHARMACOLOGICAL CONDITIONING

Since the effects of a drug are almost always signaled by environmental cues uniquely present at the time of drug administration, the administration of a drug usually satisfies the requirements of a Pavlovian conditioning trial. It follows that an understanding of drug effects requires an appreciation not only of the direct effects of the pharmacological stimulation, but also of resposnes made in anticipation of this stimulation. The study of pharmacological CRs, priamrily with animal subjects, has yielded important insights into the interaction of learning and pharmacology.

Pharmacological Conditioning and Drug Sensitization

As indicated previously, it might be expected that a pharmacological UCR may become augmented by a drug-mimicking CR displayed in anticipation of the drug effect. As the drug is administered more and more often, and the association between predrug cues and the drug is strengthened, the pharmacological CR would be expected to supplement the drug effect increasingly, thus contributing to sensitization. In fact, in Krylov's own description of his morphine-conditioning work conducted in Pavlov's laboratory (Krylov, 1933), he noted not only a salivary CR, but also the fact that the salivary effect to morphine increased over successive administrations. Krylov attributed the growth of the drug effect to a pharmacological CR, of increasing strength, adding to the pharmacological UCR. Similarly, it has been suggested (Siegel, 1977a) that the sensitization noted to the locomotor activity effects of small doses of morphine in rats (Babbini & Davis, 1972) is likely due to the conditioning of a morphine-like hyperactivity (Kamat, Dutta, & Pradhan, 1974).

Recently, persuasive evidence that some instances of drug sensitization are due to Pavlovian conditioning has been provided by studies demonstrating that nonpharmacological manipulations of predrug environmental cues similarly affect learning and drug sensitization.

ENVIRONMENTAL SPECIFICITY OF DRUG SENSITIZATION

On the basis of a conditioning analysis, it would be expected that here should be some environmental specificity to the display of the sensitized response. If the organism with a history of drug administration were administered the drug in an environment not previously associated with the drug, there would be no CR augmenting the drug effect, and little evidence of sensitization should be seen. Such context specificity in the display of sensitization to the behavioral effects of cocaine in rats has been reported (Hinson & Poulos, 1981; Post, Lockfeld, Squillace, & Contel, 1981).

EXTINCTION OF DRUG SENSITIZATION

If a CR has been acquired, presenting the CS without the UCS causes a diminution of the CR. The phenomenon is termed "extinction." If sensitization results because the predrug CS elicits a drug-mimicking CR, sensitization should be subject to extinction. In other words, it would be expected that placebo sessions would attenuate sensitization. Such a finding has recently been reported by Hinson and Poulos (1981).

OTHER EVIDENCE THAT DRUG-ANTICIPATORY RESPONSES CONTRIBUTE TO SENSITIZATION

The finding that presentation of the predrug CS during a drug-free period reverses sensitization is expected on this basis of the conditioning analysis. The analysis further predicts that no such reversal should occur if the subject is not exposed to predrug cues during abstinence. This is because CRs, although decremented by extinction, are relatively unaffected by the mere passage of time during which conditioning stimuli are not presented. That is, CRs are retained over long periods of time (see Kimble, 1961, p. 281). On ths basis of a conditioning model, therefore, it might be expected that drug sensitization, being a manifestation of a CR, would similarly be well retained. The available evidence that drug sensitization persists with little decrement over extended drug-free periods (summarized by Hinson & Poulos, 1981), then, is consistent with the suggestion that conditioning contributes to sensitization.

Finally, a study of cocaine sensitization in the Brattleboro strain of rats further supports the conditioning interpretation of sensitization. Brattleboro rats have a genetic deficiency of vasopressin, a pituitary peptide that is important in learning. Rats deficient in this peptide are (compared to littermate controls) deficient in the development of cocaine sensitization (Post, Contel, & Gold, 1980).

Pharmacological Conditioning and Drug Tolerance

Just as a drug-mimicking CR progressively augments the drug effect over the course of repeated administrations, drug-mirroring CRs progressively attenuate the drug effect. That is, drug tolerance is partially attributable to Pavlovian conditioning. Although the contribution of drug anticipation to drug tolerance has been recognized for over 100 years (Siegel, 1983b), experimental evidence implicating drug-mirroring CRs in tolerance has only recently accumulated (see review by Siegel, 1983a). A variety of drugs have been used in this research, but most experiments have assessed the contribution of conditioning to morphine tolerance.

Results of studies of morphine conditioning in rats indicate that drug-mirroring CRs are observed for many of the drug's effects. For example, the subject with a history of morphine administration, and its analgesic consequences, displays a CR of hyperalgesia (i.e., extraordinary sensitivity to nociceptive stimulation) (Krank, Hinson, & Siegel, 1981; Siegel, 1975b). Similar drug-mirroring CRs have been reported with respect to many other effects of morphine: cardiac effects (Rush, Pearson, & Lang, 1970), thermic effects[1] (Siegel, 1978c), locomotor activity (Hinson & Siegel, 1983; Mucha, Volkovskis, & Kalant, 1981), and gastrointestinal transit time (Raffa, Porreca, Cowan, & Tallarida, 1982). On the basis of the conditioning analysis of morphine tolerance, such drug-mirroring CRs displayed in anticipation of the pharmacological UCR would partially cancel the drug effect. As the drug is administered more and more often, with the same environmental stimuli signaling each drug administration, the strength of the drug-mirroring CR (and thus the degree to which the UCR is canceled) would increase. Such a progressively attenuated response to a drug defines tolerance.

The logic of the research conducted to evaluate the conditioning model of tolerance is parallel to that used to evaluate the conditioning model of sensitization.

ENVIRONMENTAL SPECIFICITY OF DRUG TOLERANCE

On the basis of the conditioning model, environmental cues consistently predicting the systemic effects of the drug should be crucial for the development of tolerance, since they enable the subject to make timely conditional drug-mirroring responses in anticipation of the drug effect. A number of experiments by Mitchell and his colleagues (e.g., Adams, Yeh,

---

1. There is controversy concerning the conditions under which a morphine-mirroring thermic CR is obtained (Eikelboom & Stewart, 1981; Sherman, 1979; Siegel, 1978c).

Woods, & Mitchell, 1969) did demonstrate that rats displayed the expected analgesic-tolerant response to the last of a series of morphine injections only if this final injection was presented in the context of the same environmental cues as the prior injections (see reviews by Siegel, 1978a, 1978b). Subsequent research has confirmed and extended Mitchell's observations concerning the situation specificity of morphine analgesic tolerance, using several experimental designs. (For a review of tolerance situation-specificity designs, see Siegel, 1979.) A range of morphine doses and a variety of analgesiometric procedures have been used in this research (Advokat, 1980; LaHoste et al., 1980; Siegel, 1975b, 1976; Siegel, Hinson, & Krank, 1978; Tiffany & Baker, 1981; Tiffany, Petrie, Martin, & Baker, 1983). Additional research has indicated the importance of drug-associated environmental cues in the display of tolerance to the thermic[2] (Siegel, 1978c) and locomotor (Hinson & Siegel, 1983 Mucha et al., 1981) effects of morphine, and the lethal effect of diacetylmorphine hydrochloride (heroin) (Siegel, Hinson, Krank, & McCully, 1982). Finally, the situational specificity of tolerance has been demonstrated with many nonopiate drugs: ethanol (Crowell, Hinson, & Siegel, 1981; Lê, Poulos, & Cappell, 1979; Mansfield & Cunningham, 1980; Melchior & Tabakoff, 1981; Parker & Skorupski, 1981), pentobarbital (Cappell, Roach, & Poulos, 1981; Hinson, Poulos, & Cappell, 1982), amphetamine (Poulos, Wilkinson, & Cappell, 1981), scopolamine (Poulos & Hinson, 1984), haloperidol (Hinson, Poulos, & Thomas, 1982; Poulos & Hinson, 1982), and chloridazepoxide (Greeley, 1981).

EXTINCTION OF DRUG TOLERANCE

If morphine tolerance is (in part) mediated by morphine-mirroring CRs, extinction of these CRs should attenuate tolerance. That is, established drug tolerance, like established drug sensitization, should be reversed by placebo administrations. Such extinction has been demonstrated with respect to the analgesic (Siegel, 1975b, 1977b; Siegel, Sherman, & Mitchell, 1980), thermic (Siegel, 1978c), and lethal (Siegel, Hinson, & Krank, 1979) effects of morphine. Extinction of tolerance has also been demonstrated with ethanol (Crowell et al., 1981; Mansfield & Cunningham, 1980) and amphetamine (Poulos, Wilkinson, & Cappell, 1981).

RETARDATION OF DRUG TOLERANCE

A variety of nonpharmacological procedures retard the acquisition of CRs. According to an associative interpretation of morphine tolerance, similar

---

2. As indicated in footnote 1, there is some controversy concerning the conditions under which a morphine-mirroring thermic CR is obtained. Similarly, there is controversy concerning the conditions that do (e.g., Rudy & Yaksh, 1977; Siegel, 1978c) and do not (e.g., Sherman, 1979; Thornhill, Hirst, & Gowdey, 1978) favor the development of tolerance to the thermic effect of morphine in the rat (see Clark & Clark, 1980).

procedures should retard the development of such tolerance. One technique for attenuating the strength of an association is to repeatedly present the CS alone prior to pairing it with the UCS. The deleterious effect of such preconditioning exposure to the CS has been termed "latent inhibition" (see review by Lubow, 1973). If drug tolerance is mediated, at least in part, by an association between predrug cues and the drug, it would be expected that rats with extensive experience with the administration cues prior to the time that these cues are paired with the drug should be relatively retarded in the acquisition of tolerance (compared to rats with minimal pre-exposure to these cues), despite the fact that the groups do not differ with respect to their histories of drug administration. Using this procedure, Tiffany and Baker (1981) and I (Siegel, 1977b) demonstrated latent inhibition of morphine analgesic tolerance.

Another procedure for decreasing the strength of a CS-UCS association is partial (as compared to consistent) reinforcement. That is, if only a portion of the presentations of the CS are paired with the UCS, CR acquisition is retarded (compared to the situation in which all presentations of the CS are paired with the UCS; see Mackintosh, 1974, p. 72). This literature has clear implications for a Pavlovian conditioning account of morphine tolerance: A group in which only a portion of the presentations of the drug administration cues are actually followed by morphine (i.e., a partial reinforcement group) should be slower to acquire tolerance than a group that never has exposure to environmental cues signaling the drug without actually receiving the drug (i.e., a continuous reinforcement group), even when the two groups are equated with respect to all pharmacological parameters. Such a finding has been reported with respect to tolerance to the analgesic, thermic, and anorexigenic effects of morphine (Krank, Hinson, & Siegel, 1984; Siegel, 1977b, 1978c).

INHIBITION OF DRUG TOLERANCE

In most Pavlovian conditioning research, the CS is paired with the UCS. As already discussed, an association established in this manner is weakened by CS-alone presentations (extinction), and the development of the association can be retarded by CS-alone presentations either prior to or interspersed among CS-UCS pairings (i.e., "latent inhibition" and partial reinforcement effects, respectively). The conditioning analysis of tolerance is supported by findings that these manipulations similarly affect the development of morphine tolerance.

Organisms can learn not only that a CS predicts the presence of the UCS, but also that a CS predicts the *absence* of the UCS. Such associations are termed "inhibitory" to distinguish them from the more commonly studied excitatory associations. An example of an inhibitory training procedure is one in which the CS signals a long period free of the UCS (Rescorla, 1969). The association between the CS and UCS *absence* is not readily detectable, because it does not result in overt CRs. However, the inhibitory association resulting from this "explicitly unpaired" procedure may be seen by subsequently arranging the CS to predict the presence of the UCS (i.e., the CS and UCS are paired). The prior inhibitory training will retard the acquisition of the excitatory association; that is, CRs will be slow to develop. This is a "retardation-of-acquistion" demonstration of inhibition (Rescorla, 1969).

If morphine tolerance is, in part, attributable to a drug-mirroring CR, it should be subject to inhibitory learning. Such inhibitory learning would be an especially dramatic and counterintuitive demonstration of the contribution of learning to tolerance, as tolerance would be retarded by a procedure involving administration of the drug.

Consider the situation in which the analgesic effect of morphine is tested, in drug-experienced subjects, in the context of a distinctive environmental cue. Subjects that receive pretest cue presentations and morphine administrations in an explicitly unpaired manner (i.e., the cue always signals a long, drug-free period) should be retarded in the acquisition of tolerance when the subjects are subsequently administered morphine in the presence of the cue. It has, in fact, recently been reported that such an explicitly unpaired technique of cue and drug presentation *does* result in an inhibitory association between the environmental and pharmacological stimuli, as evidenced by the retarded development of tolerance to the analgesic and behaviorally sedating effects of morphine (Fanselow & German, 1982; Siegel, Hinson, & Krank, 1981). The finding that the acquisition of morphine tolerance may be retarded by a treatment involving morphine injections is not readily interpretable by theories of tolerance that do not acknowledge a role for learning in the development of tolerance.

Fanselow and German (1982) further demonstrated that tolerance, once established in the presence of a distinctive environmental cue, can be eliminated by the continued presentation of the drug and that cue, but in an explicitly unpaired manner. That is, despite the fact that morphine-tolerant subjects continue to receive morphine, tolerance is eliminated if the continued morphine administrations are unpaired with a cue that was initially paired with the drug. It has previously been demonstrated, in a variety of Pavlovian conditioning situations, that unpaired CS and UCS presentations eliminate an association established by prior CS-UCS pairings (e.g., Frey & Butler, 1977). The finding that these manipulations similarly affect morphine tolerance further indicates that Pavlovian conditioning importantly contributes to such tolerance.

OTHER EVIDENCE THAT DRUG-ANTICIPATORY RESPONSES CONTRIBUTE
TO TOLERANCE

Evidence suggesting that associative processes may be involved in tolerance is provided by experiments indicating that tolerance dissipates little with the passage of time; that is, drug tolerance, like drug sensitization, is well retained. In addition, tolerance is retarded by suppressors of protein synthesis, and facilitated by vasopressin, much as these substances retard and facilitate other types of learning. Moreover, electroconvulsive shock, frontal cortical stimulation, and cortical lesions have similar effects on learning and drug tolerance, thus further suggesting a parallel between the processes. These additional findings suggesting that drug-anticipatory responses contribute to tolerance have been reviewed elsewhere (Hinson & Siegel, 1980; Siegel, 1983a).

PHARMACOLOGICAL CONDITIONING AND CROSS-DRUG EFFECTS

If a subject is presented with a cue signaling a particular drug (say, Drug A) but is actually administered an alternative drug (say, Drug B), the observed effect of Drug B would consist of an interaction between the Drug A anticipatory response and the unconditional effect of Drug B. Results illustrating such CR-UCR interactions have already been described in the discussion of the pharmacological challenge method of CR detection: The rat anticipating scopolomine is more sensitive to the adipsic effects of phenobarbital (Poulos & Hinson, 1984), and the rat anticipating pentobarbital is more sensitive to the convulsive effect of cocaine (Hinson & Poulos, 1981). Tatum and Seevers (1929) suggested that the stimulatory effect of ephedrine are enhanced, and the depressant effects of morphine antagonized, if these substances are administered in the context of cues previously associated with cocaine. Bykov (1959, pp. 82–83) claimed that such "collisions" between a CR and a UCR may be responsible for some pathological disturbances. He reported an experiment by Levitin, in which a CS was paired with acetylcholine administration in a dog. When this CS was subsequently followed by adrenalin (rather than acetylcholine) injection, "an astonishing result" was noted in the dog's electrocardiogram: The adrenalin induced paroxysmal tachycardia and extrasystoles. Bykov (1959) indicated that, at the dosage used (.5 mg), the adrenalin did not lead to such disturbed cardiac activity if its administration was not announced by an environmental signal for acetylcholine, and he suggested that these results may be relevant to some instances of pathological cardiac activity in humans.

A well-known cross-drug effect is termed "cross-tolerance." Cross-tolerance is said to occur when tolerance to one drug results in a reduced response to another drug. Results of recent research indicate that drug-anticipatory responses contribute to cross-tolerance. That is, the drug-mirroring CR not only attenuates the effect of the drug used as the UCS, but also of other drugs with the same effect (see review by Siegel, 1983a). A role for Pavlovian conditioning in cross-tolerance between ethanol and pentobarbital (Cappell et al., 1981) and between morphine and ethanol (Mansfield & Woods, 1981) has been established.

PHARMACOLOGICAL CONDITIONING AND DRUG DEPENDENCE

Pavlovian conditioning processes have been implicated in withdrawal symptoms observed when drug use is terminated. Following a period of abstinence, drug-mirroring CRs, elicited by drug-associated environmental cues, may in fact *be* so-called withdrawal symptoms; that is, in many instances, drug-withdrawal symptoms may be better characterized as drug-preparation symptoms (Siegel, 1983a; Hinson & Siegel, 1983). In addition, drug-mimicking CRs may promote continued drug use by increasing the effectiveness of drug-related stimuli and the probability of drug-related thoughts (Stewart, deWit, & Eikelboom, 1984). The literature on the experimental, clinical,and epidemiological evidence concerning the role of pharmacological conditioning in drug dependence has been summarized elsewhere (Grabowski & O'Brien, 1981; Hinson & Siegel, 1982; Siegel, 1983a; Stewart *et al.*, 1984; Wikler, 1980), as have the treatment implications of this research (Poulos, Hinson, & Siegel, 1981; Siegel, 1983a).

PHARMACOLOGICAL CONDITIONING AND PLACEBO EFFECTS

It has been suggested that some placebo effects may, in fact, be pharmacological CRs (e.g., Gliedman, Gantt, & Teitelbaum, 1957; Herrnstein, 1962; see Wickramasekera, Chapter 15, this volume). Thus, the organism with a history of drug administration may, when administered an inert substance in the context of drug-associated environmental cues, display a drug-mimicking CR. Such a response, displayed in these circumstances, may constitute some instances of placebo effects.

Since some pharmacological CRs are opposite to the drug effect, it might be expected that some conditioning-mediated "placebo effects" would be opposite to the effect of the drug that is being anticipated. Although the literature on such "reverse placebo effects" in humans is not extensive, there is evidence that they occur (Rickels, Lipman, & Raab, 1966; Storms & Nisbett, 1970).

DRUG-ANTICIPATORY RESPONSES AND DRUG EFFECTS IN HUMANS

Most of the data concerning the significance of drug-anticipatory responding have been collected with animal subjects. Although some skepticism has been expressed concerning the relevance of these data to humans (Alexander & Hadaway, 1982; Hodgson, 1980), results of those few experiments that have been conducted with humans generally confirm results obtained with animals (Beirness, 1982; Dafters & Anderson, 1982; Ferguson & Mitchell, 1969; Hinson & Siegel, 1982; Lang & Rand, 1969; Lightfoot, 1980; see review by Siegel, 1983a). It is clear that the growing literature on drug-anticipatory responses in animals has importance for an understanding of human psychopharmacology.

ACKNOWLEDGMENT

Research from my laboratory summarized in this chapter was supported by research grants from the U.S. National Institute on Drug Abuse and the Natural Sciences and Engineering Research Council of Canada.

REFERENCES

Adams, W. J., Yeh, S. Y., Woods, L. A., & Mitchell, C. L. Drug-test interaction as a factor in the development of tolerance to the analgesic effect of morphine. *Journal of Pharmacology and Experimental Therapeutics*, 1969, *168*, 251–257.

Advokat, C. Evidence for conditioned tolerance of the tail flick reflex. *Behavioral and Neural Biology*, 1980, *29*, 385–389.

Alexander, B. K., & Hadaway, P. F. Opiate addiction: The case for an adaptive orientation. *Psychological Bulletin*, 1982, *92*, 367–381.

Babbini, M., & Davis, W. M. Time–dose relationships for locomotor activity effects of morphine after acute or repeated treatment. *British Journal of Pharmacology*, 1972, *46*, 213–224.

Beirness, D. J. *Reinforcement contingencies control the development of behavioural tolerance in social drinkers.* Unpublished doctoral dissertation, University of Waterloo, 1982.

Bykov, K. M. *The cerebral cortex and the internal organs.* Moscow: Foreign Languages Publishing House, 1959.

Cappell, H., Roach, C., & Poulos, C. X. Pavlovian control of cross-tolerance between pentobarbital and ethanol. *Psychopharmacology*, 1981, *74*, 54–57.

Clark, W. G., & Clark, Y. L. Changes in body temperature after administration of acetycholine histamine, morphine, prostaglandins and related agents. *Neuroscience and Biobehavioral Reviews*, 1980, *4*, 175–240.

Crowell, C. R., Hinson, R. E., & Siegel, S. The role of conditional drug responses in tolerance to the hypothermic effect of ethanol. *Psychopharmacology*, 1981, *73*, 51–54.

Dafters, R., & Anderson, G. Conditioned tolerance to the tachycardia effect of ethanol in humans. *Psychopharmacology*, 1982, *78*, 365–367.

Demellweek, C., & Goudie, A. J. An analysis of behavioural mechanisms involved in the acquisition of amphetamine anorectic tolerance. *Psychopharmacology*, 1983, *79*, 58–66.

Deutsch, R. Conditioned hypoglycemia: A mechanism for saccharin-induced sensitivity to insulin in the rat. *Journal of Comparative and Physiological Psychology*, 1974, *86*, 350–358.

Eikelboom, R., & Stewart, J. Temporal and environmental cues in conditioned hypothermia and hyperthermia associated with morphine. *Psychopharmacology*, 1981, *72*, 147–153.

Eikelboom, R., & Stewart, J. Conditioning of drug-induced physiological responses. *Psychological Review*, 1982, *89*, 507–528.

Fanselow, M. S., & German, C. Explicitly unpaired delivery of morphine and the test situation: Extinction and retardation of tolerance to the suppressing effects of morphine on locomotor activity. *Behavioral and Neural Biology*, 1982, *35*, 231–241.

Ferguson, R. K., & Mitchell, C. L. Pain as a factor in the development of tolerance to morphine analgesia in man. *Clinical Pharmacology and Therapeutics*, 1969, *10*, 372–382.

Flaherty, C. F., Uzwiak, A. J., Levine, J., Smith, M., Hall, P., & Schuler, R. Apparent hyperglycemic and hypoglycemic conditioned responses with exogenous insulin as the unconditioned stimulus. *Animal Learning and Behavior*, 1980, *8*, 382–386.

Frey, P. W., & Butler, C. S. Extinction after aversive conditioning: An associative or nonassociative process? *Learning and Motivation*, 1977, *8*, 1–17.

Genes, S. G. *Nervnaya sistema i veotrennyaya sekretsiya* [*The nervous system and internal secretion*]. Moscow: Gosudarstuennoe Isdatelistvo Meditsinskoi Literaturii Medgiz, 1955.

Gliedman, L. H., Gantt, W. H., & Teitelbaum, H. A. Some implications of conditional reflex studies for placebo research. *American Journal of Psychiatry*, 1957, *113*, 1103–1107.

Grabowski, J., & O'Brien, C. B. Conditioning factors in opiate use. In N. Mello (Ed.), *Advances in substance abuse* (Vol. 2). Greenwich, Conn.: JAI Press, 1981.

Greeley, J. D. *Conditioning and tolerance to chlordiazepoxide*. Unpublished master's thesis, University of Toronto, 1981.

Guha, D., Dutta, S. N., & Pradhan, S. N. Conditioning of gastric secretion by epinephrine in rats. *Proceedings of the Society for Experimental Biology and Medicine*, 1974, *147*, 817–819.

Herrnstein, R. J. Placebo effect in the rat. *Science*, 1962, *138*, 677–678.

Hinson, R. E., & Poulos, C. X. Sensitization to the behavioral effects of cocaine: Modification by Pavlovian conditioning. *Pharmacology, Biochemistry and Behavior*, 1981, *15*, 559–562.

Hinson, R. E., Poulos, C. X., & Cappell, H. The effects of pentobarbital and cocaine in rats expecting pentobarbital. *Pharmacology, Biochemistry and Behavior*, 1982, *16*, 661–666.

Hinson, R. E., Poulos, C. X., & Thomas, W. L. Learning in tolerance to haloperidol-induced catalepsy. *Progress in Neuro-Psychopharmacology and Biological Psychiatry*, 1982, *6*, 395–398.

Hinson, R. E., & Siegel, S. The contribution of Pavlovian conditioning to ethanol tolerance and dependence. In H. Rigter & J. C. Crabbe, Jr. (Eds.), *Alcohol tolerance, dependence, and addiction*. Amsterdam: Elsevier/North-Holland Biomedical Press, 1980.

Hinson, R. E., & Siegel, S. Nonpharmacological bases of drug tolerance and dependence. *Journal of Psychosomatic Research*, 1982, *26*, 495–503.

Hinson, R. E., & Siegel, S. Anticipatory hyperexcitability and tolerance to the narcotizing effect of morphine in the rat. *Behavioral Neuroscience*, 1983, *97*, 759–767.

Hodgson, R. Review of "Behavioral Tolerance: Research and Treatment Implications." *British Journal of Addiction*, 1980, *75*, 101–102.

Kamat, K. A., Dutta, S. N., & Pradhan, S. N. Conditioning of morphine-induced enhancement of motor activity. *Research Communications in Chemical Pathology and Pharmacology*, 1974, *7*, 367–373.

Kimble, G. *Hilgard and Marquis' conditioning and learning*. New York: Appleton-Century-Crofts, 1961.

Konradi, G. Activity of the nervous system. In K. M. Bykov (Ed.), *Textbook of physiology*. Moscow: Foreign Languages Publishing House, 1960.

Krank, M. D., Hinson, R. E., & Siegel, S. Conditional hyperalgesia is elicited by environmental signals of morphine. *Behavioral and Neural Biology*, 1981, *32*, 148–157.

Krank, M. D., Hinson, R. E., & Siegel, S. Effect of partial reinforcement on tolerance to morphine-induced analgesia and weight loss in the rat. *Behavioral Neuroscience*, 1984, *98*, 72–78.

Krylov, V. Additional data on the study of conditioned reflexes on chemical stimuli. *Biological Abstacts*, 1933, *7*, 871.

LaHoste, G. J., Olson, R. D., Olson, G. A., & Kastin, A. J. Effects of Pavlovian conditioning and MIF-I on the development of morphine tolerance in rats. *Pharmacology, Biochemistry and Behavior*, 1980, *13*, 799–804.

Lang, W. J., Brown, M. L., Gershon, S., & Korol, B. Classical and physiologic adaptive conditioned responses to anticholinergic drugs in conscious dogs. *International Journal of Neuropharmacology*, 1966, *5*, 311–315.

Lang, W., & Rand, M. A placebo response as a conditional reflex to glyceryl trinitrate. *Medical Journal of Australia*, 1969, *1*, 912–914.

Lê, A. D., Poulos, C. X., & Cappell, H. Conditioned tolerance to the hypothermic effect of ethyl alcohol. *Science*, 1979, *206*, 1109–1110.

Lightfoot, L. O. *Behavioral tolerance to low doses of alcohol in social drinkers*. Unpublished doctoral dissertation, University of Waterloo, 1980.

Loucks, R. B. Humoral conditioning in mammals. *Journal of Psychology*, 1937, *4*, 295–307.

Lubow, R. E. Latent inhibition. *Psychological Bulletin*, 1973, *79*, 398–407.

Lynch, J. J., Stein, E. A., & Fertziger, A. P. An analysis of 70 years of morphine classical conditioning: Implications for clinical treatment of narcotic addiction. *Journal of Nervous and Mental Disease*, 1976, *163*, 47–58.

Mackintosh, N. J. *The psychology of animal learning*. London: Academic Press, 1974.

Mansfield, J. G., & Cunningham, C. L. Conditioning and extinction of tolerance to the hypothermic effect of ethanol in rats. *Journal of Comparative and Physiological Psychology*, 1980, *94*, 962–969.

Mansfield, J. G., & Woods, S. C. Cross-tolerance between the hypothermic effects of ethanol and morphine: An associative account. *Alcoholism: Clinical and Experimental Research*, 1981, *5*, 160.

Melchior, C. L., & Tabakoff, B. Modificaton of environmentally-cued tolerance to ethanol in mice. *Journal of Pharmacology and Experimental Therapeutics*, 1981, *219*, 175–180.

Mityushov, M. I. Uslovnorleflektornaya inkretsiya insulina [The conditional-reflex incretion of insulin]. *Zhurnal Vysshei Nervnoi Deiatel [Journal of Higher Nervous Activity]*, 1954, *4*, 206–212.

Mucha, R. F., Volkovskis, C., & Kalant, H. Conditioned increases in locomotor activity produced with morphine as an unconditioned stimulus, and the relation of conditioning to acute morphine effect and tolerance. *Journal of Comparative and Physiological Psychology*, 1981, *95*, 351–362.

Mulinos, M. G., & Lieb, C. C. Pharmacology of learning. *American Journal of Physiology*, 1929, *90*, 456–457.

Parker, L. F., & Skorupski, J. D. Conditioned ethanol tolerance. In A. J. Schecter (Ed.), *Drug dependence and alcoholism*. New York: Plenum, 1981.

Pavlov, I. P. *Conditioned reflexes* (G. V. Anrep, trans.). London: Oxford University Press, 1927.

Perez-Cruet, J., & Gantt, W. H. Conditional reflex electrocardiogram of bulbocapnine: Conditioning of the T wave. *American Heart Journal*, 1964, *67*, 61–72.

Post, R. M., Contel, N. R., & Gold, P. W. Impaired behavioral sensitization to cocaine in vasopressin deficient rats. *Society for Neuroscience Abstracts*, 1980, *6*, 111.

Post, R. M., Lockfeld, A., Squillace, K. M., & Contel, N. R. Drug–environment interaction: Context dependency of cocaine-induced behavioral sensitization. *Life Sciences*, 1981, *28*, 755–760.

Poulos, C. X., & Hinson, R. E. Pavlovian conditional tolerance to haloperidol catelepsy: Evidence of dynamic adaptations in the dopaminergic system. *Science*, 1982, *218*, 491–492.

Poulos, C. X., & Hinson, R. E. Interactive homeostatic regulation and Pavlovian conditioning: The development and loss of tolerance to scopolamine-induced adipsia. *Journal of Experimental Psychology: Animal Behavior Processes*, 1984, *10*, 75–89.

Poulos, C. X., Hinson, R. E., & Siegel, S. The role of Pavlovian processes in drug use: Implications for treatment. *Addictive behaviors*, 1981, *6*, 205–211.

Poulos, C. X., Wilkinson, D. A., & Cappell, H. Homeostatic regulation and Pavlovian conditioning in tolerance to amphetamine-induced anorexia. *Journal of Comparative and Physiological Psychology*, 1981, *95*, 735–746.

Raffa, R. B., Porreca, F., Cowan, A., & Tallarida, R. J. Evidence for the role of conditioning in the development of tolerance to morphine-induced inhibition of gastrointestinal motility in rats. *Federation Proceedings*, 1982, *41*, 1317.

Razran, G. The observable unconscious and the inferable conscious in current Soviet psychophysiology: Interoceptive conditioning, semantic conditioning, and the orienting reflex. *Psychological Review*, 1961, *68*, 81–147.

Reiss, W. J. Conditoning of a hyperinsulin type of behavior in the white rat. *Journal of Comparative and Physiological Psychology*, 1958, *51*, 301–303.

Rescorla, R. A. Pavlovian conditioned inhibition. *Psychological Bulletin*, 1969, *72*, 77–94.

Rickels, K., Lipman, R., & Raab, E. Previous medication, duration of illness and placebo response. *Journal of Nervous and Mental Disease*, 1966, *142*, 548–554.

Rudy, T. A., & Yaksh, T. L. Hyperthermic effects of morphine: Set point manipulation by a direct spinal action. *British Journal of Pharmacology*, 1977, *61*, 91–96.

Rush, M. L., Pearson, L., & Lang, W. J. Conditional autonomic responses induced in dogs by atropine and morphine. *European Journal of Pharmacology*, 1970, *11*, 22–28.

Russek, M., & Piña, S. Conditioning of adrenalin anorexia. *Nature*, 1962, *193*, 1296–1297.

Sherman, J. E. The effects of conditioning and novelty on the analgesic and pyretic responses to morphine. *Learning and Motivation*, 1979, *10*, 383–418.

Siegel, S. Conditioning of insulin-induced glycemia. *Journal of Comparative and Physiological Psychology*, 1972, *78*, 233–241.

Siegel, S. Conditioning insulin effects. *Journal of Comparative and Physiological Psychology*, 1975, *89*, 189–199. (a)

Siegel, S. Evidence from rats that morphine tolerance is a learned response. *Journal of Comparative and Physiological Psychology*, 1975, *89*, 498–506. (b)

Siegel, S. Morphine analgesic tolerance: Its situation specificity supports a Pavlovian conditioning model. *Science*, 1976, *193*, 323–325.

Siegel, S. Learning and psychopharmacology. In M. E. Jarvik (Ed.), *Psychopharmacology in the practice of medicine*. New York: Appleton-Century-Crofts, 1977. (a)

Siegel, S. Morphine tolerance acquisition as an associative process. *Journal of Experimental Psychology: Animal Behavior Processes*, 1977, *3*, 1–13. (b)

Siegel, S. Morphine tolerance: Is there evidence for a conditioning model? *Science*, 1978, *200*, 344–345. (a)

Siegel, S. A Pavlovian conditioning analysis of morphine tolerance. In N. A. Krasnegor (Ed.), *Behavioral tolerance: Research and treatment implications* (National Institute on Drug Abuse Research Monograph No. 18; U.S. DHEW Publ. No. ADM 78-551). Washington, D.C.: U.S. Government Printing Office, 1978. (b)

Siegel, S. Tolerance to the hyperthermic effect of morphine in the rat is a learned response. *Journal of Comparative and Physiological Psychology*, 1978, *92*, 1137–1149. (c)

Siegel, S. The role of conditioning in drug tolerance and addiction. In J. D. Keehn (Ed.), *Psychopathology in animals: Research and treatment implications*. New York: Academic Press, 1979.

Siegel, S. Classical conditioning, drug tolerance, and drug dependence. In Y. Israel, F. B. Glaser, H. Kalant, R. E. Popham, W. Schmidt, & R. G. Smart (Eds.), *Research advances in alcohol and drug problems* (Vol. 7). New York: Plenum, 1983. (a)

Siegel, S. Wilkie Collins: Victorian novelist as psychopharmacologist. *Journal of the History of Medicine and Allied Sciences*, 1983, *38*, 161–175. (b)

Siegel, S., Hinson, R. E., & Krank, M. D. The role of predrug signals in morphine analgesic tolerance: Support for a Pavlovian conditioning model of tolerance. *Journal of Experimental Psychology: Animal Behavior Processes*, 1978, *4*, 188–196.

Siegel, S., Hinson, R. E., & Krank, M. D. Modulation of tolerance to the lethal effect of morphine by extinction. *Behavioral and Neural Biology*, 1979, *25*, 257–262.

Siegel, S., Hinson, R. E., & Krank, M. D. Morphine-induced attenuation of morphine tolerance. *Science*, 1981, *212*, 1533–1534.

Siegel, S., Hinson, R. E., Krank, M. D., & McCully, J. Heroin "overdose" death: The contribution of drug-associated environmental cues. *Science*, 1982, *216*, 436–437.

Siegel, S., Sherman, J. E., & Mitchell, D. Extinction of morphine analgesic tolerance. *Learning and Motivation*, 1980, *11*, 289–301.

Stewart, J., deWit, H., & Eikelboom, R. Role of unconditioned and conditioned drug effects in the self-administration of opiates and stimulants. *Psychological Review*, 1984, *91*, 251–268.

Storms, M. D., & Nisbett, R. E. Insomnia and the attribution process. *Journal of Personality and Social Psychology*, 1970, *16*, 319–328.

Subkov, A. A., & Zilov, G. N. The role of conditioned reflex adaptation in the origin of hyperergic reactions. *Bulletin de Biologie et de Médecine Expérimentale*, 1937, *4*, 294–296.

Tatum, A. L., & Seevers, M. H. Experimental cocaine addiction. *Journal of Pharmacology and Experimental Therapeutics*, 1929, *36*, 401–410.

Thornhill, J. A., Hirst, M., & Gowdey, C. W. Changes in the hyperthermic responses of rats to daily injections of morphine and the antagonism of the actue response by naloxone. *Canadian Journal of Physiology and Pharmacology*, 1978, *56*, 483–489.

Tiffany, S. T., & Baker, T. B. Morphine tolerance in the rat: Congruence with a Pavlovian paradigm. *Journal of Comparative and Physiological Psychology*, 1981, *95*, 747–762.

Tiffany, S. T., Petrie, E. C., Baker, T. B., & Dahl, J. Conditioned morphine tolerance in the rat: Absence of a compensatory response and cross-tolerance with stress. *Behavioral Neuroscience*, 1983, *97*, 335–353.

Tiffany, S. T., Petrie, E. C., Martin, E. M., & Baker, T. B. Drug signals enhance morphine tolerance development in hypophysectomized rats. *Psychopharmacology*, 1983, *79*, 84–85.

Wikler, A. *Opioid dependence: Mechanisms and treatment.* New York: Plenum, 1980.

Woods, S. C., & Kolkosky, P. J. Classically conditioned changes of blood glucose level. *Psychosomatic Medicine*, 1976, *38*, 201–219.

Woods, S. C., Makous, W., & Hutton, R. A. Temporal parameters of conditioned hypoglycemia. *Journal of Comparative and Physiological Psychology*, 1969, *69*, 301–307.

17

Conditioned Immunopharmacological Effects in Animals: Implications for a Conditioning Model of Pharmacotherapy

ROBERT ADER

INTRODUCTION

The volume of literature dealing with placebo effects is intimidating (Turner, Gallimore, & Fox-Henning, 1980). Despite this literature and the amelioration of distress or cures effected by placebo medication, the placebo is still frequently described as "trickery," "magic," "faith healing," or, dramatically, the "lie that heals" (Brody, 1982). Gleidman, Gantt, and Teitelbaum (1957) contend that the placebo's early lack of respectability stems from the fact that "The very derivation of the word placebo, from the Latin 'I shall please,' suggests a certain superficiality and an essentially non-therapeutic intent" (p. 1103). Its current lack of respectability, I submit, may relate to the lack of a definition of the phenomena encompassed by the "placebo effect" and the lack of any theoretical position(s) within which to organize the existing data and upon which to base the design and analysis of research.

Clinical studies and drug evaluation studies have adhered to the model in which a drug or placebo is administered in order to evaluate the efficacy of pharmacotherapies or to define the pharmacological action of a drug. Clinical research has been directed primarily to the manipulation of a variety of variables, ranging from attempts at characterization of the placebo itself to characterization of the subjects or patients who respond to pharmacologically inert or pharmacologically irrelevant medication. In an effort to define the action of a drug rather than the effects of the drug on the organism, the placebo effect has become a "nuisance"—an effect that needs to be controlled in order to clarify the "real" effects of the drug.

Robert Ader. Division of Behavioral and Psychosocial Medicine, Department of Psychiatry, University of Rochester School of Medicine and Dentistry, Rochester, New York.

It is not my intent to review this literature, and it is not my intent to formulate a new model for understanding the effects of placebo administrations. I describe data that elaborate the role of conditioning processes in the study of placebo effects, and I argue that there is considerable heuristic value in adopting a conditioning model for manipulating, controlling, and predicting placebo effects in pharmacotherapeutic protocols.

Several authors have attempted to conceptualize the placebo effect as a conditioning phenomenon, or, at least, have alluded to the role of learning processes in influencing such phenomena (Beecher, 1959; Evans, 1974; Gadow, White, & Ferguson, in press; Gleidman et al., 1957; Herrnstein, 1962; Knowles, 1963; Kurland, 1957; Lasagna, Mosteller, von Felsinger, & Beecher, 1954; Petrie, 1960; Pihl & Altman, 1971; Ross & Schnitzer, 1963; Skinner, 1953; Stanley & Schlosberg, 1953; Wikler, 1973; Wolf, 1950). One of the more recent and denotative descriptions of the placebo effect as a conditioned response (CR) is given by Wickramasekera (1980), who, with others in the past, proposes that the entire ritual surrounding drug administration can become a conditioned stimulus (CS) by virtue of the repeated association of such neutral events with drug administration in the developmental history of the individual.

A few studies have been conducted directly within this framework. Herrnstein (1962), for example, noted that, under some temporal circumstances, a rat would show suppression of behavioral responding to an injection of saline that had previously characterized its response to scopolamine hydrobromide. Other studies (Pihl & Altman, 1971; Ross & Schnitzer, 1963) demonstrated that, after one or more injections of D-amphetamine, the (unconditional) increase in activity could be observed after an injection of saline, a placebo (i.e., a CS), the magnitude of the "placebo" response being a function of the number of repeated injections of the drug.

In addition to such experimental analyses of the placebo effect, there have been numerous studies and reviews (e.g., Harris & Brady, 1974; Lynch, Fertziger, Teitelbaum, Cullen, & Gantt, 1973; Miller, 1969; Siegel, 1977) dealing with the conditioning of pharmacological and physiological responses. The most recent of these, dealing specifically with drug-induced physiological responses, has been provided by Eikelboom and Stewart (1982). This literature should be considered part of the same body of data that bears on an analysis of placebo effects.

In view of the available data, to argue that a placebo response is a CR is not new. It is somewhat surprising, though, that few studies have attempted a systematic analysis of placebo effects within the context of conditioning paradigms or applied a conditioning model in pharmacotherapeutic situations. In the present chapter, I describe a conditioning paradigm used to alter immunological reactivity, describe how this conditioning paradigm was applied in a pharmocotherapeutic regimen designed to influence the development of autoimmune disease in mice, and then discuss the implications of these data for experimental and clinical research.

BEHAVIORALLY CONDITIONED IMMUNOSUPPRESSION

The application of principles and techniques of behavioral conditioning represent one of several converging lines of research indicating that central nervous system (CNS) processes are involved in the regulation or modulation of immune responses (Ader, 1981b). Indeed, the use of conditioning techniques is, perhaps, the oldest experimental approach to the study of CNS–immune system interactions (Ader, 1981a). Based on certain serendipitous observations (Ader, 1974), it was hypothesized that a suppression of immunological reactivity could be conditioned. Using a taste aversion conditioning paradigm in rats, we paired consumption of a novel, distinctively flavored drinking solution (saccharin), the CS, with the effects of an immunosuppressive drug (cyclophosphamide, or CY), the unconditioned stimulus (UCS). Subsequently, animals were immunized with sheep red blood cells (SRBC). Conditioned animals that were re-exposed to saccharin at the time of antigenic stimulation and/or 3 days later were found to have lower hemagglutinating antibody titers 6 days after the injection of SRBC than (1) conditioned animals that were not re-exposed to saccharin, (2) nonconditioned animals provided with saccharin, and (3) a placebo group (see Figure 17-1). These original data (Ader & Cohen, 1975) were taken as evidence of a conditioned immunosuppressive response and a CNS involvement in the modulation of immunological reactivity. Studies by Rogers, Reich, Strom, and Carpenter (1976) and Wayner, Flannery, and Singer (1978) have provided independent verification of these findings.

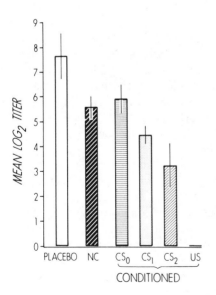

Figure 17-1. Hemagglutinating antibody titers (mean $\pm$ *SE*) measured 6 days after immunization with SRBC. NC = nonconditioned rats provided with saccharin on Day 0 (day of antigen) or Day 3; CS_0 = conditioned animals that were not re-exposed to saccharin after antigen treatment; CS_1 = conditioned animals that were re-exposed to saccharin on Day 0 or 3; CS_2 = conditioned animals re-exposed to saccharin on Days 0 and 3; US = conditioned animals injected with CY on the day of immunization. (From "Behaviorally Conditioned Immunosuppression" by R. Ader and N. Cohen. *Psychosomatic Medicine*, 1975, *37*, 333–340. Reprinted by permission of Elsevier/North-Holland, Inc.)

Conditioned immunosuppressive effects have been relatively small, but they have been quite consistent. Changing the CS or changing the magnitude of the UCS (which may alter the kinetics of the antibody response) still results in conditioned immunosuppression (Ader & Cohen, 1981). In order to control for the differential fluid intake of experimental and control groups, re-exposure to saccharin has been introduced in a preference testing situation in which animals can choose between bottles containing plain or saccharin-flavored water. Under these circumstances, the total fluid intake of experimental and control groups does not differ, but conditioned animals re-exposed to the CS previously paired with CY still show an aversion to saccharin and a conditioned immunosuppressive response (Ader, Cohen, & Bovbjerg, 1982). In other studies, lithium chloride instead of CY was used as the UCS, or an elevation of corticosterone was superimposed upon the residual immunosuppressive effects of CY. The results of these studies (Ader & Cohen, 1975; Ader, Cohen, & Grota, 1979) provided no support for the hypothesis of an adrenocortical mediation of conditioned immunosuppressive responses.

The antibody response to SRBC is a humoral response involving an interaction between T and B lymphocytes. The generality of the phenomenon of conditioned immunosuppression is evidenced by our ability to observe an attenuated antibody response to a T-cell (thymus) independent antigen in mice (Cohen, Ader, Green, & Bovbjerg, 1979) and conditioned suppression of a cell-mediated response, which is representative of the other major class of immune reactions (Bovbjerg, Ader, & Cohen, 1982). In the latter instance, the experimental protocol was modified to take advantage of the observation that multiple, low-dose injections of CY could suppress a graft-versus-host (GvH) response (Whitehouse, Levy, & Beck, 1973).

Rats werre conditioned by pairing saccharin consumption with an injection of 50 mg/kg CY 48 days before immunogenic stimulation. Nonconditioned animals also received saccharin and CY,but these stimuli were not paired. Lewis × Brown Norwegian hybrid recipients were injected subdermally in the plantar surface of a hind footpad with a suspension of splenic leukocytes obtained from Lewis donors. On that same day, conditioned recipients were re-exposed to saccharin and injected with saline. On the following day, they were again re-exposed to saccharin and injected with 10 mg/kg CY, and on the next day they were re-exposed to the CS (saccharin plus an injection of saline) for the third time. Three low-dose injections of CY markedly reduced the weight of popliteal lymph nodes harvested 5 days after injection of the cellular graft. A single low dose of CY, however, produced only a modest attention of the GvH response in nonconditioned animals (exposed to saccharin on Days 0, 1, and 2) and in conditioned animals that were not re-exposed to the CS. In contrast, conditioned rats that received a single low-dose injection of CY *and* re-exposure to the CS displayed a significant suppression of the GvH response relative to the control groups, and did not differ from animals that received three injections of the immunosuppressive drug.

The conditioned suppression of a GvH response is also subject to experimental extinction (Bovbjerg, Ader, & Cohen, 1984). Using the paradigm described above, conditioned rats were divided into subgroups that received 0, 4, 9, or 18 unreinforced CS presentations (saccharin presentation without CY injection). Relative to control groups, conditioned animals that received no extinction trials showed an attenuated GvH response, replicating the findings described above. Behaviorally, 4, 9, and 18 unreinforced CS presentations attenuated the conditioned aversion to saccharin-flavored water measured 7 weeks after conditioning, but there were no differences among these three groups. In terms of the GvH response, 4 extinction trials were not sufficient to alter the suppression of immunological reactivity, but animals that received 9 or 18 extinction trials did not differ from controls and showed a higher GvH response than animals that received either 0 or 4 extinction trials. It is particularly interesting that there appeared to be a dissociation between the behavioral and immunological effects of extinction trials—a finding reminiscent of the dissociation between conditioned motor responses and physiological responses (schizokinesis) described by Gantt (1953).

Gorczynski, Macrae, and Kennedy (1982) have also described the extinction of a conditioned immune response in a paradigm in which antigenic stimulation constituted the UCS. Such data lend support to the notion that associative processes are involved in the behavioral alteration of immune responses.

CONDITIONING PROCESSES IN THE PHARMACOTHERAPY OF AUTOIMMUNE DISEASE

As noted above, the magnitude of the effects of conditioning in altering immunological reactivity have been relatively small. They have, however, been consistent and independently reproducible. We proceeded, therefore, to evaluate the biological significance of a conditioned immunosuppressive response (Ader & Cohen, 1982). For this purpose, we chose to study the spontaneous development of autoimmune disease in New Zealand hybrid mice. The (NZB $\times$ NZW)F$_1$ female has become a standard model for systemic lupus erythematosus (SLE) in humans (Steinberg, Huston, Taurog, Cowdery, & Raveche, 1981; Talal, 1976; Theofilopoulos & Dixon, 1981). These hybrid mice develop a lethal glomerulonephritis between approximately 8 and 14 months of age. The progression of disease can be delayed or slowed, however, by treatment with immunosuppressive drugs—for example, CY (Casey, 1968; Hahn, Knotts, Ng, & Hamilton, 1975; Lehman, Wilson, & Dixon, 1976; Morris, Esterly, Chase, & Sharp, 1976; Russell & Hicks, 1968; Steinberg, Gelfand, Hardin, & Lowenthal, 1975). In this instance, suppression of immunological reactivity is in the survival interests of the organism. Based on observations that immunological reactivity can be suppressed by conditioning, we hypothesized that conditioned mice re-exposed to neutral stimuli associated with immunosuppressive medication, CY, would show a suppression of immunological reactivity that would delay the development of autoimmune disease. That is, it was hypothesized that, by pairing saccharin with injections of CY, re-exposure to saccharin could be substituted for the active drug in the course of a regimen of pharmacotherapy, and that such animals would be more resistant to the development of SLE than nonconditioned animals treated with the same amount of drug.

New Zealand hybrid mice were born in our laboratory. The females were individually caged under a 12-hour light–dark cycle and provided with food and water *ad libitum*. An 8-week chemotherapeutic regimen was begun when mice were 4 months old. On the same day of each week, all mice were administered a .15% solution of sodium saccharin in tap water by pipette (up to a maximum of 1.0 ml). CY was injected intraperitoneally (i.p.) according to the following schedule:

Group C100% received an i.p. injection of 30 mg/kg CY immediately after being given saccharin. The pairing occurred at the same time of day and on the same day of each week. This sequence of events constituted a standard pharmacotherapeutic protocol administered for a period of 8 weeks. The dose of drug and duration of treatment proved to be effective in prolonging survival, but were not sufficient to obviate the development of disease.

Group C50%, another conditioned group, also received saccharin weekly, but an i.p. injection of CY (30 mg/kg) followed saccharin on only 2 of each 4 weeks (in a random sequence). On the remaining half of the trials, mice in Group C50% received an i.p. injection of physiological saline.

A nonconditioned group (NC50%) was also exposed to saccharin weekly and i.p. injections of saline or CY on 2 of each 4 weeks, but the CY or saline injections were not paired with saccharin; they were administered on different days of the same week.

Control mice received weekly exposure to saccharin and i.p. injections of saline on a noncontingent basis, but received no immunosuppressive therapy.

Pharmacologically, there was no difference between Groups C50% and NC50%; both groups received the same amount and number of exposures to saccharin and CY. Since Group NC50% received only half the amount of drug administered to Group C100%, it was expected that animals in this group would manifest symptoms of SLE (proteinuria) and die sooner than animals in Group C100%. Group C50% also received only half the amount of drug administered to Group C100%. However, to the extent that re-exposure to the CSs paired with CY was capable of eliciting a conditioned immunosuppressive response, it was predicted that conditioned mice would show a greater resistance to the development of autoimmune disease than mice in Group NC50%, even though both groups received that same amount of drug.

As expected, weekly treatment with CY delayed the onset of proteinuria and prolonged the survival of (NZB $\times$ NZW)F_1 mice. The effects of the different chemotherapeutic regimens on the development of proteinuria and mortality are shown in Figure 17-2. There were statistically significant differences among the groups, but inclusion of the total population of each group underestimates the impact of conditioning, because virtually all of these hybrid mice could be expected to develop SLE and die. Therefore, the longer one monitors the progression of disease, the more difficult it is to discern treatment effects.

Statistically significant differences were also obtained using as a reference point the rate of development of proteinuria in the initial 50% of the animals that developed SLE or the rate at which a 50% mortality was reached. Mice treated weekly with CY developed proteinuria more slowly than animals in any of the other groups. Nonconditioned animals treated with half the amount of drug received by animals treated under a standard pharmacotherapeutic regimen did not differ from untreated controls. However, conditioned animals treated with the same cumulative amount of drug developed proteinuria more slowly than nonconditioned mice. Mortality yielded essentially the same pattern of differences. Nonconditioned mice did not differ from animals that received no immunosuppressive therapy. In contrast, conditioned animals survived significantly longer than untreated controls and did not differ from animals in Group C100%. As with proteinuria, the critical comparison is between conditioned and nonconditioned mice that received the *same* amount of drug, and, as with the difference in the rate of development of proteinuria, Group C50% survived significantly longer than Group NC50%.

Differences both in the rate of development of proteinuria and in mortality are attributable to experientially induced differences in the time of onset of disease among the groups. That is, there were significant within-group correlations between the development of proteinuria and mortality, and the interval between the development of proteinuria and mortality was relatively constant. Thus, while the progression of disease was similar in all groups, there was a clear difference in the time to onset of disease as a function of the treatment conditions. These differences were consistent with the therapeutic effects of CY in murine SLE. Although this experiment does not provide direct evidence of a conditioned immunosuppressive response per se, the findings are also consistent with previous studies of conditioned immunosuppression and with predictions derived from the application of such conditioning in the context of a pharmacotherapeutic model. In conditioned mice, re-exposure to a CS previously paired with an immunosuppressive drug delayed the onset of autoimmune disease under a regimen of immunosuppressive therapy that was not, in itself, sufficient to influence the development of disease.

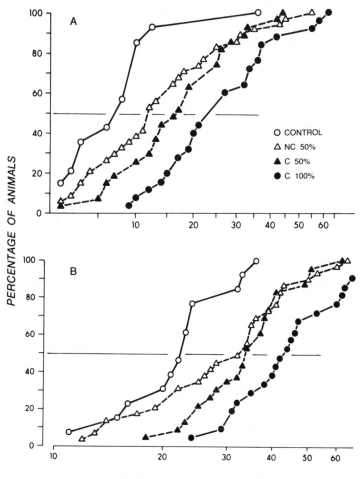

WEEKS (POST-CONDITIONING)

Figure 17-2. (A) Rate of development of an unremitting proteinuria in (NZB ×
NZW)F₁ female mice under different chemotherapeutic protocols. Group C100% (*n*
= 25) received saccharin followed by CY each week; Group C50% (*n* = 27) received
CY following half the weekly saccharin trials; Groups NC50% (*n* = 34) received the
same saccharin and CY as Group C50%, but saccharin and CY were not paired;
control mice (*n* = 14) received saccharin and unpaired injections of saline. (B)
Cumulative mortality rate in these same (NZB × NZW)F₁ female mice. (From
"Behaviorally Conditioned Immunosuppression and Murine Systemic Lupus Erythematosus" by R. Ader and N. Cohen. *Science*, 1982, *215*, 1534–1536. Reprinted
by permission of the American Association for the Advancement of Science.)

Based on these data, we suggested that there was some heuristic value in analyzing a pharmacotherapeutic regimen in terms of conditioning operations (Ader & Cohen, 1982). If a pharmacotherapeutic regimen can be structured as a conditioning paradigm, the conditioned pharmacological response should be sensitive to the manipulation of any number of experimental variables. It should, for example, be subject to experimental extinction, and resistance to extinction should be a function of the schedule of reinforcement (Kimble, 1961). Experimental extinction procedures, operationally defined as unreinforced presentations of the CS, would, in the present pharmacotherapeutic paradigm, consist of re-exposing conditioned animals to saccharin that was not followed by CY. Preliminary data on extinction were obtained in a second experiment.

During an initial period of chemotherapy, the procedures were the same as those in the study described above, except that the critical experimental group (Group C33%) was treated under a 33% reinforcement schedule; that is, CY followed saccharin on only one-third of the weekly trials on which saccharin was provided. Nonconditioned animals (Group NC33%) received the same exposures to saccharin and CY, but in an unpaired manner. At the end of the treatment period (12 weeks), Groups C100%, C33%, and NC33% were divided into three subgroups. One-third of each group continued to receive saccharin and i.p. injections of saline (CS) or CY (UCS) on the same schedule that existed during the period of chemotherapy; one-third continued to receive saccharin and i.p. injections of saline (CS), but CY treatment was discontinued; and one-third received neither saccharin nor CY. Assuming that learning processes are involved in the pairing of saccharin and CY, it was predicted that unreinforced CS presentations would influence the development of SLE in conditioned animals but not in nonconditioned mice.

Although the number of animals per subgroup was relatively small, the results conform to these predictions. Mortality was delayed in mice maintained on a continuous schedule of chemotherapy, relative to mice that were taken off CY. Mice that continued to receive saccharin and i.p. injections of saline after the termination of CY treatment, however, died more slowly than animals deprived of all "medication" (see Figure 17-3). In fact, the mortality rate of mice that continued to receive CS presentations without the UCS did not differ from that in mice that continued to receive saccharin *and* CY.

As in our initial experiment, the informative comparison is between the pattern of results obtained from conditioned and nonconditioned animals that received the same amount of chemotherapy. These data are shown in Figure 17-4. For both Groups C33% and NC33%, mice that were deprived of both saccharin and CY died relatively rapidly, compared to animals that continued to receive chemotherapy. Conditioned animals (Group C33%) that were taken off CY but continued to receive weekly exposures to saccharin died more slowly than animals deprived of both saccharin and CY,

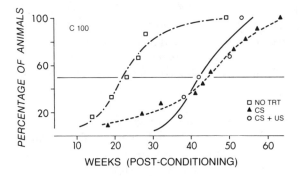

Figure 17-3. Mortality rate in (NZB × NZW)F₁ female mice treated with saccharin and CY weekly and then continued on a regimen of saccharin and CY (Group CS + US; $n = 6$), continued on placebo medication, alone (Group CS; $n = 11$), or deprived of both saccharin and CY (no treatment; $n = 6$).

Figure 17-4. Mortality rate in conditioned (C33%) and nonconditioned (NC33%) (NZB × NZW)F₁ female mice that continued to receive saccharin and CY (Group CS + US), continued to receive only saccharin (Group CS), or received neither saccharin nor CY (no treatment); n's = 11 to 20 per subgroup.

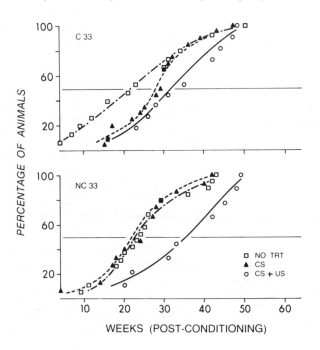

and, at least for the initial 50% of these populations, the mortality rate among mice that were re-exposed to the CS did not differ from mice that continued to receive treatment with the immunosuppressive drug. In contrast, continued exposure to saccharin in nonconditioned animals treated with the same amount of drug as conditioned animals had no effect on survival. The mortality rate in these animals did not differ from that in mice that received neither saccharin nor CY.

Again, these results do not provide direct evidence of conditioned immunosuppression, since we did not directly measure immune function. Nonetheless, these preliminary data involving the effects of drug withdrawal provide presumptive evidence for the operation of conditioning processes and are consistent with the extinction effects reported by Bovbjerg et al. (1982) and Gorczynski et al. (1982).

IMPLICATIONS FOR A CONDITIONING MODEL OF PHARMACOTHERAPY

The direct implication of the data described above is that behavioral factors may be capable of altering immune function. In contrast to current conceptualizations of an autonomous immune system, such data suggest that the immune system is subject to some regulation or modulation by the brain. In fact, there are neuroanatomical, neurochemical, neuroendocrine, and neuropharmacological data that provide grounds for expecting a relationship between behavior and immune function (Ader, 1981b). On another level, these data can be taken as an extension of the conditioning of drug-induced physiological responses (Eikelboom & Stewart, 1982). Within the present context, then, these data have implications for the conduct of placebo research.

To apply a behavioral terminology to a pharmacological treatment regimen, those physiological effects unconditionally elicited by the introduction of a drug are referred to as unconditioned responses (UCRs). The drug itself may be referred to as the UCS. Those environmental or behavioral events or stimuli that are either coincidentally or purposely associated with and reliably precede the voluntary or involuntary receipt of drug (but that are neutral with respect to the unconditioned effects of the drug) are referred to as CSs. Repeated pairing of a CS and a UCS can eventually enable the CS to elicit a CR—an approximation of the response previously evoked by the UCS.

Typically, the experimental evaluation of drug effects is based upon two groups: an experimental group (divided, perhaps, on the basis of dose, route, time, and/or frequency of administration) and a control group that does not receive the active pharmacological agent but receives an inert or chemically irrelevant substance (placebo) instead. In all other respects, the experimental and control groups are not supposed to differ; that is, the stimuli that attend the administration of either active drug or placebo are supposed to be the same. In conditioning terms, pharmacotherapeutic protocols involve continuous reinforcement. Experimental subjects voluntarily or involuntarily receive medication that is invariably followed (reinforced) by the unconditioned psychophysiological effects of the drug. In contrast, the voluntary or medically directed administration of an inert substance is never reinforced. The experimental group, then, is provided with a 100% reinforcement regimen, while the control group is under a 0% reinforcement schedule.

There is, however, an alternative to the administration of either drug *or* placebo: the administration of drug *and* placebo. This alternative represents, perhaps, a shift from a concern for defining purely pharmacological effects to a concern for the potential beneficial effects of placebo medication. Despite descriptions of the placebo effect as a conditioning phenomenon and data that suggest the utility of interspersing drug and placebo trials (e.g., Herrnstein, 1962), I know of no studies of the *therapeutic* process that have attended to schedules of pharmacological reinforcement. Pharmacotherapeutic research has never concentrated on or systematically manipulated the stimuli associated with the administration of drugs and evaluated the effects of noncontinuous or *partial* schedules of pharmacological reinforcement (i.e., schedules of reinforcement in which the receipt of "medication" and the attendant environmental stimuli are pharmacologically reinforced on some occasions but not on others).

Variation of reinforcement schedule—the "active drug:placebo ratio"— is, in effect, an alternative means of manipulating drug dose. Under a regimen of prolonged medication, for example, cumulative drug dose could be lowered by changing reinforcement schedule, rather than the concentration of drug that is actually administered in the component drug trials. Such a strategy for capitalizing on conditioned pharmacological effects could have some advantages. If it could be shown that a partial reinforcement schedule could approximate the therapeutic effects of a continuous reinforcement schedule, drug dose will have been reduced, some side effects may be reduced, problems of dependence may be lessened or alleviated more easily, and/or the duration of the effects of pharmacotherapy might be extended. The cost of medication would also be reduced.

In the studies described above, we found that the immunosuppressive effects of CY could be conditioned. In place of the immunosuppressive drug, then, we substituted CSs in a pharmacotherapeutic regimen designed to protect animals against the development of autoimmune disease. One comparison group (Group C100%) represented a standard therapeutic protocol in which the environmental stimuli associated with the receipt of the drug were invariably followed by the unconditioned immunosuppressive effects of the chemotherapeutic agents. These animals, then, were subjected to continuous pharmacological reinforcement. Animals in Group C50% were conditioned under a partial reinforcement schedule; the unconditioned effects of CY occurred on only 50% of the occasions on which animals were exposed to the complex of stimuli that defined the CS. Because these animals received only half the amount of drug received by animals in Group C100%, a nonconditioned group (NC50%) was also treated with half the amount of drug received by Group C100%. For these (nonconditioned) animals, however, the environmental contingencies were arranged so that those stimuli that were purposely associated with and reliably preceded drug administation in Group C50% were not temporally related in Group NC50%. Pharmacologically, the treatment of conditioned and nonconditioned animals was identical. The manipulation of environmental contingencies, however, resulted in a delay in the onset of SLE in conditioned animals using an amount of drug that was not, by itself, sufficient to alter the development of disease.

These studies on New Zealand mice provided no evidence that a partial schedule of reinforcement is as effective as continuous reinforcement. It must be acknowledged, though, that the selection of a 50% reinforcement schedule was essentially arbitrary.[1] Also, based on studies indicating that behavioral responses conditioned under partial reinforcement are more resistant to extinction than those acquired under continuous reinforcement (Kimble, 1961), it might be expected that the same would hold for conditioned pharmacological responses and that pharmacologically unreinforced CS presentations would extend the pharmacotherapeutic effects of a partial reinforcement schedule to a greater extent than a continuous schedule of pharmacological reinforcement. With respect to *pharmacotherapeutic* effects, however, such a prediction should be examined among subjects treated with the *same* amount of drug (Humphreys, 1943). The extinction data reported here do not meet this criterion and do not, therefore, adequately address this hypothesis. Mice treated under the continuous schedule of reinforcement (Group C100%) received three times as much drug as mice treated under the partial schedule of reinforcement (Group C33%). This prediction, then, remains to be tested. Be that as it may, comparing conditioned and nonconditioned animals that received the same cumulative amount of drug revealed different therapeutic outcomes. The substitution of CSs for active drug yielded an effect that was "as if" these conditioned animals had received a greater amount of drug than was actually administered, and our preliminary observations of extinction support the view that associative processes are involved in the effects of (conditioned) immunopharmacological responses in modifying the development of autoimmune disease in (NZB × NZW)F$_1$ mice.

It remains conceivable that, by titrating reinforcement schedule (along with other parameters of a pharmacotherapeutic protocol), one could

---

1. Nonconditioned mice injected with 30 mg/kg CY on 2 of every 3 weeks did not differ from animals treated with CY weekly. At this CY dose, then, a 67% reinforcement schedule would not provide the latitude to discriminate between conditioned and nonconditioned animals.

approximate the therapeutic effects of a continuous schedule of pharmacological reinforcement using a lower cumulative amount of drug. It is also conceivable that pharmacotherapeutic effects could be extended or the gradual withdrawal of drugs facilitated (e.g., the risk of relapse reduced) by a partial as compared to a continuous schedule of pharmacotherapy. That is, it could be hypothesized that resistance to extinction would be greater among subjects treated under partial schedules of reinforcement than subjects treated under a traditional, continuous regimen of pharmacotherapy.

Would not the conditioning of pharmacotherapeutic effects also result in the conditioning of deleterious side effects (the conditioning of noninjurious side effects might actually increase the saliency of CSs)? Indeed, there may be conditioned "side" effects. The existence of side effects illustrates the multiple effects of drugs, and, outside the clinical setting, the labeling of what are to be considered primary and secondary or "side" effects is frequently determined by the interests of the investigator. The issue is, nonetheless, a meaningful one, because even the "single" effect of a pharmacological agent may show changes over time that reflect different effects of the drug on different organ systems or responses to the initial effects of the drug. Gantt (1953) described the phenomenon of schizokinesis, in which there is a dissociation in the rate of acquisition and/or extinction of different CRs, and we have observed such a dissociation in the extinction of conditioned taste aversion and immunosuppressive responses (Bovbjerg et al., 1984). If one considers these multiple effects as resulting from different conditioning processes (Eikelboom & Stewart, 1982)—that is, as responses controlled by different CSs and UCSs—it would be reasonable to assume that acquisition and/or extinction would proceed at different rates. As such, they might also be subject to experimental interventions designed to reinforce their occurrence differentially.

It should be noted that some side effects result from the action of drugs directly on a target organ, and that some of these may not even be relevant to the restoration of homeostasis for which prescription of the drug was intended. To the extent that such drug actions are not mediated by the CNS, they do not constitute UCSs and will not directly induce CRs. They may, however, elicit changes in target organs that are subject to conditioning. Based on this analysis, Eikelboom and Stewart (1982) and Miller and Dworkin (1980) have argued that the appropriate designation of CSs and UCSs clarifies the observation of anticipatory CRs (i.e., CRs that are opposite in direction to UCRs; see Siegel, Chapter 16, this volume). Predicting the direction of drug-induced physiological (and, presumably, therapeutic) responses, then, depends upon knowledge of the site(s) of action of the pharmacological agent.

Thus, as far as the clinical relevance of conditioned side effects to the applicability of a conditioning model of pharmacotherapy is concerned, conditioned side effects that, like the therapeutic effects of the drug in question, are CNS-mediated responses could be no more prevalent than the side effects unconditionally elicited by continuous administration of that drug. Those injurious side effects elicited by the *direct* action of a drug on some organ system could, in a conditioning model, be less prevalent simply becaue fewer administrations of active drug might occur under a partial schedule of pharmacological reinforcement. As a matter of conjecture, the elicitation of anticipatory (compensatory) responses to an external CS previously associated with deleterious side effects resulting from the direct action of a drug on some target organ might have a salutary effect.[2]

In contrast to the conceptualization of placebo responses as learned responses, drug versus placebo studies have, for the most part, concentrated on the individual's initial response to inert medication. These studies that implicitly capitalize on the experiential (reinforcement) history of the individual have yielded interesting and important data, particularly with respect to individual differences. These may, however, represent only a small proportion of the variance involved in understanding and exploiting placebo effects. Indeed, the factors that contribute to initial or essentially pre-experimental responses to placebo may be no more than variables upon which subjects or patients might be matched in experiments designed to analyze the functional relationships that describe the acquistion and extinction of conditioned pharmacological responses. Observations that only some people respond to inert substances, or that there is considerable variability in the magnitude or duration of the response to placebo relative to the response to active drug, would be subsumed by a model that would exercise some explicit control over the experiential (reinforcement) history of the individual.

One of the practical consequences and advantages of adopting a conditioning perspective is the availability of animal models of disease within which to assess conditioned pharmacotherapeutic effects. Clinically, there are specific instances in which psychotherapy is conducted in conjunction with pharmacotherapy. Under these circumstances, the imposition of a partial schedule of pharmacological reinforcement might influence the interaction between these therapetuic modalities (e.g., Rounsaville, Klerman, & Weissman, 1981). For example, it would permit psychotherapeutic interventions during symptom-free periods that were not completely regulated by the continuous presence of pharmacological effects. Psychotherapy under these conditions may be more readily generalized to a subsequent drug-free period than psychotherapy conducted under the influence of drugs.

---

2. Situations in which therapeutic effects are based on the direct action of a drug on some organ system are not appropriate models for applying a simple substitution (placebo) regimen of pharmacotherapy. Under these circumstances (e.g., replacement therapies), pharmacologic substances are prescribed because the host is incapable of mounting a regulatory response. The pharmacological agent does not represent a relevant afferent stimulus to the CNS. The drug may, however, result in conditioned (compensatory) responses. Siegel (1983) has provided an elaboration of drug-anticipatory responses and other kinds of therapeutic strategies based on principles of conditioning.

More generally, the possibility of achieving short- and long-term therapeutic goals using lower maintenance levels of drug would be a worthwhile attempt to maximize benefits while reducing risks to patients.

Having accepted the descriptions of the "placebo effect" as a conditioning phenomenon, I have tried to address the issue of what one would do about it. In this respect, the data we have obtained are quite preliminary. In contrast to a standard pharmacotherapeutic protocol in which the environmental stimuli associated with drug treatment are always reinforced by the unconditioned immunosuppressive effects of the drug, a partial schedule of pharmacological treatment was introduced in order to take advantage of conditioned immunosuppressive responses to cues associated with the drug. The delay in the onset of disease in conditioned animals relative to nonconditioned animals treated with the same amount of drug, and the delay in mortality in conditioned mice effected by continued exposure to CSs after termination of active drug therapy, illustrate the heuristic value of adopting a conditioning model of the pharmacotherapeutic process.

These data suggest that there is alternative to an analysis of pharmacological and pharmacotherapetuic effects in terms of differences between groups that are treated with drug or placebo. Subjects or patients can be treated with drug *and* placebo by introducing partial schedules of pharmacological reinforcement. In addition to dose, route, frequency, duration, and other characteristics of medication, an "active drug:placebo ratio"is a relevant dimension of pharmacotherapeutic regimens. It provides an alternative means of adjusting the dose of the drug. Most particularly, though, it is an alternative that, based on a conditioning model, leads to testable hypotheses regarding the acquisition and/or extinction of the response to placebo medication, and, as such, should suggest innovative strategies for psychopharmacotherapeutic interventions. Within the context of a conditioning model, the therapeutic effect of a placebo is not something mystical, it is not a trick, and it is not a lie. As a bona fide learning phenomenon, the "placebo effect" is amenable to experimental analysis. Rather than having been overestimated, its potential therapeutic effects have probably been underestimated.

REFERENCES

Ader, R. Letter to the editor. *Psychosomatic Medicine*, 1974, *36*, 183–184.

Ader, R. A historical account of conditioned immunobiologic responses. In R. Ader (Ed.), *Psychoneuroimmunology*. New York: Academic Press, 1981. (a)

Ader, R. (Ed.). *Psychoneuroimmunology*. New York: Academic Press, 1981. (b)

Ader, R., & Cohen, N. Behaviorally conditioned immunosuppression. *Psychosomatic Medicine*, 1975, *37*, 333–340.

Ader, R., & Cohen, N. Conditioned immunopharmacologic effects. In R. Ader (Ed.), *Psychoneuroimmunology*. New York: Academic Press, 1981.

Ader, R., & Cohen, N. Behaviorally conditioned immunosuppession and murine systemic lupus erythematosus. *Science*, 1982, *215*, 1534–1536.

Ader, R., Cohen, N., & Bovbjerg, D. Conditoned suppression of humoral immunity in the rat. *Journal of Comparative and Physiological Psychology*, 1982, *96*, 517–521.

Ader, R., Cohen, N., & Grota, L. J. Adrenal involvement in conditioned immunosuppression. *International Journal of Immunopharmacology*, 1979, *1*, 141–145.

Beecher, H. K. *Measurement of subjective responses: Quantitative effects of drugs.* New York: Oxford University Press, 1959.

Bovbjerg, D., Ader, R., & Cohen, N. Behaviorally conditioned suppression of a graft-versus-host response. *Proceedings of the National Academy of Sciences USA*, 1982, *79*, 583–585.

Bovbjerg, D., Ader, R., & Cohen, N. Acquisition and extinction of conditioned suppression of a graft-versus-host response in the rat. *Journal of Immunology*, 1984, *132*, 111–113.

Brody, H. The lie that heals: The ethics of giving placebos. *Annals of Internal Medicine*, 1982, *97*, 112–118.

Casey, T. P. Immunosuppression by cyclophosphamide in NZB/NZW mice with lupus nephritis. *Blood*, 1968, *32*, 436–444.

Cohen, N., Ader, R., Green, N., & Bovbjerg, D. Conditioned suppression of a thymus independent antibody response. *Psychosomatic Medicine*, 1979, *41*, 487–491.

Eikelboom, R., & Stewart, J. Conditioning of drug-induced physiological responses. *Psychological Review*, 1982, *89*, 507–528.

Evans, F. J. The placebo response in pain reduction. *Advances in Neurology*, 1974, *4*, 289–296.

Gadow, K. D., White, L., & Ferguson, D. G. Placebo controls and double-blind conditions. In S. E. Bruening, A. D. Poling, & J. L. Matson, (Eds.), *Applied psychopharmacology: Methods for assessing medication effects.* New York: Grune & Stratton, in press.

Gantt, W. H. Principles of nervous breakdown in schizokinesis and autokinesis. *Annals of the New York Academy of Sciences*, 1953, *56*, 143–163.

Gleidman, L. H., Gantt, W. H., & Teitelbaum, H. A. Some implications of conditional reflex studies for placebo research. *American Journal of Psychiatry*, 1957 *113*, 1103–1107.

Gorczynski, R. M., Macrae, S., & Kennedy, M. Conditioned immune response associated with allogenic skin grafts in mice. *Journal of Immunology*, 1982, *129*, 704–709.

Hahn, B. H., Knotts, L., Ng, M., & Hamilton, T. R. Influence of cyclophosphamide and other immunosuppressive drugs on immune disorders and neoplasia in NZB/NZW mice. *Arthritis and Rheumatism*, 1975, *18*, 145–152.

Harris, A. H., & Brady, J. V. Animal learning—visceral and autonomic conditioning. *Annual Review of Psychology*, 1974, *25*, 107–133.

Herrnstein, R. J. Placebo effect in the rat. *Science*, 1962, *138*, 677–678.

Humphreys, L. G. The strength of a Thorndikian response as a function of the number of practice trials. *Journal of Comparative Psychology*, 1943, *35*, 101–110.

Kinble, G. A. *Hilgard and Marquis' conditioning and learning.* New York: Appleton-Century-Crofts, 1961.

Knowles, J. B. Conditioning and the placebo effect. *Behavior Research*, 1963, *1*, 151–157.

Kurland, A. A. The drug placebo: Its psychodynamic and conditioned reflex action. *Behavioral Science*, 1957, *2*, 101–110.

Lasagna, L., Mosteller, F., von Felsinger, J. M., & Beecher, H. K. A study of the placebo response. *American Journal of Medicine*, 1954, *16*, 770–779.

Lehman, D. H., Wilson, C. B., & Dixon, F. J. Increased survival times of New Zealand hybrid mice immunosuppressed by graft-versus-host reactions. *Clinical and Experimental Immunology*, 1976, *25*, 297–302.

Lynch, J. J., Fertiziger, A. P., Teitelbaum, H. A., Cullen, J. W., & Gantt, W. H. Pavlovian conditioning of drug reactions: Some implications for problems of drug addiction. *Conditional Reflex*, 1973, *8*, 221–223.

Miller, N. E. Learning of visceral and glandular responses. *Science*, 1969, *163*, 434–445.

Miller, N. E., & Dworkin, B. Different ways in which learning is involved in homeostasis. In R. F. Thompson, L. H. Hicks, & V. B. Shvyrkov (Eds.), *Neural mechanisms of goal-directed behavior and learning.* New York: Academic Press, 1980.

Morris, A. D., Esterly, J., Chase, G., & Sharp, G. C. Cyclophosphamide protection in NZB/NZW disease. *Arthritis and Rheumatism*, 1976, *19*, 49–55.

Petrie, A. Some psychological aspects of pain and the relief of suffering. *Annals of the New York Academy of Sciences*, 1960, *86*, 13–27.

Pihl, R. O., & Altman, J. An experimental analysis of the placebo effect. *Journal of Clinical Pharmacology*, 1971, *11*, 91–95.

Rogers, M. P., Reich, P., Strom, T. B., & Carpenter, C. B. Behaviorally conditioned immunosuppression: Replication of a recent study. *Psychosomatic Medicine*, 1976, *38*, 447–452.

Ross, S., & Schnitzer, S. B. Further support for the placebo effect in the rat. *Psychological Reports*, 1963, *13*, 461–462.

Rounsaville, B. J., Klerman, G. L., & Weissman, M. Do psychotherapy and pharmacotherapy for depression conflict? Empirical evidence from a clinical trial. *Archives of General Psychiatry*, 1981, *38*, 24–29.

Russell, P. J., & Hicks, J. D. Cyclophosphamide treatment of renal disease in (NZB $\times$ NZW)F$_1$ hybrid mice. *Lancet*, 1968, *i*, 440–446.

Siegel, S. Learning and psychopharmacology. In M. E. Jarvik (Ed.), *Psychopharmacology in the practice of medicine.* New York: Appleton-Century-Crofts, 1977.

Siegel, S. Classical conditioning, drug tolerance, and drug dependence. In Y. Israel, F. B. Glaser, H. Kalant, R. E. Popham, W. Schmidt, & R. G. Smart (Eds.), *Research advances in alcohol and drug problems* (Vol. 7). New York: Plenum Press, 1983.

Skinner, B. F. *Science and human behavior.* London: Macmillan, 1953.

Stanley, W. C., & Schlosberg, H. The psychophysiological effects of tea. *Journal of Psychology*, 1953, *36*, 435–448.

Steinberg, A. D., Gelfand, M. C., Hardin, J. A., & Lowenthal, D. T. Therapeutic studies in NZB/W mice: III. Relationship between renal status and efficacy of immunosuppressive drug therapy. *Arthritis and Rheumatism*, 1975, *18*, 9–14.

Steinberg, A. D., Huston, D. P., Taurog, J. D., Cowdery, J. S., & Raveche, E. S. The cellular and genetic basis of murine lupus. *Immunology Reviews*, 1981, 55, 121–154.

Talal, N. Disordered immunologic regulation and autoimmunity. *Transplanation Reviews*, 1976, *31*, 240–263.

Theofilopoulos, A. N., & Dixon, F. J. Etiopathogenesis of murine SLE. *Immunology Reviews*, 1981, 55, 179–216.

Turner, J. L., Gallimore, R., & Fox-Henning, C. An annotated bibliography of placebo research. *JSAS Catalog of Selected Documents in Psychology*, 1980, *10*(MS. No. 2063).

Wayner, E. A., Flannery, G. R., & Singer, G. The effects of taste aversion conditioning on the primary antibody response to sheep red blood cells and *Brucella abortus* in the albino rat. *Physiology and Behavior*, 1978, *21*, 995–1000.

Whitehouse, M. W., Levy, L., & Beck, F. J. Effect of cyclophosphamide on a local graft-versus-host reaction in the rat: Influence of sex, disease and different dosage regimens. *Agents and Actions*, 1973, *3*, 53–60.

Wickramasekera, I. A conditioned response model of the placebo effect: Predictions from the model. *Biofeedback and Self-Regulation*, 1980, *5*, 5–18.

Wikler, A. Dynamics of drug dependence: Implications of a conditioning theory for research and treatment. *Archives of General Psychiatry*, 1973, *28*, 611–616.

Wolf, S. Effects of suggestion and conditioning on the action of chemical agents in human subjects—the pharmacology of placebos. *Journal of Clinical Investigation*, 1950, *29*, 100.

18

Discussion

Mediational Theory of the Placebo Effect

JAYLAN S. TURKKAN
JOSEPH V. BRADY

When one considers how infrequently truly "primal" biological events occur in proportion to the total lifespan of the human organism, the amount of control over human behavior exerted by nonprimal, relatively benign events is impressive. The environment of the typical adult person is replete with visual and auditory stimuli of typically low intensity, which initially exert little lawful control over behavior, since infants are normally unreactive to signs, symbols, and language. The study of how such low-level stimuli come to generate or occasion a complex performance repertoire has been the unique domain of the behavioral scientist with special interests in conditioning and learning. It has been generally understood, whether the perspective is classical Pavlovian or more contemporary Skinnerian, that neutral stimuli acquire control over behavior after they have been paired with occurrence (or avoidance) of biologically important events, such as pain, sex, food, and/ or the intake of other chemically active substances.

Through conditioning, neutral stimuli can come to generate changes not only in the overt behavior of the organism, but also in its physiology. A partial list of conditioned physiological changes includes blood pressure, cardiac rate and rhythm, hormone levels, salivation, sweat secretion, immune response, bronchial airway resistance, respiration, electrocardiogram (EKG) waveform, blood glucose level, skin temperature, and vasomotor changes, among others. It has been well recognized by several behavior theorsists that the defining characteristics of conditioning—in particular, classical (Pavlovian) conditioning—are isomorphic with those of the placebo effect. Basically, the classical conditioning paradigm generates responses (termed "conditional responses," or CRs) to initially inert or neutral stimuli ("conditional stimuli," or CSs) after these stimuli have

Jaylan S. Turkkan and Joseph V. Brady. Department of Psychiatry and Behavioral Sciences, The Johns Hopkins University School of Medicine, Baltimore, Maryland.

been paired with other environmental events that do reliably produce such responses ("unconditional stimuli," UCSs, elicit "unconditional responses," UCRs). Such pairing can be accomplished either by contiguous or by probabilistic (contingent) methods. Fundamentally, the placebo effect is based upon the observation that initially neutral or inert substances and events can come to generate both molecular physiologial alterations (e.g., the conditioned physiological changes noted above), as well as more molar changes such as "healing," for which the precise physiological components are not well specified.

Historians of placebo (some of whom have suggested that the history of medical treatment is largely a history of the placebo effect) are fond of describing the use of, for instance, crocodile dung, fly specks, and eunuch fat as cures. Very often, however, cures were intense events, and could hardly be described as physiologically inert. Patients were bled, blistered, frozen, and shocked. The classical conditioning explanatory account retains credibility, however, since such treatments define the counterconditioning procedure (i.e., a CR is transformed after it has been paired with a different UCS). Pavlov, for example, described an experiment in which a dog came to salivate whenever it received an electric shock after shock had been repeatedly paired with food delivery (Pavlov, 1927/1960, pp. 29–30).

Some less easily dismissed constraints on the connection between classical conditioning and placebo lie in the frequent difficulty of identifying the operative UCS in situations where a placebo effect is observed to occur. What, for example, was the UCS in an experiment where patients diagnosed as neurotic were *told* they were receiving sugar pills, after which 14 out of 15 patients stated that the pills had helped their neurotic symptoms (Park & Covi, 1965)? One appeals in such cases to explanations based upon stimulus generalization effects (sugar pills, after all, look like active pills), or on references to the conditioning history of the patient (in the past, pills have led to a lessening of symptoms). In more operant Skinnerian terms, when an environmental event is observed to produce and maintain certain behaviors of a patient, for example, that event is technically labeled a reinforcement. The reinforcing agent in the Park and Covi study, then, may have been the approval of (or pleasing) the researchers, reminiscent of the famous Hawthorne effect (Roethlisberger & Dickson, 1939). Indeed, the word "placebo" itself translates as "I shall please" in Latin.

Clearly, of course, the exact determinants of placebo are not well understood, but the advantages of a broader conditioning model obviate the need for phenomenological assumptions and provide an account that makes good descriptive and predictive contact with empirically derived and generalizable principles of relevance to all behaving organisms—not just the lame, the halt, and the blind!

The four chapters to be discussed here bear directly or indirectly upon the issue of placebo response and its determinants. Those by Wickrama-sekera and Ader consider placebo effects as arising from classical conditioning principles; Plotkin offers a pre-empirical conceptualization of placebo; and Siegel reviews studies from his laboratory focusing upon conditioning, placebo, and the modulation of drug effects.

Plotkin's chapter, opening this section on mediational theory, maps out the placebo subject area from two viewpoints: the concepts of "faith" and "self-healing." Briefly, placebo effect results from faith, in that if a person believes in the cure, it works. The reason a person has faith is rooted in his or her conditioning history (although the actual term is not used) with regard to procedures, doctors, hospitals, and/or individual courses of action. The reason placebo works is that the person begins to behave in ways that counteract the health problem ("self-healing"). Plotkin goes to some pains to emphasize that the placebo effect is a "psychological phenomenon . . . as opposed to biological or even biopsychological." He nonetheless emphasizes that there is nothing "unreal" or "insubstantial" about such a description; this contention is supported by reference to, for example, biofeedback, learning, and conditioning as psychological phenomena that have "real and nonartifactual outcomes."

Unfortunately, Plotkin's reassertion of a Cartesian dualism leaves the concept of a "psychological phenomenon" hanging in the air with no underpinnings in the physical world. It is perhaps beyond the scope of this discussion to resurrect arguments regarding the involvement of psychological versus biological or psychobiological effects in biofeedback, learning, and conditioning. Even if the word "psychological" were used as a synonym for "behavior," one would be hard put to condition any behavior without accompanying changes in biochemistry or physiology—the alternative being a completely mysterious physical origin of such behaviors. Further along this line, Plotkin states that the sugar pill (i.e., the placebo) cannot be the agent of, for example, a blood pressure change, since a mechanism cannot be conceived by which a neutral stimulus can cause a change in the circulatory physiology of an organism. There is no doubt by now, just as a blush can be occasioned by a glance, that "inert" sensory stimuli can affect circulatory activity (for reviews of the operant and classical conditioning literature in this area, see Harris & Brady, 1974, and Turkkan, Brady, & Harris, 1982). Plotkin instead takes the source of control out of the environment and places it within the patient, thus terming the placebo effect "self-regulation." Some confusion here is evident in terms of which variables are being identified as independent, and which as dependent. Surely, the contextual stimuli comprise the causal independent variables of the placebo situation, with accompanying changes in behavior and physiology as the *dependent* (not causal) variables.

One further point of some practical significance is suggested by Plotkin's assertion that "we require an understanding of *what* the placebo effect is, not merely a technical understanding of how to enhance it, suppress it, or predict it." From an operational perspective, however, it should be emphasized that the requirement for an understanding of an observed biobehavioral interaction like placebo is satisfied completely by a description of the methods used to make the observation, and of the conditions under which the phenomenon is observed to occur. The concept of "faith" in this chapter, for example, takes on a quasi-metaphysical tone until one recasts faith in an operational framework as a change in verbal behavior. Although Plotkin emphasizes that his is a "pre-empirical" approach, the ideas in this chapter must be evaluated from a scientific perspective, since mediational theory can make a useful contribution only to the extent that its concepts are framed operationally.

Wickramasekera's chapter uses an explicit classical conditioning model to explain the placebo effect, and, more importantly, makes 17 specific predictions from the model. Some highlights include the description of "nocebo" as the antithesis of placebo, positing that CSs can acquire harmful effects through association with illness (voodoo may be an example of such nocebo effects). In fact, classical conditioning studies with animals have demonstrated this effect: An occluded coronary artery, for example, can result in various EKG abnormalities and arrhythmias in both monkeys (Randall & Hasson, 1977) and dogs (Corbalan, Verrier, & Lown, 1974) following presentation of CSs that had been paired previously with electric shock. Wickramasekera also recognizes clearly that the use of an active ingredient (UCS) in any biobehavioral interaction necessarily involves the potential for classical conditioning, and hence for placebo learning. This takes placebo out of the realm of "phenomenon," defines it as an orderly and systematic process, and identifies it as an expected component of the therapeutic procedure. Depending, then, upon the parameters of the CS and UCS, and the conditioning history of the subject (and therapist), "placebo" may be manifest (i.e., CRs may occur) in accordance with known principles of learning.

One point made in Wickramasekera's chapter, however, is not in good conformity with the classical conditioning literature: The cases in which CRs are opposite in direction to UCRs do not represent "a few exceptional instances." Not only does Siegel's chapter in this same section of the volume emphasize the opposite directionality of CRs and UCRs as an important source in the development of tolerance to drugs, but many other studies in the classical conditioning literature confirm this observation. Differences between the directionality and form of heart rate CRs and UCRs, for example, have been found to depend upon the species of subject (Cohen & Obrist, 1975), upon the duration of training (McDonald, Stern, & Hahn, 1963), upon pre-CS heart rate level (Ramsay, 1970), upon the CS-UCS interval (Washton, 1978), upon the presence or absence of movement during a trial (Black, Carlson, & Solomon, 1962), upon trace versus delay paradigms (Fitzgerald & Martin, 1971; Turkkan, 1979), and upon unspecified individual differences (Newton & Perez-Cruet, 1967). Thus, it would seem an oversimplification to characterize the placebo response (CR) as merely a "learned fractional component of the UCR... having a shorter latency," rather than as a complex process that will vary according to contextual and ontogenic parameters.

Shepard Siegel's chapter deals more specifically with pharmacological agents as UCSs, and explores classical conditioning as an important participant in the development of tolerance, sensitization, and withdrawal effects involved with the use of drugs. In a classical conditioning model of tolerance, for example, drugs function as UCSs, producing direct physiological UCRs. With repeated exposure to the drug under similar stimulus conditions, environmental cues that have been paired repeatedly with the drug effect come to elicit conditional responses that are frequently drug-opposite or compensatory in nature (Eikelboom & Stewart, 1982). When the CRs are drug-opposite, they counteract the direct effects of the drug, diminish their magnitude, and mediate tolerance. Studies in rats, for example, have shown that tolerance to a variety of drug effects is characterized by drug-opposite CRs. Such observations have included the analgesic effects of morphine (Siegel, 1975, 1976, 1977), and skin temperature responses to ethanol (Crowell, Hinson, & Siegel, 1981; Lê, Poulos, & Cappell, 1979; Mansfield & Cunningham, 1980). Because drug administration both in laboratory experiments and in natural settings involves environmental stimuli that become paired with the onset of drug action, the development of "conditioned compensatory responses" can provide an overarching explanation for the ubiquitous observation of tolerance to the effects of a drug. When CRs are similar to or "mimic" UCRs, a classical conditioning model of drug sensitization emerges: Increasingly larger CRs can summate with and augment the drug-induced UCRs. Though the majority of work reported in Siegel's chapter focuses upon drug-*mirroring* CRs, the relevance of this classical conditioning model to placebo effects lies, of course, in the drug-*mimicking* CRs, where CSs acquire some of the properties of the drug UCSs.

Unfortunately, the orientation of Siegel's chapter, like that of all too many theorists concerned with the classically conditioned aspects of behavior, is excessively and unnecessarily teleological. Much is made of CRs "allowing the organism to prepare for the onset of the UCS," and of "anticipatory" CRs. CRs arise, not as internal "expectations" of UCSs, but in response to external CSs after previous pairings with UCSs. There is, fortunately or unfortunately, little or no evidence in either the experimental or clinical literature that an event that has not as yet occurred can in any way control a behavioral interaction!

Drug-mimicking CRs are discussed at length by Ader, who raises the fascinating prospect of replacing medication with placebo, thereby introducing the subject of "partial reinforcement" in classical conditioning (also discussed by Wickramasekera). Partial reinforcement in the classical conditioning paradigm is represented by omission of the UCS in some proportion of training trials while continuing to present the CS alone. Although the literature is somewhat inconsistent between humans and animals in this area, continuous reinforcement (i.e., repeated pairings of both UCS and CS) generally produces stronger conditioning during acquisition, whereas conditioning with partial reinforcement tends to increase resistance to extinction relative to continuous reinforcement (for a review, see Hall, 1976, Chapter 5). Such findings suggest that once conditioned "placebo" effects to pharmacologically active substances are optimally strengthened through continuous pairing procedures, they could then be maintained on a partial schedule of drug administration, with inert substances replacing a portion of the active ingredients. Ader's research is part of the emerging area of psychoneuroimmunology, bringing into the laboratory an extensive array of anecdotal observations documenting central nervous system influences in the alteration of immune function (i.e., ways in which "perceptions" can affect "health").

Perhaps the most impressive aspect of Ader's treatment of the subject matter of primary concern in this section of the volume is the obvious appreciation shown for the rigor with which placebo conditioning variables must be experimentally parceled out. Dose, route of administration, frequency and duration of medication, and careful titration of reinforcement schedule parameters as they make contact with the "drug:placebo" ratio are all carefully and comprehensively considered in relationship to research strategies of obvious importance and highly productive potential. While the animal literature in this area is growing (see Monjan, 1981, for a review), studies with humans using appropriate double-blind procedures (such as that of Cohen, Graham, Fotopoulos, & Cook, 1977, for biofeedback efficacy) can be expected to yield results of considerable usefulness in the pragmatic setting of clinical practice.

In addition to the modulation of drug effects, changes in immune response, and the placebo effect, all outlined in the chapters of this section, classical conditioning has been recently proposed as a paradigm to explain a wide range of other behavioral interactions characterized within the framework of such terms as "aggression" and "polydipsia" (Wetherington, 1982), "drug dependence" and "substance abuse" (Wikler, 1973), "taste aversion" (Garcia & Koelling, 1966), and "sign-tracking" and "auto-shaping" (Hearst & Jenkins, 1974). This new hegemony of classical conditioning is, of course, viewed with some considerable satisfaction by those who have long been convinced that the systematic association of environmental stimuli that do not initially produce responses with more primal biological events that nearly always do can powerfully influence biochemical, physiological, and behavioral interactions.

REFERENCES

Black, A. H., Carlson, N. J., & Solomon, R. J. Exploratory studies of the conditioning of autonomic responses in curarized dogs. *Psychological Monographs*, 1962, 76, 29(Whole No. 548).

Cohen, D. H., & Obrist, P. A. Interactions between behavior and the cardiovascular system. *Circulation Research*, 1975, *37*, 693–706.

Cohen, H. D., Graham, C., Fotopoulos, S. S., & Cook, M. R. A double-blind methodology for biofeedback research. *Psychophysiology*, 1977, *14*, 603–608.

Corbalan, R., Verrier, R., & Lown, B. Psychological stress and ventricular arrhythmias during myocardial infarction in the conscious dog. *American Journal of Cardiology*, 1974, *34*, 692–696.

Crowell, C. R., Hinson, R. E., & Siegel, S. The role of conditioned drug responses in tolerance to the hypothermic effects of ethanol. *Psychopharmacology*, 1981, *73*, 51–54.

Eikelboom, R., & Stewart, J. Conditioning of drug-induced physiological responses. *Psychological Review*, 1982, *89*, 507–528.

Fitzgerald, R. D., & Martin, G. K. Heart rate conditioning in rats as a function of interstimulus interval. *Psychological Reports*, 1971, *29*, 1103–1110.

Garcia, J., & Koelling, R. Relation of cue to consequence in avoidance learning. *Psychonomic Science*, 1966, *4*, 123–124.

Hall, J. F. *Classical conditioning and instrumental learning*. Philadelphia: J. B. Lippincott, 1976.

Harris, A. H., & Brady, J. V. Animal learning—visceral and autonomic conditioning. *Annual Review of Psychology*, 1974, *25*, 107–133.

Hearst, E., & Jenkins, H. M. *Sign-tracking: The stimulus reinforcer relation and directed action*. Austin, Texas: Psychonomic Society, 1974.

Lê, A. D., Poulos, C. S., & Cappell, H. Conditioned tolerance to the hypothermic effect of ethyl alcohol. *Science*, 1979, *206*, 1109–1110.

Mansfield, J. G., & Cunningham, C. C. Conditioning and extinction of tolerance to the hypothermic effect of ethanol in rats. *Journal of Comparative and Physiological Psychology*, 1980, *94*, 962–969.

McDonald, D., Stern, J., & Hahn, W. Classical heart rate conditioning in the rat. *Journal of Psychosomatic Research*, 1963, *7*, 97–106.

Monjan, A. A. Stress and immunologic competence: Studies in animals. In R. Ader (Ed.), *Psychoneuroimmunology*. New York: Academic Press, 1981.

Newton, J. E. O., & Perez-Cruet, J. Successive-beat analysis of cardiovascular orienting and conditional responses. *Conditional Reflex*, 1967, *2*, 37–55.

Park, L. C., & Covi, L. Non-blind placebo trial: An exploration of neurotic patients' responses to placebo when its inert content is disclosed. *Archives of General Psychiatry*, 1965, *12*, 336–345.

Pavlov, I. P. *Conditioned reflexes* (G. Anrep, Ed. and trans.). New York: Dover, 1960. (Originally published, 1927.)

Ramsay, D. A. Form and characteristics of the cardiovascular conditional response in rhesus monkeys. *Conditional Reflex*, 1970, *5*, 36–51.

Randall, D. C., & Hasson, D. M. A note on ECG charges observed during Pavlovian conditioning in a rhesus monkey following coronary arterial occlusion. *Pavlovian Journal of Biological Science*, 1977, *12*, 229–231.

Roethlisberger, F. J., & Dickson, W. J. *Management and the worker*. Cambridge, Mass.: Harvard University Press, 1939.

Siegel, S. Evidence from rats that morphine tolerance is a learned response. *Journal of Comparative and Physiological Psychology*, 1975, *89*, 498–506.

Siegel, S. Morphine analgesic tolerance: Its situation specificity supports a Pavlovian conditioning model. *Science*, 1976, *193*, 323–325.

Siegel, S. Morphine tolerance acquisition as an associative process. *Journal of Experimental Psychology: Animal Behavior Processes*, 1977, *3*, 1–13.

Turkkan, J. S. Varying temporal location of a conditioned stimulus in heart rate conditioning of *Macaca mulatta*. *Pavlovian Journal of Biological Science*, 1979, *14*, 31–43.

Turkkan, J. S., Brady, J. V., & Harris, A. H. Animal studies of stressful interactions: A behavioral–physiological overview. In L. Goldberger & S. Breznitz (Eds.). *Handbook of stress*. New York: Macmillan, 1982.

Washton, A. M. *Pavlovian conditioning of heart rate in Macaca mulatta: Autonomic and stimulus control of cardiac responding as a function of CS-US interval*. Unpublished doctoral dissertation, The City University of New York, 1978.

Wetherington, C. L. Is adjunctive behavior a third class of behavior? *Neuroscience and Biobehavioral Reviews*, 1982, *6*, 329–350.

Wikler, A. Dynamics of drug dependence: Implications of a conditioning theory for research and treatment. *Archives of General Psychiatry*, 1973, *28*, 611–616.

19

Placebo Analgesia, Naloxone, and the Role of Endogenous Opioids

PRISCILLA GREVERT
AVRAM GOLDSTEIN

INTRODUCTION

Given the known pain-relieving qualities of the opiates, it is not surprising that the discovery of endogenous opioids should have led to the hypothesis that these peptides are involved in pain regulation, and therefore also in analgesia produced by acupuncture, hypnosis, or placebo administration. One or more of the three families of endogenous opioids (Cox, 1982) have been located in areas of the dorsal spinal cord known to be involved in the processing of pain, in the periventricular and periaqueductal gray matter, in specific nuclei of the mesencephalic reticular formation known to mediate analgesia, and in several nuclei of the hypothalamus, thalamus, and amygdala thought to be concerned in emotional responses to noxious stimuli.

Several experimental approaches have been used to test the hypothesis that endogenous opioids are involved in pain regulation. Most frequently, the narcotic antagonist naloxone has been administered under various conditions of pain or analgesia. In these studies, naloxone and naloxone vehicle (the pharmacologically inert solution containing the naloxone) are given in a double-blind procedure. In the better experimental designs, subjects are unaware not only of whether naloxone or vehicle is being administered, but also of whether or not an injection is being made at all. In this "hidden injection" technique, injections are made without warning and out of a subject's view into an already emplaced intravenous line. Thus, changes in behavior that might result from subjects responding to the injection procedure itself are eliminated. This precaution is especially relevant to studies on placebo analgesia. By giving placebo in full view (or nothing at all, as a control, as discussed below) and naloxone (or naloxone vehicle as a control)

Priscilla Grevert and Avram Goldstein. Addiction Research Foundation and Department of Pharmacology, Stanford University, Palo Alto, California.

as a "hidden injection," investigators can avoid confounding the "placebo effects" of a naloxone injection with the effects of a true placebo injection.

If pain increases or if analgesia is blocked or diminished more after naloxone than after vehicle, some involvement of endogenous opioids is suggested. The logic of this deduction is based upon the very high specificity of naloxone as an antagonist at opioid receptors. It should be borne in mind, however, that drug specificity is probably never absolute, so it may be impossible in principle to rule out an effect of naloxone that is unrelated to opioid receptors.

Another limitation arises from the selectivity of naloxone for opioid receptors of the μ type. Thus, failure to find a naloxone effect may be inconclusive because the naloxone doses may not have been adequate. It is now known that there are multiple types of opioid receptors (Lord, Waterfield, Hughes, & Kosterlitz, 1977; Martin, 1978), perhaps related to the several families of endogenous opioids (Goldstein, 1982). Although naloxone has a high affinity for μ receptors, its affinity for δ and κ is 10–15 times poorer. Because of the relatively low doses of naloxone used in most human studies, a negative result may only indicate that μ receptors do not mediate the phenomenon under study; endogenous opioids acting at another type of opioid receptor might be involved. Conversely, a positive effect of low-dose naloxone (e.g., exacerbation of pain)—assuming that the effect is due to blockade of opioid receptors—suggests that the pain is being attenuated in some manner by the action of an endogenous opioid on μ receptors.

Another approach used to study the possible involvement of endogenous opioids in pain regulation is to measure changes in the levels of various opioid peptides in tissues, plasma, or cerebrospinal fluid (CSF). Here, again, there are several limitations. Since these levels are usually measured by immunoassay, the validity of the conclusions is limited by the specificity of the assay. For example, in plasma, only a small part of immunoreactive (ir-) β-endorphin is authentic; several acetylated or partially degraded derivatives, which are inactive or poorly active as opioids, crossreact with the β-endorphine antisera (O'Donahue & Dorsa, 1982). Besides, the reported plasma levels of ir-β-endorphin—even if it were all authentic β-endorphin—even under conditions of stress are too low to produce activation of known opioid receptors. Moreover, passage of peptides from blood into the central nervous system, across the blood–brain barrier, is extremely limited (Rapoport, Klee, Pettigrew, & Ohno, 1980).

Given that changes in level of one or more endogenous opioids occur (and even that such changes occur within the central nervous system), major problems of interpretation remain. For example, two recent studies reported a significant negative correlation between endogenous opioid levels in CSF "Fraction I" (Tamsen, Sakurada, Wahlstrom, Terenius, & Hartvig, 1982) or plasma ir-β-endorphin (Pickar, Cohen, Naber, & Cohen, 1982) and postsurgical demand for pain medication; patients with lower Fraction I or ir-

β-endorphin levels prior to surgery required more analgesic medication after surgery. However, such correlations do not necessarily indicate causation; lower endogenous opioid levels could be a result of, a cause of, or only secondarily related to a patient's perceived pain and consequent demand for analgesic medication.

Since many of the endogenous opioids show cross-tolerance with morphine, another procedure used to test the involvement of an endogenous opioid is to determine whether the given effect is diminished or abolished in the state of morphine tolerance. Since morphine is primarily a μ agonist and since tolerance is specific to a given opioid receptor type, a negative result suggests that μ receptors are not involved, but does not rule out involvement of other opioid receptor types.

In summary, present knowledge about multiple opioid receptors makes a negative result using any of these techniques inconclusive. On the other hand, a positive result is merely suggestive of endogenous opioid involvement, and should only be considered a starting point for further research. As pointed out earlier, although exacerbation of pain by naloxone may result from a specific naloxone antagonism at the μ opioid receptors, it could also be due to nonspecific effects of naloxone on other systems. In addition, the finding that systemically administered naloxone enhances pain gives no information about what part of the pain-processing system is affected, whether the effect is low or high in the neuraxis, or whether the effect occurs directly in the main pain pathways or by a remote secondary action. These problems can often be investigated and resolved in animal experiments, where invasive techniques in the central nervous system—lesions, cannulations, microinjections, iontophoresis, implanted electrodes, sampling of brain fluid and CSF, and so on—can be readily applied. The study of placebo analgesia, however, obviously requires human subjects, in whom the range of possible experimental techniques is much more restricted, both for technical and for ethical reasons.

With all of these caveats in mind, we review critically the present state of knowledge concerning the participation of endogenous opioids in placebo analgesia. Our review consists of four sections:

1. We review briefly some studies of naloxone effects on pain and analgesia in human subjects.
2. We analyze the experimental designs that typically have been used to study placebo analgesia, illustrating by summarizing a few selected studies.
3. We review experimental studies that have used naloxone to implicate endogenous opioid involvement in placebo analgesia, and we discuss the experimental designs for those studies.
4. We discuss research approaches that might be used in the future to determine more conclusively whether placebo analgesia is mediated by endogenous opioids.

EFFECT OF NALOXONE ON PAIN AND ANALGESIA

Placebo analgesia is a procedure that attenuates pain. If the effect of naloxone upon placebo analgesia is to be studied, it is obviously essential to know and take into account any effect that naloxone itself may have upon pain. Hyperalgesic actions of naloxone in animals are well established (Berger, Akil, Watson, & Barchas, 1982; Frederickson & Geary, 1982; Sawynok, Pinsky, & LaBella, 1979); only effects in humans are considered here.

Doses of naloxone as high as 20 mg have failed to affect experimental pain produced by electric shock (El-Sobky, Dostrovsky, & Wall, 1976), ischemic arm pain (Grevert & Goldstein, 1977, 1978), or cold water pressor pain (Grevert & Goldstein, 1978; Schull, Kaplan, & O'Brien, 1981; Volavka, Bauman, Pevnick, Reker, James, & Cho, 1980). On the other hand, similar doses of naloxone have been found to increase experimental ischemic arm pain significantly when the pain was produced under stress (Frid, Singer, & Rana, 1979; Schull et al., 1981). Exacerbation of experimental pain by naloxone has been reported in certain subpopulations of subjects. Buchsbaum, Davis, and Bunney (1977) divided subjects into "pain-sensitive" and "pain-insensitive" groups, according to their responses to electric shocks of varying intensities to the forearm. The pain-insensitive subjects called shocks painful at lower levels of current and judged more of the shocks unpleasant after 2 mg of naloxone than after an injection of a salt solution. The peak amplitudes of the somatosensory evoked potentials were increased and the latencies were reduced by naloxone in the pain-insensitive subjects. There was no effect of naloxone on pain-sensitive subjects. Later, following the same procedures, these same authors found that subjects were less sensitive to the pain in the morning than in the afternoon, and that naloxone effects on the evoked potentials were present only in the morning (Davis, Buchsbaum, & Bunney, 1978). It was interesting that these changes in pain sensitivity paralleled the known circadian changes in plasma adrenocorticotropic hormone (ACTH) and β-endorphin; pain sensitivity was lowest in the morning when plasma levels of these substances are the highest.

In clinical pain, naloxone (9–10 mg) has been reported to enhance the pain resulting from tooth extraction (Gracely, Wolskee, Deeter, & Dubner, 1982; Levine, Gordon, Jones, & Fields, 1978). Lasagna (1965) had reported that low doses of naloxone (2 mg) relieved postoperative pain, while higher doses (8 mg) made the pain worse. Similarly, Levine, Gordon, and Fields (1979) found that high doses of naloxone increased pain in "placebo responders," whereas low doses had an analgesic effect. The analgesic effect of low doses and hyperalgesic effect of high doses of naloxone have also been reported when pain tolerance is measured after exercise (Haier, Quaid, & Mills, 1981).

Analgesia produced by electrical stimulation of the periaqueductal gray matter in patients suffering from chronic pain is reversed by naloxone (.2–1 mg) (Adams, 1976; Hosobuchi, Adams, & Linchitz, 1977). This analgesia is accompanied by increases in levels of ir-β-endorphin in ventricular CSF (Akil, Richardson, Barchas, & Li, 1978; Hosobuchi, Rossier, Bloom, & Guillemin, 1979). Low doses of naloxone (.4–.8 mg) partially reversed analgesia produced by transcutaneous electrical stimulation in patients undergoing dental surgery (Chapman & Benedetti, 1977) and in patients suffering from chronic back pain (Salar & Iob, 1978). However, .8 mg of naloxone did not reverse analgesia produced by transcutaneous electrical stimulation in patients with fractured ribs (Woolf, Mitchell, Myers, & Barrett, 1978). Stress-induced analgesia produced by pairing an electric shock to a signal is reversed by 5 mg of naloxone (Willer & Albe-Fessard, 1980; Willer, Dehen, & Cambier, 1981). Low doses of naloxone (.2–1.2 mg) diminished analgesia produced by acupuncture (Mayer, Price, & Rafii, 1977; Sjolund & Eriksson, 1976) but did not affect hypnotic analgesia (Barber & Mayer, 1977; Goldstein & Hilgard, 1975). However, hypnotic analgesia is partially reversed by naloxone (1 mg) when a condition of stress is introduced following the induction of hypnosis but preceding the pain procedure (Frid & Singer, 1979).

In summary, when analgesia is produced by an opioid mechanism, as in electrical stimulation of appropriate sites in the brain, naloxone, at adequate dosage, effectively opposes the analgesic effect. Analgesia produced by acupuncture or transcutaneous electrical stimulation in humans appears to fall into this category, for it is reversed by naloxone; and acupuncture analgesia in animals is clearly blocked by naloxone (Han & Terenius, 1982; Pomeranz & Chiu, 1976). Hypnosis analgesia is unaffected by naloxone, and this suggests that it is not mediated by an opioid system—at least not by endogenous μ agonists. In experimental pain, naloxone is without effect except in subjects who have intrinsically poor sensitivity to pain, or when the pain is accompanied by stress. In clinical pain, where stress is typically present, naloxone usually enhances the pain. A consistent unitary interpretation is that in most people under ordinary circumstances sensitivity to pain is not under tonic inhibition by endogenous opioids; exceptions are people who have an exceptionally low sensitivity to pain. In most people, according to this interpretation, stress accompanying pain causes release of endogenous opioids, which act to moderate the pain; and this analgesic effect is partially or wholly reversed by naloxone.

EXPERIMENTAL STUDIES ON PLACEBO ANALGESIA

Early descriptions of the ability of placebos to cause analgesia were based on studies in which the placebo served as an experimental control against which to distinguish effects of pharmacologically active substances. Typically, the placebo and a pharmacologically active analgesic were administered sequentially to the same subject. Subjects generally were patients suffering from some type of clinical pain (e.g., headache or postoperative pain), and either a placebo or an analgesic was given on demand. These studies typically were concerned with identifying characteristics of the placebo responder or the situation in which the placebo response occurred.

Two studies that used this research design and are frequently cited in the literature investigated the effects of placebos and analgesics on headache pain and postoperative pain. Jellinek (1946), following a double-blind procedure, had 200 headache sufferers self-administer tablets containing either active analgesics or an inert placebo whenever a headache occurred. At the end of each 2-week period, subjects reported to a physician the number of headaches they had had and how many of these had been relieved satisfactorily by the drug. Results indicated that those who experienced relief from the placebo did so consistently; there were individuals who definitely did respond to placebos and others who definitely did not respond.

Lasagna, Mosteller, von Felsinger, and Beecher (1954), using a double-blind technique, injected patients experiencing postoperative pain with either a saline placebo or morphine. A group of 69 patients received one placebo for every five morphine injections, while morphine and saline injections were alternated in another 93 patients. Pain relief was considered to have occurred when the patient indicated that the pain had been reduced "by more than half." Of 69 patients who received two or more placebos, only 10 consistently reported pain relief following placebo, while 38 experienced placebo analgesia inconsistently. Unlike the results of Jellinek (1946), this study revealed no identifiable group of placebo reactors or nonreactors. With respect to the inconsistency of response, the authors wrote that if one "tried to predict the efficacy of subsequent placebos by the response to the initial dose of saline, one would thus have been wrong more frequently than right" (Lasagna et al., 1954, p. 773).

These investigations were controlled drug studies but uncontrolled placebo studies. There were two fundamental design defects that made it impossible, in either study, to conclude whether (or how consistently) placebo analgesia occurred. First, there was no no-treatment control group. Subjects in such a group would have provided pain ratings at the same time as those receiving placebo or medication, thus furnishing information on the normal time course of the pain, the fluctuations in pain within subjects, and the variance in pain between subjects. Only against such a control group would it have been possible to assess the degree of placebo analgesia.

The second design defect was that all subjects received active analgesics as well as placebo. There is a tendency—called "pharmacological sophistication"—for subjects to exhibit less frequent and less marked placebo responses after they have experienced definite analgesia from a potent drug (Lasagna et al., 1954). Thus, in designing a study to demonstrate placebo analgesia, at least two groups of subjects are necessary—a no-treatment control group to monitor the normal course of the pain, and a distinct and separate placebo group that receives only the placebo. These groups could contain the same subjects, tested at different times under both conditions in a crossover design. If evaluating the analgesic potency of an active agent is also of interest, a separate drug treatment group could be included, but subjects in this group must not be the same as those in the placebo group. The schedule of drug (or placebo) administration and the method of delivery should be identical for the placebo and drug treatment groups. The ethical barrier to employing a no-treatment control group accounts for the fact that very few studies of placebo analgesia in clinical pain have been carried out according to these minimum requirements of experimental design.

One of the first studies of placebo analgesia to include both a no-treatment control group and a placebo group that only received placebo used experimental pain produced by ultrasound to the thumb (Gelfand, Ullmann, & Krasner, 1963). Subjects in the placebo group were told that the capsule they would receive was a strong and powerful agent for preventing pain. Subjects in the control group, which received no drug, were told that the purpose of the study was to measure tolerance to pain. Pain threshold was defined as the number of seconds from the onset of the stimulus to the subject's first report of pain. Pain tolerance was defined as the number of seconds between the first report of pain and the subject's removal of his or her thumb. Three trials were first carried out ("pretrials"); then the placebo group received an inert capsule; then 15 minutes later both groups were given three more trials ("posttrials"). Changes in threshold and tolerance were computed by subtracting pretrial threshold and tolerance measures from posttrial measures. A significant placebo effect occurred with both measures. Although the pain threshold in both groups decreased from pretrial to posttrial, the decrease was significantly ($p < .05$) less in the placebo than in the control group. Moreover, pain tolerance increased in the placebo group, while it decreased in the control group (difference significant, $p < .05$). These authors suggested that Beecher's (1960) frequently cited conclusion that placebos are not effective analgesics in experimental pain may have been reached because most of the studies reviewed by Beecher failed to include a no-treatment control group, thus possibly masking the presence of placebo analgesia.

In another study using both a no-treatment control group and a placebo group, Liberman (1964) examined the hypothesis that there are consistent placebo responders by testing the same subjects in two situations involving clinical pain and one involving experimental pain. The subjects were 51 obstetrical patients who were given placebos to counteract the pain of labor, postpartum pain, and ischemic arm pain. Subjects rated the clinical pain, using a linear analogue scale, 15 and 30 minutes after receiving a subcutaneous saline injection described as an effective painkiller. For the ischemic pain, a blood pressure cuff was placed on the arm and inflated to occlude the circulation. Using the hand of this occluded arm, subjects were instructed to squeeze a rubber ball until they experienced the first sign of pain. Each time the bulb was squeezed, water was displaced from a bottle to a beaker in amount proportional to the applied force. The amount of water displaced before and after ingestion of a placebo capsule was recorded. Different subjects were used as no-treatment controls. Pain was significantly less in the placebo group than in the control group for each of these pain situations. However, a given subject did not consistently experience placebo analgesia in all three pain situations. This led Liberman to conclude that "placebo reactivity should be viewed as a potential tendency that can become manifest under the right circumstances in anyone rather than as an attribute possessed by some but not by others" (1964, p. 244).

STUDIES OF PLACEBO ANALGESIA USING NALOXONE

Recently, it was suggested by Levine, Gordon, and Fields (1978) that placebo analgesia is mediated by endogenous opioids, and naloxone was administered to test this hypothesis. Naloxone (10 mg intravenously [i.v.]) or a naloxone vehicle placebo was injected in full view of the subjects, 51 patients recovering from dental surgery (extraction of impacted third molars). Subjects were told that they would receive morphine, placebo, or naloxone ("an agent that might increase the pain"). They were assigned randomly to treatment, and all drugs were administered double-blind. The first drug (Drug 1) was administered 2 hours after anesthesia for the surgery (nitrous oxide by inhalation, supplemented by diazepam i.v. and mepiva-caine as a local anesthetic); the second drug (Drug 2) was given 1 hour after Drug 1. Normally, the postoperative pain increases for several hours, then subsides. Subjects were randomly assigned to one of three sequences of drug administration: naloxone–placebo, placebo–naloxone, or placebo–placebo. Figure 19-1A summarizes the experimental design. Pain was rated both before and after each naloxone or placebo administration by means of a linear analogue scale. In the group that received placebo as Drug 1, subjects who received naloxone as Drug 2 reported a significantly greater increase of pain than the subjects given a second placebo. This finding confirmed an earlier report by Levine, Gordon, Jones, and Fields (1978): "When the groups receiving naloxone and placebo as D_1 [i.e., Drug 1] are compared, the naloxone group shows a greater increase in pain. This difference reaches significance at 60 minutes. When the effects of these drugs as D_2 are compared, the difference reaches significance at 20 minutes" (p. 827). It is not evident to what extent the same subjects may have been used in both investigations. That the postsurgical pain in this paradigm was enhanced by naloxone is an important point to which we return later in discussing these studies.

Levine, Gordon, and Fields (1978) categorized the subjects in the placebo–naloxone group as placebo responders or nonresponders on the basis of their response to the single administration of placebo as Drug 1. Placebo responders were defined as subjects whose pain did not get worse

A

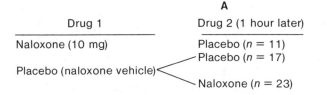

Drug 1	Drug 2 (1 hour later)
Naloxone (10 mg)	Placebo ($n = 11$)
Placebo (naloxone vehicle)	Placebo ($n = 17$) Naloxone ($n = 23$)

Design for all groups. Drug 1 was administered 2 hours after anesthesia for the surgery. Morphine was administered to some other subjects, but those data are not reported. Subjects receiving naloxone as Drug 2 reported a significantly greater increase of pain than was reported by subjects who received a second placebo.

B

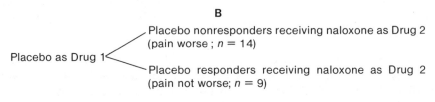

Placebo as Drug 1
Placebo nonresponders receiving naloxone as Drug 2 (pain worse ; $n = 14$)
Placebo responders receiving naloxone as Drug 2 (pain not worse; $n = 9$)

Design for subjects in the placebo–naloxone group characterized as placebo responders or nonresponders, according to their response 1 hour after placebo as Drug 1. Those characterized as responders reported a significantly greater increase of pain after receiving naloxone as Drug 2 than reported by subjects defined as placebo nonresponders.

Figure 19-1. Experimental design of naloxone study of placebo analgesia reported by Levine, Gordon, and Fields (1978).

(i.e., the pain rating 1 hour after taking placebo remained constant or decreased as compared to the rating made 5 minutes before taking placebo). The remaining subjects were defined as nonresponders. Figure 19-1B summarizes the experimental design used for this analysis. When the placebo responders received naloxone as Drug 2, their pain increased significantly more than did the pain of the other subjects. The authors concluded that these results "are consistent with the hypothesis that endorphin [i.e., endogenous opioid] release mediates placebo analgesia for dental post-operative pain" (Levine, Gordon, & Fields, 1978, p. 654). Later, this same group reported that the initial level of pain influenced the analgesic response to placebo; subjects who rated their preplacebo pain above a threshold value of 2.6 were more likely to report analgesia after placebo (Levine, Gordon, Bornstein, & Fields, 1979).

In a similar study, thus far reported only as an abstract, Gracely *et al.* (1982) administered either 10 mg of naloxone or naloxone vehicle under double-blind conditions to 93 patients 2 hours after dental surgery. These injections were made as hidden infusions out of view of subjects, through an indwelling intravenous line. Immediately thereafter, either i.v. fentanyl (.11 μg/kg) or a saline placebo was given in full view to some subjects; others received no additional treatment. Table 19-1 summarizes the experimental design of this study. Pain was measured 60 and 10 minutes before and 10

Table 19-1. Experimental Design of the Gracely, Wolskee, Deeter, and Dubner (1982) Study of the Effect of Naloxone on Placebo Analgesia

Hidden infusion	Injection in view		No treatment
	Fentanyl (.11 μg/kg)	Placebo (saline)	
Naloxone (10 mg)	X	X	X
Naloxone vehicle	X	X	X

Note. Treatments in column heads immediately followed the hidden infusions of naloxone or naloxone vehicle. The fentanyl and placebo were administered in view of the subjects. Each "X" represents a different group of subjects.

and 60 minutes after the injections, using the Pain Rating Index of the McGill Pain Questionnaire. As expected, naloxone blocked the fentanyl analgesia. A two-factor analysis of covariance (hidden infusions of naloxone or naloxone vehicle × open administration of placebo or no treatment), using the initial pain ratings as covariate, indicted that pain increased significantly after naloxone and decreased significantly after placebo. Failure to find a significant interaction between these effects led Gracely *et al.* (1982) to conclude that naloxone and placebo produce effects that are both separate and independent. There is no indication whether subjects were randomly assigned to treatments, nor are summary statistics presented that would indicate the magnitude of the placebo or naloxone effect. Finally, no statistical test is reported on the difference in pain ratings between placebo given after naloxone and placebo given after naloxone vehicle. The full report of this experiment should be of great interest.

Another experimental study of naloxone effects on placebo analgesia, also only published as a brief abstract (Mihic & Binkert, 1978), used the experimental technique of cold pressor pain. The sequence of events of the experimental design may be summarized as follows:

- Cold pressor pain 1
- Placebo (i.v. saline)
- Cold pressor pain 2
- Naloxone (.4 mg)
- Cold pressor pain 3

Although neither the type of pain rating scale nor the time interval over which pain was rated is indicated, the authors state that the pain was expressed as a function of intensity over time. Standard pain curves were obtained for each subject; then an intravenous saline placebo was administered with the suggestion that it was an analgesic. A placebo response was defined as an increase in time to reach the preplacebo peak of pain intensity. When .4 mg of naloxone (which was described as an additional dose of the "same analgesic" [placebo]) was administered, it not only failed to reverse but actually increased the placebo analgesia. The authors also state that .4 mg of naloxone failed to block placebo analgesia when it was administered to subjects who had previously shown a placebo response. Mihic and Binkert conclude that the "placebo analgesic effect is totally independent of endorphine [i.e., endogenous opioid] analgesic system" (1978, p. 19). There is no indication of the number of subjects tested, nor is it stated whether drugs were administered using a double-blind technique. Summary statistics and statistical test values also are not presented. Little weight can be given the authors' conclusions in the absence of more data, yet no full-length paper has appeared to date.

In our opinion, to determine whether naloxone attenuates placebo analgesia requires that the experimental design include all of the following:

1. A no-treatment control group to monitor the normal course of the pain. Neither the study by Levine, Gordon, and Fields (1978) nor the study by Mihic and Binkert (1978) included such a control group, and thus it is impossible in principle to determine from those studies whether the placebo significantly reduced pain.

2. Sessions during which naloxone or naloxone vehicle are administered under double-blind and hidden conditions (i.e., out of subjects' view) to demonstrate that naloxone by itself does not increase the pain. "Nonspecific biological antagonism" occurs when the effects of two agents, acting in opposite directions and by different mechanisms, tend to cancel each other. If a pharmacological agent (e.g.,naloxone) intensifies pain, and a procedure (e.g., placebo administration) ameliorates pain, it is expected that both together will result in an intermediate degree of pain, *regardless of the mechanism of action of either agent.* Under such circumstances, antagonism of placebo analgesia by naloxone would not necessarily indicate that placebo analgesia is mediated through opioid receptors, even if it were assumed that the hyperalgesic effect of naloxone is mediated at opioid receptors. Thus, the use of naloxone to establish whether placebo analgesia is due to endogenous opioids is impermissible if naloxone itself enhances the pain.

To determine that naloxone itself does not affect the particular type of pain under study, it must be administered out of the subject's view. The reason is that subjects participating in a study concerned with the testing of analgesics may well report an analgesic effect after any substance is administered; thus, any effect of naloxone in increasing pain may be obscured by subjects experiencing a placebo response to the naloxone injection.

Of the studies reviewed above, only that of Gracely *et al.* (1982) employed the hidden-infusion technique. In the investigations by Levine, Gordon, and Fields (1978) and by Levine, Gordon, Jones, and Fields (1978), naloxone itself enhanced the postsurgical dental pain. In our opinion, quite apart from other design defects noted earlier, this well-known

hyperalgesic effect of naloxone in clinical pain makes their conclusion that
endogenous opioids mediate placebo analgesia unwarranted.

3. If naloxone did block placebo analgesia, a subject might develop the
attitude that "This drug [i.e., the placebo] doesn't work," resulting in a
negative expectation concerning the next placebo experience. To avoid this
"carry-over" possibility, two different groups of subjects must be used; one
should always receive naloxone after placebo, while another receives vehicle
after placebo.

4. The dose of naloxone should be as large as possible, to ensure
antagonism of endogenous opioids; yet it must not produce subjective effects
that would allow subjects to detect when naloxone has been given, thus
frustrating the double-blind design. We have found that subjects cannot
reliably distinguish 10 mg of naloxone from naloxone vehicle (Grevert &
Goldstein, 1977, 1978), but higher doses have been found to cause
dysphoria (Cohen, Cohen, Pickar, Weingartner, Murphy, & Bunney, 1981;
Pickar et al., 1982).

Using an experimental design that incorporated all these criteria, we
recently demonstrated (Grevert, Albert, & Goldstein, 1983) a small but
significant effect of 10 mg of naloxone in diminishing the analgesic
effectiveness of a placebo administered prior to the production of experimental ischemic arm pain (Smith, Egbert, Markowitz, Mosteller, & Beecher,
1966). This is a type of pain shown previously to be unaffected by naloxone
(Grevert & Goldstein, 1977, 1978). Volunteers (18 males and 12 females)
gave informed consent, and were randomly assigned to either a vehicle group
(Group V) or a naloxone group (Group N). Subjects were told that the
purpose of the study was to test the ability of a new drug to act as a
"painkiller," and that the maximum painkilling effects should occur in
approximately 1 hour. Subjects were told that during the study they would
receive "the drug naloxone, a narcotic antagonist that at certain doses had
been shown to reduce postoperative pain" (Lasagna, 1965). All subjects
received the "painkiller" (an i.v. saline placebo given in full view) at a
placebo session, once a week for 3 consecutive weeks. This placebo injection
was followed 40 minutes later (i.e., 20 minutes before the expected time of
maximum analgesia) by a hidden injection of naloxone vehicle (Group V)
or naloxone (10 mg, Group N). The type of hidden injection (naloxone or
vehicle) remained constant throughout the study for each subject and was
determined by a subject's group assignment. Experimenters did not know a
subject's group assignment. Subjects were not only blind to the type of
injection; they also did not know that any substance other than the
"painkiller" was given, since hidden injections were made into an i.v. line
behind a screen.

Table 19-2 summarizes the experimental design and sequence of events
at each session. During each week of the study, in addition to the placebo

Table 19-2. Experimental Design and Sequence of Events for Each Session in the Study by Grevert, Albert, and Goldstein (1983)

Time (min)	Event	Placebo session	Control session	Naloxone session
−30	Start i.v. drip	X	X	X
−20	Initial POMS, DEQ, VS[a]	X	X	X
0	Ischemic pain 1	X	X	X
+10	Placebo	X		
+20	VS	X	X	X
+40	POMS, DEQ, VS	X	X	X
+50	Hidden injection	V or N[b]	V	N
+60	POMS, DEQ	X	X	X
+70	Ischemic pain 2	X	X	X
+80	Analgesic effectiveness rating	X		

Note. The order of the sessions was randomized and double-blind, but for a given subject the order remained the same during all 3 study weeks. A subject experienced all three types of session each week, thus receiving nine sessions in all. An "X" indicates that an event took place during the session.

[a]POMS = Profile of Mood States; DEQ = Drug Effects Questionnaire; VS = vital signs (pulse rate, temperature, blood pressure).

[b]V = naloxone vehicle; N = naloxone. At placebo sessions, Group V received vehicle, while Group N received naloxone; otherwise, the groups were treated identically. Vehicle and naloxone were always given into the i.v. line, out of subjects' view.

session, there was a naloxone session and a control session. During a naloxone session, naloxone (10 mg) was administered in a hidden injection, and no placebo was given. The purpose of the naloxone sessions was to replicate our previous finding (Grevert & Goldstein, 1977, 1978) that naloxone itself had no effect on the pain. During a control session, the hidden injection contained only naloxone vehicle. The purpose of the control sessions was to furnish data on the normal changes in pain ratings reported by each subject, thus providing a background each week against which to compare changes in pain following placebo. Experimental ischemic arm pain was produced twice during each session. The second time was 1 hour after placebo administration, when subjects expected maximum analgesia to occur; this was 20 minutes after the hidden administration of naloxone (Group N) or naloxone vehicle (Group V). Pain was rated for 10 minutes using a linear analogue scale (Revill, Robinson, Rosen, & Hogg, 1976). At the end of each placebo session, subject was asked to rate the analgesic effectiveness of the "painkiller," using a 5-point scale (0 = "not at all"; 4 = "extremely"). We attempted to enhance the description of the placebo as a "potent painkiller drug" by having a physician (L. H. Albert) fill the injection syringe conspicuously, in view of each subject, from a vial marked "MX 99," at the same time warning subject to report any shortness of breath, dizziness, nausea, or unusual sensations. Subjects were also told that the Profile of Mood States (McNair, Lorr, & Droppleman, 1971) and a Drug Effects Questionnaire would be administered to measure any behavioral effects of the "painkiller." Vital signs were then monitored by the physician, who remained with the subject for approximately 5 minutes after giving the injection, "in case some adverse reactions to the drug should occur."

Consistent with our previous findings, naloxone did not significantly affect the experimental pain. Placebo analgesia was demonstrated; a significantly greater decrease in pain was reported during placebo sessions than during control sessions by both groups of subjects (Group V, $p < .001$; Group N, $p < .02$). Naloxone attenuated but did not abolish the placebo response; as Figure 19-2 shows, over the 3 study weeks there was a significant trend for subjects who received hidden naloxone after placebo (Group N) to report less decrease in pain after placebo than subjects who received hidden vehicle (Group V). Here the pain score was the sum of the 10 pain ratings made at each pain procedure. The dependent variable was the change in pain score for each subject during the placebo session minus the change in pain score for the same subject during the control session of the same week. The larger the negative value, the greater the degree of placebo analgesia. Mean regression coefficients ($\pm$ *SEM*) for each subject, using the data shown in Figure 19-2, were -1.5 ± 1.9 and 2.5 ± 1.2 for Group V and Group N, respectively. The coefficients were significantly different (Wilcoxon two-sample rank test, two-tailed, $p < .02$). The difference resulted from subjects in Group N reporting less of a decrease in pain following placebo at week 3 ($p < 0.05$) than did subjects in Group V.

The ability of naloxone to diminish placebo analgesia was further supported by subjects' ratings of analgesic effectiveness. Those who received naloxone after placebo (Group N) rated the placebo as being a less effective painkiller than did those who received only vehicle after placebo (Group V). Ratings (mean $\pm$ *SEM*) for the three placebo sessions combined were as follows: Group N = 1.2 ± 0.3, Group V = 2.0 ± 0.3, median test $p < .05$.

Naloxone effects on placebo analgesia were also found in the number of subjects in each group who gave a placebo response each week. A "placebo response" was defined as a negative value obtained by subtracting a subject's change in pain score during the control sessions from the change in pain score during the placebo session of the same week. Although the two groups did not differ in the number of subjects who gave a placebo response during the first week of the study, during the second and third weeks significantly fewer ($p < .05$) subjects in Group N than in Group V reported a placebo response (week 2, 64% and 94%, respectively; week 3, 50% and 88%). It seems plausible that the expectation of analgesia from the "painkiller" dominated responses to the first placebo administration, but that more realistic reporting developed after the first week's experience. Ten (62.5%) of the subjects in

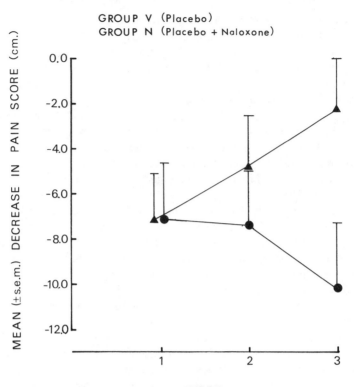

GROUP V (Placebo)
GROUP N (Placebo + Naloxone)

Figure 19-2. Mean (± *SEM*) decreases in pain scores during the three weekly placebo sessions for subjects in Group V (black circles) and Group N (black triangles). The dependent variable was the change in pain score during the placebo session minus the change in pain score during the control session of the same week. (From "Partial Antagonism of Placebo Analgesia by Naloxone" by P. Grevert, L. H. Albert, and A. Goldstein. *Pain*, 1983, *16*, 129–143. Reprinted by permission of Elsevier Biomedical Press.)

Group V experienced pain relief after all three placebo administrations; thus, under these experimental conditions, placebo analgesia could be obtained consistently in most of the subjects.

In this study, naloxone did not completely prevent placebo-induced analgesia; it only diminished the effectiveness of the placebo. A higher dose of naloxone might produce a complete blockade of placebo-induced analgesia. Another explanation of the partial efficacy of naloxone could be that both opioid and non-opioid mechanisms contribute to placebo analgesia.

IS PLACEBO ANALGESIA MEDIATED BY ENDOGENOUS OPIOIDS?: FUTURE RESEARCH

In the introduction to this chapter, we indicate that a positive naloxone effect is only suggestive of endogenous opioid involvement and should be considered as a starting point for further research. Our finding of partial antagonism of placebo analgesia by naloxone in an adequately rigorous experimental design suggests several lines of experimentation.

1. The study should be repeated using a range of naloxone doses to determine whether blockage of placebo analgesia is dose-related. The range of doses should include the 10-mg dose used here, as well as higher doses to determine whether complete blockage of placebo analgesia can be obtained. Substantially higher naloxone doses have been given safely (Cohen *et al.*, 1981; Jasinski, Martin, & Haertzen, 1967; Pickar *et al.*, 1982) than were in use when this study was initiated. However, the higher dose must not produce subjective effects that would allow subjects to detect when naloxone had been administered.

2. Our finding that naloxone did not diminish analgesia until the second or third administration of placebo suggests that the first placebo administration should be treated as a habituation session, and that only subsequent sessions should be analyzed.

3. To determine whether the effect of naloxone on placebo analgesia is mediated by opioid receptors, identical doses of the stereoisomer, (+)-naloxone, should be administered. Since this compound does not occupy opioid receptors, its failure to diminish placebo analgesia would further implicate endogenous opioids. If it were effective against placebo analgesia at the same doses as (−)-naloxone, the hypothesis of opioid mediation could be rejected decisively.

4. Antagonists that act at specific types of opioid receptors should eventually be administered to determine which type mediates placebo analgesia. Unfortunately, antagonists highly selective for one opioid receptor type have not yet been developed. Although a few partially selective antagonists have been tested on animals (Gormley, Morley, Priestley, Shaw, Turnbull, & Wheeler, 1982; Holaday, Ruvio, Robles, Johnson, & D'Amato, 1982; Von Voigtlander & Lewis, 1982), none has yet become available for human use.

5. An experimental study could be carried out to determine whether placebo analgesia is diminished or abolished in subjects who are tolerant to opiates. Since some endogenous opioids demonstrate cross-tolerance to some exogenous opiates, a positive result might point to involvement of a particular family of endogenous opioids. Opiate addicts maintained on methadone or levo-alpha-acetylmethadol (LAAM) could be used as subjects in a controlled placebo study, first while on maintenance and again after successful detoxification, each subject serving as his or her own control. If endogenous opioids are involved, placebo analgesia might be greater when subjects are no longer receiving chronic opiate medication. A negative result, however, would leave open the possibility that placebo analgesia is mediated through a different type of opioid receptor from that affected in methadone or LAAM tolerance.

In summary, at the present time there is some experimental evidence suggesting that endogenous opioids mediate placebo analgesia. However, further carefully controlled studies such as suggested in this chapter are needed before it can be concluded with confidence that the pain-relieving qualities of placebo are due to the induced release of endogenous opioids.

REFERENCES

Adams, J. E. Naloxone reversal of analgesia produced by brain stimulation in the human. *Pain*, 1976, *2*, 161–166.

Akil, H., Richardson, D. E., Barchas, J. D., & Li, C. H. Appearance of β-endorphin-like immunoreactivity in human ventricular cerebrospinal fluid upon analgesic electrical stimulation. *Proceedings of the National Academy of Sciences USA*, 1978, *75*, 5170–5172.

Barber, J., & Mayer, D. Evaluation of the efficacy and neural mechanism of a hypnotic analgesia procedure in experimental and clinical dental pain. *Pain*, 1977, *4*, 41–48.

Beecher, H. K. Increased stress and effectiveness of placebos and "active" drugs. *Science*, 1960, *132*, 91–92.

Berger, P. A., Akil, H., Watson, S. J., & Barchas, J. Behavioral pharmacology of the endorphins. *Annual Review of Medicine*, 1982, *33*, 397–415.

Buchsbaum, M. S., Davis, G. C., & Bunney, W. E. Naloxone alters pain perception and somatosensory evoked potentials in normal subjects. *Nature*, 1977, *270*, 620–622.

Chapman, C. R., & Benedetti, C. Analgesia following transcutaneous electric stimulation and its partial reversal by a narcotic anatagonist. *Life Sciences*, 1977, *21*, 1645–1648.

Cohen, M. R., Cohen, R. M., Pickar, D., Weingartner, H., Murphy, D. L., & Bunney, W. E. Behavioural effects after high dose naloxone administration to normal volunteers. *Lancet*, 1981, *2*, 1110.

Cox, B. M. Endogenous opioid peptides: A guide to structures and terminology. *Life Sciences*, 1982, *31*, 1645–1658.

Davis, G. C., Buchsbaum, M. S., & Bunney, W. E. Naloxone decreases diurnal variation in pain sensitivity and somatosensory evoked potentials. *Life Sciences*, 1978, *23*, 1449–1460.

El-Sobky, A., Dostrovsky, J. O., & Wall, P. D. Lack of effect of naloxone on pain perception in humans. *Nature*, 1976, *263*, 783–784.

Frederickson, R. C., & Geary, L. E. Endogenous opioid peptides: review of physiological, pharmacological and clinical aspects. *Progress in Neurobiology*, 1982, *19*, 19–69.

Frid, M., & Singer, G. Hypnotic analgesia in conditions of stress is partially reversed by naloxone. *Psychopharmacology*, 1979, *63*, 211–215.

Frid, M., Singer, G., & Rana, C. Interactions between personal expectations and naloxone: Effects on tolerance to ischemic pain. *Psychopharmacology*, 1979, *65*, 225–231.

Gelfand, S., Ullmann, L. P., & Krasner, L. I. The placebo response: An experimental approach. *Journal of Nervous and Mental Diseases*, 1963, *136*, 379–387.

Goldstein, A. Dynorphin and the dynorphin receptor: Some implications of gene duplication of the opioid message. In F. O. Schmitt, S. J. Bird, & F. E. Bloom (Eds.), *Molecular genetic neuroscience.* New York: Raven Press, 1982.

Goldstein, A., & Hilgard, E. R. Failure of the opiate antagonist naloxone to modify hypnotic analgesia. *Proceedings of the National Academy of Sciences USA*, 1975, *72*, 2041–2043.

Gormley, J. J., Morley, J. S., Priestley, T., Shaw, J. S., Turnbull, M. J., & Wheeler, H. *In vivo* evaluation of the opiate delta receptor antagonist ICI 154,129. *Life Sciences*, 1982, *31*, 1263–1266.

Gracely, R. H., Wolskee, P. J., Deeter, W. R., & Dubner, R. Naloxone and placebo alter postsurgical pain by independent mechanisms. *Society for Neuroscience Abstracts*, 1982, *8*, 264.

Grevert, P., & Goldstein, A. Effects of naloxone on experimentally induced ischemic pain and on mood in human subjects. *Proceedings of the National Academy of Sciences USA*, 1977, *74*, 1291–1294.

Grevert, P., & Goldstein, A. Endorphins: Naloxone fails to alter experimental pain or mood in humans. *Science*, 1978, *199*, 1093–1095.

Grevert, P., Albert, L. H., & Goldstein, A. Partial antagonism of placebo analgesia by naloxone. *Pain*, 1983, *16*, 129–143.

Haier, R. J., Quaid, K., & Mills, J. S. C. Naloxone alters pain perception after jogging. *Psychiatry Research*, 1981, *5*, 231–232.

Han, J. S., & Terenius, L. Neurochemical basis of acupuncture analgesia. *Annual Review of Pharmacology and Toxicology*, 1982, *22*, 193–220.

Holaday, J. W., Ruvio, B. A., Robles, L. E., Johnson, C. E., & D'Amato, R. J. M 154,129, a putative delta antagonist, reverses endotoxic shock without altering morphine analgesia. *Life Sciences*, 1982, *31*, 2209–2212.

Hosobuchi, Y., Adams, J. E., & Linchitz, R. Pain relief by electrical stimulation of the central gray matter in humans and its reversal by naloxone. *Science*, 1977, *197*, 183–186.

Hosobuchi, Y., Rossier, J., Bloom, F. E., & Guillemin, R. Stimulation of human periaqueductal gray for pain relief increases immunoreactive β-endorphin in ventricular fluid. *Science*, 1979, *203*, 279–281.

Jasinski, D. R., Martin, W. R., & Haertzen, C. A. The human pharmacology and abuse potential of N-allylnoroxymorphone (naloxone). *Journal of Pharmacology and Experimental Therapeutics*, 1967, *157*, 420–426.

Jellinek, E. M. Clinical tests on comparative effectiveness of analgesic drugs. *Biometrics Bulletin*, 1946, *2*, 87–91.

Lasagna, L. Drug interaction in the field of analgesic drugs. *Proceedings of the Royal Society of Medicine*, 1965, *58*, 978–983.

Lasagna, L., Mosteller, F., von Felsinger, J. M., & Beecher, H. K. A study of the placebo response. *American Journal of Medicine*, 1954, *16*, 770–779.

Levine, J. D., Gordon, N. C., Bornstein, J. C., & Fields, H. L. Role of pain in placebo analgesia. *Proceedings of the National Academy of Sciences USA*, 1979, *76*, 3528–3531.

Levine, J. D., Gordon, N. C., & Fields, H. L. The mechanism of placebo analgesia. *Lancet*, 1978, *2*, 654–657.

Levine, J. D., Gordon, N. C., & Fields, H. L. Naloxone dose dependently produces analgesia and hyperalgesia in postoperative pain. *Nature*, 1979, *278*, 740–741.

Levine, J. D., Gordon, N. C., Jones, R. T., & Fields, H. L. The narcotic antagonist naloxone enhances clinical pain. *Nature*, 1978, *272*, 826–827.

Liberman, R. An experimental study of the placebo response under three different situations of pain. *Journal of Psychiatric Research*, 1964, *2*, 233–246.

Lord, J. A. H., Waterfield, A. A., Hughes, J., & Kosterlitz, H. W. Endogenous opioid peptides: Multiple agonists and receptors. *Nature*, 1977, *267*, 495–499.

Martin, W. R. Multiple receptors: Speculations about receptor evolution. In J. Fishman (Ed.), *The bases of addiction*. Berlin: Dahlem Knoferenzen, 1978.

Mayer, D. J., Price, D. D., & Rafii, A. Antagonism of acupuncture analgesia in man by the narcotic antagonist naloxone. *Brain Research*, 1977, *121*, 368–372.

McNair, D., Lorr, M., & Droppleman, L. *Manual: Profile of Mood States*. San Diego: Educational and Industrial Testing Service, 1971.

Mihic, D., & Binkert, E. *Is placebo analgesia mediated by endorphine?* Paper presented at the Second World Congress on Pain, Montreal, August 1978.

O'Donahue, T. L., & Dorsa, D. M. The opiomelantropinergic neuronal and endocrine systems. *Peptides*, 1982, *3*, 353–395.

Pickar, D., Cohen, M. R., Naber, D., & Cohen, R. M. Clinical studies of the endogenous opioid system. *Biological Psychiatry*, 1982, *17*, 1273–1276.

Pomeranz, B. & Chiu, D. Naloxone blockade of acupuncture analgesia: Endorphin implicated. *Life Sciences*, 1976, *19*, 1757–1762.

Rapoport, S. I., Klee, W. A., Pettigrew, K. D., & Ohno, K. Entry of opioid peptides into the central nervous system. *Science*, 1980, *207*, 84–86.

Revill, S. I., Robinson, J. O., Rosen, M., & Hogg, M. I. J. The reliability of a linear analogue for evaluating pain. *Anaesthesia*, 1976, *31*, 1191–1198.

Salar, G., & Iob, I. Modification de l'action analgique de l'électrothérapie transcutanée après traitement avec naloxone. *Neurochirurgie*, 1978, *24*, 415–417.

Sawynok, J., Pinsky, C., & LaBella, F. S. Minireview on the specificity of naloxone as an opiate antagonist. *Life Sciences*, 1979, *25*, 1621–1632.

Schull, J., Kaplan, H., & O'Brien, C. P. Naloxone can alter experimental pain and mood in humans. *Physiological Psychology*, 1981, *9*, 245–250.

Sjolund, B., & Eriksson, M. Electro-acupuncture and endogenous morphines. *Lancet*, 1976, *2*, 1085.

Smith, G., Egbert, L., Markowitz, R., Mosteller, F., & Beecher, H. K. An experimental pain method sensitive to morphine in man: The submaximum effort tourniquet technique. *Journal of Pharmacology and Experimental Therapeutics*, 1966, *154*, 324–332.

Tamsen, A., Sakurada, T., Wahlstrom, A., Terenius, L., & Hartvig, P. Postoperative demand for analgesics in relation to individual levels of endorphins and substance P in cerebrospinal fluid. *Pain*, 1982, *13*, 171–183.

Volavka, J., Bauman, J., Pevnick, J., Reker, D., James, B., & Cho, D. Short-term hormonal effects of naloxone in man. *Psychoneuroendocrinology*, 1980, *5*, 225–234.

Von Voigtlander, P. F., & Lewis, R. A. U-50,488, a selective kappa opioid agonist: Comparison to other reputed kappa agonists. *Progress in Neuro-Psychopharmacology and Biological Psychiatry*, 1982, *6*, 467–470.

Willer, J. C., & Albe-Fessard, D. Electrophysiological evidence for a release of endogenous opiates in stress-induced "analgesia" in man. *Brain Research*, 1980, *198*, 419–426.

Willer, J. C., Dehen, H., & Cambier, J. Stress-induced analgesia in humans: Endogenous opioids and naloxone-reversible depression of pain reflexes. *Science*, 1981, *212*, 689–690.

Woolf, C. J., Mitchell, D., Myers, R. A., & Barrett, G. D. Failure of naloxone to reverse peripheral transcutaneous electroanalgesia in patients suffering from acute trauma. *South African Medical Journal*, 1978, *53*, 179–180.

20

Stress as a Moderator Variable in Neoplasia

HYMIE ANISMAN
LAWRENCE S. SKLAR

The potential contribution of psychological and physical insults to the promotion or exacerbation of illness has received increasing attention. In part, this interest has stemmed from the belief that traditional approaches to the analysis of etiological factors subserving disease processes have not been uniformly successful (see Depue, 1979). Additionally, it is recognized that psychological and physical stressors influence endogenous mechanisms, which may increase vulnerability to some illnesses. While it is often taken on faith that stressful events may influence the course of various pathologies, the contribution of central nervous system processes in determining vulnerability to pathologies are often overlooked. Yet, as we indicate in ensuing sections of this chapter, considerable data are available indicating that immunological, hormonal, and peripheral and central neurochemical functions represent a dynamic interactive process, and ultimately that the effectiveness of stressors in exacerbating pathology may be related to central neurochemical functioning.

In considering neoplastic disease, attributing a role to specific neurochemical and hormonal mechanisms is particularly difficult. After all, numerous types of neoplasia exist, including spontaneous tumors, those that are induced by carcinogens, and transplanted tumors (in laboratory settings), as well as diverse tumors comprised of different cell types. Some tumors are hormone-dependent, while others are not. The tumor may be syngeneic with the host (i.e., of the same genotype) or it may be allogenic, and the contribution of hormonal mechanisms in these tumors remains to be conclusively determined. If these factors were not sufficiently difficult to deal with, it should be emphasized that there is still considerable debate as to the contribution of the immune system to the cancer process, to say nothing of identification of the way in which the immune system might operate in attacking neoplastic cells. When these considerations are coupled with the

Hymie Anisman and Lawrence S. Sklar. Department of Psychology, Unit for Behavioral Medicine and Pharmacology, Carleton University, Ottawa, Ontario, Canada.

fact that the endogenous consequences of stressors will vary with a number of experiential, organismic, and environmental factors, the difficulty of assessing the stress–cancer topography is eminently clear.

STRESS-PROVOKED IMMUNOLOGICAL ALTERATIONS

The finding that some lymphocyte populations were capable of lysing tumor cells *in vitro* led to the belief that cytotoxic T cells may be essential in controlling tumor growth (Cerottini, Nordin, & Brunner, 1970). That is, such cells are responsible for the recognition and destruction of neoplastic cells (Burnet, 1970). Effector cells, such as macrophages, monocytes, and polymorphonuclear leukocytes, also play a fundamental role in immune surveillance, and have been shown to have spontaneous reactivity against some tumor lines (see review in Herberman & Ortaldo, 1981). The "immune surveillance" hypothesis was, however, challenged on the basis of several findings. In particular, depression of the immune system did not necessarily increase the occurrence of neoplasia; nude mice, which essentially lacked cytotoxic T lymphocytes, were not more vulnerable to neoplasia; and finally, tumor-specific transplantation antigens, thought to be necessary for recognition of tumor cells by cytotoxic cells, were not detected on spontaneous tumors (see Melief & Schwartz, 1975; Prehn, 1974; Stutman, 1975). Despite these inconsistencies with the immune surveillance hypothesis, the basic model is still widely accepted. The discovery of natural killer (NK) cells, a subpopulation of spontaneously occurring cytotoxic cells that may be essential in host defense against viral-infected target cells and possibly tumor cells, led to further attention being devoted to the mechanism of action and recognition by these cells. At this time there is, in fact, the belief in some quarters that these NK cells may represent a first line of defense against malignant cells (see reviews in Herberman & Holden, 1978; Herberman & Ortaldo, 1981).

Human Studies

Several investigators have evaluated the effects of various forms of stress on immune functioning in humans. A good deal of this literature has recently been reviewed (Palmblad, 1981), and thus only a very cursory overview is necessary at this time. As indicated in these reviews, immune functioning may be influenced by a variety of different stressors, including bereavement (Bartrop, Lazarus, Luckhurst, Kiloh, & Penny, 1977; Schleifer, Keller, McKegney, & Stein, 1980), sleep deprivation and/or noise (Palmblad, Cantell, Strander, Froberg, Karlsson, Levi, Granstrom, & Unger, 1976; Palmblad, Petrini, Wasserman, & Akerstedt, 1979), life change events (Cohen-Cole, Cogen, Stevens, Kirk, Gaitan, Hain, & Freeman, 1981; Greene, Betts, Ochitill, Iker, & Douglas, 1978; Locke, Hurst, Williams, &

Heisel, 1978), space flight and re-entry (Fischer, Daniels, Levin, Kimzey, Cobb, & Ritzman, 1972; Kimzey, 1975), and examination stress (Dorian, Keystone, Garfinkel, & Brown, 1981). Interestingly, in the study reported by Locke *et al.* (1978), the reduced NK cell activity was most prominent among those individuals who coped poorly with stressors. While the contribution of coping factors was not determined in the remaining studies, it should be emphasized that the immunological changes observed included reduced lymphoblast transformation, altered phagocytosis, and diminished NK activity, as well as reduced lymphocyte activity in response to a mitogen. Moreover, the immunological alterations were also evident with respect to both cellular (T-cell) and humoral (B-cell) activity.

Attempts have been made to assess immunological changes in a prospective-like paradigm. In particular, subjects were inoculated with A/ Victoria/75H3N2 virus after individuals reported their previous stress history. The immunological response to the virus was diminished among individuals who had undergone a high degree of life stress relative to those who had undergone limited life stress events (Greene *et al.*, 1978). In a subsequent experiment, Locke, Hurst, Heisel, Krause, and Williams (1979) evaluated serum antibody titers prior to and 2 weeks following swine flu (A/ NJ/76) immunization. Life events changes that had occurred in the 1-month or 1-year period prior to inoculation were unrelated to the antibody response. However, the antibody response varied with life events that occurred in the 2-week period following inoculation. In particular, a greater antibody response was evident among subjects who reported intermediate life change stress than among subjects who reported either low or high life stress. It is conceivable that while high stress may have deleterious effects, moderate levels of stress may render the individual more prepared to deal with a viral challenge.

Infrahuman Studies

Several reports are available indicating that stressors will influence immuno-logical functioning, as well as the response to viral challenge, among infrahuman animals. For example, it has been demonstrated that psycho-logical and physical insults will influence the reaction to Coxsackie B-2 (Friedman, Ader, & Glasgow, 1965; Johnson, Lavender, Hultin, & Rasmussen, 1963), rabies (Soave, 1964), herpes simplex (Rasmussen, Spencer, & Marsh, 1957), poliomyelitis (Johnsson & Rasmussen, 1965; Teodoru & Schwartzman, 1956), vesicular stomatitis (Jensen & Rasmussen, 1963), and *Trichinella spiralis* (Davis & Read, 1958). Likewise, stressors have been shown to depress the graft-versus-host response (Munster, Eurenius, Mortenson, & Mason, 1972; Munster, Gale, & Hunt, 1977), to increase resistance to passive anaphylaxis (Jensen & Rasmussen, 1963; Rasmussen, Spencer, & Marsh, 1959; Treadwell, Wistar, Rasmussen, & Marsh, 1959), to increase mortality following *Pseudomonas* infection

(McEuen, Blair, Delbene, & Eurenius, 1976), and to increase the frequency of reinfection following immunization against *Hymenolepis nana* (Hamilton, 1974).

Consistent with results involving viral challenge, stressful events have been shown to influence immunological functioning. Manipulations such as social housing conditions or simply the shipment of animals from the commercial breeders to the laboratory may result in reduced blood lymphocyte levels (Nieburgs, Weiss, Navarette, Strax, Teirstein, Grillione, & Sedlecki, 1979; Riley, Spackman, McClanahan, & Santisteban, 1979), decreased immune reactivity of peritoneal and spleen B cells (Gisler, Bussard, Mazie, & Hess, 1971), and suppression of antibody and T-cell functioning (Folch & Waksman, 1974; Lundy, Lovett, Wolinsky, & Conran, 1979; Monjan & Collector, 1977; see review in Monjan, 1981). It was recently demonstrated that a series of graded stressors resulted in a progressive increase in suppression of lymphocytes, as determined from the number of circulating lymphocytes and from the phytohemagglutinin (PHA) stimulation of lymphocytes (Keller, Weiss, Schleifer, Miller & Stein, 1981). Likewise, it has been reported that 2 hours after stress exposure the response to PHA or Concanavalin A was reduced, while 24 hours after stressor application the response to the mitogens was slightly enhanced (Shavit, Lewis, Terman, Gale, & Liebeskind, 1982). Interestingly, in this particular report it was found that the reduced response to the mitogens occurred exclusively in a stress paradigm believed to influence opioid peptides. Finally, it has been shown that exposure to a stressor (in this instance, surgery) resulted in a depression of NK cell activity, which persisted for as long as 7 days following the surgical trauma (Toge, Hirai, Takiyama, & Hattori, 1981).

It appears that the immunological changes induced by a stressor may be dependent upon the background conditions upon which the stressor is applied. For instance, Riley and his associates (Riley, 1981; Riley, Fitzmaurice, & Spackman, 1981; Riley & Spackman, 1977) reported that stress-provoked alterations of corticosterone, which results in immunosuppression, vary as a function of sex of cage mates, order in which animals were bled, noise and smells from other cages in the colony room, and so forth. Accordingly, immunological alterations invoked by the application of a stressor likewise were dependent on the social and procedural details of the experiment. Consistent with these findings, Nieburgs *et al.* (1979) found that the lymphocyte changes induced by experimental stressors were not evident among mice that had recently undergone the stress of shipment from the breeders.

Given that the effects of stressors on immune functioning vary with background conditions, it is not unexpected that immunological changes vary with the stress chronicity. It has been found, for instance, that acute exposure to sound stress resulted in depression of immune functioning, whereas chronic sound stress resulted in enhanced functioning of both B and T lymphocytes (Monjan & Collector, 1977). In accordance with these results, Monjan (1981) reported that acute sound stress (10 days) resulted in decreased thymidine incorporation of mitogen-stimulated lymphocytes, whereas a very substantial enhancement of thymidine incorporation followed 30 to 50 days of sound stress. In another experiment, Monjan (1981) reported that stress of retro-orbital bleeding resulted in a 10-fold increase of [^{3}H]thymidine incorporation of splenic lymphocytes, and that this effect was evident for 3 days *in vitro*. Among animals that had received sound stress for up to 8 days, the thymidine uptake was further enhanced; however, animals that had more than 8 days of sound stress exhibited no change or a decrease of thymidine uptake. Taken together, these two studies suggest (1) that the diminished immune responsitivity seen after acute stress is absent after chronic stress, where enhanced immunological functioning may occur; and (2) that the response to a stressor may be dependent on the animal's previous stress history.

   Finally, particularly exciting results concerning the effects of stressors have been reported by Ader and his associates (Ader & Cohen, 1975, 1981; Ader, Cohen, & Grota, 1979; Bovbjerg, Cohen, & Ader, 1980). It was found that the immunosuppressive effects of cyclophosphamide are subject to conditioning. When rats were permitted to consume a novel (preferred) saccharin solution followed by cyclophosphamide administration, later re-exposure to the saccharin solution resulted in a diminished antibody response to sheep red blood cells. This effect was not due to the presentation of the saccharin alone or to the cyclophosphamide treatment itself. Only when the two treatments were paired was the conditioned immunosuppression evident. It appears, as well, that this procedure resulted in conditioning of a cellular immune response. That is, three treatments with cyclophosphamide effectively suppressed the graft-versus-host response. A suppressant effect of virtually comparable magnitude was effected among rats that had the conditioned stimulus (saccharin) presented on 3 days following cellular graft (Bovbjerg et al., 1980). More recently, Ader and Cohen (1982) reported that presentation of the conditioned stimulus following classical pairing of saccharin and cyclophosphamide resulted in the retardation of autoimmune disease (systemic lupus erythematosus) in New Zealand mice, as indicated by the number of animals that developed a lethal glomerulonephritis over a 65-week period.

STRESS AND NEOPLASIA

Human Studies

Measurement of stressful events in humans has proven to be a particularly difficult problem, and conclusions concerning the relationship between stressful events and illness must be considered cautiously. Among other things, individuals may react to a stressor in different ways; what is stressful to one individual is not necessarily stressful to another. Moreover, other things being equal, there is no *a priori* reason to assume that stressors will influence endogenous processes equally across individuals. Human experimentation has often involved evaluation of previous life events among individuals already afflicted with cancer (i.e., retrospective analyses). However, the individual's recollection of past events, even those experienced in the preceding few months, may be inaccurate (Monroe, 1982). Furthermore, it might reasonably be expected that perceptions of past events are colored by the individual's current affective or physical state. Moreover, given that considerable time may intervene between the appearance of the first neoplastic cells and clinical identification of the illness, it is questionable whether there is any value in determining the life events encountered during the 3- to 6-month period preceding illness diagnosis (see Fox, 1978). The numerous problems encountered in such studies as they pertain to the stress–cancer topography have been detailed elsewhere (Fox, 1978; Sklar & Anisman, 1981b), and recapitulation of these shortcomings is not necessary here. It should be added, however, that the reliability and validity of the life events techniques have been questioned repeatedly, and the conclusions derived from such procedures must be regarded with caution (see Anisman & Zacharko, 1982; Rabkin & Struening, 1976).

While the shortcomings of retrospective analyses should not be disregarded, these studies have provided some support for the contention that life event changes are related to neoplastic disease. Using life events schedules such as that developed by Holmes and Rahe (1967), or less structured approaches, a relationship has been demonstrated between life changes and incidence of cancer (Bahnson & Bahnson, 1964; Greene, 1966; Horne & Picard, 1979; Jacobs & Charles, 1980; Kissen, 1967; Kissen, Brown, & Kissen, 1969; LeShan, 1966; Lombard & Potter, 1950; Murphy, 1952; Peller, 1952; Schmale & Iker, 1964, 1966; see reviews in Bloom, Asher, & White, 1978; and Fox, 1978). Demographic studies have likewise indicated that the incidence of some forms of cancer were increased among individuals who had suffered separation stress such as bereavement or divorce (Ernster, Sacks, Selvin, & Petrakis, 1979). Similarly, the incidence of lung cancer was found to be greater among individuals who had experienced early parental loss or absence (Horne & Picard, 1979; Kissen, 1967). There is reason to believe that the psychological ramifications of such insults may have contributed to the promotion of the pathology. For instance, the incidence of cancer has been found to be particularly marked among those individuals who expressed a sense of loss and hopelessness, and an inability to cope adequately (Greene, 1966; LeShan, 1966), as well as among dependent individuals (Greenberg & Dattore, 1981). Moreover, such factors as poor emotional outlet, inability to express negative emotions adequately, and diminished aggressive expression appeared to be correlated with cancer incidence (Bacon, Rennecker, & Cutler, 1952; Kissen, 1964,

1965, 1966; Kissen *et al.*, 1969; Mastrovito, Deguire, Clarkin, Thaler, Lewis, & Cooper, 1979; Stavraky, Buck, Lott, & Wanklin, 1968). Finally, it has been suggested that cancer may be related to emotional extremes—that is, either suppression or frequent emotional outbursts (Greer & Morris, 1975).

To be sure, the unstructured approaches employed in some studies to determine personality traits, as well as some of the measures taken to reflect personality characteristics, are of dubious validity. Indeed, one is often hard pressed to accept uncritically the conclusions that have been derived. Nonetheless, several prospective studies have yielded results consistent with the proposition that life event changes are associated with subsequent cancer development. In particular, it was reported that the incidence of stressful events, and psychological factors associated with these stressors, correlated with the subsequent appearance of neoplastic disease (Greer & Morris, 1975; Hagnell, 1966; Harrower, Thomas, & Altman, 1975; Thomas, 1976; Thomas & Duszynski, 1974; Thomas & Greenstreet, 1973). Indeed, it was recently reported that the risk of cancer death (over a 17-year evaluation period) was appreciably higher among individuals who had previously suffered from clinical depression than among nondepressed individuals (Shekelle, Raynor, Ostfeld, Garron, Bieliauskas, Liu, Maliza, & Paul, 1981).

Consistent with the prospective analyses, prognostic studies have provided evidence suggesting a relationship between the occurrence of cancer and incidence of stress (coupled with the coping styles that individuals adopt) (Derogatis & Abeloff, 1977; Derogatis, Abeloff, & Melisaratos, 1979; Schmale & Iker, 1964, 1966). Moreover, relapse of malignant melanoma appeared more frequently within 1 year among those individuals who exhibited difficulty in adjusting to their illness (concern) prior to the surgery (Rogentine, van Kammen, Fox, Docherty, Rosenblatt, Boyd, & Bunney, 1979). Work conducted by Greer and Morris (1975), in which women were interviewed 1 day prior to biopsy for possible breast tumors, revealed that relative to those women in which the tumors were benign, those patients with malignant tumors displayed abnormal release of emotion (e.g., suppression of anger). Likewise, in a study of women entering a hospital with suspected or confirmed malignancy of reproductive organs, Mastrovito *et al.* (1979) reported that patients with malignant tumors were more conforming, less assertive, less autonomous, and less spontaneous than were women with benign tumors. However, given that benign tumors may represent a risk factor for malignancy, the implications of these findings must be considered carefully (see discussion in Blaney, 1983).

The assumption that stressful events or personality characteristics contribute to the cancer process has not been unanimously supported. Indeed, Muslin, Gyarfas, and Pieper (1966) and Wheeler and Caldwell (1955) failed to detect differences in life events between patients with benign and malignant breast tumors. Likewise, Graham and Snell (1972) and

Graham, Snell, and Graham (1971) reported that the occurrence of breast and cervical cancer was unrelated to life stress events encountered during the preceding 5-year period. Several reports have also indicated that there was no relationship between psychological factors, such as depression, and subsequent cancer appearance (e.g., Evans, Baldwin, & Gath, 1974; Keehn, Goldberg, & Beebe, 1974; Niemi & Jaaskelainen, 1978; Tsuang, Woolson, & Fleming, 1980). A recent critical review presented by Morrison and Paffenberger (1981) questions the procedures employed in many of the aforementioned studies that suggest a relationship among stressful events, personality variables, and neoplastic disease. The Morrison and Paffenberger (1981) critique challenges the statistical methods adopted in these studies, the validity of the testing devices employed, and the reproducibility of some of the reported findings. Moreover, the necessity of using a double-blind procedure is appropriately emphasized. While it might be argued that Morrison and Paffenberger are overly conservative in their critique, it is clear from their analysis that considerable additional data, particularly well-controlled prospective and prognostic studies, are needed before it can be concluded with any degree of confidence that a relationship exists between life stress or personality variables and cancer development. In his overview of the literature, Blaney (1983) draws similar conclusions, and emphasizes as well the necessity of differentiating between different forms of cancer. Moreover, Blaney (1983) indicates the need not only of evaluating the contribution of stress events to later cancer appearance, but of assessing the effects of stressors given a backdrop of other risk factors (smoking, age, etc).

Infrahuman Studies

As in the case of the human studies, considerable variability exists among laboratories concerning the effects of stressors on tumor development in infrahuman animals. As indicated earlier, experiments conducted across laboratories have, among other things, employed different types of tumors (well-differentiated versus anaplastic; hormone-dependent and hormone-independent; transplanted, spontaneous, and carcinogen-induced), as well as different types of stress paradigms (acute vs. chronic; controllable vs. uncontrollable; stressors such as shock, sound, restraint, and social factors). Inasmuch as these varied stress parameters differentially influence immunological activity, and also have diverse effects on hormonal and neuro-chemical activity (see below), it is not particularly surprising to learn that varied alterations in tumor development are likewise observed.

Several studies have evaluated the effects of stressors on the development of carcinogen-induced tumors. Owing to the lengthy interval between application of a carcinogen and subsequent detection of the tumor, it is difficult to determine the most appropriate time at which to apply the stressor. Should the stressor be applied soon after carcinogen exposure or after a colony of neoplastic cells is present? Accordingly, in most investigations, the stressor has been repeatedly administered following application of the carcinogen. It will be recalled that such a procedure results in immunofacilitation, and thus tumor inhibition might be expected if it were assumed that immunological mechanisms contributed to tumor development. Indeed, it has been demonstrated that the repeated application of restraint stress (Bhattacharyya & Pradhan, 1979; Newberry, Gildow, Wogan, & Reese, 1976), footshock (Newberry, Frankie, Beatty, Maloney, & Gilchrist, 1972; Pradhan & Ray, 1974; Ray & Pradhan, 1974), electroconvulsive shock, and sound stress (Pradhan & Ray, 1974; see Monjan, 1981) reduced the incidence of mammary tumors in rats treated with 7,12-dimethylbenz(α)anthracene (DMBA). Likewise, some degree of inhibition of a Walker carcinoma was provided by a repeated forced daily swim (Gershben, Benuck, & Shurrager, 1974). In assessing the effects of varying amounts of stress on tumor development, Nieburgs et al. (1979) reported that 5 minutes of stress applied at 96-hour intervals over 90 days increased tumor incidence among DMBA-treated rats, whereas a similar stress regimen applied over 150 days reduced the number and size of tumors that developed. Evidently, when a stressor is chronically applied, inhibition of carcinogen-induced tumors results, and the inhibition is related to the amount of stress rats received.

As in the case of carcinogen-induced tumors, repeated application of a stressor has been found either to reduce the appearance and ultimate size of transplanted tumors relative to nonstressed animals, or to eliminate the tumor enhancement ordinarily seen after acute exposure to a stressor. For example, we (Sklar & Anisman, 1979; Sklar, Bruto, & Anisman, 1981) reported that repeated exposure to footshock inhibited the development of a transplanted P815 mastocytoma relative to that seen in mice that received acute stress exposure, while Pradhan and Ray (1974) and Ray and Pradhan (1974) observed that repeated stressor application inhibited the appearance and subsequent size of tumors provoked by 4M implants. In a similar fashion, repeated shock application was found to increase survival time among mice that received transplantation of Ehrlich ascites tumor (Kalisnik, Vraspir-Porenta, Logonder-Mlinsek, Zorc, & Pajntar, 1979; Marsh, Miller, & Lamson, 1959). Interestingly, in the Kalisnik et al. (1979) report, it was observed that among nonstressed animals death was associated with tumor invasion of the pancreas, liver, intestine, testes and seminal vesicles, and the female genital tract. In contast, among stressed mice the tumor invasion was restricted to the peritoneal cavity and pancreas. In effect, the repeated stress treatment not only had the effect of inhibiting cell proliferation, but interfered with the invasion of vital organs.

According to some investigators, the tumor inhibition appears to occur exclusively when the stressor is applied after tumor induction. For instance, Newberry (1978) reported that, contrary to the inhibition seen when the stressor was applied after tumor induction, exposure to a stressor prior to or during carcinogen application did not influence tumor development. Likewise, Baker and Jahn (1976) reported that chronic cold stress (2°C) inhibited tumor development induced by radiation, provided that animals were maintained in that environment after the carcinogen treatment. Given that the effects of the stressor were evident only after carcinogen administration, it is reasonable to suppose that the stressor interfered with the longevity or proliferation of neoplastic cells rather than with the inhibition of tumor initiation (see Newberry, 1981).

Several additional issues should be emphasized at this juncture. On the one hand, it might be considered that the reduction of tumor growth by chronic stressor application might be due, at least in part, to an adaptive change in response to a stressor (i.e., the potential of tumor enhancement by acute stress is antagonized as animals adapt to the aversive stimulation). This is, in fact, possible, given that repeated application of a stressor prior to tumor cell transplantation will result in a diminished response to the effects of subsequent stressor application on tumor growth (see Sklar & Anisman, 1981b). However, there seems to be more to the effects of chronic stressors than simple adaptation. After all, the very fact that chronic stressor application inhibits tumor development relative to that in nonstressed animals suggests that this treatment induces an active process that inhibits proliferation, or provokes changes that interfere with the mechanisms that ordinarily govern or promote tumor cell proliferation. As we indicate in ensuing sections, the available data raise the possibility that central neurochemical alterations represent active changes that might potentially participate in the tumor-inhibiting effects of chronic stressor application.

A limited number of experiments have been reported concerning the effects of acute stressor application on tumor development, and almost invariably these reports concern transplanted or viral-induced tumors. Acute stress in the form of whole-body irradiation or surgical trauma (laparotomy) was found to increase the incidence of nonimmunogenic tumors among mice that received transplants of an adenocarcinoma (CBA "NT")(Peters, 1975; Peters & Kelly, 1977). Similarly, Jamasbi and Nettesheim (1977) reported an increase of tumor takes (MSC-10) following whole-body irradiation stress. Indeed, it appears that the incidence of tumor development induced by a single lymphosarcoma cell in syngeneic mice is appreciably increased among mice exposed to whole-body irradiation (Maruyama & Johnson, 1969).

It is important to differentiate between the contribution of psychological and physical insults on alterations of tumor development. As seen in Figure 20-1, we (Sklar & Anisman, 1979) reported that exposure to a single session of escapable shock 24 hours after tumor cell (P815) transplantation did not appreciably influence the ultimate size of tumors, relative to those in nonstressed mice. However, an appreciable increase of tumor size was evident among mice that had been exposed to an identical amount of yoked inescapable shock. Since mice in the escapable and inescapable shock

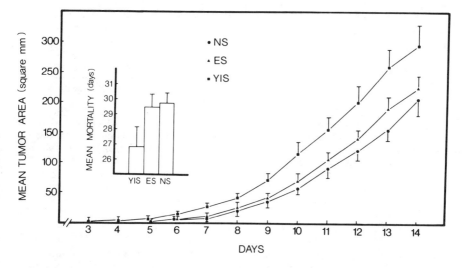

Figure 20-1. Mean tumor area (± *SEM*) over days among mice that received either 60 escapable shocks (group ES), an identical amount of inescapable shock (applied in a yoked paradigm; group YIS), or no shock (group NS). The inset denotes the mean day of mortality for each of these groups. The stress treatment was applied 24 hours following transplantation of P815 cells. (From "Stress and Coping Factors Influence Tumor Growth" by L. S. Sklar and H. Anisman. *Science*, 1979, *205*, 513–515. Reprinted by permission of the American Association for the Advancement of Science.)

received the same amount of shock, the differences detected in tumor size were probably related to the psychological dimension (and its physiological consequences) of being able to cope with the stressor through behavioral means.

In accordance with our results (Sklar & Anisman, 1979), it was recently reported (Vistainer, Volpicelli, & Seligman, 1982) that controllable and uncontrollable stressors differentially influenced rejection of a Walker 256 tumor preparation. Rats were injected with Walker 256 cells at a dose that would result in tumor rejection in about half the animals (54%). Whereas escapable shock was found to increase slightly the number of animals that rejected the tumor (63%), an identical amount of inescapable shock significantly reduced tumor rejection (27%). In effect, uncontrollable aversive events decreased the probability of a small number of cells being rejected, hence increasing the proportion of animals in which the tumor flourished. While these data are entirely consistent with our previous report (Sklar & Anisman, 1979), it should be indicated that in an earlier study using a P815 mastocytoma, we (Sklar & Anisman, 1981b) were unable to detect effects comparable to those of Visintainer *et al.* (1982). As seen in Table 20-1, mice received transplantation of a small number of cells that produced

Table 20-1. Proportion of Mice in Which Tumors Developed as a Function of Dosage and Shock Treatment

Cell dosage	Yoked inescapable shock	Escapable shock	No shock
40 cells	22/40	23/40	23/40
60 cells	34/40	28/40	31/40
100 cells	39/40	36/40	34/40

From "Contributions of Stress and Coping to Cancer Development and Growth" by L. S. Sklar and H. Anisman. In K. Bammer and B. H. Newberry (Eds.), *Stress and Cancer.* Toronto: Hogrefe, 1981. Reprinted by permission.

tumors in only a portion of the animals. Neither exposure to escapable nor exposure to inescapable shock was found to influence the number of animals that subsequently developed tumors. It is difficult to assess the source for the differences between the effects reported by us (Sklar & Anisman, 1981b) and by Visintainer *et al.* (1982), given the differences in tumor system employed, the rate of tumor development, the amount of stress animals received, and the phase of cell division when stress was applied. Nonetheless, it does appear that an amount of uncontrollable stress that induces an increase in tumor size following transplantation of a large number of cells will not necessarily have a similar effect following transplantation of a relatively small number of cells. It is certainly conceivable that the mechanisms operative during the early phases of tumor development (i.e., when only a small number of cells are present) differ from the mechanisms operative when a larger colony of cells is present. Differential effects of stressful events might be expected if the treatment selectively acts on an endogenous process that is operative during one phase and not another (e.g., potential contribution of hormones and steroids).

In evaluating the effects of stressors on a Moloney murine sarcoma virus, Amkraut and Solomon (1972) found that 3 days of shock applied prior to viral inoculation inhibited tumor development, while 3 days of stress commencing on the day of inoculation enhanced tumor development. It is almost as if prior stress application increases the preparedness of the organism to deal with subsequent insults in the form of the murine sarcoma virus, whereas stressor application following virus inoculation leaves the organism less prepared to deal with the viral insult. In accordance with such a supposition, Burchfield, Woods, and Elich (1978) reported that cold stress applied over a 3-week period prior to inoculation with either the (C58NT)D or PW7410 viral tumors reduced the maximal size to which tumors developed. However, application of the stressor following tumor inoculation did not result in inhibition. It will be noted that these results directly contradict those of Newberry (1981). Unfortunately, the source for these different results cannot readily be deduced, given the differences in the type of tumors employed, as well as the stress regimen to which animals were subjected. Nonetheless, the data are consistent in that they suggest that the effect of a repeated stress regimen is that of inhibiting tumor growth, whereas the aforementioned studies involving acute stressors indicate enhancement of tumor development.

In addition to the effects of stressors on the growth rate of a primary neoplasm, it is important to emphasize potential effects on metastases. The invasion of tumor cells and the subsequent development of secondary neoplasms in regions not immediately adjacent to the primary tumor represent a major problem in the treatment of human cancer (Fidler, 1978). As such, it is imperative to determine whether stressful events influence the metastatic processes, particularly since the treatments for the primary neoplasm are stressful (as is simply the individual's knowing that he or she is afflicted with the disease), and might thereby offset potential benefits derived from the therapy. Few studies are available that have examined the effects of stressors on the formation of metastases. Inasmuch as metastases represent the formation of tumors following the migration of a few cells from the main tumor mass to distant sites, the aforementioned studies that assessed tumor development following transplantation of a small number of cells may represent a model of metastases. These data provisionally suggest that acute stressor application influences cell proliferation, given the presence of a small cell colony. However, these experiments do not speak to the possibility of stressful events' influencing cell survival over the fairly arduous voyage from the primary tumor to a distant site. Several studies, however, have revealed that acute stressors, such as restraint, tumbling, and surgery, increased liver and pulmonary tumors following intravenous injection of malignant cells (e.g., Fisher & Fisher, 1959; Saba & Antikatzides, 1976; Van den Brenk, Stone, Kelly, & Sharpington, 1976). Moreover, it was reported that surgical stress increased the formation of secondary neoplasms in a spontaneously metastasizing tumor (Lundy et al., 1979), while repeated stressor application inhibited the formation of metastases (Zimel, Zimel, Petrescu, Ghinea, & Tasca, 1977).

A recent series of experiments conducted by Hattori and colleagues (Hattori, Hamai, Ikeda, Harada, & Ikeda, 1978; Hattori, Hamai, Ikeda, Takiyama, Hirai, & Miyoshi, 1982; Hattori, Hamai, Takiyama, Hirai, & Ikeda, 1980) revealed that stress in the form of laparotomy, thoracotomy, or laparothoracotomy increased the incidence of Sato lung cancer after intraperitoneal inoculation with tumor cells. Moreover, the surgical procedures were found to increase the number of metastatic nodules on the lungs. Interestingly, the effectiveness of the surgical procedures in decreasing survival time was evident when surgery was performed within 2 days of tumor inoculation (before or after). Evidently, a stressor such as surgery will enhance tumor development even if the stressor is applied prior to malignant cells being transplanted (of course, the aftereffects of the stressor probably persist for 2 days). A potential role for immunological mechanisms in provoking the enhanced tumor development and metastases is gleaned from the finding that the adverse consequences of the surgical trauma were largely abrogated if rats were treated with immunopotentiators prior to or after tumor cell transplantation (Hattori *et al.*, 1982).

Social Stressors

Just as physical and psychological stressors may influence tumor size, it appears that psychosocial factors will alter the course of tumor development. For instance, the social conditions in which mice are housed will affect tumor development, and ultimately the survival time of the organism. Mice housed individually typically exhibit a greater incidence of spontaneous and carcinogen-induced tumors, relative to animals housed in small groups (Andervont, 1944; Dechambre, 1981; Dechambre & Gosse, 1973; Truhaut & Dechambre, 1972). With respect to transplanted tumors, it has been demonstrated that tumor mass is increased in isolated mice following transplantation of P815 cells (Sklar & Anisman, 1980), as well as L1210, B16 melanoma, and Krebs-2 cells (Dechambre, 1981; Dechambre & Gosse, 1973). Interestingly, in the studies of Dechambre and Gosse (1973), the isolated mice were found to survive *longer* than the grouped animals. It was suggested (Dechambre, 1981) that in the isolated mice the volume of ascites fluid was increased, relative to that in grouped animals. Given that the ascites tumor cell lysate is toxic, any immunosuppressant effect of the isolation condition, which reduces this lysate, would actually favor survival time, while permitting greater proliferation of tumor cells.

Several experiments have shown that the effects of social housing conditions on tumor development are dependent on the previous and concurrent experiences of the animal. As seen in Figure 20-2, relative to mice raised in grouped cages, tumor development was unaltered in mice that had been raised in isolation since weaning. However, tumor development was enhanced among mice that had been raised in groups and then transferred to isolated conditions. Transfer from isolated cages to the grouped conditions, in contrast, did not have an overall effect on tumor development; however, it was observed that when transferred to the grouped condition, some mice engaged in fighting while others did not. Tumor enhancement was evident in mice that did not engage in fighting, whereas tumor development was slightly retarded among mice that engaged in fighting (see inset of Figure 20-2). Amkraut and Solomon (1972) similarly observed that tumor size following inoculation with Moloney murine sarcoma virus was reduced among female mice that had engaged in spontaneous fighting. Together, these data suggest that change in housing conditions was the fundamental factor determining altered tumor development, and that

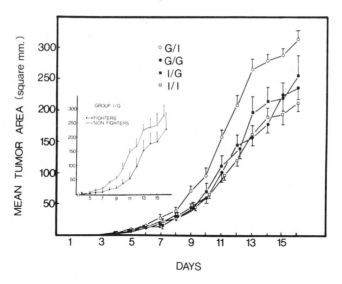

Figure 20-2. Mean tumor area ($\pm$ *SEM*) over days among mice that had been raised in communal cages and then transferred to isolation (G/I), raised in isolation from weaning and then transferred to communal cages (I/G), or housed throughout in isolation (I/I) or groups (G/G). The inset shows the tumor area of mice in group I/G categorized with respect to whether they exhibited persistent fighting after transfer to communal cages. (From "Social Stress Influences Tumor Growth" by L. S. Sklar and H. Anisman. *Psychosomatic Medicine*, 1980, *42*, 347–365. Reprinted by permission.)

engaging in fighting (which one might intuitively have considered maladaptive) had the effect of inhibiting the effects of the social change. It is conceivable that the fighting acted as a coping mechanism (much as escape from shock does), thereby militating against the effects of change in social conditions (see Sklar & Anisman, 1981b; Stolk, Conner, Levine, & Barchas, 1973).

A series of studies reviewed by Dechambre (1981) revealed that any number of variables that alter social equilibrium would influence the rate of tumor development among mice that had received grafted tumors. Moreover, stressful events such as early maternal deprivation (weaning at 15 rather than 21 days of age) decreased the survival time of mice that received tumor grafts in adulthood, and also decreased antibody-forming cells in such animals. It should be underscored, however, that the effectiveness of such manipulations carried out in young animals may be dependent on a number of variables, including the precise developmental stage at which the treatment is applied, and the tumor system employed (cf. Ader & Friedman, 1965; LaBarba & White, 1971; Newton, Bly, & McCrary, 1962; see discussion in Sklar &

Anisman, 1981 a). It is significant as well, that social housing conditions may influence the effects of other forms of stress on tumor development. It will be recalled that the immunological consequences of stressors were dependent on the background upon which the stressor was superimposed (Monjan, 1981; Nieburgs et al., 1979). In a similar fashion, we (Sklar & Anisman, 1980) observed that the enhancement of tumor growth seen after acute shock exposure was not evident among mice that had been housed in isolation. In fact, among these animals, the stress treatment resulted in tumor inhibition. Clearly, fairly complex interactions exist that determine the effects of stressors on immunological processes and on the development of tumors.

Summarizing briefly, experiments conducted in infrahumans have yielded diverse effects of stressors on tumor growth. Nevertheless, it seems that several tentative conclusions can be drawn:

1. There is reason to believe that the effectiveness of stressors in exacerbating tumor development may be dependent on the animal's ability to control the stressor through behavioral means.
2. In considering the effects of uncontrollable stressors, it is essential to distinguish between acute and chronic insults. Whereas acute stressors appear to have the effect of enhancing tumor growth, repeated applications of a stressor either will inhibit tumor development or will, at least, minimize the effects otherwise induced by acute application of the stressor.
3. The time of stressor application may be essential in determining effects on tumor development. It seems that stressors may not be instrumental in determining whether or not neoplastic cells will be evident, but rather will modify their proliferation.
4. Stressors not only will influence growth of a primary tumor, but may also influence the occurrence of secondary tumors (metastases) and tumor cell rejection.
5. It is important to distinguish between the effects of psychological stressors associated with the ability to control aversive stimulation and the effects of psychosocial stressors. In contrast to the former type of stressor, it seems that psychosocial stressors, even if chronically applied, will enhance tumor development.
6. The effectiveness of stressors in promoting tumor change will be dependent upon the backdrop upon which the stressor is applied.

There certainly remain a great number of unanswered questions concerning the fundamental features and consequences of the stressors that lead to cancer exacerbation or inhibition. Among other things, it is essential to determine whether the effects of stressors are dependent on the nature of the tumor being examined, as well as the phase of tumor development during which the stressor must be applied in order to detect changes of development.

MEDIATING MECHANISMS FOR STRESS-PROVOKED
TUMOR ENHANCEMENT

Although stressors modify immune functioning, it remains to be conclusively demonstrated whether stress-provoked tumor exacerbation is due to a weakened ability of the immune system to detect or react to neoplastic cells. If one accepts the supposition that the stressors influence tumor development via immunological alterations, one is still left with the question of the mechanism by which stressors come to have such an effect. One of the most often cited accounts for the effects of stressors on tumor development is that the application of physical or psychological insults provokes secretion of adrenal corticoids, which induce immunosuppression, thereby enhancing the tumor development. Indeed, it is well established that stressors will provoke secretion of corticoids in rodents (corticosterone) and in humans, and it is known that corticoids act as effective immunosuppressants. Moreover, it has been established that administration of corticoids will enhance tumor development and decrease the frequency of tumor regression (see reviews in Riley, 1981; Riley et al., 1981). According to Riley (1981), stressors will influence tumor development only if the tumor is under partial or complete control of the immune system. In effect, it is suggested that the release of corticosterone will induce immunosuppression, thereby enhancing tumor development (or conversely preventing rejection), provided that the immune system ordinarily limits tumor growth. Riley and his associates have provided an impressive body of evidence in favor of such an interpretation. Among other things, it was demonstrated that in two substrains of C3H mice, exposure to a stressor (rotation) enhanced the growth of a transplanted lymphosarcoma only if the tumor and host animal were nonhistocompatible. In another study, it was demonstrated that within a single strain of mouse (C57Bl/6), stress in the form of exposure to an LDH virus enhanced the growth of a nonpigmented melanoma, but did not influence the development of a more histocompatible nonpigmented melanoma (see Riley, 1981).

   While the data provided by Riley and his associates are fairly convincing, alternative explanations are available to account for the observed results. For instance, the stress treatment aside, it was found that growth rate of a histocompatible tumor was marked, relative to that seen when the tumor was nonhistocompatible with the substrain of mouse. Thus, the lack of effect of stressor application may have been related to the particularly rapid rate of growth of the histocompatible tumor, preventing detection of a further stress-provoked increase. It might have been advantageous to assess the effects of stressors on tumor change following administration of a small number of cells, thereby permitting the assessment of tumor growth during a relatively early phase of tumor development. In the experiment where tumor development was assessed in two different strains of mice, it should also be considered that these strains may have been differentially reactive or sensitive to the stressor, thus accounting for the differences in tumor development. It has, after all, been demonstrated that strains of mice differ in reactivity to an aversive stimulus, and that a given stressor may differentially influence neurochemical and hormonal activity across mouse strains (see review in Anisman, 1978). Finally, it should be noted that stress effects on tumor development have been demonstrated when syngeneic tumors were employed, and in addition, immunological reconstitution by transplantation of syngeneic spleen cells after animals had been exposed to the stressor did not alter the effects of the stressor (Jamasbi & Nettesheim, 1977). Likewise, the effects on tumor development induced by surgical stress were unaffected by adrenalectomy, a treatment that would have been expected to eliminate the immunosuppression that might otherwise have been engendered by corticosterone release from the adrenal engendered by the stressor (Peters & Kelly, 1977). Paradoxically, the latter investigators found that treatment with adrenocorticotropic hormone (ACTH) or dexamethasone enhanced tumorigenicity in nonstressed animals. It would appear from these results that stress-induced release of corticosterone may influence tumor development; however, the fact that adrenalectomy did not prevent the enhanced tumor development indicates that some other stress-induced mechanism, unrelated to circulating adrenal steroids, also contributes to the tumor changes.

There is reason to believe that alterations of central neurotransmitter activity may also contribute to the effects of stressors on tumor development. Although the potential role of neurotransmitters on immune mechanisms has frequently been ignored, it has become clear that central neurochemical activity influences immune functioning, and vice versa. The recent volume edited by Ader (1981) contains several reviews indicating that these systems are interdependent in many respects (see Hall & Goldstein, 1981; Spector & Korneva, 1981; Stein, Schleifer, & Keller, 1981). Likewise, considerable evidence exists relating neuroendocrine and immune functioning (Besedovsky & Sorkin, 1981; Maclean & Reichlin, 1981). Several approaches have been adopted to evaluate the interrelationships among neurochemical, neuroendocrine, and immunological functioning. It has been demonstrated, for instance, that lesions of the anterior hypothalamus protect animals from death due to either passive or active anaphylaxis (Macris, Schiavi, Camerino, & Stein, 1972; Schiavi, Macris, Camerino, & Stein, 1975). Likewise, lesion of the anterior hypothalamus reduced antibody titers in response to the hapten picryl chloride (Macris, Schiavi, Camerino, & Stein, 1970). While these investigators found that lesion of other regions of the hypothalamus did not influence either antibody titers or the anaphylactic reaction, others have reported that lesions of the posterior ventral hypothalamus depressed antibody production (Korneva & Khai, 1964), while stimulation of this region enhanced antibody production (Korneva, 1966, cited in Stein et al., 1981). Still others, however, were unable to detect alterations of immune activity following a variety of hypothalamic lesions (Ado & Goldstein, 1973; Thrasher, Bernardis, & Cohen, 1971).

Hypothalamic manipulations not only will influence humoral immunity, but will also affect the cellular immune response. Anterior hypothalamic lesions reduced the tuberculin reaction and reduced the blood lymphocyte stimulation by PHA and tuberculin-purified protein derivative (Keller, Stein, Camerino, Schleifer, & Sherman, 1980). Likewise, anterior hypothalamic lesions suppressed immune functioning as determined by inhibition of delayed cutaneous hypersensitivity (Janakovic & Isakovic, 1973; Macris *et al.*, 1970), while stimulation of the hypothalamus enhanced the delayed cutaneous hypersensitivity reaction (Janakovic, Jovanova, & Markovic, 1979). Just as surgical manipulation of hypothalamic sites influences immunological functioning, it appears that exposure to an antigen will influence unit activity in specific nuclei of the hypothalamus (Klimenko, 1975, cited in Spector & Korneva, 1981). Moreover, the hypothalamic unit activity change in hypothalamus corresponded with the course of the immunological changes induced by the antigen. Furthermore, just as secretion of adrenal steroids will influence immune functioning, it has been demonstrated that exposure to an antigen will provoke changes in adrenal steroids as indicated by changes in 11-oxycorticosteroid (see Spector & Korneva, 1981). It should be underscored at this juncture that it has been demonstrated that viral-induced increases of interferon production are also associated with production of an ACTH-like substance from lymphocytes. Unlike the suppression of corticosterone seen after dexamethosone treatment in hypophysectomized mice, the interferon production is unaffected. Thus, it appears that the consequences of viral exposure on interferon and steroid production are subserved by independent mechanisms (Smith, Meyer, & Blalock, 1982). Moreover, the fact that the corticoid increase was noted in hypophysectomized mice raises the possibility that in addition to a pituitary–adrenal axis, there may exist a lymphoid–adrenal axis controlling steroid production (Smith *et al.*, 1982). While these investigators suggest that this axis may be stimulated by factors other than those related to central nervous system functioning (i.e., the cognitive correlates of stressors), the possibility cannot be dismissed that central nervous system activity, quite independent of pituitary involvement, contributes to the lymphocyte production of steroids and interferon.

The supposition that neurochemical and hormonal factors influence immunological functioning is supported by the findings that lymphocytes carry receptors on their surface that are sensitive to several neurotransmitters, including epinephrine, norepinephrine (NE), and acetylcholine (ACh), as well as receptors sensitive to hormones and steroids (see reviews in Besedovsky & Sorkin, 1981; Hall & Goldstein, 1981; Spector & Korneva, 1981). In their review of the literature, Hall and Goldstein (1981) provide a strong case for the central and peripheral neurotransmitters, as well as steroids in influencing immunological functioning. Among other things, it is indicated that drug-provoked neurochemical alterations will result in immunological variations. In general, treatments that increase serotonin (5-

HT) concentrations decrease antibody production, whereas reductions of 5-HT increase antibody production (e.g., Bliznakov, 1980; Devoino, Eremina, & Ilyutchenok, 1970). Moreover, the latent phase of antibody production in rabbits immunized with typhoid vi-antigen was associated with decreased hypothalamic 5-HT concentrations. The influence of 5-HT activity on immunological functioning may be modulated or subserved by neuroendocrine functioning, given that hypophysectomy prevented the immunological consequences otherwise induced by the 5-HT precursor, 5-hydroxytryptophan (Devoino et al., 1970).

In their analysis of the role of dopamine (DA) on immune functioning, Hall and Goldstein (1981) indicate that there is reason to believe that this amine has a stimulatory influence on the immune system. For instance, they note that individuals suffering from neurological disturbances associated with reduced DA functioning exhibit reduced lymphocyte functioning. Similarly, it has been reported (Cotzias & Tang, 1977) that brain concentrations of DA were reduced in mice with a high propensity for mammary tumors. Along the same line, it has been shown that reserpine-induced depletion of biogenic amines resulted in immunosuppression (Dukor, Salvin, Dietrich, Gelzer, Hess, & Loustalot, 1966), while stimulation of DA receptors had an opposite effect (Cotzias & Tang, 1977; Tang & Cotzias, 1977; Tang, Cotzias, & Dunn, 1974). Finally, several studies have revealed that catecholamine stimulants, such as levodopa (L-dopa) or amphetamine, inhibited the development of DMBA-induced tumors and transplanted syngeneic tumors (Driscoll, Melnick, Quinn, Lomax, Davignon, Ing, Abbott, Congleton, & Dudeck, 1978; Quadri, Kledzik, & Meites, 1973; Wick, 1977, 1978, 1979), whereas reductions of catecholamines tended to exacerbate tumor development (Lacassagne & Duplan, 1959; Lapin, 1978; Sklar & Anisman, 1981a; Welsch & Meites, 1970). Indeed, it was recently reported (Sarkar, Gottschall, & Meites, 1982) that prolactin-secreting pituitary tumors (in old female rats and in younger rats treated chronically with estrogen) were accompanied by damage of tuberinfundibular DA neurons. Thus, these data suggest that the pituitary tumors may be related to hypothalamic DA changes, particularly involving the arcuate nucleus. It should be underscored, however, that several reports are available showing the treatment with DA receptor blockers reduced tumor development (Belkin & Hardy, 1957; Driscoll et al., 1978; Gottlieb, Hazel, Broitman, & Zamcheck, 1960; Kanzawa, Hoshi, & Kuretani, 1970; Van Woert & Palmer, 1969). Particularly high drug doses were used in some of these studies (which led to 70–80% mortality), while in other studies animals received repeated drug administration (a treatment known to result in receptor supersensitivity). Accordingly, it is not clear that the effects observed in these studies, in fact, suggest that DA receptor blockade leads to tumor reduction. To the contrary, it is perfectly predictable that the receptor supersensitivity that follows chronic treatment with a DA receptor blocker would result in diminished tumor development (see discussion in Sklar &

Anisman, 1981b). At any rate, none of the aforementioned data conclusively suggest a causal relationship between DA status and immune functioning, but the possibility certainly warrants further attention.

The data suggesting a role for central NE in modulating immunological functioning and tumor development are less impressive than the data suggesting a role for peripheral NE in these processes. To be sure, some of the aforementioned drugs that influence DA neuronal functioning also influence NE activity. Moreover, the previously mentioned studies showing that hypothalamic lesions influence immune functioning may represent the consequences of NE alterations. Peripherally, it has been shown that β-NE receptors are present on the surface of T and B cells and on macrophages (Bourne, Lichtenstein, Melmon, Henney, Weinstein, & Shearer, 1974), and as indicated earlier, immune functioning is associated with alterations of NE concentrations (Besedovsky & Sorkin, 1981). Furthermore, chemical sympathectomy by systemic injection of the neurotoxin 6-hydroxydopamine has been found to depress antibody production (Hall, McClure, Hu, Tick, Seales, & Goldstein, 1980; Kasahara, Tanaka, Ito, & Hamashima, 1977) and to reduce the response to a mitogen (see Hall & Goldstein, 1981). When these factors are taken together, there appears reason to assume that alterations of peripheral catecholamine activity (and possibly central catecholamine functioning, as well) may influence immunological functioning, and hence may affect the course of illnesses related to immune processes.

STRESS AND NEUROCHEMICAL CHANGE

Acute Effects

If it is assumed that alterations of immunological functioning are promoted, or at least modulated, by central neurotransmitter activity, then it would be of value to determine the course of the neurochemical changes induced by stressors, as well as the limiting conditions for such alterations. We have reviewed this literature on several occasions (e.g., Anisman, 1978, 1983; Anisman, Kokkinidis, & Sklar, 1981, 1983), and thus only a limited overview is provided at this time.

A variety of stressors have been shown to increase the synthesis and utilization of NE in several brain regions (e.g., Korf, Aghajanian, & Roth, 1973; Thierry, Blanc, & Glowinski, 1971; see Stone, 1975). Soon after stress inception or after exposure to a mild stressor concentrations of NE increase, possibly reflecting a transient inhibition of monoamine oxidase (Welch & Welch, 1970). Following fairly severe or somewhat protracted stress, the utilization of NE may come to exceed the rate of synthesis, and consequently concentrations of the amine may decline (e.g., Anisman & Sklar, 1979; Kvetnansky, Mitro, Palkovits, Brownstein, Torda, Vigas, & Mikulaj, 1976; Thierry, 1973; Weiss, Glazer, & Pohorecky, 1976). It appears that a fundamental feature in determining whether NE reductions will be provoked concerns the organism's ability to deal with the stressor through behavioral methods. As depicted in Figure 20-3, exposure to escapable shock was not found to influence NE concentrations appreciably. However, exposure to an identical amount of inescapable shock, applied in a yoked paradigm, resulted in a pronounced depletion of NE (Anisman, Pizzino, & Sklar, 1980; Weiss *et al.*, 1976; Weiss, Goodman, Losito, Corrigan, Charry, & Bailey, 1981).

It has been our contention that upon exposure to a stressor, the organism attempts to meet environmental demands through behavioral methods. Concurrently, several neurochemical and hormonal changes take place, whose functions may include facilitating behavioral responses, modulating peripheral sympathetic tone (e.g., modulating heart rate), blunting the impact of the aversive stimulation, and so forth. When behavioral mechanisms of dealing with a stressor are available, the neurochemical systems will not be overly taxed. However, when behavioral attempts to deal with the stressor

Figure 20-3. Mean concentrations of norepinephrine ($\pm$ *SEM*) in hypothalmus and in hippocampus plus cortex among mice exposed to 60 escapable shocks, an identical amount of inescapable shock applied in a yoked paradigm, or no shock. Mice were decapitated immediately after the last shock trial. (From "Coping with Stress, Norepinephrine Depletion and Escape Performance" by H. Anisman, A. Pizzino, and L. S. Sklar. *Brain Research*, 1980, *191*, 583–588. Reprinted by permission.)

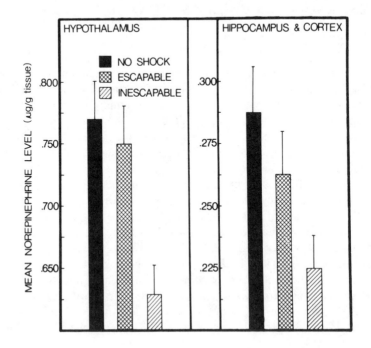

are unsuccessful (or appear to be ineffective), then further neurochemical changes occur, presumably to meet the demands placed on the organism. Under such conditions the utilization of neurotransmitters increases further, eventually exceeding the rate of synthesis and hence resulting in a net decline of transmitter levels.

In the case of DA, the available data are far less extensive than those for NE. Some investigators insist that DA activity is only slightly affected by stressors. In fact, it appears that pronounced DA alterations will occur in response to physical insults, but that these alterations are restricted to a limited number of brain regions. For instance, discrete analysis of individual hypothalamic nuclei has revealed that stressors may provoke substantial reductions of DA (in excess of 50%) in the arcuate nucleus, while in other nuclei, such as the ventral dorsomedial nucleus, DA concentrations are increased (Kobayashi, Palkovits, Kizer, Jacobowitz, & Kopin, 1976; Kvetnansky et al., 1976). In the DA-rich substantia nigra, turnover of the amine is hardly influenced by stressors, but several investigators have demonstrated profound increases of DA activity in the nucleus accumbens and in the mesolimbic frontal cortex (e.g., Blanc, Herve, Simon, Liso-prawski, Glowinski, & Tassin, 1980; Fadda, Argiolas, Melis, Tissari, Onali, & Gessa, 1978; Fekete, Szentendrei, Kanyicska, & Palkovits, 1981; Herman, Guillonneau, Dantzer, Scatton, Semerdjian-Rouquier, & LeMoal, 1982; Lavielle, Tassin, Thierry, Blanc, Herve, Barthelemy, & Glowinski, 1978; Thierry, Tassin, Blanc, & Glowinski, 1976), and reductions of DA concentrations have been detected as well (e.g., Blanc et al., 1980). Finally, Saavedra (1982) recently reported that stress exposure reduces DA concentrations in the lateral septal nucleus, without affecting concentrations of DA in other septal nuclei. The fact that the DA alterations are not as widespread as those of NE certainly does not imply lesser importance of this amine. To the contrary, the intimate relationship between the arcuate nucleus and the pituitary leads one to suspect that stress-induced alterations of pituitary hormones may be influenced by the DA alterations within the arcuate. Likewise, the potential role of the mesolimbic DA system in emotional behaviors raises the possibility that altered DA functioning may be responsible for emotional and behavioral consequences provoked by stressors.

Typically, investigators who have been concerned with evaluating the contribution of coping factors to the alterations of DA activity have evaluated brain regions where DA alterations are minimal or where DA concentrations increase. Conversely, investigators who have evaluated DA alterations in appropriate discrete brain regions have not assessed the contribution of coping factors. Nevertheless, data reported by Cherek, Lane, Freeman, and Smith (1980) suggest that DA neuronal activity is influenced by coping factors. These investigators found that, relative to exposure to escapable shock, exposure to yoked inescapable shock over four sessions of 8 hours altered the sensitivity of low-affinity DA receptors in the mesolimbic frontal cortex of rats. Owing to the fairly protracted stress regimen employed, it is not certain to what extent the particular receptor changes observed were related to the chronicity of the stress treatment applied (see below). This notwithstanding, it does appear that controllable and uncontrollable aversive stimulation may differentially affect DA receptor sensitivity, just as such treatments differentially influence NE neuronal functioning.

Alterations of 5-HT activity, like those of NE and DA activity, have been observed following application of stressors (e.g., Bliss, Thatcher, & Ailion, 1972; Curzon, Joseph, & Knott, 1972); however, it appears that the severity of the stressor needed to engender increased 5-HT turnover is appreciably greater than that required to promote alterations of NE turnover (see Thierry, 1973). Concentrations of 5-HT have been shown to decrease within 10 minutes of a stressor (formalin injection), after which concentrations of the amine increase above control values (Palkovits, Brownstein, Kizer, Saavedra, & Kopin, 1976). Others, however, have noted only the increase of 5-HT concentrations following stress exposure (Morgan, Rudeen, & Pfeil, 1975). Likewise, in some two dozen experiments conducted in our laboratory, where 5-HT concentrations have been determined, we have noted either no change or increases of 5-HT concentrations (using various stress parameters and times after stress), but have yet to observe a decline of this amine in either the hypothalamus, hippocampus, cortex, or locus ceruleus plus raphe nuclei. It is not unlikely, however, that the 5-HT alterations induced by stressors are restricted to a limited number of brain regions. Indeed, Petty and Sherman (1982) reported reductions of 5-HT in the septum and in the anterior cortex following footshock—a finding that contrasts with that of Palkovits *et al.* (1976), who examined 5-HT concentrations in other brain regions. It should be emphasized, as well, that in their particular experiment Petty and Sherman (1982) observed that the reduction of 5-HT was seen only in rats that received inescapable shock, and not in rats that had received escapable shock.

ACh activity and concentrations, like those of other amines, have been found to vary with stress conditions. Costa, Tagliomonti, Brunello, and Cheney (1980) reported that 20–25 minutes following 1 hour of cold exposure, turnover of ACh was reduced in the frontal cortex. The altered turnover was not evident after 4 or 24 hours of such treatment. In the hypothalamus, both 1 and 23 hours of stress resulted in reduced ACh turnover. Recently, Schmidt, Cooper, and Barrett (1980) observed that the effects of stress on high-affinity choline uptake and on ACh turnover could be increased by shock stress; however, the occurrence of such an effect was dependent on the strain of rat employed. In particular, the cholinergic alterations were noted in the reactive (motor-suppressing) Zivic–Miller line of rat, but not in the less reactive F-344 Wistar line. Evidence presented by Zajaczkowska (1975) indicates that the effects of stressors on ACh differs during the stress period (or immediately thereafter) versus during the poststress exhaustion period. Immediately after stress, application ACh concentrations were reduced; however, within 40 minutes, during which rats appeared to be immobile owing to exhaustion, levels of ACh increased well above those of control rats. Thus, it is likely that the differential effects of stressors on ACh activity may be related to the time at which the cholinergic determinations are made and to the amount of stress animals receive, as well as the strain of animal employed.

There is reason to believe that the psychological dimension of coping with the stressor may determine the nature and magnitude of the ACh changes. In particular, Karczmar, Scudder, and Richardson (1973) reported that in a study where mice received avoidable/escapable shock, ACh concentrations were not altered, while in a second experiment, where mice received inescapable shock, ACh concentrations were increased. Unfortunately, the purpose of the two studies was not to evaluate coping factors, and consequently a yoked control procedure was not employed. Nonetheless, these data are suggestive of the potential importance of controllability in determining ACh activity and concentrations. In accordance with this supposition, Cherek et al. (1980) observed that relative to rats exposed to escapable shock, increased ACh receptor binding was evident in rats that received inescapable shock. As in the case of the DA data described earlier, shock was applied over several days; hence it is not certain to what extent the chronicity of the stress regimen contributed to the precise alterations of ACh receptor sensitivity.

The discovery of endogenous opioids has led to increased evaluation of these peptides in psychological dysfunction, as well as of the potential effects of stressors on these endogenous substances. Stressors have been shown to increase endorphin secretion from the anterior pituitary, thereby decreasing concentrations in this region (Baizman, Cox, Osman, & Goldstein, 1979; Barta & Yashpal, 1981; Millan, Tsang, Przewlocki, Hollt, & Herz, 1981; Przewlocki, Millan, Gramsch, Millan, & Herz, 1982; Vuolteenaho, Leppaluoto, & Mannisto, 1982) while increasing β-endorphin concentrations in blood (e.g., Przewlocki et al., 1982). The alterations of endogenous opioids induced by stress are not restricted to the pituitary, but have been noted in several brain regions. Some investigators have observed that stressors produce a decrease of immunoreactive endorphin or leu-enkephalin concentrations in the hypothalamus (Rossier, French, Rivier, Ling, Guillemin, & Bloom, 1977; Rossier, Guillemin, & Bloom, 1978), while others have found increases of β-endorphin or dynorphin in the hypothalamus (Barta & Yashpal, 1981; Madden, Akil, Patrick, & Barchas, 1977; Millan et al., 1981; Przewlocki et al., 1982). Furthermore, several investigators have reported that stress exposure provokes decreased binding of exogenous [3H]leu-enkephalin, possibly due to increased availability of the endogenous opioid (Chance, White, Krynock, & Rosecrans, 1978; Christie, Chesher, & Bird, 1981; DeVries, Chance, Payne, & Rosecrans, 1979). The source for the differential effects observed among laboratories has yet to be deduced; however, the report of Barta and Yashpal (1981) may prove important in this respect. In particular, following stress of moderate severity, increased endorphin concentrations were noted in several brain regions, while decreased endorphin concentrations were evident in the anterior and intermediate posterior lobes of the pituitary. Following acute severe stress the central endorphin increases were much more pronounced, while in the anterior pituitary the extent of the endorphin reduction was minimized, and the reduction was entirely absent in the intermediate posterior lobe. Following repeated application of moderate stress over 21 days, adaptation occurred with respect to the endorphin changes in the pituitary and in brain; however, following repeated application of the severe stressor, adaptation was not seen in brain, and endorphin levels increased still further. Clearly, the effectiveness of stressors in determining endorphin alterations is dependent on the severity of the stressor, as well as on the organism's previous stress history.

Organismic, Environmental, and Experiential Factors

The rate of neurotransmitter turnover not only is dependent upon the availability of behavioral coping methods, but is also influenced by the backdrop upon which the stressor is applied. Indeed, several organismic, environmental, and experiential variables have been shown to have a pronounced influence in this respect. For instance, the rate of amine turnover, the magnitude of the depletion of NE, and the time course of the NE alterations vary with the age of the organism. In general, it seems that stress has more pronounced and longer-lasting effects among older rats than among young adult animals (Ritter & Pelzer, 1978). Not surprisingly, catecholamine and ACh concentrations and turnover have also been shown to differ among strains of mice and rats, and exposure to stressors will differentially influence the course and extent of the amine changes (e.g., Schmidt et al., 1980; Wimer, Norman, & Eleftheriou, 1973). Similarly, it has been shown that housing mice in isolation (which may itself be considered a form of stress) results in alterations of NE turnover (Modigh, 1976; Welch & Welch, 1970) and increases vulnerability to NE reductions upon exposure to other forms of stressors (Anisman & Sklar, 1981). Likewise, social housing conditions have been shown to influence the DA variations induced by stressors (Blanc et al., 1980). Finally, even the time of day at which the stressor is applied will influence the course of neurochemical variations (e.g., Irwin, Bowers, Zacharko, & Anisman, 1982).

In addition to the aforementioned variables, the neurochemical response to stressors varies considerably as a function of the organism's prior stress history. In this respect, two fundamental treatments should be distinguished from each other: specifically, the differential effects of acute and chronically applied stressors, and the consequences of a single stress experience on vulnerability to neurochemical alterations upon re-exposure to the stressor. Considering the latter issue first, it has been demonstrated that exposure to an uncontrollable stressor will increase vulnerability to later alterations of NE neuronal functioning. Figure 20-4 shows that within 24 hours of stress termination, amine levels returned to control values. Among naive mice, exposure to 10 shocks had minimal effects on NE levels; however, among mice that had received 60 inescapable shocks 24 hours earlier, the amine reduction was re-established upon subsequent exposure to 10 shock presentations (Anisman & Sklar, 1979; Anisman, Kokkinidis & Sklar, 1981). Likewise, as seen in Figure 20-5, among mice that had not previously been stressed, exposure to limited shock or restraint did not appreciably reduce amine concentrations. In contrast, among mice that had received inescapable shock 24 hours earlier, a decline of NE concentrations was evident upon re-exposure to limited shock or upon exposure to restraint stress. Experiments conducted by Cassens, Roffman, Kuruc, Orsulak, and Schildkraut (1980) also revealed that presentation of cues that had previously been paired with shock increased NE utilization. Evidently,

Figure 20-4. Mean concentrations of norepinephrine ($\pm$ *SEM*) in hypothalamus and in hippocampus among mice that received either no shock on two consecutive days (N/N), 60 shocks on one day followed by no shock on the second day (60/N), no shock on the first day and 10 shocks on the second day (N/10), or 60 shocks on the first followed by 10 shocks on the second day (60/10). Mice were decapitated immediately following the second session. Note that immediately following 60 shocks a marked reduction of NE was noted (see Figure 20-3), but that levels approached control values within 24 hours of the stress session. (From "Contribution of Neurochemical Change to Stress-Induced Behavioral Deficits" by H. Anisman, L. Kokkinidis, and L. S. Sklar. In S. J. Cooper (Ed.), *Theory of Psychopharmacology.* London: Academic Press, 1981. Reprinted by permission.)

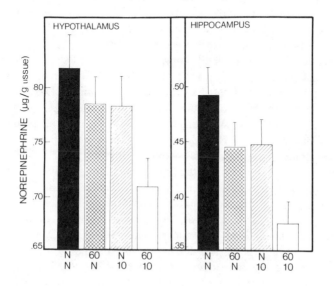

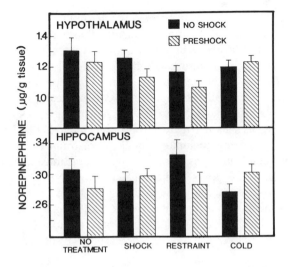

Figure 20-5. Mean concentration of norepinephrine ($\pm$ *SEM*) in hypothalamus and in hippocampus among mice that received either 60 inescapable shocks or no shock. Twenty-four hours afterward, mice were subdivided and given either no treatment other than brief handling, a single 30-second footshock, 30 minutes of restraint, or 5 minutes of cold exposure ($2°C$). Mice were decapitated immediately after the second session. (From "Stress-Induced Alterations of Norepinephrine: Cross-Stressor Sensitization" by J. Irwin, W. Bowers, R. M. Zacharko, and H. Anisman. *Society for Neuroscience Abstracts*, 1982, *8*, 359. Reprinted by permission.)

experience with a traumatic stressor will result in the sensitization or conditioning of the mechanisms responsible for NE alterations. In effect, an aversive experience leaves the organism more vulnerable to neurochemical alterations upon subsequent exposure to a stressor.

The occurrence of a conditioning/sensitization effect is not restricted to variations of NE activity. It was recently shown (Herman *et al.*, 1982) that cues associated with a stressor will increase mesolimbic DA activity, while stimuli paired with shock have been shown to increase ACh concentrations (Hingtgen, Smith, Shea, Aprison, & Gaff, 1976) and enkephalin receptor binding (Chance *et al.*, 1978). Moreover, it seems that exposure to a stressor will also influence the behavioral response ordinarily elicited by a pharmacological treatment, such as the catecholamine stimulant amphetamine (Antelman, Eichler, Black, & Kocan, 1980). Taken together, these findings lead to the obvious implication that aversive events not only may have immediate adverse consequences, but may dispose the organism to later neurochemical alterations, and consequently to pathology related to these neurochemical alterations (see discussion in Anisman & Zacharko, 1982).

With respect to the effects of chronic stress application, increasing evidence has accumulated showing that the effectiveness of stressors in modifying neurochemical change varies with repeated exposure to physical insults. Whereas acute exposure to a stressor results in a depletion of NE, owing to utilization rates' exceeding synthesis, the depletion is absent or limited among mice that receive repeated exposure to the stressor (Roth, Mefford, & Barchas, 1982; Weiss *et al.*, 1976, 1981). Indeed, even within a single protracted stress session, adaptation may be observed with respect to NE alterations (Kvetnansky *et al.*, 1976; Saavedra, 1982), while adaptation of DA neuronal activity is not evident as readily (Saavedra, 1982). It appears that with repeated exposure to a stressor an increase of tyrosine hydroxylase and dopamine-β-hydroxylase activity occurs, thereby resulting in amine synthesis keeping pace with utilization, and thereby preventing the amine depletion (see Kvetnansky, 1980).

Recent data collected in our laboratory (Irwin *et al.*, 1982) revealed an interesting series of neurochemical changes following chronic stress application, which may have considerable adaptive value. As seen in Figure 20-6, the depletion of NE ordinarily seen after acute inescapable shock was not evident among mice that were decapitated immediately after the last of 15 sessions of shock. Among mice that were decapitated 24 hours after the last stress session, NE levels in several regions actually exceeded those of nonstressed mice. A subsequent experiment revealed that during the last stress session, amine utilization rate exceeded control values, and levels remained constant, presumably owing to a complementary increase of synthesis. Over the 24-hour period following the last stress session, the rate of amine utilization declined below that of nonshocked mice. These data suggest that two independent processes were operative. During shock, amine utilization increased in order to meet the immediate demands placed on the organism, and the increased synthesis assured availability of adequate amine supplies. Following termination of the stressor, it would be adaptive for amine supplies to be increased (in this instance, by decreased utilization coupled with a relatively sustained increase of synthesis) in order for the animal to be prepared to deal with impending threats.

In addition to the altered rates of amine utilization and synthesis, repeated application of a stressor may induce subsensitivity of β-NE receptors (Nomura, Watanabe, Ukei, & Nakazawa, 1981; Stone, 1978, 1979a, 1979b, 1981; Stone & Platt, 1982). It is possible that with the sustained increase of NE utilization and synthesis following repeated stress treatments, receptor down regulation may occur in order to prevent the occurrence of maladaptive neuronal changes. In particular, excessive neuronal stimulation could potentially lead to physical pathologies (e.g., cardiovascular effects). Accordingly, reduction of the sensitivity of NE receptors in both the central and peripheral nervous systems may prevent some of the potentially hazardous consequences of excessive neuronal activity. Indeed, Stone and Platt (1982) reported that the anorexic and ulcerogenic effects of stressors diminished with chronic application of the physical insult, and the loss of β-NE receptors was positively correlated with reduction of pathology.

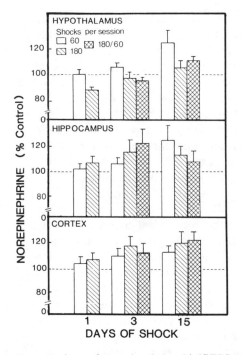

Figure 20-6. Mean concentrations of norepinephrine ($\pm$ *SEM*) as a percentage of control animals (nonshocked) in hypothalamus, hippocampus, and cortex as a function of the shock regimen to which mice were exposed. Independent groups of mice received either 1, 3, or 15 shock sessions. For one group of mice, each session consisted of 60 shocks (open bars); in a second condition, each session involved 180 shocks (striped bars); and in the third condition, each session but the last involved 180 shocks, while the last session involved only 60 shocks (cross-hatched bars). Note that, following repeated shock, the amine depletion ordinarily provoked by a single session of 180 shocks was absent, and actually exceeded control levels. (From "Stress-Induced Alterations of Norepinephrine: Cross-Stressor Sensitization" by J. Irwin, W. Bowers, R. M. Zacharko, and H. Anisman. *Society for Neuroscience Abstracts*, 1982, *8*, 359. Reprinted by permission.)

    The diverse effects of chronic stressor application have several implications concerning potential effects on pathology. First, it is possible that the adverse effects of acute stressors will be eliminated or minimized with repeated application. This does not imply, of course, that a treatment for a disorder brought about by acute stress is to have the stress continue. Rather, the possibility should be considered that interindividual differences in response to a stressor may stem not only from the way in which the individual initially responds to the stressor (in neurochemical terms), but also from the adaptive changes that occur with repeated stressor application. It might be expected that among most individuals, neurochemical adaptation will occur and pathology will not arise. However, just as individuals may differ with respect to the immediate impact of the stressor, individuals may also differ with respect to the effectiveness of their adaptive systems. Hence, pathology may be more marked among those individuals in whom the adaptive processes are least effective.

Second, stressors may have the immediate effect of leading to one sort of pathology, and could potentially lead to a second form of pathology with repeated stress exposure, owing to excessive neurochemical utilization. Here again, one might expect that interindividual differences may exist with respect to the development of receptor subsensitivity. Thus, some individuals may be more prone to the secondary pathology than other individuals. Finally, in considering the consequences of repeated stress, it is important perhaps to examine not only the immediate neurochemical consequences of the stressor, but also those that occur some time following termination of the stressor. It will be recalled that we (Sklar *et al.*, 1981), in fact, have suggested provisionally that some of the effects of stressors on tumor development may reflect alterations of endogenous substances that take place 24 hours or so after stressor termination, rather than neurochemical alterations that occur soon after stress exposure. Likewise, Smith *et al.* (1982) have indicated that variations of ACTH-like substances (possibly released from lymphocytes) may be maximal as long as 8 hours after stress exposure. Thus, the possibility exists that the induction of pathology—or, conversely, protection from pathology—may be related to some of the delayed endogenous chemical changes associated with the insult.

OVERVIEW

A considerable literature exists suggesting that stressful events may influence the development of several types of tumors. Such variables as stressor controllability, chronicity, and background conditions on which the stressor is applied will influence the nature and magnitude of the pathological changes that result. At this juncture, it is premature to attempt a detailed analysis of the precise mechanisms operative in the provocation of the tumor changes. Yet, it is known that manipulations that influence immunological functioning and tumor development likewise affect central and peripheral neurotransmitters and some hormones. Conversely, hormonal and neurochemical manipulations may influence immune functioning. Accordingly, as a working hypothesis, it would not be unreasonable to suppose that modulation of tumor development may be determined, at least in part, by the variations of central neurochemical activity. This should not be misconstrued to imply that central nervous system functioning is either more or less important than hormonal or immunological alterations that might occur upon exposure to a stressor. Rather, it is our contention that the variations of central neurotransmitters represent one of a great number of factors that ultimately influence tumor development.

Essentially, it is our contention that when an organism is confronted with adverse stimuli, behavioral and neurochemical changes occur in order to enable the organism to meet environmental demands. These neurochemical alterations, in turn, influence hormonal and immunological mechanisms that may be essential in dealing with environmental insults. The application of a moderate stressor, which results in mobilization of resources without overly taxing them (e.g., depletion), may have beneficial effects, in that this experience may prepare the organism for impending insults. However, if the stress is uncontrollable or sufficiently protracted, the excessive utilization of resources and their ultimate depletion may leave the organism less well prepared to deal with pathogens that might subsequently be encountered. Furthermore, after an encounter with a traumatic stressor, re-exposure to the stressor at a later date may influence the organism's neurochemical responsivity and hence its ability to deal with pathogenic stimuli. Likewise, the vulnerability of an organism to stress-related pathology may be influenced by a series of organismic variables (interindividual differences, age, social background, etc.).

Most stressors encountered by humans are of a chronic nature, at least when one considers rumination over the initial trauma to represent a stressor. Given the prevalence of stressful stimulation coupled with the chronicity of such stimulation, one might wonder why the incidence of stressor-related pathology is not far greater than it actually is. One possibility, in this respect, is that the organism has available adaptive processes that counteract the primary neurochemical alterations provoked by stressors. Among other things, the synthesis of brain amines increases, thus assuring adequate supplies of the neurotransmitters, and when stimulation of receptors eventually becomes excessive, receptor subsensitivity may ensue. It is conceivable that these adaptive alterations are fundamental in protecting the organism from pathology. In effect, the heightened neurochemical activity assures adequate supplies of the amine, at least over the short run, thereby maintaining the organism's ability to deal with environmental insults. According to such a formulation, chronic exposure to stressors will have pathological effects when the system is finally overly taxed, or among those individuals in whom the adaptive neurochemical systems are not adequate.

The proposition that we are entertaining is not a radical departure from an intuitive appreciation of the way in which the central and peripheral nervous systems operate, nor of the way in which the immunological mechanisms might interact with the nervous systems. Essentially, the assertion is simply being made that it may be inappropriate to consider alterations of one of these systems at the expense of considering the contribution of other systems. To be sure, if the final step in controlling neoplastic transformation, cell proliferation, and the occurrence of metastases involves immunological functioning, then it would be most appropriate to deal with such a system in attempts to achieve a positive therapeutic outcome. At the same time, it should be considered that if central and peripheral neurotransmitters contribute to immunological functioning, it would be appropriate to deal with these systems in order to achieve maximal benefits of therapy. Given the psychological repercussions descending from the knowledge that the individual is afflicted with cancer, coupled with the fact that the treatments for neoplastic disease may be stressful, the possibility exists that central neurochemical changes would reduce the potential benefits of the therapy. Accordingly, attempts to minimize stress-induced neurochemical alterations by pharmacological treatments, or to use stress management techniques (e.g., cognitive therapies) to minimize the cognitive components of the stressor, may ultimately enhance the effectiveness of traditional therapies.

ACKNOWLEDGMENTS

The research by our laboratory reported in this chapter was supported by Grants MT-6486 from the Medical Research Council of Canada and A9845 from the Natural Sciences and Engineering Research Council of Canada. The advice and help provided by Robert M. Zacharko, Jill Irwin, Wayne Bowers, Angela Corradini, and Christine Beauchamp are gratefully acknowledged.

REFERENCES

Ader, R. (Ed.). *Psychoneuroimmunology*. New York: Academic Press, 1981.
Ader, R., & Cohen, N. Behaviorally conditioned immunosuppression. *Psychosomatic Medicine*, 1975, *37*, 333–340.
Ader, R., & Cohen, N. Conditioned immunopharmacologic responses. In R. Ader (Ed.), *Psychoneuroimmunology*. New York: Academic Press, 1981.
Ader, R., & Cohen, N. Behaviorally conditioned immunosuppression and murine systemic lupus erythematosus. *Science*, 1982, *215*, 1534–1535.
Ader, R., Cohen, N., & Grota, L. J. Adrenal involvement in conditioned immunosuppression *International Journal of Immunopharmacology*, 1979, *1*, 141–145.
Ader, R., & Friedman, S. B. Differential early experiences and susceptibility to transplanted tumor in the rat. *Journal of Comparative and Physiological Psychology*, 1965, *59*, 361–364.
Ado, A., & Goldstein, M. M. The primary immune response in rabbits after lesion of the different zones in the medial hypothalamus. *Annals of Allergy*, 1973, *31*, 585–589.
Amkraut, A., & Solomon, G. F. Stress and murine sarcoma virus (Moloney)-induced tumors. *Cancer Research*, 1972, *32*, 1428–1433.
Andervont, E. B. Influence of environment on mammary cancer in mice. *Journal of the National Cancer Institute*, 1944, *4*, 579–581.
Anisman, H. Neurochemical changes elicited by stress. In H. Anisman & G. Bignami (Eds.), *Psychopharmacology of aversively motivated behavior*. New York: Plenum Press, 1978.
Anisman, H. Vulnerability to depression. In R. M. Post & J. C. Ballenger (Eds.), *Neurobiology of mood disorders*. Baltimore: Williams & Wilkins, 1983.

Anisman, H., Kokkinidis, L., & Sklar, L. S. Contribution of neurochemical change to stress-induced behavioral deficits. In S. J. Cooper (Ed.), *Theory in psychopharmacology.* London: Academic Press, 1981.

Anisman, H., Kokkinidis, L., & Sklar, L. S. Neurochemical consequences of stress: Contributions of adaptive processes. In S. Burchfield (Ed.), *Physiological and psychological interactions in response to stress.* New York: Hemisphere, 1983.

Anisman, H., Pizzino, A., & Sklar, L. S. Coping with stress, norepinephrine depletion and escape performance. *Brain Research,* 1980, *191,* 583–588.

Anisman, H., & Sklar, L. S. Catecholamine depletion in mice upon reexposure to stress: Mediation of the escape deficits produced by inescapable shock. *Journal of Comparative and Physiological Psychology,* 1979, *93,* 610–625.

Anisman, H., & Sklar, L. S. Social housing conditions influence escape deficits produced by uncontrollable stress: Assessment of the contribution of norepinephrine. *Behavioral and Neural Biology,* 1981, *32,* 406–427.

Anisman, H., & Zacharko, R. M. Depression: The predisposing influence of stress. *Behavioral and Brain Sciences,* 1982, *5,* 89–137.

Antelman, S. M., Eichler, A. J., Black, C. A., & Kocan, D. Interchangeability of stress and amphetamine in sensitization. *Science,* 1980, *207,* 329–331.

Bacon, C. L., Rennecker, R., & Cutler, M. A psychosomatic survey of cancer of the breast. *Psychosomatic Medicine,* 1952, *14,* 453–460.

Bahnson, C. B., & Bahnson, M. B. Denial and repression of primitive impulses and of disturbing emotions in patients with malignant neoplasms. In D. M. Kissen & L. L. LeShan (Eds.), *Psychosomatic aspects of neoplastic disease.* London: Pitman, 1964.

Baizman, E. R., Cox, B. M., Osman, O. H., & Goldstein, A. Experimental alterations of endorphin levels in rat's pituitary. *Neuroendocrinology,* 1979, *28,* 403–424.

Baker, D. G., & Jahn, A. The influence of chronic environment stress on radiation carcinogenesis. *Radiation Research,* 1976, *68,* 449–458.

Barta, A., & Yashpal, K. Regional redistribution of β-endorphin in the rat brain: The effect of stress. *Progress in Neuro-Psychopharmacology,* 1981, *5,* 595–598.

Bartrop, R. W., Lazarus, L., Luckhurst, E., Kiloh, L. G., & Penny, R. Depressed lymphocyte function after bereavement. *Lancet,* 1977, *1,* 834–836.

Belkin, M., & Hardy, W. G. Effect of reserpine and chlorpromazine on sarcoma. *Science,* 1957, *125,* 233–234.

Besedovsky, H. O., & Sorkin, E. Immunologic–neuroendocrine circuits: Physiological approaches. In R. Ader (Ed.), *Psychoneuroimmunology.* New York: Academic Press, 1981.

Bhattacharyya, A. K., & Pradhan, S. N. Effects of stress on DMBA-induced tumor growth, plasma corticosterone and brain biogenic amines in rats. *Research Communications in Chemical Pathology and Pharmacology,* 1979, *23,* 107–116.

Blanc, G., Herve, D., Simon, H., Lisoprawski, A., Glowinski, J., & Tassin, J. P. Response to stress of mesocortical–frontal dopaminergic neurons in rats after long-term isolation. *Nature,* 1980, *284,* 265–276.

Blaney, P. H. Physiological considerations in cancer. In N. Schneiderman & J. T. Tapp (Eds.), *Behavioral medicine: A multi-systems approach.* Hillsdale, N.J.: Erlbaum, 1983.

Bliss, E. L., Thatcher, W., & Ailion, J. Relationship of stress to brain serotonin and 5-hydroxyindoleacetic acid. *Journal of Psychiatric Research,* 1972, *9,* 71–80.

Bliznakov, E. G. Serotonin and its precursors as modulators of the immunological responsiveness in mice. *Journal of Medicine,* 1980, *11,* 81–105.

Bloom, B. L., Asher, S. J., & White, S. W. Marital disruption as a stressor: A review and analysis. *Psychological Bulletin,* 1978, *85,* 867–894.

Bourne, H. R., Lichtenstein, L. M., Melmon, K. L., Henney, C. S., Weinstein, Y. S., & Shearer, G. M. Modulation of inflammation and immunity by cyclic AMP. *Science,* 1974, *184,* 19–28.

Bovbjerg, D. H., Cohen, N., & Ader, R. Conditioned suppression of a cellular immune response. *Psychosomatic Medicine*, 1980, *42*, 73.

Burchfield, S. R., Woods, S. C., & Elich, S. E. Effects of cold stress on tumor growth. *Physiology and Behavior*, 1978, *21*, 537–540.

Burnet, F. M. The concept of immunological surveillance. *Progress in Experimental Tumor Research*, 1970, *13*, 1–27.

Cassens, G., Roffman, M., Kuruc, A., Orsulak, P. J., & Schildkraut, J. J. Alterations in brain norepinephrine metabolism induced by environmental stimuli previously paired with inescapable shock. *Science*, 1980, *209*, 1138–1140.

Cerottini, J. C., Nordin, A. A., & Brunner, K. T. Specific *in vitro* cytotoxicity of thymus derived lymphocytes sensitized to alloantigens. *Nature*, 1970, *228*, 1308–1309.

Chance, W. T., White, A. C., Krynock, G. M., & Rosecrans, J. A. Conditional fear-induced antinociception and decreased binding of [3H]N-leu-enkephalin to rat brain. *Brain Research*, 1978, *141*, 371–374.

Cherek, D. R., Lane, J. D., Freeman, M. E., & Smith, J. E. Receptor changes following shock avoidance. *Society for Neuroscience Abstracts*, 1980, *6*, 543.

Christie, M. J., Chesher, G. B., & Bird, K. D. The correlation between swim-stress induced antinociception and [3H]leu-enkephalin binding to brain homogenates in mice. *Pharmacology, Biochemistry and Behavior*, 1981, *15*, 853–857.

Cohen-Cole, S., Cogen, R., Stevens, A., Kirk, K., Gaitan, E., Hain, J., & Freeman, A. Psychosocial, endocrine, and immune factors in acute necrotizing ulcerative gingivitis ("trenchmouth"). *Psychosomatic Medicine*, 1981, *43*, 91. (Abstract)

Costa, E., Tagliomonti, A., Brunello, N., & Cheney, D. L. Effect of stress on the metabolism of acetylcholine in the cholinergic pathways of extrapyramidal and limbic systems. In E. Usdin, R. Kvetnansky, & I. J. Kopin (Eds.), *Catecholamines and stress: Recent advances*. New York: Elsevier, 1980.

Cotzias, G.C., & Tang, L. An adenylate cyclase of brain reflects propensity for breast cancer in mice. *Science*, 1977, *197*, 1094–1096.

Curzon, G., Joseph, M. H., & Knott, P. J. Effects of immobilization and food deprivation on rat brain tryptophan metabolism. *Journal of Neurochemistry*, 1972, *19*, 1967–1974.

Davis, D. E., & Read, C. P., Effect of behavior on development of resistance in trichionosis. *Proceedings of the Society of Experimental Biology and Medicine*, 1958, *99*, 269–272.

Dechambre, R. P. Psychosocial stress and cancer in mice. In K. Bammer & B. H. Newberry (Eds.), *Stress and cancer*. Toronto: Hogrefe, 1981.

Dechambre, R. P., & Gosse, C. Individual versus group gaping of mice with grafted tumors. *Cancer Research*, 1973, *33*, 140–144.

Depue, R. A., *The psychobiology of depressive disorders*. New York: Academic Press, 1979.

Derogatis, L. R., & Abeloff, M. D. Psychological aspects of management of primary and metastatic breast-cancer. In A. C. W. Montague, G. L., Stonesifer, & E. F. Lewinson (Eds.), *Breast cancer: Progress in clinical and biological research* (Vol. 12). New York: Alan R. Liss, 1977.

Derogatis, L. R., Abeloff, M. D., & Melisaratos, N. Psychological coping mechanisms and survival time in metastatic breast cancer. *Journal of the American Medical Association*, 1979, *242*, 1504–1508.

Devoino, L. V., Eremina, O. F. N., & Ilyutchenok, R. Y. The role of the hypothalamopituitary system in the mechanism of action of reserpine and 5-hydroxytryptophan on antibody production. *Neuropharmacology*, 1970, *9*, 67–72.

DeVries, G. H., Chance, W. T., Payne, W. R., & Rosecrans, J. A. Effect of autoanalgesia on CNS enkephalin receptors. *Pharmacology, Biochemistry and Behavior*, 1979, *11*, 741–744.

Dorian, B. J., Keystone, E., Garfinkel, P. E., & Brown, G. M. Immune mechanisms in acute psychological stress. *Psychosomatic Medicine*, 1981, *43*, 84. (Abstract)

Driscoll, J. S., Melnick, N. R., Quinn, F. R., Lomax, N., Davignon, J. P., Ing, R., Abbott, B. J., Congleton, G., & Dudeck, L. Psychotropic drugs as potential antitumor agents: A selective screening study. *Cancer Treatment Reports*, 1978, *62*, 45–73.

Dukor, P., Salvin, S. B., Dietrich, F. M., Gelzer, J., Hess, R., & Loustalot, P. Effect of reserpine on immune reactions and tumor growth. *European Journal of Cancer*, 1966, *2*, 253–261.

Ernster, V. L., Sacks, S. T., Selvin, S., & Petrakis, N. L. Cancer incidence by marital status: U.S. Third National Cancer Survey. *Journal of the National Cancer Institute*, 1979, *63*, 567–585.

Evans, N. J. R., Baldwin, J. A., & Gath, D. The incidence of cancer among in-patients with affective disorders. *British Journal of Psychiatry*, 1974, *124*, 518–525.

Fadda, F., Argiolas, A., Melis, M. R., Tissari, A. H., Onali, P. L., & Gessa, G. L. Stress-induced increase in 3,4-dihydroxyphenylacetic acid (DOPAC) levels in the cerebral cortex and in the nucleus accumbens: Reversal by diazepam. *Life Sciences*, 1978, *23*, 2219–2224.

Fekete, M. I. K., Szentendrei, T., Kanyicska, B., & Palkovits, M. Effects of anxiolytic drugs on the catecholamine and DOPAC (3,4-dihydroxyphenylacetic acid) levels in brain cortical areas and on coticosterone and prolactin secretion in rats subjected to stress. *Psychoneuroendocrinology*, 1981, *6*, 113–120.

Fidler, I. J. Tumor heterogeneity and the biology of cancer invasion and metastasis. *Cancer Research*, 1978, *38*, 2651–2660.

Fischer, C. L., Daniels, J. C., Levin, S. L., Kimzey, S. L., Cobb, E. K., & Ritzman, W. E. Effects of the spaceflight environment on man's immune system: II. Lymphocyte counts and reactivity. *Aerospace Medicine*, 1972, *43*, 1122–1125.

Fisher, B., & Fisher, E. R. Experimental studies of factors influencing hepatic metastases: II. Effect of partial hepatectomy. *Cancer*, 1959, *12*, 929–932.

Folch, H., & Waksman, B. H. The splenic suppressor cell: I. Activity of thymus-dependent adherent cells. Changes with age and stress. *Journal of Immunology*, 1974, *113*, 127–137.

Fox, B. H. Premorbid psychological factors as related to cancer incidence. *Journal of Behavioral Medicine*, 1978, *1*, 45–133.

Friedman, S. B., Ader, R., & Glasgow, L. A. Effects of psychological stress in adult mice inoculated with Coxsackie B virus. *Psychosomatic Medicine*, 1965, *27*, 361–368.

Gershben, L. L., Benuck, I., & Shurrager, P. S. Influence of stress on lesion growth and on survival of animals bearing parenteral and intracerebral leukemia L1210 and Walker tumors. *Oncology*, 1974, *30*, 429–435.

Gisler, R. H., Bussard, A. E., Mazie, J. C., & Hess, R. Hormonal regulation of the immune response: I. Induction of an immune response *in vitro* with lymphoid cells from mice exposed to acute systemic stress. *Cellular Immunology*, 1971, *2*, 634–645.

Gottlieb, L. S., Hazel, M., Broitman, S., & Zamcheck, N. Effects of chlorpromazine on transplantable mouse mastocytoma. *Federation Proceedings*, 1960, *19*, 1981. (Abstract)

Graham, S., & Snell, L. Social trauma as related to cancer of the breast. *British Journal of Cancer*, 1972, *25*, 721–734.

Graham, S., Snell, L., Graham, J. B., & Ford, L. Social trauma in the epidemiology of cancer of the cervix. *Journal of Chronic Diseases*, 1971, *24*, 711–725.

Greenberg, R. P., & Dattore, P. J. The relationship between dependency and the development of cancer. *Psychosomatic Medicine*, 1981, *43*, 35–43.

Greene, W. A. The psychosocial setting of the development of leukemia and lymphoma. *Annals of the New York Academy of Sciences*, 1966, *125*, 794–801.

Greene, W. A., Betts, R. F., Ochitill, H. N., Iker, N., & Douglas, R. Psychosocial factors and immunity: Preliminary report. *Psychosomatic Medicine*, 1978, *40*, 87. (Abstract)

Greer, S., & Morris, T. Psychological attributes of women who develop breast cancer: A controlled study. *Journal of Psychosomatic Research*, 1975, *19*, 147–153.

Hagnell, O. The premorbid personality of persons who develop cancer in a total population investigated in 1947 and 1957. *Annals of the New York Academy of Sciences*, 1966, *125*, 846–855.

Hall, N. R., & Goldstein, A. L. Neurotransmitters and the immune system. In R. Ader (Ed.), *Psychoneuroimmunology*. New York: Academic Press, 1981.

Hall, N. R., McClure, J. E., Hu, S. H., Tick, N. T., Seales, C. M., & Goldstein, A. L. Effects of chemical sympathectomy upon thymus dependent immune responses. *Society for Neuroscience Abstracts*, 1980, *26*, 4.

Hamilton, D. R. Immunosuppressive effects of predator induced stress in mice with acquired immunity to *Hymenolepis nana*. *Journal of Psychosomatic Research*, 1974, *18*, 143–153.

Harrower, M., Thomas, C. B., & Altman, A. Human figure drawings in a prospective study of six disorders: Hypertension, coronary heart disease, malignant tumor, suicide, mental illness, and emotional disturbance. *Journal of Nervous and Mental Disease*, 1975, *161*, 191–199.

Hattori, T., Hamai, Y., Ikeda, H., Harada, T., & Ikeda, T. Enhancing effect of thoracotomy on tumor growth in rats. *Gann*, 1978, *69*, 401–406.

Hattori, T., Hamai, Y., Ikeda, T., Takiyama, W., Hirai, T., & Miyoshi, Y. Inhibitory effects of immunopotentiators on the enhancement of lung metastases induced by operative stress in rats. *Gann*, 1982, *73*, 132–135.

Hattori, T., Hamai, Y., Takiyama, W., Hirai, T., & Ikeda, T. Enhancing effect of thoracotomy on tumor growth in rats with special reference to the duration and timing of the operation. *Gann*, 1980, *71*, 280–284.

Herberman, R. B., & Holden, H. T. Natural cell-mediated immunity. In G. Klein & S. Weinhouse (Eds.), *Advances in cancer research* (Vol. 27). New York: Academic Press, 1978.

Herberman, R. B., & Ortaldo, J. R. Natural killer cells: Their role in defense against disease. *Science*, 1981, *214*, 24–30.

Herman, J. P., Guillonneau, D., Dantzer, R., Scatton, B., Semerdjian-Rouquier, L., & LeMoal, M. Differential effects of inescapable footshocks and stimuli previously paired with inescapable footshocks on dopamine turnover in cortical and limbic areas of the rat. *Life Sciences*, 1982, *30*, 2207–2214.

Hingtgen, J. N., Smith, J. E., Shea, P. A., Aprison, M. H., & Gaff, T. M. Cholinergic changes during conditioned suppression in rats. *Science*, 1976, *193*, 332–334.

Holmes, T. H., & Rahe, R. H. The Social Readjustment Rating Scale. *Journal of Psychosomatic Medicine*, 1967, *11*, 213–218.

Horne, R. L., & Picard, R. S. Psychosocial risk factors for lung cancer. *Psychosomatic Medicine*, 1979, *41*, 503–514.

Irwin, J., Bowers, W., Zacharko, R. M., & Anisman, H. Stress-induced alterations of norepinephrine: Cross-stressor sensitization. *Society for Neuroscience Abstracts*, 1982, *8*, 359.

Jacobs, T. J., & Charles, E. Life events and the occurrence of cancer in children. *Psychosomatic Medicine*, 1980, *42*, 11–24.

Jamasbi, R. J., & Nettesheim, P. Non-immunological enhancement of tumor transplantability in x-irradiated host animals. *British Journal of Cancer*, 1977, *36*, 723–729.

Janakovic, B. D., & Isakovic, K. Neuro-endocrine correlates of immune response: I. Effects of brain lesions on antibody production, Arthus reactivity, and delayed hypersensitivity in the rat. *International Archives of Allergy and Applied Immunology*, 1973, *45*, 360–372.

Janakovic, B. D., Jovanova, K., & Markovic, B. M. Effect of hypothalamic stimulation on the immune reaction in the rat. *Periodicals of Biology*, 1979, *81*, 211–212.

Jensen, M. M., & Rasmussen, A. F. Stress and susceptibility to viral infection. I. Response of adrenals, liver, thymus, spleen and peripheral leukocyte counts to sound stress. *Journal of Immunology*, 1963, *90*, 17–20.

Johnsson, T., Lavender, J. F., Hultin, E., & Rasmussen, A. F. The influence of avoidance-learning stress on resistance to Coxsackie B virus in mice. *Journal of Immunology*, 1963, *91*, 569–575.

Johnsson, T., & Rasmussen, A. F. Emotional stress and susceptibility to poliomyelitis virus infection in mice. *Archives Gesamte Virusforschung*, 1965, *18*, 393–396.

Kalisnik, M., Vraspir-Porenta, O., Logonder-Mlinsek, M., Zorc, M., & Pajntar, M. Stress and Ehrlich ascites tumor in mouse. *Neoplasma*, 1979, *26*, 483–491.

Kanzawa, F., Hoshi, A., & Kuretani, K. Relationship between antitumor activity and chemical structure in psychotropic agents. *Gann*, 1970, *61*, 529–534.

Karczmar, A. G., Scudder, C. L., & Richardson, D. L. Interdisciplinary approach to the study of behavior in related mice types. In S. Ehrenpries & I. J. Kopin (Eds.), *Chemical approaches to brain function*. New York: Academic Press, 1973.

Kasahara, K., Tanaka, S., Ito, T., & Hamashima, Y. Suppression of the primary immune response by chemical sympathectomy. *Research Communications in Chemical Pathology and Pharmacology*, 1977, *16*, 687–694.

Keehn, R. J., Goldberg, I. D., & Beebe, G. W. Twenty-four year mortality follow-up of army veterans with disability separations for psychoneurosis in 1944. *Psychosomatic Medicine*, 1974, *36*, 27–46.

Keller, S. E., Stein, M., Camerino, M. S., Schleifer, S. J., & Sherman, J. Suppression of lymphocyte stimulation by anterior hypothalamic lesions in the guinea pig. *Cell Immunology*, 1980, *52*, 334–340.

Keller, S. E., Weiss, J. M., Schleifer, S. J., Miller, N. E., & Stein, M. Suppression of immunity by stress: Effect of a graded series of stressors on lymphocyte stimulation in the rat. *Science*, 1981, *213*, 1397–1400.

Kimzey, S. L. The effects of extended spaceflight on hematologic and immunologic systems. *Journal of the American Medical Women's Association*, 1975, *30*, 218–232.

Kissen, D. M. Lung cancer, inhalation and personality. In D. M. Kissen & L. L. LeShan (Eds.), *Psychosomatic Aspects of Neoplastic Disease*. London: Pitman, 1964.

Kissen, D. M. Possible contribution of the psychosomatic approach to prevention of lung cancer. *Medical Officer*, 1965, *114*, 343–345.

Kissen, D. M. Psychosocial factors, personality and prevention of lung cancer. *Medical Officer*, 1966, *116*, 135–138.

Kissen, D. M. Psychosocial factors, personality and lung cancer in men aged 55–64. *British Journal of Medical Psychology*, 1967, *40*, 29–43.

Kissen, D. M., Brown, R. I. F., & Kissen, M. A further report on personality and psychosocial factors in lung cancer. *Annals of the New York Academy of Sciences*, 1969, *164*, 535–545.

Kobayashi, R. M., Palkovits, M., Kizer, J. S., Jacobowitz, D. M., & Kopin, I. J. Selective alterations of catecholamines and tyrosine hydroxylase activity in the hypothalamus following acute and chronic stress. In E. Usdin, R. Kvetnansky, & I. J. Kopin (Eds.), *Catecholamines and stress*. Oxford: Pergamon Press, 1976.

Korf, J., Aghajanian, G. K., & Roth, R. H. Increased turnover of norepinephrine in the rat cerebral cortex during stress: Role of locus coeruleus. *Neuropharmacology*, 1973, *12*, 933–938.

Korneva, E. A., & Khai, L. M. Effect of destruction of hypothalamic areas on immunogenesis. *Federation Proceedings of the American Society of Experimental Biology*, 1964, *23*, 88–92.

Kvetnansky, R. Recent progress in catecholamines under stress. In E. Usdin, R. Kvetnansky, & I. J. Kopin (Eds.), *Catecholamines and stress: Recent advances*. New York: Elsevier, 1980.

Kvetnansky, R., Mitro, A., Palkovits, M., Brownstein, M., Torda, T., Vigas, M., & Mikulaj, L. Catecholamines in individual hypothalamic nuclei in stressed rats. In E. Usdin, R. Kvetnansky, & I. J. Kopin (Eds.), *Catecholamines and stress*. Oxford: Pergamon Press, 1976.

LaBarba, R. C., & White, J. L. Maternal deprivation and the response to Ehrlich carcinoma in Balb/c mice. *Psychosomatic Medicine*, 1971, *33*, 458–460.

Lacassagne, A., & Duplan, J. F. Le mécanisme de la cancerisation de la mamelle chez les souris, considéré d'après les résultats d'expérience au moyen de la reserpine. *Comptes Rendus Hebdomadaires des Séances de l'Académie des Sciences*, 1959, *249*, 810–812.

Lapin, V. Effects of reserpine on the incidence of 9,10 dimethyl-1,2-benzanthracene-induced tumors in pinealectomised and thymectomised rats. *Oncology*, 1978, *35*, 132–135.

Lavielle, S., Tassin, J. P., Thierry, A. M., Blanc, G., Herve, D., Barthelemy, C., & Glowinski, J. Blockade by benzodiazepines of the selective high increase in dopamine turnover induced by stress in mesocortical dopaminergic neurons of the rat. *Brain Research*, 1978, *168*, 585–594.

LeShan, L. L. Psychological states as factors in the development of malignant disease: A critical review. *Journal of the National Cancer Institute*, 1959, *22*, 1–18.

LeShan, L. L. An emotional life history pattern associated with neoplastic disease. *Annals of the New York Academy of Sciences*, 1966, *125*, 780–793.

Locke, S. E., Hurst, M. W., Heisel, J. S., Krause, L., & Williams, M. *The influence of stress and other psychosocial factors on human immunity*. Paper presented at the 36th Annual Meeting of the American Psychosomatic Society, Dallas, March 1979.

Locke, S. E., Hurst, M. W., Williams, M., & Heisel, J. S. *The influence of psychosocial factors on human cell-mediated immune function*. Paper presented at the Annual Meeting of the American Psychosomatic Society, Washington, 1978.

Lombard, H. L., & Potter, E. A. Epedemiological aspects of cancer of the cervix: Hereditary and environmental factors. *Cancer*, 1950, *3*, 960–968.

Lundy, J., Lovett, E. J., Wolinsky, S. M., & Conran, P. Immune impairment and metastatic tumor growth. *Cancer*, 1979, *43*, 945–951.

Maclean, D., & Reichlin, S. Neuroendocrinology and the immune response. In R. Ader (Ed.), *Psychoneuroimmunology*. New York: Academic Press, 1981.

Macris, N. T., Schiavi, R. C., Camerino, M. S., & Stein, M. Effects of hypothalamic lesions on immune processes in the guinea pig. *American Journal of Physiology*, 1970, *219*, 1205–1209.

Macris, N. T., Schiavi, R. C., Camerino, M. S., & Stein, M. Effect of hypothalamus on passive anaphylaxis in the guinea pig. *American Journal of Physiology*, 1972, *222*, 1054–1057.

Madden, J., Akil, H., Patrick, R. L., & Barchas, J. D. Stress-induced parallel changes in central opioid levels and pain responsiveness in the rat. *Nature*, 1977, *265*, 358–360.

Marsh, J. T., Miller, B. E., & Lamson, B. G. Effect of repeated brief stress on growth of Ehrlich carcinoma in the mouse. *Journal of the National Cancer Institute*, 1959, *22*, 961–977.

Maruyama, Y., & Johnson, E. A. Quantitative study of isologous tumor cell inactivation and effective cell fraction for the LSA mouse lymphoma. *Cancer*, 1969, *23*, 309–312.

Mastrovito, R. C., Deguire, K. S., Clarkin, J., Thaler, T., Lewis, J. L., & Cooper, E. Personality characteristics of women with gynecological cancer. *Cancer Detection and Prevention*, 1979, *2*, 281–287.

McEuen, D. D., Blair, P., Delbene, V. E., & Eurenius, K. Correlation between *Pseudomonas* burn wound infection and granulocyte antibacterial activity. *Infectious Immunology*, 1976, *13*, 1360–1362.

Melief, C. J. M., & Schwartz, R. S. Immunocompetence and malignancy. In F. F. Becker (Ed.), *Cancer: A comprehensive treatise* (Vol. 1). New York: Plenum, 1975.

Millan, M. J., Tsang, Y. F., Przewlocki, V., Hollt, V., & Herz, A. The influence of foot-shock stress upon brain, pituitary and spinal cord pools of immunoreactive dynorphin in rats. *Neuroscience Letters*, 1981, *24*, 75–79.

Modigh, K. Influence of social stress on brain catecholamine mechanisms. In E. Usdin, R. Kvetnansky, & I. J. Kopin (Eds.), *Catecholamines and stress*. Oxford: Pergamon Press, 1976.

Monjan, A. A. Psychosocial factors, stress, and immune processes. In R. Ader (Ed.), *Psychoneuroimmunology.* New York: Academic Press, 1981.

Monjan, A. A., & Collector, M. I. Stress-induced modulation of the immune response. *Science,* 1977, *196,* 307–308.

Monroe, S. M. Assessment of life events: Retrospective versus concurrent strategies. *Archives of General Psychiatry,* 1982, *39,* 606–610.

Morgan, W. W., Rudeen, P. K., & Pfeil, K. A. Effect of immobilization stress on serotonin content and turnover in regions of the rat. *Life Sciences,* 1975, *17,* 143–150.

Morrison, F. R., & Paffenberger, R. A. Epidemiological aspects of biobehavior in the etiology of cancer: A critical review. In S. M. Weiss, J. A. Herd, & B. H. Fox (Eds.), *Perspectives on behavioral medicine.* New York: Academic Press, 1981.

Munster, A. M., Eurenius, K., Mortenson, R. F., & Mason, A. D. Ability of splenic lymphocytes from injured rats to induce graft-versus-host reaction. *Transplantation,* 1972, *14,* 106–108.

Munster, A. M., Gale, G. R., & Hunt, H. H. Accelerated tumor growth following experimental burns. *Journal of Trauma,* 1977, *17,* 373–375.

Murphy, D. P. *Heredity in uterine cancer.* Cambridge, Mass.: Harvard University Press, 1952.

Muslin, H. L., Gyarfas, K., & Pieper, W. J. Separation experience and cancer of the breast. *Annals of the New York Academy of Sciences,* 1966, *125,* 802–806.

Newberry, B. H. Restraint induced inhibition of 7,12-dimethylbenz(a)anthracene-induced mammary tumors: Relation to stages of tumor development. *Journal of the National Cancer Institute,* 1978, *61,* 725–729.

Newberry, B. H. Stress and mammary cancer. In K. Bammer & B. H. Newberry (Eds.), *Stress and cancer.* Toronto: Hogrefe, 1981.

Newberry, B. H., Frankie, G., Beatty, P. A., Maloney, B. D., & Gilchrist, J. C. Shock stress and DMBA-induced mammary tumors. *Psychosomatic Medicine,* 1972, *34,* 295–303.

Newberry, B. H., Gildow, S., Wogan, J., & Reese, R. C. Inhibition of Huggins' tumors by forced restraint. *Psychosomatic Medicine,* 1976, *38,* 155–162.

Newton, G., Bly, C. G., & McCrary, C. Effects of early experience on the response to transplanted tumor. *Journal of Nervous and Mental Disease,* 1962, *134,* 522–527.

Nieburgs, H. E., Weiss, J., Navarette, M., Strax, P., Teirstein, A., Grillione, G., & Sedlecki, B. The role of stress in human and experimental oncogenesis. *Cancer Detection and Prevention,* 1979, *2,* 307–336.

Niemi, T., & Jaaskelainen, J. Cancer morbidity in depressive persons. *Journal of Psychosomatic Research,* 1978, *22,* 117–120.

Nomura, S., Watanabe, M., Ukei, N., & Nakazawa, T. Stress and B-adrenergic receptor binding in the rat's brain. *Brain Research,* 1981, *224,* 199–203.

Palkovits, M., Brownstein, M., Kizer, J. S., Saavedra, J. M., & Kopin, I. J. Effects of stress on serotonin and tryptophan hydroxylase activity of brain nuclei. In E. Usdin, R. Kvetnansky, & I. J. Kopin (Eds.), *Catecholamines and stress.* Oxford: Pergamon Press, 1976.

Palmblad, J. Stress and immunologic competence: Studies in man. In R. Ader (Ed.), *Psychoneuroimmunology.* New York: Academic Press, 1981.

Palmblad, J., Cantell, K., Strander, H., Froberg, J., Karlsson, C. G., Levi, L., Granstrom, M., & Unger, P. Stressor exposure and immunological response in man: Interferon-producing capacity and phagocytosis. *Journal of Psychosomatic Research,* 1976, *20,* 193–199.

Palmblad, J., Petrini, B., Wasserman, J., & Akerstedt, T. Lymphocyte and granulocyte reactions during sleep deprivation. *Psychosomatic Medicine,* 1979, *41,* 273–278.

Peller, S. *Cancer in man.* New York: International Universities Press, 1952.

Peters, L. J. Enhancement of syngeneic murine tumor transplantation by whole body irradiation—A nonimmunologic phenomenon. *British Journal of Cancer,* 1975, *31,* 293–300.

Peters, L. J., & Kelly, H. The influence of stress and stress hormones on the transplantability of a non-immunogenic syngeneic murine tumor. *Cancer*, 1977, *39*, 1482–1488.

Petty, F., & Sherman, A. A neurochemical differentiation between exposure to stress and the development of learned helplessness. *Drug Development Research*, 1982, *2*, 43–45.

Pradhan, S. N., & Ray, P. Effects of stress on growth of transplanted and 7,12-dimethyl-benz(α)anthracene-induced tumors and their modification by psychotropic drugs. *Journal of the National Cancer Institute*, 1974, *53*, 1241–1245.

Prehn, R. T. Immunologic surveillance: Pro and con. In F. H. Bach & R. A. Good (Eds.), *Clinical immunobiology* (Vol. 2). New York: Academic Press, 1974.

Przewlocki, R., Millan, M., Gramsch, C., Millan, M. H., & Herz, A. The influence of selective adeno- and neurointermedio-hypophysectomy upon plasma and brain levels of β-endorphin and their response to stress in rats. *Brain Research*, 1982, *242*, 107–117.

Quadri, S. K., Kledzik, G. S., & Meites, J. Effects of L-dopa and methyldopa on growth of mammary cancers in rats. *Proceedings of the Society for Experimental Biology and Medicine*, 1973, *142*, 759–761.

Rabkin, J. G., & Struening, E. L. Life events, stress and illness. *Science*, 1976, *195*, 1013–1020.

Rasmussen, A. F., Spencer, E. S., & Marsh, J. T. Increased susceptibility to herpes simplex in mice subjected to avoidance-learning stress or restraint. *Proceedings of the Society for Experimental Biology and Medicine*, 1957, *96*, 183–184.

Rasmussen, A. F., Spencer, E. S., & Marsh, J. T. Decrease in susceptibility of mice to passive anaphylaxis following avoidance-learning stress. *Proceedings of the Society for Experimental Biology and Medicine*, 1959, *100*, 878–879.

Ray, P., & Pradhan, S. N. Growth of transplanted and induced tumors in rats under a schedule of punished behavior. *Journal of the National Cancer Institute*, 1974, *52*, 575–577.

Riley, V. Psychoneuroendocrine influences on immunocompetence and neoplasia, *Science*, 1981, *212*, 1100–1109.

Riley, V., Fitzmaurice, M. A., & Spackman, D. H. Psychoneuroimmunologic factors in neoplasia: Studies in animals. In R. Ader (Ed.), *Psychoneuroimmunology*. New York: Academic Press, 1981.

Riley, V., & Spackman, D. H. Cage crowding stress: Absence of effect on melanoma within protective facilities. *Proceedings of the American Association of Cancer Research*, 1977, *18*, 173.

Riley, V., Spackman, D., McClanahan, H., & Santisteban, G. A. The role of stress in malignancy. *Cancer Detection and Prevention*, 1979, *2*, 235–255.

Ritter, S., & Pelzer, N. L. Magnitude of stress-induced norepinephrine depletion varies with age. *Brain Research*, 1978, *152*, 1701–1775.

Rogentine, G. N., van Kammen, D. P., Fox, B. H., Docherty, J. P., Rosenblatt, J. E., Boyd, S. C., & Bunney, W. E. Psychological factors in the prognosis of malignant melanoma: A prospective study. *Psychosomatic Medicine*, 1979, *41*, 647–655.

Rossier, J., French, E., Rivier, C., Ling, N., Guillemin, R., & Bloom, F. Foot shock induced stress increases β-endorphin in rat blood but not brain. *Nature*, 1977, *270*, 618–619.

Rossier, J., Guillemin, R., & Bloom, F. Foot-shock induced stress decreases leu-enkephalin immunoreactivity in rat hypothalamus. *European Journal of Pharmacology*, 1978, *48*, 465–466.

Roth, K. A., Mefford, I. M., & Barchas, J. D. Epinephrine, norepinephrine, dopamine and serotonin: Differential effects of acute and chronic stress on regional brain amines. *Brain Research*, 1982, *239*, 417–424.

Saavedra, J. M. Changes in dopamine, noradrenaline and adrenaline in specific septal and preoptic nuclei after acute immobilization stress. *Neuroendocrinology*, 1982, *35*, 396–401.

Saba, T. M., & Antikatzides, T. G. Decreased resistance to intravenous tumor cell challenge during reticuloendothelial depression following surgery. *British Journal of Cancer*, 1976, *34*, 381–389.

Sarkar, D. K., Gottschall, P. E., & Meites, J. Damage to hypothalamic dopaminergic neurons is associated with development of prolactin-secreting pituitary tumors. *Science*, 1982, *218*, 684–686.

Schleifer, S. J., Keller, S. E., McKegney, F. P., & Stein, M. *Bereavement and lymphocyte function*. Paper presented at the annual meeting of the American Psychiatric Association, San Francisco, 1980.

Schiavi, R. C., Macris, N. T., Camerino, M. S., & Stein, M. Effect of hypothalamic lesions on immediate hypersensitivity. *American Journal of Physiology*, 1975, *228*, 596–601.

Schmale, A. H., Jr., & Iker, H. P. The effect of hopelessness in the development of cancer: I. The prediction of uterine cancer in women with atypical cytology. *Psychosomatic Medicine*, 1964, *26*, 634–635.

Schmale, A. H., Jr., & Iker, H. P. Psychological setting of uterine–cervical cancer. *Annals of the New York Academy of Sciences*, 1966, *125*, 807–813.

Schmidt, D. E., Cooper, D. O, & Barrett, R. J. Strain specific alterations in hippocampal cholinergic function following acute footshock. *Pharmacology, Biochemistry and Behavior*, 1980, *12*, 277–280.

Shavit, Y., Lewis, J. W., Terman, G. W., Gale, R. P., & Liebeskind, J. C. Opioid peptides may mediate the immunosuppressive effect of stress. *Society for Neuroscience Abstracts*, 1982, *8*, 71.

Shekelle, R. B., Raynor, W. J., Ostfeld, A. M., Garron, D. C., Bieliauskas, L. A., Liu, S. C., Maliza, C., & Paul, O. Psychological depression and 17-year risk of death from cancer. *Psychosomatic Medicine*, 1981, *43*, 117–125.

Sklar, L. S., & Anisman, H. Stress and coping factors influence tumor growth. *Science*, 1979, *205*, 513–515.

Sklar, L. S., & Anisman, H. Social stress influences tumor growth. *Psychosomatic Medicine*, 1980, *42*, 347–365.

Sklar, L. S., & Anisman, H. Contributions of stress and coping to cancer development and growth. In K. Bammer & B. H. Newberry (Eds.), *Stress and cancer*. Toronto: Hogrefe, 1981. (a)

Sklar, L. S., & Anisman, H. Stress and cancer. *Psychological Bulletin*, 1981, *89*, 369–406. (b)

Sklar, L. S., Bruto, V., & Anisman, H. Adaptation to the tumor enhancing effects of stress. *Psychosomatic Medicine*, 1981, *43*, 331–342.

Smith, E. M., Meyer, W. J., & Blalock, J. E. Virus-induced corticosterone in hypophysectomized mice: A possible lymphoid adrenal axis. *Science*, 1982, *218*, 1311–1312.

Soave, O. A. Reactivation of rabies virus in guinea pigs to the stress of crowding. *American Journal of Veterinary Research*, 1964, *25*, 268–269.

Spector, N. H., & Korneva, E. A. Neurophysiology, immunophysiology and neuroimmunomodulation. In R. Ader (Ed.), *Psychoneuroimmunology*. New York: Academic Press, 1981.

Stavraky, K. M., Buck, C. W., Lott, S. S., & Wanklin, J. M. Psychological factors in the outcome of human cancer. *Journal of Psychosomatic Research*, 1968, *12*, 251–259.

Stein, M., Schleifer, S. J., & Keller, S. E. Hypothalamic influences on immune responses. In R. Ader (Ed.), *Psychoneuroimmunology*. New York: Academic Press, 1981.

Stolk, J. M., Conner, R. L., Levine, S., & Barchas, J. D. Brain norepinephrine metabolism and shock-induced fighting behavior in rats: Differential effects of shock and fighting on the neurochemical response to a common footshock stimulus. *Journal of Pharmacology and Experimental Therapeutics*, 1973, *190*, 193–209.

Stone, E. A. Stress and catecholamines. In A. J. Friedhoff (Ed.), *Catecholamines and behavior* (Vol. 2). New York: Plenum Press, 1975.

Stone, E. A. Effect of stress on norepinephrine-stimulated accumulation of cyclic AMP in rat brain slices. *Pharmacology, Biochemistry and Behavior*, 1978, *8*, 583–591.

Stone, E. A. Reduction by stress of norepinephrine-stimulated accumulation of cyclic AMP in the rat cerebral cortex. *Journal of Neurochemistry*, 1979, *32*, 1335–1337. (a)

Stone, E. A. Subsensitivity to norepinephrine as a link between adaptation to stress and antidepressant therapy: An hypothesis. *Research Communications in Psychology and Psychiatric Behavior*, 1979, *4*, 241–255. (b)

Stone, E. A., & Platt, J. E. Brain adrenergic receptors and resistance to stress. *Brain Research*, 1982, *237*, 405–414.

Stutman, O. Immunodepression and malignancy. *Advances in Cancer Research*, 1975, *22*, 261–422.

Tang, L. C., & Cotzias, G. C. Quantitative correlation of dopamine-dependent adenylate cyclase with responses to levodopa in various mice. *Proceedings of the National Academy of Sciences USA*, 1977, *74*, 1242–1244.

Tang, L. C., Cotzias, G. C., & Dunn, L. Changing the action of neuroactive drugs by changing protein synthesis. *Proceedings of the National Academy of Sciences USA*, 1974, *71*, 3350–3354.

Teodoru, C. V., & Schwartzman, G. Endocrine factors in pathogenesis of experimental poliomyelitis in hamsters: Role of inoculating and environmental stress. *Proceedings of the Society of Experimental Biology and Medicine*, 1956, *91*, 181–187.

Thierry, A. M. Effects of stress on the metabolism of serotonin and norepinephrine in the central nervous system of the rat. In S. Nemeth (Ed.) *Hormones, metabolism and stress: Recent progress and perspectives*. Bratislava, Czechoslovakia: Slovak Academy of Sciences, 1973.

Thierry, A. M., Blanc, G., & Glowinski, J. Effect of stress on the disposition of catecholamines localized in various intraneuronal storage forms in the brainstem of rats. *Journal of Neurochemistry*, 1971, *18*, 449–461.

Thierry, A. M., Tassin, J. P., Blanc, G., & Glowinski, J. Selective activation of the mesocortical DA system by stress. *Nature*, 1976, *263*, 242–244.

Thomas, C. B. Precursors of premature disease and death: The predictive potential of habits and family attitudes. *Annals of Internal Medicine*, 1976, *85*, 653–658.

Thomas, C. B., & Duszynski, K. R. Closeness to parents and the family constellation in a prospective study of five disease states: Suicide, mental illness, malignant tumor, hypertension and coronary heart disease. *Johns Hopkins Medical Journal*, 1974, *134*, 251–270.

Thomas, C. B., & Greenstreet, R. L. Psychobiological characteristics in youth as predictors of five disease states: Suicide, mental illness, hypertension, coronary heart disease and tumor. *Johns Hopkins Medical Journal*, 1973, *132*, 16–43.

Thrasher, S. G., Bernardis, L. L., & Cohen, S. The immune response in hypothalamic lesioned and hypophyectomized rats. *International Archives of Allergy and Applied Immunology*, 1971, *41*, 813–820.

Toge, T., Hirai, T., Takiyama, W., & Hattori, T. Effects of surgical stress on natural killer cell activity, proliferative response of spleen cells, and cytostatic activity of lung macrophages in rats. *Gann*, 1981, *72*, 790–794.

Treadwell, P. E., Wistar, R., Rasmussen, A. F., & Marsh, J. T. The effect of acute stress on the susceptibility of mice to passive anaphylaxis. *Federation Proceedings of the American Society of Experimental Biology*, 1959, *18*, 602.

Truhaut, R., & Dechambre, R. P. Modalités de l'induction chez la souris de tumeurs pulmonaires par le benzo(α)pyrène: Influence de la dose d'hydrocarbure aromatique et de facteurs écologiques. *Comptes Rendus de l'Académie des Sciences de Paris*, 1972, *18*, 426–435.

Tsuang, M. T., Woolson, R. F., & Fleming, J. A. Premature deaths in schizophrenia and affective disorders. *Archives of General Psychiatry*, 1980, *37*, 979–983.

Van den Brenk, H. A. S., Stone, M. G., Kelly, H., & Sharpington, C. Lowering of innate resistance of the lungs to the growth of blood-borne cancer cells in states of topical and systemic stress. *British Journal of Cancer*, 1976, *33*, 60–78.

Van Woert, M. H., & Palmer, S. H. Inhibition of the growth of mouse melanoma by chlorpromazine. *Cancer Research*, 1969, *29*, 1952–1955.

Visintainer, M. A., Volpicelli, J. R., & Seligman, M. E. P. Tumor rejection in rats after inescapable or escapable shock. *Science*, 1982, *216*, 437–439.

Vuolteenaho, O., Leppaluoto, J., & Mannisto, P. Effect of stress and dexamethasone on immunoreactive β-endorphin levels in rat hypothalamus and pineal. *Acta Physiologica Scandinavica*, 1982, *114*, 537–541.

Weiss, J. M., Glazer, H. I., & Pohorecky, L. A. Coping behavior and neurochemical changes: An alternative explanation for the original "learned helplessness" experiments. In G. Serban & A. Kling (Eds.), *Animal models in human psychobiology*. New York: Plenum, 1976.

Weiss, J. M., Goodman, P. A., Losito, B. G., Corrigan, S., Charry, J. M., & Bailey, W. H. Behavioral depression produced by an uncontrollable stressor: Relationship to norepinephrine, dopamine and serotonin levels in various regions of rat brain. *Brain Research Reviews*, 1981, *3*, 161–191.

Welch, B. L., & Welch, A. S. Control of brain catecholamines and serotonin during acute stress and after *d*-amphetamine by natural inhibition of monoamine oxidase: An hypothesis. In E. Costa & S. Garattini (Eds.), *Amphetamines and related compounds*. New York: Raven Press, 1970.

Welsch, C. W., & Meites, J. Effects of reserpine on development of 7,12-dimethylbenzanthracene-induced mammary tumors in female rats. *Experientia*, 1970, *26*, 1133–1134.

Wheeler, J. I., & Caldwell, B. M. Psychological evaluation of women with cancer of the breast and cancer of the cervix. *Psychosomatic Medicine*, 1955, *17*, 256–268.

Wick, M. M. L-Dopa methyl ester as a new antitumor agent. *Nature*, 1977, *269*, 512–513.

Wick, M. M. L-Dopa methyl ester: Prolongation of survival of neuroblastoma-bearing mice after treatment. *Science*, 1978, *199*, 775–776.

Wick, M. M. Levodopa and dopamine analogs: Melanin precursors as antitumor agents in experimental human and murine leukemia. *Cancer Treatment Reports*, 1979, *63*, 991–997.

Wimer, R. E., Norman, R., & Eleftheriou, E. Serotonin levels in hippocampus: Striking variations associated with mouse strain and treatment. *Brain Research*, 1973, *63*, 397–401.

Zajaczkowska, M. N. Acetylcholine content in the central and peripheral nervous system and its synthesis in the rat brain during stress and post-stress exhaustion. *Acta Physiologica Polska*, 1975, *26*, 493–497.

Zimel, H., Zimel, A., Petrescu, R., Ghinea, E., & Tasca, C. Influence of stress and endocrine imbalance on the experimental metastasis. *Neoplasma*, 1977, *24*, 151–159.

21

Discussion

Growing Pains in Psychobiological Research

JON D. LEVINE
NEWTON C. GORDON

Research in the area of mechanisms in psychobiology has been plagued by inadequate operational definitions, as well as by only limited attempts at correlation with clinical disease. The chapters by Grevert and Goldstein and by Anisman and Sklar explore these two areas in detail. Since a general overview providing a complementary perspective might be helpful, we restrict our comments to some of the broader issues relating to operational definitions and to animal models of clinical disease in psychobiological research.

Derived from the Latin "to please," the term "placebo" acquired a medical meaning almost two centuries ago, at a time when there was little or no scientific basis to clinical practice. Over the years, medical use of the placebo has accrued a large number of negative connotations. A physician who administers a placebo may be considered unethical, and the patient who responds to it may be regarded as a malingerer with no real disease. In contemporary research, the placebo functions as an experimental control against which "active" therapies must be compared. Modern scientific method and governmental regulatory agencies both require that a placebo be administered as a control in the evaluation of new therapeutic modalities.

It is necessary to develop an operational definition of the placebo effect in order to study its physiological mechanisms and to develop its therapeutic role. Since an operational definition must pertain to the variable being

Jon D. Levine. Section of Rheumatology and Clinical Immunology, and Division of Clinical Pharmacology and Experimental Therapeutics, Department of Medicine, University of California School of Medicine, San Francisco, California; Division of Oral and Maxillofacial Surgery, Department of Stomatology, University of California School of Dentistry, San Francisco, California.

Newton C. Gordon. Division of Oral and Maxillofacial Surgery, Department of Stomatology, University of California School of Dentistry, San Francisco, California.

studied (i.e., a placebo for pain may be quite different from a placebo for high blood pressure), this discussion focuses on placebo analgesia. It is probably the most common and well-recognized use of the placebo in clinical practice, as well as the only one for which we have data suggesting the physiological mechanism mediating its action.

Operationally, a placebo for pain is an intervention that has no known action on the underlying noxious pathological process, does not inhibit pain transmission, and does not affect a neural pain modulation circuit such as the endogenous opioid-mediated analgesia system. A placebo effect is a consistent change following placebo administration that is not predicted by the "natural history" of the condition being treated. It has been assumed that placebo effects are produced by the "psychological" interaction between the physician and the patient, for lack of a physiological explanation. However, such a narrow construct ignores the fact that there is a group of physiologically active placebos that can markedly increase the potency of the physician–patient interaction without having a direct physiological effect on the underlying pathology, and without inhibiting pain transmission or directly activating pain modulation circuits. Therapeutic agents having physiological effects that do not act directly via one of these mechanisms, but by other means (such as gustatory stimulation or gastrointestinal irritation), exemplify such therapies. Placebos therefore can be divided into two physiological categories: "inactive" and "active." An "inactive" placebo is a therapeutic intervention that has no known physiological action. An "active" placebo, for pain, is one that induces some physiological or pharmacological action—that serves as a potent physiological stimulus for analgesia—while its direct action involves no inhibition of pain transmission pathways or activation of pain modulation circuits.

That the mind is derived from activity in the brain implies that there exists a physiological basis for placebos. If placebos function by activating physiological circuits that function to re-establish normality or homeostatic balance, one might expect that the variable controlled (in this case, pain) would itself be an important cue to activate such a circuit. If this were true, then what we refer to as an "active" placebo might indirectly modulate this variable and be more potent than an inactive placebo. Such may be the mode of action of the analgesia produced by low-dose naloxone and the numerous counterirritant-type therapies (acupuncture, transcutaneous electrical nerve stimulation, tiger balm, mustard plaster, etc.). The demonstration of an endogenous analgesia system also suggests the possibility that some forms of placebo could inhibit the functioning of this system and exacerbate pain. The existence of such negative placebos is an additional variable that needs to be controlled for in scientific studies of the placebo effect.

Considerably more difficult to approach is the question of what constitutes the natural history against which to compare a placebo treatment. Does giving no treatment produce a natural history group? Since the expectations of both investigator and subject are thought to influence the response obtained, a no-treatment group alone—to whom care providers might communicate the expectation of no improvement—probably does not constitute an adequate "natural history" group. To get around this problem, investigators sometimes attempt to preserve the positive expectations of those attending the patient by administering a "hidden placebo" (i.e., the blind administration of an inert substance out of the sight of the patient via an indwelling intravenous line), so that neither patient nor physician knows whether treatment is being given. However, unless carefully designed, this approach may cause the opposite problem: The experimenter may communicate implicitly to the patient an expectation that improvement should occur. Similarly, we have seen large differences in the "natural history" of postoperative pain, depending on whether patients were managed by experienced postoperative recovery room nurses or by doctoral candidates in the School of Nursing involved in unrelated research of their own. Thus, use of a "no-treatment" group, by itself, may not provide an adequate baseline against which to evaluate placebo effects. Another method of demonstrating a placebo effect is based on the premise that there are placebo "responders." If some patients respond to placebo and others do not, the reported pain intensities of patient populations whose pain has been described by a unimodal distribution should become bimodal after placebo administration while staying unimodal in untreated groups. Such a bimodal distribution occurs after placebo administration to patients with postoperative pain. However, this approach requires one to assume that the natural history, over the same period of time, will not be bimodal.

The definition of the placebo is appropriately a definition of exclusion; that is, the placebo effect is all those actions of a therapeutic intervention—physiologically inactive or active—that are not specific effects on the pathophysiology of that condition. This definition appropriately returns to active therapies the requirement of proof that an observed response is produced by that treatment and is not a placebo effect.

Anisman and Sklar point out the numerous circuits known to integrate neural function with non-neural physiological systems. The interaction between the nervous system and the immune system is one such area that is of current interest. Like the nervous system, the immune system functions to distinguish self fron nonself; it maintains the integrity of the self as separate and individual, while allowing homeostatic balance within the self. Among many other known functions, surveillance against the establishment of malignant growth is thought to be a domain of the immune system, and is probably the least understood of its functions. This function is so much more difficult to study because our understanding of the processes of malignant transformation and metastatic spread and of the mechanism of action of chemotherapeutic agents remains inadequate. Investigating the neural control of this phenomenon adds a third tier of complexity.

It is no longer possible to maintain—as many immunologists might wish—that the immune system is an entity unto itself, not integrated with other physiological organ systems. On the clinical front, recognition that psychological factors are associated with some diseases accompanied or even preceded the understanding of other pathophysiological factors of the disease. Thus, diseases such as rheumatoid arthritis, inflammatory bowel disease, and thyrotoxicosis are now thought to involve immune mechanisms, but are, classically, psychosomatic illnesses. The relationship of stress to ulcers and asthma is also well known. The list of immunological diseases whose onset or clinical course is thought to be related to stresses in the patient's life includes diabetes, multiple sclerosis, malignancies, and numerous infections.

Studies of the interaction between the nervous system and the immune system have followed three main avenues of investigation: (1) the effect of noxious stressors on disease states and immune function, (2) the effect of lesions or stimulation of the nervous system on immune function, and (3) the effect of behavioral conditioning paradigms on immune function. In general, these studies either have produced conflicting results or have shown consistent but only small effects of the nervous system on immune functions. This small magnitude of effect might have occurred either because the nervous system really does influence the immune system only slightly, or because we have not been posing the correct questions. In light of the overwhelming, though mostly anecdotal, clinical literature supporting a much larger influence, it is reasonable to assume that more appropriate research protocols would demonstrate a larger effect.

Our inability to discover the locus of control at which the nervous system influences immune function is not due to a lack of possible mechanisms or circuits. It is known that the nervous system directly innervates organs of immune function; that the cells of the immune system have receptors for neural humors, and vice versa; and that neuroendocrine circuits can potently affect immune function. Both the thymus and the spleen receive neural innervation, and termination of neurons on immunocytes in immune organs has been reported. Similarly, neurectomy has been shown to produce atrophy of these organs and alteration in immune function. The number of neural humors for which receptors have been identified on immunocytes is growing rapidly, and some are found only on subsets of immunocytes. Conversely, receptors for immunoglobulins have been demonstrated on pituocytes, and vasoactive amines function both as mediators of inflammation and as neurotransmitters, providing an additional mechanism by which the immune system may selectively activate neural circuits. Finally, glucocorticoids, a class of potently immunosuppressive hormones, are under the control of the hypothalamic–putuitary–adrenal axis; and growth and thyroid hormones, which are also at least partly under neural control, may produce immunoenhancing effects.

Rather than a lack of mechanisms and methods of searching for new mechanisms, it appears to be our incomplete understanding of the pathophysiology of diseases that hinders our efforts to develop the field of neuroimmunology. In no area of medical research is this more apparent than in the area of oncology. Although the inciting agent has been discovered for a limited number of malignancies, it remains unknown for most tumors. Even less is known about the mechanism of unregulated growth, and still less about the mechanism by which tumors invade locally and metastasize to distant sites. It is this lack of pathophysiological mechanisms that leaves us poorly equipped to study the role of the nervous system in the pathogenesis of malignancy. The difficulties posed by the study of the neuroimmunology of malignancy may represent an extreme example. However, the opportunity to apply knowledge gained from studies of disease mechanisms or from "experiments of nature" has been surprisingly unexploited.

Psychobiology has undergone many growing pains in its infancy and childhood. This period of its development may now be subsiding, giving rise to a more mature period when the wide diversity of available scientific information will be used more systematically, so that truly rigorous physiological insights into what has been termed the "mind–body" problem will be made. The contributions to this endeavor made here by Grevert and Goldstein and by Anisman and Sklar may foreshadow the end of these growing pains.

PLACEBO IN CLINICAL TRIALS AND CLINICAL PRACTICE

22

Truth-Telling and Paternalism in the Clinic: Philosophical Reflections on the Use of Placebos in Medical Practice

MARY CRENSHAW RAWLINSON

Every practitioner must find himself occasionally in circumstances of very delicate embarrassment, with respect to the contending obligations of veracity and professional duty: And when such trials occur, it will behoove him to act on fixed principles of rectitude, derived from previous information, and serious reflection—PERCIVAL, Medical Ethics (1803/1975)

In recent decades the long-established therapeutic use of placebos in medical practice has come under increasingly vociferous attack by ethicists of all persuasions, utilitarians and deontologists alike. These criticisms of placebo therapy are generally based upon the assumption that the use of placebos necessarily involves some degree of deception. In fact, this critical attitude toward placebos reflects a broader challenge to the traditional hierarchy of values governing medical practice. For the most part in the history of medicine, beneficence has far outweighed any other duty, including that of veracity. The relation between doctor and patient has typically been defined by physicians as one of benevolent paternalism, and few writers in the history of medicine have denied that the physician's duty to benefit and guard the patient may sometimes require that he or she deceive the patient or override the patient's expressed wishes.

Contemporary ethical theories, however, deriving largely from Kant or Mill, tend to accord a respect for personal autonomy first place in any hierarchy of duties. Thus, the traditional benevolent paternalism of the medical practitioner has come to be viewed as an offense against the patient's fundamental and indefeasible right of self-determination. The principle of beneficence, the age-old foundation of the medical relationship, has given way to the principle of informed consent (Beauchamp & Childress, 1983; Veatch, 1972, 1982).

Mary Crenshaw Rawlinson. Department of Philosophy, State University of New York at Stony Brook, Stony Brook, New York.

Any discussion of the ethical dimensions of the therapeutic use of placebos in medical practice, therefore, must be informed by an adequate analysis of the nature and foundation of the doctor–patient relationship itself. This chapter constitutes in part a defense of the principle of beneficence as a foundation for medical practice. I argue that one of the essential effects of illness is precisely an undermining of the patient's autonomy, and that it ought always to be the physician's first aim to restore this loss. I show, however, that the achievement of this global aim may require in the interim some degree of benevolent paternalism.

A second aspect of modern medicine that differentiates it from that of former eras is its skepticism regarding the influence of symbolic factors in therapeutic practice. This difference, too, is relevant to any consideration of the ethics of placebo therapy. Contemporary medical science aims to define illness and treatment in strictly material terms, and it conceptualizes the object of its practice more as a set of organ systems, a functioning physiology, than as an embodied person. It is not surprising, then, that contemporary medicine has given little attention to the impact of illness on the form and structure of the patient's experience—the way it alters his or her experience of time or relationships with others, for example—or to therapies that are efficacious, though pharmacologically inert with respect to a given condition. In this climate, placebo therapy has been labeled a form of charlatanism or quackery, an unscientific procedure, and, therefore, an irresponsible medical practice (Preston, 1982). This challenge to the validity of placebo therapy and to the significance of the symbolic in medicine generally indicates that not only the moral foundations of the doctor–patient relationship, but the very concepts of illness and treatment, are at issue in any discussion of the ethics of placebo.

In order to situate my discussion of the ethics of placebo therapy properly, I begin with a brief history of paternalism and benevolent deception in medical practice. Secondly, I show how a failure to appreciate the real therapeutic effects of placebos has perpetuated certain misconceptions and prejudices regarding their use, especially the assumption that deception is necessary to their successful employment. Finally, granting that deception may be required in specific cases, I consider both formalist and consequentialist arguments against the use of placebos, in order to demonstrate that there are cases in which the duty of beneficence outweighs that of truthfulness so as to justify the benevolent deception of placebo therapy.

PATERNALISM AND BENEVOLENT DECEPTION IN THE HISTORY OF MEDICINE

The administration of placebos and the practice upon the patient of various forms of benevolent deception constitute a well-established tradition in the history of medicine. Physicians from Hippocrates to Oliver Wendell Holmes have not only recognized the healing power of certain symbolic elements in the relationship of doctor to patient, such as the mere naming of the disease, the act of prescription itself, or the patient's faith in the physician, but have also vigorously asserted the responsibility of the physician to protect the patient from knowledge that may be harmful to him or her and to practice such deception as may be essential to a cure.

Throughout the Hippocratic corpus, reticence, reserve, and brevity of speech were repeatedly proposed as cardinal virtues of the physician. Nowhere in the corpus do we find any recognition of truthfulness as a duty that a physician may owe to a patient; rather, practitioners were enjoined to perform their art

> calmly and adroitly, concealing most things from the patient while ... attending him. Give encouragement to the patient to allow himself to be treated, turning his attention away from what is being done to him; sometimes reprove sharply and emphatically, and sometimes comfort with solicitude and attention, revealing nothing of the patient's future or present condition. (Hippocrates, *Decorum*, XVII)

Certainly, there was no room here for anything like the modern doctrine of informed consent; rather, the attitude of the Hippocratic physician toward the patient was clearly paternalistic. The patient was often described as being "under orders" (e.g., see Hippocrates, *Precepts*, IX, also *The Art*, VII), and this relinquishing of his or her autonomy to the physician was seen to be essential to the success of any course of treatment, and, ultimately to the patient's recovery. Moreover, the Hippocratic texts explicitly recognized that it is "sometimes simply in virtue of the patient's faith in the physician that a cure is effected" (Hippocrates, *Regimen*, II); physicians were urged to exploit their position of authority, the mystery of their esoteric knowledge, and the symbolic power of the language and implements of their art in obtaining the necessary compliance on the part of their patients. Not truthfulness, but a proper paternalism, was the first duty of the Hippocratic physician.

During the medieval and Renaissance periods, principles governing the behavior of physicians derived almost entirely from the Hippocratic corpus via the Galenic texts; thus, the physician continued to conceive of the relationship with the patient as one of benevolent paternalism. The importance of the patient's attitude in effecting a cure continued to be emphasized. Thus, in 1628, Robert Burton wrote,

> A third thing to be required in a patient is confidence, to be of good cheer, and have sure hope that his Physician can help him. Damescen, the Arabian requires likewise ... that (the Physician) be confident he can cure (the Patient) or at least make the patient believe so, otherwise his Physick will not be effectual ... and, as Galen holds, confidence and hope do more good than Physick. ... Paracelsus assigned it for an only cause why Hippocrates was so fortunate in his cures, not for any extraordinary skill he had, but because the common people had a most strong conceit of his worth. (Burton, 1628/1955)

The physician of this period, whose scientific attention was sufficiently occupied in accurately describing and distinguishing specific diseases, as well as by an empirical study of anatomy (finally freed from the biblical authority of the Galenic texts), does not seem to have been especially attuned to the project of describing the specific mechanisms of therapeutic agents. Certainly, the distinction between placebos and other therapies does not appear to have been clearly drawn. As Paracelsus (quoted by Burton) remarked, "It matters not whether it be God or the Devil, Angels or unclean Spirits [which] cure him, so that he be eased" (Burton, 1628/1955).

In the 18th century, the physician's responsibility to protect the patient from the truth was expanded to include a more pointed account of the therapeutic efficacy of the lie. Peter Shaw wrote in 1750 that "the principal Quality of a Physician, as well as of a Poet, (for Apollo is the God of Physic and Poetry) is that of fine lying, or flattering the Patient. . . . And it is doubtless as well for the Patient to be cured by the Workings of his Imagination or a Reliance upon the Promise of his Doctor, as by repeated Doses of Physic" (Shaw, 1750). Deception became a duty for the physician in those cases where it could be expected to have therapeutic efficacy. A somewhat more reserved view than Shaw's was developed in John Gregory's *Lectures on the Duties and Qualifications of a Physician* (1773), yet here, too, the physician was urged to practice benevolent deception when indicated and "to tell his patient only that much about his remedy as shall be good for him." By 1787, "placebo" could be defined in Quincy's *Lexicon* as "a commonplace method in medicine," indicating that the practice of prescribing therapies that were expected to benefit the patient only via their symbolic value, rather than in virtue of any physiological effects, had become well recognized (Shapiro, 1959).

Modern theories of medical ethics, in fact, derive not so much from the Hippocratic writings that exerted such a profound influence over the medieval and Renaissance periods as they do directly from Thomas Percival's *Medical Ethics*, published in 1803 (King, 1971). Percival's text constitutes the first systematic justification of a variety of ethical attitudes and behaviors that had become traditional in medical practice. The text is an amplification of a code of laws regulating physicians' conduct drawn up by Percival in 1792 at the request of the staff of the Manchester Infirmary in England, and concerns both relationships among physicians and the relationship of physician to patient. Percival, convinced that "it is the characteristic of a wise man to act on determinate principles; and of a good man to be assured that they are conformable to rectitude and virtue," intended "to frame a general system of *medical ethics*; that the official conduct, and mutual intercourse of the faculty, might be regulated by precise and acknowledged principles of urbanity and rectitude" (Percival, 1803/ 1975).

Percival was the first author in the history of medicine who not only asserted that the physician is sometimes obliged to practice benevolent deception upon patients, but also attempted to defend this position against counterarguments. During the composition of his text, Percival engaged in an extended correspondence with the Rev. Thomas Gisborne, author of a work in practical ethics entitled *Enquiries into the Duties of Man.* Gisborne's criticism of Percival's claim that the physician may on occasion be required to deceive his patient was based on what are in fact Augustinian and Pauline grounds—namely, that an evil means may not be employed even for the purpose of achieving a good end. Gisborne's underlying assumption, which can also be found at work in contemporary arguments against the use of placebos, was that deception is always evil. Percival pointed out that what may *in abstracto* be considered evil may not be so, given a specific intentional context. For example,

> [I]t is evil to hazard life without a view to some good; but when it is necessary for a public interest it is very lovely and honourable. It is criminal to expose a man to danger for nothing; but it is even just to force him into the greatest dangers for his country. It is criminal to occasion any pains to innocent persons without a view to some good; but for restoring of health we reward chirurgeons for scarifyings, burnings, and amputations. (Percival, 1803/1975)

Percival considered deception to be just such an instance of something ordinarily evil and morally reprehensible that, given the right circumstances, becomes morally obligatory. In two cases, according to Percival, deception is warranted in medical practice: (1) when full disclosure of the facts of his or her condition would be injurious to the patient, and (2) when some ruse is necessary in order to insure the success of treatment. Clearly, "we must not do, for a good end, such actions as are evil even when done for a good end"; however, the question is whether or not deception is, as philosophers such as Augustine and Kant have argued, intrinsically evil. I return shortly to this question; here, I simply record Percival's answer that it is so far from being intrinsically evil as to be positively required of physicians in certain cases.

The second counterposition that Percival addressed was advanced by Dr. Johnson, and concerned the way in which deception injures the patient by insulting and usurping his or her autonomy. Of the physician, Dr. Johnson remarked, "You have no business with consequences, you are to tell the truth. . . . Of all lying I have the greatest abhorrence [of that practiced in medicine], because I believe it has been frequently practiced against myself" (Boswell, 1791/1851). Certainly, benevolent deception, like any form of paternalism, involves some offense against a person's right to make decisions for himself or herself. Generally, one's failure to respect the sphere of another's autonomy is a form of injustice, in which the other is reduced to an object of manipulation in one's own world, rather than being recognized as *like oneself,* a self-determining agent organizing his or her own sphere of interest and activity. Again, however, Percival appealed to the special features of the medical relationship for a justification of benevolent deception. First, he emphasized that physicians must carefully evaluate the characters of their patients, so that they may avoid offending against those independent spirits for whom, as for Dr. Johnson, any deception would inevitably prove a noxious instance of disrespect. Thus, Percival was sensitive to a consideration that is one of the most often cited in contemporary arguments against the therapeutic use of placebos—namely, the damage to the relationship between doctor and patient that may result from the deception. Secondly, however, Percival pointed out that it is the trust that a patient reposes in his or her physician that constitutes the substance of the doctor–patient relationship, and that this trust derives from the patient's confidence that by the physician he or she will be "guarded against whatever would be detrimental to him" (Percival, 1803/1975). Thus, in those cases where full disclosure of his or her condition is likely to be injurious to the patient, or where successful treatment depends upon withholding the truth, it is the moral substance binding doctor to patient that requires the paternalistic practice of benevolent deception.[1]

By the 19th century, the prescription of placebos had certainly become commonplace. In a letter to Casper Wistar written in 1807, Thomas Jefferson remarked, "One of the most successful physicians I have ever known, has assured me, that he used more of bread pills, drops of colored water, and powders of hickory ashes, than of all other medicines put together" (quoted in Brody, 1982, p. 112). Moreover, the practice of benevolent deception continued to be a well-accepted part of physicians' decorum. Oliver Wendell Holmes, famous for his views on the deleterious consequences of most medical treatments, remarked, "Your patient has not more right to all the truth you know than he has to all the medicine in your saddlebags. . . . He should get only as much as is good for him" (Holmes, 1883). Holmes also commented upon what was apparently a time-honored practice: the use of extravagant and imaginative language to impress upon the patient the power of a remedy or to answer his or her need for a diagnosis when none was possible or no physical illness was manifested. To insure the success of the placebo that was prescribed, one physician would name it "tincture of Condurango," another "fluid-extract of *Cimicifuga nigra*." Holmes exhibited a keen awareness of the degree to which the mere naming of the disease conveys to the patient that the physician has taken his or her complaint seriously and that the physician, having recognized the illness, will be competent to deal with it. Holmes's favorite diagnoses for the purposes of obfuscation, allaying the patient's anxieties, and instilling confidence in the physician seem to have been "spinal irritation" and "congestion of the portal

1. The first concerted attack by a physician upon Percival's position came half a century later from Worthington Hooker (1849) (see Reiser, 1980). Further counterarguments were offered by Richard C. Cabot in 1903. Both Brody (1982) and Reiser (1980) provide excellent summaries of Cabot's views, which are remarkably similar to contemporary arguments against placebos and benevolent deception. Cabot remarked succinctly, "Placebo giving is quackery."

system." His deep appreciation for the symbolic power of medical language led him to view such deceptive phrases as useful therapeutic tools.

CONTEMPORARY ATTITUDES AND THE PROBLEM OF DECEPTION

Given the long and well-established tradition of benevolent deception in medical practice, it is perhaps surprising that paternalism and placebos have fallen under such heavy attack in the 20th century. There are at least three reasons for this shift. First, modern scientific medicine emphasizes the specification of any treatment's physiological or biochemical mechanisms of effect, and views any proposed therapy as dubious that cannot be so explained. Thus, placebos are frequently condemned as "unscientific." Secondly, the use of placebos as controls in drug trials in the past several decades has led to an identification of the term with the notion of an ineffective treatment. Thirdly, the professionalization of medicine in the 19th century and the advent of the legal regulation of medicine, along with an increase in dialogue between ethicists and physicians, have made the specification of the physician's responsibility to the patient, as well as the limitations placed upon the physician's actions by his or her obligation to respect the patient's autonomy, a more urgent issue. Moreover, the employment of placebos in medical practice has come to be viewed as the thin end of a wedge of deception and disrespect that, if admitted at all into the therapeutic arena, will inevitably proceed to overrun and crush the trust, confidence, and responsible regard essential to the relation of doctor and patient. Sissela Bok (1974), in her well-known paper "The Ethics of Giving Placebos," states this domino theory of deception clearly:

> I have tried to show that the benevolent deception exemplified by placebos is widespread, that it carries risks not usually taken into account, that it represents an inroad on informed consent, that it damages the institution of medicine and contributes to the erosion of confidence in medical personnel. (Bok, 1974, p. 23)

In light of this new skepticism and fear surrounding the use of placebos in medical practice, a further analysis of the moral dimensions of this paternalistic procedure is required, despite its venerable tradition.

Before addressing the moral arguments opposing the therapeutic employment of placebos in medical practice, let us review certain relatively well-established facts concerning their nature and efficacy—facts that are not irrelevant to the moral issue. Placebos appear to be therapeutically beneficial in approximately 35% of patients, and to produce negative effects in approximately 10% (Beecher, 1955; Byerly, 1976; Ross & Buckalew, 1979; Vogel, Goodwin, & Goodwin, 1980). It is not the case that placebos are effective only against pain or psychologically generated symptoms; rather, they have been found effective in cases of nausea, cough, hay fever, and even warts, as well as headache, angina, rheumatoid and degenerative arthritis, peptic ulcer, hypertension, insomnia, anxiety, and depression (Benson & Epstein, 1975; Frank, 1973; Vogel et al., 1980). Moreover, placebos produce measurable physiological changes, including antitussive effects, antiemetic effects, changes in gastric acid production, and the release of endorphins (Vogel et al., 1980).

There seems to be little evidence that the efficacy of placebo therapy can be correlated with a particular personality type (Buckalew, Ross, & Starr, 1981; Shapiro, 1964). Interestingly, the only consistent findings in this regard seem to be that those patients who benefit from placebo therapy tend to be more communicative, more socially responsive, and more trusting in and confident of their physicians than those who do not react to the placebo (Hankoff, Freedman, & Engelhardt, 1958; Lasagna, Mosteller, von Felsinger, & Beecher, 1954). Social isolation, skepticism about others' motives and competencies, and a general sense of uneasiness, doubt, and mistrust are reported as significantly more frequent in nonreactors.

Finally, and most importantly for present purposes, some research indicates that deception is not a necessary feature of the successful therapeutic employment of placebos (Brody, 1982; Frank, 1973). The assumption that deception is essential in placebo therapy derives from two sources. First, deception traditionally *has* been associated with the use of placebos. Secondly, to the degree that physicians view placebo therapy as "unscientific" and akin to quackery, they will be inclined (if they do not ignore the placebo altogether) either to misuse them, employing them only to quiet the complaints of patients who have been labeled "troublesome" or "hypochondriacal," or to assume that their efficacy depends upon the fact that the patients believe they are receiving a pharmacologically potent substance (e.g., see Goldberg, Leigh, & Quinlan, 1979; Gray & Flynn, 1981; Shapiro & Struening, 1973; Vogel et al., 1980). Of course, there is nothing unscientific about a treatment that is effective in 35% of patients suffering from a variety of conditions; nor is there any reason to believe that patients would lack faith in it if properly informed of its efficacy. Here it is the physicians' unscientific disbelief and their firm conviction that only pharmacologically active agents can be truly useful therapeutically that generate the assumption that deception will be necessary in the use of placebos.

Were the general efficacy of placebos well accepted, and, in particular, were it well recognized that successful treatment by placebo does not indicate that an illness is merely imaginary or that the patient is of a peculiarly gullible or dependent personality type, there would be no reason for deception in their administration. In those cases where placebos may reasonably be expected to be useful, and where pharmacologically active agents are ineffective or contraindicated, a physician could simply report to a patient that the prescribed agent appears to be pharmacologically inert with respect to his or her disorder, but that, *in fact*, it has been shown to be therapeutically effective in other patients suffering from the condition. On this basis, the physician could urge the patient to give the placebo a try. Of course, to the degree that the physician communicates skepticism regarding the placebo's efficacy, or suggests that the patient will be proven a fool or a hypochrondriac if it works, he or she is likely to undermine the treatment. Were deception omitted from the therapeutic employment of placebos, they would thereby become no more morally problematic than any other treatment. Placebos would still be subject to misuse and misprescription, but so is any other drug or medical procedure.

THE ETHICS OF THE BENEVOLENT LIE

Let us assume, however, in order to represent the case against placebos as strongly as possible, that deception is essential in at least some, if not all, cases of placebo therapy. Can this benevolent deception be justified? Are the arguments against it incontrovertible?

First, let us note that the arguments advanced against this form of benevolent deception are of two kinds, and that their difference, which often goes unrecognized in discussion of this issue, is critical. Formalist arguments against the benevolent deception involved in placebo therapy advance the claim that deception is intrinsically bad, because it entails the violation of a moral rule that is without exception. Consequentialist arguments against this benevolent deception oppose it on the ground that it results in bad effects. Let us review each argument in turn.

There are two kinds of formalist arguments that may be advanced against the benevolent deception of placebo therapy. The first appeals to a universal duty of veracity; the second asserts the inviolability of the principle of informed consent.

The first position is well represented by Augustine and Kant. Both thinkers attempt to establish the injuction to tell the truth as a universal moral law, and to establish it on the grounds of the same two reasons. First, lying or deception is determined as morally wrong, insofar as it is intrinsically self-contradictory and thus cannot be willed consistently or as a universal law. The purpose of language, Augustine (1961) remarks, is to establish understanding between men; therefore, lying corrupts the very thing out of which it is constituted, thereby annihilating itself. Similarly, Kant argues,

> Should I really be content that my maxim [the maxim of getting out of a difficulty by a false promise] should hold as a universal law [one that is valid for myself and others]? And, could I really say to myself that everyone may make a false promise if he finds himself in a difficulty from which he can extricate himself in no other way? I then become aware at once that I can indeed will to lie, but I can by no means will a universal law of lying; for by such a law there would properly be no promises at all, since it would be futile to profess a will for

future action to others who would not believe my profession or who, if they did
so over-hastily, would pay me back in like coin, and consequently my maxim, as
soon as it was made a universal law, would be bound to annul itself. (Kant,
1785/1958)

Note first that in seeking to establish a universal duty of veracity, both Kant
and Augustine assume that all cases of deception are qualitatively the same;
however, as we have seen in the discussion of Percival, the intentional
context of an action (here we may not have to do with consequences) may be
so significant as to effect a substantial qualitative differentiation of it from
another action, which *in abstracto* would be the same. In deceiving the
patient, the physician's purpose is not actually to deceive, but to cure. The
deception is or should be practiced only to the degree that it is therapeutically
necessary. And the physician's allegiance to his or her duty to benefit
the patient distinguishes him or her morally from the individual who merely
lies out of self-interest.

Moreover, both Kant and Augustine assume that specific cases of
deception will lead to a general skepticism of language, promise, and
contracts. (It is, in fact, from Augustine that Bok [1974] derives her own
domino theory of deception.) Only on this basis can it be argued that lying,
even when done for a good end, is a "wrong done to mankind generally"
(Kant, 1797/1949). It seems no less plausible to assume, however, that
specific cases of deception would lead to a specific skepticism regarding the
veracity and reliability of the deceiver, rather than to a generalized
impeachment of the validity of any promise or utterance.

The second reason that Kant and Augustine, as well as Aristotle,
advance in support of a universal duty of veracity concerns the corruption to
which the deception exposes the deceiver himself or herself. In arguing
against the benevolent lie, Kant considers the famous case of the murderer
who is seeking to learn if his intended victim is at home. Even here, Kant
insists, the truth must be told; by way of justification for this claim, he
advances only the reasoning that by lying one becomes responsible, both
legally and morally, for the unforeseen, possibly deleterious consequences of
one's action, while, if one adheres to the truth, one cannot under any
circumstances be reproached. In telling the truth "one does not do harm to
him who suffers as a consequence; accident causes this harm" (Kant, 1797/
1949). Thus, one must refuse to commit even the benevolent lie, according to
Kant, not only because it too would undermine the foundations of communication and contract generally, but also because such a lie would put one
morally "at risk."

Moreover, the commission of even the benevolent lie vitiates one's very
status as a moral agent.

Man's duty to himself insofar as he is a moral being alone . . . is formal, and
consists in the conformity of the maxims of his will with the dignity of humanity
in his person. Accordingly, such virtue consists in the prohibition against
depriving himself of a moral being's excellence. (Kant, 1797/1964)

First among the vices that are opposed to this duty is lying. In fact, "the greatest violation of man's duty to himself considered only as a moral being [the humanity in his person] is the opposite of veracity: lying" (Kant, 1797/ 1964). To Kant, the individual who so corrupts his or her own soul is the most contemptible of creatures.

Kant's ethic has often been criticized, perhaps most vigorously by Hegel (1807/1979, 1840/1974), for its focus on the cultivation of a "beautiful soul" rather than on an analysis of moral action. In fact, in the Kantian scheme, moral valuation can apply only to motives and intentions, not to actions. The end of this ethic, strictly speaking, is not moral *behavior* and right action, but the production of a good *will*. Kant's moral agent must identify himself or herself with the purely formal freedom of reason. Yet the self can identify itself with the abstract, universal "I" of reason only at the cost of taking as untrue the empirical self and its natural order. Kant leaves us with a diremption between freedom and nature, in which freedom is taken as essential and nature as inessential. Thus, the Kantian moral self is defined by a striving to overcome and discard its natural or animal self in order to achieve a realization of the universal freedom latent within it. The categorical imperative is necessarily divorced from life, and the formal principle of reason is itself incapable of generating any content or providing the source of a concrete moral action. Thus, the problem with Kant's moral world view is that, as nature is negated, duty can be only an empty form; for the self can *act*, and so concretely embody its moral worth, only in the natural order.

Regarding specifically the use of benevolent deception in medical practice, we need only note that the foundation of Kant's opposition to this deception consists entirely in reasons that relate to the deceiver himself or herself, not to the one deceived. No consideration of the harm done to the deceived figures in Kant's argument; in fact, we are specifically enjoined to ignore this aspect of the case. How, then, should a physician proceed in those cases where deception seems essential to the protection and successful treatment of the patient—where the duties of veracity and healing conflict?

> In such a situation . . . the only point at issue is, whether the practitioner shall sacrifice that delicate sense of veracity, which is so ornamental to, and indeed forms the characteristic excellence of the virtuous man, to this claim of professional and social duty [that of protecting and benefiting the patient]. Under such a painful conflict of obligations, a wise and good man must be governed by those which are the most imperious, and *will therefore generously relinquish every consideration referable only to himself.* (Percival, 1803/ 1975; *italics added*)

In short, the physician will set the welfare of the patient above his or her own moral cleanliness. Certainly, the physician ought to be sensitive to the damage that can be done to the trust the patient has in him or her by the deception. Such a practice ought only to be undertaken in an attitude of reluctance, and only in those cases where its necessity can be clearly demonstrated. From the moral point of view, however, Percival's call for this noble sacrifice on the part of the physician is at least as defensible as Kant's insistence on protecting one's beautiful soul at whatever cost.

The second formalist argument to be considered relies upon the principle of informed consent. Deception, so the argument goes, is impermissible in medical practice, insofar as it usurps the patient's right to give consent for his or her own treatment, and thereby undermines the patient's autonomy. This argument enjoys great currency in the legal literature: Even in those cases where "therapeutic privilege" permits the carefully controlled disclosure and even withholding of information that may hamper a patient's cure, such action "must be consistent with the *full disclosure of facts necessary for an informed consent*" (Simmons, 1978, p. 174). Moreover no consideration of therapeutic benefit alone is sufficient to override this injunction: "A doctor might well believe that an operation or form of treatment is desirable or necessary, but the law does not permit him to substitute his own judgment for that of the patient by any form or artifice or deception" (*Natanson v. Kline*, 1960).

This view runs counter to the traditional paternalistic conception of the doctor–patient relationship in medicine, insofar as it interprets that relationship as more contractual than fiduciary. It assumes either that the individual is the most competent judge of what will be in his or her own best interest, or that the individual's autonomy is of paramount value and outght not to be qualified. Of course, this requires the further assumption that the patient is capable of autonomous function, and that the free exercise of his or her rational will has not been usurped by, for example, an addicting agent or a psychotic episode. In fact, all illness to some degree undermines the autonomy of the sufferer. Even in a relatively innocuous illness (e.g., a mild case of the flu), one's embodiment becomes unreliable and unpredictable, so that it is difficult to project a future and carry out one's plans. One's will is subjected to the contingencies of the sickness, confined, and constricted. And the more serious the illness, the more the patient becomes dependent on others—not only for treatment, but also for assistance in meeting ordinary responsibilities and in carrying out the usual functions of daily life. This impairment of the capacity to possibilize and pursue one's worldly involvements, this disruption of the self-direction of one's own life history, and this extraordinary loss of self-sufficiency constitute some of the most painful features of illness. This loss of autonomy due to illness can be exacerbated by deception, as when, for example, Tolstoy's fictional character Ivan Ilych finds the lying reassurances of those around him to be the most painful element of his deeply painful situation (Tolstoy, 1886/1960). Yet, it must always be the physician's task to restore autonomy in the patient by releasing him or her from the bondage of illness. In those cases where successful treatment depends upon a degree of deception, the physician must measure the damage done to the paitent's autonomy by the deception against that exacted by the illness, and act accordingly. The physician can make such a judgment only by putting himself or herself in the patient's place—not only identifying with the patient's suffering and incapacitation, but also attempting to think from within the patient's own system of values. The principle of informed consent and the duty of the physician to respect and restore autonomy in the patient present the greatest challenge to the practice of benevolent deception in medicine; nevertheless, even here, it would be unreasonable to foreclose exceptions.

The second kind of argument advanced against placebo therapy, insofar as it involves benvolent deception, concerns the consequences of such an action. Encouraging belief in medicine as a cure-all, to the neglect of solving problematic personal issues; pill dependency; the neglect of "real" illness whose symptoms may be temporarily masked by relief derived from placebos; damage to the trust between doctor and patient; and the cancerous spread of deceptive practices—these are some of the deleterious effects possibly attending the benevolent deception of placebo therapy that are most often cited by its critics (Bok, 1974; Simmons, 1978).

Certainly, the use of benevolent deception in medical practice requires strict regulations—to wit:

1. That it never be employed for the convenience of the health care team, but only for the therapeutic benefit of the patient.
2. That it be used only in cases where substantial evidence indicates that it is necessary.
3. That the physician be able to make the case for the necessity of the deception to any reasonable observer.
4. That the physician determine whether or not any physical or psychophysical condition for which other treatment is indicated would be masked by reliance on the placebo.
5. That the physician consider carefully the character and value system of the patient and the effect of such deception on his or her self-respect and attitude toward the physician.

If it can be shown, however, that deception is necessary to the success of a treatment (something, recall, that we have granted in the case of placebos only for the sake of argument), and if this deception is practiced properly—in an attitude of reluctance, after weighing its costs and in accordance with the controls specified above—there is simply no reason to assume, as Bok and others do, that this benevolent lie will function as the seed of a widespread and self-interested system of deception in medicine. The use of deception in medical practice always ought to be viewed as exceptional and to be permitted only on the basis of the sort of careful justification and control outlined here; however, to prohibit this practice altogether on the basis of overzealous speculations about the remote effects of its abuse seems unwise, unnecessary, and a flagrant denial of the substantial evidence in the history of medicine that it is sometimes therapeutically indicated and efficacious.[2]

In summary, I have argued that neither formalist nor utilitarian reasoning succeeds in justifying an absolute prohibition against the therapeutic use of placebos in medical practice; rather, the moral and medical validity of their use can only be determined by judgments in specific cases. Moreover, the use of placebos in clinical practice becomes morally problematic only when some deception is necessitated, and I have outlined some of the "fixed principles of rectitude," the controls and considerations, that ought to inform and regulate the physician's judgment when the duties of beneficence and veracity conflict. The therapeutic value of the placebo, "whose beneficial effects must lie in its symbolic power" (Frank, 1973), will only be understood when medicine achieves a more adequate conceptualization of the doctor–patient relationship itself, including the recognition that the patient is more than a mechanical, physical entity and that such factors as expectation, confidence, social setting, and language are significant elements in the course of illness and treatment. Meanwhile, it is to be hoped that recent reinterpretations of this relationship as a contract, as well as the contemporary physician's understandable concern with liability, will not altogether undo the age-old foundation of medicine in a principle of beneficence, nor be responsible for the dismissal of the powerful placebo from the *materia medica*.

REFERENCES

Augustine. *Enchiridion* (H. Paolucci, Ed.). Chicago: Henry Regnery, 1961.

Beauchamp, T. L., & Childress, J. F. *Principles of biomedical ethics* (2nd ed.). New York: Oxford University Press, 1983.

Beecher, H. K. The powerful placebo. *Journal of the American Medical Association*, 1955, *159*, 1602–1606.

Benson, H., & Epstein, M. D. The placebo effect: A neglected asset in the care of patients. *Journal of the American Medical Association*, 1975, *232*, 1225–1227.

Bok, S. The effects of giving placebos. *Scientific American*, 1974, *231*, 17–23.

Boswell, J. *The life of Samuel Johnson, LL.D.* (Vol. 2). New York: Routledge & Sons, 1851. (Originally published, 1791.)

Brody, H. The lie that heals: The ethics of giving placebos. *Annals of Internal Medicine*, 1982, *97*, 112–118.

Buckalew, L. W., Ross, S., & Starr, B. J. Nonspecific factors in drug effects: Placebo personality. *Psychological Reports*, 1981, *48*, 308.

Burton, R. *The anatomy of melancholy* (F. Dell & P. J. Smith, Eds.). New York: Tudor, 1955. (Originally published, 1628.)

Byerly, H. Explaining and exploiting placebo effects. *Perspectives in Biology and Medicine*, 1976, *19*, 423–435.

2. For clinical illustrations, see Case #46 in Veatch (1977) and Case #4 in Beauchamp and Childress (1983).

Cabot, R. C. The use of truth and falsehood in medicine: An experimental study. *American Medicine*, 1903, *5*, 344–49.

Frank, J. D. *Persuasion and healing*. Baltimore: Johns Hopkins University Press, 1973.

Goldberg, R. J., Leigh, H., & Quinlan, D. The current status of placebo in hospital practice. *General Hospital Psychiatry*, 1979, *1*, 196–201.

Gray, G., & Flynn, F. A survey of placebo use in a general hospital. *General Hospital Psychiatry*, 1981, *3*, 199–203.

Gregory, J. *Lectures on the duties and qualifications of a physician*. 1773.

Hankoff, L. D., Freedman, N., & Engelhardt, D. M. The prognostic value of placebo response. *American Journal of Psychiatry*, 1958, *115*, 549–550.

Hegel, G. W. F., Kant. In E. S. Haldane & F. H. Simson (trans.), *Lectures on the history of philosophy* (Vol. 3). New York: Humanities Press, 1974. (Originally published, 1840.)

Hegel, G. W. F. *The phenomenology of spirit* (A. V. Miller, trans.). New York: Oxford University Press, 1979. (Originally published, 1807.)

Hippocrates. The art. In *Hippocrates* (Vol. 2). Cambridge, Mass.: Harvard University Press, 1979.

Hippocrates, Decorum. In *Hippocrates* (Vol. 2). Cambridge, Mass.: Harvard University Press, 1979.

Hippocrates. Precepts. In *Hippocrates* (Vol. 1). Cambridge, Mass.: Harvard University Press, 1979.

Hippocrates. Regimen, II. In *Hippocrates* (Vol. 4). Cambridge, Mass.: Harvard University Press, 1979.

Holmes, O. W. *Medical essays*. Boston: Houghton Mifflin, 1883.

Hooker, W. *Physician and patient*. New York: Baker & Scribner, 1849.

Kant, I. On a supposed right to lie from benevolent motives. In L. W. Beck (Ed. and trans.), *Critique of practical reason and other writings in moral philosophy*. Chicago: University of Chicago Press, 1949. (Originally published, 1797).

Kant, I. *Groundwork of the metaphysic of morals* (H. J. Paton, trans.). New York: Harper & Row, 1958. (Originally published, 1785.)

Kant, I. *The metaphysical principles of virtue* (J. Ellington, trans.). New York: Bobbs-Merrill, Library of Liberal Arts, 1964. (Originally published, 1797.)

King, L. S. *The medical world of the eighteenth century*. Huntington, N.Y.: Robert E. Krieger, 1971.

Lasagna, L., Mosteller, F., von Felsinger, J. M., & Beecher, H. K. A study of the placebo response. *American Journal of Medicine*, 1954, *16*, 770–79.

Natanson vs. Kline. 1960, 186 Kan. 393, 350, P_2d, 1093.

Percival, T. *Medical ethics*. New York: Robert E. Krieger, 1975. (Originally published, 1803.)

Preston, T. A. Placebos: Letter to the editor. *Annals of Internal Medicine*, 1982, *5*, 781.

Reiser, S. J. Words as scalpels: Transmitting evidence in the clinical dialogue. *Annals of Internal Medicine*, 1980, *92*, 837–842.

Ross, S., & Buckalew, L. W. On the agentry of placebos. *American Psychologist*, 1979, *34*, 277–278.

Shapiro, A. K. The placebo effect in the history of medical treatment. *American Journal of Psychiatry*, 1959, *116*, 298–304.

Shapiro, A. K. Factors contributing to placebo effect. *American Journal of Psychotherapy*, 1964, *18*, 73–88.

Shapiro, A. K., & Struening, E. L. The use of placebos: A study of ethics and physicians attitudes. *Psychiatry in Medicine*, 1973, *4*, 17–29.

Shaw, P. *The reflector: Representing human affairs as they are, and may be improved*. London: Longman, 1750.

Simmons, B. Problems in deceptive medical procedures: An ethical and legal analysis of the administration of placebos. *Journal of Medical Ethics*, 1978, *4*, 172–181.

Tolstoy, L. The death of Ivan Ilych (A. Maude, trans.). In *The death of Ivan Ilych and other stories*. New York: Signet, 1960. (Originally published, 1886.)

Veatch, R. M. Models for ethical medicine in a revolutionary age. *Hastings Center Reports*, 1972, *2*, 5–7.

Veatch, R. M. *Case studies in medical ethics*. Cambridge, Mass.: Harvard University Press, 1977.

Veatch, R. M. *A theory of medical ethics*. New York: Basic Books, 1982.

Vogel, A. V., Goodwin, J. S., & Goodwin, J. M. The therapeutics of placebo. *American Family Physician*, 1980, *22*, 106–109.

23

Placebo Controls Are Not Always Necessary

The value of the controlled clinical trial in the determination of the safety and effectiveness of a new intervention is largely undisputed. Current U.S. Food and Drug Administration (FDA) regulations list four types of comparative trials:

1. No treatment, which involves a comparison of the results in comparable concurrent groups of treated and untreated patients. This type of control is utilized when objective measurements of effectiveness are available and placebo effect or spontaneous improvement of the disease or condition is negligible.
2. Placebo control, which involves a comparison of the results of a particular therapy with an inactive preparation or a sham procedure. Dose-ranging studies, although usually considered as another form of controlled clinical trial, can perhaps best be included as a variant of the placebo control in that effectiveness at the low dosage levels cannot always be presumed, at least in an individual study.
3. Active treatment control, which involves a comparison of the results from the new intervention with those from a treatment known to be effective.
4. Historical control, which involves comparison of the results from a new intervention with prior experience obtained in a comparable group of patients receiving no therapy or a known effective regimen. The use of this type of control may be appropriate in the study of a new treatment for a disease with high and predictable mortality or, in the case of prophylaxis, where morbidity is predictable. It is also appropriate when the effect of a therapy is self-evident.

For most new therapies, the drawbacks of the historical control and no-treatment control designs are generally such that they are not commonly employed, except to provide preliminary information on safety and effec-

Marion J. Finkel. Office of Orphan Products Development, U.S. Food and Drug Administration, Rockville, Maryland.

tiveness. This chapter is devoted to the place of the active treatment design in the study of a new drug or a new use for a marketed drug. Before doing this, however, it is well to state that in almost all plans for the study of the effectiveness of a new drug, it is desirable to include some placebo-controlled studies unless it is considered unethical to do so (e.g., in treatment of a life-threatening disease; in the presence of infection where a treatment known to be effective is available; in contraceptive studies). Placebo-controlled studies are cost-effective. In studies smaller than those with active controls, one can ascertain the effectiveness of a new drug early in the process and thereafter not have to worry about whether one is dealing with a useful drug. Studies with active controls can then be used primarily to determine whether the drug is effective for prolonged periods, how effective or safe it is in comparison with known active agents, and how useful it is with patients who are poorly responsive or are losing their response to known agents. Leaving ethical considerations aside, I believe that the three instances where trials with active controls might substitute wholly for any placebo-controlled trial are (1) where it is reasonably certain that a new therapy will be more effective than other agents known to be effective; (2) where the effectiveness of the new therapy is self-evident; or (3) where the nature of the therapy or procedure is such that it is not possible to blind the patients or the observers.

This is not to say, however, that, in other instances, a company could not obtain approval of a new drug for marketing on the basis of active control studies alone. These studies need to be large enough to establish that the drug under investigation and the known active drug are reasonably similar in effectiveness; in addition, the patient populations involved in the studies need to be sufficiently similar and the conduct of the studies sufficiently rigorous that one can be confident of the validity of the results. Temple (1982) has noted that, unlike the situation that prevails in placebo-controlled studies, the motive in designing studies with active controls is to demonstrate a lack of difference between treatments; therefore, the striving for study excellence that marks placebo-controlled trials may be less apparent in trials with active controls. It is difficult to know whether disincentives to a well-conducted active control study are such that they play a significant role in many such trials. Perhaps the potential investigator bias introduced by the use of two presumed active agents in the study may be more of a factor in failing to show a difference between treatments. For example, when two topical cortico-steroids are compared to each other, the percentage of patients showing major improvement in their skin disease is commonly higher than when one of those drugs is compared to placebo.

Although many active control studies are performed merely with the hope of showing that the substance under investigation is at least as effective as a known active substance, drug company sponsors are always pleased when they can point to a significant beneficial difference for their products, and investigators themselves have the intellectual curiosity to determine whether there is a difference. To the extent that these factors play a part in the design and execution of a study, the study using an active control has the potential for being performed with the same rigor as a placebo-controlled trial.

When the goal is, however, to demonstrate the equivalence of two therapies, it is well to keep in mind that even though comparable effectiveness appears to be demonstrated in a study, the reality may in fact be that neither of the drugs is effective in this study. The U.S. FDA has seen many analgesic studies including both active and placebo controls in which patient response was similar in the placebo control, active control, and investigational drug groups. Had the placebo not been included, it would not have been apparent that these were "failed" studies.

Temple (1982) has suggested that if a drug company wishes to demonstrate that its new drug is effective on the basis of its equivalence to a known effective agent, it should do the following: (1) Show that the proposed active control has regularly been demonstrated to be superior to placebo; (2) design studies similar to those in which the proposed active control was shown to be effective; and (3) determine the magnitude of the placebo response in the studies that were of similar design to those to be used in the new studies, and specify a level of response in the treatment groups that would be beyond what could be attributed to a placebo effect.

Certain drugs (e.g., certain antihypertensives and antilipemics) lend themselves nicely to Temple's suggestions, but others do not. In some cases, the disease to be treated is characterized by great variation in placebo response, a high placebo response rate, or considerable fluctuations in the disease process; in other cases, the drug to be investigated and the active control are not sufficiently powerful to be regularly distinguished from placebo. In these cases, it is evident that placebo-controlled studies are required. An alternative to Temple's (1982) suggestions, useful in certain cases—for example, in the treatment of moderate to severe pain—is the active control study employing multiple dose levels in which the ability to distinguish between dose levels readily permits the conclusion that the control drug is active in the study under consideration.

There are certain cases where effectiveness is self-evident; in such cases, active control studies can substitute entirely for any placebo control trials. In many of these situations, of course, the active control studies are used mainly to confirm what can be observed from historical control studies and to provide information on the comparability or superiority of the new drug with known effective therapy. For example, a powerful diuretic that results in an increase in urinary excretion of 3 liters or more per day does not require placebo or active control studies for proof of effectiveness, but such studies are useful to answer other questions or provide other information about the drug.

Most drug companies are not interested in marketing drugs that are less effective or less safe than other available agents, although the U.S. FDA would certainly approve for marketing drugs that are less effective than and as safe as other drugs. In addition, the FDA would approve drugs that are both less effective and less safe when they have been shown to be useful in patients who cannot tolerate or do not respond to other drugs. In those cases where differences can be detected with certitude, labeling will inform the physician of the information obtained about the drugs.

Lasagna (1979) has asked whether it is not unethical to place on the market new drugs that are less effective than other available agents, thus at least temporarily depriving patients of the benfits of older and better treatments. This question is asked in the context of his argument that it is not conscionable to retreat to the era of the uncontrolled clinical trial, with the consequence that some drugs would be marketed that may (unbeknownst to physicians or consumers) be less effective. If physicians are fully aware, however, that these drugs are less effective, and if there is a defined population that would benefit from them, then the marketing of such drugs is not unethical.

Except for situations where the degree of therapeutic response to available agents is well established and quite predictable, the use of placebo-controlled trials alone will not provide information on whether a new agent is more or less effective than older drugs. Even studies with active controls are usually not sufficiently large to provide other than a reasonable conclusion that there are no major differences in effectiveness. If, however, the results of comparative studies almost always point in the same direction (i.e., there is a consistent trend for one drug to be superior to another), the confidence that there is a real difference in effectiveness (or safety) is enhanced, even if the difference is not always statistically significant. Because active control studies of the type usually performed with a new drug are generally able to detect only major differences in effectiveness between therapies, the U.S. FDA is conservative in permitting labeling claims for drug superiority. permitting labeling claims for drug superiority.

Studies with active controls have been widely used by drug companies in the study of their new drugs. In fact, few new drugs are not made the subject of active control studies prior to marketing. Properly designed, such studies provide valuable information.

REFERENCES

Lasagna, L. Editorial: Placebos and controlled trials under attack. *European Journal of Clinical Pharmacology*, 1979, *15*, 373–374.

Temple, R. Government viewpoint of clincial trials. *Drug Information Journal*, 1982, *16*, 10–17.

24

Discussion

The Ethics of Placebo

MAX FINK

The need for the statements in the chapters by Rawlinson and Finkel symbolizes a dramatic shift in public attitudes toward the medical profession—from acceptance of the physician's beneficent paternalism to the insistent demand for individual responsibility for one's welfare. This shift is well described by Rawlinson, but, in addition to the roots that she describes, I would argue for additional factors in psychiatric practice. Disappointment with the therapies of the 1930s, the need to justify the use of the psychoactive drugs with severe neurotoxic potential, and the abuse of the psychiatric authority to force incarceration of political prisoners and protesters in some countries, each contributed to the change in the public's perception and acceptance of the authoritarian psychiatrist.

At the turn of the century, neurosyphilis remained one of the most devastating mental diseases. The introduction of arsenical chemotherapy by Ehrlich and the development of fever therapy elicited waves of enthusiasm, which culminated in the awarding of the Nobel Prize in medicine to Wagner-Jauregg for fever therapy in 1928. Following this enthusiastic reception, other invasive "therapies," such as the psychoanalytic therapies, insulin coma, leucotomy, and convulsive therapy, became popular prior to World War II. These were practiced by an authoritarian band of therapists, who asserted that they understood these complicated therapies, and that only trained acolytes could have the sophistication to carry these out successfully.

In the postwar liberation movements, the right of nations to beneficent guardianship of colonies and the divine right of monarchies were questioned. The authoritarian positions of other elements of society, including psychiatric practitioners with their privileges of forced hospitalization, were also questioned. Descriptions of mental hospital "snakepits" made it clear that incarceration in hospitals was not always done for the benefit of the patients.

Max Fink. Department of Psychiatry and Behavioral Sciences, School of Medicine, State University of New York at Stony Brook, Stony Brook, New York.

With the appearance of phenothiazine antipsychotic agents and tricyclic antidepressants between 1953 and 1958, relative efficacy among these interventions became economic, as well as scientific, concerns. Psycho- therapy clinicians, faced with the threat of a simpler and less expensive therapy in medications, strenuously insisted that proof of efficacy and mode of action was needed before they would give up their "curative, interpretive" therapies for the presumed "symptomatic, palliative" approach of drug therapy. The introduction of antipsychotic drugs allowed comparisons of insulin coma with chlorpromazine (Boardman, Lomas, & Markowe, 1956; Fink, Shaw, Gross, & Coleman, 1958) and barbiturate sedation (Ackner, Harris, & Oldham, 1957). The drug therapies were clearly safer than insulin coma, leading to the rapid cessation of the use of insulin coma throughout the world by 1960.

Comparisons of drug therapies with psychotherapy and convulsive therapy yielded less dramatic conclusions, with convulsive therapy usually found to be more effective than drug therapies (Fink, 1979). The psycho- therapy comparisons foundered on attitudinal and technical issues, such as selection criteria, dropouts, outcome criteria, role of training of the therapist, and the like. The effect of expectation and attitude was demonstrated when practices of different hospitals with different therapeutic orientations were studied (Fink, 1979). Not only did the classifications of the illnesses differ, but the outcome criteria were so different as to make comparisons difficult.

The need to compare the relative efficacy of newly introduced drug treatments with existing treatments (psychotherapy and somatic therapies) had a dramatic effect on evaluation methods. This need for sensitive evaluation methods led to the development of behavioral rating scales, new classification schemes, discussions of balanced samples (achieved by random assignment of patients), and arguments that efficacy could not be defined without a comparison group, usually one that was untreated or treated by a pharmacologically inert substance or procedure. These attitudes, and the dramatic events in the evaluation of the neurotoxicity of thalidomide, strengthened the role of governmental agencies in medical treatment and scientific evaluation, culminating in the present power of the U.S. Food and Drug Administration to regulate the introduction of new medical treatments. An example of these regulations and attitudes is seen in the discussion by Finkel, who argues that placebo trials are not always necessary.

Medical paternalism was also put under stress by the public's distrust of governments that suppressed dissent and silenced opposition by using psychiatrists and psychiatric institutions to detain and "treat" dissenters. These efforts came into prominence in the 1960s. The misuse of psychiatric hospitalization by the Soviet government, and the interrogation methods employed by the Iranian, Chilean, and Ugandan governments, encouraged a loss of faith in the integrity of psychiatrists. They also popularized a misinterpretation that the "electric shock" used in interrogation and punishment was the same as the "electroshock" (convulsive therapy, or ECT) used in the treatment of patients with affective disorders. In our nation, the brouhaha regarding psychosurgery in criminals, the threat of forced detention of dissidents by the Nixon government, and the abuse of power by Presidents Kennedy, Johnson, and Nixon to carry on an undeclared and illegal war in Vietnam, each confirmed fears of governmental paternalism as harmful.

It is in this climate of distrust—distrust of medical judgment and of governmental power—that an emphasis on scientific methodology in the evaluation of treatments became a strong force in our culture. This emphasis on scientific methodology was also encouraged by the influence of governmental agencies as they came to dominate our national research effort. General excellence and academic position were no longer accepted as a basis for awarding grants, being replaced by peer review committees demanding detailed methodologies designed to prove a conclusion.

With the demand for certainty, numerous technical innovations designed to improve the likelihood of a conclusion became elevated to the status of minimum standards of evidence of treatment efficacy. Thus, the need for placebos in treatment evaluation became established—first as a useful device for certain types of studies, then as a necessary part of the evaluation. So onerous has this requirement become that it is useful for Finkel, a responsible officer of the U.S. Food and Drug Administration, to write that, after all, placebo controls are not *always* necessary. Her general statement will not give solace to many sponsors of new entities for treatment, but it does serve notice that slavish adherence to a single model of evaluation may not be necessary.

In my own laboratory, there are two points at which placebo controls seem useful. In assessing the pharmacodynamic effects of new psychoactive entities on the human electroencephalogram (EEG), we ordinarily undertake open, dose-ranging trials. When we have defined a dose that affects the EEG and behavior, we undertake a double-blind, matched-placebo, crossover study (Fink & Irwin, 1979). The doses we assess are threshold doses, and to define a minimum difference, we use the difference between drug and placebo at numerous time points after dosing. In subsequent classification trials, the effects of the new entity are compared to those of an established substance, and to a placebo, to determine the activity of the standard compound on our measures in a new sample of subjects.

In clinical drug evaluations, placebos seem useful to determine the safety of compounds (the incidence of side effects for the selected sample of subjects). In the evaluation of new psychiatric therapies, particularly the evaluation of antidepressants, it is often stated that a placebo control is necessary. But such is not usually feasible. What is a suitable placebo control for human verbal psychotherapeutic interventions, or for an induced seizure? In the first instance, waiting lists have been used, but the more desperate patients or the more sophisticated have simply not waited, but have sought help elsewhere; this has resulted in biased populations in such studies. Or, therapists have been asked to use a different mode of psychotherapy, but how can one control for the enthusiasm of the therapist assigned to carry out the "new" intervention—the one that already carries enough interest to warrant funding of the research or the enrollment of therapist/researchers? In the instance of ECT research, anesthesia alone has been used, without the passage of currents. But from the work of many authors, we know that repeated administration of sedatives alone may be therapeutic (Ackner *et al.*, 1957).

In discussing contemporary attitudes, Rawlinson notes that the placebo is often interpreted as an ineffective treatment. While this may have been popular at one time, studies of psychiatric populations find placebos to be particularly effective in some population samples. The effects may be dramatic in ambulatory populations, especially those with symptoms of anxiety or depression, where the efficacy of placebos may range from 30% to 50% of a sample. The insistence on a placebo control for studies of drug treatments and psychotherapies has developed, not because placebos are seen as ineffective, but because they *are* effective. We now ask that a new treatment, particularly one that society will sanction and pay for, demonstrate a specificity of effect that is greater than that of a placebo. A compelling example of the important information given by placebo controls is seen in a recent study of the convulsive therapy process, where the effects of sham ECT were compared to the effects of standard ECT (Johnstone, Lawler, Stevens, Deakin, Frith, McPherson, & Crow, 1980). Patients treated with sham ECT showed a similar reduction in depression ratings to the patients treated with ECT. There was a statistical advantage for ECT over sham ECT only at the end of 8 treatments (week 4 of the schedule), but not 1 and 6 months after the last treatment. The improvement rate of patients treated with standard ECT was only slightly greater than that of sham ECT, a rate much lower than others reported for the same treatment (Fink, 1979). Reviews of the protocol allowed explanations of the differences in observations from the work of others to emerge. In the sham ECT group, the unusual dedication of the therapist and the widespread use of sedative drugs improved the results; in the treated group, or the other hand, the numbers of seizures were minimal, the durations were not measured, and the role of missed seizures was not assessed, minimizing its efficacy.

Much of the improvement with placebos is generated from the relationship between therapist and patient, in which the authority of the therapist and his or her expectations for a successful conclusion are powerful factors in the outcome. The patient's desire to please the therapist is a contributory factor. One of the losses resulting from the change in attitude toward medical authority has been the decreased reliance by practitioners on the use of placebos. As Rawlinson notes, placebo use is deemed "unscientific," and few practitioners are willing to assert the usefulness of placebo therapy, even in cases where no effective specific therapy is known. The litiginous environment in which the doctor–patient relationship now finds itself also influences practitioners' attitudes toward placebos. Faced with an inability to defend the use of placebos as safe and effective therapy for a patient, physicians eschew their use.

To these practical issues must be added the ethical questions that Rawlinson raises. We are in the midst of dynamic changes in medical practice and research, in the relationship between the citizen and the state, and in the awesome power of big government. The problem of informed consent, which Rawlinson discusses well, is a side issue of the relationship between authority and the individual. Where the needs of the patient are clear, and where the options among a series of interventions are well defined, consent is neither an ethical nor a practical problem. The explanations given by the therapist are often sufficient when combined with a reasoned examination and evaluation of the state of the patient. It is when an economic or legal issue is interposed that the ethical issues become sticky. Where the therapist has a financial stake in the decision, as in the recommendation of an elective surgical procedure, or in the selection of patients to become participants in controlled trials in which the therapist is paid by an industrial sponsor on a case-by-case basis, the ethical concerns become central to the interaction. The present system of institutional review boards is a partial answer to the dilemma, but their usefulness is clearly dependent on the good faith of the investigator. It would be better if treatment evaluations were done by specialists who have no financial stake either in the outcome or in the number of cases included in the trial.

The issues are further complicated by the view of some public bodies that free and informed consent cannot be given by prisoners, mental patients, children, and the impoverished (who may be unduly influenced by economic factors). Informed consent is also of limited value in subjects with mental deficiency, language handicaps, and other impediments to the full understanding of the explanations given them. These issues arise in the present climate of loss of faith in authority.

Finally, the desire for certainty leads to demands for evidence that is hardly likely to be found in our present state of medical knowledge. We live in a world filled with uncertainty and hostility, in imminent danger of annihilation and slavery. Families, churches, social groups, and political organizations no longer protect us, and more often are destructive rather than protective of the good will of the individual. In this climate, the ethical issues in the use of placebos are a small concern in the conflict between governmental authority and individual liberty.

REFERENCES

Ackner, B., Harris, A., & Oldham, A. J. Insulin treatment of schizophrenia: Controlled study. *Lancet*, 1957, *2*, 607–611.

Placebo in Clinical Trials and Clinical Practice

Boardman, R. H., Lomas, J., & Markowe, M. Insulin and chlorpromazine in schizophrenia: Comparative study in previously untreated cases. *Lancet*, 1956, *2*, 487–494.

Fink, M. *Convulsive therapy: Theory and practice.* New York: Raven Press, 1979.

Fink, M., & Irwin, P. CNS effects of the antihistamines, diphenhydramine and terfenadine (RMI-9918). *Pharmakopsychiatrie/Neuro-Psychopharmakologie*, 1979, *12*, 34–44.

Fink, M., Shaw, R., Gross, G., & Coleman, F. S. Comparative study of chlorpromazine and insulin coma in the therapy of psychosis. *Journal of the American Medical Association*, 1958, *166*, 1846–1850.

Johnstone, E. C., Lawler, P., Stevens, M., Deakin, J. F. W., Frith, C. D., McPherson, K., & Crow, T. J. The Northwick Park electroconvulsive therapy trial. *Lancet*, 1980, *2*, 1317–1319.

SUMMARY

25

Proposed Synthesis of Placebo Models

LEONARD WHITE
BERNARD TURSKY
GARY E. SCHWARTZ

Although the abundance of information contained in the preceding chapters cannot be adequately summarized without significant omission, several themes do reappear that warrant comment. In trying to highlight these themes, we note only limited places where these issues are discussed in the text, and apologize in advance to our colleagues for any slight or misrepresentation.

DEFINITION

One of the objectives of this examination of placebo issues has been to arrive at a definition of the term; Section II of the volume is devoted to this purpose. We would begin our comments by seconding Borkovec's endorsement of two conceptual clarifications made in Grünbaum's analysis of the placebo concept. The two points noted are (1) recasting the definition of "placebo" so that it is made relative to the theoretical framework of the speaker; (2) replacing the term "nonspecific causes" that appears in previous definitions of "placebo" with "incidental causes." It follows from these two points that placebo effects are effects that, when examined from a given theoretical framework, are due to unidentified causes. These causes are *not*, however, intrinsically unknowable. Placebo effects, after all, have in common with other unexplained phenomena problems of inadequate theory and/or procedures, but they are amenable to scientific inquiry.

Brody's critique of Grünbaum's generic definition is an attempt to ground the definition of placebo in a historical/clinical context. In this

Leonard White. Department of Psychiatry and Behavioral Science, School of Medicine, State University of New York at Stony Brook, Stony Brook, New York; Department of Psychology, Pilgrim Psychiatric Center, West Brentwood, New York.

Bernard Tursky. Department of Political Science, State University of New York at Stony Brook, Stony Brook, New York.

Gary E. Schwartz. Department of Psychology, Yale University, New Haven, Connecticut.

context, the role of symbolic processes, imagination, beliefs, and emotions in the healing processes has long been recognized. Even in Western medicine, the empirical practitioner has traditionally been concerned with the role of psychological processes in the healing arts, and Brody suggests that it has been an error to exclude such considerations from current practice. Brody's analysis focuses on the fundamental importance of the disciplinary matrix in determining whether symbolic processes are recognized as significant causal factors in health and illness or precluded from consideration. The present exclusion of placebo effects from contemporary medical practice and research, according to this perspective, derives from the dominance of a biological reductionist matrix that necessarily dismisses symbolic processes. Brody suggests that a systems approach may provide a more comprehensive disciplinary matrix (metatheory) for contemporary health care practice. We have more to say on this point later on.

Borkovec stresses that the designation of a placebo effect, since it denotes an effect from essentially unknown or poorly conceptualized causes, is a starting point for further theory building and data collection. The goal of science is to enlarge knowledge by transforming the unknown into the known, and in this process theory has a central role in summarizing previous data and guiding new research. As knowledge expands in a particular area, the term "placebo" may be replaced by designated procedural variables or particular laws of behavior. The term "imagination" itself is one alternative explanation of placebo effects that lends itself to further experimental study.

Although each of the chapters in this volume emphasizes a different aspect of the definitional problems, they are consistent in their endorsement of the need for further scientific exploration of effects currently designated "placebo effects." This scientific explanation necessarily involves methodological considerations, some of which are considered in the next section of the volume.

METHODOLOGY

The issues under detailed consideration in Section III, "Research Methods," are as follows:

1. The interaction between drug effects and psychological effects (Ross and Buckalew).
2. The differentiation of efficacy research from mechanism research (Wilkins).
3. Quantification and summary of placebo effects (Rosenthal).
4. Control-group solutions, research design, and hypothesis testing (Paul).

Ross and Buckalew consider the extent and determinants of response to placebo preparations as encountered in the traditional double-blind comparison studies. They note the false dichotomy between drug and placebo effects, in part maintained by the two-group comparison (drug vs. placebo) methodology. Since both groups are subjected to the same healing environments and develop similar expectancies, the two-group design confounds drug and placebo effects in the drug group. The two-group double-blind design may be seen as an application of Mill's "method of difference" (Gadow, White, & Ferguson, 1985), which states that if an instance in which the phenomenon under investigation occurs and an instance in which it does not occur have every circumstance in common save one, that occurring in the former, the circumstances in which alone the two instances differ is the effect, or the cause, or an indispensable part of the cause of the phenomenon (J. S. Mill, cited by Cohen & Nagel, 1934, p. 256).

According to Ross and Buckalew, the effects obtained in the drug group may in part be due to psychological influences. In order to disentangle drug, placebo, and interactive effects adequately, these authors recommend a four-group research design employing a "disguised" drug group and a no-treatment control. Their chapter contains a summary of their own studies that have used such a design. These studies find that drug effects are altered by instructions and that when a drug is administered surreptitiously, the usual clinical effects are altered. The disguised drug technique yields a telling demonstration of the significant interaction between context and instructional variables and drug effects in clinical settings.

The uncritical acceptance of the drug versus placebo research methodology has contributed to the neglect of the experimental examination of psychological influences upon biological processes. Ross and Buckalew have, with these potential confounds in mind, surveyed the literature. They conclude that the following dependent variables are responsive to placebo manipulations: reaction time, grip strength, pulse rate, blood pressure, pain, short-term rote memory, and self-perceptions of relaxation and activation. These conclusions are tempered, however, by the lack of replication and comparability of studies. This compilation differs from previous listings of placebo-responsive variables, because it primarily considers dependent variables rather than disorders per se. As such, it may hold more interest for researchers than for clinicians.

Wilkins's chapter emphasizes the distinction between efficacy research and mechanisms research. Efficacy research addresses the question of whether an intervention causes improvement in a given disorder, whereas mechanisms research seeks to define and understand the cause or mechanisms whereby change is effected. According to Wilkins, this distinction in the characteristic of the research hypothesis necessitates a change in emphasis from a search for a reliable association between independent and dependent variables to an interest in intervening variables that are inferred from observable events. Wilkins additionally discriminates between the domains of chemotherapy, psychotherapy, and placebo research. In chemotherapy research, the psychological factors are, in fact, only noted as contributing to the placeo effect and are exluded from further consideration, while, by definiton, these psychological factors are the primary focus of psychotherapy research. Psychotherapy research, to the degree that is modeled after chemotherapy research, is in error on two counts: a search for an inert control manipulation, and an accompanying premature focus on determination of psychological mechanisms. Placebo procedures employing "inactive" treatment components are not appropriate for psychotherapy research, because they do not control for observer bias as they do in chemotherapy research. Wilkins's recommendations concerning the utility of studies in which active therapies are compared are reinforced by Paul.

We find Paul's comments on the issue of research design particularly astute. It is of overriding importance that any research be designed to maintain internal validity so that *plausible* rival hypotheses are ruled out. Table 25-1 summarizes the domains of variables Paul indicates as requiring manipulation, measurement, description, or control in clinical research.

When domains of variables are delineated according to Paul's schema, many of the important determinants of the "placebo response" too often excluded from consideration when a narrow chemotherapy perspective dominates become included as significant specified variables, and lethal threats to internal validity are unlikely. These lethal disruptions of internal validity, if overlooked, lead to misinterpretation of data and the drawing of false conclusions. Paul's framing of the "ultimate question" for clinical researchers (i.e., "What treatment, by whom, is most effective for this individual with that specific problem, under which set of circumstances, and how does it come about?") has often been repeated, because it concisely establishes the multidimensional nature of clinical research. When placebo effects are incorporated into a multivariate conceptualization in which

Table 25-1. Domains of Variables to Be Accounted for in Clinical Research with Representative Examples

---

  I. Clients or patients
     A. Problem behaviors
     B. Stable personal–social characteristics
     C. Physical–social life environments
 II. Staff or therapists
     A. Therapeutic techniques
     B. Personal–social characteristics
     C. Physical–social treatment environments
III. Time
     A. Time window during which information is obtained
     B. Period of time to which such information applies

Note. Summarized from Paul (Chapter 8, this volume).

factorial research designs explore plausible alternative hypotheses, placebo effects may be demystified.

It has been suggested that the primary objective of clinical medicine and perhaps of all healing professions is the individualization of treatment (Pellegrino & Thomasma, 1981). We are of the opinion that progress toward this clinical objective requires a research perspective such as that delineated by Paul, which explores the multidimensional question he proposes and plausible psychosocial hypotheses that may answer it in part.

Paul also endorses the use of no-treatment control groups in clinical studies. Since most estimates of placebo effects are derived from retrospective analysis of drug versus placebo comparisons, it is important to note that such studies may provide an inadequate basis for such estimates, because they lack controls for spontaneous fluctuations in the natural course of the disorder that may be independent of unique "placebo manipulations." Since disorders may spontaneously improve or worsen, the true magnitude of placebo effects may be incorrectly gauged without adequate controls, either through underestimating or overestimating of effects that are due to the unique conditions of the placebo manipulation. In the "placebo" group, the experimental manipulations may not be the cause of changes observed, and the estimates of placebo effects may be biased in unknown ways. It may be noted that the term "spontaneous fluctuation" or "spontaneous improvement," like "placebo," is an expression of ignorance of the mechanisms involved.

An often-cited statistic in the placebo literature is the one taken from Beecher (1955) to the effect that placebo effects occur in 30–40% of treated patients (see Brody, Chapter 3, this volume). More recently (Shapiro, 1981), it has been suggested that placebo effects are relatively small and account for only a small proportion of the variance in organic illnesses. In his chapter, Rosenthal presents some of the more recently developed statistical methods for (1) selecting theoretically driven contrasts in factorial studies and summarizing variance and effect size across studies, and (2) estimating size of treatment and placebo effects. An important point illustrated by Rosenthal is that effects that account for only 10% of the variance may alter rates of successful treatment from 34% to 66%. If these effects are only evaluated by more traditional statistical methods, their clinical significance may readily be overlooked.

Paul introduces a cautionary note about the use and interpretation of various effect size indices. Alternative measures of effect size computed on the same data may yield markedly different estimates. Additionally, effect size estimates are altered by design-specific influences, such as unequal sample size and distriubtion of scores, as well as metric characteristics and the relationship between pretreatment and posttreatment measures. In view of these statistical considerations, and in view of Grünbaum's admonition that placebo effects be made relative to particular disorders, overview summaries of the magnitude of placebo effects (such as those of Beecher and Shapiro) are probably unwarranted.

CLINICAL PHENOMENA

As noted by Bakan, who serves as the first discussant in Section IV, the chapters by Hahn and by Bootzin are attempts to apprehend placebo procedures and placebo responses. "Apprehension" may be defined as the act of grasping something with the understanding, recognizing the meaning of it; in this sense, apprehension of a phenomenon may alter basic conceptualization of the phenomena under consideration. In a substantive way, the task of apprehension of placebo effects is a preoccupation of this volume. Hahn's focus is on cultural influences upon belief systems and their ultimate effects upon biological functioning. A dramatic example of such influences may occur during voodoo death, the evidence for which Hahn discusses in detail. Such dramatic harmful effects of belief systems ("nocebo effects") underscore the potency of belief in effecting health. Hahn describes how belief systems are framed by culturally transmitted modes of thought, and he goes to some length to demonstrate a mind–body unity.

Bootzin's chapter examines developments in cognitive theories of behavior change, and briefly reviews the literature on the efficacy and mechanisms of psychotherapy. At present, behavioral therapies are generally found to be superior to insight therapies, but with regard to specific mechanisms, the effectiveness of therapy has not been disentangled from expectancy effects. Indeed, Bootzin notes that expectancy effects are only one of the many cognitive variables that have been investigated, and he suggests that cognitive variables are interrelated in organized schemas that have cognitive, behavioral and autonomic nervous system consequences. At this level, the cultural and cognitive perspectives appear to be converging. Both Bootzin and Hahn are concerned with the determinants and behavioral and physiological consequences of the "assumptive world" of the individual. Although Hahn and Bootzin are considering quite disparate literatures, they acknowledge the importance of mental influences upon physiological processes and the existence of a functional interrelationship among various components of mental processes.

Bakan reminds us that mental processes are a directly experienced reality, independent of laboratory findings or theory. The challenge is to evolve a position that avoids both "materialistic" and "mentalistic" reductionism. To that end, it also remains to test empirically the circumstances under which mental and biological processes interact, as well as the magnitude and nature of these effects.

The early history of medicine may be summarized by a search for methods of pain relief, and placebo effects have long been a consideration in the development of analgesics. Evans's review comprises a detailed study of the personality determinants and the magnitude of placebo analgesia. A notable finding of his studies is that there is a constant effectiveness ratio of 55–60% when placebo is compared with a drug of known efficacy. This finding of a constant drug : placebo effect ratio has been replicated for insomnia and for tricyclic and lithium treatment of depression. In Evans's studies, this ratio of placebo response to standard drug response holds even when the potency of the standard varies (i.e., morphine or codeine). This finding is in accordance with a prediction from a conditioning interpretation of placebo (see Wickeramasekera, Chapter 15, this volume) that placebo effects become more potent as the potency of the medications increases. However, from a strictly biologically based classical conditioning model, the subjects would require prior exposure to the drug, while from a cognitive expectancy model, only prior information is necessary. Evans reviews further evidence indicating that placebo analgesia is mediated by expectancy effects, is moderated by situational anxiety, and is independent of hypnotizability.

In his discussion of Evans's chapter, Tursky points out that the constant ratio between the analgesic effects of drugs versus placebos may be an artifact, due to the unidimensional and rough-grained characteristics of classical techniques for measuring clinical pain responses. Tursky recommends the use of psychophysically scaled response systems, which are more precise than other methods for evaluating subjective responses. Pain responses have also been found to have three components, each of which may be differentially responsive to drug or placebo.

MEDIATIONAL THEORIES

Plotkin's chaper, "A Psychological Approach to Placebo: The Role of Faith in Therapy and Treatment," presents another effort to apprehend placebo phenomena. It is included with other mediational concepts as a contrast to the biological orientation of the other chapters in Section V. As a psychological perspective, it is an effort to conceptualize an important aspect of the assumptive world of the individual, as does the concept of expectancy effects (see Bootzin, Chapter 10). Plotkin designates the concept of faith as the focus of his approach. "Faith" is characterized as a condition of absolute certainty, free from all doubt. In this formulation, faith has primarily indirect consequences in the healing process, in that it facilitates acquisition and performance of prescriptive behaviors, even in the face of contradictory evidence. The literature on expectancy effects also provides a psychological perspective on placebo effects. However, by choosing faith as the central concept in his formulation—a term that historically is associated with religious contexts—Plotkin has touched upon sensitive issues.

In a religious context, faith is not amenable to analysis and has often been juxtaposed against empirical science. The absolute certainty demanded by faith contrasts with an empirical science that begins with doubt. An important component of empirical science is the statement of the null hypothesis, which is an expression of an attitude of doubt. Perhaps from the point of view of the patient, treatment is undertaken because of confidence or belief or faith in the practitioner. The practitioner, however, is obligated to base his or her treatment on empirically determined evidence whenever possible. It is in this way that the concerned practitioner guards against quackery.

The next three chapters in Section V are concerned with the presentation of noncognitive, biologically conceived conditioning models of placebo effects. A clear advantage of this model is that it leads to testable hypotheses, as specified by Wickramasekera. In their discussion of the first four chapters in this section, Turkkan and Brady note important consequences of an explicit classical conditioning model of placebo: "This takes placebo out of the realm of 'phenomenon,' [and] defines it as an orderly and systematic process . . . [dependent] upon the parameters of the CS and UCS, and the conditioning history of the subject and therapist" (Turkkan & Brady, Chapter 18, p. 327). The conditioning model may account for harmful effects (nocebo effects) of placebo administration, as well as therapeutic effects. Following presentations of conditional stimuli (CSs) that had previously been paired with an aversive stimulus, cardiac irregularities have been conditioned in laboratory animals. Although such demonstrations offer a reasonable model for nocebo effects, there remains the alternative that cognitive processes and symbolic meanings (see Hahn, Chapter 9) as considered in expectancy models (see Bootzin, Chapter 10) may modulate or mediate such nocebo responses in humans.

Conditioned responses (CRs) may not only replicate unconditioned responses (UCRs) to a drug (drug-mimicking responses), but may also be antagonistic to or in the opposite direction to the drug responses (drug-mirroring responses). The conditions favoring the expression of the two forms of CRs are not entirely clear. These "drug-mirroring" responses and their role in moderating drug responses and determining drug tolerance and cross-tolerance are examined in detail by Siegel.

Ader's contribution reviews a rigorously controlled series of animal studies, in which adminsitration of a placebo preparation subsequent to the administration of potent immunosuppressant drugs resulted in a sustained drug-mimicking response. This conditioned placebo response paradigm may have significant therapeutic application, but human clinical trials have not yet been conducted. One area of clinical interest in which conditioned placebo response might have significant application is psychophysiological insomnia. Currently available hypnotics are both addictive and habituating (Institute of Medicine, 1979); however, patients often report placebo responses when involved in insomnia management procedures (Steinmark & Borkovec, 1974). If a placebo preparation were to be periodically substituted for a potent sleep inducer, perhaps a sustained therapeutic response with minimal side effects would be obtained.

Grevert and Goldstein's chapter reviews the available evidence concerning the hypothesis that endogenous opioids mediate placebo analgesia. Their summary conclusion is that present experimental evidence does suggest that endogenous opioids play a significant role in the mediation of placebo analgesia. This conclusion is made possible by a series of rigorously conducted studies that have sought to avoid the many potential pitfalls of human clinical research. It is apparent from reading this chapter that knowledge of fundamental mechanisms contributes to research methodology and ensures that rigorous scientific standards are adhered to. It is possible that these studies of pain response might be enhanced by multidimensional measures of pain response (see Tursky, Chapter 13, this volume), which may be differentially responsive to experimental manipulations. Multidimensional subjective measures may help in clarifying alternative pain mechanisms, particularly in differentiating changes in sensitivity from affective components.

It is apparent in reading Anisman and Sklar's chapter that the role of stress in modulating neoplasia is more firmly established in laboratory animals than in humans. As suggested in their chapter, efficacy of stress reduction therapy for neoplasia in humans has yet to be established, although the work summarized establishes this as a plausible hypothesis. As a final comment on this area, Levine and Gordon's remarks in their discussion chapter bear repeating: "Psychobiology has undergone many growing pains in its infnacy and childhood. This period of its development may now be subsiding, giving rise to a more mature period when the wide diversity of available scientific information will be used more systematically, so that truly rigorous physiological insights into what has been termed the 'mind–body' problem will be made" (Chapter 21, p. 399).

ETHICAL ISSUES

The practicing physician who employs information sharing and patient encouragement as part of his or her therapeutic armamentarium may be considered to be enhancing placebo effects, but would not be subject to censure (Brody, 1982). However, the intentional use of a placebo preparation by a physician confronts ethical issues. In an influential paper (Bok, 1974) exporing these ethical concerns, the administration of placebo preparations is identified as a fundamentally deceptive practice that cannot have any specific effect on a patient's condition. In this analysis, ethical considerations lead to restricted sets of conditions in which placebo preparations may be justified: (1) Placebos should be used only after a careful diagosis; (2) no active placebos should be employed, merely inert ones; (3) no outright lie should be told, and questions should be answered honestly; (4) placebos should never be given to patients who have asked not to receive them; (5) placebos should never be used when other treatment is clearly called for or all possible alternatives have not been weighed. Bok's position on the ethics of placebo administration incorporates a definition based upon the distinction between nonspecific and specific effects. In so doing, Bok may have underestimated real clinical effects of placebo administration from unspecified causes (see Grünbaum, Chapter 2, this volume). Not considered in discussions on the ethics of placebos are the diagnostic uses of placebo preparations (Evans, Chapter 12, this volume; Shapiro, Struening, & Shapiro, 1980).

Rawlinson's chapter is a re-examination of the medical and philosophical roots of attitudes toward the administration of placebos. Following Percival's *Medical Ethics* (1803), Rawlinson examines the role of paternalism and benevolent deception in clinical practice. Percival maintained that the specific intentional context needed to be considered in evaluating the ethics of deception. He defended the position that in medical practice a ruse may be employed if it is necessary to insure the success of treatment, and that the patient's trust and confidence in the doctor—essential elements in the doctor–patient relationship—are not thereby eroded. Additionally, Rawlinson notes the evidence suggesting that deception is not always necessary in order to obtain therapeutic results from the administration of a placebo preparation. The use of benevolent deception does require strict regulation, and Rawlinson enumerates five tests to be met before placebos may be used clinically; she further advises the cautious and reluctant use of benevolent deception.

These cautions are to be particularly noted. Rawlinson is not endorsing widespread use of placebos and is aware of the potential for corruption of medical responsibility. An essential consideration in the ethical consideration of placebo use is its potential for eroding the patient's trust in the treating physician. Some of the determinants of this relationship are indeed complex. Fink, in his discussion, reviews recent events that have led to a current breach in the traditional doctor–patient relationship. Prominent among these are authoritarian excesses in political policies, leading to a public climate in which confidence in authority per se has been undermined and individual autonomy idealized. Within the field of psychiatric practice, the apparent success of biological psychiatry therapy for syphilis and the subsequent development of convulsant therapies reinforced public perceptions of the potency of medical practice. However, the potential for enhancement of a trusting doctor–patient collaboration was undermined by authoritarian pretensions among psychiatric practitioners. According to this analysis, the insistence upon drug studies with placebo controls arose in part as a scientific safeguard against authoritarian abuse of trust. However, slavish adherence to the double-blind placebo research methodology may be in part a reactive response and may reflect an unrealistic need for illusory certainty.

Finkel's contribution reflects upon those circumstances in drug studies in which much is to be gained by active treatment comparisons. She particularly notes that there are three conditions in which trials employing active controls might substitute wholly for placebo-controlled trials. The chapters of Rawlinson and Finkel have in common a challenge to generally well-established attitudes toward placebos in clinical practice and research studies (i.e., intentional clinical use of placebos is unethical; placebo controls in drug studies are mandatory). It would be a desirable outcome if the presentation of these challenges would stimulate a re-examination and an enlarged understanding of the clinical uses of placebo preparations and placebo double-blind research methodology.

NEED FOR INCLUSIVE THEORY

It is apparent that in the search for effective treatments, current research findings are altering the traditional meaning of placebo, and that in the process models of clinical research are being altered. In the search for effective treatments, it is necessary first to establish that an effect on a specific disorder is obtained as the result of experimental manipulation. Subsequent controlled studies may find that theoretically specified causes are either unnecessary or insufficient in order to obtain the effect. Under conditions in which adequate safeguards to internal validity of the study obtain, there may then be a placebo effect in the generic sense of the term. In these circumstances, the effect is not illusory or insubstantial or nonspecific; rather, the causes are unspecified.

The "placebo preparation" and the double-blind method represent a specific experimental control that seeks to meet the criteria for the "method of difference," as discussed above. Reliance upon retrospective analysis of these drug versus placebo studies for determination of the magnitude of the placebo response is methodologically unsound. Such studies do not control for such factors as spontaneous fluctuations in the disorder, or for such research artifacts as observer bias. Additionally, uncritical acceptance of a drug versus placebo methodology obscures the interaction between physiological and psychological processes, as well as the effect of physiological processes upon mental processes, which has traditionally been a concern of Western clinicians (Brody, Chapter 3, this volume; Rather, 1965). The double-blind placebo-controlled methodology implicitly recognizes the validity of placebo-induced changes in specific disorders, but, due to theoretical bias, excludes these observations from further consideration. The "deeply rooted" nature of these biases has been traced by Karasu (1982). As designated by Grünbaum (Chapter 2), it is the perspective of a given therapeutic theory that determines which elements of the treatment process are identified as essential characterists and which are considered incidental. Theory or "disciplinary matrix" legitimizes treatments in addition to determining plausible research hypotheses, and in this function it may lead an investigator/clinician to dismiss or fail to identify potent or moderator constituents of a treatment process. The apparent success of pharmacology combined with a reductionist disciplinary matrix has led many to dismiss inadvertent placebo components prematurely. A more comprehensive model of treatment may ultimately facilitate clinical efficacy and critical research. There is no single placebo effect having a single mechanism and efficacy, but rather a multiplicity of effects, with differential efficacy and mechanisms. Table 25-2 contains a summary of nominated placebogenic variables derived from the chapters in this volume, schematically ordered from macro to micro levels. This ordering is necessarily arbitrary at this time.

One of the difficulties facing an integrative theory of health is the number of the nominated variables rather than an absence of candidates. The list comprises concepts derived from cultural influences, social-psychological theory, cognitive theory, classical conditioning, and psychophysiology. A challenge for the social-psychological sciences is the attainment of a greater

Table 25-2. Biopsychosocial Determinants of Placebo Response

Cultural context
  A. Belief system
  B. Faith
Environmental milieu
Instruction
Suggestion
Preparation characteristics
Doctor–patient relationship
Patient's expectations and needs
Patient's personality
Psychological state
Symptom severity
Discomfort severity
Anxiety/stress
  A. Central evaluative processes
  B. Cognitive processes
Cognitive schema
Self-schema
Self-control
Expectancy
Outcome expectancy
Efficacy expectations
Operant behavior
Symbolic processes
Imagination
Covert rehearsal
Emotions
Central nervous system influences upon physiology
  A. Immune system
  B. Stress mechanisms
  C. Endogenous opiates
Classical conditioning
Spontaneous remissions

---

degree of clarity and consolidation of fundamental variables. The placebo effect paradigm may be seen as a special case of a biopsychosocial effect. An appreciation of the significance of placebo effects may serve as a departure for an integrative theory leading to a sustained program of research in which mechanisms will become specified and magnitude of effects will be delimited. The chapters in this volume attest to the potential of this approach for generating new knowledge and improving clinical efficacy. This context would provide an arena for testing a biopsychosocial model for health and illness. An integrated theory would facilitate such an enterprise.

Three criteria for a useful integrative macro-level theory have been proposed (Schwartz, 1983a):

1. The macro-level theory should *integrate seemingly disparate and/or competing findings*. This includes the fact that data disregarded by more specific, micro-level theories (e.g., findings viewed as anomalous results that are not predicted and are not consistent with a given theory) should be viewed as important and even essential from the perspective of the macro-level theory.
2. The macro-level theory should stimulate *new predictions and discoveries* that would not be derived from the more micro-level theories. Hence, the effective macro-level theory should not only integrate more data (criterion 1), but should also uncover new data (criterion 2).
3. The macro-level theory should be *friendly* to the mciro-level theories, illustrating how the micro-level theories are special cases of the macro theory and are appropriate to specific levels of processes. Hence, micro-level theories should not be discarded because they appear wrong at certain levels. Rather, the micro-level theories should be appreciated and incorporated to the extent that they reflect novel emergent processes occurring at specific levels (Schwartz, 1983a).

A systems theory perspective (Miller, 1978; von Bertalanffy, 1968) has been proposed as a metatheoretical framework for integrating biological, psychological, and social influences on health and illness (Schwartz, 1979, 1980, 1981, 1982, 1983a, 1983b). A detailed examination of the etiology and treatment of hypertension as organized by systems theory has been conducted by Schwartz, Shapiro, Redmond, Ferguson, Ragland, and Weiss (1979).

CHARACTERISTICS OF SYSTEMS

A system is an entity (a whole) composed of subsystems that interact at all levels via a complex network of feedback and feed-forward loops. A characteristic of such a system is that effects occurring at one level have consequences upon other levels. If the system is an open system, then the system is also regulated by its environment. Out of this interaction of the parts, there emerge new properties that are unique to the system or entity as a whole. Emergent properties are more than the simple, independent sum of the properties of the parts studies in isolation.

A classic example of emergent property is water—a chemical (a molecule) that is composed of hydrogen and oxygen, two basic atoms. These atoms, at room temperature, themselves have a set of system/whole properties: They are both gases, they both have no smell, and cannot be tasted. However, when these two atoms (and only these two atoms) are connected under the right circumstances, a new, molecular system is formed, called water. Water has unique emergent properties that are very different from the individual properties of hydrogen and oxygen: At room temperature water is a liquid, has no obvious smell, and can be tasted. It is impossible to predict from the individual properties of hydrogen and oxygen all the unique emergent properties of water.

What systems theorists propose is that emergent phenomena are universal in nature, and occur at all levels of complexity. Atoms combine to form new molecules; molecules combine to form new, more complex molecules; some of these complex molecules combine to form new living cells; living cells combine to form new organ systems and organisms; organisms combine to form new social groups; and so forth. The different disciplines of knowledge reflect the study of emergent phenomena that occur at each of these levels. Organized hierarchically, the disciplines emerge from philosophy and mathematics, to physics and physical chemistry, to chemistry and biochemistry, to cellular biology and organ physiology, to psychophysiology and psychology, to social psychology and sociology, to political science and economics, to government and ecology, and so forth.

Cannon (1932), in his description of the body's homeostatic processes, anticipated the principles of positive and negative feedback later developed by Weiner (1948) in his cybernetic control theory (a subset of systems theory). Homeostasis is the process whereby the brain and the body interact in mutual regulation to maintain the internal milieu at critical levels when faced with environmental stress. This stability requires multiple levels of self-regulation between brain and body. For example, human body temperature is maintained at 98.6°F despite wide changes in external temperature. This stability requires multiple levels of feed-forward and feedback control between body and brain, including the evolution of new behavioral strategies such as clothing, housing, and systems of heating and cooling.

Table 25-3 presents a schematic representation of levels of processes in which there is a linking of biological, psychological, and social systems. The variables are arranged in hierarchical order in accordance with systems theory principles. These levels, it must be remembered, are interconnected

Table 25-3. Nine Major Levels of Processes Linking Biological, Psychological, and Social Systems

9. Social interactions
8. Motivation and belief
7. Education and insight
6. Cognitive–emotional–behavioral–environmental self-control
5. Discrimination training
4. Motor skills learning
3. Operant conditioning
2. Classical conditioning
1. Homeostatic–cybernetic self-regulation

Note. From "Psychophysiology of Imagery and Healing: A Systems Perspective" by G. E. Schwartz. In A. Sheikh (Ed.), *Imagination and Healing.* New York: Baywood, 1983. Reprinted by permission.

Note. The levels are synthesized using a systems perspective. The processes are organized from micro to macro levels. Note that each higher-numbered process incorporates processes described by the lower-numbered processes.

via feedback and feed-forward loops such that intervention at one level has consequences at other levels. The determinants of placebo response (as shown in Table 25-2) may be seen to map on to the level of processes shown in Table 25-3.

An important methodological implication of the concept of emergent properties is that new, unpredicted effects may arise out of the interaction of component susbsystems. It would follow from this formulation that factorial research strategies that uniquely allow for the examination of interaction effects may yield the discovery of new, potent combinations that cannot be predicted from a consideration of the variables taken in isolation. Significant interactive effects may occur when two independent variables individually have negligible effects. Even when independent variables have effects, a statistically significant interaction indicates more than a summation of the variables taken independently.

SUMMARY

We begin this chapter by summarizing some of the more salient points of preceding chapters. Placebo phenomena may be seen as clinical effects upon a variety of disorders produced by unspecified causes. The determination of the magnitude of these effects and the incorporation of these effects into clinical regimens has been frustrated by methodological errors, the search for a single mechanism, and a narrowly conceived model of health care. Some estimates of the therapeutic significance of these effects have been exaggerated. However, their clinical significance can no longer be in question. Our analysis has led us to view placebo effects as a subset of biopsychosocial interactions. We have concluded by proposing a systems theory perspective that may provide for the integration of disparate data and competing theories, and may lead to the generation and testing of new hypotheses. In fostering a synthetic integration, we hope that the analytic study of health care will continue to prosper, and we see the two approaches as interdependent.

REFERENCES

Beecher, H. K. The powerful placebo. *Journal of the American Medical Association*, 1955, *159*, 1602–1606.

Bok, S. The ethics of giving placebos. *Scientific American*, 1974, *231*, 17–23.

Brody, H. The lie that heals. *Annals of Internal Medicine*, 1982, *97*, 112–118.

Cannon, W. B. *The wisdom of the body*. New York: Norton, 1932.

Cohen, M. R., & Nagel, E. *An introduction to logic and scientific method*. New York: Harcourt, Brace, 1934.

Gadow, K. D., White, L., & Ferguson, D. G. Placebo controls and double-blind conditions: Experimenter bias, conditioned placebo response and drug psychotherapy comparisons. In S. E. Bruening, A. D. Poling, & J. L. Matson (Eds.), *Applied psychopharmacology: Methods for assessing medication effects*. New York: Grune & Stratton, 1985.

Institute of Medicine. *Sleeping pills, insomnia, and medical practice*. Washington, D.C.: National Academy of Sciences, 1979.

Karasu, T. B. Psychotherapy and pharmacotherapy: Toward an integrative model. *American Journal of Psychiatry*, *139*(9), 1982, 1102–1113.

Miller, J. G. *Living systems*. New York: McGraw-Hill, 1978.

Pellegrino, E. D., & Thomasma, D. C. *The philosophy of medicine. A philosophical basis of medical practice*. New York: Oxford University Press, 1981.

Rather, J. L. *Mind and body in eighteenth century medicine; A study based upon Jerome Garb's De regimine mentis*. Berkeley: University of California Press, 1965.

Schwartz, G. E. The brain as a health care system. In G. Stone, N. Adler, & F. Cohen (Eds.), *Health psychology*. San Francisco: Jossey-Bass, 1979.

Schwartz, G. E. Behavioral medicine and systems theory: A new synthesis. *National Forum*, 1980, *4*, 25–30.

Schwartz, G. E. A systems analysis of psychobiology and behavior therapy: Implications for behavioral medicine. *Psychotherapy and Psychosomatics*, 1981, *36*, 159–184.

Schwartz, G. E. Biofeedback as a paradigm for health enhancement and disease prevention: A systems perspective. In J. Matarazzo, N. E. Miller, S. Weiss, A. J. A. Herd, & S. M. Weiss (Eds.), *Behavioral health: A handbook of health enhancement and disease prevention*. New York: Wiley, 1982.

Schwartz, G. E. Psychophysiology of imagery and healing: A systems perspective. In A. Sheikh (Ed.), *Imagination and healing*. New York: Baywood, 1983. (a)

Schwartz, G. E. Social psychophysiology and behavioral medicine: A systems perspective. In J. T. Cacioppo & R. E. Petty (Eds.), *Social psychophysiology*. New York: Guilford Press, 1983. (b)

Schwartz, G. E., Shapiro, A. P., Redmond, D. P., Ferguson, D. C., Ragland, D. R., & Weiss, S. M. Behavioral medicine approaches to hypertension: An integrative analysis of theory and research. *Journal of Behavioral Medicine*, 1979, *2*, 311–363.

Shapiro, A. K. [Review of H. Brody's *Placebos and the philosophy of medicine*]. *Social Science and Medicine*, 1981, *15E*, 96–97.

Shapiro, A. K., Struening, E. L., & Shapiro, E. The reliability and validity of a placebo test. *Journal of Psychiatric Research*, 1980, *15*, 253–290.

Steinmark, S. W., & Borkovec, T. D. Active and placebo treatment effects on moderate insomnia under countermand and positive demand instructions. *Journal of Abnormal Psychology*, 1974, *83*, 157–163.

von Bertalanffy, L. *General systems theory.* New York: Braziller, 1968.

Weiner, N. *Cybernetics or control and communication in the animal and machine.* Cambridge, Mass.: MIT Press, 1948.

NAME INDEX

Italicized page numbers refer to material in tables.

Cohen, M. R., 333, 343, 347, 348*n*., 350*n*., 433, 446*n*.
Cohen, N., 262, 282*n*., 283*n*., 308, *308*, 309–311, *313*, 314, 322*n*., 355, 383*n*., 385*n*.
Cohen, R. M., 333, 343, 348*n*., 350*n*.
Cohen, S., 368, 393*n*.
Cohen-Cole, S., 352, 385*n*.
Cole, J. O., 13, 35*n*.
Coleman, F. S., 424, 428*n*.
Collector, M. I., 354, 355, 390*n*.
Collins, B. E., 87, 106*n*.
Collins, W. F., Jr., 268, 286*n*.
Compas, B. E., 88, 103*n*.
Congleton, G., 370, 386*n*.
Conner, R. L., 365, 392*n*.
Conran, P., 354, 389*n*.
Contel, N. R., 294, 295, 303*n*.
Cook, M. R., 256, 283*n*., 329, 330*n*.
Cook, T. D., 140, 147, 161*n*.
Cooper, D. O., 374, 392*n*.
Cooper, E., 357, 389*n*.
Cooper, H. M., 118, 134*n*., 153, 161*n*.
Cooper, S. J., *377*
Corbalan, R., 327, 330*n*.
Cordray, D. S., 197, 208*n*.
Corrigan, S., 372, 394*n*.
Costa, E., 374, 385*n*.
Cotzias, G. C., 370, 385*n*., 393*n*.
Covi, L., 10, 17, 18, 22, 36*n*., 45, 58*n*., 76, 81*n*., 325, 330*n*.
Cowan, A., 295, 304*n*.
Cowdery, J. S., 310, 323*n*.
Cox, B. M., 332, 348*n*., 375, 384*n*.
Craighead, L. W., 98, 104*n*.
Crimmings, A. M., 96, 106*n*.
Critelli, J. W., 19, 20, 35*n*., 100, 102, 104*n*.
Crocker, J., 206, 208*n*.
Crockett, J. E., 216, 227*n*., 255, 283*n*.
Cronbach, L. J., 140, 161*n*.
Crow T. J., 426, 428*n*.
Crowell, C. R., 296, 301*n*., 328, 330*n*.
Cullavi, S., 86, 104*n*.
Cullen, J. W., 307, 322*n*.
Culver, C. M., 52, 58*n*.
Cunningham, C. L., 296, 303*n*., 328, 330*n*.
Curzon, G., 374, 385*n*.
Cutler, M. A., 356, 384*n*.
Cutler, R., 92, 105*n*.

Dafters, R., 301, 301*n*.

Dahl, J., 293, 305*n*.
D'Amato, R. J. M., 347, 349*n*.
Daniels, J. C., 353, 386*n*.
Dantzer, R., 373, 387*n*.
Darley, J. M., 98, 104*n*.
Dattore, P. J., 356, 386*n*.
Davidson, R. J., 266, 273, 283*n*.
Davignon, J. P., 370, 386*n*.
Davis, D. E., 353, 385*n*.
Davis, G. C., 335, 348*n*.
Davis, J. M., 13, 35*n*.
Davis, K. E., 239, 242*n*., 252*n*.
Davis, W. M., 294, 301*n*.
Davison, G. C., 198, 208*n*.
Deakin, J. F. W., 426, 428*n*.
Dechambre, R. P., 364, 365, 385*n*., 393*n*.
Deeter, W. R., 335, *341*, 349*n*.
Deguire, K. S., 357, 389*n*.
Dehen, H., 336, 350*n*.
Delbene, V. E., 354, 389*n*.
Del Giudice, J., 91, 104*n*.
Demarr, E. W. J., 72, 76, 80*n*.
Demellweek, C., 293, 301*n*.
Demers, R. Y., 178, 191*n*.
Depue, R. A., 351, 385*n*.
Derogatis, L. R., 357, 385*n*.
DeRubeis, R. J., 98, 106*n*., 146, 161*n*.
Descartes, R., 186, 191*n*.
DeSilva, R., 176, 193*n*.
Deuschle, K. W., 179, 193*n*.
Deutsch, R., 291, 301*n*.
Devoino, L. V., 370, 385*n*.
DeVries, G. H., 375, 385*n*.
DeWit, H., 300, 305*n*.
Diamond, E. G., 216, 227*n*., 255, 283*n*.
Dickman, S., 266, 272, 286*n*.
Dickson, W. J., 325, 330*n*.
Dietrich, F. M., 370, 386*n*.
Dillard, D. H., 255, 283*n*.
DiMascio, A., 91, 106*n*., 107*n*.
Dinnerstein, A. J., 74, 80*n*., 88, 93, 104*n*.
Dixon, F. J., 310, 322*n*., 323*n*.
Dixon, N. F., 272, 283*n*.
Docherty, J. P., 357, 391*n*.
Dohan, J. L., 74, 81*n*.
Doherty, G., 89, 107*n*.
Dohrenwend, B. P., 176, 191*n*.
Dohrenwend, B. S., 176, 191*n*.
Dorian, B. J., 353, 385*n*.
Dorsa, D. M., 333, 350*n*.
Dostrovsky, J. O., 335, 348*n*.
Douglas, R., 352, 386*n*.
Downing, R. W., 93, 104*n*.

SUBJECT INDEX